W9-ADW-863

Sri Lanka

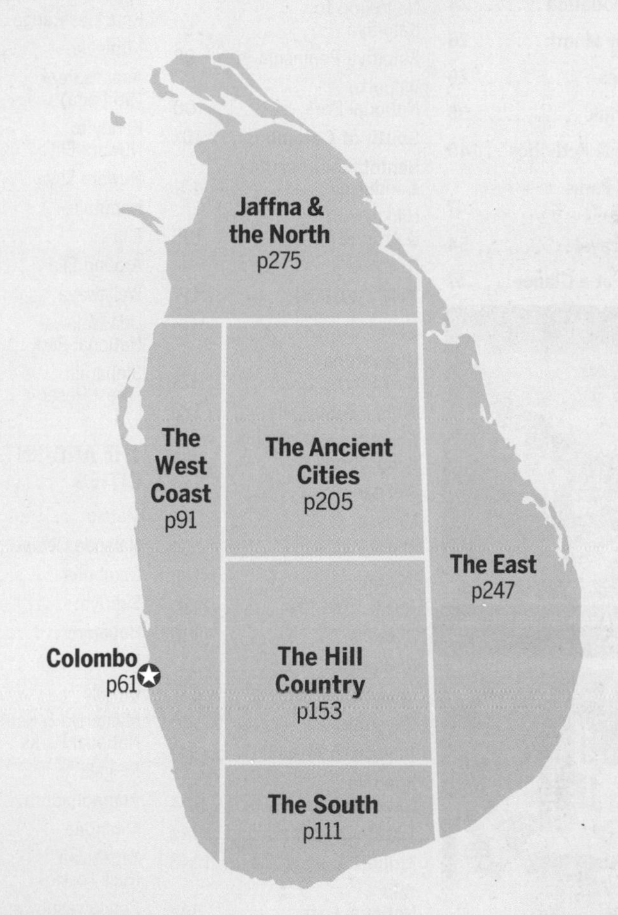

Joe Bindloss, Stuart Butler, Bradley Mayhew, Jenny Walker

PLAN YOUR TRIP

UTOPIA_88/GETTY IMAGES ©

KUMANA NATIONAL PARK P259

JONATHON STOKES/LONELY PLANET ©

JAFFNA P277

ON THE ROAD

Contents

UNDERSTAND

SURVIVAL GUIDE

SPECIAL FEATURES

COVID-19

We have re-checked every business in this book before publication to ensure that it is still open after the COVID-19 outbreak. However, the economic and social impacts of COVID-19 will continue to be felt long after the outbreak has been contained, and many businesses, services and events referenced in this guide may experience ongoing restrictions. Some businesses may be temporarily closed, have changed their opening hours and services, or require bookings; some unfortunately could have closed permanently. We suggest you check with venues before visiting for the latest information.

Right: Temple of the Sacred Tooth Relic (p156)

MATT MUNRO/LONELY PLANET ©

WELCOME TO

Sri Lanka

You could say Sri Lanka is in my blood. My grandfather was a stoker on a navy warship and I grew up with stories of what was then Ceylon, inspiring me to devote my working days to travel. Sri Lanka has been struck by civil war, communal conflict and natural disasters, but its people have an amazing ability to bounce back from crisis. Package this positive thinking with gorgeous beaches, delicious food and lost civilisations, and it's hard to resist any opportunity to return.

By Joe Bindloss, Writer
joe_planet
For more about our writers, see p352

Sri Lanka

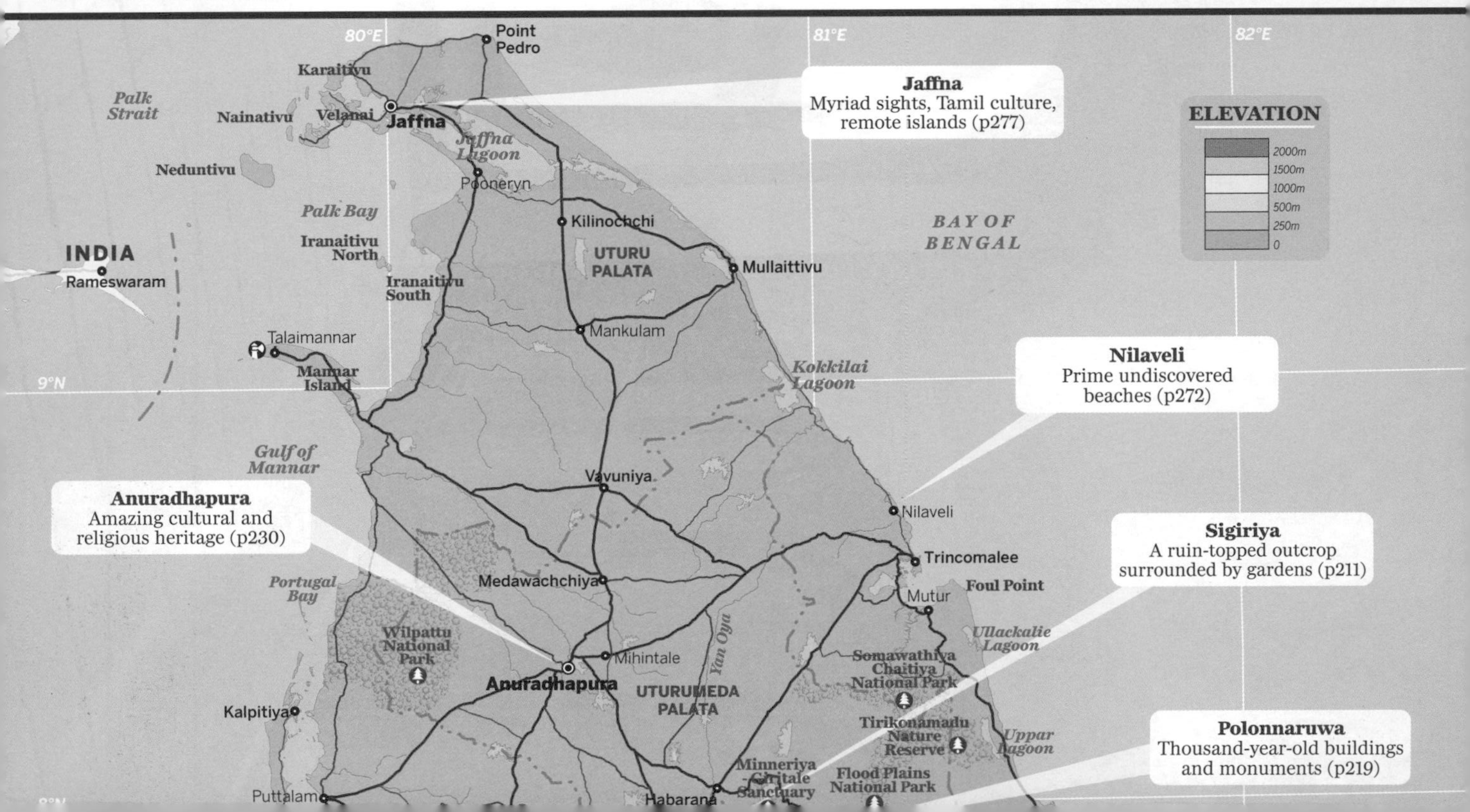
0 50 km
0 25 miles
ELEVATION
2000m
1500m
1000m
500m
250m
0
80°E
81°E
82°E
9°N
Jaffna
Myriad sights, Tamil culture, remote islands (p277)
Nilaveli
Prime undiscovered beaches (p272)
Sigiriya
A ruin-topped outcrop surrounded by gardens (p211)
Polonnaruwa
Thousand-year-old buildings and monuments (p219)
Anuradhapura
Amazing cultural and religious heritage (p230)
Point Pedro
Karaitivu
Palk Strait
Nainativu
Velanai
Jaffna
Jaffna Lagoon
Neduntivu
Pooneryn
Palk Bay
Kilinochchi
BAY OF BENGAL
INDIA
Rameswaram
Iranaitivu North
Iranaitivu South
UTURU PALATA
Mullaittivu
Mankulam
Talaimannar
Mannar Island
Kokkilai Lagoon
Gulf of Mannar
Vavuniya
Nilaveli
Trincomalee
Foul Point
Mutur
Portugal Bay
Medawachchiya
Ullackalie Lagoon
Wilpattu National Park
Yan Oya
Mihintale
Somawathiya Chaitiya National Park
Anuradhapura
UTURUMEDA PALATA
Kalpitiya
Tirikonamadu Nature Reserve
Uppar Lagoon
Minneriya-Giritale Sanctuary
Flood Plains National Park
Puttalam
Habarana

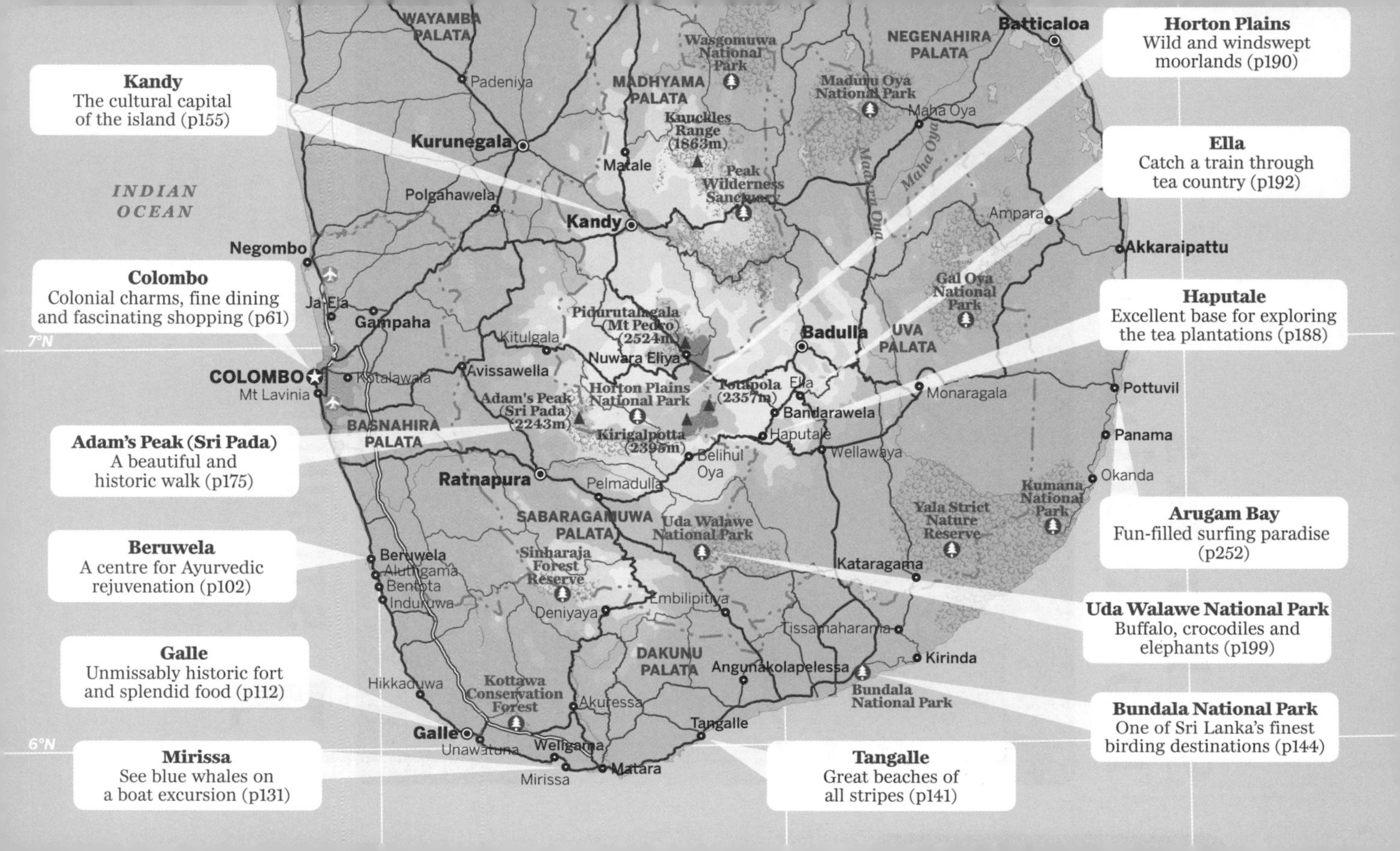
Kandy
The cultural capital of the island (p155)
Colombo
Colonial charms, fine dining and fascinating shopping (p61)
Adam's Peak (Sri Pada)
A beautiful and historic walk (p175)
Beruwela
A centre for Ayurvedic rejuvenation (p102)
Galle
Unmissably historic fort and splendid food (p112)
Mirissa
See blue whales on a boat excursion (p131)
Tangalle
Great beaches of all stripes (p141)
Horton Plains
Wild and windswept moorlands (p190)
Ella
Catch a train through tea country (p192)
Haputale
Excellent base for exploring the tea plantations (p188)
Arugam Bay
Fun-filled surfing paradise (p252)
Uda Walawe National Park
Buffalo, crocodiles and elephants (p199)
Bundala National Park
One of Sri Lanka's finest birding destinations (p144)
INDIAN OCEAN
WAYAMBA PALATA
MADHYAMA PALATA
NEGENAHIRA PALATA
UVA PALATA
BASNAHIRA PALATA
SABARAGAMUWA PALATA
DAKUNU PALATA
Batticaloa
Kurunegala
Kandy
Badulla
Ratnapura
Galle
COLOMBO
Negombo
Padeniya
Polgahawela
Matale
Ja-Ela
Gampaha
Kotalawala
Mt Lavinia
Avissawella
Kitulgala
Nuwara Eliya
Bandarawela
Haputale
Ella
Wellawaya
Belihul Oya
Pelmadulla
Monaragala
Ampara
Maha Oya
Akkaraipattu
Pottuvil
Panama
Okanda
Kataragama
Tissamaharama
Kirinda
Angunakolapelessa
Embilipitiya
Deniyaya
Akuressa
Tangalle
Matara
Weligama
Mirissa
Unawatuna
Hikkaduwa
Beruwela
Aluthgama
Bentota
Induruwa
Wasgomuwa National Park
Maduru Oya National Park
Knuckles Range (1863m)
Peak Wilderness Sanctuary
Gal Oya National Park
Pidurutalagala (Mt Pedro) (2524m)
Horton Plains National Park
Totapola (2357m)
Adam's Peak (Sri Pada) (2243m)
Kirigalpotta (2395m)
Uda Walawe National Park
Sinharaja Forest Reserve
Kottawa Conservation Forest
Yala Strict Nature Reserve
Kumana National Park
Bundala National Park
Maduru Oya
Maha Oya
7°N
6°N

Sri Lanka's Top Experiences

1 STUNNING SANDS

Beaches are what put Sri Lanka on the travel map. Long, palm-backed sweeps, exposed to the Indian Ocean swell. Dainty coves with soft, powder-white sand. Fishing beaches crowded with colourful boats. City beaches thronging with people, and isolated strands without a footprint. Some beaches offer sublime tranquillity, some are party central but whichever you choose, the coast is every bit as gorgeous as you've heard.

JOHN CRUX PHOTOGRAPHY/GETTY IMAGES ©

Sands for all at Tangalle

This south-coast jewel has beaches of all flavours, some gorgeous and accessible and close to the action, and some mostly untouched and far from the crowds. Ramble along the shore and take your pick. p141

JONATHCN STOKES/LONELY PLANET ©

DAILY TRAVEL PHOTOS/SHUTTERSTOCK ©

Serene Uppuveli & Nilaveli

The blissful beaches of Uppuveli and Nilaveli add extra magic to a quiet eastern corner of the country. Escapers are lured here by the small, friendly travellers' scene and beautiful seascapes to admire. p270

Wild northern sand

Most of the beaches in the far north-east are totally isolated, offering a sublime escape for explorers, dreamers and silence seekers. Arrange transport in Jaffna to explore this untouched strip of coast and seek out your own strip of sand. p274

Above: Point Pedro beach (p287)

2 CAPTIVATING CULTURE

Sri Lanka has been a seafaring hub for at least 2500 years, and centuries of trade and conquest have created a mesmerising melting pot of cultures and customs. Buddhism, Hinduism, Islam and Christianity have all played a part in shaping the island's rich history; wherever you go, you'll never be far from an ancient ruin, towering temple or historic entrepôt.

Exploring glorious Anuradhapura

Against competition from the likes of Polonnaruwa and Sigiriya, Anuradhapura emerges as the greatest of Sri Lanka's ancient cities – a vast sprawl of dagobas (stupas), carvings, temples and palaces, some ruined, some restored, but all magnificent and evocative. p230

Below: Isurumuniya Vihara (p239)

A PHOTO BY BHAGIRAJ SIVAGNANASU ©

RUWAN WALPOLA/SHUTTERSTOCK ©

EFESENKO/SHUTTERSTOCK ©

Living faith in Colombo

Culture in Sri Lanka is no musty museum exhibit. In the historic capital, Colombo, the faithful queue daily at carving-filled Buddhist and Hindu temples, historic mosques and colonial-era churches, in a timeless display of devotion that brings Sri Lanka's cultural melting pot vividly to life. p60

Above left: Wolvendaal Church (p65)

Wonderful poya days

Full moon day is always something special at Sri Lanka's Buddhist temples. Pilgrims dressed in immaculate white flock to sacred sites to make offerings, chant mantras and connect with the divine. Even crumbling ruins come alive with rituals and activity. p28

3 WONDERFUL WILDLIFE

Even if there were no beaches, temples or surf breaks, encounters with the local wildlife would be reason enough to come to Sri Lanka. Hornbills, kingfishers and flycatchers fill the skies with noise and colour; whales and dolphins splash in the briny blue; elephants and leopards stalk the island's spectacular national parks. With Sri Lanka's manageable scale, it would take real effort to not bump into the island's wonderful wildlife!

Jumbo-sized encounters

Magnificent herds of elephants rumble through Minneriya National Park, particularly during the annual 'Gathering' from June to September. p229

UTOPIA_88/SHUTTERSTOCK ©

Looking for leopards at Yala

Slinking leopards stalking through the undergrowth are the top spot at famous Yala National Park (though you'll see leopards without the crowds at nearby Kumana). p148

Whale watching at Mirissa

Spotting elephants on land is nothing compared to sighting a blue whale – the largest animal to ever live – gambolling off Dondra Head. p131

4 CATCHING A WAVE

THOMAS WYNESS/SHUTTERSTOCK ©

For thousands of travellers to Sri Lanka, it's all about the surf. The Indian Ocean crashes magnificently against the Sri Lankan coastline, and easy-going surf centres dot the shore, with boards for hire, cheap digs, warm waters and consistent breaks that are perfect for surfers just finding their feet. Make a beeline for Arugam Bay, Weligama or Hikkaduwa and start the surf safari.

Arugam's laid-back breaks

Come to this chilled-out surf centre for accessible breaks (pictured), cheap accommodation among the palms, and a barefoot traveller vibe that buzzes after dark. p251

Working the surf at Weligama

This sweet surf town down south is a prime spot to learn to catch a wave, but it's just as appealing to loll on the lovely sands. p129

Spectacular kitesurfing at Kalpitiya

The calm, flat Kalpitiya Lagoon is one of the top spots to learn to kitesurf, with plenty of surf camps to teach you the ropes. p98

5 EPIC RAIL JOURNEYS

The British-built railways that rattle along the coast and rumble into the hills offer a perfect vantage point for observing this idyllic island – particularly when sitting in a train doorway with your feet dangling nonchalantly in the breeze. Some journeys are genuinely epic – the hill train from Kandy to Badulla warrants special mention – but even a short hop on the coast will leave rail enthusiasts grinning from ear to ear.

MARTIN SILVA COSENTINO/SHUTTERSTOCK ©

JANE SWEENEY/ROBERTHARDING ©

Travelling the coast line

The scenic train line from Colombo to Matara (via Hikkaduwa and Galle; above left) hugs the coast so closely that sea spray wafts into the carriages. p88

Riding the rails to Kandy

The perfect train travel taster (above right) – a gentle trundle from the heat of the coast to the cool of the hills, ending in cultured Kandy. p166

Kandy to Badulla through tea country

Sri Lanka's most beautiful train journey (below left) trundles through emerald tea plantations on its way from Kandy to Badulla. p166

6 SEEING IT ALL FROM ABOVE

CRISTI POPESCU/SHUTTERSTOCK ©

DUDAREV MIKHAIL/SHUTTERSTOCK ©

Sublime views from Sigiriya

Rising above the terrain like a rocky exclamation mark, the ruin-capped plateau of Sigiriya looks out over a landscape of timeless history, tropical gardens and verdant jungles (left). p214

Climbing Adam's sacred summit

Join pilgrims on the hike to the summit of sacred Adam's Peak (Sri Pada; left) and you'll gain a glimpse of Sri Lanka's soul. p178

Landmark views from World's End

The rugged, lonely highlands of Horton Plains National Park plunge suddenly away towards the coastal plain at this appropriately named viewpoint. p190

The best way to appreciate Sri Lanka's tropical topography is to view it all from above. Landmark viewpoints, both natural and constructed, offer sublime vistas over dense, green jungles, sprawling townships and relics from Sri Lanka's ancient past. A bit of effort is required to earn the views, but that's part of the fun of exploring Sri Lanka's cooler, calmer higher ground.

7 EATING LIKE A SRI LANKAN

Hunting down an authentic plate of rice and curry is one of the great pleasures of travel in Sri Lanka. The nation's most sensational meals are served in simple canteens, where 'rice and curry' manifests as heaped mounds of rice served with a dozen different sides and sauces, prepared with rich spices and local fish, meats and vegetables (including plenty of coconut, jackfruit and other exotic ingredients).

The Pilawoos experience

Colombo's most authentic dining experience is not in its fine dining restaurants but in no-frills Pilawoos, purveyors of the best *kotthu* (fried chopped *rotti*; below) in town. p84

JONATHON STOKES/LONELY PLANET ©

Jaffna's curry sensations

Jaffna's cooks create the best food on the island, drawing on a rich palate of spices influenced by neighbouring India. For authentic Jaffna cuisine, Mangos is cream of the kitchens. p283

Tea tasting in the Hill Country

Sri Lankan tea is famously full-flavoured and visiting a tea estate such as the Handunugoda Tea Estate (right) near Koggala for a tasting is almost mandatory. p127

8 RELICS OF COLONIAL EMPIRES

EFESENKO/SHUTTERSTOCK ©

Few Sri Lankans were sorry to see the departure of Europe's colonial empires, but local people have made good use of the monuments, infrastructure and architecture the interlopers left behind. Explore Colombo's historic government precincts, Galle's Dutch-era fortifications or the Portuguese and Dutch relics along the coast at Trincomalee, Jaffna, Mannar, Negombo and Batticaloa, and you'll get a powerful sense of the island's complex, layered history.

Whitewashed grandeur in old Colombo

The Dutch and British left a lasting mark on Colombo, where once-crumbling colonial buildings are being reborn as shopping arcades, eating hubs and centres for civic life. p60

Dutch days in historic Galle

Lovely Galle (above) earned a Unesco World Heritage listing for its beguiling mix of Dutch-colonial buildings, ancient mosques and churches, grand mansions and museums. p112

Jaffna's cultural fusion

Empire-builders from South India and Portugal shaped Jaffna's historic downtown, studded with ancient churches, rainbow-hued Hindu temples and fabulous places to eat. p277

Need to Know

For more information, see Survival Guide (p321)

Currency

Sri Lankan Rupee (Rs)

Language

Sinhala, Tamil and English

Visas

Most tourists travel with an Electronic Travel Authorisation (ETA), obtained online before visiting at www.eta.gov.lk. It costs US$35 to $40 for a 30-day visit, depending on your nationality. Two-day transit visas are free, and Sri Lankan missions overseas offer visas for longer stays.

Money

ATMs are widespread in cities and large towns. Credit cards are accepted at midrange and top-end hotels.

Mobile Phones

Local SIM cards for voice and data are cheap; bring an unlocked phone.

Time

Sri Lanka Standard Time (GMT/UTC + 5½ hours)

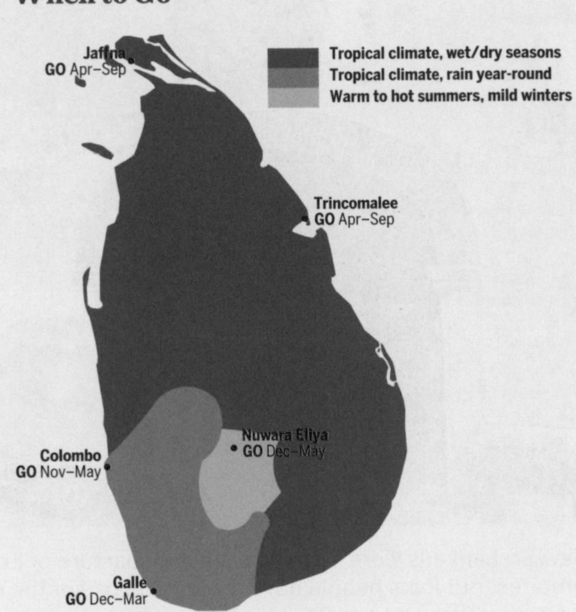

High Season

(Dec–Mar)

- Dry weather in the Hill Country, and on the west and south coast beaches.
- Heavy demand for beds and peak prices.
- The Maha monsoon season (October to January) keeps the East, North and ancient cities wet.

Shoulder

(Apr & Sep–Nov)

- April and September offer the best chance of good weather countrywide.
- New Year's celebrations in mid-April cause transport troubles as people move around the country.

Low Season

(May–Aug)

- The Yala monsoon season (May to August) brings rain to the south and west coasts and the Hill Country.
- Drier weather lures visitors to the North and the east coast.
- Room rates fall nationwide.

Useful Websites

Lonely Planet (www.lonelyplanet.com/sri-lanka) Destination information, hotel bookings, traveller forum and more.

Ceylon Today (www.ceylontoday.lk) News, sports and entertainment from a top English-language newspaper.

Info Lanka (www.infolanka.com/news) Aggregated news from Sri Lanka's leading news sources.

Yamu (www.yamu.lk) Excellent restaurant reviews, sights listings and more.

Meteo (www.meteo.gov.lk) Weather forecasts nationwide.

Man in Seat 61 (www.seat61.com/srilanka) Comprehensive information on all aspects of Sri Lankan rail travel.

Important Numbers

All regions have a three-digit area code followed by a six- or seven-digit number. Mobile numbers usually begin with 07 or 08 and have up to 12 digits.

Country code	94
International access code	00
Emergencies (Police hotline)	118/ 119

Exchange Rates

Australia	A$1	Rs 154
Canada	C$1	Rs 160
Europe	€1	Rs 241
Japan	¥100	Rs 184
New Zealand	NZ$1	Rs 143
UK	UK£1	Rs 277
USA	US$1	Rs 201

For current exchange rates, see www.xe.com.

Daily Costs

Budget: Less than Rs 6000

- Hostel bed or guesthouse: Rs 1200–4000
- Local rice and curry: Rs 150–350
- Bus fares: under Rs 300 per day

Midrange: Rs 6000–20,000

- Double room in a midrange hotel: Rs 4000–14,000
- Restaurant meal: Rs 1000–3000
- Train travel, bike hire and occasional use of a car and driver: per day Rs 3000

Top End: More than Rs 20,000

- Top-end hotel: Rs 14,000 and up
- Meals at top-end places: from Rs 3000
- Daily use of car and driver: from Rs 9000

Opening Hours

Apart from tourist areas much is closed on Sunday.

Bars Usually 5pm to midnight; last call is often a sobering 11pm

Restaurants and cafes 8am to 9pm daily, later in areas popular with travellers

Offices 9am to 5.30pm Monday to Friday, 9am to 1pm Saturday

Shops and services 9am to 8pm (daily in tourist areas)

Arriving in Sri Lanka

Bandaranaike International Airport (Colombo) Sri Lanka's one main airport is 30km north of Colombo. From the airport, prepaid taxis cost Rs 2800 to Rs 3650 depending on destination; driving time to Fort is 30 to 45 minutes via the toll road (Rs 300 toll). Pre-arranged rides with Colombo hotels cost Rs 3000 to Rs 5000. Air-con buses via the toll road to Central Bus Station cost Rs 150 to Rs 200 and take one hour upwards, but stop 750m south of the airport at Awariwatta, a Rs 150 three-wheeler ride from the terminal.

Getting Around

Bus Buses are the country's main mode of transport. They connect most towns and charge low fares but are often crowded. Only major routes have air-con buses. Private buses offer a bit more comfort than government buses.

Car Many travellers use a hired car with a driver for all or part of their trip. This allows maximum flexibility and is the most efficient way to access the interior from the coast. Drivers are very helpful and founts of local knowledge.

Train The improving railway network serves major towns and can be more comfortable than buses (excepting third-class carriages). Some train journeys such as the trip from Haputale to Ella and Colombo to Galle are renowned for the epic scenery en route.

For much more on **getting around**, see p327

First Time Sri Lanka

For more information, see Survival Guide (p321)

Checklist

- Make sure your passport is valid for at least six months after your arrival date
- Check which vaccinations and medications are recommended
- Arrange for appropriate travel insurance
- Check the airline baggage restrictions
- Inform your debit-/credit-card company of your travel plans
- Arrange your visa online at least a week before you depart

What to Pack

- A good pair of earplugs
- Effective mosquito repellent – hard to find in Sri Lanka (unlike mosquitoes)
- Sunscreen – another surprisingly hard-to-find item
- Tampons – nearly impossible to find outside Colombo
- Extra camera cards and a spare phone-charging cable

Top Tips for Your Trip

- If you see a road heading towards the coast, take it and see what you find; there could be a stunning beach at the end.
- Ride the trains: you'll have great views of the scenery and a comfy seat, and you'll meet lots of locals.
- Eat where locals eat; a busy downtown 'hotel' (cafe) will serve rice and curry that's properly spicy and full-flavoured.
- *Poya* (full moon) nights see celebrations across the country, so time temple visits to coincide.

What to Wear

Shorts and a T-shirt will work most of the time, but bathing suits and bikinis are never appropriate away from tourist beaches. Bring a long-sleeved cotton top or shirt and a long skirt, sarong or light pants to cover up shoulders, arms and legs when visiting temples. Sandals are good for slipping off quickly when visiting religious sites. Bring a lightweight waterproof jacket or poncho or an umbrella in case of sudden downpours, and a warm fleece or sweater for the temperate mountains.

Sleeping

Sri Lanka has accommodation to suit all tastes and budgets. See p24 for more information

Guesthouses Inexpensive family-run guesthouses are found everywhere, offering a great way to interact with locals.

Hostels Geared to backpackers; numbers are growing in the main tourist centres.

Hotels From bargain basement to five star, found everywhere.

Resorts Offering one-stop luxury, found on all coasts and even near national parks.

Ayurvedic spas Many spas offer accommodation so you don't have to travel far to the massage table.

Rented villas From simple homes to grand places with a pool and private beach.

Transport Tips

Getting around Sri Lanka can be cheap, and occasionally uncomfortable, or expensive, and very comfortable. There isn't much cost difference between buses and trains, but trains offer a better vantage point and an easier ride. Hire a car and driver for maximum flexibility and air-conditioned comfort.

Bargaining

Unless you are shopping at a fixed-price shop, you must bargain. Generally, if someone quotes you a price, counter with half that. The seller will come down about halfway towards your price, and the last price will be a little higher than half the original price. Try and keep a sense of perspective; there's little point arguing over tiny amounts.

Tipping

Although a 10% service charge is added to food and accommodation bills, this usually goes straight to the owner rather than the worker.

Restaurants and bars 10% in cash to servers on top of the 'service charge'

Drivers 10%

Room cleaners Up to Rs 100 per day

Bag carriers/porters Rs 50 per bag

Shoe minders at temples Rs 30

Guides Varies greatly; agree to a fee *before* you set out

ADITYA SINGH/GETTY IMAGES ©

Leather goods for sale, Kandy (p164)

Etiquette

Sri Lankan cultural mores are easy to navigate if you remember a few key points.

Temple footwear Remove shoes and hats at temples. Socks are OK when walking scorching pavements.

Clothing Cover shoulders, arms and legs at temples as directed.

Buddha statues Never pose beside or in front of a statue (ie with your back to it), as this is considered disrespectful.

Buddha images Displaying body art or wearing clothing that includes an image of the Buddha can get you arrested and deported.

Photography Ask permission before photographing people. A few business-orientated folk like the stilt fishermen at Koggala will ask for payment.

Beach attire Nude and topless sunbathing are not allowed on beaches.

Modesty Overt displays of affection are frowned upon.

Shaking hands The left hand is used for ablutions and considered unclean; when shaking hands or passing things, just use your right hand.

Language

Many Sri Lankans speak English, but efforts to speak Sinhala or Tamil are always appreciated. In tourist areas, English is all you really need. See Language (p335) for more information.

What's New

The years since the end of Sri Lanka's long civil war have seen rapid change. New resorts are mushrooming along the shoreline, and formerly derelict districts are bursting back to life. Nowhere is Sri Lanka's renaissance more obvious than in Colombo, where showy new hotels and malls are pushing onto the skyline. What is less clear is whether this newfound optimism can survive the economic fallout of the global coronavirus pandemic.

Best in Travel

Sri Lanka was awarded first place in Lonely Planet's list of top 10 countries in 2019, in recognition of the country's impressive revival after years of conflict. Across the country, new resorts, hotels and restaurants are opening, transport links are expanding and the welcome for travellers is friendlier than ever.

Soaring Colombo

Colombo's skyline is climbing ever higher with towering developments like the new Colombo Lotus Tower (p75), the glass-walled Cinnamon Life (p66), and glamorous new hotels bursting up on every corner.

Colombo's Cafes

The cafe scene in Colombo is going from strength to strength too, with cool neighbourhood hideaways such as Café Kumbuk (p85) and Kiku (p85) leading the charge. Pull up a cappuccino and a slice of chocolate cake and exhale.

Megamalls, Everywhere!

New malls are springing up all over Colombo, hosting ritzy retail outlets from around the world, plus good food courts, clean toilets and icy air-conditioning. Try One Galle Face (p86) and Colombo City Centre (p86).

LOCAL KNOWLEDGE

WHAT'S HAPPENING IN SRI LANKA

Joe Bindloss, Lonely Planet Writer

Since the end of Sri Lanka's civil war, the island has seen peace and prosperity creeping in to replace conflict. Despite setbacks such as the deadly bombings of April 2019, new resorts are appearing all around the coast, colonial-era buildings have been restored from ruin, and new shopping malls are springing up all over the island. How Sri Lanka will weather the effects of the global coronavirus pandemic, however, remains to be seen. The government closed the island's borders early, and Sri Lanka has experienced a fraction of the cases seen by its near neighbours, but even with proposals for strict testing of future arrivals, the future for tourism is uncertain.

Against this backdrop, political controversy rumbles on. A commanding win in the 2020 parliamentary elections by the ruling coalition – led by Prime Minister Mahinda Rajapaksa and his brother, President Gotabaya Rajapaksa – was largely welcomed by Sinhalese Sri Lankans, but condemned by Tamils and other marginalised minority groups. In general though, in spite of the politics and the tumultuous events of 2020, most Sri Lankans are enjoying what looks to be a period of relative calm.

Kitesurfing Kalpitiya

What started as a secret scene has exploded, with more and more kitesurfing camps opening up in the lanes south of Kalpitiya town, and new places on often-overlooked Mannar Island, including Vayu Resort (p296).

Extra Sinharaja

Bird paradise Sinharaja Forest Reserve (p201) has expanded its borders to 360 sq km, with a string of new jungle lodges where birders can relax between safaris.

Domestic Flights

Slowly but surely, domestic flights are expanding, with new routes around the country offered by Cinnamon Air and Fits Air, including easy hops to Jaffna.

Airport Arrangements

Since the 2019 bombings, airport security is tighter than ever. You can still reach the airport by bus for a bargain price, but buses stop 750m south of the terminal at Awariwatta, where three-wheelers wait to take you to the airport gates.

More Ways to Explore Wilpattu

Long the backwater of Sri Lankan national parks, despite being the largest, Wilpattu National Park is easier to appreciate than ever, with a growing number of cool places to stay, including stylish Wilpattu Corridor (p100).

New Treats in the East

There are lots of new openings on the east coast, from herbal-cocktail-specialist Local Bar (p256) at Arugam Bay to caketastic bakery Taste & Treats (p264) in Batticaloa and colonial-cottage eatery Key Ceylon (p248) in Monaragala.

Fast Travels Down South

The opening of the southern expansion of Hwy E01 in February 2020 has cut journey times between Matara and Hambantota, speeding up access to Bundala National Park (p144) and other sights in the southwest of the country.

LISTEN, WATCH & FOLLOW

For inspiration and up-to-date news, visit www.lonely planet.com/sri-lanka/articles.

insta @srilanka Lots of pretty pictures of Sri Lanka for inspiration.

insta @destination_srilanka Posts from the government tourism department.

twitter #srilanka Captures a wide range of topics, including news and traveller posts.

twitter @tourismlk More news and tips from Sri Lanka's tourism department.

FAST FACTS

Food trend Cheese *kotthu* (*rotti* chopped up and mixed with fillings)

Number of World Heritage Sites 8

Language 87% of Sri Lankans speak Sinhala

Population 22.9 million

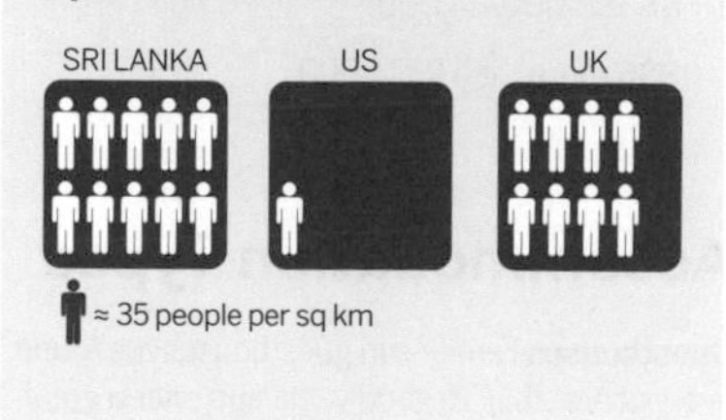

More of the North

With the lifting of military restrictions, it is now possible to follow the northern coastline all the way from Kankesanturai to Valvettiturai and on to Point Pedro. Fort Hammenhiel (p291) is now open to visitors, with a four-room hotel for overnight guests.

Ancient City Guesthouses

Dozens of new family-run guesthouses are opening in places such as Sigiriya, Polonnaruwa and Anuradhapura in the ancient cities area, meaning lots of options for budget travellers.

Finally a Ferry Route?

If plans go ahead, there will finally be a ferry route between Sri Lanka and India, linking Kankesanturai near Jaffna to either Karaikal or Sidambaranagar in Tamil Nadu. Watch this space!

Accommodation

Find more accommodation reviews throughout the On the Road chapters (from p59)

PRICE RANGES

The following price ranges refer to a double room with bathroom in high season. Unless otherwise stated, rooms come with a fan, and tax is included in the price.

$ less than Rs 4000

$$ Rs 4000–14,000

$$$ more than Rs 14,000

Accommodation Types

Guesthouses Family-run guesthouses are found everywhere; they're good value and offer a great way to interact with locals.

Hostels Geared to backpackers, these are less common but numbers are growing in the main tourist centres.

Hotels Ranging from bargain-basement to grand and expensive, found everywhere from back roads to beachfronts.

Resorts Offering one-stop luxury, the best resorts are found on the west and south coasts and around national parks.

Ayurvedic spas Many spas offer accommodation so you don't have to travel far to the massage table.

Rented villas Offer grand accommodation; some even have a private beach.

Best Places to Stay

Best on a Budget

Sri Lanka has a huge range of inexpensive guesthouse accommodation, from simple rooms in family homes in the hills to basic lodging near the sand. You might not get air-con or a bathroom in every room, but the home-cooked food can be spectacular. Hostels are also popping up in tourist towns across the island, offering dorm beds with curtains for privacy and lockers for valuables. Most places have a rooftop terrace or some outside space.

- Bunkyard Hostel (p76), Colombo
- D'Villa Garden House (p282), Jaffna
- Clock Inn (p161), Kandy
- Chamodya Homestay (p197), Ella
- Thisara Guest House (p219), Polonnaruwa
- Roy's Villa (p213), Sigiriya
- Ranga's Beach Hut (p254), Arugam Bay
- Nature House (p200), Uda Walawe

Best for Families

Families are well catered for in Sri Lanka. Most hotels can provide family rooms, or extra beds, but not everywhere has cots, so consider bringing a travel cot from home. Dedicated kids clubs are rare, except at all-inclusive resorts, but many places offer family-friendly activities, such as water sports and mangrove boat tours. With kids in tow, seek out places with a pool and beach access, either directly, or a short walk down the road. Rental villas can also be a good bet for families.

- Colombo Court Hotel & Spa (p75), Colombo
- Villa Araliya (p94), Negombo
- Zion View (p194), Ella
- Sharon Inn (p162), Kandy
- Hotel Susantha Garden (p103), Bentota
- Tree Tops Jungle Lodge (p250), Yudaganawa
- Riviera Resort (p263), Batticaloa

Best for Solo Travellers

Like birds, solo travellers have the best time when they flock together. The best hotels, guesthouses, hostels and resorts for solo travellers have shared spaces – roof terraces, gardens, beach bars, lounges, reading rooms – where you can connect with other travellers and swap tips from the road. The best options tend to be at the lower end of the price range, with a sociable vibe that usually makes up for the less luxurious facilities. You'll find plenty of like-minded travellers at dive or kitesurfing resorts and water-sport hubs.

➡ Clock Inn (p74), Colombo

➡ Ice Bear Guest House (p94), Negombo

➡ JJ's Hostel (p131), Mirissa

➡ Milano Tourist Rest (p231), Anuradhapura

➡ That's Why (p273), Nilaveli

➡ Kitesurfing Lanka (p99), Kalpitiya

➡ Upali Beach Surf Café and Resort (p253), Arugam Bay

➡ Dyke Rest (p269), Trincomalee

Best Beach Resorts

An incredible range and variety of beach resorts hug the idyllic Sri Lankan coast, from lavish, design-mag-worthy retreats with Ayurvedic spas and antiques in every room, to rustic, sand-floored cabanas beneath the palms. At all price points, you'll normally get beach access, loungers on the sand, a beachside restaurant, and often a beach-facing pool. Ocean-facing rooms invariably cost more than rooms further back from the surf.

➡ Ging Oya Lodge (p97), Waikkal

➡ Paradise Road – The Villa (p103), Bentota

➡ Barberyn Reef Ayurveda Resort (p104), Beruwela

➡ Aditya Resort (p108), Hikkaduwa

➡ Mangrove Beach Cabanas (p143), Tangalle

➡ Upali Beach Surf Café and Resort (p253), Arugam Bay

➡ Uga Jungle Beach Resort (p273), Nilaveli

Booking

Book well ahead for the peak tourist season, from December to March. At peak times, some beach resorts have a minimum stay, and prices everywhere are at their highest. When booking through websites such as Booking.com, some travellers have reported bookings not being honoured; it may be safer to book directly with hotels.

Lonely Planet (www.lonelyplanet.com/hotels) Find independent reviews, as well as recommendations on the best places to stay – and then book them online.

Airbnb (www.airbnb.com) This global rooms site is a good source for cheap (and not so cheap) rooms, villas and apartments for rent, including in major cities.

Booking.com (www.booking.com) Most hotels and guesthouses can be booked here, though some places are not enrolled and have to be booked directly.

Agoda (www.agoda.com) Most accommodation can be booked here, and some cheaper hostels and hotels take all their bookings through the site.

Holiday Lettings (www.holidaylettings.co.uk/sri-lanka) A wide range of villas for rent, brought to you by the folks at Tripadvisor.

Villa Sri Lanka (www.villainsrilanka.co.uk) Luxury villas for rent across the country, most with pools and other glam features.

JONATHON STOKES/LONELY PLANET ©

Uga Jungle Beach Resort, Nilaveli (p273)

Month by Month

TOP EVENTS

Duruthu Perahera, January

Maha Sivarathri, March

Avurudu (New Year), April

Vesak Poya, May

Kandy Esala Perahera, August

January

The peak of the tourist season. Crowds are at their largest, but many popular towns have special events such as the respected literary festival at Galle.

Duruthu Perahera

Held on the *poya* (full moon) day in the month of Duruthu, at the Kelaniya Raja Maha Vihara in Colombo, this lavish festival of lights, dances, parades and drumming celebrates the first of the Buddha's three visits to Sri Lanka. (p79)

Thai Pongal

Held in mid-January, this Hindu winter-harvest festival honours the sun god Surya. It is important to Tamils in Sri Lanka and South India. Hindu families prepare the special dish, *pongal* – rice cooked with palm sugar, nuts and spices.

February

Visitor numbers are still high, with wintering Europeans baking themselves silly on the beaches in the dry winter weather. This is a busy time for Sri Lankans, with Independence Day early in the month.

Independence Day

Sri Lanka gained independence from Britain on 4 February 1948 and this day is commemorated every year with festivals, parades, fireworks and sporting events across the nation. In Colombo, motorcades rush politicians from one ceremony to the next.

Navam Perahera

First celebrated in 1979, Navam Perahera is one of Sri Lanka's biggest and most flamboyant *peraheras* (processions). Held on the February *poya,* the parade starts from Colombo's Gangaramaya Temple and travels around Viharamahadevi Park and South Beira Lake.

March

Visitor numbers decline but early March (or late February) is an important time for Sri Lankan Hindus. You'll see devotees honouring Shiva at Hindu temples across the island.

Maha Sivarathri

In late February or early March the Hindu festival of Maha Sivarathri commemorates the marriage of Shiva to Parvati with all-night vigils and more. It's the most important day for Shaivites, who comprise the majority of Sri Lanka's Hindus.

April

Although Christians comprise only 6% of Sri Lanka's population, Christian festivals are still celebrated with gusto. Don't be surprised if you see the Easter bunny adorning shop windows for Easter.

Avurudu (New Year)

New Year's Eve (13 April) and New Year's Day (14 April) are nonreligious holidays. There is a period of a few hours between the old and new year called the 'neutral period' (*Nonagathe*) when all activities are meant to cease. Over the days before and after, buses and trains are jammed as people go to their home villages.

May

The Yala monsoon blows in for five months, bringing heavy rains from the Indian Ocean that drench the Hill Country and the beach towns in the southwest.

Vesak Poya

This two-day holiday commemorates the birth, enlightenment and death of the Buddha. Alongside public festivities, paper lanterns and displays of coloured lights adorn every Buddhist home, shop and temple. Night-time Colombo is a riot of colours.

Ramadan

Muslims make up a small percentage of Sri Lanka's population, but their prominence in commercial enterprises means that Muslim holidays are conspicuously observed. Islamic holidays move with the lunar calendar; in coming years, the annual Muslim fast (ending with the Id ul-Fitr feast) takes place on or around the following dates: 2 April to 1 May 2022, 22 March to 20 April 2023.

June

Sri Lanka's Buddhists barely have a chance to catch their breath after Vesak before another major religious event hits the calendar.

Poson Poya

The Poson *poya* day celebrates the introduction of Buddhism to Sri Lanka by the monk Mahinda. In Anuradhapura there are festivities in the famous temples, while in nearby Mihintale thousands of white-clad pilgrims ascend the calf-busting 1843 steps to the topmost temple.

July

Light-bulb vendors do lively business as Buddhists gear up for Esala Perahera, which begins at the end of the month. Light displays are an integral part of the Kandy festivities.

Vel

This Hindu festival is celebrated in Colombo and Jaffna in July and August. In Colombo the gilded chariot of Murugan (aka Skanda or Kartikeya), the Hindu god of war, is ceremonially hauled from Pettah to Bambalapitiya. In Jaffna, the Nallur Kandaswamy Kovil has a 25-day festival.

Esala Poya

This day celebrates the Buddha's first sermon as well as the arrival of the tooth relic in Sri Lanka. This latter milestone is why the ceremonies in Kandy – home of the relic – are especially vibrant and intense.

Kataragama Skanda Festival

Another important Hindu festival is held in July at Kataragama, where devotees put themselves through a whole gamut of acts of ritual self mortification. It commemorates the triumph of the six-faced, 12-armed war god Murugan over evil demons.

Eid ul-Adha

A three-day Islamic festival and part of the Haj or the pilgrimage to Mecca. It recalls Abraham's willingness to sacrifice his son for God. Islamic holidays move with the lunar calendar; in coming years, Eid ul-Adha falls on or around the following dates: 10 July 2022, 29 June 2023.

August

The Kandy Esala Perahera is legendary, but smaller parades are held across Sri Lanka. Many celebrations feature dancers, drummers and stilt-walkers who practise all year for the occasion.

Kandy Esala Perahera

The Kandy Esala Perahera (p163), Sri Lanka's most spectacular and prominent festival, is the climax of 10 days and nights of celebrations during the month of Esala. This great procession honours the sacred tooth relic of Kandy and festivities run from July into August.

Nallur Festival

Jaffna's Nallur Kandaswamy Kovil is the focus of an enormous and spectacular Hindu festival running over 25 days in July and August, which climaxes on day 24 with parades of juggernaut floats and gruesome displays of self-mutilation by entranced devotees.

POYA

Every *poya* (full moon) day is a holiday, and buses, trains and accommodation fill up, especially if the full moon falls on a Friday or Monday. No alcohol is supposed to be sold on *poya* days and many bars close, though some hotels discreetly provide cold beer 'under the table'.

Note that the official full-moon day for *poya* does not always coincide with the same designated full-moon day in Western calendars. Because of the religious time used to calculate the exact moment of full moon, the *poya* day may be a day earlier or later than that shown on regular lunar calendars.

September

The main tourist season comes to an end as the northern hemisphere summer ends. It's a good time to enjoy a less-crowded Sri Lanka. On the east coast the waves are also abating.

October

This is a time of meteorological change, as the Yala monsoon fades and conditions build towards the Maha monsoon. In many areas, thunderstorms arrive in the afternoons, and rain is common, but there's still good surfing on the east coast.

November

November continues October's storms and rain, particularly in the north and the ancient cities. The south and west get drier as the month moves on.

Deepawali

The Hindu festival of lights takes place in early November (or late October). Fireworks burst and thousands of flickering oil lamps celebrate the triumph of good over evil and the return of Rama after his period of exile.

European Film Festival

Sri Lanka's nascent film industry gets its chance to show off during this festival (www.facebook.com/EuropeanFilmFestival) held at various venues in Colombo, usually in October.

December

Sri Lanka's second annual monsoon season, the Maha, brings heavy rains to the northeast part of the island. This is not the time to plan a Jaffna beach holiday.

Adam's Peak Pilgrimage

The pilgrimage season, when pilgrims of all faiths (and the odd tourist) climb Adam's Peak (p175) near Ella, starts in December and lasts until May. The trek begins shortly after midnight so that everyone can reach the sacred footprint at the summit for sunrise.

Unduvap Poya

Moving around the month of December depending on the timing of the full moon, this festival commemorates Sangamitta, daughter of the Indian emperor Ashoka, who in 288 BCE brought a cutting from the sacred Bodhi Tree in India to Anuradhapura. Thousands flock to pay their respects at the Sri Maha Bodhi, cultivated from that same cutting and nurtured for over 2000 years.

Christmas

Sri Lanka's Christian communities – mostly around Colombo – celebrate Christmas enthusiastically, and followers of other faiths also join in secular events over the holidays. Local versions of Western Christmas traditions can be found everywhere, from bone-thin Santas in strange masks to garish artificial trees.

Itineraries

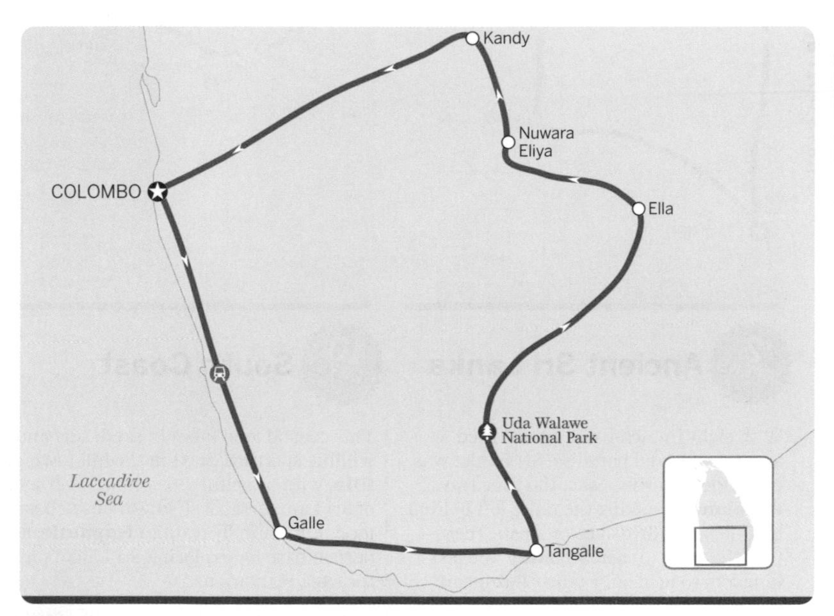

Essential Sri Lanka

This compact trip covers a core selection of Sri Lanka's must-see sights.

Start in **Colombo**, exploring the markets and visiting the city's revitalised Fort district. Then take the train south along the shore to beguiling **Galle**, avoiding the often traffic-clogged road on the west coast.

After Galle, you've earned some beach time. The **Tangalle** region has a growing selection of beachfront places to stay on its beautiful and uncrowded ribbon of sand. Head inland and grab your camera for plentiful photo-ops in elephant-filled **Uda Walawe National Park**. Take the winding road on up into the heart of the Hill Country and put down roots for a few days in **Ella**, a cool mountain town with a fun traveller feel.

To see more of the high country, take one of the world's most beautiful train rides to the stop for the British colonial heritage town of **Nuwara Eliya**, where you'll enter a time warp. Amble and taste at historic tea plantations and stop in iconic **Kandy** to pay your respects at the temple housing a tooth of the Buddha. From here it's an easy jaunt back to Colombo or the airport.

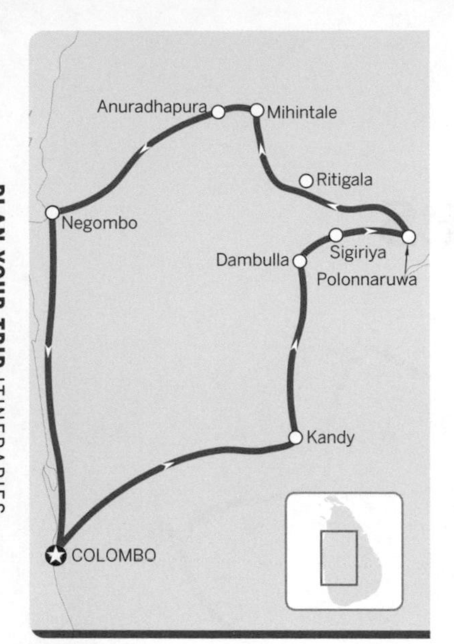

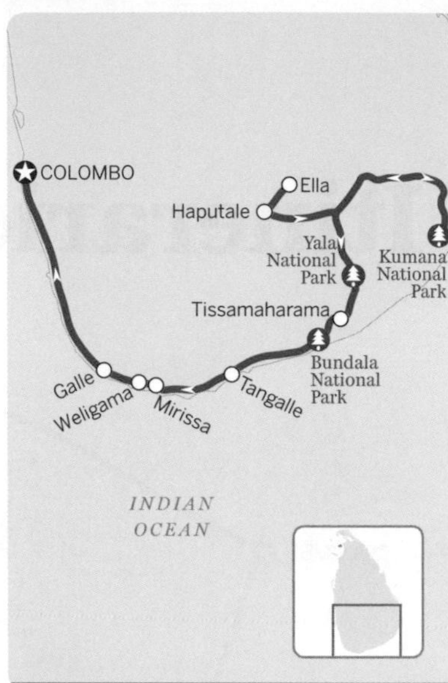

2 WEEKS Ancient Sri Lanka

With eight Unesco-listed sites dotted around an island paradise, Sri Lanka was made for exploring. Start the time travel in **Colombo**, visiting the relics left behind by Dutch and British colonialists, then take the train to sacred **Kandy**, the last kingdom to hold out against European invaders.

Next, take a bus north to **Dambulla**, where vividly painted statues and murals fill a network of rocky caverns. Next stop, **Sigiriya**; explore the gardens at the base of the outcrop before climbing to the summit for epic views. Onwards to **Polonnaruwa**, where the carvings and statues mark the high point of ancient Sri Lankan art. Consider a bonus detour to ruined **Ritigala** before moving on from the centre of the island.

Head on to **Mihintale**, the spot where the king of Sri Lanka converted to Buddhism. One more hop will take you to sprawling, wonderful **Anuradhapura**, where towering dagobas (stupas) mark the extents of Sri Lanka's first Buddhist kingdom. Finally, drop down to the coast, with a little easy-going beach time in **Negombo** before closing the circle in Colombo.

10 DAYS South Coast

This coastal loop takes in sand, surf and wildlife spotting. Start in the hill town of **Ella**, with peaceful forest hikes, and some of Sri Lanka's tastiest, guesthouse-cooked food. Flit south by train to **Haputale**, a perfect base for exploring Sri Lanka's historic tea plantations.

Now the big fun begins. Tumble downhill to seek leopards in **Yala National Park** – or in nearby **Kumana National Park** (formerly Yala East National Park), with half the crowds. Continue just a little further to the temple town of **Tissamaharama**, where a gleaming stupa rises near a scenic lake. Hit the coast by the wetlands of **Bundala National Park**, to spy flamingos and eagles, then take a well-earned day at the beach at **Tangalle**. A short hop west will take you to **Mirissa**, where you can spot blue whales offshore.

For the final run to the capital, try a day of starter surfing at **Weligama**, before exploring gorgeous, historic **Galle**. One last easy train ride will deposit you in **Colombo**, Sri Lanka's pulsing capital city.

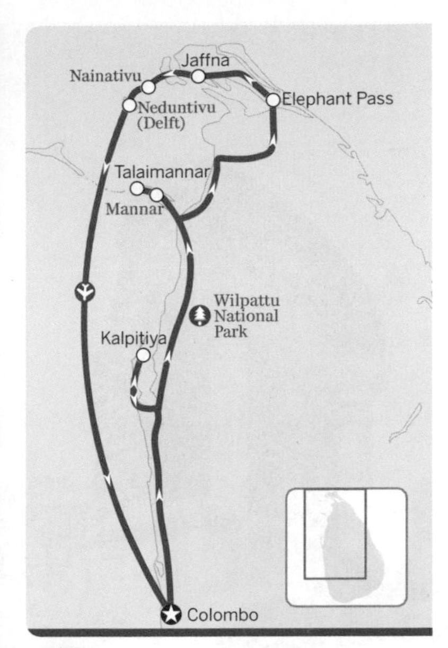

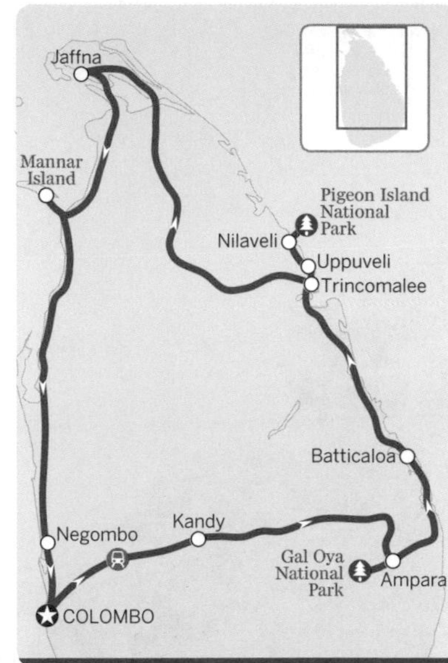

1 WEEK Emerging North

With prolonged peace and restoration of road and train links in Sri Lanka's north, visitors are discovering the beauty, beaches and culture of this fascinating region.

Start in **Colombo**, for fine food, fascinating museums and culture, then head quickly north to **Kalpitiya**, for dolphin-spotting safaris and kitesurfing on the Kalpitiya Lagoon. Roll north, with a detour inland to under-explored **Wilpattu National Park**, a haven for leopards with none of the crowds seen further south. Next, head to **Mannar**, an island that looks to be thumbing a ride to India. Remote **Talaimannar** looks out at Adam's Bridge, a chain of reefs and islets said to have been created by the Hindu monkey god Hanuman.

Continue north through **Elephant Pass**, with its bombastic war memorials, to **Jaffna**, where Tamil culture and cuisine thrives amidst the colonial backstreets. Head off the map to **Nainativu**, a tiny speck of an island with Buddhist and Hindu temples, and **Neduntivu (Delft)**, a windswept place where wild ponies roam. Flights wait to whisk you back to Colombo to close the circle.

2 WEEKS Off-Season Sojourn

Peak-season crowds can be overwhelming but visit out of season and a new Sri Lanka emerges, with a lively, local vibe, plus the weather is still good in the north and east.

Kick off in **Colombo**, then when you've drunk your fill of city life, board the train for **Kandy**, Sri Lanka's spiritual heart, and take in ancient temples and the tea museum. Continue over the hump of the island to **Ampara**, a backwater town with some interesting Buddhist sites, and consider a detour to uncrowded **Gal Oya National Park**. Access the coast at **Batticaloa**, with its beaches, Dutch fort and diverse religious heritage.

Follow the coast north to **Trincomalee**, with its Hindu temples and Dutch relics, then kick back on the sands of **Uppuveli** and **Nilaveli**, and scuba dive or snorkel nearby in peaceful **Pigeon Island National Park**. Loop back though Trincomalee to **Jaffna**, for a taste of vibrant Tamil culture. Circle onwards to **Mannar Island**, for views over romantically remote shorelines. There's time for one more stop on the sand for a spa treat at **Negombo**, before zipping back to Colombo.

ATTILA JANDI/SHUTTERSTOCK ©

Top: Vatadage, Polonnaruwa (p223)

Bottom: National Museum, Colombo (p67)

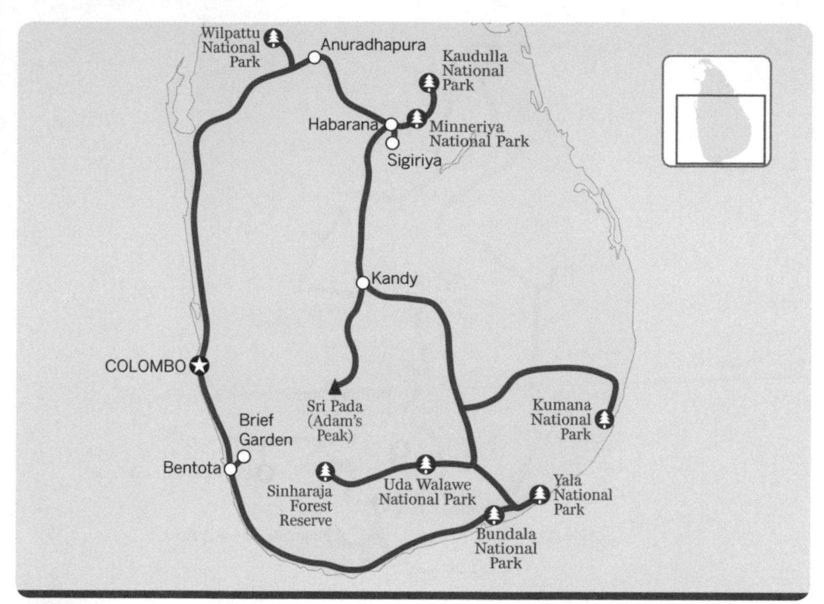

Wildife Wonders

Sri Lanka's amazing biodiversity is a reason to visit all by itself, and you'll want to bring plenty of camera cards for pics of wild elephants, leopards, blue whales and other beasties in their natural habitat.

Flying into **Colombo**, leave the city smog behind quickly and follow the coast north to little-explored **Wilpattu National Park**, for a crowd-free introduction to Sri Lankan wildlife. Connect inland through stupa-studded **Anuradhapura**, before crossing to equally historic **Sigiriya**, to learn the lie of the land looking out over the centre of the island.

Stop over in **Habarana**, and use it as a base for exploring **Minneriya National Park** and adjacent **Kaudulla National Park**, both thronged by elephants, particularly during the Gathering from June to September. Hightail it south to spiritual **Kandy**, and loop to **Sri Pada (Adam's Peak)** for more epic views over the island.

Make your next stop **Uda Walawe National Park**, staying at one of the lodges inside this lush, green elephant habitat (and watch for crocodiles in the park's watering holes). From here, you have two choices: go wegct itst to **Sinharaja Forest Reserve**, for foot safaris in one of Asia's top birding habitats, or join the hordes heading east to **Yala National Park**, where you have a good chance of seeing leopards, though photos will most likely include lots of other animal spotters. You'll see similar wildlife and fewer people closer to the coast at **Kumana National Park**.

For bonus wildlife, follow the coast west to lovely **Bundala National Park**, whose dunes and lagoons provide a home for crocodiles, wild boar and abundant birdlife, amongst other critters. As you loop back via the southwest, drop in on the lush gardens and art collection at **Brief Garden** near **Bentota**, then back up your camera cards in Colombo before heading home.

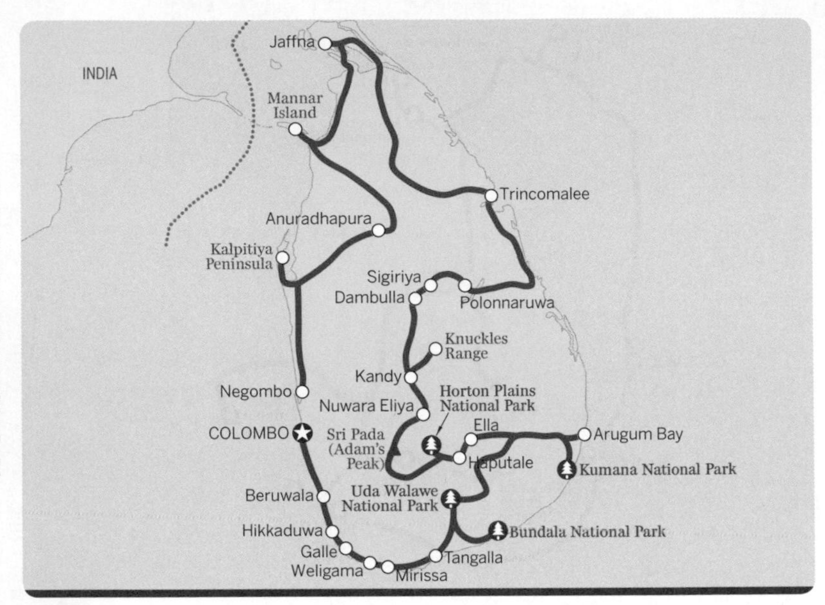

Almost Everything

With several weeks at your disposal, you can explore the island in real depth. Start in **Colombo**, with its museums, monuments and fantastic food. After the city crush, recharge at an Ayurvedic spa just south along the coast in **Beruwela**, then pause for sand and surf nearby at **Hikkaduwa**.

Next, roll into historic **Galle**, Sri Lanka's most charming coastal city, to soak up the history vibe, then tackle the easy-to-conquer surf breaks at **Weligama**. Go whale watching from **Mirissa**, then find your own isolated stretch of sand near **Tangalle**. Detour inland to **Uda Walawe National Park**, for your first elephant encounter in Sri Lanka. Another short hop along the coast will take you to the birdwatching playground of **Bundala National Park**, and the chance of leopard encounters at **Kumana National Park**. Put up your feet for a few days in the fun surf hub of **Arugam Bay**.

Next head for the hills, starting off in **Ella**, departure point for the scenic train ride to **Haputale**. Continue west to trek over the exposed plateau of **Horton Plains National Park**, then try hiking of a different kind on the busy pilgrimage route to the summit of **Sri Pada (Adam's Peak)**. Next, check into a colonial-era hotel in **Nuwara Eliya** and explore the tea country. Roll north to cultured **Kandy**, and visit the **Knuckles Range** on your way towards the ancient cities.

Start the history lesson in the cave temples of **Dambulla**, then climb to the rock-top palace/fortress of **Sigiriya** and drop down to carving-filled **Polonnaruwa**. Drop back down to the coast at **Trincomalee** and feel the change from Sinhalese to Tamil culture as you journey north to **Jaffna**.

Swing by remote islands, then turn south to **Mannar Island**, for views towards India, and swing inland to stunning, temple-covered **Anuradhapura**. Take a dolphin safari back on the coast on the **Kalpitiya Peninsula**, then wind up your trip in **Negombo**, a short hop from Bandaranaike International Airport.

Plan Your Trip

Eat & Drink Like a Local

A melting pot of Indian, Southeast Asian and Arabic flavours, incredibly fresh herbs and spices and the bounty of the land and sea, Sri Lankan cooking is a feast for the senses. Eating out here is a delight, whether tucking into an authentic roadside rice and curry, a plate of *kotthu* (fried chopped *rotti*) at a downtown hole-in-the-wall or surf-fresh seafood at an oceanfront restaurant. Eat where the locals eat to enjoy Sri Lankan food at its most fiery and full-flavoured.

Food Experiences

From the Sea

Ministry of Crab, Colombo (p79) A temple to crustaceans, with crabs served an amazing variety of ways.

Bu Ba, Colombo (p82) Seafood served at candle-lit tables right on Mt Lavinia beach.

Bambini's Cafe & Restaurant, Hikkaduwa (p108) A thatched-roofed hut serving the freshest seafood around at bargain prices.

AQUA Forte, Galle (p120) Sublime, modern Italian seafood rich with the tastes of the Indian Ocean.

Galaxy Lounge, Arugam Bay (p255) Rice and curry so good the Sri Lankan cricket team came back for seconds.

Riviera Resort, Batticaloa (p263) Crab curries that make a great overture to a coda by the town's famous singing fish.

Intense Flavours

Nihonbashi Honten, Colombo (p81) Gourmet Japanese that's one of Colombo's most stylish dining experiences.

Fort Printers, Galle (p117) A historic setting for a modern, inventive East-meets-West menu.

The Year in Fruit

Sri Lanka's diverse topography means that the variety of fruit is staggering.

Year-Round

Many fruits – including bananas (over 20 varieties!), papayas and pineapples – are available year-round, as are jackfruit and breadfruit, which are often made into savoury dishes. Also look out for varieties of knobbly and bag-like *anoda* (soursop).

Apr–Jun

The first mangoes appear in April in the north: the Karuthakolamban (or Jaffna) mango thrives in dry parts of the island and is prized for its golden flesh and juicy texture. Rambutans (a red-skinned fruit with hairy skin) are at their best in June.

Jul–Sep

It's peak season for durian, that huge, spiky, love-it-or-hate-it fruit that smells so pungent that it's banned from public transport in some countries – you won't find this one on the breakfast buffet. Mangosteens, delicately flavoured purple-skinned fruit, are also harvested at this time.

Cafe C Ella, Ella (p195) Shack in the hills where flavours are authentic to the max.

Bedspace Kitchen, Unawatuna (p125) Deceptively casual garden restaurant where the cooking is highly accomplished and contemporary.

Coconut Beach Lodge, Uppuveli (p271) Sleep off the authentic Sri Lankan breakfast under the garden palms.

Peninsula Restaurant, Jaffna (p284) Tops for curried crab, cuttlefish and *odiyul khool* (seafood stew thickened with palmyrah root flour).

Meals with a View

Church Street Social, Galle (p117) Dine on the street-facing veranda or in the atmospheric colonial dining room.

Sharon Inn, Kandy (p162) This place offers stupendous views of the Kandy hills and richly spiced local cuisine.

Hill Club, Nuwara Eliya (p184) Classic, baronial-style dining room with British menu and adjacent billiards room.

Farm Resorts, Adam's Peak (p177) Artfully prepared Asian and western dishes with a view out over stacked-up tea fields.

Hideaway Restaurant, Arugam Bay (p255) This international eatery is buried in a garden of tropical vines.

Crab, Uppuveli (p272) Taste the surf in this romantic beachside fish restaurant.

Dining with Class

Governor's Restaurant, Colombo (p82) A historic hotel-restaurant that's perfect for Sunday lunch.

Paradise Road Gallery Cafe, Colombo (p81) Alfresco dining in a gorgeous courtyard villa, once the office of architect Geoffrey Bawa.

Empire Café, Kandy (p164) An old favourite in atmospheric colonial premises.

Royal Dutch Cafe, Galle (p118) Sip fine teas and coffees or enjoy a meal in this elegant colonnaded structure.

Sanctuary at Tissawewa, Anuradhapura (p240) Refined dining in the former residence of a British governor.

Key Ceylon, Monaragala (p248) Proof that colonial relics can be cute, set in a bygone-era cottage.

Cafe Cool

Barefoot Garden Cafe, Colombo (p80) Stylish courtyard cafe in the Barefoot gallery.

Commons, Colombo (p81) Laid-back and popular, with big flavours – the beef curry here is simply spectacular.

Old Railway Cafe, Galle (p120) Fine cafe well worth venturing outside the Fort's walls for.

Main Bites, Arugam Bay (p120) If jaggery doesn't do it for you, the Nordic cheesecakes here might!

Dutch Bank Cafe, Trincomalee (p269) Urban chic opposite Trinco's famous harbour.

Time for Tea

High Tea at the Grand, Nuwara Eliya (p185) For cucumber sandwiches, dainty cakes and a vast selection of different teas.

T-Lounge by Dilmah, Colombo (p79) An atmospheric setting for a cuppa in a colonial building in the historic Fort.

Handunugoda Tea Estate, Ahangma (p127) Tour the tea estate, sip 40 different brews and dive into some homemade chocolate cake.

Cheap Treats

Kotthu A spicy stir-fried combo of chopped *rotti* bread, vegetables and cheese, meat or egg. Try it at the Hotel De Pilawoos (p84), Colombo.

Paratha A filling flatbread that's pan-fried on a hotplate, particularly popular in Hindu quarters.

Vadai Generic term for disc- or doughnut-shaped deep-fried snacks, usually made from lentil flour.

Coconut rotti Locals eat this toasted minibread, sold by street vendors and also known as *pol rotti*, with a chilli-salt topping.

Samosa A ubiquitous snack: fried pastry pyramids, stuffed with spicy cooked vegetables.

Cooking Classes

Growing numbers of cooking courses in towns popular with travellers offer an introduction to Sri Lankan cooking, and an invaluable explanation of how to prepare unfamiliar ingredients. In a morning or afternoon, you'll learn to make your own rice and curry spread. Good options include the following:

RICE & CURRY

The national dish, rice and curry is an umbrella term for a broad family of complex, intricately spiced vegetable (and often meat and fish) dishes, served with rice. A meal might consist of half a dozen curries, with at least one based on meat, poultry, fish, seafood or egg, and one made from *dal* (lentils). On the side, pickles, chutneys and *pol sambol* (a condiment made from coconut pounded with chilli) add extra heat. Curries made for the tourist market are toned down; eat local for full-on fiery flavours.

Virtually all Sri Lankan curries are based on coconut milk and a blend of spices, including – but not limited to – chilli, turmeric, cinnamon, cardamom, coriander, lemongrass, *rampe* (pandanus leaves), curry leaves, mustard and tamarind. Dried fish is also frequently used as a seasoning.

Chicken and mutton form the foundation of Sri Lankan meat-based cooking, with plenty of beef dishes outside of Tamil Hindu regions and some pork dishes in non-Muslim areas.

As you travel around the country, you'll often have occasion to pull over at a local restaurant for a rice and curry feed. Some of the best places are simple family-owned restaurants by the roadside, offering a daily selection of meat, fish and veg dishes (sometimes with as many as 10 choices). It's a vastly more exciting introduction to Sri Lankan cuisine than eating at a tourist restaurant.

Many restaurants only serve rice and curry at lunchtime. Guesthouses will often prepare it for dinner but you'll need to order it early in the day to give cooks time to work their magic.

Aunty's, Colombo (p83)

Best Kandy Kitchen, Kandy (p161)

East N' West On Board, Batticaloa (p263)

Lanka's Restaurant & Cooking Classes, Ella (p193)

Matey Hut Cooking Classes, Ella (p193)

Wasantha's Sri Lankan Cuisine, Unawatuna (p123)

Sri Lankan Specialities

Rice is the bedrock of Sri Lankan cuisine and a key part of the national dish (rice and curry). Rice flour is also a basis for all sorts of unique local fried staples and snacks. Many Sri Lankans are vegetarian, so meat-free eating is easy and vegetable dishes are varied and abundant. Coconut is another core ingredient added to most dishes. 'Devilled dishes' are any type of meat or fish cooked in a spicy, sweet-and-sour-style sauce with onion and peppers.

Rice

Hoppers Bowl-shaped pancakes (also called *appa* or *appam*) made from rice flour, coconut milk and palm toddy. If eggs are added it becomes an egg hopper. *Sambol* (spicy coconut relish) is often added for flavouring.

String hoppers The *other* hoppers; rice noodles, steamed into tangled nests and served for breakfast.

Dosas (Thosai) Paper-thin pancakes made from rice and lentil flour batter, often stuffed with spiced vegetables.

Kola kanda A nutritious porridge of rice, coconut, green vegetables and herbs.

Rice and curry The national dish could be any of a hundred different spiced stews made from vegetables, meat or fish.

Biryanis Fragrant basmati rice cooked with plenty of turmeric, garlic and cardamom, often with chunks of chicken or lamb.

Vegetable Dishes

All sorts of vegetables are cooked into spicy sauces, soups and curries. Look out for the following specialities:

Mallung Slightly like tabbouleh, this salad combines chopped local greens (such as kale), shredded coconut and onion.

Wambatu moju (brinjal pickle) Not so much a pickle as a stir-fry; eggplants fried together with sweet shallots, spices, vinegar and, often, anchovies.

Jackfruit curry The world's biggest fruit combines beautifully with rich curry sauces, as its flesh actually has quite a meaty texture.

Breads

Bakeries are common throughout the country, but Western-style bread and cakes can be disappointing; local-style 'short eats' (spiced pastries) are much more rewarding.

Rotti Thick flatbreads cooked on a hotplate and served with sweet or savoury fillings. Seek out *pol rotti*, prepared with grated coconut.

Kotthu Chopped *rotti* fried with vegetables and/or egg, cheese or meat on a hotplate. The 'dolphin' version uses a doughier *rotti*, but no dolphin!

Uttapam A Tamil speciality, this thick rice and lentil pancake is prepared with onion, chillies, peppers and vegetables.

Seafood

Fish, crabs and other seafood is used extensively in soups, sauces, grills and curries. Local delicacies include the following:

Devilled tuna Devilled in Sri Lanka means 'cooked in a sweet, sour and spicy sauce', and tuna is one of the most popular starting points.

Jaffna crab Recipes vary but tamarind and coconut are key ingredients to bring out the flavour of this unique dish.

Ambulthiyal A southern speciality, this rich, fish curry is made with *goraka*, a fruit that gives it a sour flavour.

Condiments

Pol sambol Shredded coconut, lime juice, red onions, chilli and spices, often served with hoppers.

Lunu miris Red onions, salt, chilli powder, lime juice and dried fish.

Achcharu Local spicy pickles, made from carrot, onions, beans, peppers and chilli.

Gotukola sambol A green, tabbouleh-like salad made from the Pennywort plant.

Desserts & Sweets

Wattalappam (*vattalappam* in Tamil) A coconut milk and egg pudding with jaggery and cardamom.

Pittu Cylindrical cakes made from flour and coconut, steamed in bamboo.

Curd Natural yoghurt; it's often served drizzled with *kitul* treacle made from raw palm sugar.

Pani pol A small pancake made with a sweet topping of cinnamon and cardamom-infused jaggery.

Bolo fiado A layered cake said to have been first introduced by the Portuguese.

Ice cream Widely available in exotic local flavours, including Indian-influenced *kulfi* with pistachios.

Eating in Sri Lanka

When to Eat

Sri Lankans generally eat three meals a day, and the type of food consumed at each meal is quite distinct, so you usually won't find lunch foods (like rice and curry) available at dinner time.

Breakfast A typical Sri Lankan breakfast is served (for locals) around sunrise and consist of hoppers (or string hoppers) and some fruit. In hotels and guesthouses popular with tourists, Western-style breakfasts are almost always available. Milky tea is usually taken with breakfast; in the cities some favour coffee.

Lunch Eaten between midday and 2.30pm. Rice and curry, the definitive Sri Lankan meal, is an essential experience – this staple meal can be a lavish banquet with multiple elements, or a simple pit-stop canteen meal, depending on the place.

Dinner Usually eaten between 7pm and 9pm. If you really don't fancy more chilli and spice for dinner, seafood and fish dishes are often lightly spiced, and fried rice is usually mild.

Where to Eat

Sri Lanka is quite unusual by Asian standards in that most locals prefer to eat at home. Things are different in beach resorts and the capital, but in many towns there are actually very few restaurants, or even street-food stalls. Often, you'll eat in your guesthouse or hotel rather than out on the street.

Accommodation Most travellers eat breakfast where they are staying. Evening meals are often available too, though guesthouses will ask you to order ahead, so they can purchase ingredients. Larger hotels usually offer buffet lunches and dinners with a mix of Western and (toned-down) local food.

'Hotels' When is a hotel not a hotel? When it's in Sri Lanka. Restaurants here are also called 'hotels', and these urban eateries are the default restaurant for locals. Many are simple, verging on scruffy, with a counter at the front selling snacks and drinks to go and tables at the rear for sit-down meals. Rice and curry is the lunchtime staple; for dinner *kotthu*, fried rice, biryani and noodle dishes are popular.

Restaurants In Colombo, beach resorts and tourist-geared towns (like Galle), you'll find excellent restaurants offering everything from curried local crabs to Mexican burritos and pizza. Seek out local restaurants offering authentic rice and curry amidst the generic places aimed at tourists.

Bakeries Local bakeries specialise in 'short eats', essentially an array of meat- or fish-stuffed rolls, meat-and-vegetable patties (called cutlets), pastries and *vadai*. At some places, a plate of short eats is placed on your table and you're only charged for what you eat. Many bakeries (and some restaurants) also offer a 'lunch packet', basically some rice and a couple of small portions of curry. A similar preparation baked together in banana leaves is *lamprais*; if you see it anywhere, order it, as it's invariably delicious.

Drinks

Sri Lanka's heat means that refreshing beverages are an important – if not vital – part of the day's intake.

Tea & Coffee

Sri Lankans enjoy the island's famous tea, usually served hot, with spoonfuls of sugar. If you don't have a sweet tooth, be very assertive about lowering the sugar dose. You'll find both 'plain' versions, and Indian-style spiced tea, often pepped up with ginger. To appreciate Sri Lankan tea in all it's complexity, seek out upmarket cafes, which serve leaves from local estates the way nature intended: black, with no sugar.

Coffee has become a hot commodity in Colombo and areas popular with tourists. Cafes with espresso machines are catching on, though are not as widespread as in most Western nations – if all else fails, Italian-run pizza restaurants will make you a decent cup. Out in the sticks be prepared for instant coffee whisked up from a tin with minimum fuss.

Soft Drinks

You'll want to keep topped up with purified water, but lime juice is also highly refreshing. Locals mix it with still water or soda water and salt and/or sugar, making an isotonic electrolyte replenisher. Indian restaurants and sweet shops are a good spot for a *lassi* (drinking yoghurt). Ginger beer is an old-school, British-inspired beverage, offering fizz and zing – look out for the Elephant or Lion brands. *Thambili* (king coconut) water served in the husk can be found on sale at roadside stalls everywhere.

Beer

Locally brewed Lion Lager is a crisp and refreshing brew, found everywhere. Lion also sells a very good 8.8% stout (also known as Sinha Stout) with coffee and chocolate flavours. Three Coins and Anchor are less delicious local lagers. Licensed versions of international brands like Carlsberg and Heineken are also available.

Craft beer can be found in Colombo, but it's very rare elsewhere. The Three Coins brewery makes some tasty lagers, ales and *witbiers*.

Toddy & Arrack

Toddy is a lightly alcoholic drink made from the sap of palm trees. It has a sharp taste, a bit like cider. There are three types: toddy made from coconut palms, toddy from *kitul* palms and toddy from palmyra palms. Toddy shacks are found throughout the country, but are very much a male preserve. Arrack is a fermented and (somewhat) refined toddy. It can have a powerful kick and give you a belting hangover. The best mixer for arrack is the local ginger ale.

Hiriketiya (p1

Plan Your Trip

Beaches & Activities

As the quintessential tropical island, Sri Lanka is blessed with astonishing beaches, from wave-lashed surf beaches to sheltered sandy coves. Water-based activities include scuba diving, surfing and whale watching, but if horizontal lounging is more your thing, you've come to the right place.

MARIUS DOBILAS/SHUTTERSTOCK ©

Best Beaches For...

Diving & Snorkelling

Pigeon Island off Nilaveli beach offers crystal waters, shallow reefs, colourful fish, and diving and snorkelling that's great for divers of all levels.

Whale Watching

Whales can be seen all along the Sri Lankan coast but Mirissa is the best base for seeing the blue whales that surge past Dondra Head.

Exploring

Jaffna's islands offer a stunning array of white-sand bays and remote coves, where you can leave the crowds far behind, travelling by scooter or bicycle.

Indulgence

Bentota beach has an unrivalled collection of lavish and lovely boutique hotels. When you're done with pampering, the beach itself isn't bad.

Solitude

We almost want to keep this one to ourselves, but seeing as you asked nicely...Talalla beach is utterly empty and utterly divine – for the time being at least. Treat it gently!

When to Go

The main tourist season coincides with the northeast or Maha monsoon, which runs from December to March, leaving the east coast wet but the west coast sunny and dry. Between May and September, the stronger southwest or Yala monsoon hits the island and the southwest coast is drenched, while the east coast is drier, thanks to the rain shadow of the highlands.

As a general guide, the beaches of the west coast are the most developed, but the south coast is catching up fast. Things get quieter as you head east, and development fizzles out almost entirely if you head to the far north of the country.

Safe Swimming

As elsewhere in South Asia, currents, rip currents and undertows are a fact of life in Sri Lanka. Every year, there are drownings, so it pays to respect the water. If you aren't an experienced swimmer or surfer, look to sheltered beaches such as those at Unawatuna, Passekudah and Uppuveli, which offer calm waters for less confident swimmers and children. There are few full-time lifesaving patrols, so take charge of your own safety; ask locally about water conditions and swim cautiously.

Beach Culture

Even on popular beaches in the South and West, remember that the vast majority of Sri Lankans are socially conservative. Topless sunbathing is a no-no anywhere and few local women would go so far as to wear a bikini. Keep skimpy swimwear for the water, and use a shirt or sarong to cover up if you head off the sand into any village or town. Attitudes can be even more conservative in the East and North; consider wearing shorts and a T-shirt to swim in these areas. Most resort hotels have pools where you can sunbathe freely without fear of giving offence or being hassled.

Best Beaches

Talk about opening a can of worms, but in the interest of sun-lounger debates across Sri Lanka here's our pick of the nation's finest stretches of sand.

Ahangama (p128) Centre of the serious surf scene, with consistent breaks, and a low down, easy mood.

Arugam Bay (p251) One of the best surf spots in the country, with a fun traveller buzz.

Bentota (p101) A long and lovely sweep of golden sand backed by design-savvy boutique hotels.

Hiriketiya (p137) Once peaceful, now hip and buzzing, but still utterly tropical, and not blighted by traffic noise.

Mirissa (p131) Idyllic south-coast beach with something of a party scene and the best base for whale watching.

Passekudah (p266) An upscale escape for those who like a little luxury with their sand, sea and sun.

Tangalle (p141) A fine collection of sands, from buzzy town beaches to isolated coves, and pieces of perfection such as Marakolliya Beach.

Thalpe (p126) The stunning beaches of Thalpe are some of the quietest on the south coast.

Uppuveli & Nilaveli (p270 & p272) Two favourite sandy stretches for independent travellers on the east coast.

Surfing

Sri Lanka has consistent surf year-round, but the quality of waves is variable compared to nearby Maldives and Indonesia. On the other hand, Sri Lanka is a superb place to learn how to surf or for intermediate surfers to get their first reef-break experiences. Many of the best waves break very close to shore so surf access couldn't be easier.

On the east coast, surf's up from April to October. On the west and south coasts, the best surfing is from November to April. Boards can be hired (expect to pay Rs 1200 to Rs 1500 per day) and lessons are available at most beach towns; courses start at around Rs 2500.

Best Surf Spots

Ahangama & Midigama (p128) The best spots along the south coast, with a mellow left point, a consistent beach break and a short and sharp right reef, which frequently hollows.

Arugam Bay (p252) Sri Lanka's best-known wave is at Arugam Bay on the east coast. Surfers crowd this long right point from April to October.

Weligama (p129) A prime spot for learning to surf, and a number of surf schools and camps have recently sprung up there.

Surfing, Hikkaduwa (p106)

Hikkaduwa (p106) This west-coast resort is a long-time favourite, although more for the resort buzz than the quality of waves.

White-Water Rafting, Kayaking & Boating

Currently Sri Lanka's best-known white-water rafting river is the Kelaniya Ganga near Kitulgala, with both gentle stretches and descents on Class IV to V rapids. However, new dams under construction may curtail the white-water fun here. Rates with operators such as Action Lanka (p72) start at US$65 per person.

Kayaking is possible at many spots along the coast, including the lagoons around Batticaloa (p260), Tangalle (p141) and Bentota (p102). Boat or catamaran trips for sightseeing, birdwatching and fishing are offered from most west-coast, east-coast and south-coast beach resorts.

SAIKO3P/SHUTTERSTOCK ©

Top: White-water rafting, Kelaniya Ganga (175)

Bottom: Kitesurfing, Kalpitiya (p99)

Dolphin, Mirissa (p131)

Windsurfing & Kitesurfing

Sri Lanka isn't famous for windsurfing but that doesn't mean there's no action. Most beach resorts can arrange windsurfing equipment (from US$15 per hour) and lessons for beginners (from US$75 for a three-hour course). Bentota has plenty of water sports centres (p102).

Further north, the Kalpitiya Peninsula (p99) has gained a reputation as one of the best kitesurfing spots in South Asia, with numerous kitesurfing schools offering gear hire (prices usually quoted in euro; from €60 per day), lessons on Kalpitiya Lagoon (nine-hour courses over two or three days start from €240) and laid-back accommodation.

Whale & Dolphin Watching

Sri Lanka is a world-class whale-watching location. The big attraction is big indeed – blue whales cruise past Dondra Head near Mirissa (p133), the best place to organise a whale-watching trip. On the east coast, Uppuveli and Nilaveli offer quieter but less-reliable whale watching.

In the northwest, the Kalpitiya Peninsula (p98) is another possible base; enormous pods of dolphins are often encountered, along with (less reliably) sperm whales and Bryde's whales.

The season off the south coast and Kalpitiya is from December to April, while on the east coast it runs from May to October.

Diving & Snorkelling

There are plenty of opportunities to splish like a fish in Sri Lanka. However, don't expect the endless, crystal-clear blue waters of Southeast Asia. Visibility is variable, but it's still worth diving in to see impressive wrecks, and everything from angelfish, butterfly fish, surgeon fish and scorpion fish to black- and white-tip reef sharks.

Along the west coast, the best time to dive and snorkel is November to April. On

Snorkelling, Pigeon Island National Park (p272)

the east coast, the seas are calmest from April to September. Dive centres offer two-dive boat trips from US$70, and open-water certification dive courses range from US$325 to US$390. Popular dive schools Include the following:

Poseidon Diving Station (p105), Hikkaduwa

Kalpitiya Diving Center (p99), Kalpitiya

Unawatuna Diving Centre (p123), Unawatuna

Weligama Bay Dive Center (p130), Weligama

Sri Lanka Diving Tours (p263), Batticaloa

Poseidon Diving Station (p272), Nilaveli

Angel Diving (p271), Uppuveli

Colombo Divers (p94), Negombo

Responsible Diving

Please consider the following tips when diving to help preserve the ecology and beauty of reefs:

➡ Discourage boat operators from anchoring on the reef or grounding boats on coral.

➡ Avoid touching or standing on living marine organisms or dragging equipment across the reef.

➡ Be conscious of your fins. The surge from fin strokes near the reef can damage delicate organisms and smother coral polyps with sand.

➡ Practise and maintain proper buoyancy control to avoid colliding with the reef.

➡ Spend as little time as possible in underwater caves as air bubbles can get trapped inside, leaving organisms high and dry.

➡ Resist the temptation to collect or buy corals or shells or take objects from shipwrecks.

➡ Ensure that you take home all your rubbish and collect any litter you find as well.

➡ Don't feed fish; it creates dependency and can disrupt the natural ecosystem.

➡ Try not to disturb marine animals, and never grab onto turtles or dolphins.

BEST DIVE SPOTS

Great Basses reefs (p148) Offshore from Kirinda and great for eagle rays and white-tip reef sharks, but for expert divers only.

Bar Reef (p98) Off the Kalpitiya Peninsula, this pristine reef system has masses of fish, plus dolphins and whales.

Pigeon Island (p272) Around 300 species of fish and other marine life have been recorded here.

Unawatuna (p123) It's all about wreck diving here, with dives for all levels of experience.

Batticaloa (p263) Calm waters for exploring the wreck of HMS *Hermes*, a WWII British naval ship.

Negombo (p94) Don't judge the diving by the rather brown waters at the beachside; the reefs offshore bustle with fish.

Plan Your Trip

National Parks & Safaris

Sri Lanka is one of the best locations in Asia for wildlife-watching; national parks are dotted around the country and the variety of habitats and the diversity of wildlife is exceptional. Even on a short trip, it's easy to see great herds of elephants and buffalo, hordes of monkeys, enormous whales, schools of dolphins, thousands of colourful birds and rainbow-coloured tropical fish, and leopard sightings are frequent. The Sri Lankan tourism industry hasn't been slow to cotton on to the country's wildlife-watching potential. Good infrastructure means easy access to the island's many national parks and protected zones; indeed the issue sometimes is not that wildlife is hard to find, but that it can be hard to see through the crowds of wildlife-spotters. Seek out smaller, less-visited reserves for a more peaceful experience.

Wildlife

For its size, Sri Lanka boasts an incredible diversity of animals: 125 mammal species, 245 butterflies, 463 birds, 96 snakes and more than 320 species of tropical fish. Given the fragility of the environment in which they live, however, it should come as no surprise that quite a few are vulnerable.

Mammals

Some of Sri Lanka's most endangered mammals are easy to spot because of their size, while many smaller creatures are missed by animal-spotters itching for a photograph of the big hitters. On land, the top spot is taken by the majestic Asian elephant, with vast herds visible in parks such as Minneriya National Park, particularly during the event known as the Gathering in June to September.

Harder to spot are the solitary and mostly nocturnal leopard, Sri Lanka's top

Best Wildlife Experiences

The West

The West serves up the best marine life, but Wilpattu National Park has large mammals and birders will be in spotting heaven in Muthurajawela Marsh.

South & East

Boat trips from the south coast offer the chance to spot whales and dolphins, while Yala National Park is one of the best places in Asia to see leopards. Parks in the East host myriad bird species.

The Hill Country & Ancient Cities

The hills have rainforests, moorlands and savanna parks with everything from elephants to endemic high-country birds. The Ancient Cities area is home to national parks filled with big-ticket mammals, and birdlife amid the ruins.

FIELD GUIDES & WILDLIFE BOOKS

There are plenty of good field guides out there. These are some of our favourites:

- *A Photographic Guide to Mammals of Sri Lanka* (Gehan de Silva Wijeyeratne) A comprehensive guide from a well-known Sri Lankan naturalist
- *A Selection of the Birds of Sri Lanka* (John and Judy Banks) A slim, well-illustrated tome that's perfect for amateur birdwatchers.
- *A Field Guide to the Birds of Sri Lanka* (John Harrison) A detailed hardback with lots of colour illustrations.
- *The Nature of Sri Lanka* (Luxshmanan Nadaraja) An impressive collection of essays about Sri Lanka by eminent writers and conservationists.

predator, also found in its melanistic form. Smaller predators include the scavenging golden jackal; the shaggy sloth bear; the civet (a catlike hunter related to the weasel); the mongoose; and the shy, armour-plated Indian pangolin, with overlapping scales made from modified hair.

Prey species include the omnivorous and tusked wild boar, large maned sambar deer and smaller white-spotted Axis deer. The bushy-tailed, five-striped palm squirrel is commonly seen scurrying around gardens and town parks. In any part of the country, look for colonies of Indian flying foxes (large fruit-eating bats) taking flight in the late afternoon and evening.

Sri Lankan primates abound; look out for common langurs (also known as Hanuman or grey langurs), endemic purple-faced langurs, hairy bear monkeys, and toque macaques, notable for their distinctive thatch of middle-parted hair. The slow movements of the slender loris belie its ability to snatch its prey with a lightning-quick lunge.

The biggest of all mammals are to be found in the waters off Sri Lanka. Blue whales, sperm whales, fin whales and Bryde's whales swim along migration corridors off the coast around Mirissa and neighbouring Dondra Head. Various species of dolphins are commonly encountered on whale-watching trips, including megapods of spinner dolphins at Kalpitiya.

Birds

A tropical climate, long isolation from the Asian mainland and a diversity of habitats have gifted Sri Lanka with an astonishing abundance of birdlife. Some 463 species have been recorded, 26 of which are unique to Sri Lanka. Of the 200 migrant species, most of which take up residence from August to April, the waders (sandpipers, plovers etc) are the long-distance champions, making the annual journey from their breeding grounds in the Arctic tundra.

Birders may wish to contact the **Field Ornithology Group of Sri Lanka** (http://fogsl.cmb.ac.lk), the national affiliate of Birdlife International.

Tips for Birdwatchers

- Visit a variety of habitats – rainforest, urban parks and bodies of water in the dry zone – to see the full diversity of birdlife in Sri Lanka.
- February to March is the best time for birdwatching. You'll miss the monsoons, and the migrant birds are still visiting.
- Morning is the best time to go birdwatching, but evenings see noisy flocks of birds preparing to roost.
- Consider taking a tour with a specialist if you're keen to tot up a healthy birdwatching tally.

Planning Your Safari

Where to Go

Where to go depends entirely on what you want to see and what kind of safari you want to take. Yala National Park in the far southeast is the most popular overall park and is fantastic for leopards, but it's also very busy and can become something of a circus with minibuses chasing each other around in search of big cats. If you want your leopard-spotting quieter (and less certain), try Kumana National Park (formerly Yala East National Park) or Wilpattu.

National Parks & Reserves

More than 2000 years ago, enlightened royalty declared certain land areas off limits to any human activity. Almost every

MAJOR NATIONAL PARKS & RESERVES

PARK	AREA	FEATURES	BEST TIME TO VISIT
Bundala National Park	62.2 sq km	coastal lagoon, migratory birds, elephants	year-round
Gal Oya National Park	629.4 sq km	grasslands, evergreen forest, deer, Senanayake Samudra (tank), elephants, sloth bears, leopards, water buffaloes	Dec-Sep
Horton Plains National Park	31.6 sq km	Unesco World Heritage Site, montane forests, marshy grasslands, World's End precipice, sambars	Dec-Mar
Kaudulla National Park	66.6 sq km	Kaudulla Tank, evergreen forest, scrub jungle, grassy plains, elephants, leopards, sambars, fishing cats, sloth bears	Aug-Dec
Knuckles Range	175 sq km	Unesco World Heritage Site, traditional villages, hiking trails, caves, waterfalls, montane pygmy forest, evergreen forest, riverine forest, grasslands, scrub, paddy fields, over 30 mammal species	Dec-May
Kumana National Park	356.6 sq km	grasslands, jungle, lagoons, mangrove swamp, waterfowl	May-Sep
Minneriya National Park	88.9 sq km	Minneriya Tank, toque macaques, sambars, elephants, waterfowl	May-Sep
Sinharaja Forest Reserve	360 sq km	Unesco World Heritage Site, sambars, rainforest, leopards, purple-faced langurs, barking deer, 147 recorded bird species	Aug-Sep, Jan-Mar
Sri Pada Peak Wilderness Reserve	224 sq km	Unesco World Heritage Site, Adam's Peak, hiking trails, melanistic leopards	Dec-May
Uda Walawe National Park	308.2 sq km	grasslands, thorn scrub, elephants, spotted deer, water buffaloes, wild boar	year-round
Wilpattu National Park	1317 sq km	dry woodland, scrub, saltgrass, leopards, sloth bears, deer, crocodiles	Jan-Mar
Yala National Park	141 sq km	tropical thorn forest, lagoons, leopards, elephants, sloth bears, water buffaloes, lesser flamingos	Nov-Jul

province in the ancient kingdom of Kandy had such *udawattakelle* (sanctuaries). All animals and plants in these reserves were left undisturbed, preserving populations from hunting and habitat loss.

Today's system of parks and reserves is mostly an amalgamation of these

BEST PLACES FOR ELEPHANTS

Uda Walawe National Park (p199) With around 500 elephants in attendance year-round.

Minneriya National Park (p229) From July to September, huge herds come together in a spectacle known as 'the Gathering'.

Kaudulla National Park (p229) Over 250 elephants call this park home.

Bundala National Park (p144) Consistent elephant sightings in a beautiful watery setting.

Yala National Park (p148) Lots of elephants but forest cover can make spotting them tricky.

Top: Langur, Bundala National Park (p144)

Bottom: Green bee-eater, Yala National Park (p148)

MATT MUNRO/LONELY PLANET ©

traditional protected areas, reserves established by the British and newly designated areas set aside as wildlife corridors. There are more than 100 of these areas under government guard, covering approximately 8% of the island.

Protected areas are divided into three types: strict nature reserves (no visitors allowed), national parks (visitors allowed under fixed conditions) and nature reserves (human habitation permitted). Sri Lanka also has two marine sanctuaries – the Bar Reef (west of Kalpitiya peninsula) and Hikkaduwa National Park near Hikkaduwa – as well as dozens of protected island and coastal zones.

Off the Beaten Track

A full 82% of Sri Lanka's land is controlled by the state in some form or another, and is therefore subject to a raft of legislation to protect sensitive areas like natural forests. There are 63 sanctuaries in the country, a long list of forest reserves and countless wetlands both with and without official titles.

Given the overcrowding at some of the better-known natural areas, attention is turning to other minor national parks, such as Lunugamvehera (which serves as a migration corridor between Yala and Uda Walawe National Parks), and Wasgomuwa instead of Minneriya.

Sri Lanka is a signatory to the Ramsar Convention on Wetlands, which currently recognises six zones in the country. These include Bundala National Park, the 915-hectare Madu Ganga Estuary near Balapitiya and the Anawilundawa Wetland Sanctuary, just about 100km north of Colombo.

For further listings of out-of-the-way green escapes, contact the government conservation departments or consult **LOCALternative Sri Lanka** (www.localternative.com) for information on small, local projects.

BEST PLACES FOR BIRDS

Sinharaja Forest Reserve (p201) A slab of rainforest with around 160 bird species.

Knuckles Range (p173) Little-known montane forests filled with hill-country and forest birds.

Bundala National Park (p144) This wetland park is the classic Sri Lankan birdwatching destination.

Kumana National Park (p259) Superb low-country birdwatching with around 150 species present.

Muthurajawela Marsh (p95) Excellent wetland birding close to Colombo.

Pottuvil Lagoon (☎075-824 1432, 076-307 5516; 2hr tour per 2 people Rs 4000) Numerous migratory waders and waterbirds in this little-visited east-coast wetland.

When to Go

Sri Lanka is a year-round wildlife-watching destination but generally the best times to spot fauna align with the main November-to-April tourist season. At this time of year all the big parks are open and the dry conditions mean that animals start to gather around waterholes, making them easier to spot (especially so between February and early April). If you come in the May-to-October southwest monsoon season, head to the parks around the Ancient Cities and in the east of the island.

How to Book

For all the major national parks and protected areas, organising a safari couldn't be easier. Groups of safari jeep drivers can normally be found in the nearest town or gathered outside the gates, and hotels can also organise safaris. Entry fees to all parks are paid directly at entrance gates.

Plan Your Trip
Ayurveda

Ayurveda, Sri Lanka's ancient art of herbal and holistic healing, is attracting more and more visitors to these sun-kissed shores. Whether you dedicate a whole trip to traditional therapies, or just dip in with an Ayurvedic treatment at a hotel spa, experiencing Ayurveda is an integral part of the Sri Lankan experience.

Top Ayurvedic Spas

Ayurvedic centres are found across Sri Lanka, from casual hotel spas to serious Ayurvedic hospitals. Top spas include:

Siddhalepa Ayurveda (p69) You can enjoy a full range of treatments in this authentic spa with highly trained Ayurvedic doctors.

Spa Ceylon (p69) Upscale treatments and beautifully packaged Ayurvedic products; branches nationwide, with a flagship in Colombo.

Sanctuary Spa (p123) Follow a hard day swimming in Unawatuna's surf by getting your inner balance restored.

Jetwing Ayurveda Pavilions (p95) In Negombo, Pavilions offers rooms with spa treatments included in the rates.

Barberyn Reef Ayurveda Resort (p104) A complete health resort in Beruwela, this place offers lavish packages that include yoga and meditation.

Heritance Ayurveda Maha Gedara (p104) A west-coast retreat where the quality of the resort matches the quality of the treatments.

Introducing Ayurveda

Ayurveda (eye-your-veda) is an ancient system of medicine using herbs, oils, metals and animal products to heal and rejuvenate. Influenced by the system of the same name in India, Ayurveda has been used in Sri Lanka for a range of ailments for thousands of years.

Ayurveda postulates that the five elements (earth, air, ether, water and light) are linked to the five senses, which in turn shape the nature of an individual's constitution – his or her *dosha* (life force). Illness occurs when the *dosha* is out of balance. The purpose of Ayurvedic treatment is to restore the balance.

Digging deeper, *dosha* is believed to be made up of three elements: *vayu*, *pita* and *kapha*. Commonly translated as 'wind', 'bile' and 'phlegm', these terms are often poorly understood by people new to Ayurveda. *Vayu* refers not to air or gas, but motion and the transmission of energy through the body, while *pita* encompasses metabolism and heat production within the body and *kapha* covers the balance of fluids within body tissues.

When consulting an Ayurvedic specialist, patients may be informed that they must undergo treatments designed to balance any one of these elements, or even all three. For full-on therapeutic treatments, patients must be prepared to make a commitment of weeks or months. This can be a gruelling regimen featuring frequent enemas and a bare minimum diet of simple vegetable-derived calories. It's not for everyone.

Much more commonly, tourists treat themselves at Ayurvedic massage centres attached to major hotels and in popular tourist centres. Full treatments take up to three hours and include such relaxing therapies as herbal saunas, steam baths and dripping oil treatments.

The History of Ayurveda

Ayurveda has a history dating back at least 2000 years in Sri Lanka. Folklore dictates that the tradition arrived on the island with Buddhist missionaries in the 3rd century BCE, but it's likely that imported traditions from India were melded with existing traditions of herbal medicine known as *deshiya chikitsa*, practised by the indigenous Veddah people.

What is certain is that there was flow in both directions between Sri Lanka and India in the ancient period, with mentions of visiting sages from Sri Lanka in historic Ayurvedic texts. The monastic hospital founded by King Sena II at Mihintale in the 8th century C almost certainly employed Ayurvedic treatments, as evidenced by archaeological discoveries on the site.

Common Ayurvedic Treatments

Among the many treatments on offer, tourists commonly encounter the following therapies, often as part of a single spa package.

Herbal saunas (Sweda Karma) Based on a 2500-year-old design, these hot rooms feature plaster walls infused with herbal ingredients, including honey and sandalwood powder, and a floor covered with medicinal herbs. Like a European sauna, a steady mist of steam is maintained with water sprinkled onto hot coals, carrying herbal compounds into the skin.

Steam baths (Vashpa Swedanam) These devices look like a cross between a coffin and a torture chamber. Patients lie stretched out on a wooden platform, and a giant hinged door covers the body with only the head exposed. From the base of the wooden steam bath, up to 50 different herbs and spices infuse the pores.

Third Eye of the Lord Shiva Treatment (Shiro Dhara) This relaxing head massage is the highlight for many patients. For up to 45 minutes, a delicate flow of warm oil is poured slowly onto the forehead from a special jar and then smoothed gently into the temples by the masseuse.

Panchakarma (Five Actions) As the name suggests, this is a package of five separate treatments designed to flush the body of toxins, often administered over the space of five days. Treatments may include herbal saunas, steam baths, warm-oil massage, herbal enemas (*basti*) and the administering of herbal drops to the nose (*nasya*).

Finding an Ayurvedic Spa

There are Ayurvedic clinics all over Sri Lanka, from dedicated Ayurvedic hospitals offering intensive, long-term treatments for patients with chronic complaints, to beach resort spas offering Ayurveda alongside more familiar spa treatments. If you stay anywhere with a spa, the chances are some Ayurvedic treatments will be on offer.

SPA SAFETY

While there are numerous spas with good international reputations, the standards at some smaller Ayurvedic centres are variable. The massage oils may be simple coconut oil and the practitioners may be unqualified, and in some instances may even be sex workers.

For massage, enquire whether there are both male and female therapists available; we've received complaints from female readers about sexual advances from some male Ayurvedic practitioners. In general, it's not acceptable Ayurvedic practice for males to massage females, and vice versa.

As poisoning cases have resulted from herbal treatments being misadministered, it pays to enquire precisely what any medicine contains and then consult with a conventional physician.

Dambulla Cave Temples (p.

Plan Your Trip

Family Travel

Like a good rice and curry meal, Sri Lanka offers a dazzling array of choices for families. However, if this is a first family trip to the developing world, some adjustment will be needed to local conditions, particularly the heat and noise. Focus on beaches and wildlife and you'll keep the kids on side, and the Sri Lankan love of children will help with any bumps along the way.

NILA NEWSOM/SHUTTERSTOCK ©

Keeping Costs Down

Accommodation

Most places can provide an extra bed for a small extra charge, and some offer cots for free. Generally, the closer you stay to the beach, the higher the cost; stay somewhere with a pool a short way inland and you have the best of both worlds.

Transport

Trains are family-friendly (and provide a sense of adventure), and hiring a car and driver gives you maximum control (bring a car seat from home). Buses are slow, crowded and uncomfortable; stick to air-con services.

Eating

Restaurants targeting tourists serve plenty of Western dishes, as an alternative to spicy local food. In tourist areas, you can always find inexpensive family-run places among the posher eateries.

Activities

The beach is the obvious free activity. Most resorts offer boat rides, snorkelling and other water sports, but prices can add up. Renting a mask and snorkel to splash around in the shallows is cheaper than going out to the reef. Many attractions charge half rates to children aged five to 12.

Children Will Love...

Beaches

Negombo (p92) A good first or last port of call, close to the airport and easy for first timers.

Hikkaduwa (p105) Highly developed, but with good options for families, and snorkelling offshore.

Bentota (p101) Family-friendly resorts and loads of water sports so there's never a dull moment.

Arugam Bay (p251) Good for older kids, with lots of places to learn to surf and a hip feel.

Unawatuna (p121) Good shallow beaches that are safer for little ones, and watery activities.

Wildlife-Spotting

Uda Walawe (p199) One of the best national parks for wildlife-spotting safaris.

Sinharaja Forest Reserve (p201) Seek out exotic birdlife on foot, breaking to swim in natural waterfalls.

Minneriya (p229) A national park renowned for its herds of elephants, with almost guaranteed sightings.

Whale-watching, Mirissa (p133) Long boat rides, but good chances of spotting blue whales for patient kids.

Pigeon Island National Park (p272) Off beautiful Nilaveli beach, this island has great snorkelling.

Historic Sites

Anuradhapura (p230) Amazing ruins to explore, loads of birdlife and no crazy crowds.

Sigiriya (p214) Climbing to the top of this ruin-crowned outcrop is a great family adventure.

Dambulla (p208) For sheer colour, these mural- and carving-filled caverns tick all the boxes.

Polonnaruwa (p219) Kids can run themselves silly at this vast and car-free ancient heritage site.

Mihintale (p241) A bigger adventure, made more exciting by clambering up rocky outcrops.

Adventures

Train rides (p330) Air-con carriages offer easy thrills, especially on the way to Kandy and Badulla.

Three-wheelers (p330) The best way to explore; you could even rent a three-wheeler to drive everyone around.

Kitesurfing (p99) Teens can take the first steps to becoming a kitesurfer on the calm lagoon at Kalpitiya.

Weligama (p129) A great place for older kids to conquer their first wave, with schools offering tuition for first timers.

Boat rides (p102) Bentota and other resorts offer boat trips onto mangrove-filled lagoons.

Region by Region

Colombo Not easy for small travellers; use Mt Lavinia as a beach base and explore with a car and driver.

The West Coast Brilliant, family-friendly beach resorts at Negombo, Bentota and Hikkaduwa.

The South More fine family-friendly stretches of sand, with added surf appeal; great national parks near the coast.

The Hill Country Slow, uncomfortable bus rides are the down side; tea plantation tours and hikes to viewpoints are pluses.

The Ancient Cities Oodles of history and some good national parks; explore Anuradhapura or Polonnaruwa on foot and feel like Indiana Jones.

The East Bigger distances to cover, but fine sand and surf at Arugam Bay, Batticaloa and near Trincomalee.

Jaffna & the North Off the family tourism map, but with wild beaches for real Robinson Crusoes.

Good to Know

Accommodation Sri Lankan hotels and guesthouses often have triple and family rooms; extra beds can be supplied on demand, though cots are in short supply. 'Kids clubs' are rare outside of all-inclusive resorts.

Eating Most tourist-orientated places offer Western-style dishes, though children's menus are rare. Highchairs are uncommon; consider bringing a portable infant seat that fixes to a table or chair.

Transport Renting a car and driver is a great family option but car seats can be hard to find; bring your own from home. Trains are much more kid-friendly than buses.

Toilets Public toilets are best avoided; use the ones at restaurants or in hotels.

Prams & Strollers Pavements, where they exist, are not great for pushchairs. Bring an all-terrain model, or a backpack baby-carrier or sling.

Babies & Toddlers Imported baby food and disposable nappies/diapers are easy to find, but sizes tend to be small. Breastfeeding in public is accepted, but there are few baby-changing rooms.

Health Sunburn and mosquito bites are big issues; bring sunscreen, repellent and antiseptic, and a mosquito net in case the hotel doesn't have one. Rabies is a risk, so keep children away from cats, dogs and monkeys.

Useful Resources

Lonely Planet Kids (www.lonelyplanetkids.com) Loads of activities and great family travel blog content.

World Travel Family (www.worldtravelfamily.com/sri-lanka-with-kids) A handy guide to family travel to Sri Lanka from parents who have done it.

Regions at a Glance

Colombo

Sunsets
History
Shopping

Sunset Colours

Pushed up against the Indian Ocean, Colombo proudly faces west towards the setting sun. Clear evenings begin with an explosion of magenta and purple on the horizon, best viewed from a hotel bar or along the shoreline at Galle Face Green.

Rich History

Colombo's colonial history is written large on the streets. Gleaming white British and Dutch buildings recalling the vainglory of empire have been reinvented as brilliant museums, heritage hotels and dynamic public spaces for eating, drinking and boutique browsing.

Pettah Market

Almost getting run down by a madman with a cart full of goods in the markets of Pettah is just part of the experience of shopping in Sri Lanka's colourful capital. Leave space in your luggage for colourful crafts and fine teas.

p61

The West Coast

Beaches
Activities
Luxury Lodging

Sand for All

From all-inclusive beach resorts to hippy hang-outs and remote strips of sand, the west coast will keep everyone happy. Start at family-friendly Hikkaduwa or find serenity on the wild sands at Kalpitiya.

Watery Pleasures

There's more to the west than sunbathing. Ride the waves and dive the reefs, birdwatch on the marshes, spot the dolphins in the north, or take a wildlife-spotting boat safari around Bentota.

Top Resorts

Bentota is home to some breathtaking design-mag-worthy boutique hotels, including top Ayurvedic spas. Negombo also has accommodation to remember, conveniently close to the airport.

p91

The South

Beaches
Wildlife
Cities

Stunning Strands

There are beaches here with a buzzing traveller vibe and beaches with barely a footprint on the sand. And the south is a surf playground, with fun-filled breaks at Ahangama, Midigama and Weligama.

Wildlife

Wildlife lovers congregate at Bundala National Park and Yala National Park for glimpses of elephants, leopards, monkeys and more. In the ocean, tropical fish teem close to shore, while whales and dolphins cruise near Mirissa.

Cities

Gorgeous Galle is the highlight of any visit to the southern shores. This Unesco-listed city is a captivating sprawl of terracotta-tiled colonial buildings, historic mansions and museums.

p111

The Hill Country

Walking
Wildlife
Eating

Verdant Hikes

Trek your way through jungles, shiver over high plains, traipse to vertigo-inspiring viewpoints, tiptoe through tea plantations or walk in the very footsteps of the gods.

Elephants & More

Wildlife encounters abound in steamy rainforests filled with chattering birds, grassland savannas ruled by mighty elephants, and highland forests covered in moss.

Guesthouse Dining

In the Hill Country, the preparation of Sri Lankan food becomes an art form. Enjoy fine dining on a budget in guesthouse kitchens, or signature dining experiences such as high tea at the Grand Hotel in Nuwara Eliya.

p153

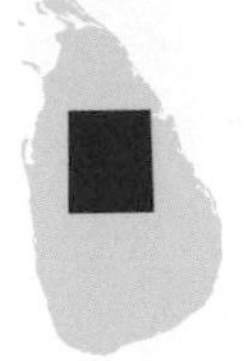

The Ancient Cities

Monuments
Culture
Cycling

Ancient Treasures

The Polonnaruwa Quadrangle, the ancient stupas of Anuradhapura, the jaw-dropping rock palace at Sigiriya, the Technicolour caves at Dambulla: the region is a treasure trove of history.

Sacred Sri Maha Bodhi

Amid the leaf-shrouded ruins of Anuradhapura you'll find Sri Maha Bodhi, a sacred tree that has been tended by devotees for more than 2000 years.

Peaceful Pedalling

The ruins of the Ancient Cities are set within peaceful parks and reserves, and you can pedal from temple to temple and ruin to ruin along palm-shaded paths and never see a car.

p205

The East

Beaches
Activities
Wildlife

Lonely Sands

The east coast's endless stretches of beach are starting to emerge as traveller destinations, with just the right mix of palm trees, white sands and low-key traveller buzz.

Snoozing & Diving

The ocean isn't just warm and gorgeous, it also has reefs and wrecks for snorkelling and diving, and a string of fine breaks for surfing, especially south around Arugam Bay.

Kumana National Park

Tucked away in the far south, Kumana National Park (formerly Yala East National Park) is smaller and less famous than its neighbour, Yala, but on the plus side it lacks Yala's tourist population, which means the leopards, elephants and birds here are all yours.

p247

Jaffna & the North

Discovery
Culture
Seashores

Off the Beaten Path

Shut down to travel for years, the North is now one of the best places in Sri Lanka for aimless exploring. It has never been easier to discover surprises like Fort Hammenhiel and surreal Mannar Island.

Tamil Culture

Deities painted in hyper-real colours animate towering Hindu temples all over the North. This is the heartland of Tamil culture and customs, best experienced in revitalised Jaffna, with its colonial relics.

Islands & Coasts

Beaches and isolated coves curl around the mainland near Jaffna, but there's even more to discover on the islands that sprawl offshore, calling out to adventurous explorers.

p275

On the Road

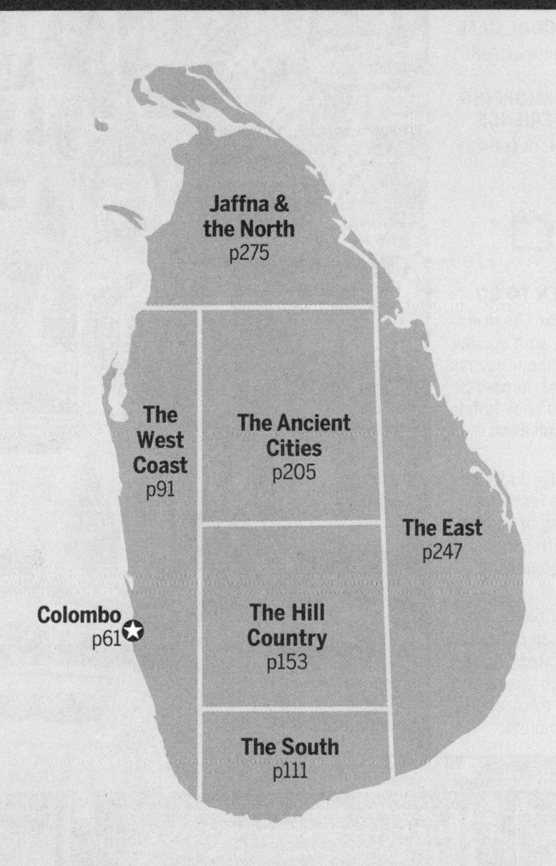
Jaffna & the North
p275
The West Coast
p91
The Ancient Cities
p205
The East
p247
Colombo
p61
The Hill Country
p153
The South
p111

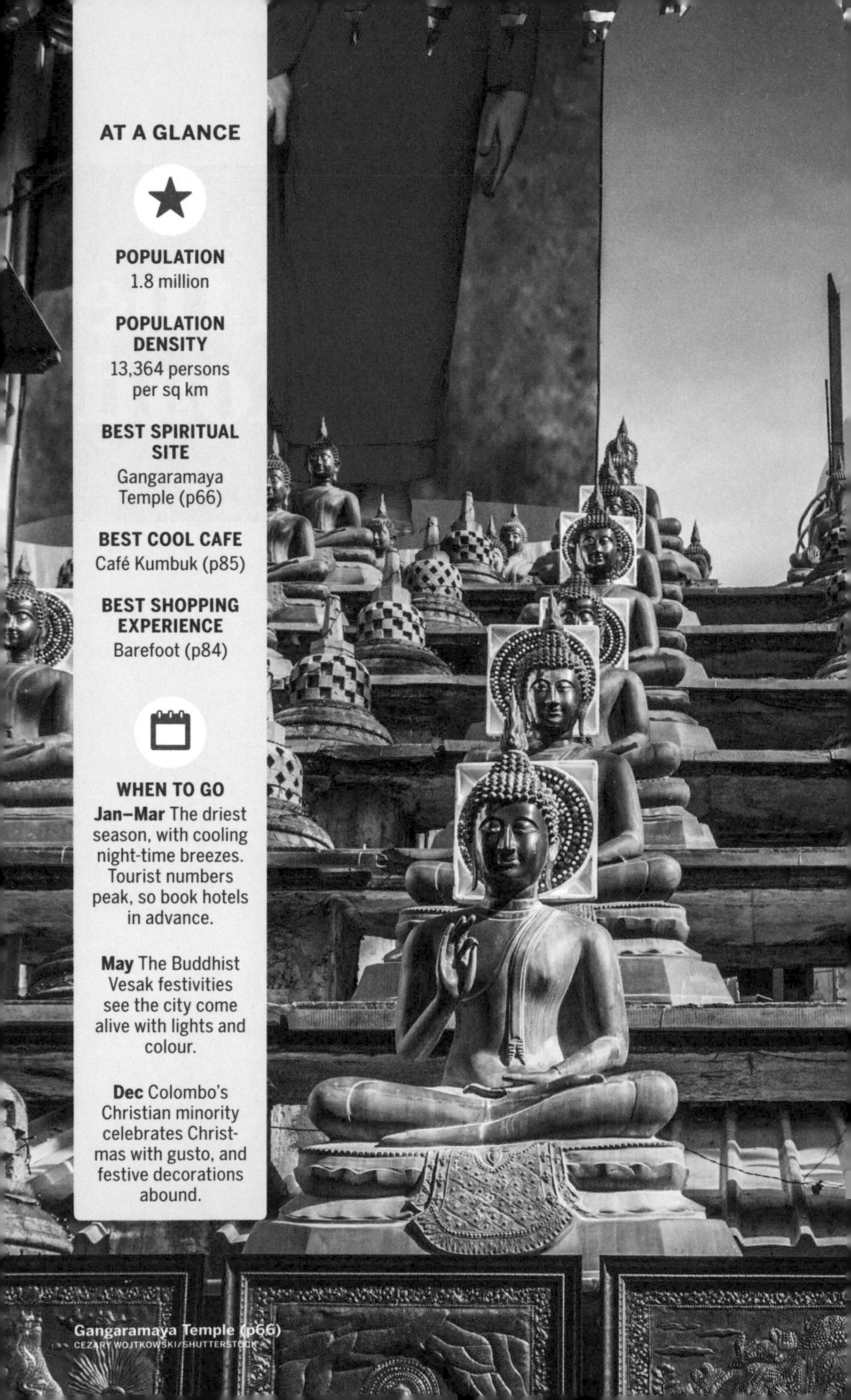

AT A GLANCE

POPULATION
1.8 million

POPULATION DENSITY
13,364 persons per sq km

BEST SPIRITUAL SITE
Gangaramaya Temple (p66)

BEST COOL CAFE
Café Kumbuk (p85)

BEST SHOPPING EXPERIENCE
Barefoot (p84)

WHEN TO GO

Jan–Mar The driest season, with cooling night-time breezes. Tourist numbers peak, so book hotels in advance.

May The Buddhist Vesak festivities see the city come alive with lights and colour.

Dec Colombo's Christian minority celebrates Christmas with gusto, and festive decorations abound.

Gangaramaya Temple (p66)
CEZARY WOJTKOWSKI/SHUTTERSTOCK ©

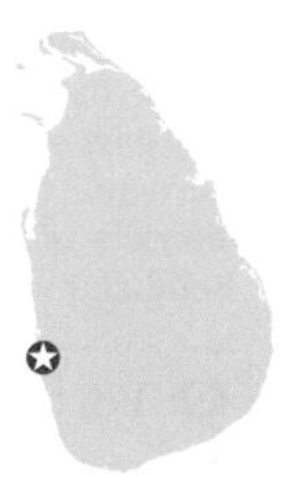

Colombo

Many people overlook Sri Lanka's historic capital in the rush to the coast, but there's plenty to explore, if you can get used to the city's rather disjointed layout. The British were responsible for the railway tracks that cut the city off from much of its ocean shoreline, and they also dotted the city with its landmark buildings, particularly in the Fort district.

Explore beyond the noisy arterial roads running north–south through the centre, and you'll find centuries-old churches, colourful temples, atmospheric accommodation, ritzy shopping malls and manic markets, as well as some of Sri Lanka's finest food. While you explore, duck into some of Colombo's cool cafes, which dot the backstreets and dish out cake, espresso and calm.

INCLUDES

History

Colombo was a busy sea port for trade between Asia and the West by the 5th century, inspiring Arab merchants to set up their own trading posts. The Portuguese arrived in 1505, only to be ousted in the mid-17th century by the Dutch, who seized control of the cinnamon trade, establishing plantations at Cinnamon Gardens. But it was when the British arrived that the town was formally designated as a city, becoming the capital of Ceylon in 1815.

The Brits were the most enthusiastic remodellers of Colombo, building breakwaters, laying the railway line and creating the Fort district by flooding surrounding wetlands. After independence, the government shifted the Sri Lankan parliament to Sri Jayawardenepura-Kotte, an outer suburb on the site of the 15th-century kingdom of Kotte, in 1982.

Repeated bomb attacks in Fort during the civil war caused Colombo's businesses and institutions to disperse across the city, but with the end of the conflict, work began to reclaim and restore the old colonial quarter. However, the peace was shattered again on 21 April 2019 as Islamist suicide bombers targeted three luxury hotels, the Cinnamon Grand, the Shangri-La and the Kingsbury, and St Anthony's Church in Kotahena.

Despite the economic impact of the attacks, Colombo's building boom continues, though some projects have slowed to a snail's pace. Spurred by Chinese investment, new hotels, shopping malls and condominium towers have appeared all over the city, but it remains to be seen if the economic fallout from the coronavirus pandemic will put a dent in the city's appetite for lavish living.

Sights

Colombo doesn't pack in the must-see sights. Instead, get the best out of the city by exploring neighbourhood by neighbourhood. Start in the historic Fort district, and work your way east to Pettah and inland to Cinnamon Gardens, then roam south to the coastal districts of Kollupitiya (kolu-pity-yah) and Bambalapitiya (bamba-la-pity-yah).

Fort

During the British era Fort was indeed a fort, surrounded by the sea on two sides. Most signs of the old fortifications are gone, but the grand civic buildings still remain. Two lighthouses, one colonial, one built after independence, serve as reminders that this was the seafront of Colombo before land was reclaimed to build the new **Colombo Port City** (Map p64; www.colomboportcity.lk).

Many buildings fell into disuse or were taken over by the army during the civil war, but with the end of the conflict, landmark buildings are returning to life as cafes, offices and hotels, joined by some rather incongruous skyscrapers.

★**Dutch Hospital** HISTORIC BUILDING
(Map p64; Bank of Ceylon Mw, Col 1) This terracotta-tiled, Dutch-era structure dates back

COLOMBO IN...

One Day

Start in Fort with a wander around the colonial streets, and take a tea break at the **Old Dutch Hospital** (p62). Wander over to Pettah to soak up the bazaar frenzy, then take a three-wheeler to Cinnamon Gardens for lunch at a hip cafe such as **Commons** (p81).

Suitably refreshed, take your time exploring the fascinating **National Museum** (p67), and stroll around **Viharamahadevi Park** (p68) before dropping into the offering-filled **Gangaramaya Temple** (p66). Later, as the sun sets, take a stroll along the oceanfront at **Galle Face Green** (p78) then zip south for a lavish dinner at **Paradise Road Gallery Cafe** (p81) in Bambalapitiya. Perfection!

Two Days

On day two, start with a local breakfast of string hoppers at **Curry Pot** (p80), then fill the morning with a three-wheeler ride to the lavishly decorated **Kelaniya Raja Maha Vihara** (p79) in the northeast suburbs.

Return to Fort, for a filling *lamprais* (rice and curry baked in banana leaves) lunch at **Pagoda Tea Room** (p79), then head south to Bambalapitiya to souvenir shop at well-stocked **Barefoot** (p84) or **Laksala** (p85). For dinner, dig into seafood by the seashore at **Bu Ba** (p82).

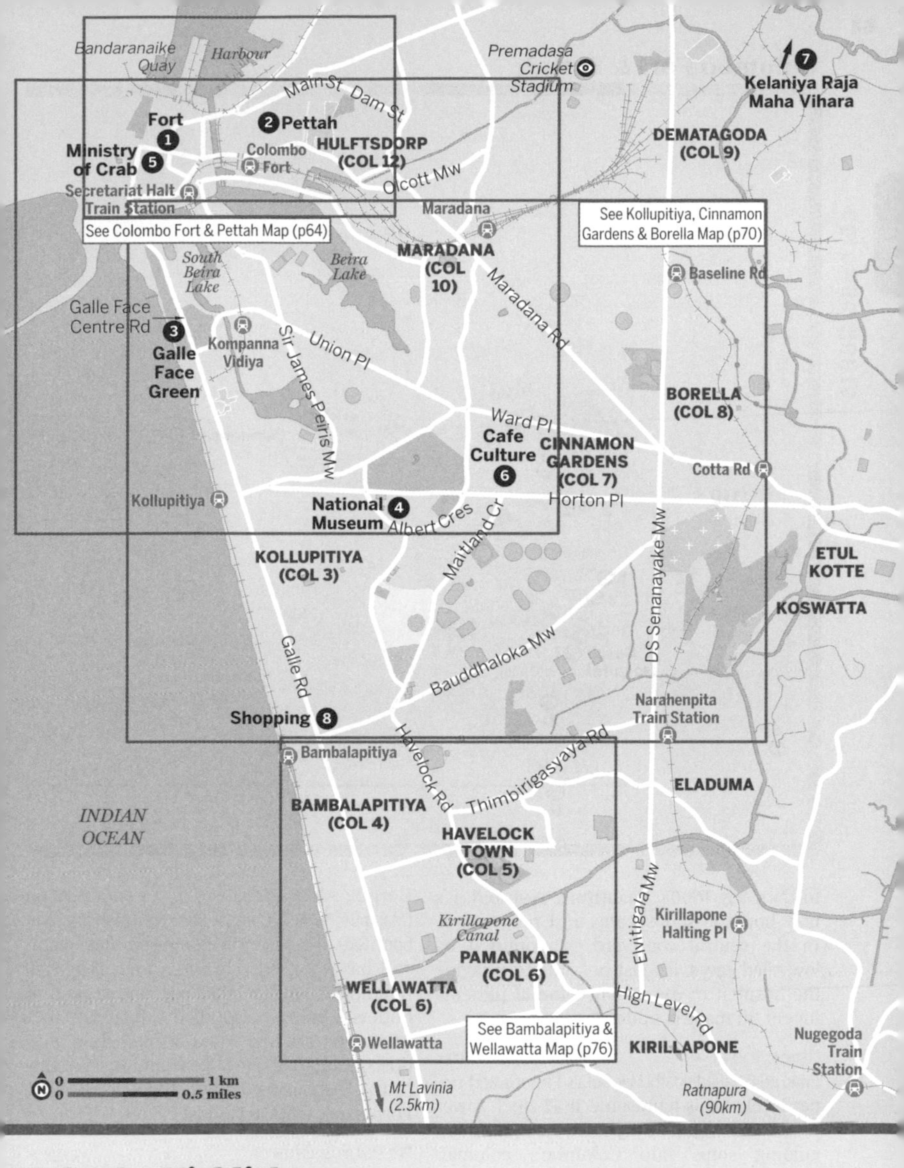

Colombo Highlights

1. **Fort** (p62) Stepping back in time in this compelling colonial quarter.
2. **Pettah** (p65) Plunging into the mercantile madness of this district.
3. **Galle Face Green** (p78) Taking a sunset promenade on Colombo's front lawn.
4. **National Museum** (p67) Walking through two millennia of history in this colonial-era edifice.
5. **Ministry of Crab** (p79) Feasting on crawling ocean critters at Sri Lanka's most famous seafood restaurant.
6. **Cafe culture** (p85) Enjoying fine Sri Lankan brews in one of Colombo's hip cafes.
7. **Kelaniya Raja Maha Vihara** (p79) Day-tripping to this historic, mural covered Buddhist temple.
8. **Shopping** (p84) Browsing landmark stores such as Barefoot, filled with local artistic creativity.

Colombo Fort & Pettah

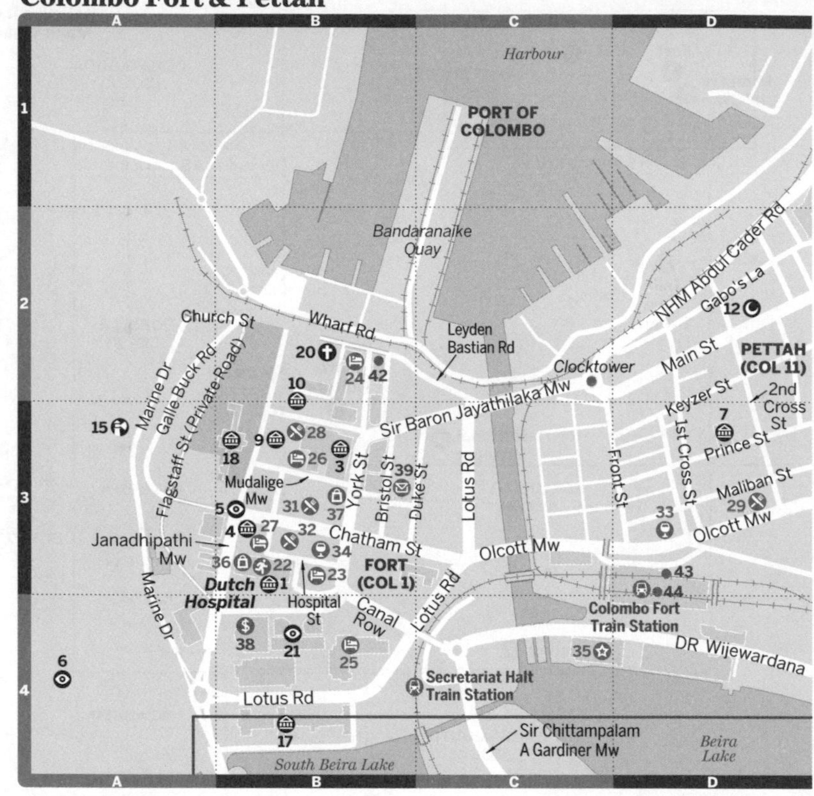

to the early 1600s. Beautifully restored, it's now home to shops, cafes and restaurants. In the central courtyard, surrounded by low, tiled eaves, it's just possible to imagine the hospital in use, when colonial patients fought off malaria under the stars.

Clock Tower LANDMARK

(Map p64; Janadhipathi Mw, Col 1) The glazed upper level of this handsome 1857 clock tower reveals its original purpose as a lighthouse, guiding ships into Colombo's colonial-era port, before it was marooned by land reclamation.

Central Point HISTORIC BUILDING

(Map p64; Chatham St, Col 1; museum 9am-4.45pm Mon-Fri) FREE Built in 1914, the handsome, colonnaded Central Bank building, known locally as Central Point, features a riot of Greco-Roman detailing and the tallest chandelier in Asia.

Cargills Main Store HISTORIC BUILDING

(Map p64; York St, Col 1; 8am-7pm Mon-Fri, 8am-5pm Sat) The Cargills supermarket chain still has a presence in the grand, red-brick building on York St that was one of its first outlets. Dating to 1906, the historic store retains its original wood-framed shop windows, and signboards proclaiming 'Cargills Ltd – Dispensing Drugs, Toilet Requisites, Perfumery, Optical Goods'.

St Peter's Church CHURCH

(Map p64; Church St, Col 1; 7am-5pm Tue-Sun) Reached along the arcade on the north side of the Grand Oriental Hotel, this converted Dutch governor's banquet hall was first used as a church in 1821. Inside are lines of plaques commemorating sons (and daughters) of empire; consider the fates of William Dumaresq Wright (thrown from a cart), Alice Mary Gordon (died at sea just off Colombo) and Charles Wallet (killed by an elephant).

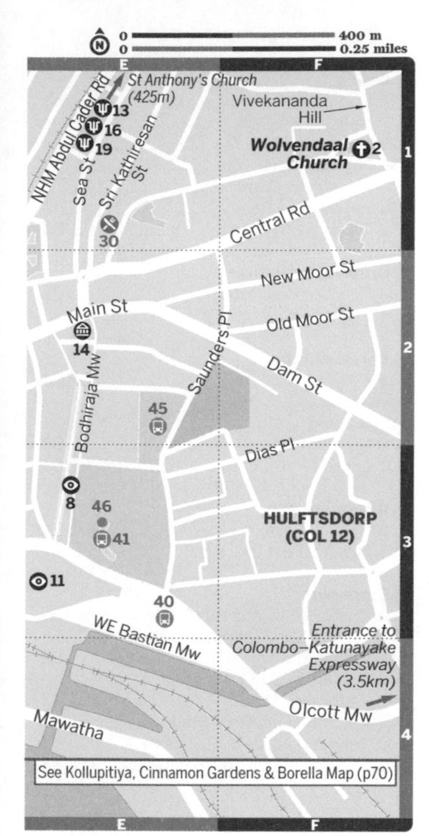

Pettah

Immediately inland from Fort, the frantic bazaar quarter of Pettah is a maze of markets, mosques, Hindu temples and Christian churches. Start your explorations from Olcott Mawatha, opposite Fort railway station and just dive on in.

Dutch Period Museum MUSEUM
(Map p64; ☎011-244 8466; 95 Prince St, Col 11; Rs 500; ⏲9am-5pm Tue-Sat) This handsome, column-fronted museum was originally the 17th-century residence of the Dutch governor. Today, it's undergoing a long overdue renovation (due to finish in 2021), which should put its fascinating collection of Dutch-era artefacts in the spotlight.

Old City Hall HISTORIC BUILDING
(Map p64; Main St, Col 11; ⏲hours vary) FREE Dating to 1865, this municipal building from the British era is today used as a market for household goods. A mouldering museum inside is open periodically, displaying old machines and vehicles.

Masjid Jami-Ul-Alfar MOSQUE
(Red Mosque; Map p64; Main St, Col 11) In the heart of Pettah, the Jami-Ul-Alfar Mosque is a showstopper from 1909, executed in candy-striped brickwork. It's one of the most striking buildings in the city, but only worshippers can enter.

★ **Wolvendaal Church** CHURCH
(Christian Reformed Church; Map p64; Wolvendaal Lane, Col 11; ⏲8.30am-4pm Tue-Thu & Sat, 8.30am-1.30pm Fri) Erected in 1749, the fading Wolvendaal Church is the most important Dutch building in Sri Lanka. Most of the woodwork inside the interior is original, and the floor is a patchwork of Dutch-period grave-slabs decorated with coats of arms, cherubs and symbols of mortality.

Federation of Self Employees Market MARKET
(Map p64; off Olcott Mw, Col 11; ⏲7am-4pm) The manic commerce of Pettah goes into overdrive in this partly covered market, following the line of 5th Cross St. The front part of the market is all clothes, toys and accessories, but further back, fruit and household items take over. Walk through the bazaars to reach the Old Town Hall and the Pettah Hindu temples.

Manning Market MARKET
(Map p64; Olcott Mw, Col 11; ⏲6am-2pm) East of Fort train station, Manning Market is the city's fragrant – in good ways and bad – wholesale fruit and veg market. A new market is under construction outside the centre at Peliyagoda, but for now, the old market is piled high with towers of papayas, mountains of watermelons and whole stalks of bananas.

Pettah Hindu Temples
Pettah has a sizeable Hindu population, and lined up near the junction of Sea St and St Paul's Mawatha are the multicoloured **Sri Muthu Vinayagar Swamy Kovil** (Map p64; Sea St, Col 11; ⏲6am-6pm); the **Old Kathiresan Kovil**, which was built in 1830 and is one of Colombo's oldest religious buildings; and the similarly revered **New Kathiresan Kovil**.

The temples are dedicated to the Hindu war god Murugan (Skanda), and form the starting point for the chariot procession that marks the Hindu festival of Vel in July/August. The streets nearby are lined with shops selling flower garlands, Hindu statues and other religious paraphernalia.

Colombo Fort & Pettah

Top Sights
1 Dutch Hospital B3
2 Wolvendaal Church F1

Sights
3 Cargills Main Store B3
4 Central Point B3
5 Clock Tower B3
6 Colombo Port City A4
7 Dutch Period Museum D3
8 Federation of Self Employees Market E3
9 General Post Office B3
10 Lloyd's Buildings B2
11 Manning Market E3
12 Masjid Jami-Ul-Alfar D2
13 New Kathiresan Kovil E1
14 Old City Hall E2
15 Old Galle Buck Lighthouse A3
16 Old Kathiresan Kovil E1
17 Presidential Secretariat B4
18 President's House B3
19 Sri Muthu Vinayagar Swamy Kovil E1
20 St Peter's Church B2
21 World Trade Centre B4

Activities, Courses & Tours
22 Spa Ceylon B3

Sleeping
23 City Rest Fort B3
24 Grand Oriental Hotel B2
25 Hilton Colombo Hotel B4
26 Star Anise Boutique Capsule B3
27 Steuart B3

Eating
28 Commons B3
Heladiv Tea Club .... (see 1)
29 Hotel de Norris D3
30 Mayura Hotel E1
Ministry of Crab .... (see 1)
31 Pagoda Tea Room B3
32 T-Lounge by Dilmah B3

Drinking & Nightlife
33 New Colonial Hotel D3
34 Re.Pub.Lk B3

Entertainment
35 Bally's C4

Shopping
36 Barefoot B3
37 Laksala B3

Information
38 Bank of Ceylon B4
39 General Post Office B3

Transport
40 Bastian Mawatha Bus Station E3
41 Central Bus Station E3
42 Cinnamon Air B2
43 Colombo Fort Left-luggage Storage D3
44 Colombo Fort Train Station D3
45 Saunders Place Bus Station E2
46 Sri Lanka Transport Board E3

Galle Face Green

Colombo's front porch is immediately south of Fort. More dust-yellow than actually green, this open park is where Colombo comes to unwind as the afternoon turns to sunset. Kids play cricket and fly kites, *paan* vendors shake bottlecap rattles and couples stroll arm in arm, making the most of the cooling sea breezes. There's a tiny beach where locals paddle, but joining in is not recommended.

Just inland. Galle Face Center Rd is erupting into a garden of new skyscrapers, malls and five-star hotels, dominated by the conjoined **Sapphire Residencies** towers.

Slave Island & South Beira Lake

Bordering South Beira Lake, Slave Island is perhaps Colombo's oldest neighbourhood, and the Dutch, shamefully, did keep slaves here during colonial times. With Colombo's construction boom, the few remaining historic buildings are being replaced by luxury hotels, condos and malls.

You'll still find a lone row of **colonial storefronts** (Map p70; Union Pl, Col 2) on Union Pl, and the grand old **Sri Sivasubramania Swami** (Map p70; Kew Rd) *kovil* (Hindu temple) nearby. Of the new buildings bursting skywards, the eye-catching **Altair** (Map p70; www.altair.lk; 121A Sir James Peiris Mw, Col 2), a pair of futuristic twin towers toppling into one another, and the sheer cliff wall of glass that is **Cinnamon Life** (Map p70; www.cinnamonlife.com; off Glennie St, Col 2) deserve special mention.

★ **Gangaramaya Temple** BUDDHIST TEMPLE
(Map p70; ☎011-232 7084; www.gangaramaya.com; Sri Jinarathana Rd, Col 2; Rs 400; ⏰6am-11pm) Run by one of Sri Lanka's most powerful monks, this revered complex is not so much a temple as a treasure vault, packed floor to ceiling with offerings left by Buddhist devotees. Alongside thousands of Buddha images in

every imaginable material and style, you'll see cabinets full of jewels, cameras, wristwatches, crystals and coral, plus an impressive collection of luxury cars (including two early Rolls-Royces).

Also here is the stuffed body of the temple's late elephant, Ganga. Gangaramaya is the focus of the Navam Perahera on the February *poya* (full moon) day each year, and Vesak celebrations are also extravagant.

Seema Malakaya Meditation Centre RELIGIOUS SITE
(Map p70; South Beira Lake, Col 2; Rs 400; ⌚7.30am-10pm) This small but atmospheric spiritual centre was designed by Geoffrey Bawa in 1985 and administered by the Gangaramaya Temple. The statue-filled pavilions are popular with devotees as a place for peaceful reflection and look especially striking when illuminated at night.

Kollupitiya

Geoffrey Bawa House MUSEUM
(Number 11; Map p70; ☎011-433 7335; www.geoffreybawa.com; 11 33rd Lane, Col 3; tours Rs 1000; ⌚tours 10am, noon, 2pm & 3.30pm Mon-Fri, 11am & 4pm Sat, 11am Sun) At the end of this quiet cul-de-sac is the house where the renowned architect Bawa lived from 1960 to 1970. The house combines his usual mix of traditional forms and stark white modernist architecture. Book ahead for tours (cash only) of the interior; you can also arrange to stay in one part of the house (p75).

St Andrew's Kirk CHURCH
(Map p70; www.scotskirk.lk; 73 Galle Rd, Col 3; ⌚7am-7pm) This castle-like church from 1834 is an island of calm on Galle Rd. Inside the cool interior, the walls are lined with fulsome memorials to long-forgotten colonial Scots.

Cinnamon Gardens

About 5km southeast of Fort, inland from Kollupitiya, Cinnamon Gardens is Colombo's most upscale area. A century ago it was covered in cinnamon plantations, but the British added mansions, sporting facilities and grand civic buildings, some of which live on as embassies, cafes, boutiques and galleries.

At the centre is Viharamahadevi Park (p68), bookended by Colombo's grand, domed, White House–like **Old Town Hall** (White House; Map p70; FR Senanayaka Mw, Col 7) and other colonial-era buildings. At the south end of the park are the striking National Museum and the basket-like Nelum Pokuna Mahinda Rajapaksa Theatre (p84), used for major cultural events.

★ **National Museum** MUSEUM
(Map p70; ☎011-269 4366; www.museum.gov.lk; Albert Cres, Col 7; adult/child Rs 1000/500, with Natural History Museum Rs 1200/600; ⌚9am-5pm) Offering a captivating walk through Sri Lankan history, this delightful museum sprawls across a gleaming white, neo-Baroque building constructed for the purpose by William Henry Gregory, Governor of Ceylon, in 1877. Rooms take you through each of Sri Lanka's historical kingdoms, with display boards

GEOFFREY BAWA'S ARCHITECTURE

The most famous and best-loved Sri Lankan architect, Geoffrey Bawa (1919–2003) created a landmark style, fusing ancient and modern influences. Using courtyards and pathways, Bawa linked the interior and exterior of his buildings, bringing the outdoors inside, and vice versa, with contemplative spaces between functional rooms, and portals offering glimpses of spaces yet to be entered.

Don't miss the following standout Bawa buildings in Colombo and beyond.

Paradise Road Gallery Cafe (p81) With its atrium, courtyards and pools, this modified colonial villa used to be Bawa's office.

Seema Malakaya Meditation Centre (p67) This jewel-like pavilion floats on an island on South Beira Lake.

Geoffrey Bawa House (p67) This graceful but enigmatic house is where Bawa once lived, and it is open to visitors on guided tours.

Parliament of Sri Lanka (☎011 277 7100; www.parliament.lk; Parliament Approach Rd, Kotte; ⌚9am-3.30pm Mon-Fri, till 7pm on sitting days) Bawa's grandest construction is located on a lake island in Sri Jayawardenepura-Kotte, 11km southeast of Fort. Visits to this pavilion-like building require a complex series of approvals as outlined on the website.

ARTY COLOMBO

Colombo's chaotic urban sprawl might not seem immediately conducive to creativity, but the city has some excellent galleries and art spaces, supporting a vibrant creative arts scene. Make time for the following galleries and exhibition spaces.

Lionel Wendt Theatre (p84) A busy centre for visual arts and theatre; check the website for coming shows and events.

Saskia Fernando Gallery (Map p70; ☎ 011 742 9010; www.saskiafernandogallery.com; 41 Horton Pl, Col 7; ⏲10am-6pm) A happening small art space showcasing some of the best contemporary Sri Lankan artists. The owner is the daughter of local design maven Shanth Fernando, of Paradise Road fame.

Museum of Modern & Contemporary Art (Map p76; www.mmca-srilanka.org; 17th fl, Colombo Innovation Tower, 58 Lauries Rd, Col 4; ⏲11am-5pm Wed, & Thu, 11am-8pm Fri, 11am-5pm Sat & Sun) Colombo's best art space, this urban gallery looms over the city on the 17th floor of the Colombo Innovation Tower. There's some genuinely interesting work on show, and the views over the city are stupendous.

Nelum Pokana Art Street (Map p70; Green Path, Col 7; ⏲10.30am-6.30pm) The lane beside the National Museum serves as a street-side gallery space for local artists to sell paintings of elephants, historic sights and Sri Lankan life.

explaining interesting details such as the significance of the *mudras* (gestures and poses) of Sri Lanka's Buddha statues.

Upstairs galleries are devoted to Sri Lankan arts, crafts and culture. In the banyan tree-shaded grounds are a good cafe serving Sri Lankan meals, a branch of the **Laksala** ☎ 011-269 8263; ⏲8.30am-8pm) gift shop and the modest **Natural History Museum**, with a collection of wonky stuffed animals and skeletons.

★Viharamahadevi Park PARK

(Map p70; Col 7; ⏲24hr) The lungs of Colombo, this huge park was originally called Victoria Park, but was renamed in the 1950s after the mother of King Dutugemunu. It's notable for its flowering trees, which fill the walkways with colour from March to May. During the day, couples and families promenade, and snake charmers wander the paths looking for tourists to charm out of a few rupees.

A reflecting pool at the northeast end of the park frames a golden seated Buddha statue within the dome of the adjacent Old Town Hall (p67).

De Soysa (Lipton) Circus LANDMARK

(Map p70; Col 7) Just east of the park, this busy gyratory is flanked by an impressive collection of colonial-period buildings. The **Cinnamon Gardens Baptist Church** dates to 1877, and backs onto the **Cinnamon Gardens Post Office** (Srimath Anagarika Dharmapala Mw; ⏲7.30am-6.30pm Mon-Sat), from 1905, and the **Dewatagaha Jumma Mosque**, a rambling structure built in 1820. Across the road to the northeast is the former **Victoria Memorial Eye Hospital**, a strikingly striped brick structure with strong similarities to Kuala Lumpur's Jamek Mosque.

Independence Memorial Hall MONUMENT

(Map p70; ⏲24hr) Beside the broad, green Independence Square, this temple-like pavilion was built to mark Sri Lanka's 1948 independence from Britain. It's loosely based on Kandy's Audience Hall, which in turn was influenced by the *mandapas* (columned halls) found in Hindu temples.

Southern Colombo

Traditional Puppet Art Museum MUSEUM

(☎ 011-271 4241; www.puppet.lk; Anagarika Dharmapala Mw, Col 5; adult/child Rs 500/250; ⏲9am-5pm Tue-Sun) This engaging museum keeps the traditional art of Sri Lankan puppetry alive, with dozens of colourful traditional puppets displayed in atmospheric dioramas (check out the errant Buddhist monk being dragged to hell). With advance notice, performances can be arranged for groups. The museum is about 200m east of Galle Rd, midway between Wellawatta and Mt Lavinia.

Mt Lavinia

Colombo's closest beach retreat, Mt Lavinia provides some respite from the city's cacophony and fumes. The cafe-lined beach isn't bad, although some murky rivers empty to the north and there's an undertow. It's only 15 minutes by train from Fort (Rs 25).

Kotahena

Immediately northeast of Pettah, the culturally diverse district of Kotahena is closely linked to Colombo's port, which forms the western boundary.

St Anthony's Church CHURCH
(www.kochchikade.churchlk.com; St Anthony's Mw, Col 13; 6am-6pm) Historic St Anthony's Church was propelled into the world's press in 2019 as one of the targets for the Easter Sunday attacks, which killed more than 90 of the congregation. While security is tight, worshippers are doing their best to return to normal, filling the pews and venerating a wish-fulfilling statue of St Anthony.

Activities

★**Spa Ceylon** SPA
(Map p70; 011-233 7111; www.spaceylon.com; 103 Galle Rd, Col 3; treatments from Rs 4900; 10am-11pm) This is the most lavish branch of this chain of luxury spas, and the shop at the front is an Aladdin's cave of stunningly presented Ayurvedic creams and lotions. Therapies range from massages to sirodhara drizzled-oil treatments. There are branches all over town, including at the **Dutch Hospital** (Map p64; 011-233 4208; Bank of Ceylon Mw, Col 1, on **Park St** (Map p70; 011-243 2603; Parkland, 33 Park St, Col 2), and on Galle Rd in **Bambalapitiya** (Map p70; 011-511 6609; cnr Galle Rd & Glen Aber Pl, Col 4), plus shops in most malls.

Kemara SPA
(Map p70; 011-269 6498; www.kemaralife.com; Lakpahana Complex, 14 Phillip Gunawardena Mw, Col 7; therapies from Rs 2500; 10am-8pm) Come to this spa in the Lakpahana complex for holistic health treatments and luxurious beauty and health products, many based on fruits and herbs.

Siddhalepa Ayurveda SPA
(Map p70; 011-269 8161; www.siddhalepa.com; 33 Wijerama Mw, Col 7; therapies from Rs 3200; 8.30am-5.30pm) This full-service Ayurvedic spa offers all manner of treatments and therapies, plus consultations with Ayurvedic doctors. It runs a small pharmacy (also offering consultations) in the **One Galle Face** (Map p70; Galle Face Center Rd, Col 2; consultations Rs 2000; 10am-10pm) mall.

Kanduboda Siyane Meditation Center MEDITATION
(011-240 2306; www.insight-meditation.org; Delgoda-Pugoda Rd, Kanduboda, Delgoda; by donation) This is a major centre for meditation instruction in the style of the late Mahasi Sayadaw. Accommodation and meals are offered free of charge, but donations are expected, and most stay for at least three weeks to train. The centre is located 25km east of Colombo in Delgoda.

Tours

As well as guided tours of the city, it's easy to arrange activities such as white-water rafting, canyoning, trekking and more in the interior of the island with local operators such

COLOMBO'S MAIN NEIGHBOURHOODS

Colombo is split into 15 postal-code areas, which are often used to identify the specific districts, many of them crossed by Galle Rd, one block inland from the seashore. Street numbers start again each time you move into a new district, so there will be a '100 Galle Rd' in several different neighbourhoods. Note that traffic runs north along Galle Rd for most of its length within the city limits. To head south, follow parallel RA de Mel Mawatha, one block inland.

The main areas of interest are as follows:

DISTRICT	SUBURB
Col 1	**Fort** The restored and bustling centre of the city.
Col 2	**Slave Island** Not an island at all, with colonial-era buildings and huge new developments.
Col 3	**Kollupitiya** The dense commercial heart of the city, good for shopping, eating and sleeping.
Col 4	**Bambalapitiya** An extension of Col 3 with some good restaurants and hotels.
Col 6	**Wellawatta** More commercial sprawl south along Galle Rd, with gentrified Pamankada just inland.
Col 7	**Cinnamon Gardens** Colombo's swankiest district, home to the National Museum and Viharamahadevi Park.
Col 11	**Pettah** Old quarter just east of Fort, with thriving markets.
Col 13	**Kotahena** Historic quarter flanking the port north of Pettah.

Kollupitiya, Cinnamon Gardens & Borella

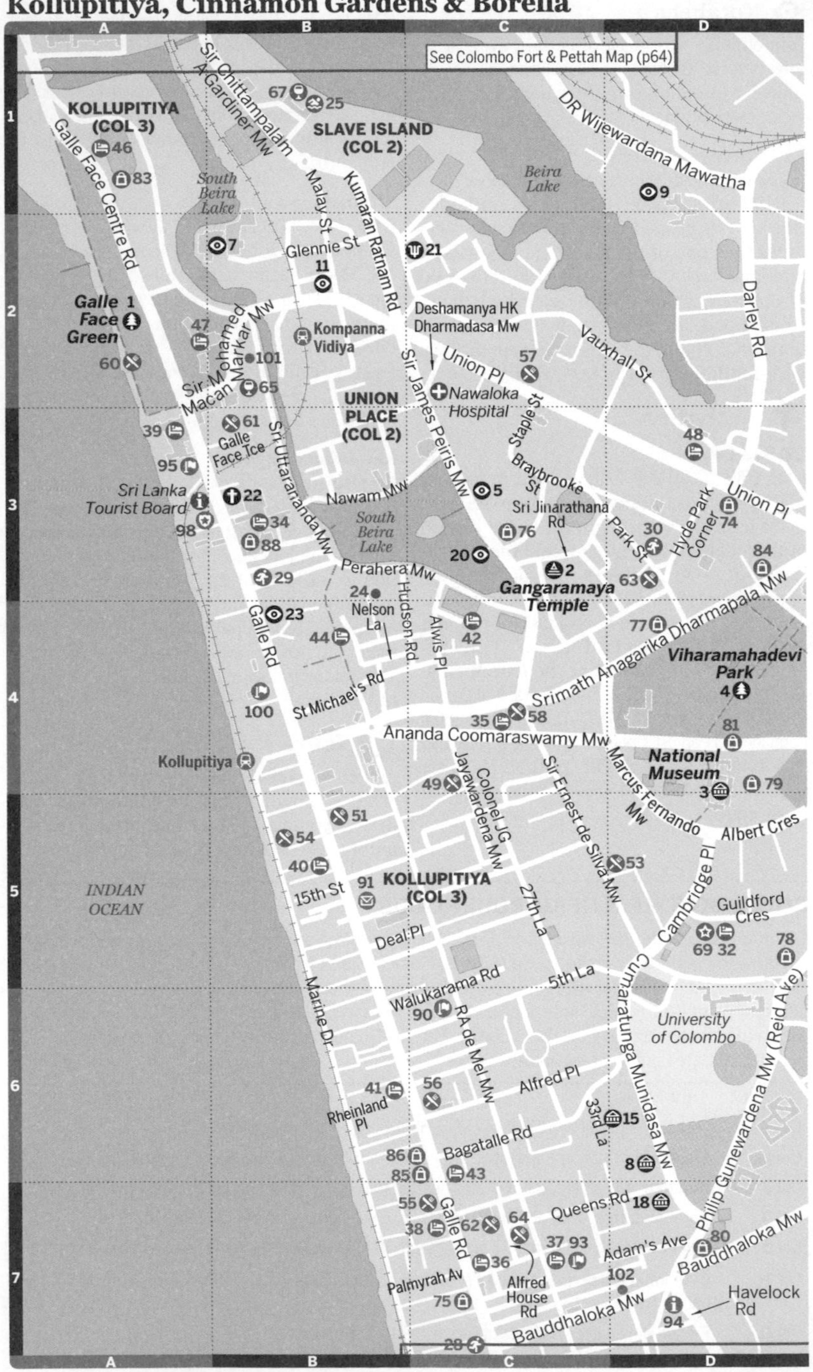

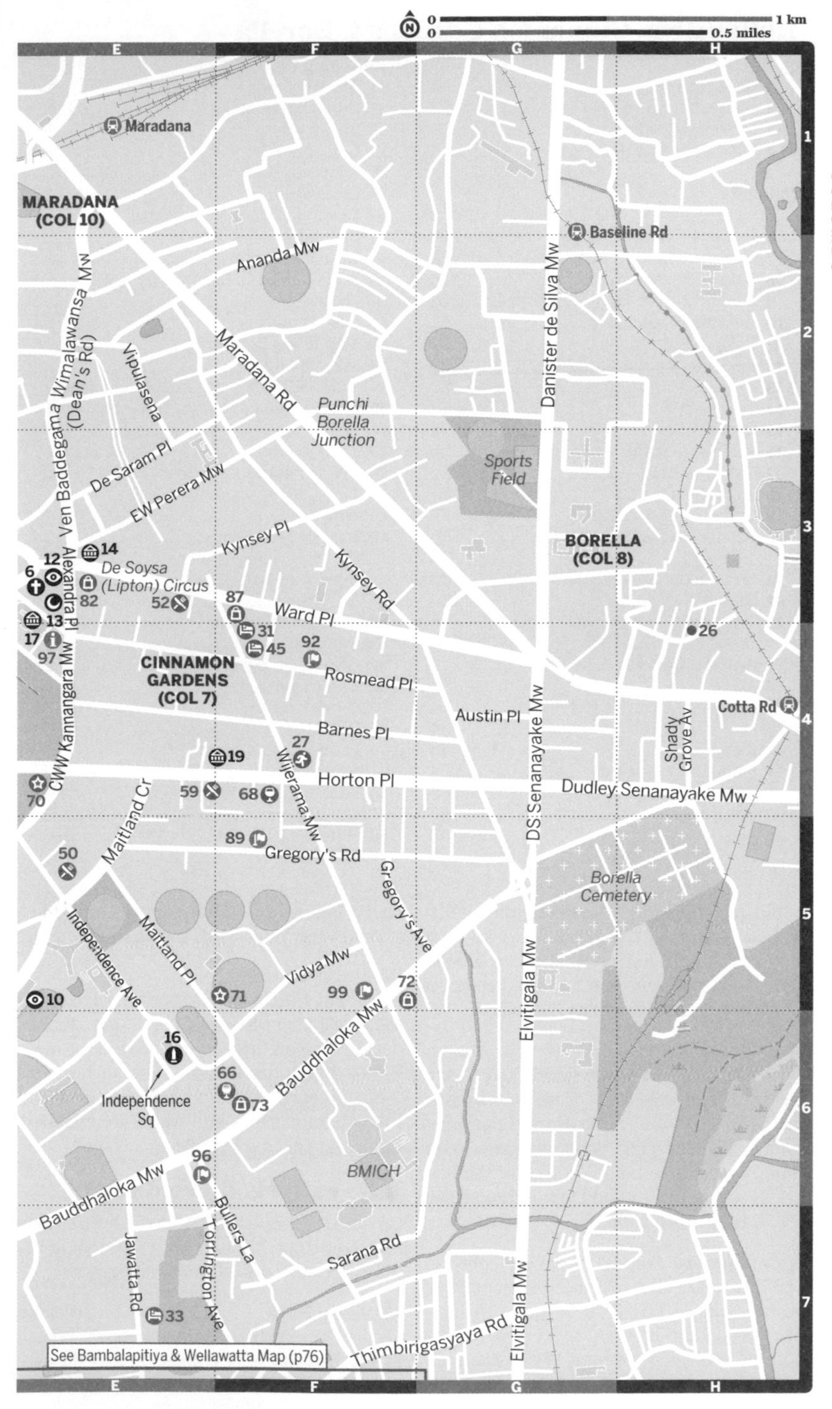

0 1 km
0 0.5 miles
Maradana
MARADANA (COL 10)
Baseline Rd
Ananda Mw
Danister de Silva Mw
Ven Baddegama Wimalawansa Mw (Dean's Rd)
Vipulasena
Maradana Rd
Punchi Borella Junction
Sports Field
De Saram Pl
EW Perera Mw
Kynsey Pl
Kynsey Rd
BORELLA (COL 8)
De Soysa (Lipton) Circus
Alexandra Pl
Ward Pl
CINNAMON GARDENS (COL 7)
Rosmead Pl
CWW Kannangara Mw
Austin Pl
Cotta Rd
Barnes Pl
Shady Grove Av
Wijerama Mw
Horton Pl
Dudley Senanayake Mw
DS Senanayake Mw
Maitland Cr
Gregory's Rd
Gregory's Ave
Borella Cemetery
Independence Ave
Maitland Pl
Vidya Mw
Elvitigala Mw
Baudhaloka Mw
Independence Sq
BMICH
Bauddhaloka Mw
Bullers La
Torrington Ave
Jawatta Rd
Sarana Rd
Thimbirigasyaya Rd
See Bambalapitiya & Wellawatta Map (p76)

Kollupitiya, Cinnamon Gardens & Borella

Top Sights
1 Galle Face Green A2
2 Gangaramaya Temple C3
3 National Museum D4
4 Viharamahadevi Park D4

Sights
5 Altair C3
6 Cinnamon Gardens Baptist Church E3
7 Cinnamon Life B2
8 College House D6
9 Colombo Lotus Tower D1
10 Colombo Racecourse E5
11 Colonial Storefronts B2
12 De Soysa (Lipton) Circus E3
13 Dewata-Gaha Mosque E3
14 Eye Hospital E3
15 Geoffrey Bawa House D6
16 Independence Memorial Hall E6
17 Old Town Hall E3
18 Saifee Villa D7
19 Saskia Fernando Gallery F4
20 Seema Malakaya Meditation Centre C3
21 Sri Sivasubramania Swami Kovil C2
22 St Andrew's Kirk B3
23 Temple Trees B4

Activities, Courses & Tours
24 Aunty's B3
25 Cinnamon Lakeside Hotel B1
26 Eco Team Sri Lanka H4
Kemara .... (see 78)
27 Siddhalepa Ayurveda F4
28 Spa Ceylon C7
29 Spa Ceylon B3
30 Spa Ceylon D3

Sleeping
31 Black Cat Bed & Breakfast F4
32 Bunkyard Hostel D5
33 Ceilão Villas E7
34 Cinnamon Grand Hotel B3
35 Cinnamon Red C4
36 Clock Inn C7
37 Colombo Court Hotel & Spa C7
38 Drift B&B C7
39 Galle Face Hotel A3
40 Hotel Renuka & Renuka City Hotel B5
41 Ivy Lane B6
42 Lake Lodge C4
43 Mandarina Colombo C6
44 Miracle City Inn B4
Number 11 .... (see 15)
45 Paradise Road Tintagel Colombo F4
46 Shangri-La Hotel A1
47 Taj Samudra A2
48 YWCA International Guest House D3

Eating
49 Bakes by Bella C4
Barefoot Garden Cafe .... (see 75)
Black Cat Cafe .... (see 31)
Boulevard .... (see 82)
50 Café Kumbuk E5
51 Carnival B5
52 Coco Veranda Cafe E3
53 Commons D5
54 Curry Pot B5
55 Dao Krua Thai C7
Food Studio, Colombo City Centre .... (see 76)
Food Studio, One Galle Face .... (see 83)
Good Market .... (see 78)
56 Hotel De Pilawoos C6
Keells .... (see 83)

as the recommended **Borderlands** (011-441 0110; www.discoverborderlands.com; activities from US$45) and **Action Lanka** (011-450 3448; www.actionlanka.com; 366/3 Rendapola Horagahakanda Lane, Talangama, Koswatta).

★Colombo Walks WALKING
(077-560 0333; www.colombowalks.com; tours adult/child from US$27/10; tours at 6.45am, 11am, 4pm) Colombo expert Harold Sandrasagara leads engaging daily walking tours lasting up to three hours, exploring the historic precincts of Fort and Pettah. Tours leave from the Dutch Hospital; book in advance.

★Colombo by Jeep DRIVING
(077-733 0900; www.colombobyjeep.com; 3½hr tour for 1-3 people US$140) Tour guide Nishantha Abeysekara is even more interesting than his vehicle, a restored WWII jeep; expect a highly entertaining romp around just about everything worth seeing in Colombo.

Colombo City Tour BUS
(011-281 4700; www.colombocitytours.com; tour adult/child from US$20/12) Open-top double-deckers run on three routes around the main sights and tours depart daily, including a weekend early evening tour. Narration is in English and snacks and water are included. Book and check schedules in advance.

Festivals & Events

Colombo's festival calendar is overwhelmingly religious, though big cricket matches fill the streets with riotous celebrations.

★Vesak Poya RELIGIOUS
(May) The birth, enlightenment and death of the Buddha is celebrated across the city, but the festivities around Gangaramaya

Temple (p66) are mind-blowing. The streets are filled by light displays and *dansala* stands, where food and treats are given away.

Vel RELIGIOUS
(Jul or Aug) During the Vel, the gilded chariot of Murugan (Skanda), the Hindu war god, is ceremonially hauled from the two Kathiresan *kovils* (temples) in Pettah (p65) to Bambalapitiya.

Navam Perahera RELIGIOUS
(Feb) Held on the February *poya* and led by 50 elephants; the parade starts from Gangaramaya Temple (p66) and visits Viharamahadevi Park and South Beira Lake.

Duruthu Perahera RELIGIOUS
(Jan) A spirited celebration held at the Kelaniya Raja Maha Vihara (p79) on the January *poya* (full moon).

Sleeping

Ritzy new five-star hotels are shooting up around Fort and along Galle Rd, and there's a fast-growing selection of high-quality budget and midrange places. The best range of budget accommodation is further south in Kollupitiya and Bambalapitiya.

Fort & Pettah

Historic Fort has several high-glam five-star hotels plus a decent scattering of budget guesthouses and hostels.

★Star Anise Boutique Capsule HOSTEL $
(Map p64; 011-245 1777; www.thestaranise.com; 15/1-1 Mudalige Mw, Col 1; pod dm/r from Rs 3310/5520;) With a dream location in the heart of Fort, this hidden-away place is just yards from the President's House. The hostel's stock in trade is boutique capsule beds

in four- or 20-bed dorms, but there are also private rooms. It's calm and quiet, and there's a rooftop terrace.

City Rest Fort HOTEL $$
(Map p64; ☎011-233 9340; fort@cityrest.lk; 46 Hospital St, Col 1; dm/r from US$22/55; ❄📶) This very professionally managed hotel and hostel is just east of the Dutch Hospital. The enthusiastic manager runs a tight ship, and the private rooms and dorms (male, female and mixed) are clean and comfy, with splashes of colour. There's a restaurant and rooftop terrace.

Grand Oriental Hotel HOTEL $$
(Map p64; ☎011-522 1100; www.grandoriental.com; 2 York St, Col 1; r from US$50; ❄📶) Opposite the harbour, this was Colombo's finest hotel a century ago, and the worn corridors, wooden elevator and cavernous rooms with four-poster beds still have a certain faded charm. Staying here is a bit like holidaying in the 1960s. Ask for a room facing the quiet inside of the block. Restaurants on the ground floor and 4th floor, and a bar and nightclub round off the package.

Hilton Colombo Hotel HOTEL $$$
(Map p64; ☎011-249 2492; www.hilton.com; 2 Sir Chittampalam A Gardiner Mw, Col 2; r from US$115; ❄@📶🏊) This large international business-class hotel is the cock of the walk in Fort, though the new Ritz-Carlton will give it a run for its money. It offers the full luxury package: smart rooms with big windows and the latest amenities, multiple restaurants, tight security and a superior lobby cake shop. The attractive pool and gym are reached via a walkway over the road.

Steuart BOUTIQUE HOTEL $$$
(Map p64; ☎011-557 5575; www.citrusleisure.com; 45 Hospital Lane, Col 1; r US$90-130; ❄📶) The Steuart is set in a renovated colonial-era building that dates from 1835. The lobby with its tartan trim, coats of arms and old woodwork sets the scene for more modern rooms upstairs with a similar Scots flavour. The reason for all this Scottishness is the original owner of the building, George Steuart, one of the first traders to set up in British-administered Ceylon.

Kollupitiya

Colombo's best range of accommodation can be found near Galle Rd and RA de Mel Mawatha. Lavish, five-star chain hotels worth considering include the garden-framed **Taj Samudra** (Map p70; ☎011-244 6622; www.tajhotels.com; 25 Galle Face Centre Rd, Col 3; s/d from US$175/185; ❄@📶🏊) and the gleaming **Shangri-La Hotel** (Map p70; ☎011-788 8288; www.shangri-la.com; 1 Galle Face Centre Rd, Col 2; r incl breakfast from US$180; ❄@📶🏊), both just back from Galle Face Green.

Miracle City Inn HOSTEL $
(Map p70; ☎077-002 3747; www.colombocityhostel.com; 177 RA de Mel Mw, Col 3; dm/r from US$10/30; ⏱reception 7am-9pm; ❄📶) This well-located hostel has a rooftop lounge/kitchen/chill-out space with great views over the city, including over nearby Temple Trees, home of the prime minister. Beds in 4- to 8-bed dorms come with curtains and lockers and there are also compact private rooms.

It's easiest to reach following the alley on the east side of the president's house from Perahera Mw (officially, the entrance is on Muhandiram's Rd).

Clock Inn HOTEL $
(Map p70; ☎011-250 0588; www.clockinn.lk; 457 Galle Rd, Col 3; dm/s/d from US$8/33/38; ❄📶) Many long-staying guests are lured to this good-value hotel by the friendly staff, tidy rooms and central location. Choose from four- to six-bed dorms or private rooms with TVs, air-con and hot showers. Breakfast is served on the terrace and you can help yourself to tea and coffee throughout the day.

★ **YWCA International Guest House** GUESTHOUSE $$
(Map p70; ☎011-232 4181; www.ywcacolombo.com; 393 Union Pl, Col 2; r with cold water & fan from Rs 4700, with hot water & air-con from Rs 6750; ❄📶) Set in a huge compound of buildings associated with the 'Y', this nostalgic colonial bungalow features plain but airy guest rooms opening onto a central lounge with whirring ceiling fans. It's a setting straight from an EM Forster novel, and in the evening, you can relax on rattan planters' chairs on the veranda.

Drift B&B B&B $$
(Map p70; ☎011-250 5536; www.facebook.com/driftbnb; 646 Galle Rd, Col 3; dm US$12-15, r from US$55; ❄@📶) In a mural-covered courtyard building on Galle Rd, this flashpacker special looks a little like a 1950s motel from the outside, but rooms inside are full of arty touches and pot plants. Bags are hauled upstairs with a mechanical hoist.

Ivy Lane GUESTHOUSE $$
(Map p70; ☎011-257 5733; www.ivylane.lk; 538 Galle Rd, Col 3; s/d from Rs 6300/7200; ❄📶) A real urban retreat, Ivy Lane offers 15 rooms decorated in subtle colours, with sleek bathrooms and lots of natural light. Some have balconies, and communal spaces are livened up by colourful pieces of art.

Hotel Renuka & Renuka City Hotel HOTEL $$
(Map p70; ☎011-257 3598; www.renukahotel.com; 328 Galle Rd, Col 3; s/d from US$60/70; ❄📶🏊) The well-run Renuka is split across two different buildings on Galle Rd, but both blocks contain well-maintained rooms, accessed via businesslike wooden corridors. Ask for a room not facing noisy Galle Rd. The staff are attentive, and there's a good basement restaurant, known for its Jaffna dishes.

★**Galle Face Hotel** HERITAGE HOTEL $$$
(Map p70; ☎011-254 1010; www.gallefacehotel.com; 2 Galle Rd, Col 3; r from US$175; ❄@📶🏊) The grande dame of Colombo hotels faces Galle Face Green to the north and the ocean to the west. Behind cream-coloured walls, the atmospheric lobby is filled with columns and creaking wooden floorboards, and a wood-panelled lift (or a sweeping wooden staircase) whisks guests to rooms that are decorated just as you'd want them to be in a hotel dating from 1864.

★**Lake Lodge** GUESTHOUSE $$$
(Map p70; ☎011-232 6443; www.taruvillas.com; 20 Alvis Tce, Col 3; r from US$120; ❄📶🏊) Set in a whitewashed modernist villa near South Beira Lake, the rooms at Lake Lodge are full of designer furniture, abstract artworks and polished concrete. Rooftop terraces have lake views, service is excellent and you can easily walk to the sights.

★**Cinnamon Grand Hotel** HOTEL $$$
(Map p70; ☎011-243 7437; www.cinnamonhotels.com; 77 Galle Rd, Col 3; r US$125; ❄@📶🏊) Colombo's best five-star hotel has a prime location just south of Galle Face Green but sits well back from Galle Rd. It buzzes with life as there always seems to be an elite wedding on or some high-profile politician strolling the huge, airy lobby. The tasteful rooms have massive windows looking over the ocean, the lake or the city.

All traces of the 2019 bombing have been erased, and there's Fort Knox–level security. The hotel has a fitness centre, a stunning outdoor swimming pool and numerous top-notch restaurants.

★**Colombo Court Hotel & Spa** BOUTIQUE HOTEL $$$
(Map p70; ☎011-464 5333; www.colombocourthotel.com; 32 Alfred House Ave, Col 3; s/d incl breakfast US$82/94; ❄📶🏊) A surprising find on busy RA de Mel Mawatha, offering a real escape from the city crush. Colombo Court spills across greenery-filled atriums and ponds, with a delightful pool, calm lounge spaces and the popular rooftop bar Cloud Cafe (p83). Rooms are large, and ice-cool, with natural wood furniture and chic moulded concrete bathrooms.

Cinnamon Red HOTEL $$$
(Map p70; ☎011-214 5145; www.cinnamonhotels.com; 59 Ananda Coomaraswamy Mw, Col 3; s/d from US$78/94; ❄@📶🏊) Popular from the day it opened, this towering 26-floor hotel from the Cinnamon Group feels modern, cool and international, with a red, black and white colour scheme that extends from the lobby to the smart rooms, all with floor-to-ceiling windows framing the view. There's a sleek bar (p83) and pool on the top floor.

Number 11 INN $$$
(Map p70; ☎011-433 7335; www.geoffreybawa.com; 11 33rd Lane, Col 3; s/d/tr incl breakfast US$275/300/375) Geoffrey Bawa fans can stay in his stylish former Colombo home (p66), a graceful modernist villa with plenty of signature Bawa touches. Only one group of guests can stay at a time, and the apartment has stylish bedrooms, a sitting room and access to a 3rd-floor loggia and open-air deck.

Mandarina Colombo HOTEL $$
(Map p70; ☎011 255 0660; www.mandarinacolombo.com; 433 Galle Rd, Col 3; s/d from

COLOMBO LOTUS TOWER

Without doubt, the most eye-catching building on the Colombo skyline is the green and purple **Colombo Lotus Tower** (Map p70; DR Wijewardana Mw, Col 2), rising in obvious flower-like form above Slave Island. Topping 350m, the Lotus Tower is 24m taller than the Eiffel Tower, and when open will host an array of tourist attractions, including an observation deck at the top. Like most other megaprojects in Sri Lanka, it is being financed by China, and is running behind schedule. At the time of research, opening was projected for late 2021 or beyond.

Bambalapitiya & Wellawatta

Bambalapitiya & Wellawatta

Sights
1 Museum of Modern & Contemporary Art A1

Sleeping
2 Hotel Sunshine A2
3 Ozo Colombo A3

Eating
4 Beach Wadiya A4
5 Bombay Sweet Mahal B4
6 Chana's B4
7 ID: Kiku B2

Drinking & Nightlife
8 Kopi Kade D4
9 Rhythm & Blues A1

Shopping
10 Gandhara D4
11 Selyn D2
12 Vijitha Yapa Bookshop A1

US$80/90; ❄☒) A smart new addition on Galle Rd, this neat and tidy tower is crowned by a rooftop pool and restaurant with enviable views. Rooms below have ritzy carpets, dark-wood tones and a good selection of hotel mod cons. Bathrooms are compact, but prices are good value for the facilities.

Cinnamon Gardens

Away from the main thoroughfares, there are some superior places to stay along the tree-lined side streets.

★**Bunkyard Hostel** HOSTEL $
(Map p70; ☎077-730 2865; www.bunkyardhostels.com; 20A Guildford Cres, Col 7; dm/r from US$10/40; ❄@☎) Colombo's hippest hostel, this cool spot by the Lionel Wendt Theatre

has upbeat staff, inviting chill-out areas, colourful murals and smart dorms with bunk beds, set in a modernist concrete villa with an upstairs terrace. Dorms are female-only or mixed and there are a handful of private rooms.

Black Cat Bed & Breakfast B&B **$$**
(Map p70; ☎011-267 5111; www.blackcatcolombo.com; 11 Wijerama Mw, Col 7; r from US$45; ❄📶) One of Colombo's best cafes also rents out five rooms with stylish four-poster beds in a lovely old house east of Viharamahadevi Park. Guests can make use of a shared lounge and breezy balcony. Bookings can be made through Airbnb.

★**Paradise Road Tintagel Colombo** BOUTIQUE HOTEL **$$$**
(Map p70; ☎011-460 2060; www.tintagelcolombo.com; 65 Rosmead Pl, Col 7; r incl breakfast from US$200; ❄@📶🏊) Set inside a gorgeous old mansion that was the former home of Sri Lankan prime minister SWRD Bandaranaike (and also where he was assassinated), this stunningly stylish hotel dazzles with its dark, atmospheric interiors, chandeliers and candelabras. The blend of old and new is note perfect and each of the 10 rooms is unique (some even include a private splash pool).

Bambalapitiya, Havelock Town & Wellawatta

Bambalapitiya station provides access to this area of inexpensive hotels and good Indian food.

Hotel Sunshine HOTEL **$$**
(Map p76; ☎011-401 7676; www.hotelsunshine.lk; 5A Shrubbery Gardens, Col 4; r with fan/air-con from Rs 2500/3500; ❄📶) This small budget hotel is hemmed in by even taller neighbours, but it's chintzy and cheap, with a vibe like a 1980s living room. Rooms are reached via mazelike corridors but are tiled and clean, and the address will appeal to Monty Python fans everywhere.

★**Ceilão Villas** BOUTIQUE HOTEL **$$$**
(Map p70; ☎011-723 5232; www.ceilaovillas.com; 47/1 Jawatta Rd, Col 5; r from US$75; ❄📶🏊) Isolated from the street mayhem, this stylish designer home has a hint of Geoffrey Bawa in its architecture. Portals through white concrete walls reveal hidden shared spaces, there are pools on two floors, and guests stay in huge, atmospheric rooms with parquet floors and designer furniture.

Ozo Colombo HOTEL **$$$**
(Map p76; ☎011-255 5570; www.ozohotels.com; 36-38 Clifford Pl, Col 4; r from US$80; ❄@📶🏊) Offering calm, high-rise comfort right on Colombo's waterfront, this striking tower hotel climbs 14 floors close to Wellawatta train station. Well-appointed rooms are bright and modern and the rooftop pool seems to merge with the ocean.

Mt Lavinia

Best known by locals for its exclusive private schools, Mt Lavinia is a 30-minute drive (or a Rs 25 train ride) from Fort and has a low-key, beachy charm.

Colombo Beach Hostel HOSTEL **$**
(Map p80; ☎077-787 1393; www.colombobeachhostel.com; De Saram Rd; dm Rs 1200, r with fan/air-con Rs 3500/4500; ❄📶) You get what it says on the tin at this simple but calm hostel: tidy concrete dorms and rooms with aquamarine trim, wifi, a rooftop terrace and a small courtyard cafe, yards from the beach.

★**Cottage Gardens Bungalows** HOTEL **$$**
(Map p80; ☎077-794 7804; www.cottagegardenbungalows.com; 42-48 College Ave; r from US$35; ❄📶) True to its name, this walled tropical garden contains five inviting bungalows with terraces, kitchenettes, air-conditioning and TVs, though you'll probably spend more time sitting outside enjoying the garden. Rates are a bargain and it's seconds from the surf on the road by St Thomas' College.

Blue Seas Guest House GUESTHOUSE **$$**
(Map p80; ☎011-271 6298; blueseas.mt@gmail.com; 9/6 De Saram Rd; r with fan/air-con from Rs 3500/4500; ❄📶) This well-managed guesthouse has rooms that are chintzy but clean and spacious, some with balconies. There's a large shared sitting room and garden, and welcoming staff. It's down a short lane at the north end of the strip.

Mount Lavinia Hotel HOTEL **$$$**
(Map p80; ☎011-271 1711; www.mountlaviniahotel.com; 100 Hotel Rd; s/d from US$110/130; ❄📶🏊) The main wing of this grand seafront hotel on the headland at the south end of the beach dates to 1806, when it was the residence of the British governor. The appropriately named 'governor's wing' has all the prerequisite colonial trim, but rooms are larger and arguably grander in the modern annexe. The beautifully positioned pool and terrace have sweeping ocean views.

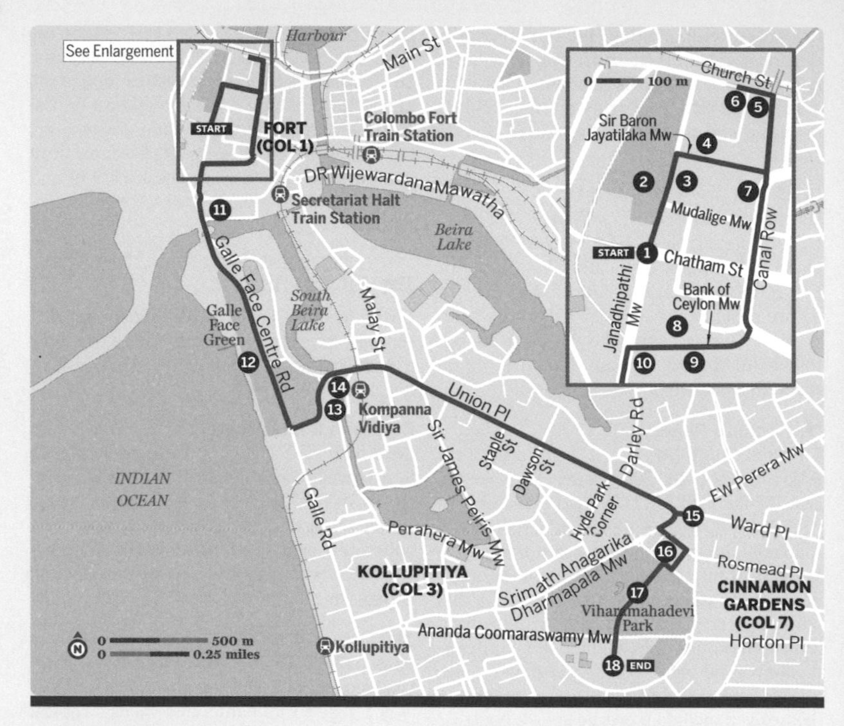

Walking Tour
Fort to Cinnamon Gardens

START CLOCK TOWER
END NATIONAL MUSEUM
LENGTH 9KM; FIVE HOURS

The best place to get a feel for Colombo in its trading heyday is the British-built Fort, flanking Colombo harbour and the new, under-construction Colombo Port City. Start at the **1 Clock Tower** (p64), a former lighthouse, on Janadhipathi Mawatha, and stroll past the imposing, fortress-like **2 President's House**, facing the once grand **3 General Post Office**. Turn right onto Sir Baron Jayathilaka Mawatha, passing the handsome **4 Lloyd's Buildings** and turn left to duck round the back of the **5 Grand Oriental Hotel** (p74) to reach **6 St Peter's Church** (p64) with its mournful memorials to sons of empire.

Return to York St and wander past the historic frontage of the original **7 Cargills Main Store** (p64), with its nostalgic signboards. Continue south to Bank of Ceylon Mawatha to see the old, in the shape of the gorgeously restored **8 Dutch Hospital** (p62; a great place to pause for a restorative drink and snack), juxtaposed with the new, in the form of the looming **9 World Trade Centre** and **10 Bank of Ceylon** (p87) tower. Reconnect with Janadhipathi Mawatha and follow it south to meet Galle Face Centre Rd, passing the handsome, tobacco-coloured **11 Presidential Secretariat**, another British-era heirloom.

Pause to catch a sea breeze with the strolling couples on **12 Galle Face Green**, then head inland on Sir Mohamed Macan Markar Mawatha, passing the venerable **13 Christ Church** from 1853, and the **14 Victoria Masonic Lodge**, a suitably grand construction from 1901. To reach Cinnamon Gardens, you'll have a long walk (or easy three-wheeler ride) along Union Pl, ending at **15 De Soysa (Lipton) Circus** (p68), with its eclectic collection of colonial relics. Turn southwest on Srimath Anagarika Dharmapala Mawatha, passing the White House–like **16 Old Town Hall** (p67), and cross **17 Viharamahadevi Park** (p68) to finish off in the **National Museum** (p67) – phew, that's a lot of history!

Sunday lunch at the hotel's Governor's Restaurant (p82) is hugely popular.

Eating

Colombo has the best variety of restaurants on the island, with everything from local-style rice and curry to five-star fine dining. However, there are more options at the middle and top of the price range than cheap eats.

The websites www.yamu.lk and www.tasty.lk are good resources for the fast-changing Colombo dining scene.

Fort & Pettah

Hordes of office workers flock into Fort by day and flock out again by night, so things are busy at lunchtime and just after work, but quieter later. Nearby Pettah is busy day and night, with 'hotels' (inexpensive rice and curry restaurants) serving blisteringly authentic local meals.

★Pagoda Tea Room BAKERY $

(Map p64; ☎011-232 5252; 105 Chatham St, Col 1; mains Rs 90-500; ⏲7.30am-5.30pm Mon-Fri, 7.30am-1.30pm Sat) Hungry like the wolf? Duran Duran filmed the classic 1980s video for that very song in this venerable colonial-era tea room, which opened in 1884. It's now run by the Green Cabin bakery and offers tasty and inexpensive short eats, *lamprais* (curry and rice baked in banana leaves), packed curry and rice meals and lime juice or iced coffee.

Hotel de Norris SRI LANKAN $

(Map p64; Olcott Mw, Col 11; mains Rs 180-500; ⏲6am-10.30pm) For a quick bite while waiting for a train, you can do a lot worse than this brightly coloured canteen just up the road from Fort station. Surrounded by vivid yellow and red wall panels, you can enjoy tasty fried rice, rice and curry plates and biryani, plus freshly baked short eats and juices.

Mayura Hotel SRI LANKAN $

(Map p64; 46 Sri Kathiresan St, Col 11; mains Rs 250-750; ⏲noon-3.30pm & 6.30-9.30pm) This tiny hole-in-the-wall canteen on a back lane near Pettah's Old Town Hall looks dingy, but the rice and curry here is fabulously spicy and full of flavour, with a choice of fish, chicken, cuttlefish, crab, prawn or egg as the main curry.

★T-Lounge by Dilmah CAFE $$

(Map p64; ☎031-227 2874; www.dilmaht-lounge.com; Chatham St, Col 1; teas & snacks from Rs 350; ⏲8am-11pm; 📶) Run by Sri Lanka's most famous tea producer, Dilmah, this upmarket cafe is a temple to tea, with iPad menus of fine Sri Lankan brews (including superior Silver Tips) plus scrummy cakes and light meals. Whole-leaf teas come with a timer to ensure the perfect cuppa.

There's a branch at the front of the One Galle Face (p86) mall.

Heladiv Tea Club CAFE $$

(Map p64; ☎011-575 3377; www.heladivteaclub.com; Old Dutch Hospital, Col 1; mains Rs 350-1300; ⏲8am-midnight; 📶) Spicy local nibbles, fat burgers, fresh salads and more are served at this casual cafe in the Dutch Hospital. It also serves a mean cup of tea, with a range of single-estate brews.

★Ministry of Crab SEAFOOD $$$

(Map p64; ☎011-234 2722; www.ministryofcrab.com; Dutch Hospital, Col 1; mains Rs 2500-39,400; ⏲6-11pm Mon-Fri, noon-11pm Sat & Sun) This high-profile restaurant – often celebrated as Colombo's best – is a cathedral to crabs, serving the delectable crustaceans in a stunning variety of peparations, from chilled butter crab to Sri Lankan-style pepper and chilli crab. Prices are based on size, ranging from Rs 6100 for a modest 500g crawler to Rs 23,400 for a 2kg 'crabzilla'. On a smaller budget, try the baked crab for Rs 2500.

JOINING THE PILGRIMS AT KELANIYA RAJA MAHA VIHARA

Thronged by pilgrims dressed in immaculate white, Colombo's most impressive religious sight is 9km from the centre in Kelaniya. **Kelaniya Raja Maha Vihara** (☎011-291 1505; www.kelaniyatemple.org; Biyagama Rd; ⏲5am-10pm) was reputedly founded by the Buddha on his third visit to Sri Lanka, making the temple more than 2500 years old, though the current building dates to the 18th century.

Flanked by vendors selling lotus bloom offerings, the main shrine is lavishly decorated inside with murals, some added more recently by Sri Lankan artist Solias Mendis, including an elaborate depiction of Mahinda and Sanghamitta bringing Buddhism to Sri Lanka on what looks like a European galleon.

Several buses run this way from southern Colombo, but it's much easier to come by three-wheeler (bank on Rs 1000 upwards with waiting).

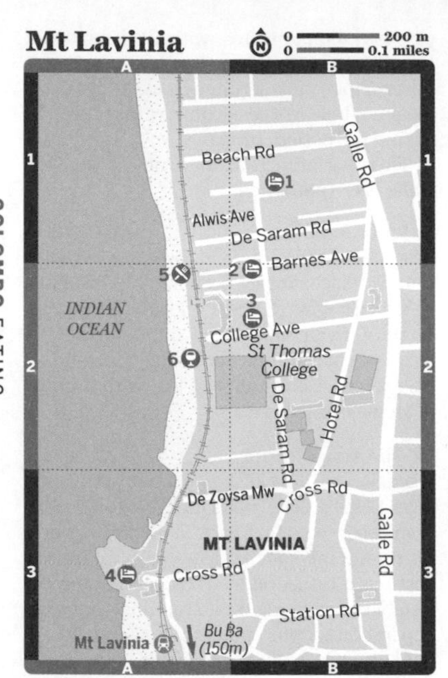

Mt Lavinia

Activities, Courses & Tours
Mount Lavinia Hotel .... (see 4)

Sleeping
1 Blue Seas Guest House B1
2 Colombo Beach Hostel B2
3 Cottage Gardens Bungalows B2
4 Mount Lavinia Hotel A3

Eating
Governor's Restaurant .... (see 4)
5 Sugar Beach LVB A2

Drinking & Nightlife
6 Shore By O A2

Kollupitiya, Slave Island & Union Place

Galle Rd is studded with veteran eateries that pull in a local crowd, plus some posher fine-dining restaurants on the backroads between Galle Rd and RA de Mel Mawatha.

★Nana's STREET FOOD $
(Map p70; Galle Face Green, Col 3; dishes Rs 250-600; 4pm-midnight) Easily spotted amongst the vendors on Galle Face Green, Nana's has a loyal following for its grilled meats, *kotthu* and rice dishes. Expect no frills – choose a battered plastic stool and wonky table and enjoy a filling meal served in double-quick time by the glow of sunset.

Curry Pot SRI LANKAN $
(Map p70; 011-237 0119; www.currypotlk.com; 314/1/A Marine Dr, Col 3; mains Rs 150-500; 6.30am-4.30pm;) With the splashing of the Indian Ocean against the seawall across the street, settle back for some superior local food at this little eatery that serves some of the most authentic Sri Lankan flavours in the city. Mornings are all about string hoppers and sauces, whereas lunchtimes are about rice and curry.

Carnival ICE CREAM $
(Map p70; 011-257 6265; 263 Galle Rd, Col 3; ice cream from Rs 130; 10am-11pm) Unchanged in decades, Carnival serves extremely creamy ice cream, in all the usual international flavours, plus local variations like mango, durian and coconut. Set in a historic villa with original Victorian floor tiles, it's a big hit with Colombo families.

★Barefoot Garden Cafe CAFE $$
(Map p70; 011-258 9305; www.barefootceylon.com; 704 Galle Rd, Col 3; mains Rs 750-1950; 10am-7pm Mon-Sat, 11am-6pm Sun;) Located in the courtyard of the excellent Barefoot (p84) gift shop, this casual garden cafe is a favoured hangout for expat ladies – and gents – who lunch. Come for ciabatta, bagels, sandwiches, wraps and good breakfasts; on Sunday there's popular live jazz at lunchtime.

★Dao Krua Thai THAI $$
(Map p70; 077-960 3760; 618 Galle Rd, Col 3; mains Rs 700-1500; 11am-4pm & 6.30-10.30pm Tue-Sun) This streetwise cafe serves full-flavoured Thai dishes, prepared with gusto by the energetic Dao, who bustles around the kitchen like a whirlwind. Diners eat at shared tables, and the menu covers everything from green curries to *pad kraprao* (stir-fried mince with Thai basil) with sticky rice.

Park Street Mews Cafe CAFE $$
(Map p70; 011-230 0133; www.parkstreetmews.com; 50/1 Park St, Col 2; mains Rs 700-3650; 11am-11pm;) The flagship eatery in an upmarket mews filled with cafes and bars, this cavernous, lantern-lit space feels very European, and the menu runs to healthy Continental-style salads, pepper steaks, burgers and deli sandwiches with parma ham and sun-dried tomatoes.

★Nihonbashi Honten JAPANESE **$$$**
(Map p70; ☎011-232 3847; www.nihonbashi.lk; 11 Galle Face Tce, Col 3; sushi from Rs 600, mains Rs 4400-21,000; ⏰noon-2.30pm & 6-10.30pm) Gird the expense account for a feast at Colombo's best Japanese restaurant. The sushi, *donburi* and Kobe beef (at the usual stratospheric Wagyu prices) are as good as you can find anywhere in Asia, and the sleek interior spills into a Japanese garden, where you can savour sake and cocktails.

★Paradise Road Gallery Cafe ASIAN **$$$**
(Map p70; ☎011-258 2162; www.paradiseroad.lk; 2 Alfred House Rd, Col 3; mains Rs 1125-5150; ⏰10am-midnight; 📶) In the courtyard garden of a colonial villa on a quiet lane east of Galle Rd, this stylish indoors-outdoors restaurant is easily the most romantic place for dinner in Colombo. At night, candles light up the tables and the courtyard beneath the *flamboiã* tree fills with couples staring into each others' eyes and enjoying superior Asian fusion and modern European cuisine. We strongly recommend the lemongrass chicken served over spinach mash.

The courtyard-filled space used to be the office of Sri Lanka's most famous architect, Geoffrey Bawa. A small shop sells gifts from the Paradise Road (p84) design shop.

Mango Tree INDIAN **$$$**
(Map p70; ☎011-762 0620; 82 Srimath Anagarika Dhamapala Mw, Col 3; mains Rs 875-1300; ⏰noon-3pm & 7-11pm) One of the best Indian restaurants in town, serving authentic flavours from North and South India in a tidy modern dining room with plush purple chairs, just west of Viharamahadevi Park. It's great for tandoori dishes, kebabs and meaty curries, and fully licensed.

Thai Cuisine Boulevard THAI **$$$**
(Map p70; ☎011-205 5425; 33 Queens Rd, Col 3; mains Rd 650-1750; ⏰11.45am-2.15pm & 6.45-10.15pm) This cool, celadon-coloured Thai restaurant oozes class. Walls are dotted with Thai ornaments and the menu takes in delicious dishes from all over Thailand. There's no liquor license, but the owners are working on it.

Cinnamon Gardens

Many of Colombo's best eateries can be found along the genteel streets of the city's classiest district. As well as the proper restaurants, check out the area's many cool cafes (p85).

★Commons BISTRO **$$**
(Map p70; ☎011-269 4435; 39A Sir Ernest de Silva Mw, Col 7; mains Rs 400-1030; ⏰9.30am-11am Sun-Thu, to midnight Fri & Sat; 📶) Our favourite Colombo cafe, in part for its spectacular Sri Lankan curries and *rotti* and rice meals, on top of a huge menu of coffees, cakes, burgers and international dishes. It's a charmingly laid-back space, sprawling over several dining rooms and a shady rear garden; come for breakfast and you might not leave all day.

There's a more workaday **branch** (Map p64; Chatham St, Col 1; ⏰8am-6.30pm Mon-Fri) in Fort.

Good Market MARKET **$$**
(Map p70; ☎077-276 4455; www.goodmarket.lk; Lakhapana Complex, 14 Phillip Gunawardena Mw, Col 7; light mains from Rs 350; ⏰8am-8pm) This organic and artisan food market fills a store in the same complex as the Lakpahana (p85) souvenir emporium, and on Saturdays, it spills out into an open-air market in the old Colombo Racecourse across the road (from 9am to 5pm). On non-market days, Colombo's middle classes hang out in the cafe area for soy lattes, fried rice, wraps and hoppers.

Paradise Road Cafe CAFE **$$**
(Map p70; ☎011-268 6043; www.paradiseroad.lk; 213 Srimath Angarika Dharmapala Mw, Col 7; mains Rs 395-1325; ⏰10am-7pm) Part of the Paradise Road design empire, this small but smart cafe serves posh teas, coffees, milkshakes, luscious cakes and light lunches on the 2nd floor above the popular design shop.

Wellawatta

A good area for Indian food, south from Bambalapitiya along Galle Rd, with hip Pamankada just inland.

PLACES TO SPLASH

The nearest place you might consider an ocean dip is at Mt Lavinia or Negombo. If you're happy with a pool, many upper-range hotels let guests use the facilities for a fee. Try the pools at the **Cinnamon Lakeside Hotel** (Map p70; ☎011-216 1161; 115 Sir Chittampalam A Gardiner Mw, Col 2; nonguests adult/child Rs 2500/2000; ⏰6am-9pm) and the grand **Mount Lavinia Hotel** (Map p80; ☎011-271 1711; 100 Hotel Rd, Mt Lavinia; nonguests Rs 2500; ⏰8am-8pm).

SUPERIOR FAST FOOD

For a quick meal in air-conditioned comfort, hit Colombo's malls and department stores. The following food courts are top spots to lunch without breaking a sweat.

Food Studio, Colombo City Centre (Map p70; Sir James Pieris Mw, Col 2; mains Rd 200-1500; ⌚10am-10pm) Looking out on South Beira Lake, the globetrotting food court at Colombo City Centre is a relaxed, family-friendly place to graze.

Food Studio, One Galle Face (Map p70; Galle Face Centre Rd, Col 2; mains from Rs 500; ⌚10am-11pm) The lower ground level of this shimmering new mall has eating options from every corner of the globe.

Boulevard (Map p70; Odel, 5 Alexandra Pl, Col 7; meals Rs 200-1400; ⌚10am-8pm) The slick outdoor food court at Odel serves up top-class world food, in a handy, central Cinnamon Gardens location.

Bombay Sweet Mahal SWEETS $

(Map p76; 161 Galle Rd, Col 6; sweets per 100g from Rs 80; ⌚9am-9pm Mon-Sat, 9am-4pm Sun) This Indian sweet shop sells everything from *gulab jamun* (milk curd balls in syrup) to thick and chewy nut *musket* (sweet syrup, thickened into a sticky cake). It has a **branch** (331 Galle Rd, Col 6) a short way down the street.

Yaal Restaurant SRI LANKAN $$

(☎077-222 0022; 56 Vaverset Pl, Marine Dr, Col 6; mains Rs 400-1000; ⌚7am-9.30pm, to 10.30pm Sat & Sun) The spicy Tamil cuisine of Jaffna is the drawcard at this simple but highly regarded restaurant across from the seashore. The house speciality is *odiyal kool*, a famous Jaffna dish consisting of vegetables and seafood combined in a creamy porridge, but the menu also includes filling 'rice meal' specials and a mean crab curry.

Chana's INDIAN $$

(Map p76; ☎011-328 8788; www.chanas.lk; 50 WA Silva Mw, Col 6; mains Rs 400-1250; ⌚11am-11pm) A superior North Indian restaurant on WA Silva Mawatha, with a smart, bright dining room and a full menu of tandoori dishes and kebabs. The house special is the *dum biryani* (Hyderabadi-style spiced rice with meat) but we strongly recommend the *harilyali* chicken – kebabs marinated with mint, coriander and chilli.

Beach Wadiya SEAFOOD $$$

(Map p76; ☎011-258 8568; www.beachwadiya.com; 2 Station Ave, Col 6; mains Rs 850-3000; ⌚11am-3.30pm & 6-11pm) Cross the tracks north of Wellawatta train station and enter a sand-floored enclave lit by romantic lights. Waiters describe what's fresh – there's always crab, prawns and lobster – then you can order something cold and watch the sunset while your meal is cooked. It's quiet for lunch, busier for dinner.

Mt Lavinia

The beachfront strip at Mt Lavinia is lined with cafes – some cool, some ramshackle – offering drinks, Western-style snack meals and local seafood.

Sugar Beach LVB CAFE $$

(Map p80; ☎011-703 5135; www.facebook.com/sugarbeachsl; mains Rs 700-2100; ⌚9am-11.30pm) At this smart beachside cafe, a row of iconic palm trees wafts over a white picket fence, fronting a gleaming, white pavilion dining room. The drinks list is long and the menu runs to posh sandwiches, pasta and seafood.

Surfboards and sun loungers are available for rent. Look for the cafe across the tracks behind the Mount Breeze Hotel.

★**Bu Ba** SEAFOOD $$$

(☎011-273 2190; www.bubabeach.com; 42/1 Vihara Rd; mains Rs 480-3200; ⌚9am-1am) With candlelit tables right on the sandy beach, this kick-off-your-shoes seafood restaurant is a hidden treat. In the heat of the day you can retreat into a grove of pandanus and palm trees; at night, sit out under the stars and enjoy the breeze. The menu covers everything from crabs, prawns and cuttlefish to marlin and seer (Spanish mackerel).

★**Governor's Restaurant** BUFFET $$$

(Map p80; ☎011-271 1711; www.mountlaviniahotel.com; Mount Lavinia Hotel, 100 Hotel Rd; buffet lunch/dinner from Rs 2500/3500; ⌚6.30-10.30am, 12.30-3pm & 7-10.30pm) The main restaurant at the Mount Lavinia Hotel has buffets three times a day, with themes that change daily. The special Sunday lunch is a local legend: there's live jazz and blues, and patrons get to use the hotel's beautiful pool.

Drinking & Nightlife

Hotel bars abound, and there are some hip hidden nightspots, many hosting live bands or DJs. Note that the last orders call comes early: technically 11pm, although many places keep pouring much later.

★Cloud Red LOUNGE

(Map p70; ☎011-214 5175; www.cinnamonhotels.com; Cinnamon Red, 59 Ananda Coomaraswamy Mw, Col 3; ⌚5pm-midnight) The rooftop bar high on the 26th floor of the popular Cinnamon Red (p75) hotel has stellar views, and for once, the drinks at this particular eyrie match the sights, as do the snacks and small meals. It's a perfect spot to say goodbye to Colombo on your last night.

★Inn... on the Green BAR

(Map p70; ☎011-254 1010; Galle Face Hotel, Galle Rd, Col 3; ⌚4pm-midnight) The wood-lined bar at the Galle Face Hotel (p75) has a lively buzz at weekends, when a post-office crowd gathers to sing along with the live band and there's barely standing room at the bar. Drinks are half price during the 5.30pm to 7.30pm happy hour.

Re.Pub.Lk LOUNGE

(Map p64; ☎011-744 6654; www.facebook.com/therepublk; 57 Hospital St, Col 1; ⌚12.30-11pm Sun-Thu, to 2.30am Fri & Sat) This property was a bar back in colonial times, but it's been thoroughly reinvented as a cool modern cocktail lounge. The cocktail list is long and creative – and reasonably priced, with long drinks starting from Rs 800 – and various snack plates are on hand to keep hunger at bay.

Asylum LOUNGE

(Map p70; ☎011-406 1761; www.asylum.lk; Arcade Independence Sq, 30 Bauddhaloka Mw, Col 7; ⌚11am-late Mon-Fri, 8am-late Sat & Sun) Sleek cocktail bar Asylum takes its name from the original use of this historic building before it became a modern mall. The bar is moodily lit and sophisticated, with excellent cocktails made by talented bartenders and upscale bites to go with the drinks.

Cloud Cafe COCKTAIL BAR

(Map p70; ☎011-464 5333; www.colombocourthotel.com; Colombo Court Hotel, 32 Alfred House Ave, Col 3; ⌚5.30pm-midnight Sun-Thu, to 1am Fri & Sat) The rooftop bar atop the three-storey Colombo Court Hotel is a relaxing spot to watch the city slow down over a cold beer or a cocktail. It's only a few floors up, but feels high above the street-level hustle and bustle.

New Colonial Hotel BAR

(Map p64; Olcott Mw, Col 11; ⌚11am-3pm & 5-11pm) With swinging saloon doors and a pasted up menu of 'beer & liquour' that could have been plucked from the Prohibition era, this dimly-lit locals hangout by Fort station has a certain shabby charm. Pull up a chair and join the solitary male drinkers, sheltering from the noise – and possibly heartbreak – outside.

Rhythm & Blues LOUNGE

(R&B; Map p76; ☎077-802 0690; www.facebook.com/rhythmandbluescolombo; 19/1 Daisy Villa Ave, Col 4; admission Rs 1000; ⌚8.30pm-3am) A moody, upholstered spacc on the corner with busy RA de Mel Mawatha, Rhythm & Blues offers cool cocktails whipped up by cool bartenders beneath a light fitting made from clustered umbrellas. From about 11pm at weekends, dancing takes over from drinking.

ColomBar COCKTAIL BAR

(Map p70; ☎011-249 1000; Cinnamon Lakeside Hotel, 115 Sir Chittampalam A Gardiner Mw, Col 2; ⌚4pm-1am Thu-Sat, 4pm-midnight Sun-Wed) The one compelling reason to visit this otherwise unremarkable hotel is the stylish bar that overlooks Beira Lake. You can watch skullers out rowing at sunset then sip expertly mixed cocktails and dozens of varieties of arrack (liquor distilled from toddy) under the stars.

★Curve Bar BAR

(Map p70; ☎011-230 0183; www.curvebarcolombo.com; Park Street Mews, 50/1 Park St, Col 2; ⌚11am-11pm Sun-Thu, 11am-1am Fri & Sat) The sleek, vivid purple bar at Park Street Mews pulls in an energetic, post-work crowd with a menu of tapas-style bar food, expertly mixed cocktails and live bands from 8pm onwards from Thursday to Saturday.

Love Bar BAR

(Map p70; ☎077-859 7766; www.facebook.com/thelovebarcolombo; 58A Horton Pl, Col 7; ⌚6pm-midnight Sun-Thu, 6pm-3.30am Fri & Sat) Upstairs above the Baz Luhrmann–esque Flamingo House restaurant (worth a visit in

COOKING WITH AUNTY

After sampling Sri Lanka's fabulous, fiery rice and curry, why not learn to cook some of the delectable dishes that go into it on a cooking course with **Aunty's** (Map p70; ☎076-694 1540; www.auntys.lk; 39/28 Nelson Lane, Col 3; cooking course from US$59)? This small, family-run cooking school will guide you through the essentials, on courses that can be combined with visits to local markets to buy ingredients.

DON'T MISS

HOTEL DE PILAWOOS

Known locally just as **Pilawoos** (Map p70; 077-741 7417; 417 Galle Rd, Col 3; meals Rs 200-700; 24hr), this open-fronted, nofrills purveyor of short eats is renowned for what may be the best *kotthu* in town. This uniquely Sri Lankan dish is prepared using left-over *rottis*, mixed with spices, vegetables and meat or cheese and chopped dramatically on a griddle with two scraper-like knives (you'll hear the clatter of *kotthu* knives long before you reach the doors).

Note that this is the true and original Pilawoos. The restaurant's success has inspired dozens of competitors along Galle Rd to adopt some version of the Pilawoos name.

its own right as a spot for a posh dinner and drink), Love Bar blends a strange mix of 'love you' teddy bears, flowers in vases and moody neon. It's compact and crowded, with young folk who rave about the DJs and vibe.

Ask for Fern BAR
(Map p70; 077-805 0330; www.facebook.com/askforfer; 32B Sir Mohammed Macan Markar Mw, Col 3; 6pm-midnight Tue-Thu, 6pm-2am Fri & Sat) The kind of place you have to be in the know to know about, Ask for Fern is hidden behind an anonymous doorway just north of the Ramada hotel. Mounted animal skulls guide you upstairs to a sleek polished concrete bar and club, where the drinks are as cool as the clientele.

Shore By O BAR
(Map p80; 011-272 6638; www.facebook.com/theshorebyo; College Ave, Mt Lavinia; 11am-2pm & 5-11pm) Feel the sand between your toes at this upscale beach bar in prime place on the sand at Mt Lavinia. Tables and loungers are set over two levels facing the waves, and there's a vaguely Balearic feel to the weatherboard architecture. Note that alcohol is not served from 2pm to 5pm because of the schools nearby, but soft drinks are still available.

Entertainment

After-dark entertainment is limited in Colombo. Sri Lankans love cricket, so if you can get into a match, it will be memorable.

Good cinemas include **PVR Cinemas** (Map p70; 076-644 7664; www.pvrcinemas.lk; Galle Face Centre Rd, Col 2; tickets from Rs 900) in the One Galle Face mall and **Scope Cinemas** (Map p70; 011-208 3064; www.scopecinemas.com; Sir James Peiris Mw, Col 2; tickets Rs 600-1100) at Colombo City Centre.

Nelum Pokuna Mahinda Rajapaksa Theatre THEATRE
(Map p70; 011-266 9019; www.nelumpokuna.com; Ananda Coomaraswamy Mw, Col 7) Colombo's flagship venue dominates the landscape at the south end of Viharamahadevi Park. Its stunning design is based on the Nelum Pokuna, the 12th-century lotus pond in Polonnaruwa. Scan the local press for news of upcoming productions here.

Lionel Wendt Theatre CULTURAL CENTRE
(Map p70; 011-269 5794; www.lionelwendt.org; 18 Guildford Cres, Col 7) Alongside art shows and cultural events, this gallery hosts regular live theatre performances at night.

Sri Lanka Cricket CRICKET
(Map p70; 011-267 9568; www.srilankacricket.lk; 35 Maitland Pl, Col 7; tickets from Rs 300; ticket office 8.30am-5pm Mon-Fri, 9am-4pm Sat, 9am-5pm Sun) The top sport in Sri Lanka is, without a doubt, cricket. You can buy tickets for major games from Sri Lanka Cricket from this street-side office near the oval. Major matches are played at Premadasa Cricket Stadium, northeast of the centre.

Shopping

The markets of Pettah are fun to explore but not great for souvenirs. Instead, try Colombo's one-stop souvenir emporiums, fairtrade stores and mega malls.

★**Barefoot** CRAFTS, BOOKS
(Map p70; www.barefootceylon.com; 704 Galle Rd, Col 3; 10am-7pm Mon-Sat, 11am-5pm Sun) Designer Barbara Sansoni's beautifully laid-out shop, set in an old villa, is famed for its vivid, primary-coloured hand-loomed textiles, fashioned into bedspreads, cushions and more (or sold by the metre). Barefoot also sells books about Sri Lanka, toys, ceramics, paper products and clothing. There's also a lovely courtyard cafe (p80).

There's a branch in the **Dutch Hospital** (Map p64; Bank of Ceylon Mw, Col 1; 10am-7pm Mon-Sat, 10am-6pm Sun) in Fort.

Paradise Road HOMEWARES
(Map p70; www.paradiseroad.lk; 213 Srimath Anagarika Dharmapala Mw, Col 7; 10am-7pm) In addition to colonial and Sri Lankan collectables,

you'll find a vast selection of original homewares and designer items in this crammed-to-the-rafters boutique, owned by famous designer Shanth Fernando.

It runs a small gift store adjoining the Paradise Road Gallery Cafe (p81).

Laksala ARTS & CRAFTS
(Map p70; www.laksala.gov.lk; 215 Bauddhaloka Mw, Col 7; ⌚9am-9pm) Part of a large government-run chain of arts-and-crafts shops, Laksala offers pretty much every craft and product made in Sri Lanka, from tea and cashew nuts to carved elephants, dance masks and handmade jewellery and clothing. There's another outlet in the National Museum (p68) and one near the **Dutch Hospital** (Map p64; York St, Col 1; ⌚9am-6pm).

Selyn HOMEWARES
(Map p76; www.selyn.lk; 102 Fife Rd, Col 5; ⌚10am-7pm Mon-Sat, 10am-3pm Sun) Selyn specialises in fair-trade goods made on local handlooms, with all sorts of clothes, ornaments and homewares made from colourful, vivid fabrics. The shop works exclusively with Sri Lankan producers.

Plâté HOMEWARES
(Map p70; www.platelimited.com; 580 Galle Rd, Col 3; ⌚9am-5.30pm Mon-Fri, 9am-2pm Sat) Set behind a popular photo studio, this wood-panelled store is an engrossing treasure trove of antiques, old photos, art, books and more; it's like browsing in the attic of an eccentric uncle.

Lakpahana ARTS & CRAFTS
(Map p70; www.lakpahana.lk; Lakpahana Complex, 14 Phillip Gunawardena Mw, Col 7; ⌚9am-6.30pm) The place to buy carved elephants in bulk so you can show *everyone* back home you care. Traditional souvenirs are sold in profusion and this vast store is a cathedral of unintentional kitsch.

COLOMBO'S CAFE CULTURE

You might not notice at first glance, but Colombo has a vibrant cafe scene, with a fine collection of cool places where you can sit back with an espresso or a wedge of chocolate cake, catch up on emails, and exhale, away from the city noise and bustle. Top spots to unwind include the following:

Milk & Honey Cafe (Map p70; ☎011-523 4347; 44 Horton Pl, Col 7; meals Rs 600-1200; ⌚9am-6.30pm Mon-Sat) Behind a colourful kids toy and book shop, this groovy little cafe has an ever-changing menu of fresh, healthy food, such as smashed avocado on sourdough, and many dishes are vegetarian or vegan.

Coco Veranda Cafe (Map p70; ☎011-763 5635; www.cocoveranda.co; 32 Ward Pl, Col 7; mains Rs 600-1400; ⌚7am-midnight Mon-Sat, 8am-midnight Sun; 📶) Sharing a building with hip designer-clothing shops, this tidy cafe has an extraordinarily long menu of teas, coffees, juices and main courses, from burgers and pasta to stir-fried mutton and tuna steaks.

Black Cat Cafe (Map p70; ☎011-267 5111; www.blackcatcolombo.com; 11 Wijerama Mw, Col 7; dishes from Rs 400; ⌚8am-10pm; 📶) A cool escape in a mansion from 1920, with fine coffee, tasty, international-flavoured snack meals and various soothing spaces to relax in.

Kopi Kade (Map p76; ☎077-055 2233; www.facebook.com/thekopikade; 15/3 Stratford Ave, Col 6; mains from Rs 800; ⌚noon-8pm Wed & Thu, to 9pm Fri-Sun; 📶) Regulars are drawn to this classy but unpretentious cafe at Pamankada by great organic coffee, and a small but imaginative lunch menu.

Bakes by Bella (Map p70; ☎011-230 1588; www.facebook.com/bakesbybella; 26 Colonel TG Jayawardena Mw, Col 3; cakes & snacks from Rs 450; ⌚8.30am-9pm; 📶) Those with a sweet tooth seek out Bakes by Bella for the layer cakes and buttercream-topped cupcakes, as well as tea served in proper cups and saucers.

Café Kumbuk (Map p70; ☎011-268 5310; www.cafekumbuk.com; 3/1 Thambiah Ave, Col 7; snacks from Rs 500; ⌚8am-5.30pm Tue-Sun; 📶) A great place to retreat with your laptop and catch up on blog entries, this hipster cafe serves healthy light lunches and good coffee in bright dining spaces or two gravel-floored courtyards.

Kiku (Map p76; ☎077-108 7123; www.facebook.com/kikucolombo; Dr Lester James Peries Mw, Col 5; snacks & light lunches from Rs 400; ⌚7am-9pm Tue-Sun; 📶) Very Japanese and oozing design chic, this cool, quirky cafe is the place to come for homemade *mochi* (Japanese rice cakes), glazed doughnuts and mini *katsu* (cubrioche burgers.

Sri Lanka Tea Board Shop TEA
(Map p70; 574 Galle Rd, Col 3; ⌚9am-6.45pm Mon-Sat) For one-stop tea shopping, this one-trick shop is stacked wall to wall with Sri Lankan teas, from low-cost fannings to the finest whole-leaf silver tips from the top estates. Many teas are gorgeously presented in easily transportable tins.

Tropic of Linen CLOTHING
(Map p70; www.tropicoflinen.com; 1 Wijerama Mw, Col 7; ⌚10am-7pm, 10am-5pm Sun) You'll find plenty of stylish apparel here made from the namesake fabric, as well as cool cotton wear that's ideal for the tropics. There are lots of bright colours as well as colonial-style whites.

Cotton Collection CLOTHING
(Map p70; www.cotton-collection.com; 143 Srimath Anagarika Dharmapala Mw, Col 7; ⌚10am-8pm) Spread over two floors, this sleek store specialises in casual but stylish, high-quality clothes for ladies and gents, made from the perfect fabric for the Sri Lankan climate.

PR CLOTHING
(Map p70; www.pr.lk; 41 Horton Pl, Col 7; ⌚10am-6pm) The fashion wing of the swish Paradise Road design group is run by Annika Fernando and shares a building with her sister Saskia Fernando's gallery. All the clothing is from local designers.

Gandhara HOMEWARES
(Map p76; www.gandharacrafts.com; 28 Stratford Ave, Col 6; ⌚10am-7pm) This stylish designer shop on the trendy stretch of Stratford Ave sells everything from candles and lamps to carvings and coffee tables. It's a great place to browse.

SUPERMARKET STAPLES

Everyone craves the tastes of home sooner or later while on the road, and Colombo has some excellent supermarkets, stocking everything from Marmite and Mars Bars to sunscreen. Try **Keells** (Map p70; 199 Union Pl, Col 2; ⌚9am-9.30pm) on Union Pl – or the branches in **Crescat Boulevard** (Map p70; 89 Galle Rd, Col 3; ⌚10am-9pm) or **One Galle Face** (Map p70; Galle Face Centre Rd, Col 2; ⌚9am-10pm) – or the city-block-sized **Arpico** (Map p70; 62 Hyde Park Corner, Col 2; ⌚8am-10pm), which stocks pretty much everything.

Vijitha Yapa Bookshop BOOKS
(Map p76; www.vijithayapa.com; Unity Plaza, Galle Rd, Col 4; ⌚9.30am-6pm Mon-Fri, to 7pm Sat, 10am-6pm Sun) This store stocks an impressive range of foreign and local novels, magazines and pictorial tomes on Sri Lanka. There's a second branch in **Crescat Boulevard** (Map p70; 89 Galle Rd, Col 3; ⌚10am-7.15pm Mon-Thu, 10am-7.45p Fri-Sun).

All Ceylon Buddhist Congress Bookshop BOOKS
(Map p70; 380 Bauddhaloka Mw, Col 7; ⌚10am-6pm Mon-Sat) This shop is filled with books on Buddhism and guides for practitioners; about a third of the stock is in English, the rest in Sinhala.

Malls & Department Stores

One Galle Face MALL
(Map p70; www.onegalleface.com; Galle Face Centre Rd, Col 2; ⌚10am-11pm) Colombo's ritziest mall has airport-level security outside, and the most upmarket brands in town inside, including a branch of the Odel department store. The basement level is good for fast-food meals and there's an ultra-modern cinema (p84) on the fifth. It also has the smartest toilets in town.

Colombo City Centre Mall MALL
(Map p70; www.colombocitycentre.lk; 137 Sir James Peiris Mw, Col 2; ⌚10am-10pm) This gleaming new mall is awash with posh local and international brands, including Odel and Spa Ceylon. There's a superior food court with a terrace overlooking South Beira Lake, and there's a good cinema (p84) on the top floor.

Arcade Independence Square MALL
(Map p70; www.arcadeindependencesquare.com; 30 Bauddhaloka Mw, Col 7; ⌚10am-11pm) A massive restoration of Colombo's colonial-era 'hospital for the insane', this posh retail space spreads across whitewashed buildings, courtyards and gardens, with some good places to eat and drink.

Crescat Boulevard MALL
(Map p70; https://crescat-boulevard.business.site; 89 Galle Rd, Col 3; ⌚10am-9pm) Small upscale mall next to the Cinnamon Grand Hotel with plenty of tea shops and a handy branch of the Keells supermarket chain.

Odel DEPARTMENT STORE
(Map p70; www.odel.lk; 5 Alexandra Pl, Col 7; ⌚10am-9pm) This high-profile department store is great for stylish clothes and souvenirs

from the Luv-SL outlet, and there's the upscale Boulevard (p82) food court out front.

Information

SAFE TRAVEL

Colombo is a very safe city by international standards, and crime against foreigners is uncommon, although you should take the usual safeguards.

- Solo women should be careful when taking taxis and three-wheelers at night; if your ride turns up with two men inside, find another.
- Colombo has its share of touts and con artists. People who strike up conversations at tourist sites may be warming you up for a scam. Street offers for guides and 'special' tours (particularly trips to see 'temples with elephants') should also be shunned.
- Some three-wheeler drivers try to steer male travellers towards spas that are actually brothels. Ignore any offers to take you to any spa you haven't picked out yourself.

EMERGENCY

Ambulance & Fire	☎110, ☎011-242 2222
Medi-Calls Private Ambulance	☎011-255 6605
Police	☎119, ☎011-243 3333
Tourist Police	☎1912, ☎011-242 1052

INTERNET ACCESS

Pretty much every hotel, cafe and restaurant in Colombo offers free wi-fi, and local SIM cards with mobile data packages are cheap and easy to get hold of from any phone shop, or at the airport.

MEDICAL SERVICES

Avoid government hospitals, such as Colombo General; stick to private operators.

Nawaloka Hospital (Map p70; ☎1514, 011-557 7111; www.nawaloka.com; 23 Deshamanya HK Dharmadasa Mw, Col 2) This private hospital has a good reputation and English-speaking doctors.

MONEY

There are banks and ATMs everywhere. Numerous foreign exchange services can be found along York St in Fort, as well as in the arrivals hall at Bandaranaike International Airport, and along Galle Rd.

Bank of Ceylon (Map p64; Bank of Ceylon Mw, Col 1; ⏲24hr) This branch has a 24-hour foreign exchange desk.

POLICE

Tourist Police (Map p70; ☎011-242 1052, 1912; 80 Galle Rd, Col 3; ⏲24hr) A helpful wing of the police service, close to the Sri Lanka Tourist Board office.

> **DON'T MISS**
>
> **SUNSETS**
>
> The Indian Ocean can yield up sunsets so rich in vivid colours that your eyes and brain can't quite cope. The best vantage point for admiring the view is Galle Face Green (p66), but the beachfront cafes of Mt Lavinia come a close second. Note that the day's weather is no indication of sunset quality: a dreary grey day can suddenly erupt in crimson and purple at dusk.

POST

General Post Office (Map p64; 27 Bristol St, Col 1; ⏲7am-6pm Mon-Sat) The Fort post office is the best place to send parcels.

DHL (Map p70; 307 Galle Rd, Col 3; ⏲9am-6pm Mon-Fri, 9am-5pm Sun) Good for shipping larger items.

TOURIST INFORMATION

Tourist Office (Map p70; ☎077-228 5400; SN Senanayake Mw, Col 7; ⏲8.30am-4.15pm Mon-Fri) Beside the Old Town Hall, the municipal tourist office is a handy source of local information and offers free city and country maps.

Sri Lanka Tourist Board (SLTB; Map p70; ☎011-242 8600; www.srilanka.travel; 80 Galle Rd, Col 3; ⏲8am-9pm) The country's national tourism office has maps and shiny brochures and can answer questions about the rest of the country.

Getting There & Away

Note that the roads in and around Colombo are very congested; allow plenty of time for any journey.

AIR

Although **Bandaranaike International Airport** (CMB; ☎011-226 4444; www.airport.lk) is 30km north of Colombo in Katunayake, it is called Colombo (CMB) in airline schedules. If you're arriving by air – especially late at night – it may be easiest to spend your first night near the airport in Negombo.

A few domestic services use the tiny **Colombo International Airport Ratmalana** (☎011-262 3030; www.airport.lk/rma; Ratmalana), an airforce base southeast of Mt Lavinia. Expect to pay around Rs 2000 for a taxi from Fort.

BUS

Colombo's bus stations are chaotic, but buses run to most destinations throughout the day. The city has three main bus terminals, all just east of Fort train station on the south edge of Pettah.

CASINOS

Gaming is legal in Colombo, but only for holders of foreign passports. The casinos themselves, though, are fairly lacklustre, despite adopting Vegas-style names. If you fancy a flutter, large, showy **Bally's** (Map p64; ☎011-555 6555; www.ballyscolombo.com; 34 DR Wijewardana Mw, Col 10; ⏲24hr) is the biggest player in town, with a full range of slots, card tables and roulette wheels.

Red buses operated by the **Sri Lanka Transport Board** (SLTB; Map p64; ☎077-287 2877; www.sltb.express.lk) run to destinations all over Sri Lanka from the busy and hectic **Central Bus Station** (Map p64; Olcott Mw, Col 11). There are services to most destinations at least hourly during daylight hours, but air-con services are less frequent. Stands are fairly clearly marked with the destinations for each numbered route, but the number refers to the route, not the destination, so while most No 2 buses run from Colombo to Galle, only some continue on to Matara.

Private bus companies mainly use the large, and slightly more organised **Bastian Mawatha Bus Station** (Map p64), a short walk away along Olcott Mawatha. Private companies offer services on the same numbered routes as SLTB buses, with very frequent buses to most destinations, and a greater proportion of air-con services, often using small minibuses.

A handful of buses use the small **Saunders Pl Bus Station** (Map p64; Saunders Pl, Col 11), also known as Gunasinghapura, behind the Central Bus Station, including private buses to Aluthgama, and air-con minibuses to Negombo.

TRAIN

The main train station, **Colombo Fort** (Map p64; Olcott Mw, Col 11), is a major landmark, and within walking distance of Fort. Trains run from here to every corner of the country, but often stop only for two or three minutes to pick up passengers, so don't dally.

Tickets are purchased at different ticket windows for different destinations; advance reservations (for 1st- and 2nd-class seats) are only taken at counter No 17. The inquiry counter is efficient and helpful and will tell you which counter to go to. There's also a private train information desk in front of the station whose staff are honest and helpful.

When crossing between platforms, there's track-level crossing at the west end of the platforms that is easier than taking the stairs. The **left-luggage storage** (Map p64; per bag per day Rs 62; ⏲5.30am-8.30pm) desk is at the extreme east end of the station on the street (not platform) side.

Getting Around

Like most big cities, Colombo can grind to a halt due to traffic congestion during the weekday morning and evening rush hours; if you want to see a lot of Colombo fast, explore on a Saturday or Sunday.

TO/FROM THE AIRPORT

Travelling via the Colombo–Katunayake Expressway, you can reach the airport from Fort in 45 minutes, but taxi drivers will only take this road if you commit to paying the Rs 300 toll. However, it beats travelling via the old Colombo–Negombo Rd, which can take up to two hours.

Bus The No 187 airport bus departs from the Bastian Mawatha bus station in Pettah every 15

LONG-DISTANCE BUSES FROM COLOMBO

DESTINATION	ROUTE NUMBER	PRICE (RS) ORDINARY/AIR-CON	DURATION (HR)
Anuradhapura	4, 15	250/610	6
Galle	2, EX001	170/300	2-3¼
Hikkaduwa	2	150/300	3
Jaffna	15	820/1700	8-10
Kandy	1	175/350	3-4
Kataragama	32	600/1000	6-8½
Kurunegala	5, 6	140/280	3½
Matara	2, 32	200-510	2½-5
Negombo	4, 7	65-100/150	1-2
Nuwara Eliya	79	410/445	6
Polonnaruwa	48	310 (ordinary)	6
Tangalle	32	220/1020	3-6
Trincomalee	49	535/750	7

LONG-DISTANCE TRAINS FROM COLOMBO

DESTINATION	PRICE (RS) 1ST/2ND/3RD CLASS	DURATION (HR)	FREQUENCY (TRAINS PER DAY)
Anuradhapura	215/380/800-1200	5	8-9
Batticaloa	330/570/1500	9	2-3
Galle	135/240/600	2¼-3½	10
Jaffna	350/630/1700	6-8	6
Kandy	140/250/800	2½-3	10-12
Trincomalee	280/500/1500	8	1-2

to 30 minutes around the clock, taking about 45 minutes, for a fare of Rs 150 (or Rs 200 air-con). Because of the security situation, buses are not permitted to enter the airport compound and stop instead at Awariwatta, about 750m south of the terminal in Katunayake, where waiting three-wheelers can transfer you to the terminal gate (Rs 150).

Taxi As you enter the arrivals hall, you'll see the government taxi desk on the right, along with numerous private travel agencies. You'll pay around Rs 1500 to Negombo, Rs 3000 to Fort, and Rs 3860 to Mt Lavinia. Let the desk know if you want to use the expressway and pay the Rs 300 toll. In the opposite direction, it's easiest to ask your hotel to book a cab (fares from Colombo are Rs 3000 to 5000). If you arrange a hotel-pick the driver will meet you at arrivals; if you order an Uber, the driver will pick you up outside the terminal.

BUS

Buses zip all over town from Olcott Mawatha in Pettah, and buses usually have an English-language destination sign, but working out routes can be confusing. The website www.routemaster.lk can help. The best way to find out which bus to take is just to ask people at the nearest stop.

Heading between Fort and the southern suburbs, buses run northbound along Galle Rd and southbound along RA de Mel Mawatha; the No 100 bus runs every 10 minutes or so in both directions. Fares vary from Rs 10 to 50, depending on distance.

TAXI

You won't see taxi cabs to flag down in the street, but you can call ahead for a radio cab, or ask your hotel or a travel agency to arrange a taxi, including for multiday trips. Fares are expensive compared to other means of transport; expect to pay Rs 3000 upwards to reach the airport from central Colombo.

In addition, Uber is active in Colombo and pick-ups are reliable; fares are lower than standard taxi fares, but the vehicle that arrives may be a three-wheeler instead of a car. Local ride-sharing, PickMe, is also popular.

Reliable dispatch taxi companies (with actual cars) include the following:

Kangaroo Cabs (☎ 011-258 8588; www.kangaroocabs.com) Offers service in comfortable air-con cars.

Ace Cabs (☎ 011-281 8818; www.acecabs.lk) A reliable radio cab company.

THREE-WHEELER

Also known as tuk-tuks and tri-shaws, three-wheelers are ubiquitous and an essential part of the Colombo experience. Increasingly, three-wheelers have meters, either installed in the cab, or on the drivers' mobile phone, and many are also enrolled on ride-sharing apps such as Uber. Gratifyingly, many drivers are willing to use their meters, with rides starting from Rs 50 or 60.

However, the drivers who park around Fort railway station, the bus stands and tourist hotels may refuse to the use the meter, so you'll have to bargain for a fair price. Alternatively, flag down a passing rickshaw on the road; moving drivers are much more likely to play by the rules.

From Fort, travelling on the meter, expect to pay around Rs 200 to get to Cinnamon Gardens, Rs 300 to Bambalapitiya and Rs 800 to Mt Lavinia. Note that drivers will often agree to a journey even if they aren't 100% clear on the destination. If may be easier to ask to be taken to a nearby landmark or road junction, rather than a specific address.

TRAIN

Commuter trains pass through Kollupitiya, Bambalapitiya, Wellawatta, Dehiwala and Mt Lavinia en route between Galle and Colombo's Fort station, so they can be a handy way to get between the south of the city and the centre. However, not every train stops at all of these stations, though most visit Mt Lavinia.

Generally, there are more services into Fort in the morning, and more trains heading south in the afternoon, but you'll rarely wait long for a train. You won't pay more than Rs 25 (3rd class) to reach any of the suburban stations from Fort.

AT A GLANCE

POPULATION
Hikkaduwa: 114,700

GATEWAY CITY
Hikkaduwa (p105)

BEST MANGROVE GETAWAY
Ging Oya Lodge (p97)

BEST LUXE RESORT
Saman Villas (p103)

BEST RICE & CURRY
Bookworm (p109)

WHEN TO GO

Jan Schools of dolphins party daily in Dutch Bay; backpackers party nightly in Hikkaduwa.

Mar–Apr Sri Lanka's Christians stage Easter passion plays in Negombo and Talawila.

Nov Beaches are (mostly) free of tourists; accommodation bargains abound, but restaurants are very quiet.

Main Fish Market, Negombo (p92)
ANGELO CORDESCHI/SHUTTERSTOCK ©

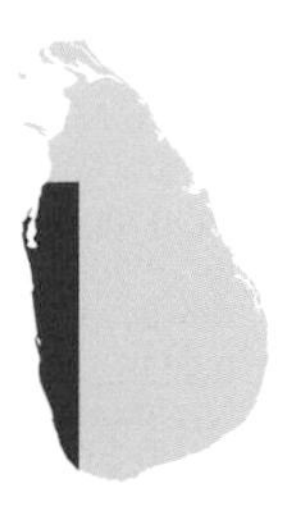

The West Coast

The west coast of Sri Lanka can feel like the most touristed part of the country, or the least, depending on which way you turn after leaving Colombo. Head south and the beach developments continue in an almost unbroken line all the way to Galle. But there are still pockets of charm, particularly at smaller beach resorts such as Bentota and Induruwa. At the end of the strip is boisterous Hikkaduwa, which offers good surfing and diving, friendly backpacker vibes and plenty of family fun.

Go north from Colombo and you'll hit Negombo, a long-established resort that offers airport-handy accommodation and historic appeal as compensation for its so-so beach. North of Negombo things get wilder and more interesting, with some delightfully secluded resorts hidden amongst the mangroves and a long, wild strip of coast riding up the Kalpitiya peninsula – a playground for kitesurfers and dolphin spotters.

INCLUDES

NORTH OF COLOMBO

Having exhausted the sights of Colombo most travellers look south, but the coastline to the north of the capital has seen only a fraction of the development that has eroded the charm – and beaches – of the resort strip between Colombo and Galle. With time on your hands, the A3 highway provides an intriguing back route to Anuradhapura, taking in low-key resorts, old Dutch canals, and a coastline that becomes increasingly wild and wildlife-filled as you head away from the capital.

Negombo

☎031 / POP 142,000

Negombo – abbreviated to 'neegoh' by bus conductors – is the closest beach town north of Colombo, tucked in just 10km north of the runway for Bandaranaike International Airport. With a stash of decent hotels and restaurants on the beach, and an interesting and historic downtown area, it's a popular place to spend the first or last night of a trip.

Negombo was one of the most important sources of cinnamon during the Dutch era, which explains the historic churches dotted along this stretch of coastline. Most places to stay are on the beachside road starting about 2km north of the town centre. The Hamilton Canal provides a quiet back route linking the two.

Sights

Negombo is dotted with historic churches – so many locals converted to Catholicism that the town is sometimes known as 'Little Rome'.

Negombo Beach BEACH

Even though it can't compete with Sri Lanka's best beaches and the water isn't crystal blue, the sandy strip at Negombo is a perfectly pleasant place to spend a few days. Outrigger boats haul up on the sand, fishermen offer boat trips and the road behind the beach is lined with cafes, bars and restaurants.

Main Fish Market MARKET

(Esplanade; ⏲4am-5pm) Each day, fishers take their *oruvas* (outrigger canoes) and go out in search of the fish for which Negombo is famous, selling the day's catch in the atmospheric fish market near the old Dutch fort. It's a pungent affair, and tables are piled high with tuna, barracuda, sailfish, snappers and mounds of semi-translucent anchovies.

Hamilton Canal CANAL

To whisk cinnamon to markets overseas, the Dutch and British created a network of canals linking Negombo to Colombo and Puttalam, covering a total distance of over 120km. You can hire a bicycle from many hotels and ride the canal-side paths of the Hamilton Canal, picking up the waterway on Anderson Rd, inland from the beach strip.

Dutch Fort RUINS

(Circular Rd) Close to the seafront near the lagoon mouth are the ruins of the old Dutch fort, which has a fine gateway inscribed with the date 1678. The fort grounds are now occupied by the town's prison; the people milling around the gatehouse are here to see friends and relatives serving sentences inside.

Angurukaramulla Temple BUDDHIST TEMPLE

(Temple Rd; Rs 1000; ⏲5am-10.30pm) East of the town centre, the Angurukaramulla Temple has a pavilion entered through the mouth of a concrete lion at the feet of a large sitting Buddha. Inside, a hall of statues and murals tells the story of the Buddha's life, but attendants ask for a steep fee to view it (an explanatory booklet is included in the price). A three-wheeler from town will cost Rs 300.

St Mary's Church CHURCH

(Main St; ⏲5.30am-8pm) Behind Dutch eaves, the grand interior of St Mary's Church, which towers over the town centre, has numerous statues of saints and some thunderous ceiling paintings of the Virgin Mary covering the nave.

Activities & Courses

Boatmen on the beach offer 30 minute trips around the bay and lagoon for Rs 3000. By the public beach, the small **Negombo Water Park** (☎077-716 7151; Porutota Rd; adult/child Rs 700/500; ⏲10.30am-7pm) will appeal to families with little ones in tow.

The **Jetwings Ayurveda Pavilions Spa** (☎031-227 6719; Porutota Rd; treatments from US$40; ⏲8am-5pm) offers a full range of revitalising treatments for walk-ins. **Spa Ceylon** (☎031-227 6067; www.spaceylon.com; 25 Porutota Rd; ⏲10am-10pm) is another recommended spa on the strip.

★**Ceylon Adventure Tours** ADVENTURE SPORTS

(☎077-717 3007; www.ceylonadventuretours.com; 117 Lewis Pl) A recommended operator of expertly guided motorbike and car tours, plus camping and trekking trips. You can also rent bikes and tuk-tuks for DIY touring. Drop by to see what is on offer.

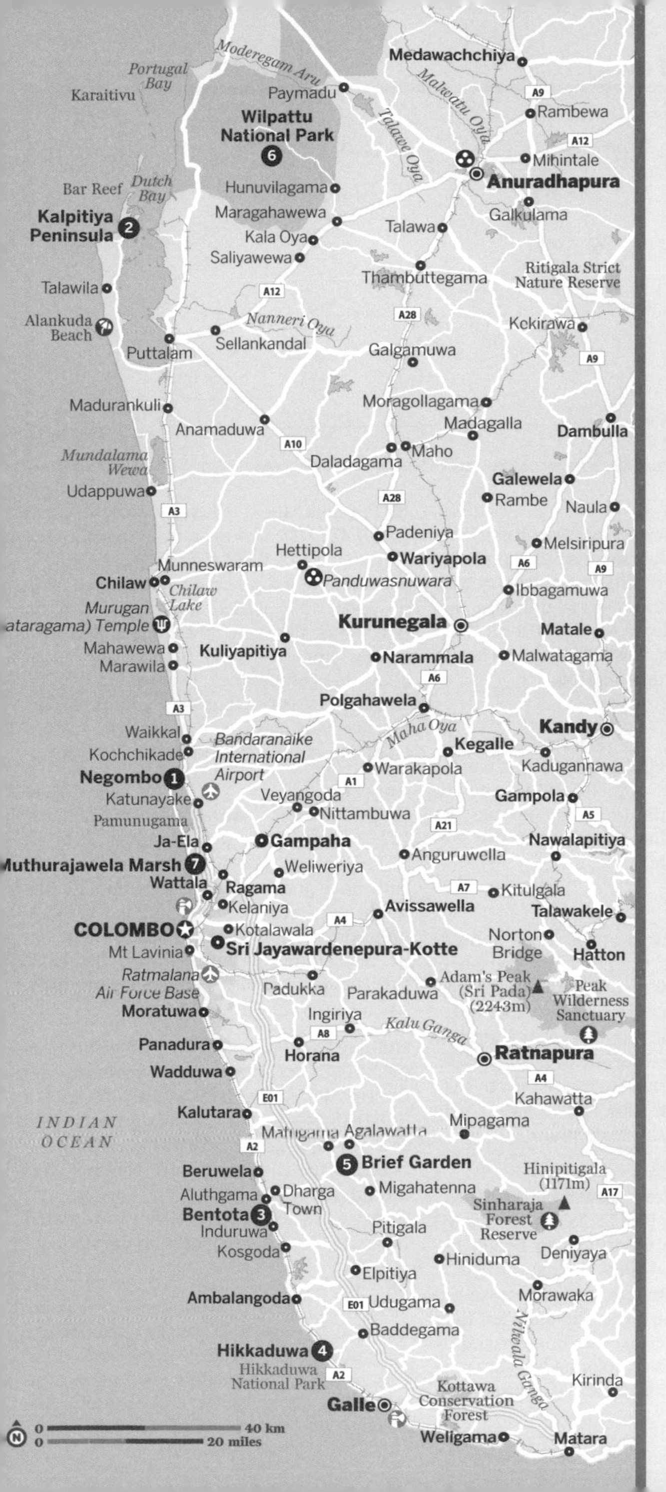

The West Coast Highlights

❶ **Negombo** (p92) Finding your feet and strolling in the surf after a long flight in this oh-so-easy resort town.

❷ **Kalpitiya Peninsula** (p98) Boat-tripping in search of dolphins or learning to kitesurf on the protected lagoon.

❸ **Bentota** (p101) Living the design magazine life in the boutique resorts of this gorgeous beach escape.

❹ **Hikkaduwa** (p105) Diving, surfing and sunbathing by day, and living it up by night in this backpacker hangout.

❺ **Brief Garden** (p101) Admiring the greenery, artworks and bohemian architecture of Bevis Bawa's former home.

❻ **Wilpattu National Park** (p100) Scouring the undergrowth for leopards, sloth bears and deer from the back of a safari jeep.

❼ **Muthurajawela Marsh** (p95) Spotting egrets, herons, kingfishers and monitor lizards on a birdwatching safari.

Negombo (Town)

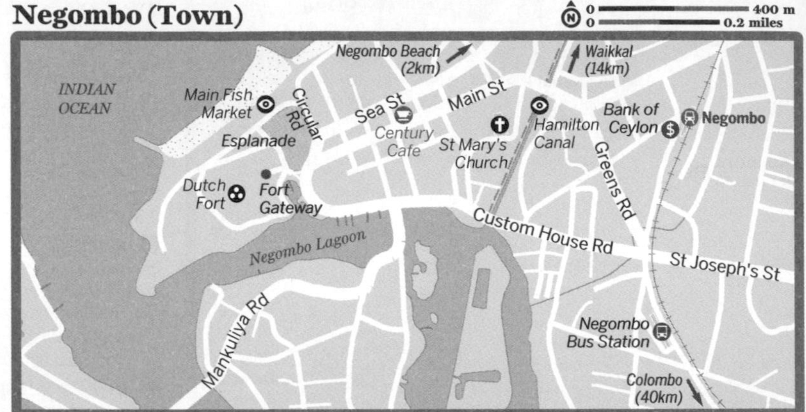

Colombo Divers DIVING
(077-736 7776; www.colombodivers.com; Porutota Rd) Negombo has surprisingly good diving and this well-regarded agency can take you to meet the fish at over 40 different reef sites. A two-tank dive costs US$70, or a PADI open-water course costs US$450. They're based at the Jetwing Blue Hotel.

Lucky's Tours BIRDWATCHING
(077-357 8487; www.facebook.com/luckytour55; 146 Lewis Pl) Specialist birdwatching tours in the Negombo region, including half-day tours (one/two people Rs 5000/7200, including transport) to the Muthurajawela Marsh.

Sleeping

It pays to book ahead at the more popular places. As well as the hotels on the strip, inexpensive rooms can be found in simple guesthouses on Rosary Rd and Peter Mendes Rd, inland from the south end of the beach – **Villa Rodrigo** (077-378 7030; www.villa-rodrigo-lk.book.direct; 38/3 Peter Mendis Rd, Cemetery 2nd Lane, Kudapaduwa; r from US$25;) is one decent option.

Hotel Silver Sands HOTEL $
(031-222 2880; silversands@sltnet.lk; 229 Lewis Pl; r with fan/air-con from RS 2500/4900;) A calm and clean Christian-run beach hotel that offers good value for money, if you can get over the strange, tent-like mosquito nets that cover the beds. The angular, tiled rooms spill over several buildings linked by Arabian-style arched colonnades, but the hotel can feel a little austere if there isn't a crowd in.

★**Ice Bear Guest House** GUESTHOUSE $$
(071-423 7755; www.icebearhotel.com; 95 Lewis Pl; s from US$24, d US$34-78;) A delightful oddball on a generally mainstream strip of coast, this garden guesthouse has no two rooms the same, but all are filled with quirky, homey details that elevate them above the competition. The owners emphasise the 'Swissness' but we'd emphasise the lovely shady garden, dotted with mature trees and pot plants, and the breezy cafe.

Angel Inn GUESTHOUSE $$
(031-223 6187; www.angel-inn-negombo.com; 189/17 Lewis Pl; r with fan/air-con from Rs 3500/5000;) This is one of the best-run cheap guesthouses in Negombo. Rooms might not have sea views, but the beach is only 20m away and the hotel is excellent value, with simple but immaculately clean and tidy rooms with shady terraces set around a small courtyard.

Holiday Fashion Inn GUESTHOUSE $$
(031-223 7550; festuskmf@hotmail.com; 109 Cemetery Rd; s/d incl breakfast Rs 5000/5500, f Rs 11,000;) There's a friendly family vibe at this simple guesthouse just back from the beach strip. Tiled rooms are spotless with a mini kitchenette (minus the cooker), and there's a small pool in a garden with potted bougainvilleas and loungers on the lawn.

★**Villa Araliya** BOUTIQUE HOTEL $$$
(031-227 7650; www.villaaraliya-negombo.com; 154/10 Porutota Rd; s/d/ste US$65/75/105;) On a quiet lane lined with villas, this standout choice offers spotless modern rooms with high ceilings and a tasteful mix of moulded concrete and wooden furniture,

spread across a garden shaded by frangipani trees. The buildings surround an attractive swimming pool and rates include breakfast.

The hotel is family-friendly (it has children's toys, cots and high chairs) and the suites can comfortably accommodate four.

★Jetwing Ayurveda Pavilions AYURVEDA RESORT $$$
(☎031-227 6719; www.jetwinghotels.com; Porutota Rd, Ethukala; s/d full-board plus spa treatments US$260/310, villa from US$317/407;) The one place in Negombo executed with real imagination, this upscale spa resort is a maze of linked courtyards and herb gardens spilling into private villas, each with a walled garden and massage pavilion. The Ayurvedic treatments here are the real deal, and most guests visit on a package that includes a pure vegetarian or vegan meal plan and in-room treatments.

Goldi Sands Hotel RESORT $$$
(☎031-227 9021; www.goldisands.com; Porutota Rd; r from US$125;) The rooms at this tidy, modern resort at the north end of the strip are full of local fabrics and colourful art, with big windows facing the sea that let in loads of light. There's a large and inviting pool area, and a broad stretch of palm-backed sand.

Eating

Ocean 14 SRI LANKAN $
(off Porutota Rd; mains Rs 300-750; ⏲11am-11pm) This rustic, palm-thatched restaurant down by the surf (take the track opposite the police station) pulls in a crowd daily with cheap, tasty Sri Lankan meals and freshly-caught seafood at bargain prices.

★Koththamalli by Rohan VEGETARIAN $$
(☎031-227 6719; Jetwings Ayuveda Pavilions, Porutota Rd; mains from Rs 670) The vegetarian and vegan restaurant at the Jetwings Ayurveda Pavilions hotel offers up a menu with real flair. Dishes are prepared following traditional Ayurvedic principles. Tempt your palate with such delights as coconut *rotti* stuffed with banana blossom.

Dolce Vita ITALIAN $$
(☎031-227 4968; 27 Porutota Rd; mains Rs 900-1200; ⏲8am-10pm Tue-Sun) This casual Italian-owned beachside cafe and restaurant is full of lovely pizza smells. The tables under the trees on the beachfront arc a popular place to while away an afternoon, munching pizzas, sipping good espresso and slurping homemade gelato.

★Lords Restaurant FUSION $$$
(☎077-285 3190; www.lordsrestaurant.net; 80B Porutota Rd, Ethukala; dishes Rs 770-2390; ⏲1-10.30pm) By far Negombo's most creative eating experience, Lords takes Sri Lankan cooking uptown, bringing in plenty of European and world food influences. Stylishly presented dishes range from Sri Lankan pork curry served in a coconut to grilled ocean-fresh seafood, Thai curries, and steaks. Credit cards are accepted.

Tusker Restaurant SEAFOOD $$$
(☎031-222 6999; 83 Ethukala Rd; mains Rs 900-2500; ⏲noon-9.30pm) The airy, elephant-adorned Tusker is one of the smarter places to eat in town, and there's a globetrotting menu that shines brightest if you order the seafood dishes. Crab with pol *rotti* and salad is a bargain for Rs 900.

Drinking & Nightlife

T-Lounge by Dilmah CAFE
(112 Porutota Rd; ⏲8am-9pm) A slick cafe serving a superior menu of teas from the Dilmah estates; order from the iPad menu and be sure to let your tea brew for the recommended time!

WORTH A TRIP

MUTHURAJAWELA MARSH

At the southern end of Negombo's lagoon, Muthurajawela Marsh, which evocatively translates as 'Supreme Field of Pearls', is home to some 75 bird species, including purple herons, cormorants and kingfishers, as well as crocodiles, monkeys and otters, attracting large flocks of birdwatchers.

The **Muthurajawela Visitor Centre** (☎011-403 0150; boat trip per person Rs 1300; ⏲7am-4pm) is at the southern end of the narrow belt of land between the gulf and the lagoon, next to the Hamilton Canal. There are moth-eaten displays but the highlight is a 90-minute boat trip through the wetlands. Call and reserve a spot in advance as it gets busy at weekends and on holidays; prime wildlife-spotting time is 7am to 9am.

Negombo (Beach Area)

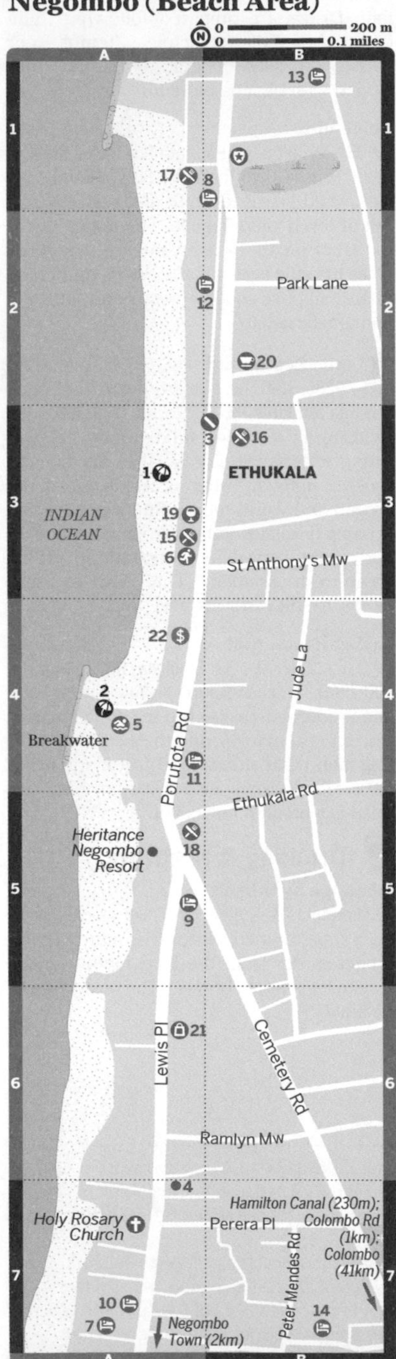

Negombo (Beach Area)

Sights

1 Negombo Beach A3
2 Negombo Beach Park A4

Activities, Courses & Tours

3 Colombo Divers B3
Jetwings Ayurveda Pavilions Spa .... (see 11)
4 Lucky's Tours A7
5 Negombo Water Park A4
6 Spa Ceylon A3

Sleeping

7 Angel Inn A7
8 Goldi Sands Hotel B1
9 Holiday Fashion Inn A5
10 Hotel Silver Sands A7
11 Jetwing Ayurveda Pavilions A4
12 Jetwing Beach B2
13 Villa Araliya B1
14 Villa Rodrigo B7

Eating

15 Dolce Vita A3
Koththamalli by Rohan .... (see 11)
16 Lords Restaurant B3
17 Ocean 14 .... A1
18 Tusker Restaurant A5

Drinking & Nightlife

19 Rodeo Pub A3
20 T-Lounge by Dilmah B2

Shopping

21 Selyn A6

Information

22 ATMs A4

Century Cafe CAFE

(25 Main St; 9am-5pm) In a lovingly restored whitewashed colonial-era townhouse, this quiet retreat in the heart of Negombo offers Sri Lankan teas, homemade cakes and lunch specials.

Rodeo Pub PUB

(031-227 4713; 35 Porutota Rd; 9am-1am) A graffiti-sprayed bar busy with expats and tourists. There's a long list of cocktails with beach-bar names, plus live music and DJs several times a week. The pub also serves classic Western and Sri Lankan bar food (from Rs 700). Drinks are three for two from 3pm to 7pm.

Shopping

Aside from supermarkets borrowing the names of famous European chains (Coop,

Sainsbury, Tecso), there's a useful branch of the fair-trade store **Selyn** (www.selyn.lk; 190 Lewis Pl; ⏲8am-7pm). A busy afternoon **street market** fills DS Senanayaka Mawatha near the train station on Saturdays.

Information

There are **ATMs** (Porutota Rd) on the main beach strip by the Topaz Beach Hotel.

Bank of Ceylon (Broadway; ⏲8.30am-3pm Mon-Fri, 8.30am-1pm Sat) Changes cash in the centre of town.

Tourist Police (☎031-227 5555; Porutota Rd, Ethukala; ⏲24hr) At the northern end of the hotel strip.

Getting There & Away

Government and private buses zip back and forth all day between **Negombo bus station** and Colombo (Rs 65 to 100, two hours, every 20 minutes). A faster and more comfortable air-con bus goes via the toll highway to Colombo's Saunders Pl Bus Station (Rs 150, one hour) until 8pm. Buses also run four times a day to Kandy (Rs 185, four hours) and every half hour to Kurunegala (Rs 115 to 230, two hours).

Two or three buses leave for Kalpitiya between 4am and 5.45am (Rs 250, four hours) – don't mix these up with buses to the nearby town of Kuliyapitiya. Buses to Chilaw can drop you near the hotels in Waikkal.

Trains run every hour or so from the central train station to Colombo (2nd/3rd class Rs 80/50, two hours), but they're slower than the buses.

To reach the airport, bus 240/3 leaves from the bus station every 15 minutes between about 6am and 6.30pm (Rs 30 to 50, 40 minutes), dropping passengers at Arawiwatta, a short three-wheeler ride from the terminal. Take a three-wheeler all the way from Negombo for Rs 800; travel agencies can arrange a taxi for about 1500.

Getting Around

Kochchikade-bound No 905 buses run from Negombo bus station every 20 minutes or so, following the beach strip (Rs 20). Alternatively take a three-wheeler for Rs 200 to Rs 300.

Waikkal

☎031

North of Negombo the tourist development dissipates, apart from some slightly eccentric resorts hidden away in the mangroves west of the A3 highway near Kammala. You'd never know they were there, but the beaches are long and uncrowded and the surrounding forests are alive with birdsong and wriggling monitor lizards.

Sleeping & Eating

★Ging Oya Lodge LODGE **$$**
(☎031-227 7822; www.gingoya.com; Kammala North; s/d/tr incl breakfast US$66/78/97; ❄@🛜🏊) One of the west coast's loveliest lodges, Ging Oya emerges from the mangroves just south of Waikkal. Elegant, comfortable cottages with high ceilings, filigree windows, dark-wood furniture and four-poster beds with mosquito nets are spread across tropical grounds on the edge of a lagoon, with an inviting central pool and restaurant. Bathrooms are partly outdoors, bringing in the sounds of the mangrove forest.

Set three-course dinners (US$13) are served in the open-sided dining room. The beach is a shady 1km walk away, or you can borrow a bike or kayak to reach the shoreline. It's the kind of place you only tell your best friends about.

Ranweli Holiday Village RESORT **$$$**
(☎031-227 7359; www.ranweli.com; s/d with full board from US$225/250; ❄@🛜🏊) Ecofriendly Ranweli Holiday Village sits on an island in the mangroves, and a boatman in a straw hat waits to punt you across the channel when you arrive. At the end of a mangrove walkway are tidy brick cottages decorated with bird prints and oriented to face the sea, a big central restaurant facing onto pools, and a pretty beach bound by stone breakwaters.

Getting There & Away

Many come with a car and driver, but buses between Negombo and Chilaw can drop you at the junction in Kammala (Rs 20, 30 minutes), a Rs 300 to 400 three-wheeler ride from the resorts.

Negombo to Kalpitiya

Although the A3 stays close to the coast, there are few ocean views between Negombo and Kalpitiya. About 30km north of Negombo at **Madampe**, pop into the roadside **Murugan (Kataragama) Temple** (A3 Hwy; ⏲8.30am-1.30pm & 5-8pm), a vast Hindu shrine with building-sized statues of Vishnu, Ganesh, Hanuman and Shiva. Respectful visitors can enter, minus shoes and hats.

Nearby is the **Thaniwella Devalaya** (A3; ⏲dawn-dusk) FREE, a revered Buddhist shrine fronted by a stucco statue of a rearing horse, which devotees honour by smashing coconuts as offerings. The temple is dedicated to

Thaniwelle Bandara Deviyo, a divine incarnation of the Kotte-era king Thaniya Wallabha.

About 7km north, the fishing town of **Chilaw** has a strong Roman Catholic flavour. Travel 5km east on the road to Wariyapola to reach **Munneswaram**, crowned by the tall *gopurams* (deity-covered temple gateways) of the **Sri Munneswaram Devasthanam** (Chilaw-Wariyapola Rd; ⏲dawn-dusk) FREE. Dedicated to Shiva, this important Hindu temple is centred on a stone shrine constructed in the 10th century. Outbuildings house the giant chariots used to parade the temple deities during festivals.

The tiny village of **Udappuwa**, 12 km north of Chilaw, has another important Hindu temple with a large *gopuram*. In August devotees here and at Munneswaram prove their devotion by walking on red-hot coals.

Kalpitiya Peninsula

Watery activities lure travellers to the flat, windswept and sparsely developed Kalpitiya peninsula. Huge megapods of spinner dolphins can often be seen playing offshore, low-key resorts trace the western shoreline at Alankuda, and local scuba centres offer boat trips to some of the best dive sites in Sri Lanka.

Kitesurfers, on the other hand, flock to the enclosed lagoon at the far end of the peninsula, where steady and sustained winds provide ideal conditions for learners. Dozens of kitesurfing camps offer accommodation, gear rental, training, and a shoes-off, Robinson Crusoe vibe.

CHANGING KALPITIYA?

Changes are afoot in the Kalpitiya peninsula. The government has plans to turn the peninsula and its offshore islands into one of Sri Lanka's prime beach-tourism destinations. Blueprints call for huge self-contained resorts, a domestic airport, golf courses and more.

Environmentalists are concerned about the impact these projects will have on local populations of dolphins, sperm whales and dugongs, while many locals are angered by the banning of fishing in certain areas and allegations of corruption in the development process.

The full impact of the plan may only become apparent when – or if – it comes to fruition. For now the peninsula slumbers in what may be a last period of calm before the hordes descend.

Sights & Activities

Kalpitiya feels like a sleepy backwater, for the time being. There are a handful of low-key resorts at **Alankuda Beach**, an attractive strip of sand about halfway up the isthmus, marred only slightly by a large boat jetty and a line of wind turbines just inland.

There are more wild, rugged beaches at the end of the peninsula, near the quiet fishing town of **Kalpitiya**, which has a crumbling **Dutch fort** (Main Rd; ⏲9am-5pm) FREE, occupied by the navy, but open to visitors for free tours (present your passport at the security post). The fort is linked by secret tunnels to the seashore and the nearby **Dutch Reformed Church** (Bazar Rd), whose dusty graveyard is full of tilting Dutch tombstones. West of Kalpitiya town is the **Kalpitiya Lagoon**, surrounded by dozens of kitesurfing camps, reached by tiny dirt tracks branching west off the main road.

Off the main road in the village of **Talawila**, the revered Catholic **St Anne's Shrine** (⏲6am-9pm) is set in a tree-filled compound that spills onto a broad fishing beach. The church is the centre for major festivals in March and August, when thousands of pilgrims attend healing services to honour a wish-fulfilling statue of St Anne, patron saint of women and childless couples. A three-wheeler will charge Rs 170 from the main road.

Dolphin & Whale Watching

Boat safaris to spot megapods of hundreds of spinner dolphins run most mornings from 7am to 9am during the prime spotting period from November to March. Your chances of a dolphin encounter are excellent during the season. Every hotel can organise a safari and prices start from US$40 per person, which includes a US$9 wildlife conservation fee.

Diving & Snorkelling

There are some spectacular reefs off the peninsula with plenty of big marine fauna (large rays, small sharks, turtles, moray eels and the like), including the stunning **Bar Reef** at a depth of 3m to 8m. There are several dedicated diving centres hidden away on the sandy tracks south of Kalpitiya town, offering boat trips with two scuba dives for US$85 (plus the conservation fee).

Accessible by three-wheeler from the highway, **Ocean Lanka** (☎071-082 2231; ww.scubadivingkalpitiya.com;), by the fishing beach in Kudawa, and **Kalpitiya Diving Center** (☎077-663 6255; www.kalpitiyadivingcenter.com) on the shore near the church at Kandakuliya, are both reliable operators. Most hotels can organise half-day snorkelling trips for about US$60. You'll also have to pay the US$9 local conservation fee.

Sleeping & Eating

Development at Kalpitiya so far mostly consists of small resorts around Alankuda and kitesurfing camps around the Kalpitiya Lagoon.

Alankuda

Omeesha Beach CABANAS **$$**
(☎076-292 3289; www.omeeshabeach-kalpitiya.com; r with fan/air-con incl breakfast Rs 5500/7500;) This friendly, family-run place looks out onto a fine section of beach. Sand paths lead to comfortable bungalows (the best have partly outdoor bathrooms with water spouts made from seashells) and an airy beachfront restaurant where you can rest between trips out to spot dolphins with the resort boatmen.

Guests can use the pool at the nearby Ocean Wind resort, run by the same owners.

Roshanne Beach Resort RESORT **$$**
(☎032-720 0434; www.roshannebeach.lk; s/d incl breakfast Rs 7700/9900;) About 100m back from the spray, this stylish and friendly place has nine whitewashed, thatched cottages huddled in a sandy compound under the palms. The vibe is Robinson Crusoe but with all mod cons.

Ocean Wind RESORT **$$**
(☎076-292 3289; www.oceanwindkalpitiya.com; Ilanthiadiya; s/d from Rs 6500/7500;) Run by the same team as the popular Omeesha Beach hotel, and just down the road, this smart place has a lovely pool and immaculate bungalows with partly outdoor showers with seashell spouts, in a sandy garden 100m from the beach.

Kalpitiya Lagoon

Dozens of kitesurfing camps are hidden away on the lanes south of Kalpitiya town; call ahead for directions.

KITESURFING KALPITIYA

With reliable and sustained winds that blow like clockwork during the season, Kalpitiya is fast gaining a reputation as South Asia's best kitesurfing location. Dozens of laid-back kitesurfing camps have sprung up along the west coast of the peninsula, in the sandy lanes south of Kalpitiya town. Most are run by mixed teams of European and local kitesurfers, and are busy when the wind is up (the best conditions are during the monsoon months from May to October) and very quiet when conditions are calm.

All offer lagoon-side accommodation in simple beach cabins, gear rental for experienced kitesurfers (from US$55/70 for a half/full day) and training for beginners on the protected waters of the lagoon. A nine-hour (two or three days) course should be enough to start you surfing solo; expect to pay around US$420 for individual tuition, or US$290 upwards for group lessons. For advanced surfers the exposed Indian Ocean coast awaits.

Kitesurfing Lanka KITESURFING CAMP **$$**
(☎077-114 5096; www.kitesurfinglanka.com; Kandakuliya; tent per person full board US$42, bungalow with beach/lagoon/garden view full board from US$290;) This French–Sri Lankan kitesurfing camp sprawls over a huge, palm-tree-filled compound near the south end of the lagoon. There's a barefoot tropical vibe, and the resort offers lessons for all levels and gear rental. Between outings on the lagoon relax in the beach bar, read in the driftwood library or take the bridge across the inlet to the long, gorgeous beach on the ocean shore.

To reach the resort, turn off the Kalpitiya road towards Kandakuliya and bear north towards the beachfront just before the village mosque.

Margarita Kite School KITESURFING CAMP **$$**
(☎in Spain +34 687439690; www.margaritakiteschool.com; Sethawadiya; r US$24-72;) Down a maze of confusing tracks southwest of Kalpitiya town, this Spanish-run place is aimed squarely at kitesurfers. It has several sites around the village of Sethawadiya, with everything from simple backpacker rooms to private beach bungalows, covering all budgets – alongside lessons and gear rental.

To get here turn off the main road onto Main St about 1km before the navy base, and follow winding lanes behind the Grand Mosque towards the southern end of the lagoon.

Surfpoint KITESURFING CAMP **$$**
(☎072-596 7564; www.surfpoint-srilanka.com; Kudawa; r US$25-80) This appealing and easy-to-find kitesurfing camp sits just by the fishing beach at Kudawa. As well as the usual gear rental and lessons, the camp has a beach bar that's perfect for sundowners and a palm-thatched block of comfortable hotel-style rooms at the back of the tidy compound.

Getting There & Away

Getting to Kalpitiya by public transport can be complicated. Buses run to Kalpitiya town from Colombo (Rs 210, five hours) and Negombo (Rs 250, four hours) but most services leave early in the morning. Consider instead taking one of the three to four daily trains from Colombo to Puttalam (2nd/3rd class Rs 270/155, five hours) and jumping on the No 901 bus to Kalpitiya (Rs 90, half-hourly, 1½ hours).

Most people ask to be dropped off south of Kalpitiya town, near the junctions for the small villages where the kitesurfing camps and resorts are based. Three-wheelers charge about Rs 300 for transfers from the main road, but it may be easier to call the resort or camp to make arrangements. For Alankuda Beach get off at Norochcholai.

Heading inland from Kalpitiya, the best option is to head to Puttalam and take a three-wheeler from the bus stand to the highway (Rs 100) to pick up a bus to Anuradhapura (Rs 168, half-hourly, two hours).

Wilpattu National Park

Wilpattu means 'natural lakes' in Sinhala and '10 lakes' in Tamil and that's exactly what you'll find at **Wilpattu National Park** (☎025-385 5691; adult/child US$15/8, jeep Rs 250, service charge per group US$8, plus overall tax 8%; ⏲6am-6.30pm, last entry 4.30pm). Visitor numbers remain low, even in high season, which gives it a genuine sense of wilderness.

At 1317 sq km Wilpattu is Sri Lanka's largest national park, preserving a vast swath of dense, dry woodland and scattered wetlands. Look carefully and you may spot leopards (this is the second-best park after Yala), sloth bears, spotted deer, wild pigs and crocodiles. For birders, the mix of dry forest and wetlands provides a habitat for everything from vivid green bee-eaters to Malabar pied hornbills.

Note, however, that the dense forest means that actually sighting wildlife is less of a sure thing than in the country's more-visited parks. The park headquarters has various stuffed and preserved specimens (including a pickled manatee) and some Buddhist relics uncovered inside the park.

Activities

Any of the lodges around the park access road can arrange jeep safaris for Rs 4500 upwards for a half-day tour, and Rs 8500 upwards for a full day. You can also make arrangements directly through the staff at the park headquarters.

The best time to visit is early morning, right after the park opens. Much of the wildlife lays low during the heat of the day, only to become more active again towards sunset.

Sleeping & Eating

Teal Cottage HOTEL **$$**
(☎025-490 1500; www.wilpattutealcottage.com; Wilpattu Junction, Pahala Maragahawewa; d Rs 3500-7500; ❄📶) On the highway just east of the park access road, this friendly place has a large, inviting restaurant by the roadside and rooms in several blocks behind, offering a quieter night's sleep the further back you go. The more expensive and flashier back rooms have lake views of Timbire Wewa.

Wilpattu Corridor LODGE **$$$**
(Tree House Hotel; ☎077-376 7113; www.wilpattucorridor.lk; Wilpattu Park Headquarters; r incl breakfast US$80, r in treehouse incl breakfast US$90-120) Right beside the park headquarters, this appealing place has four attractive, wood-lined air-con rooms in wooden stilt houses in a tropical garden, plus simpler hotel rooms. The staff can arrange safaris (making it easy to be first into the reserve) and bike tours of local villages. Rooms 3 and 4 face out over a bird-filled wetland.

Mahoora Safari Camp LODGE **$$$**
(☎Colombo 011-533 0581; www.mahoora.lk; per person full board from US$215; 📶) This is safari the old-fashioned, decadent way, at an appropriately exclusive price point. Mahoora's upscale tented camp on the edge of Wilpattu Park offers proper bush-chic luxury and guests visit on packages that include safaris, activities, meals and accommodation for one night and two days.

It's essential to book in advance – not only does it not accept walk-ins, but the camp itself may not even be set up.

HATCHING TURTLES

Five species of sea turtle lay their eggs on the west and south coasts of Sri Lanka: green turtles, olive ridleys, hawksbills, leatherbacks and loggerheads. During their long lives (turtles can live for over a century unless killed by humans or predators), females make numerous visits to the coast to lay eggs in the sand of the same beach where they were born.

A huge proportion of the tiny turtles that hatch on Sri Lanka's beaches are quickly gobbled up by birds, sharks, dogs and other predators, and many never hatch at all, as poachers harvest nests for human consumption. Other hatchlings are fooled into heading away from the water by the lights of houses and resorts, where they quickly perish. In response to this crisis a number of turtle hatcheries have been established around Bentota and Kosgoda, buying eggs from fishermen and reburying them to be released under safer conditions, under cover of darkness.

While survival rates are increased, some of the hatcheries are little more than money-making turtle petting zoos. There are also concerns about hatcheries delaying release so that they have a supply of cute babies to show off to tourists, which may affect the turtle's ability to 'imprint' on their birth beach. For more on the issues see www.responsibletravel.com/holidays/turtle-conservation/travel-guide/sea-turtle-hatcheries.

The following hatcheries at Kosgoda follow good practices, limiting handling and providing a home for vulnerable adult turtles who have been injured by sharks or boat propellors.

Kosgoda Sea Turtle Conservation Project (☎091-226 4567; www.kosgodaseaturtle.org; 13A Galle Rd, Mahapalana; Rs 1000; ⏲8.30am-5.30pm) Easy to find on the beachside just north of Kosgoda, this volunteer-run operation has been here (with a tsunami hiatus) for 30 years, and has the highest standards of the west-coast hatcheries.

Victor Hasselblad Sea Turtle Research & Conservation Century (☎077-326 2553; off Galle Rd; Rs 500; ⏲8am-6pm) Down a small track by the Kosgoda police post, this operation faces a pristine beach. As well as hatchlings it has a number of rescued adults, including albino turtles, which rarely survive long in the wild.

Getting There & Away

The park headquarters is 7.7km off the Puttalam–Anuradhapura highway (A12). Lodges are clustered around the junction, 45km northeast of Puttalam and 26km southwest of Anuradhapura.

Any bus between Anuradhapura and Puttalam can drop you by the turn-off, and three-wheelers can transfer you to the park HQ for Rs 350.

SOUTH OF COLOMBO

Most independent travellers make a beeline for surf-focused Hikkaduwa, with its busy strip of hotels, guesthouses and restaurants, but the Bentota area offers quieter and even more stunning beaches with a sprinkling of boutique hideaways amid the luxury resorts. Hire a scooter for a day and you'll quickly find your own stretch of private deserted sand.

Bentota, Aluthgama & Induruwa

☎034

A long ribbon of golden sand at the mouth of the Bentota Ganga, **Bentota Beach** is a sun-and-fun playground, with a huge range of water sports and activities possible on the ocean and lagoon. Big resorts have snapped up the best strips of seafront on the spit, but inexpensive resorts on the riverbank in **Aluthgama** offer boat transfers across the inlet, so you can access the same stunning sands on a smaller budget.

South of the river mouth a number of extremely stylish beach resorts offer maximum exclusivity. Even further south, **Induruwa** marks the start of a long, wild beach that runs for miles along the highway, with some very swanky, and very unswanky, places to stay dotted along the shore.

Sights

Brief Garden GARDENS

(☎034-227 4462; Rs 2000; ⏲8am-5pm) Hidden away along dirt roads, about 10km inland from Bentota, the Brief Garden is a barely controlled riot of greenery, surrounding the eccentric, bohemian house of Bevis Bawa, brother of renowned architect Geoffrey Bawa. This was once a rubber plantation, before the owner set to work creating a fantasy garden on the estate. After wandering the lovely grounds you'll be led around the house, preserved much as its former owner left it when he died in 1992.

An enthusiastic artist and collector, Bevis filled his home with interesting artworks and functional objects, many inspired by the nude male form. He also hosted a string of high-society house guests, including Vivien Leigh, Laurence Olivier, Agatha Christie and Australian artist Donald Friend, who came for a weekend and stayed for six years.

To get here follow the Mathugama road inland from Aluthgama and turn left just past Dharga Town. Follow the road and turn right just before the large white mosque, then after 1.5km look out for the sign saying 'Brief', where a winding dirt track on the right will eventually lead you to the garden. A three-wheeler will cost around Rs 1000 return from Aluthgama.

Galapata Raja Temple BUDDHIST TEMPLE
(dawn-dusk) FREE About 3km inland from Bentota, on the south bank of the Bentota Ganga, this venerable temple hides behind a time-worn stone gateway from the 12th century. The main chapel has some fine old Buddha effigies and murals (particularly on the ceiling). Note the Romanesque murals depicting Jains from India.

The 2500-year-old dagoba in front is said to hold the canine tooth of the Buddha's main disciple, Kasyapa. To get here turn inland from the coast on the Elpitiya road and look for the white sign as the road turns sharply right after 1.5km, then go straight ahead for a further 1km.

Activities

Operators on the main beach and on the riverside road in Aluthgama can arrange a staggering range of water sports, from windsurfing, waterskiing and jet-skiing to kayaking, scuba diving, snorkelling and deep-sea fishing. Prices start from US$10 for a banana boat ride, or US$15 for one-hour rental of windsurfing equipment or a surfboard.

Boat tours (US$40 to US$70 for up to four people) through local mangroves are a peaceful and popular way to pass half a day, traversing intricate coves and islands on the lower stretches of the river, which is home to more than a hundred bird species.

All the operators have long menus of activities, with special packages combining several ways to get entertainingly drenched. **Sunshine Water Sports Center** (034-428 9379; www.sunshinewatersports.net; River Ave; 8am-dusk) and **Diyakawa Water Sports** (034-454 5105; www.srilankawatersports.lk; 10 River Ave; 8am-dusk) are close together on the riverfront road in Aluthgama.

Sleeping

Big resorts have snaffled up the prime stretches of Bentota Beach, but cheap guesthouses on the river in Aluthgama provide boat transfers to the same strip of sand. South of Bentota train station are some of

AYURVEDA IN PARADISE

For over 2500 years the inhabitants of India and Sri Lanka have proclaimed the virtues of Ayurveda, a complex system of herbal treatments, massage, controlled breathing, yoga and specialist foods, designed to balance the forces in the body to combat illness and improve well-being.

The area around Beruwela, a short way north of Bentota, has some of Sri Lanka's finest Ayurvedic resorts, from serious centres offering weeklong intensive treatments to lavish resort spas offering a toe in the water for the curious. Consider booking into the following:

Barberyn Reef Ayurveda Resort (p104) One of the best-regarded Ayurveda resorts, with an extensive program of treatments.

Heritance Ayurveda Maha Gedara (p104) Top-notch treatments at a Geoffrey Bawa–designed resort.

Ayurveda Pavilions (p95) A lovely Jetwing-owned retreat with a fine vegetarian restaurant and villas with their own gardens.

Saman Villas (p103) Top of the line, exclusive retreat set on a headland south of the Bentota resort strip, with a superior Ayurvedic spa.

Aditya Resort (p108) A top-end escape, orientated toward pampering rather than purification; just south of Hikkaduwa.

Sri Lanka's most stylish resorts, at predictably steep price-tags.

Bentota

The fine beach of Bentota has a good mix of all-inclusive resorts towards the north end of the spit, and smaller boutique places running south from Bentota train station.

Hotel Susantha Garden GUESTHOUSE **$$**
(034-227 5324; www.hotelsusanthagarden.com; Bentota; s/d with fan from Rs 5900/6900, with air-con from Rs 6500/6950;) Shady gardens, cheery staff, easy access to the public part of Bentota Beach and an array of colourful, comfortable rooms make this a very popular place to drop your pack. There's a bright blue pool, a good restaurant and you can access the hotel from the end of the platform at Bentota (not Aluthgama) train station.

★**Paradise Road – The Villa** BOUTIQUE HOTEL **$$$**
(034-227 5311; www.paradiseroadhotels.com; 138/18 Galle Rd, Bentota; r/ste incl breakfast from US$135/200;) From the design-obsessed minds at Paradise Road, The Villa looks like the private pad of a diplomat who retired to a life of leisure surrounded by Asian antiques and art. Courtyards open onto courtyards, fish splash in quiet pools, peaceful pavilions spill over with designer furniture and every one of the opulent rooms is different and unique.

Other perks include fine dining and a lovely beach, sheltered by greenery beyond the rail tracks at the bottom of the garden.

★**Saman Villas** BOUTIQUE HOTEL **$$$**
(034-227 5435; www.samanvilla.com; Aturuwella; r from US$485;) Words hardly describe the sheer opulence of this beachfront hotel complex. How opulent? Well, some of the rooms have private swimming pools – inside the bathroom! Everything, from rooms to shared spaces, is lavish beyond belief and the hotel edges onto a stunning, empty strip of sand.

Other highlights include a heavenly infinity pool that merges into an ocean horizon, one of the island's best Ayurvedic spas, and fine dining at a single table set up on a deck above the rocky headland.

Club Villa BOUTIQUE HOTEL **$$$**
(034-227 5312; www.clubvillabentota.com; 138/15 Galle Rd, Bentota; s/d/tr incl breakfast from US$160/180/250;) Travellers who insist on privacy and style escape the crowds at this effortlessly elegant, Bawa-designed masterpiece. From the antique furniture to the blissed-out Buddha and Shiva statues, everything about this place says design magazine chic.

Courtyards and fishponds lead to rooms with steps to a second level and theatrically flamboyant drape-like mosquito nets. There's a lovely beach accessed by crossing the rail tracks at the bottom of the garden.

BOAT LIVING

A few kilometres inland from Bentota, but feeling like a million miles away, Jetwing's **Yathra Houseboat** (Colombo 011-470 9400; www.jetwinghotels.com; Dedduwa Junction; houseboat room from U$120. incl cruise from US$180;) is another world. This thatched, Keralan-style houseboat floats on Dedduwa Lake, offering accommodation that gets more expensive and romantic if you take the vessel for a cruise along the bird-thronged Benthara River. The two air-con cabins have basket-weave walls and stylish en suite bathrooms, and dinner is served out on deck.

Amal Villa BOUTIQUE HOTEL **$$$**
(034-227 0747; www.amal-villa.com; 135 Galle Rd, Bentota; s/d with half board Rs 15,500/19,000, in villa Rs 18,500/22,000;) On the ocean side of the road, this attractive villa is set in garden grounds beside a gorgeous infinity pool. Rooms are large and airy, with four-poster beds and tasteful artworks on the walls. If you want a more conventional beach stay, cross the road to linked Amal Beach Hotel.

There's also a good Ayurvedic spa.

Aluthgama

The town of Aluthgama has a few small guesthouses that line the road beside the river, all offering boat transfers across to the lovely beach on the far side of the spit that encloses the inlet.

Hotel Hemadan GUESTHOUSE **$$**
(034-227 5320; www.hotelhemadan.com; 25 River Ave, Aluthgama; s/d from Rs 5500/6500;) A cosy Danish-owned guesthouse with a waterfront restaurant wafted by riverside breezes and its own dock for transfers to the ocean shore. Rooms are simple tiled affairs;

BALAPITIYA

About 25km south of Bentota, the small village of Balapitiya straddles the mouth of the mangrove-fringed Maduganga lagoon. The lake teems with birdlife and boat operators by the main bridge over the inlet offer family-friendly boat trips for Rs 2500 per person, taking in the mangroves, an island temple, cinnamon workshops and more. Get an early morning start for the best wildlife-spotting opportunities.

While you're here it's worth dropping into the interesting **Sri Pushparama Maha Vihara** (Galle Rd; by donation; dawn-dusk), with its church-shaped chapel dating from 1871, and a striking 1950s temple containing statue-filled dioramas.

Any bus between Bentota and Ambalangoda or Hikkaduwa can drop you at Balapitiya.

some have balconies and only deluxe rooms have air-con.

High Rich River View Resort GUESTHOUSE **$$**
(034-227 4050; highrichresort@gmail.com; 97 Riverside Rd, Aluthgama; r/ste from Rs 5000/7200;) This long-established riverside hotel's six old-fashioned rooms have comfy beds, colourful cushions, wooden dressing tables and hot-water showers, but it's the pleasant deck and riverfront restaurant that make a stay here worthwhile.

★**Barberyn Reef Ayurveda Resort** RESORT **$$$**
(034-227 6036; www.barberynresorts.com; Beruwela; s/d with full board from US$115/205, plus Ayurveda treatments per person per day US$100;) One of the best-regarded Ayurveda resorts in Sri Lanka, Barberyn serves up a full menu of treatments, therapies and Ayurvedic meals, administered by highly trained doctors. Most people stay for a minimum of a week, and rates include airport transfers, yoga and activities such as Ayurvedic cooking demonstrations. Cheaper rooms are fan cooled but all have wooden furniture, flowing drapes and day beds. The resort is 4km north of central Aluthgama.

Heritance Ayurveda Maha Gedara RESORT **$$$**
(034-555 5000; www.heritancehotels.com; Beruwela; s/d with full board from US$230/359;) At the Heritance not only are the treatments first-rate, with highly experienced doctors on-site, but the Bawa-designed hotel is a wonderful luxury retreat tucked among the frangipani trees. Rates include treatments and yoga, and most visit as part of one- or two-week therapeutic programs.

Induruwa

Induruwa lies at the quieter southern end of Bentota Beach; it's a great strip of sand but there are few shops or restaurants.

Temple Tree Resort & Spa BOUTIQUE HOTEL **$$$**
(034-227 0700; www.templetreeresortandspa.com; 660 Galle Rd; r/ste incl breakfast from US$120/300;) Picture a minimalist loft apartment transported to a tropical beach and you get the Temple Tree Resort. The polished-concrete and stone rooms are decorated in soothing tones, and deluxe rooms have a whirlpool bathtub that you can soak in while staring at the ocean. All rooms have balconies overlooking the two pools and a superb strip of beach.

Eating & Drinking

Most hotels and guesthouses double as restaurants, and there are a handful of independent restaurants in Bentota and Aluthgama town.

Randholee SRI LANKAN **$$**
(Galle Rd, Bentota; mains Rs 700-2300; 11am-9.30pm) For a change of scene from the hotel restaurants, this Bentota cafe offers real espresso and a good range of Sri Lankan and international dishes, served in an attractive old building opposite the lilypond in Bentota.

Wunderbar Hotel and Restaurant SEAFOOD **$$**
(034-227 5908; Galle Rd, Bentota; mains Rs 750-1700; 7.30am-10.30pm) The Wunderbar Hotel and Restaurant has an inviting 1st-floor cabana-style restaurant that is open to nonguests and catches cooling sea breezes, and a broad menu of seafood and Western dishes.

Getting There & Away

Most trains running between Colombo and Galle stop at Aluthgama, but only slower, local trains stop at Beruwela and Bentota.

For Colombo (2nd/3rd class Rs 140/75, 1½ to two hours), morning trains leave Aluthgama every 30 minutes or so, with two or three services in the afternoon. For Hikkaduwa (one hour, 2nd/3rd class Rs 90/50), there are two or three morning trains, and numerous trains in the afternoon and evening. A single train runs to Kandy at 3.40pm (five hours, 2nd/3rd class Rs 340/195).

Aluthgama is also the best place to pick up a bus, although it's easy to hop *off* any Colombo–Galle bus at any point along the highway. From Aluthgama, very frequent buses stop on the main road bound for Colombo (regular/air-con Rs 100/400, three hours) and Hikkaduwa (regular/air-con Rs 65/200, one hour) until 5pm.

The easiest way to get between the hotels of Aluthgama, Bentota and Induruwa is by three-wheeler.

Hikkaduwa & Around

091

The surf resort of Hikkaduwa has been a firm fixture on the Sri Lankan tourist map since the 1970s, and long exposure to tourism has left this lively beach town a little worn round the edges. Guesthouses, shops and restaurants hug the sand, but erosion at the northern end of the strip has almost sucked some of the older resorts into the surf; things get better, and cheaper, as you go south.

On one level Hikkaduwa is an extremely easy-going place for a beach holiday, and it's perennially popular with backpackers and families. Peace and quiet is somewhat marred by the frantic Colombo–Galle highway, however, which runs the length of the resort strip.

To get the best out of Hikkaduwa rent a moped or a three-wheeler (or taxi) to visit interesting sights just along the coast towards Aluthgama.

Sights

Hikkaduwa Lake LAKE

Hikkaduwa Lake, which teems with birds and super-sized monitor lizards, makes for a calming excursion away from the busy beach strip. Speak to your hotel or local travel agencies about arranging a boat trip. To reach the lake turn off Baddegama Rd as the town starts to thin out, just after the pedestrian crossing, and follow the brick-paved track, then Lane 3 (or take a three-wheeler for Rs 300).

Seenigama Vihara BUDDHIST TEMPLE

(Galle Rd, Seenigama; dawn-dusk) About 2km north of Hikkaduwa, the Seenigama Vihara is perched on its own island, with a partner shrine on the mainland. It's one of only two temples in the country where victims of theft can seek retribution. Devotees purchase specially prepared lamp oil made with chilli and pepper, which they light in their homes while reciting a mantra. A short time later the thief will be identified when they're struck down with misfortune.

Kumara Maha Vihara BUDDHIST TEMPLE

(Kumarakanda; by donation; dawn-dusk) South of the Hikkaduwa strip, just inland from the main junction at Kumarakanda, this handsome whitewashed temple was founded in 1765. The gleaming frontage manages to look a little bit Dutch, a little bit Portuguese and a little bit British, and inside is a 4m-long reclining Buddha.

Jananandharamaya Vihara BUDDHIST TEMPLE

(off Baddegama Rd; by donation; dawn-dusk) This interesting Buddhist temple is spread over a cluster of colonial-era buildings in a sandy courtyard, with a central chapel full of statues and murals telling the life story of theBuddha, created by one monk over nearly a decade.

Activities

The most appealing stretch of beach at Hikkaduwa extends south from the huge Cinnamon Hikka Tranz resort to **Narigama Beach**. Most of the sun loungers here belong to hotels, but nonguests can use them if you order a drink or food.

Local travel agencies offer boat safaris on the lagoons north of Hikkaduwa (US$50 per person), snorkelling trips offshore (Rs 4500 per person) and land-based tours of the surrounding area, taking in sights such as the tsunami museums and the underwhelming moonstone mines at Mitiyagoda.

As an alternative, rent a scooter to explore; traffic isn't too heavy and there are some lovely wild beaches scattered along the highway between Hikkaduwa and Aluthgama.

Diving

Hikkaduwa has dozens of dive centres running trips out to sections of reef and the wrecks of the *Conch*, a well-preserved 19th-century steam-tanker, and *The Earl of Shaftesbury*, a four-masted sailboat from 1892. Visibility is at its best from November to April.

Novices can learn the ropes on PADI open-water dive courses (from US$375) and all the usual options are open to qualified divers. A two-dive boat trip costs US$75.

Most of the dive schools have their own gear and training pools. One professional operation is **Poseidon Diving Station** (091-227 7294; www.divingsrilanka.com; 304

Hikkaduwa & Around

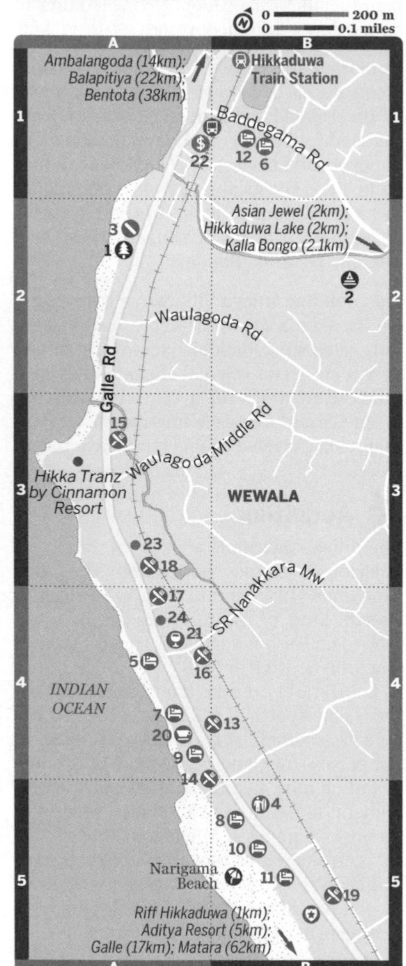

Hikkaduwa & Around

Sights

1 Hikkaduwa National Park A2
2 Jananandharamaya Vihara B2

Activities, Courses & Tours

3 Poseidon Diving Station A2
4 Reef End Surf School B5

Sleeping

5 Blue Ocean Villa A4
6 Camellia Dwellings B1
7 Dewasiri Beach Restaurant & Hotel A4
8 Drifters Hotel B5
9 Hotel Moon Beam A4
10 Hotel Ritas B5
11 Neela's B5
12 Sena's Place B1

Eating

13 Bambini's Cafe & Restaurant B4
14 Bookworm A4
15 Cool Spot A3
16 Home Grown A4
17 No 1 Roti Restaurant A4
18 Sandagiri Supermarket A3
19 Spaghetti & Co B5

Drinking & Nightlife

20 Coffee Shop A4
21 Sam's Bar A4

Information

22 Bank of Ceylon A1

Transport

23 International Travels A3
24 Sri Lanka Travels & Tours A4

Galle Rd; 8am-6pm), which has a dedicated teaching campus with a restaurant and accommodation for divers.

Snorkelling

Horseshoe-shaped Hikkaduwa Beach at the northern end of the strip has a section of coral reef just offshore in around 3m of water, right in front of the **Hikkaduwa National Park** (adult/child Rs 30/15; 8am-5.30pm) office, where you may be asked to pay the nominal entry fee. Kiosks on the beach rent out masks, snorkels and fins for Rs 700 to 800, but watch out for speeding dive boats.

Surfing

Hikkaduwa rose to fame as a surf beach and remains a magnet for surfers, though these days it's more a place to learn than test your long-honed skills. Conditions for surfing are at their best from November to April, when consistent rather than spectacular waves break along the Wewala and Narigama sections of the beach.

Most guesthouses and several dedicated surf shops rent out surfboards for around US$3 per hour, and there are several places offering surf lessons. Pick carefully because some 'teachers' are more interested in looking cool than teaching. **Reef End Surf School** (077-704 3559; www.reefendsurfschool.com; 593 Galle Rd; lessons per hour from US$20) has a more professional attitude than most.

Sleeping

Virtually all of Hikkaduwa's accommodation is strung out along Galle Rd, in the narrow space between the sand and the highway. What this means in most cases is a big beachfront restaurant with sun loungers, a small front row of sea-facing rooms, and a block of less exciting rooms at the back that cop a fair bit of traffic noise.

Sena's Place HOSTEL $

(☎077-101 4099; info@senasplace.com; 28/6 Baddegama Rd; dm from Rs 1250, cabin US$16; 📶) Hidden away off Baddegama Rd, this cheerful hostel offers dorm beds in clean, fan-cooled rooms (six or eight bed) with lockers and mosquito nets in a small courtyard garden. There's a single private room in a treehouse cabin.

Dewasiri Beach Restaurant & Hotel HOTEL $

(☎091-227 5555; 472 Galle Rd; r with fan/air-con Rs 2500/3500; 📶) A simple option for surfers on a budget, this white, crenellated block overlooks Main Reef and has a variety of simple but clean budget (ie cold-water) rooms, the priciest of which face the breakers.

★**Camellia Dwellings** GUESTHOUSE $$

(☎071-227 7999; www.camelliadwellings.com; Baddegama Rd; d from US$30; ❄📶) Ringed by an immaculate garden of tidily trimmed topiary, this colonial-style villa is a lovely retreat from the Hikkaduwa chaos. Rooms lead off a central lounge that opens at both ends, letting in fresh air from the garden. Major pluses are the friendly staff and peaceful mood – rather amazing considering the proximity to the train and bus stations.

Neela's GUESTHOUSE $$

(☎091-438 3166; www.neelasbeachinn.com; 634 Galle Rd; r with fan/air-con from Rs 4500/8500; ❄📶) This well-run place has plenty of foliage shading the grounds and the live-in owners are extremely welcoming. Even the cheapest rooms are spotlessly clean and come with a balcony or terrace for sitting out. Breakfast in the beachside restaurant is included.

Blue Ocean Villa HOTEL $$

(☎091-227 7566; blueoceanvilla420@gmail.com; 420 Galle Rd; r with fan/air-con from US$20/40; ❄📶) This blue and white, deco-style guesthouse has attractive upper-floor air-conditioned rooms overlooking the beach, with mismatched furniture and vintage trim, and cheaper, darker side rooms with fans, that have more of a budget feel.

Asian Jewel BOUTIQUE HOTEL $$

(☎091-493 1388; www.asian-jewel.com; Lane 3, Field View, Baddegama Rd; r incl breakfast from US$70; ❄📶🏊) This small boutique hotel close to Hikkaduwa Lake has characterful rooms with carved furniture, a beautiful pool and excellent food. Staff bend over backwards to make guests welcome. It's just inland from the lake, 3km inland of Hikkaduwa, off Baddegama Rd just before the lakeshore.

REMEMBERING THE TSUNAMI

The coastline just north of Hikkaduwa was one of the areas worst affected by the Indian Ocean tsunami on 26 December 2004, which swept across the Indian Ocean, killing some 35,000 Sri Lankans and ravaging swaths of Sri Lanka, India, Thailand, Maldives and Indonesia.

Beyond the colourful boatyards at the north end of Hikkaduwa, the **Tsunami Education Centre and Museum** (☎077-731 6664; Galle Rd, Telwatta; Rs 500; ⊙8am-8pm) focuses on tsunami education for locals, and also has some harrowing photos. A small pavilion contains one of the carriages from the packed commuter train that was washed off the tracks by the second wave, with the loss of over 1200 lives.

Just to the north is the ramshackle **Tsunami Photo Museum** (☎091-390 0884; Galle Rd, Telwatta; by donation; ⊙7am-7pm), with more powerful images and handwritten notes from those affected, as well as the torn tent which sheltered the owner after the disaster – a humbling reminder of human resilience in the face of tragedy.

Just south of the museums in Peraliya is a small stone **memorial** (Galle Rd) to those lost in the tsunami. Further south is the **Tsunami Honganji Vihara** (Galle Rd) memorial, centred on a tall standing Buddha facing the waves with his hands in the *abhaya mudra* pose conveying fearlessness and protection. The statue is a replica of Afghanistan's Bamiyan Buddha, which was destroyed by the Taliban in 2001.

WORTH A TRIP

AMBALANGODA'S DEVIL MASKS

North of Hikkaduwa, sleepy Ambalangoda is Sri Lanka's leading centre for the production of masks for *kolam* devil-dances. Accompanied by frenzied drumming, these masked dances are believed to drive away the demons responsible for physical ailments, and are still sometimes practised in rural villages under cover of night.

Ambalangoda has several busy mask-making workshops, with attached museums showcasing the history of *kolam* masked dances. At the north end of town **Ariyapala & Sons** (091-225 8373; www.masksariyapalasl.com; cnr Galle Rd & Main St; 8.30am-5.30pm) FREE has the most interesting museum, and the highest quality masks for sale.

The town has also grown into a busy hub for the trade in antiques, with a string of Aladdin's cave emporiums piled high with carvings, old crockery and genuine treasures hidden amongst the junk. **Southern Antiques & Reproductions** (091-225 8640; 32 Galle Rd, Urawatte; 8am-5.30pm) and **Sujeewa Antiques** (075-834 2243; 460 Galle Rd; 7.30am-5.30pm), at the south and north ends of town respectively, are great places to browse.

Most buses and many trains between Colombo and Galle stop in Ambalangoda. Pause for lunch at **Gold Win Restaurant** (56/3 Galle Rd; rice & curry from Rs 400; 11am-11pm) – a superior rice and curry place hidden behind a shopfront just south of the bus stand.

Hotel Moon Beam HOTEL **$$**
(091-505 6800; hotelmoonbeam@hotmail.com; 548/1 Galle Rd; r from US$40;) A smart midrange option down a greenery covered path, with spick-and-span rooms enlivened by pictures, colourful cushions and bed covers. The beachfront restaurant with its faux driftwood chairs is a pleasant place to while away the hours.

Drifters Hotel HOTEL **$$**
(077-706 7091; www.driftershotel.com; 602 Galle Rd; d with fan/air-con from US$45/70;) The small but well-kept pool at this beachside property makes it worth the money all by itself, but add in large, nicely presented rooms and a decent patch of beach and you have a solid proposition. Deluxe seafront rooms have space for two or three.

★ **Aditya Resort** RESORT **$$$**
(091-226 7708; www.aditya-resort.com; 719/1 Galle Rd, Devenigoda; r incl breakfast from US$400;) This sublime escape is crammed with Buddhist statues, zen-like pools, tropical blooms and decked out throughout with fine antiques. The huge rooms have carved wooden beds, heirloom furniture, and partly open-air bathrooms with a private koi pond and a plunge-pool bath that doubles as a jacuzzi. The Ayurvedic spa is also recommended. It's 6km south of Hikkaduwa.

★ **Kalla Bongo** BOUTIQUE HOTEL **$$$**
(091-438 3234; www.kallabongo.com; Lane 3, Field View, Baddegama Rd; lakeshore/poolside r incl breakfast from Rs 15,500/17,500;) A serene Buddha greets new arrivals at this beautiful hideaway on Hikkaduwa Lake. Set in pristine grounds, large, subtly stylish rooms look out over the placid waters, either on the lakeshore or from the garden beside the pool. Staff are delightful, and there are free kayaks for a sunset paddle.

Eating

Most of Hikkaduwa's hotels have their own (unremarkable) beachfront restaurants that are OK for a drink and snack.

No 1 Roti Restaurant SRI LANKAN **$**
(373 Galle Rd; snacks Rs 200-450; 9.30am-9.30pm) Away from the beach restaurant scene, this local roadside joint sells over 60 kinds of *rotti* (folded crepe-like pancakes), ranging from garlic chicken and cheese to banana and honey. Order two to make a meal.

★ **Bambini's Cafe & Restaurant** SEAFOOD **$$**
(Galle Rd; mains Rs 1000-2000; 11am-11pm) A thatch-roofed traveller spot on the main drag that pulls in a crowd nightly with some of the cheapest seafood on the strip – displayed in an ice-box out front and served grilled with a big plate of rice and salad. Canned beer is available off menu, but there's a big markup.

★ **Home Grown** SRI LANKAN **$$**
(072-440 7858; 140/A Wewala; curries Rs 500-750; 1pm-10pm) Half-buried under palm trees and flowering plants, this cosy little garden-terrace restaurant is tucked away near the rail tracks. The family who run it are as lovely as the setting, and dish up fresh, tasty homemade Sri Lankan curries at reasonable rates. There's no alcohol license.

★Bookworm SRI LANKAN **$$**
(☎077-622 5039; Galle Rd; rice & curry Rs 700; ⏰6.30-8.30pm) For some of the best home-cooked Sri Lankan food in town swing by early in the afternoon to order dinner in this simple, family-run place behind a bookshop on the strip. The setting is humble and there's no beer, but the selection of well spiced vegetable curries is a feast.

Cool Spot SEAFOOD **$$**
(☎077-233 4900; 327 Galle Rd; mains Rs 650-1650; ⏰10am-10.30pm) This family-run place has been serving up fresh seafood (and other local and international dishes) from a vintage roadside house since 1972. There's an upstairs balcony where you can perch looking out over the bustle of Galle Rd.

★Spaghetti & Co ITALIAN **$$$**
(☎077-669 8114; 587/2 Galle Rd; meals Rs 900-1900; ⏰11am-3pm & 5-10.30pm) Lush gardens screen this colonial-style villa from busy Galle Rd, which enhances the enjoyment of the ultra-thin-crust pizzas and creamy pastas. It's Italian-owned, so the menu also runs to good salads and *secondi piatti*.

Drinking & Nightlife

For takeaway wine, beers and spirits, and other supermarket essentials, head to **Sandagiri Supermarket** (Galle Rd; 8am-10pm) opposite the Citrus hotel.

Coffee Shop CAFE
(536 Galle Rd; ⏰8.30am-8.30pm; 📶) Proper coffee smells linger around this low-key coffee shop on the main drag, serving a full range of espresso treats, plus cakes, breakfasts and light snacks.

Sam's Bar BAR
(Roger's Garage; 403 Galle Rd; ⏰5pm-midnight) An old-school bar on the main strip that pulls in a mixed crowd of expats and migratory drinkers, drawn here by the international flags on the wall, sport on TV, inexpensive bar food and cold Lion beer on draught.

ℹ Information

Bank of Ceylon (Galle Rd; ⏰8.30am-3pm Mon-Fri) One of several banks on the main strip; offers forex and has an ATM that doesn't charge for foreign transactions.

Tourist police station (☎091-227 5545; Galle Rd; ⏰24hr) At the southeastern end of the tourist strip.

ℹ Getting There & Away

BUS

Bus 388/3 buzzes back and forth every 15 minutes between Hikkaduwa **bus station** (Galle Rd) and Galle (Rs 30, 30 minutes). Alternatively wait at the bus stand in front of the station for one of the frequent No 2 or No 32 buses from Colombo to Galle (ordinary/air-con Rs 30/100). In the opposite direction, buses stop at a bus shelter across from the bus station bound for Colombo (ordinary/air-con Rs 150/330, three hours).

For local exploring take bus 188/1 for Ambalangoda (Rs 50, 35 minutes) or any Colombo-bound bus for Aluthgama (ordinary/air-con Rs 65/200, one hour).

CAR

If you come with a car and driver or rented vehicle, save time by taking the Southern Expressway, a toll road that runs 15 minutes inland from slow, busy Galle Rd on the coast.

TRAIN

During the morning trains run every half hour or so towards Colombo (2nd/3rd class Rs 190/105), and there are two or three afternoon trains. The only 1st-class train leaves at 3.38am. Most trains go via Aluthgama and Ambalangoda. For Galle (Rs 40/25, 30 minutes) there are a couple of morning trains, and numerous trains in the afternoon and evening.

Avoid the slow trains that stop everywhere; check at the station for express departure times. There's also a single daily train at 3.05pm for Kandy (2nd/3rd class Rs 390/220, five hours).

ℹ Getting Around

A three-wheeler from the train or bus stations to Wewala or Narigama costs about Rs 300, though you may be able to bargain down.

A scooter or motorbike gives you wonderful freedom to explore the sights around Hikkaduwa. Several agencies rent out mopeds and larger bikes from Rs 1000 per day, though there may be a minimum rental period at busy times – **International Travels** (☎077-790 4220; 363/A Galle Rd; ⏰9am-9pm) and **Sri Lanka Travels & Tours** (☎091-227 7354; kingslyperera@hotmail.com; 321/395A Galle Rd; ⏰9am-9pm) are reliable operators.

AT A GLANCE

POPULATION
Galle: 133,000

GATEWAY CITY
Galle (p112)

BEST HISTORIC RELIC
Dutch Reformed Church (p115)

BEST-KEPT SECRET
Mulkirigala Rock Temples (p144)

BEST SUNSET VIEWPOINT
Tissa Wewa (p145)

WHEN TO GO

Dec–Apr Whales roll through the sea, the beaches buzz and everything is open.

Jul & Aug Pilgrims perform acts of self-mortification at the unforgettable Kataragama festival.

Nov The monsoon rains die out, beach resorts wake up and crowds are yet to arrive.

Galle (p112)
ANTON PETRUS/GETTY IMAGES ©

The South

The South is Sri Lanka at its most sultry and enticing: a glorious sweep of dazzling white beaches set against emerald-forested hills. This stretch of coastline is a delight to explore, with each bend in the coastal highway revealing another idyllic cove to investigate.

No matter what you're after, you'll find it here. Surfers return year after year in pursuit of the perfect wave. Blue whales and dolphins surge through offshore swells, and turtles crawl onto moonlit beaches. In the national parks inland, leopards creep like spirits in the night and elephants trumpet across the forest to greet the first light of day.

Then there are human-made creations, including Galle, an utterly captivating walled city that swims with history – undoubtedly the South's cultural highlight.

INCLUDES

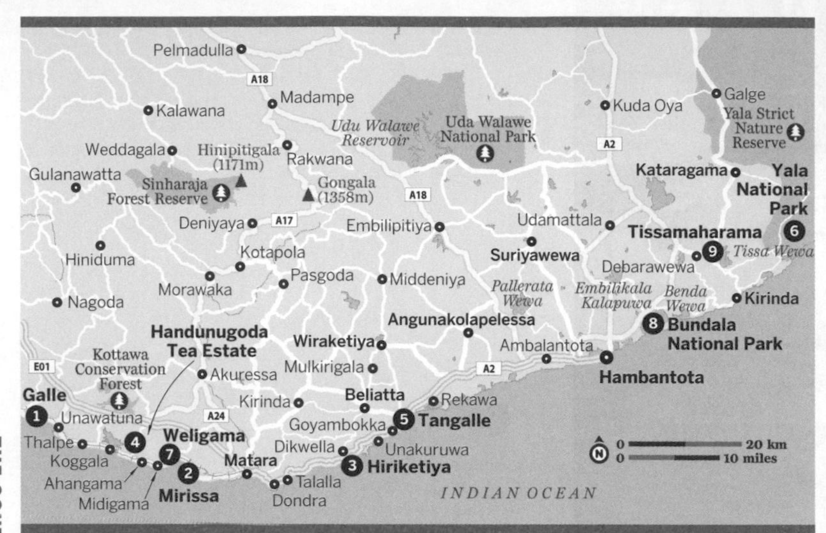

The South Highlights

❶ **Galle** (p112) Strolling the lanes of this uniquely atmospheric Unesco World Heritage Site.

❷ **Blue-whale tours** (p133) Achieving the dream of a lifetime: seeing the world's largest living creatures on a boat tour out of Mirissa.

❸ **Hiriketiya** (p137) Discovering that most perfect of beaches.

❹ **Handunugoda Tea Estate** (p127) Learning about the gourmet tea trade at this famous white-tea plantation.

❺ **Tangalle** (p141) Enjoying long walks along empty oceanic beaches.

❻ **Yala National Park** (p148) Spotting a leopard or camera-snapping a croc in this famous reserve.

❼ **Weligama** (p129) Learning to surf in a backpacker-friendly town.

❽ **Bundala National Park** (p144) Scanning these wetlands for flamingos, ibis and eagles.

❾ **Tissamaharama** (p145) Watching the mist rise off Tissa Wewa in the pink glow of sunset.

Galle

☎091 / POP 133,000

Galle enchants all who visit. A Unesco World Heritage Site, this historic city is a delight to explore on foot, an endlessly exotic old trading port blessed with imposing Dutch-colonial buildings, ancient mosques and churches, grand mansions and museums. Wandering its rambling lanes, you'll pass stylish cafes, quirky boutiques and impeccably restored hotels owned by local and foreign artists, writers, photographers and designers.

Built by the Dutch, beginning in 1663, Galle's core is the Fort, a walled enclave surrounded on three sides by the ocean. A key part of the Fort's appeal is that it isn't just a pretty place. Sure, tourism now dominates the local economy, but this unique city remains a working community: there are administrative offices and courts, export companies, schools and colleges.

Most travellers are utterly seduced by Galle's ambience, and it's undoubtedly southern Sri Lanka's one unmissable sight.

History

Some historians believe Galle may have been the city of Tarshish – where King Solomon obtained gems and spices – though many more argue that a port in Spain seems a more likely candidate. Either way, Galle only became prominent with the arrival of the Europeans. In 1505 a Portuguese fleet bound for the Maldives was blown off course and took shelter in the harbour. Apparently, on hearing a cock (*galo* in Portuguese) crowing, they gave the town its name. Another slightly less dubious story is that the name is derived from the Sinhala word *gala* (rock).

In 1589 during one of their periodic squabbles with the kingdom of Kandy, the Portuguese built a small fort, which they named Santa Cruz. Later they extended it with a series of bastions and walls, but the Dutch, who took Galle in 1640, destroyed most traces of the Portuguese presence.

After the construction of the Fort in the 17th century, Galle was the main port in Sri Lanka for more than 200 years, and was an important stop for boats and ships travelling between Europe and Asia. However, by the time Galle passed into British hands in 1796, commercial interest was turning toward Colombo. The construction of breakwaters in Colombo's harbour in the late 19th century sealed Galle's status as a secondary harbour, though it still handles some shipping and yachts.

Sights

The Fort area is home to about 400 historic houses, churches, mosques, temples and many old commercial and government buildings. Galle is an experience to savour, taste and touch; revel in its surprises. And don't neglect the new town, where you'll find interesting shops and markets.

A large Muslim community lives and works inside the Fort, particularly at the southern end of the walled town. Some businesses close for a couple of hours around noon on Friday for prayers.

The Fort Walls

Ambling along the Fort's ramparts at dusk is a quintessential Galle experience. As the daytime heat fades away, you can walk almost the complete circuit of the Fort along the top of the wall in an easy hour or so. You'll be in the company of lots of residents, shyly courting couples, and plenty of kids diving into the protected waters or playing cricket.

Note that you can tell which parts of the walls were built by the Portuguese and which by the Dutch: the latter designed much wider walls to allow for cannons to be mounted. If you examine the walls closely you can make out chunks of coral mixed in with the stone and mortar.

★Flag Rock HISTORIC SITE

(Rampart St) Flag Rock, at the southernmost end of the Fort, was once a Portuguese bastion. Today it is easily the most popular place to catch a sunset. During daylight hours you may see daredevil locals leaping into the water from the rocks. Numerous vendors sell good street food here such as fresh papaya with chilli powder from carts.

During the Dutch period, approaching ships were signalled from the bastion atop Flag Rock, warning them of dangerous rocks – hence its name. Musket shots were fired from Pigeon Island, close to the rock, to further alert ships to the danger. Later, the Dutch built a lighthouse here; since removed, the nearby street name survives.

★Old Gate HISTORIC SITE

A beautifully carved British coat of arms tops the entrance to the Old Gate on the outer side. Inside, the letters VOC (standing for Verenigde Oostindische Compagnie; Dutch East India Company), are inscribed in the stone with the date 1669, flanked by two lions and topped by a cockerel. A section of the fortifications here also served as a spice warehouse.

Main Gate HISTORIC SITE

(Lighthouse St) The Main Gate in the northern stretch of the wall is a comparatively recent addition – it was built by the British in 1873 to handle the heavier flow of traffic into the old town. This part of the wall, the most intensely fortified because it faced the land, was originally built with a moat by the Portuguese. It was then substantially enlarged by the Dutch who, in 1667, split the wall into separate Star, Moon and Sun Bastions.

Point Utrecht Bastion HISTORIC SITE

(Hospital St) The eastern section of Galle's wall ends at the Point Utrecht Bastion, close to the powder magazine, which bears a Dutch inscription from 1782. Today this is the location of Galle's **lighthouse** and the views across the Indian Ocean are wonderful.

Lighthouse Beach BEACH

(off Hospital St) A slim swath of sand right on the east side of the Fort. It's popular with locals in the evenings and at weekends – however, it's not that great for a dip as there are rocks offshore.

Inside the Fort

Most of the older buildings within the Fort date from the Dutch era, and many of the streets still bear their Dutch names, or are direct translations. The Dutch also built an intricate sewer system that was flushed out daily by the tide. With true efficiency, they

Galle

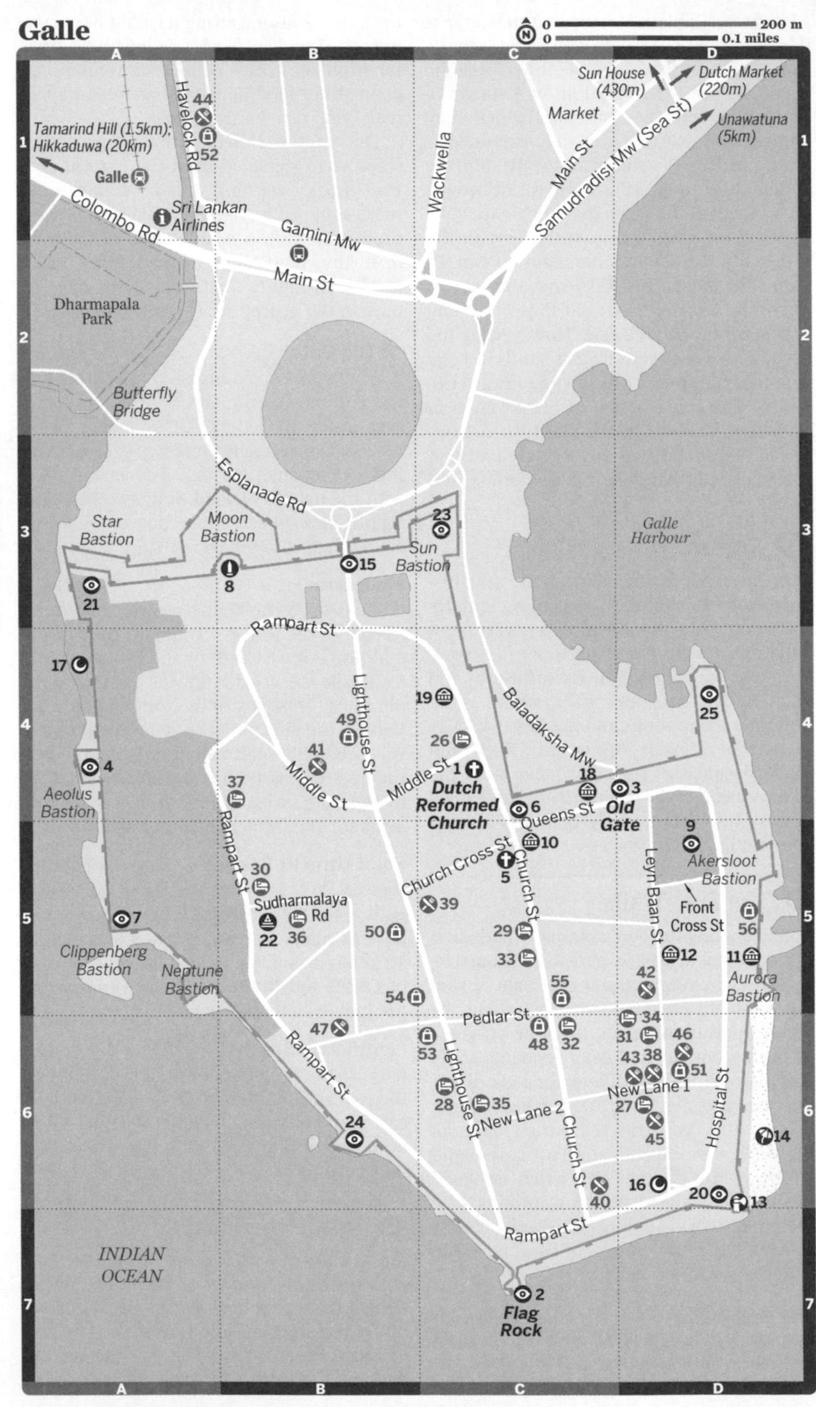

0 200 m
0 0.1 miles
Sun House (430m)
Dutch Market (220m)
Unawatuna (5km)
Market
Main St
Samudradisi Mw (Sea St)
Tamarind Hill (1.5km); Hikkaduwa (20km)
Havelock Rd
Galle
Wackwella
Colombo Rd
Sri Lankan Airlines
Gamini Mw
Main St
Dharmapala Park
Butterfly Bridge
Esplanade Rd
Star Bastion
Moon Bastion
Sun Bastion
Galle Harbour
Rampart St
Lighthouse St
Baladaksha Mw
Aeolus Bastion
Middle St
Dutch Reformed Church
Queens St
Old Gate
Church Cross St
Church St
Leyn Baan St
Akersloot Bastion
Front Cross St
Sudharmalaya Rd
Clippenberg Bastion
Neptune Bastion
Aurora Bastion
Pedlar St
New Lane 1
New Lane 2
Hospital St
INDIAN OCEAN
Flag Rock

Galle

bred musk rats in the sewers, which were exported for their musk oil.

Visitors to Galle 20 years ago would be surprised by what they find today: crumbling streets resurfaced with tidy paving stones and myriad historic building renovations both completed and ongoing. And just when it all seems a bit chi-chi, a screaming monkey will go leaping overhead.

★Dutch Reformed Church CHURCH
(Groote Kerk, Great Church; cnr Church & Middle Sts; 8.30am-5pm Tue-Sun) Originally built in 1640, the present building dates from 1752. Its floor is paved with gravestones from Dutch cemeteries, while other impressive features include the organ and an imposing pulpit made from calamander wood and topped by a grand hexagonal canopy. The friendly caretaker will likely point out the (slightly bizarre) carved wooden memorial dedicated to a former Commander of Galle, Abraham Samlant – the tiny cotton shirt is said to be the one he was baptised in.

Galle's small Christian community attend Sunday worship at 9.30am, which is a nice time to listen to the hymns.

National Maritime Museum MUSEUM
(Queens St; adult/child US$5/2.50; 8am-5pm Tue-Sat) Nestled in the old walls, this small museum is worth a quick look for its skeleton of a Bryde's whale and a very useful model that explains how tsunamis occur. There are also some dusty displays demonstrating old fishing techniques and examples of local boats.

Historical Mansion HISTORIC BUILDING
(077-792 1555; 31-39 Leyn Baan St; 9am-6pm Sat-Thu, 9am-noon & 1.30-6pm Fri) FREE This Fort townhouse (which dates back to the Dutch days) displays the private collection of a

long-time local family. It's an Aladdin's cave of treasures washed in, dug up and dusted down from the waters, streets and houses of Galle, with oodles of colonial artefacts, including antique typewriters, VOC china, spectacles and jewellery, all displayed in a haphazard, but absorbing manner. Also, look out for craftspeople busy polishing gems and weaving lace in the shops attached to the museum.

Amangalla HISTORIC BUILDING
(10 Church St) The Amangalla was built in 1684 to house the Dutch governor and officers. Later, as the New Oriental Hotel, it was the lodging of choice for 1st-class P&O passengers travelling to and from Europe in the 19th century. For much of the 20th century, it was in a decades-long decline and was run by the legendary Nesta Brohier, a grand lady who was actually born in room 25.

Dutch Hospital HISTORIC BUILDING
(Hospital St) Now fully restored and home to myriad upmarket boutiques and restaurants, this vast, colonnaded colonial landmark dates from the 18th century. Its size was necessary as both the voyage to Ceylon and life in the tropics proved very unhealthy to the Dutch, who died in droves from various diseases and the tropical heat. There are fabulous bay views from its upper balcony.

National Museum MUSEUM
(☎091-223 2051; Church St; adult/child Rs 300/150; ⊙9am-5pm Tue-Sat) This museum is housed in what's thought to be the oldest Dutch building in Galle, dating back to 1686. Displays are somewhat dusty and dated but include information on the lace-making process, traditional masks and religious items, including a relic casket.

Activities & Tours

★Galle Fort Walks WALKING
(☎077-683 8659; julietcoombe@yahoo.com.au; Serendipity Arts Cafe, 60 Leyn Baan St; tours from US$25) Author and photographer Juliet Coombe leads excellent walking tours of the Fort. These include a Mystical Fort Tour, which delves into local legends and myths; a Meet the Artists tour, taking in an optional mask-making course (24 hours' notice required); and evening walks exploring the city's black magic traditions and legends. Great culinary tours are also offered.

Coffee & Stories with Fazal WALKING
(☎077-177 4949; 72 Leyn Baan St; tours Rs 3500) Fazal, the owner of the Royal Dutch Cafe (p118), has a hundred stories to tell and he'll get through as many as he can during a morning walk through the city or, better, a moonlit night walk that includes coffee on the ramparts.

Sleeping

Spending a night or two in Galle is a pleasant change from the sandy beach towns and resorts – and if you thought Galle was nice in the day just wait until you see it in the relative cool of night. The Fort has a fast-expanding selection of places to stay, including some outstanding heritage hotels, though few really good budget places. Definitely book ahead in high season as demand keeps spiralling upward.

The surrounding region also has several options, including resort-style hotels with pools.

Fort

Mrs ND Wijenayake's Guest House GUESTHOUSE $
(Beach Haven; ☎091-223 4663; www.beachhaven-galle.com; 65 Lighthouse St; r with/without air-con from Rs 4000/3000; ❄📶) The wonderful Mrs Wijenayake and her family have been hosting grateful backpackers since 1968 and their hospitality shows in this comfy guesthouse. The rooms range from the clean and simple with shared bathrooms to fancier air-con rooms; all beds have mosquito nets. Lonely Planet cofounder Tony Wheeler had an extended stay here in 1977.

Seagreen Guest House GUESTHOUSE $
(☎091-224 2754; www.seagreen-guesthouse.com; 19B Rampart St; s/d US$40/45; ❄📶) A simple elegance defines this fine guesthouse. Its five whitewashed, air-conditioned rooms feature colourful Indian textiles and a splash of artwork, while some have excellent ocean views. The bathrooms are some of the best in this price range and the rooftop terrace has sublime sunset views over the ramparts and the salt-spraying Indian Ocean. Breakfast is $6 extra.

There are a couple of plain but clean downstairs budget rooms that are very good value at just Rs 4000.

★Antic Guesthouse BOUTIQUE HOTEL $$
(☎077-766 3664; https://antic-guesthouse-lk.book.direct; 3 New Lane 1; r incl breakfast US$45-65; ❄📶) This historic property has been sympathetically converted into an inviting guesthouse by

the friendly, artistic hosts who have a keen eye for design. Rooms have stylish lighting, rainbow-stained ceilings, painted floorboards and seaside appeal, as well as mod cons including air-con, flat-screen TVs and hairdryers. A delicious breakfast is included.

Curry Leaf Hostel HOSTEL $$
(☎077-635 3353; https://curryleafhostelrestaurant.business.site; 62 Lighthouse St; dm Rs 1500, d incl breakfast US$32; ❄📶) A busy little hostel with solid-value private rooms that are bright and have attractive stained-wood dressers and decent beds. The dorms are also good, but each dorm does have a lot of beds crammed into it. Staff offer walking tours, onward transport, surf lessons and more.

Fort Dew Guesthouse GUESTHOUSE $$
(☎091-222 4365; www.fortdew.com; 31 Rampart St; r from Rs 7000; ❄📶) Set close to the ancient city walls, this small but impressive guesthouse has a simple yet tasteful theme of white walls and dark wood, and rooms enjoy shared balconies overlooking the ramparts towards the sea. Listen to the thwack of cricket balls from the parkland opposite as you enjoy the sunset from the rooftop terrace restaurant and bar.

★Fort Bazaar HERITAGE HOTEL $$$
(☎077-363 8381; www.teardrop-hotels.com; 26 Church St; r/ste incl breakfast from US$175/295; ❄📶) An outstanding nine-year renovation has transformed this 17th-century townhouse into one of Galle's most evocative hotels, with 18 gorgeous, large rooms and suites, each with espresso machines, wonderful bathrooms and finished in natural tones. It's also home to the excellent Church Street Social restaurant and bar (www.teardrop-hotels.com; Fort Bazaar Hotel, 26 Church St; meals Rs 1200-3500; ⏲7am-10pm; 📶), and boasts a small library and a spa.

Fort Printers BOUTIQUE HOTEL $$$
(☎091-224 7977; www.thefortprinters.com; 39 Pedlar St; r US$187; ❄📶🏊) In the heart of the Fort, this imposing 1825 structure once housed printing presses and, later, school classrooms. Today it's divided into two sections: rooms in the older part have enormous wooden beams and are supremely spacious, while the other wing houses more contemporary rooms with sleek, modern decor. The in-house restaurant (p120) is one of the best in Galle.

Amangalla BOUTIQUE HOTEL $$$
(☎091-223 3388; www.amanresorts.com; 10 Church St; r incl breakfast from US$550; ❄📶🏊) One of the Fort's most famous buildings, this Aman hotel has an abundance of colonial opulence. Its reception rooms (all polished teak floors and period furnishings) are quite something: witness spiffily dressed staff waltzing around bearing gifts (cocktails) to guests. There are several categories of room – all luxurious and immaculately presented, and with four-poster beds – though the least expensive are smallish.

★Le Jardin du Fort BOUTIQUE HOTEL $$$
(☎076-676 7704, 076-722 7142; www.lejardindufort.com; 52 Leyn Baan St; d incl breakfast US$80; ❄📶) This French-owned place has more character than almost any other Galle guesthouse. The communal areas are squashed full of random objets d'art, including giant string puppets, leafy tropical plants and Hindu statues, while the five rooms are more simply stated with refreshing colour schemes and great bathrooms.

There's also a wonderful cafe, Puppets, where crêpes and other French snacks are served – all while being stared at by more puppets.

Galle Fort Hotel BOUTIQUE HOTEL $$$
(☎091-223 2870; www.galleforthotel.com; 28 Church St; r/ste incl breakfast from US$311/373; ❄📶🏊) Following a Unesco-commended renovation, this former 17th-century Dutch merchant's house is now a breathtaking boutique hotel. The rooms are all different: some have two levels and others stretch across an entire floor. Linens are exquisite and you won't find any distractions such as TVs – rather, you can enjoy the courtyard pool and serenity.

🛏 Around Galle

Tamarind Hill BOUTIQUE HOTEL $$$
(☎091-222 6568; www.asialeisure.lk; 288 Galle Rd; r incl breakfast from US$270; ❄📶🏊) This 19th-century former British admiral's mansion is now a terrific boutique hotel with 10 luxurious rooms, fine service and a jungle-fringed pool. Rooms are set in long colonnaded wings and are furnished with antiques, oil paintings and oriental rugs. Guests get the run of a high-ceilinged guest lounge, dining room and bar. It's 2km west of the new town.

Sun House BOUTIQUE HOTEL $$$
(☎091-438 0275; www.thesunhouse.com; 18 Upper Dickson Rd; incl breakfast r US$125-225, ste US$280; ❄📶🏊) This gracious old villa, built in the 1860s by a Scottish spice merchant, is located on the shady hill above the new town. The eight rooms vary in size, although even the smallest is crisply decorated.

There's a good collection of books to browse in the lounge, a lovely garden to enjoy and fine dining in the restaurant.

Eating

The Fort has fine restaurants and cafes, but be sure to find a table before 9pm as the town gets sleepy fast. Also, many places do not serve any alcohol.

Fort

You can't beat dining inside the Fort for atmosphere. Note, however, that few places are air-conditioned, so dinner is usually a better option for a relaxed, romantic meal, rather than sweaty lunch.

Dairy King DESSERTS **$**
(091-222 5583; 69A Church St; from Rs 250; 11am-10pm) The King family have been whipping up Galle's best ice cream for many years from their window-front outlet. The crunchy cashew and passionfruit flavours are simply divine, and satisfyingly rich cakes are also sold.

★ **Spoon's Cafe** SRI LANKAN **$$**
(077-938 3340; 100 Pedlar St; meals from Rs 650; noon-9pm) For authentic Galle-style rice and curry (from Rs 850), this minuscule place (there are only four tables) can't be beaten. Chef Shamil Roshan Careem hails from one of the Fort's oldest families and he prepares traditional family recipes. Save room for dessert and try his superb 'Silk Route Toffee'.

Mom's Hidden Kitchen SRI LANKAN **$$**
(077-901 9324; 3 New Lane; mains Rs 650-950; noon-9pm Mon-Sat) This no-frills, side-street place might only have three tables, but the ever-smiling owner puts endless care into her delicious seafood *kotthu* (Rs 950), *rotti* and hoppers (bowl-shaped pancakes). It's a real tonic against all Galle's fancy chi-chi places.

Royal Dutch Cafe CAFE **$$**
(077-177 4949; 72 Leyn Baan St; meals Rs 550-850; 8am-7pm;) The sign says 'Relax Zone' and this is a fine place to sit back and enjoy the company of cafe owner Fazal Badurdeen, who has a million stories to tell. He also seems to have almost that many teas and coffees, from cinnamon to cardamom to ginger. There's a small menu of curries and good banana pancakes for breakfast.

Serendipity Arts Cafe INTERNATIONAL **$$**
(077-102 0063; 65 Leyn Baan St; meals Rs 500-900; 8am-9pm;) This boho cafe has a

Town Walk
The Historic Fort

START CLOCK TOWER
FINISH CLOCK TOWER
LENGTH 2.75KM; THREE TO FOUR HOURS

This walk will take you past many of Galle's highlights as you cover over four centuries of history. One of the Fort's great charms is that detours and aimless wanderings are rewarded, so don't hesitate to stray from the following route.

Start at the ❶ **Clock Tower**, which, unlike so many worldwide, actually displays the correct time thanks to the fine engineering of the 1882 British mechanism inside. Stop to look out across the cricket stadium to the new town, with its ceaseless bustle. Walk down along the inside of the wall and pause at the British-built ❷ **Main Gate** (p113). Avoid the careening three-wheelers and cross Lighthouse St, following the walls to the ❸ **Sun Bastion**, with its fine views of the harbour.

Head back down off the wall and proceed up Church St to the heart of old Dutch Galle. Admire the deep porches of the ❹ **Amangalla** (p116) hotel, then cross Middle St to the cool confines of the ❺ **Dutch Reformed Church** (p115). Across from the church is a 1901 ❻ **bell tower**, which rings for tsunami warnings. Continue south on Church St to ❼ **All Saints Anglican Church** (www.allsaintsgalle.org; 8am-8pm) at the corner of Church Cross St. Constructed between 1868 and 1871, its solid rock structure would look right at home in an English village. Leave some money in the donation box, as relentless repairs are necessary to preserve the building. Just further south is the impressive facade of the 17th-century ❽ **Fort Bazaar** (p117) hotel.

Retrace your steps and turn east on Queens St. Admire the 1683 ❾ **Dutch Governor's House**. A slab over the doorway bears the date 1683 and Galle's ubiquitous cockerel symbol. Walk down the gentle hill and stop to admire both sides of the ❿ **Old Gate** (p113).

Now make your way back up the walls to the Fort's northeast corner and the ⓫ **Zwart Bastion** (Black Bastion), thought to be Portuguese built. It is the oldest of

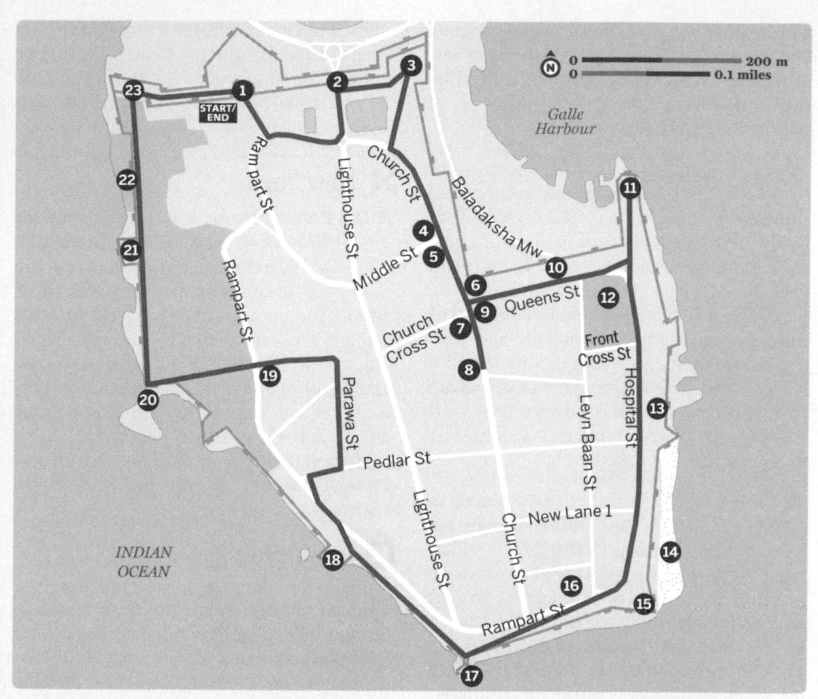

the Fort bastions, with some portions dating to 1580.

Make your way down to the vast leafy expanse of **12 Court Sq**. Various courts and related offices ring the sides. On weekdays you'll see people in the shade of the huge banyan trees awaiting their turn in court. At weekends there's a small market when stalls set up under the trees and sell art, antiques and a lot of things pretending to be antiques. Follow Hospital St south and you'll encounter the lavishly restored **13 Dutch Hospital** (p116), which was once filled with victims of the plague, but now has a slew of smart cafes. It's not ideal for swimming but to cool off you might want to dip your toes in the sea alongside masses of families at **14 Lighthouse Beach** (p113).

At the southeast corner of the Fort you can't miss the British-built **15 lighthouse** (p113). Just west along Rampart St is the shining white and imposing **16 Meeran Mosque**, the centre of Galle's vibrant Muslim community. Continue west to the fun and frolic at **17 Flag Rock** (p113), a good place to see so many of the submerged rocks that have claimed dozens of ships through the centuries. Walk the walls northwest to **18 Triton Bastion** on Rampart St, a great place to be at sunset.

Come down off the wall to cafe-lined Pedlar St and make a quick turn north on Parawa St. These two narrow blocks have some of the most typical of the old Dutch colonial houses. Curve west and at the corner of Rampart St you'll find **19 Sudharmalaya Temple** (⏲8am-8pm) with its compact dagoba and large reclining Buddha. If you're here on a full-moon day, you can expect to see all sorts of ceremonies, many featuring coloured lights and candles after dark.

Head back up onto the wall at **20 Clippenberg Bastion**. In the usually gentle surf surging around the rocks and sand below you may well see sea turtles feeding at dusk. Head north along the walls and enjoy the vast grassy expanse that until very recently was part of Galle's modern-day army base. Today you're more likely to see a cow chewing its cud or locals knocking a cricket ball about than a recruit standing at attention.

North of **21 Aeolus Bastion**, look for the small **22 tomb** of the Muslim saint Dathini Ziryam outside the wall. At the northwest corner of the Fort, pause at the **23 Star Bastion**, which has ample evidence of the area's dark past; the fortifications were used at various times by the Dutch as a prison and slave quarters. Now complete your circuit at the Clock Tower.

fusion menu that includes Western sandwiches and Eastern curries, fresh juices and shakes, bacon-and-egg hoppers and filter coffee. It's a very casual place, with a pretty patio and lots of artwork to enjoy.

★ AQUA Forte ITALIAN **$$$**
(☎ 091-454 9650; www.aquaforterestaurant.com; 62 Leyn Baan St; mains Rs 2900-4600; ⊙ noon-10pm) Simply fabulous Italian cuisine and arguably the best Italian restaurant on the island. Head chef Roberto and his team artfully mix the finest Sri Lankan seafood and influences with time-honoured Italian ingredients and ideas to produce dishes such as squid-ink tortellini stuffed with prawns or slow-cooked rolled pork in herbs. The sophisticated setting, with trickling water features and classical music, is as memorable as the food.

★ Crab & Co SEAFOOD **$$$**
(☎ 076-985 4693; https://crab co.business.site; 3 Church Cross St; mains Rs 800-2900; ⊙ 10am-10pm) A classy new seafood restaurant where you can dine on Sri Lanka's delicate tropical seafood bounty under the sweeping branches of a great old tree out in the courtyard. The Jaffna-style prawn curry and the Mediterranean seafood stew are small triumphs.

Fort Printers INTERNATIONAL **$$$**
(☎ 091-224 7977; www.thefortprinters.com; 39 Pedlar St; meals Rs 1000-1800; 📶) The ideal venue for a memorable meal, this hotel restaurant offers a concise menu featuring fresh seafood and organic local produce. It's especially good for Mediterranean-inspired dishes (such as slow-roasted leg of goat or Moroccan tajine), while traditional Sri Lankan rice and curry is also excellent. Dine in the frangipani-shaded courtyard at the rear or in the imposing dining room.

Elita Restaurant SEAFOOD **$$$**
(☎ 077-242 3442; www.facebook.com/elita.restaurant; 34 Middle St; mains Rs 2100-2900; ⊙ 8am-11pm) Thirteen years of work as a chef in Belgium gave Krishantha Suranjith myriad skills in preparing seafood. His buttercup yellow restaurant has recently moved to a new location in a quiet corner of the Fort, but the quality of the local saltwater bounty served here remains as good as ever. Opt for a table out on the terrace.

Hoppa SRI LANKAN **$$$**
(20 Pedlar St; 3 hoppers from Rs 1090; ⊙ Noon-9.30pm) Only in a town like Galle would that humble Sri Lankan staple, the hopper, be whizzed through a hipster mixer and turned into a creative gourmet delight. Grab a chair at one of the couple of tables at this tiny cafe and enjoy delicious chicken, cheese or fish hoppers. Finish up with a coconut pancake.

New Town

★ Old Railway Cafe CAFE **$$**
(☎ 077-626 3400; 42 Havelock Rd; mains Rs 600-900; ⊙ 9am-6pm Mon-Sat; 📶) Right across the small canal from the namesake station, this fashionable upstairs cafe has artfully mismatched furnishings and a boho vibe. You'll find an enticing menu of creative soups, salads and mains, with dishes such as pesto-crusted chicken patties with coleslaw, as well as espresso and good juices.

After you've eaten, browse the offbeat clothes, jewellery and bags in the store downstairs.

Shopping

Galle's history makes it a natural spot for antique shopping. You'll also find an incredible number of designer-owned shops and upmarket boutiques. Many stores in the new town close on Sundays, but in the Fort the shopping never stops.

★ Withered Leaves TEA
(☎ 077-225 0621; Dutch Hospital, Hospital Rd) Specialist tea store with an amazing range of top-quality green teas, white teas, Ceylon garden teas, blended teas and single-estate teas. There's no hard sell and staff are highly informed. It's on the upper level of the Dutch Hospital.

★ Mr Ellie Pooh's Poo Poo Paper Shop STATIONERY
(www.ecomaximus.com; 75 Leyn Baan St; ⊙ 9am-7.30pm) Not just does this little shop have an unbeatably brilliant name, but it's also won a BBC World Challenge for Sustainable Entrepreneurship and it's an ideal place to pick up some unique and fun gifts. As the name suggests, every item it sells (notebooks, postcards, artist paper) is made from recycled elephant poo!

Chilli Dragon Spice Shop SPICES
(☎ 077-337 4488; https://chilli-dragon.business.site; 34 Lighthouse St; ⊙ 9am-8.30pm) High-quality spice shop run by a friendly family. They create their own special curry powder blends and the owner has written a cookbook (sold here). The artfully presented spices make for good gifts.

Old Railway CLOTHING
(☎077-626 3400; 42 Havelock Rd; ⊙10am-6pm Mon-Sat) An eclectic, interesting store where most of the clothing, jewellery, bags, toys and gifts are designed in-house, made from locally sourced materials, and created right on the premises. Check out the upstairs cafe, too.

Stick No Bills ART
(☎091-224 2504; www.sticknobillsonline.com; 35 Church St; ⊙8am-8pm) Super-stylish reproduction posters (Rs 3000) and postcards (Rs 350) covering Sri Lanka through the decades. Many of the beautiful vintage airline images for Ceylon sell a tropical paradise of fantasy. The classic film posters are also superb.

Exotic Roots ARTS & CRAFTS
(☎091-224 5454; 50 Lighthouse St; ⊙9am-6pm) Hindu inspired art, amazing ironwork, standout paintings, locally designed clothing and even a rusty old dentist's chair. This eclectic gallery contains a little bit of everything as well as a cool cafe serving juices, herbal teas and more.

Shoba Display Gallery ARTS & CRAFTS
(☎091-222 4351; www.shobafashion.org; 67A Pedlar St; ⊙7.30am-10pm) Beautiful lacework made right here. The shop teaches local women dyeing crafts and ensures them a fair price for their work. Even if you're not buying, pop in to witness the process of making lace, or sign up to a lace-making (Rs 2500) or papermaking (Rs 1500) class. There's a small cafe, too.

Barefoot ARTS & CRAFTS
(☎091-222 6299; www.barefootceylon.com; 41 Pedlar St; ⊙10am-6pm) Chic boutique selling colourful local clothing, jewellery, linen and rugs, crafts and gifts. The book section has a small selection of English-language Sri Lanka–related titles.

Spa Ceylon HEALTH & WELLNESS
(☎091-223 5944; www.spaceylon.com; 54A Lighthouse St; ⊙10am-8pm) You've never seen a shop as colourful as this one-stop emporium for all things health and wellness. Body creams, oils and make-up – you name it. It's all here and all made in Sri Lanka. Massages and spas are also available but they recieve mixed feedback.

ℹ Getting There & Away

BUS

There are plenty of local buses linking the towns along the coastal road, though very few air-con services. Buses leave from the **bus station** (Main St) in the new town and operate roughly every 10 to 20 minutes between 4.30am and 8pm on all routes. Destinations include the following:

Colombo (via coastal road) Rs 240, 3¼ hours

Hikkaduwa Rs 38, 30 minutes

Matara Rs 65, 1¼ hours

Weligama Rs 50, 40 minutes

EX001 air-conditioned buses using the Southern Expressway from Colombo to Galle (Rs 400 to 550, 1½ hours, every 20 minutes) use a terminal in the southern Colombo suburb of Maharagama; there are also buses from Kadawatha. Buses that take the expressway save at least two hours compared with the coastal road.

CAR

Galle is an exit on the Southern Expressway, a toll road. Allow around 2½ hrs from the international airport to Galle.

TRAIN

The railway route along the coast from Colombo Fort to Galle is easily the most scenic and atmospheric way to journey between the two cities.

The website www.seat61.com is far more user-friendly for checking services and prices than the official Sri Lanka Railways one.

There are at least six express trains a day on the Colombo–Matara line, which all stop at Galle. There's also one daily 5.10am service from Kandy to Galle (2nd/3rd class Rs 320/175, 6½ hours), returning from Galle at 2.45pm. A new line opened in 2019 between Matara and Beliatta (inland of Tangalle) and some of the Colombo trains travel all the way to Beliatta. Eventually, it's hoped that the rail network will extend all the way to Kataragama, but at the time of research work had yet to begin on this section of line.

Destinations include the following:

Colombo Fort 2nd/3rd class Rs 180/100, 2¼ to 3½ hours, seven to nine daily

Hikkaduwa 2nd/3rd class Rs 40/25, 30 minutes, six to nine daily

Matara 2nd/3rd class Rs 90/50, one to 1½ hours, five to seven daily

Unawatuna & Around

☎091 / POP 4800

With palm-lined beaches, turquoise waters and a good selection of guesthouses and restaurants, Unawatuna is very popular with travellers. The resort's location is superb, with the historic city of Galle just 6km away and a wooded headland to the west dotted with tiny coves.

Unawatuna

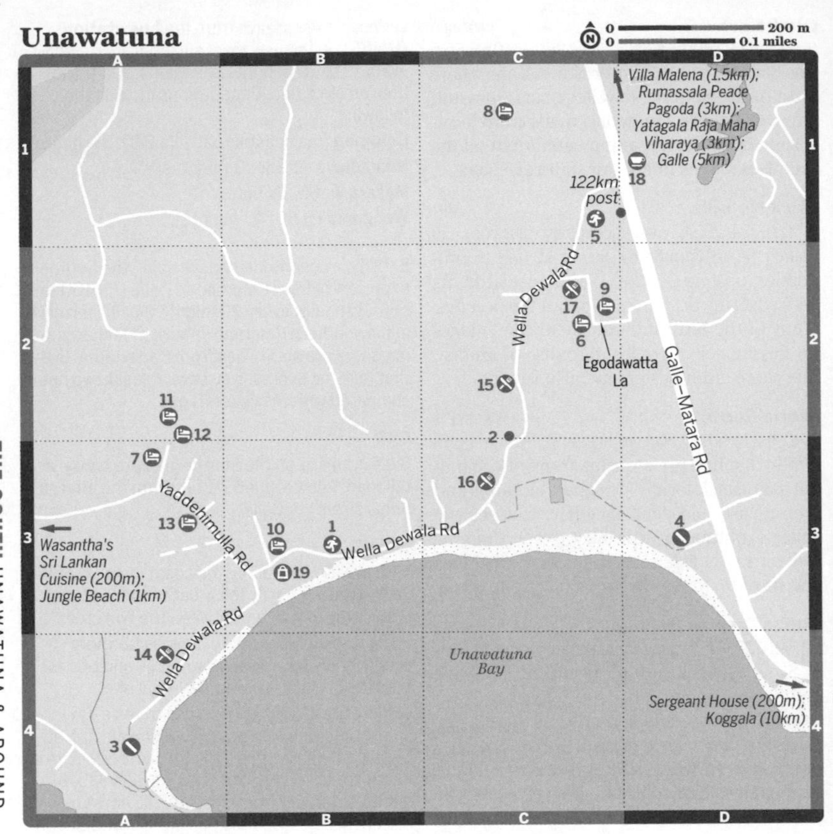

Unawatuna

Activities, Courses & Tours

1 Sanctuary Spa B3
2 Sonjas Health Food Restaurant C2
3 Submarine Diving School A4
4 Unawatuna Diving Centre D3
5 Yoga with Asiri C1

Sleeping

6 Bedspace Guesthouse C2
7 Dream House A3
8 Nooit Gedacht C1
9 Palm Grove C2
10 Secret Garden B3
11 Thambapanni Retreat A2
12 Unawatuna Singha Lounge A2
13 Weliwatta House A3

Eating

14 Bedspace Beach A4
Bedspace Kitchen .... (see 6)
15 Jina's Vegetarian and Vegan Restaurant C2
16 Koha Surf Lounge C3
17 Mati Gedara C2

Drinking & Nightlife

18 Kat's Coffee D1

Shopping

19 Made in Ceylon B3

Years of insensitive development, however, have resulted in an unappealing sprawl of concrete hotels and restaurants packed together right on the shore, blocking views of the bay in many spots.

Erosion caused by the construction of ill-advised breakwaters have also hit Unawatuna hard, causing massive loss of sand to its fabled beaches. By 2012 the resort was in a poor state. But since then initiatives have certainly improved things, as the authorities have pumped sand from deep water offshore to widen the beach, which is now looking in better shape than it has for years. Unawatuna is, once again, an enjoyable beach hangout. The calm waters make it an especially good bet for families with younger children. However, those gains might turn out to be undone thanks to the ongoing construction of a massive 13-storey hotel with a rumoured thousand rooms right on the western headland. The construction of this hotel is generally deeply opposed by locals and is undeniably a monstrous eyesore that's visible from miles around.

Atmosphere-wise, Unawatuna is lively without being rowdy: think sunset drinks rather than all-night raves.

Sights & Activities

Unawatuna doesn't have a lot in the way of surf breaks thanks to a fringing reef, though there is a gentle break right at the western end of the bay that a few locals ride. The main beach is fine for frolicking and body-surfing.

You can easily rent gear to **snorkel** the reefs a short distance from the west end of the beach.

There are several interesting **wreck dives** around Unawatuna, as well as reef and cave diving. Wrecks include the *Lord Nelson,* a cargo ship that sank in 2000; it has a 15m-long cabin to explore. The remains of a 100-year-old British steamer, the 33m *Rangoon,* are a 30-minute boat ride south of Unawatuna.

Less beach focused activities include yoga and cookery courses.

Yatagala Raja Maha Viharaya BUDDHIST TEMPLE
(Rs 500) Just 4km inland from Unawatuna, the Yatagala Raja Maha Viharaya is a quiet rock temple with a 9m reclining Buddha. The mural-covered walls are painted in the typical style of the Kandyan period. Monks have been living here for at least 1500 years. You'll seldom find crowds here, which only adds to the appeal. As you ascend the long flights of stairs, there are good views over the rice fields.

★ Sri Yoga Shala YOGA
(077-569 1672; www.sriyogashala.com; Durage Watta, Metaramba; 90min classes Rs 1900; wi-fi) This incredible rural retreat, 3km inland from Unawatuna is one of Sri Lanka's very best, with amazing facilities including a yoga studio with jungle views and a gorgeous saltwater pool. There are three daily yoga sessions (in vinyasa, Iyengar, hatha, slow-flow and yin styles); workshops, teacher training and treatments are also available. Three-day packages (including meals and beautiful accommodation) cost US$239 for one person and US$346 for two. Longer packages are also available.

Various accommodation packages with local hotels are possible; consult the website for details. Sri Yoga Shala is Rs 400 in a three-wheeler from Unawatuna.

Yoga with Asiri YOGA
(077-176 4662; www.yogawithasiri.net; 6 Wella Dewala Rd; classes from Rs 1500; classes 9.30am daily, also 4.30pm Dec-Apr) Asiri is a popular instructor who wins plaudits for his teaching style and general enthusiasm. Treatments and massages (Rs 3000 per hour) are also available.

Sanctuary Spa SPA
(077-307 8583; www.sanctuaryspaunawatuna.com; 136 Wella Dewala Rd; 1hr full body massage Rs 3300; 9am-6pm) If a holiday means doing nothing more strenuous than being utterly pampered, the Sanctuary Spa should be music to your knotted muscles. Reflexology, aromatherapy and a good variety of massages are offered.

Unawatuna Diving Centre DIVING
(076-760 8597; www.unawatunadiving.com; off Galle-Matara Rd; 2-tank boat dives €60, PADI Open Water €320; 8am-7pm mid-Oct–mid-Apr) The only dive shop with a decompression unit. It offers refresher programmes (€40) and discovery dives and rents out underwater cameras. Booking online secures a 10% discount.

Submarine Diving School DIVING
(077-719 6753, 077-704 4886; www.submarinediving.center; discovery dive US$50, PADI Open Water US$300) Unawatuna's original dive school runs dive trips for qualified divers to underwater wonders around Unawatuna (from US$30) as well as dive courses for newbies. Fun snorkelling trips (suitable for children) cost from US$50 for two people and take in reefs that are reached by a short boat ride.

Wasantha's Sri Lankan Cuisine COOKING
(077-288 6761; Rs 4000) The highly regarded cookery classes on offer at this hidden-away wooden cabin will reveal the secrets behind grinding your own spices, creating coconut milk, shopping for the best ingredients in Galle market and then turning it all into a taste sensation. Half-day classes run from 10am. Book ahead.

SHORT WALKS AROUND UNAWATUNA

There are numerous good walks in and around Unawatuna.

For views to the other side of the promontory with Galle Fort far in the distance, head up the hill behind Yaddehimulla Rd.

Another pleasant option is to walk north around the rocky outcrop at the west end of the beach to **Rumassala**, known for its protected medicinal herbs. Legend has it that Hanuman, the monkey god, dropped herbs here that had been carried from the Himalayas.

You can also wander up to the **Rumassala Peace Pagoda** on top of the hill. This impressive pagoda was built by Japanese Buddhist monks of the Mahayana sect in 2005, as part of their scheme to build peace temples in conflict zones (the Sri Lankan war was raging at the time). It's a (steep) 20-minute hike from the west end of Unawatuna beach.

Isolated **Jungle Beach** on the north side of the peninsula is also a popular destination. If you don't feel up for the 2km walk over the hill through dense forest to this bay, you can access it by scooter or three-wheeler via the Galle-Matara Rd. One of those 'secret' spots that everyone seems to know about, it has a couple of slimline sandy coves, some snorkelling offshore (though the reef is degraded) and a cafe (the venue for excellent DJ-driven parties on Wednesdays in high season).

Sonjas Health Food Restaurant COOKING
(091-224 5815, 077-961 5310; Wella Dewala Rd; half-day course Rs 3000) These enjoyable cookery courses involve you preparing five different curry dishes and will have you mixing your own curry powder in no time. The course is led by the lovely Karuna and a trip to Galle market is included in the price. Book ahead.

Sleeping

Unawatuna is home to a good number of small budget and midrange guesthouses. Many of the beachside hotels are uninspiring. Better deals are available in the quiet side lanes inland of the sands.

There are also budget places right on busy Galle-Matara Rd: avoid them unless you enjoy being serenaded by honking buses and trucks.

Unawatuna Singha Lounge HOSTEL $
(091-224 8014; www.facebook.com/unasinghalounge; dm Rs 2700;) There's a great social scene at this easy-going small hostel, which is housed inside an attractive old villa on a leafy side road. The dorms themselves are fairly basic but the barbecue nights, cooking classes, cinema nights, free bikes, surf lessons and more easily make up for that.

Bedspace Guesthouse HOTEL $$
(076-541 7001, 077-534 0130; www.bedspaceuna.com; Egodawatta Lane; r US$54-68, f US$75;) A superb guesthouse run by two expat mates (one from the UK, one from New Zealand), located down a quiet lane set back from the beach. Rooms are spacious and well presented, all with air-con and iPod docks, and some with colossal beds. It's perfect for foodies, as the owners are top chefs: breakfast is a magnificent spread, while dinner is a memorable occasion.

Palm Grove GUESTHOUSE $$
(091-225 0104; www.palmgrovesrilanka.com; off Wella Dewala Rd; r US$50-65;) This lovely little English-run guesthouse has five spacious rooms, all with air-con and ceiling fans, that are very comfortable and have nice private outdoor porches. Upstairs there is a roof terrace filled with hammocks. Breakfast is extra, but worth the US$5 charged.

Secret Garden GUESTHOUSE $$
(091-224 1857; www.secretgardenunawatuna.com; off Wella Dewala Rd; r incl breakfast from US$75;) This renovated 140-year-old house has a range of colour-coordinated rooms, suites and good-value bungalows, but do be aware that some rooms are much darker and more cave-like than others. There are twice-daily yoga sessions during the main holiday season and Ayurvedic treatments are also available.

It's very close to the beach, but the spacious grounds full of tropical flowers give a welcome sense of being a long way from anywhere.

Dream House GUESTHOUSE $$
(091-438 1541; www.dreamhouse-srilanka.com; off Yaddehimulla Rd; d from US$55;) This Italian-owned house has four intimate rooms that have been decorated in a Rome-meets-the-tropics fusion. It's got a large terrace that's great for relaxing while you count the monkeys leaping overhead; there's a good in-house Italian restaurant, too. There are substantial discounts during low season.

Nooit Gedacht HISTORIC HOTEL $$
(091-222 3449; www.nooitgedachtheritage.com; Galle-Matara Rd; r incl breakfast from US$50;

) Pass through the big entrance gates and slip into an oasis of calm. The heart of this compound is an atmospheric 1735 Dutch colonial mansion, which is slightly tumble-down but perfectly enchanting. Rooms are divided between an old wing and a newish two-storey block. Ayurvedic treatments can be arranged, and there are two pools in the lush, beautiful garden.

Weliwatta House GUESTHOUSE **$$**
(091-222 6642; Yaddehimulla Rd; r Rs 5500-6500;) Offering character and charm, this attractive buttercup-yellow villa was built in 1900 and has a lush garden to enjoy (where you may spot monkeys, monitor lizards and woodpeckers). There are a couple of spacious and tidy rooms with hot-water bathrooms in the main building and newer and more comfortable rooms behind.

Sergeant House BOUTIQUE HOTEL **$$$**
(077-356 5433; www.sergeanthouse.com; 381 Galle-Matara Road; r US$90-136, bungalow US$329;) Set well back from the busy road, these very comfortable and charmingly old-fashioned rooms (there's also a three-bedroom bungalow) all have a homely ambience thanks to rugs, carvings, art and the American owner's decorative taste. There's a supremely fecund tropical garden, with a 20m pool, plus a games room, a small gym and a spa.

Thambapanni Retreat HOTEL **$$$**
(091-438 1722; www.thambapannileisure.com; d incl breakfast from US$90;) One of Unawatuna's more upmarket options, this lovely place is built into and around great granite boulders that even protrude into the very chic rooms. There's a decent in-house restaurant and a lovely pool surrounded by jungle foliage. It's a five-minute walk down a quiet country lane from the beach.

Eating & Drinking

★Wasantha's Sri Lankan Cuisine SRI LANKAN **$$**
(077-288 6761; rice & curry Rs 750) From the wooden terrace of this tiny, secluded restaurant you can listen to the distinctive crow of the peacocks traipsing through the undergrowth while relishing the multitude of flavours of Unawatuna's best traditional rice and curry. It aso serves quality devilled dishes and seafood. If you're a fan of the food sign up to one of the chef's cooking courses (p123).

Jina's Vegetarian and Vegan Restaurant VEGETARIAN **$$**
(091-222 6878; Wella Dewala Rd; meals Rs 600-800; 11am-9pm) This fine place offers a wide array of Indian food (thalis and masala dosas) as well as great falafel, wholesome soups, Indonesian dishes like *gado-gado*, and Mexican-style dishes such as *huevos rancheros* (eggs in a spicy tomato sauce). Cold-pressed juices are superb, too. As everything is freshly prepared, you may have to wait a while – enjoy the garden setting.

Mati Gedara SRI LANKAN **$$**
(077-790 6723; Egodawatta Lane; meals Rs 350-500; 8am-9.30pm;) For inexpensive, authentic rice and curry, this appealingly rustic place is well worth seeking out. *Mati gedara* refers to the large earthenware pots the food is served in; a full veggie buffet is just Rs 350; meat and fish dishes are also available. The rich curd and honey is a treat for dessert.

Kat's Coffee CAFE
(076-856 8495; www.katscoffee.com; 235 Galle-Matara Rd; 8.30am-5.30pm;) For the best cafe in Unawatuna, head to Kat's. The German owner only uses premium arabica beans and though prices aren't cheap (a flat white is Rs 500) the coffee is excellent, as are the homemade cakes. It also serves porridge which must be a tough sell in steamy, hot Unawatuna! It's on the badass-busy main highway.

★Bedspace Kitchen INTERNATIONAL **$$$**
(091-225 0156; www.bedspaceuna.com; Egodawatta Lane; mains Rs 900-1600; noon-4pm & 6-10pm;) Unawatuna's most progressive restaurant, Bedspace Kitchen has it all right. Around 95% of the ingredients used are sourced in Sri Lanka, with most organic and local. Standout dishes include chicken pad thai, and the coconut lemongrass soup; lunch is more casual. Make sure you try one of the homemade craft sodas (Rs 400) in a range of bubbly flavours.

Bedspace Beach SRI LANKAN **$$$**
(Skinny Tom's; 091-225 0156; www.bedspaceuna.com; 147 Wella Delaya Rd; meals Rs 600-1600; 8am-10pm;) This great place offers a mod take on Sri Lankan cooking, with perfect hoppers available all day (including fusion versions of this dish – try the eggs Benedict hoppers with smoked salmon), a huge selection of authentic curries (including gluten-free and vegan choices) and a dozen or so sambals and relishes. There's great coffee and half of the attractive premises is air-conditioned.

Shopping

Unawatuna is overshadowed by nearby Galle as a shopping centre, but there are a few interesting shops along the main tourist drag. **Made in Ceylon** (077-519 9199; 9am-10pm) is a colourful, beachside shop that sells locally sourced, fair-trade products such as quirky bags, vintage tourism posters, elephant dung paper, devil masks, statues and more.

Getting There & Away

Coming by bus from Galle (Rs 21, 10 minutes) you can get off at the beach access lane (Wella Dewala Rd) at the 122km post, or get off at the next stop, where the ocean meets the main road. A three-wheeler to or from Galle costs about Rs 500.

Thalpe & Koggala

091

Beyond Unawatuna, the road runs close to the coast through Thalpe, Dalawella and Koggala, and on to Ahangama and beyond. This is posh country, with beautiful albeit narrow beaches and a long stretch of walled estates and hotels. Many times the beaches around here can be largely deserted, but that's only because the hotels act as something of a physical barrier and access lanes are few and far between.

Along this part of the coast you will see **stilt fishermen** perching precariously like storks above the waves at high tide. Each fisherman has a pole firmly embedded in the sea bottom, close to the shore, on which they perch and cast their lines. Stilt positions are passed down from father to son and are highly coveted. You'll be amazed at how fast they can get off those stilts and run up to you for payment if you even vaguely wave a camera in their direction.

Sights

Martin Wickramasinghe Folk Art Museum MUSEUM

(www.martinwickramasinghe.info; off Galle-Matara Rd, Koggala; Rs 250; 9am-5pm) This interesting museum includes the house where respected Sinhalese author Martin Wickramasinghe (1890–1976) was born (the traditional southern structure dates back 200 years and has some Dutch architectural influences). Exhibits are well displayed, with information in English. There's a good section on dance (including costumes and instruments), puppets, *kolam* (masked dance-drama) masks (including one of a very sunburned British officer), carriages and Buddhist artefacts. Look for the turn near the 131km post, across from the Fortress Hotel.

Koggala Lake LAKE

(boat trips 8am-4.30pm) Next to the road, Koggala Lake is alive with birdlife and dotted with islands, one of which features a Buddhist temple that attracts many visitors on *poya* (full moon) days, another that contains an interesting cinnamon plantation and also an (overpriced and touristy) herb-garden island.

Kataluwa Purwarama Temple BUDDHIST SITE

(24hr) Rarely crowded, this feels like the temple time forgot. Dating from the 13th century, it has some recently restored murals, including some large ones depicting foreigners in flowing robes. A friendly monk will open the building and explain the murals. Some of the Jataka tales (stories of the Buddha's previous lives) painted here are 200 years old. Turn inland and drive for 1.2km right at the 134km post; there are some signposts to help you navigate the way.

Sleeping & Eating

This stretch of shoreline is dotted with villas, upmarket hotels and Airbnb rentals (many of which are suitable for travelling families), though there's almost nothing for budget travellers.

There are very few independent restaurants, but virtually all of the large hotels have a fine choice of dining options.

Thalpe

Thalpe is popular with those looking for a more sedate and much more upmarket alternative to nearby Unawatuna. The beaches are largely hidden from the road by a solid line of villas, houses and hotels, each with thick walls and massive gates, and even when you can get onto the sand, the water isn't always safe for swimming because of currents and waves. **Wijaya beach** is by far the most popular, especially with Russian visitors. There's a calm, reef-fringed lagoon ideal for children and turtles (don't touch or otherwise harass the turtles) and at the western end is a distinctive rock and palm-tree swing that's a popular evening selfie spot.

★ **Why House** BOUTIQUE HOTEL $$$

(091-222 7599; www.whyhousesrilanka.com; off Galle-Matara Rd; r from US$250;) This dreamy place is exactly what you imagine a holiday in Sri Lanka would be like. Set in

DON'T MISS

HANDUNUGODA TEA ESTATE

The exquisite **Handunugoda Tea Estate** (☎091-228 6364, 077-771 3999; www.hermanteas.com; Tittagalla; ⏲8am-4.30pm; 📶) plantation in the hills above Koggala offers (free) highly informative tours of the estate.

During the tour, you'll walk through shady tea fields to a cafe for a free cuppa and a slice of very moreish homemade chocolate cake. Afterward, there's a (fairly brief) factory tour and then a visit to the tasting room where you can taste test 42 different kinds of tea. It's almost certainly the single best tea estate tour in Sri Lanka. There's also a well-stocked shop and horse rides around the estate are available (from US$10).

Handunugoda is owned by Herman Gunaratne, one of the legends of the island's tea industry. Be sure to pick up a copy of Gunaratne's autobiography, *The Suicide Club: A Virgin Tea Planter's Journey* (sold in the on-site shop), which is a remarkably entertaining and insightful read about his life, tea and Sri Lanka, from the waning days of the British Raj to today.

The estate is best known for producing the fabled virgin white tea, a delicate brew made from the tiniest and newest leaves. Where the average large plantation worker will pick 23kg of black tea in a day, the workers here manage but 150 grams of virgin white leaves.

It's 6km inland from the coastal highway; signposted from the 131km post.

expansive grounds, the rooms in a colonial house (or cottages) are the very definition of understated elegance. Personal service is emphasised, children are catered for, and all manner of meals can be prepared.

It's a kilometre inland from the shore – look for the turn-off from the main road at the 124km post – which some might see as a disadvantage but we see as a positive. This far back from the beach things are quieter, greener and generally just more Sri Lankan.

Frangipani Tree BOUTIQUE HOTEL **$$$**
(☎077-040 4040; www.edwardscollection.com/the-frangipani-tree; 182 Galle-Matara Rd; ste from US$219; ❄📶🏊) Cement, of all things, is the basis for this starkly modern vision of contemporary architecture on the coast. There are nine suites in three houses: all are named after turtle species and have soaring ceilings, private verandas and ocean views. There's a lovely infinity pool and a semi-private, palm-fringed beach.

Wijaya INTERNATIONAL **$$$**
(☎077-790 3431, 077-697 0649; www.wijayabeach.com; Galle-Matara Rd; mains Rs 900-2300; ⏲9am-11pm; 📶) This boutique hotel's restaurant is one of southern Sri Lanka's most renowned places to dine out, famed for its pizza cooked in wood-burning ovens. Bar staff whip up mean cocktails and the seafood specials also win rave reviews. No reservations by phone; use the website to book a table. It also does a comprehensive takeaway service.

Koggala

Koggala is home to a long, wide, but wave-lashed stretch of beach. The road runs quite close to the shore, but most of the time it remains just out of sight, hidden by the high walls of estates. When you do find somewhere to access the beach, you may well find that you've got the sands all to yourself. And lucky you because there's some gorgeous beaches here.

KK Beach BOUTIQUE HOTEL **$$$**
(☎091-494 4582; www.kkbeach.com; Habaraduwa; d incl breakfast US$204; ❄📶🏊) Urban luxury living on the beach is all the rage at this small resort with white cube-shaped rooms with ocean-blue pillows, bed sashes and furnishings. The floor-to-ceiling windows look across a breathtaking and near-deserted beach that ticks all the lazy, tropical beach fantasies (though be careful of dangerous undertows). There's also a flawless pool and good food.

Surf 'n' Turf INTERNATIONAL **$$**
(☎071-922 0622; www.facebook.com/surfandturfkoggala; mains Rs 900-1500; ⏲11am-10pm) This modern, open-fronted beachside (but with road views rather than beach views) place has striking art, lots of leafy plants and even a dartboard to use while you wait for your meal. The menu is crammed with creatures that just a short time earlier were swimming in the ocean. Good pasta too.

Getting There & Away

Buses between Galle and Matara pass through Thalpe and Koggala every 10 to 15 minutes during daylight hours.

Cinnamon Air (Map p64; 011-247 5475; www.cinnamonair.com; 2nd fl, 11 York St, Col 1; 8.30am-5pm Mon-Fri) runs a daily scheduled flight between Colombo's Bandaranaike International Airport and the airstrip at Koggala (one-way US$223). There are also daily flights to Kandy (Victoria reservoir; US$166).

Tuk-tuks are locally available for short journeys, and car rentals (with driver) are convenient for excursions.

Ahangama, Midigama & Gurubebila

041

Home to what is arguably the most consistent, and best, surf in Sri Lanka, the Ahangama and Midigama area has recently become one of the hippest beach areas in the country. What were, only a few short years ago, fairly quiet beaches have now been utterly consumed by international surf culture and the beaches around here are backed by dozens of surf camps and schools.

In many respects, there's very little that's truly Sri Lankan left about the area. That said, the atmosphere is fun and relaxed and there are still a few hidden corners where stilt fishermen cast lines to the sea and turtles haul themselves onto the beach.

The shoreline around here generally consists of slim sandy bays and rocky outcrops, though the highway often runs very close to the shore. The swimming is often dangerous.

Activities & Courses

Don't expect a peaceful, solitary surf in these parts. It's not at all unusual to find over 50 people battling it out on a single peak.

The first main surf spot heading east is the consistent beach break at **Kabalana Beach**, which normally has something to ride even when waves are tiny elsewhere.

In **Midigama** itself, a pint-sized village built beside a curve of sand, there are a couple of reef breaks. Lazy Left is the aptly named wave that bends around the rocks and into the sandy bay – it's perfect for that first reef experience. A few hundred metres further down is Ram's Right, a hollow, shallow and unpredictable beast. It's not suitable for beginners. Plantations is a popular reef break that sits somewhere in between the other two spots in terms of quality and difficulty.

There are surf schools on almost every beach around here. Prices are a pretty standard Rs 2500 for an hour lesson.

Note that just below sea level there are loads of rocks, coral and other hazards. Plantation Surf Inn offers ding repairs, surf lessons and board rental.

Sleeping & Eating

Accommodation sprawls along the coast from Ahangama to Midigama though real value for money can be hard to find. An increasing number of quality (and often foreign-owned) Airbnbs can be found nestled among the rice fields in the sweet, green countryside inland of Ahangama.

Ahangama

★**The Kip** BOUTIQUE HOTEL **$$**
(076-263 4610; www.thekipsrilanka.com; Mahavidana Gedara; r US$59-89;) You only have to open the door to one of the four understated rooms, which are set around the interior courtyard of a restored colonial villa, to know that everything at the Kip was put together with a designer's eye and the heart of someone in love with Sri Lanka. It's in a peaceful rural zone inland of the beach.

As well as having some of the south's best rooms, there's a superb cafe (open to nonguests; 8am to 3pm Tuesday to Sunday) serving an all-day brunch of vegetarian, organic and gluten-free homegrown dishes.

The Deco House BOUTIQUE HOTEL **$$$**
(076-140 4288; www.thedecohousesrilanka.com; Munidasa Mw; r from US$100;) One of the few upmarket places in these parts and it's a good one. This utterly divine boutique guesthouse, set a couple of quiet kilometres inland of the beach, is housed in an art-deco style building and has tasteful rooms that follow the period style. It's set within flowering gardens complete with a magnificent pool. Some of the units are suitable for families.

Follow The White Rabbit Restaurant INTERNATIONAL **$$$**
(077-310 1167; 76 Matara Rd; mains Rs 900-1800; noon-10pm) This bizarrely named restaurant (we looked but definitely couldn't find any white rabbits) is part restaurant, part art gallery and a totally relaxed place to sit on bean cushions eating crab curry, king prawns served in arrack (liquor distilled from coconut sugar) or an arty burger while watching the waves roll onto the quiet beach below the terrace.

Midigama

This tiny town has a few basic services and a few worthwhile cheap guesthouses.

Subodinee Guesthouse GUESTHOUSE $
(041-225 2383, 077-765 9933; www.subodinee.com; off Galle-Matara Rd; r from Rs 1000, cabanas from US$45;) Long-time owners Jai and his wife Sumana alongside their daughter offer 19 very different rooms, from hot concrete cubes with shared bathrooms to pleasing individual cabanas and rooms in a modern building over the road. Turn inland off the main road at the 139km post and go just past the clock tower and the train station.

Ram's Surfing Beach Guesthouse GUESTHOUSE $
(076-166 5600; ramssurfingbeach@gmail.com; Galle-Matara Rd; r with/without air-con Rs 4500/3000;) An old favourite with budget surfers, the rooms here are as basic as you'll get in Sri Lanka and the road noise is invasive, but it's certainly cheap and there's a good community spirit among guests. It's located just west of the 140km post, right in front of the best wave on the island: Rams Right (advanced surfers only).

Plantation Surf Inn GUESTHOUSE $$
(077-643 8912; www.plantationsurfinn.com; off Galle-Matara Rd; r from US$40;) This attractive family-run surf inn has a pretty garden and pleasingly simple but colourful rooms. The food here is excellent as the owner worked as a chef for years in Colombo. It's set just back from the highway and beach, on the inland side and a couple of minutes' walk from the waves.

Gurubebila

At the 140km post, look for a tiny road heading 100m towards the water from the main road. At the end, you'll discover a cluster of guesthouses and restaurants and a large grassy area where impromptu cricket games take place in the evenings, although these are slowly being pushed out in favour of makeshift cafe-bars, music and even the occasional fire juggler. The Plantation and Coconuts surf spots are here along with some narrow, rocky beaches.

This area is called Gurubebila, but it's really just an offshoot of Midigama.

Surfing Life GUESTHOUSE $
(077-740 1667; 32 Kadabeddagama; r Rs 3500-6000;) Small and personable guesthouse offering spotless rooms with hot-water bathrooms and an enjoyably low-key courtyard restaurant.

Lion's Rest GUESTHOUSE $$$
(041-225 0990; www.lions-rest.com; 5A Kadabeddagama; r US$70-110, f US$140;) Directly opposite the Coconuts break, this attractive, but pricey, hotel draws surfers and yogis for its daily classes. It has pleasant, modern rooms set in a two-storey complex surrounding a pool; upper-floor units have ocean views across the green, while the decor is all whitewashed plaster and dark wood. There's a small seafood restaurant.

Shirani Homemade Rice & Curry SRI LANKAN $$
(077-920 6951; 36 Kadabaddagama; rice & curry from Rs 500) This no-frills, semi-open-air restaurant on a leafy street serves the most authentic rice and curry (with five curries and pickles) in the Midigama area.

Getting There & Away

Buses run every 15 minutes along the busy coastal road connecting Ahangama and Midigama with Galle (Rs 50) and Matara (Rs 40). Many Colombo–Galle–Matara trains stop at Ahangama. Only a few local trains stop at Midigama.

Weligama

041 / POP 22,337

Weligama (meaning 'Sandy Village') is an interesting blend of lively fishing town and beach resort. The sprawling main settlement and coastal road is somewhat scruffy and not that easy on the eye, but you'll find the sandy beach is reasonably attractive once you're away from the main section – there's a couple of far more attractive cove beaches west of the centre. At the east end of the beach, there's an enormous Marriott hotel, which towers over the surrounding buildings and looks completely out of place.

Weligama's benign beach break is ideal for novice surfers and many independent travellers learn to ride their first waves here. At times there can be hundreds of people in the water (a situation which can present its own set of dangers). There are surf shacks almost all the way along the beach where instructors rent boards (from Rs 1000 per half-day) and offer lessons (from Rs 2500). After fun in the ocean, you can marvel at (and feast on) the denizens of the deep, who end their days being sold from roadside fish stalls.

Sights & Activities

Bandrawatta Beach BEACH

This lovely natural cove beach is well away from the main highway, has sheltered swimming and also a surf break further offshore. Look out for stilt fishermen in the sea just below the Cape Weligama hotel. It's 3km southwest of Weligama.

Taprobane ISLAND

(☎091-438 0275; www.taprobaneisland.com; island rental per day from US$1000; 📶) Just offshore – you can walk out to it at low tide – is this tiny island. It looks like an ideal artist's or writer's retreat, which it once was: novelist Paul Bowles wrote *The Spider's House* here in the 1950s. The island was developed in the 1920s by the French Count de Mauny Talvande who perched his mansion on the tiny rock. You can stay or dine on the island with advance planning; five staff are allocated to cater for your stay.

Weligama Bay Dive Center DIVING

(☎041-225 0799; www.scubadivingweligama.com; 126 Kapparathota Rd; discover dive US$70, PADI Open Water US$350) Snorkelling and diving around Weligama is quite good. This very professional and long-running operation, just off the highway at the western end of the beach, runs PADI courses as well as night dives and wreck dives. It also organises whale- and dolphin-watching trips and snorkelling excursions (Rs 3000 per person for a group boat trip).

Freedom Surf & Travel SURFING

(☎077-717 7422; www.freedomsrilanka.com; lessons Rs 2500, half-day board rental Rs 1000; ⏰5.30am-6pm) One of the more reputable and better organised of the many, many surf schools in Weligama.

Sleeping

Accommodation is spread out along the main beach road and inland towards the town centre. There are a growing number of funky hostels popular with people wanting to learn how to surf.

Hangtime Hostel HOSTEL $

(☎071-415 6135; www.hangtimehostel.com; 540 Weligama Rd; dm with/without air-con Rs 2000/1500, r with/without air-con Rs 5500/4500; ❄📶) Take a dated concrete hotel on the seafront, pimp it up with backpacker-geared appeal (yoga deck, rooftop bar-resto, surfboard racks) and end up with the Hangtime Hostel. The private rooms are on the ground level and have private verandas, while dorms have attached hot-water bathrooms, mosquito nets, reading lights and individual fans and lockers.

Excursions are offered, including booze cruises and safaris. Yoga classes are Rs 1000.

Coco Hostel HOSTEL $

(☎076-679 2156; 620 Matara Rd; dm with/without air-con US$9/6, r with/without air-con Rs 5000/3500; ❄📶) Super friendly and sociable new hostel with six-bed dorms and a couple of functional private rooms. Only the air-con dorm has an attached bathroom. There's a big bar-cafe which is a great place for an evening drink, but a bit of a hot suntrap during the day. It's just over the street from the main concentration of surf schools.

★**Cape Weligama** RESORT $$$

(☎041-225 3000; www.resplendentceylon.com; Abimanagama Rd; r incl breakfast from US$456; ❄📶🏊) Perched on a promontory above the Indian Ocean, this astonishing hotel has stunning vistas and a sublime 60m crescent-shaped infinity pool (should you get bored of your own private pool that many of the villas are equipped with, or indeed the huge kid-friendly 'cove pool'). There's a spa, a dive school and several restaurants, including a cliff-edge steakhouse.

Eraeliya Villas & Gardens VILLA $$$

(☎077-771 6779; www.eraeliya.com; 299 Walliwala; villas from US$265; ❄📶🏊) Located in Weligama's most attractive and peaceful location, this stunning villa complex enjoys a delightful oceanfront situation and its air-conditioned villas (sleeping two to eight) are very spacious and are kitted out with flat-screen TVs and kitchenettes. There's a spa, a lovely pool and a restaurant, gorgeous gardens and a secluded, dreamy beach.

Eating & Drinking

Along the seafront strip various food stalls set up in the afternoon and evening. They do a roaring trade in fresh seafood. Otherwise there are a growing number of traveller-oriented cafes.

AVM Cream House INTERNATIONAL $

(3 Samaraweera Pl; meals Rs 250-350; ⏰9am-9pm) A bustling little place serving filling meals, including noodle and fried-rice dishes as well as tasty snacks (the shawarmas are superb). There's good ice cream and fresh fruit juices; a delicious soursop (custard apple) juice is Rs

150. It's opposite the bus station in the town centre and has a menu in English.

Nomad Boutique Cafe INTERNATIONAL **$$**
(www.nomadsrilanka.com; 640 Matara Rd; mains Rs 600-1200; ⌚8am-3pm) Dishing up organic tofu poke bowls, vegan cakes and designer tacos (including the delicious jackfruit taco) as well as detox juices and smoothies, this is a fine example of the new wave of foreign-owned cafes sprouting across southern Sri Lanka where everything is designed and presented to be perfectly Instagrammable. Fortunately, it all tastes as good as it looks!

The only let-down about this cool place is the busy road right out front.

Tiki Clifftop BAR
(☎071-200 1483; www.facebook.com/tikiweligama; 1 Awariyawaththa; ⌚10am-late; 📶) Tucked away in a remote cliff-side spot 3km southwest of the centre, this cool bar-resto is well worth a tuk-tuk ride. The ocean views are mesmerising and DJs pump up the dance floor with house and party vibes, and reggae on Wednesdays.

Getting There & Away

There are buses every 15 minutes to both Galle (Rs 50, one hour) and Matara (Rs 40, 30 minutes).

Weligama is on the Colombo–Matara train line, with four to six trains stop daily. Destinations includes the following:

Colombo 2nd/3rd class Rs 280/160, 2½ to four hours

Galle 2nd/3rd class Rs 70/40, 40 minutes to one hour

Matara 2nd/3rd class Rs 40/20, 20 to 30 minutes

Mirissa

☎041 / POP 4695

Mirissa is a stunning crescent beach of ivory sand bookended by rust-red cliffs. This scenic perfection hasn't gone unnoticed though and in recent years Mirissa's popularity has soared. Today it's one of the biggest and busiest beach resorts on the south coast and it's developed a reputation as a party destination for young travellers. In high season DJs spin pumping tunes till late several nights a week. If you're looking for solitude and zen-like calm, this may not be the beach for you, but if you want to dance and drink the night away, and then collapse into a hammock or sunlounger in the day, then Mirissa ticks all the boxes.

Sights & Activities

Mirissa Beach BEACH
Mirissa Beach boasts powdery pale sand and azure waters. The west side is the nicest and has the broadest expanse of sand; as the bay curves gently around to the east it meets up with the roar of the Galle-Matara Rd. Close to the centre of Mirissa Bay is a much-photographed sandbar that connects to a tiny island that you can walk to at low tide. The western end also has a reasonable right point break for surfers.

The far eastern section of the beach has been lost to coastal erosion and is lined with unsightly concrete sea defences. There's very little shade on the beach thanks to much of the original fringe of palm trees being chopped down to make way for beachfront cafes and hundreds of sunloungers.

Secret Root Spa SPA
(☎077-329 4332; www.secretrootspa.com; off Galle-Matara Rd; massage per hour Rs 3000; 📶) Just inland from the east end of the beach is this family-run sanctuary of calm. It's an Ayurvedic centre with male and female therapists who are experts in relieving tension. Try a herbal steam bath after your massage.

Cinnamon Plantation Tour TOURS
(☎041-225 0980; www.mirissahills.com; Mirissa Hills Hotel, Henwalle Rd, off Galle-Matara Rd; 45min tour Rs 1650; ⌚9am-4.30pm) Tours of this magnificent 24-hectare hilltop estate are an excellent introduction to the cultivation and harvesting of cinnamon, the queen of spices. You get to examine the bushes, which can be up to 40 years old, and see how a skilled worker removes the bark by hand using a specialist brass instrument. You can also stay for a meal and make a free tour of the hotel's remarkable contemporary art gallery. It's essential to book ahead.

Sleeping

You'll find a thicket of good-value guesthouses and modest beach hotels at the west end of Mirissa, on and off tiny Gunasiri Mahimi Mawatha. Inland, there are some excellent family-run places along tiny lanes a short walk from the beach. Beware of road noise at the east end of the beach and loud and late music near the beach cafes.

★ **JJ's Hostel** HOSTEL **$**
(☎041-226 0710; www.jjshostelmirissa.com; Yatipila Rd; dm Rs 2000, r with/without air-con Rs 7000/5000; ❄📶) Mirissa's best hostel – and

one of the best in southern Sri Lanka – JJ's is a super sleek offering with quality dorms (including a female-only dorm) and rooms that would be the envy of many a much smarter and pricier hotel. Each dorm has two bathrooms, a big locker for each guest and super thick mattresses on the beds.

Twice-daily yoga sessions, good breakfasts and a switched-on management help round the deal out. It's a fiveminute walk to the beach.

Hangover Hostel Mirissa HOSTEL **$**
(☎077-791 7916; www.hangoverhostels.com; Udupila; dm/r US$9/40; ❄📶) One for the night owls. This hostel is bang on the main drag right at the eastern end of the beach and (as the name implies) it's party central for a young international backpacker crew. The accommodation is very basic and there's a fair bit of road noise but nobody seems to mind and everyone loves the instant beach access.

★**Palm Villa** GUESTHOUSE **$$**
(☎041-225 0022; www.palmvillamirissa.com; Galle-Matara Rd; r incl breakfast US$84; ❄📶) Each of the lovely rooms in this colonial-style manor is uniquely decorated in a bright and modern fashion and represents good value. The more expensive are set right on a quiet patch of beach (expect some passing people traffic). There's a two-night minimum, and a fine restaurant.

Espirit d'ici Hotel HOTEL **$$**
(☎075-377 9200; www.espritdicihotel.com; Galle-Matara Rd; r from US$45; ❄📶🏊) Formerly a dated concrete hotel in an architecturally challenging building, this place has been reinvented as a contemporary French-run abode. The bright rooms are very spacious, with modern furnishings and some with sea views. In the huge bar-restaurant you'll find a pool table, table tennis and board games. The huge family rooms (US$90) are solid value.

Poppies GUESTHOUSE **$$**
(☎077-794 0328; www.poppiesmirissa.com; off Galle-Matara Rd; s/d with fan US$30/40, with air-con US$50/60; ❄📶) Offering good value, the pristine rooms here are set around a pretty, shady courtyard full of trees that squirrels race up and down. Each room has a nice outside sitting area and hammock. It's just inland from the eastern end of the beach, though expect some traffic noise from the highway.

Mirissa Hills BOUTIQUE HOTEL **$$$**
(☎041-225 0980; www.mirissahills.com; Henwalle Rd, off Galle-Matara Rd; r US$90-300; ❄📶🏊) One of southern Sri Lanka's most remarkable places to stay, this working cinnamon farm has a selection of fine accommodation (though cheaper rooms can be a little dingy), including a renovated estate house and a spectacular hilltop retreat. Meals are excellent, with dramatic coastal views from the dining terrace, while the contemporary art gallery contains many important sculptures.

Spice House HOTEL **$$$**
(☎077-351 0147; www.thespicehousemirissa.com; Galle-Matara Rd; r US$90-130; ❄📶🏊) Set back from the road, a short walk from Mirissa's east shoreline, this attractive hotel has nine well-appointed and inviting rooms, and three more family rooms in a separate villa at the rear. It's owned by a welcoming British–Sri Lankan couple and you'll find plenty of chill-out areas for relaxing, and a lovely garden and pool to enjoy.

Eating & Drinking

Numerous places set up tables and chairs right up to the tide line day and night. Wander and compare which one has the freshest seafood. All are good for a beer; some also serve espresso.

★**No1 Dewmini Roti Shop** SRI LANKAN **$**
(☎071-516 2604; www.dewminirotishop.wordpress.com; off Udupila Rd; meals Rs 200-550; ⏲8am-9pm; 📶) The original and still the best local *rotti* (flatbread) shop. It also makes *kotthu* (*rotti* chopped up and mixed with veggies) and delicious, more substantial rice-and-curry-style dishes. The ever-smiling chef and owner also offers **cooking classes** (Rs 2500 for six curries). It's 350m north of the coastal highway in an attractive semi-rural setting.

Milky Wave Mirissa INTERNATIONAL **$$**
(Udupila Rd; mains Rs 600-1000; ⏲8am-10pm) Snappy new, open-air cafe with a huge whale wall mural and tables set out under the trees. The menu has an urban edge with fruit bowl breakfasts, pasta and rice salads for lunch; and they even make their own gelato. Plus there's decent coffee and juices.

Papa Mango INTERNATIONAL **$$**
(☎041-454 5341, 077-772 6546; www.facebook.com/papamangomirissasl; off Galle-Matara Rd; meals Rs 650-1200; ⏲8am-10pm or later; 📶) This restaurant has a prime beachfront location on the east side of Mirissa with tables dotted around a large garden shaded by palms. The menu takes in seafood, local curries and Western

BLUE-WHALE TOURS

It's only in the past 15 years that marine biologists realised that blue whales – the world's largest living mammal – are remarkably similar to many holidaying humans: they like Sri Lanka's coast. In fact, the waters off Mirissa and Dondra Head to the east often host some of the world's largest number of blue whales.

The stats for blue whales are as extraordinary as their size: 30m long and weighing up to 200 tonnes (which makes them heavier than any known dinosaur by a significant amount). They are thought to live for more than 80 years, but this is not well understood as research has been scant, primarily because there were so few blue whales left – an estimated 5000 (just 1% of the population from 200 years ago) – after whaling finally ended in the 1970s. Since then, numbers have recovered slightly and there are now an estimated 10,000 to 25,000 spread around the world's oceans.

Mirissa-based boat tours to spot blue whales are a major draw for visitors and there are many competing operators. Besides the blues, it's common to spot their (slightly) smaller cousins: fin whales (the world's second-largest at up to 27m), sperm whales, Bryde's whales and various dolphins. Megapods of spinner dolphins, numbering over 500, are regularly encountered. A few points to consider:

- Although blue whales have been spotted throughout the year, December and April seem to be the peak months.
- Avoid May to July as monsoon season makes the waters very rough.
- It's very rare to see the whales leap out of the water. Normally you will only get a quick glimpse of a whale coming up for air or its tail rising into the sky as it starts to dive.
- Most tours depart around 6.30am and generally last from two to five hours, depending on how long it takes to find whales. This can make for a long day if seas are rough.
- Look for tours that respect international conventions about approaching whales. Ask about this before you book.
- Avoid rogue operators or chartered fishing boats as many of these are known to harass whales, for example by boxing one animal between two boats.
- The long day and potentially rough seas mean that this is not a suitable trip for younger children (below the age of around 10).
- Some operators advertise swimming with the whales. You should not do this because of the dangers it can present to the whales (and you!).

Recommended operators:

Raja and the Whales (☎071-333 1811; www.rajaandthewhales.com; Mirissa Harbour; adult/child US$54/27) Uses a two-level trimaran for trips and follows international guidelines for approaching whales.

Kumara and Whales (☎077-2050719; www.kumaraandwhales.com; Matara Rd; adult/child US$50/25) This operator gets good feedback for its well-run whale-spotting tours.

Jetwing Eco (☎Colombo 011-238 1201; www.jetwingeco.com/whale-watching-mirissa; adult/child Rs 7500/37,500) The team at Jetwing Eco (and offshoot of the acclaimed and very environmentally aware Jetwing group) are among the leaders in Sri Lankan whale watching and did much to help call attention to the whales. They offer customised whale-watching trips. Book in advance through the Colombo office.

F-Airways (☎077-444 5830; hwww.f-air.lk; per person US$150) Taking to the air in order to see an underwater creature might seem like an odd way of doing things, but from above you can actually see the whole bulk of the whale whenever it comes up to surface and, for photographers, this often gives more interesting shots. F-Airways offer 45-minute scenic flights in small planes departing from Koggala. Advance bookings essential.

dishes and it regularly hosts parties with live bands and DJs.

Getting There & Away

Very regular buses, running about every 15 minutes, connect Mirissa with Galle (Rs 70 to 80, one hour) and Matara (Rs 45, 25 minutes). If you're heading to Colombo by bus, head to Matara or Galle and take an express service from there.

The bus fare to/from Weligama is Rs 20 (10 minutes); a three-wheeler costs Rs 400 to 500.

Drivers charge Rs 10,000 for a one-way ride to Colombo airport; the journey time is around 2½ hours.

Matara

041 / POP 74,193

Matara is a busy, booming, sprawling commercial town that owes almost nothing to tourism – which can make it a fascinating window on modern Sri Lankan life. Matara's main attractions are its ramparts, Dutch architecture, a well-preserved fort and its street life.

Sights

You can spend half a day wandering Matara. The long strip of **beach** along Sea Beach Rd is somewhat tatty and commercial and not a place a foreign tourist is likely to want to sunbathe but in the evenings, when locals throng the sands for a paddle and an ice cream, it's a colourful slice of authentic Sri Lankan life that's far removed from the glossy beach resorts.

Star Fort FORT

(Main St; 8.30am-4.30pm Wed-Mon) FREE This fort was built by the Dutch to compensate for deficiencies in the neighbouring rampart, but it's so small it could only have protected a handful of bureaucrats. Look out for the construction date (1765) embossed over the main gate, along with VOC insignia and the coat of arms of the governor of the day. Inside there's a small **museum** with modest displays about the history of Matara, and you can view former soldiers' sleeping quarters and prisoners' cells.

Old Dutch Trade Centre HISTORIC BUILDING

(Nupe Market; Anagarika Dharmapala Mw) FREE On the western side of town, this magnificent T-shaped building (once the town's market) will fascinate architectural buffs: it has an imposing, steeply pitched roof, three conical towers and a grand gabled entrance. It's open-sided and supported by colossal wooden beams and columns.

Matara Fort AREA

This historic, though run-down, district was once the heart of Dutch, and later British, Matara. There are no real sights, but it's an intriguing area architecturally, and a quick wander will reveal many fine old colonial mansions in various states of disrepair. The riverbank at the west corner is serene; see if you can spot one of the rumoured crocodiles.

Polhena Beach BEACH

(Polhena Rd) The best beach in the area is a small sandy cove that's sheltered by a reef offshore. There's good snorkelling in the bay, and though visibility is not that great, turtles are very regularly spotted here. It's popular with locals at weekends who rent goofy inflatable toys and frolic in the surf, but it's usually quiet on weekdays.

Sleeping & Eating

Sunil Rest Guest House & Restaurant GUESTHOUSE $

(076-318 1548, 041-222 1983; sunilrestpolhena@yahoo.com; 16/3A Second Cross Rd; r from Rs 3000;) Run by Sunil and Ureka, a charming local couple, this fine guesthouse is about 150m from the beach. Rooms in the main building are simple and clean, or there are other options managed by the family close by. Ureka is an excellent cook, too. As they

LONG-DISTANCE BUSES FROM MATARA

DESTINATION	PRICE (RS)	DURATION (HR)	FREQUENCY
Colombo (via coastal road)	350	5	every 15min
Colombo (via expressway)	600 (air-con luxury)	2½	hourly, 4am-7pm
Galle	65	1	every 15min
Kataragama	235	4	hourly
Ratnapura	246	2½	6.20am, 7am, 12.40pm
Tangalle	73	1	every 15min

Matara

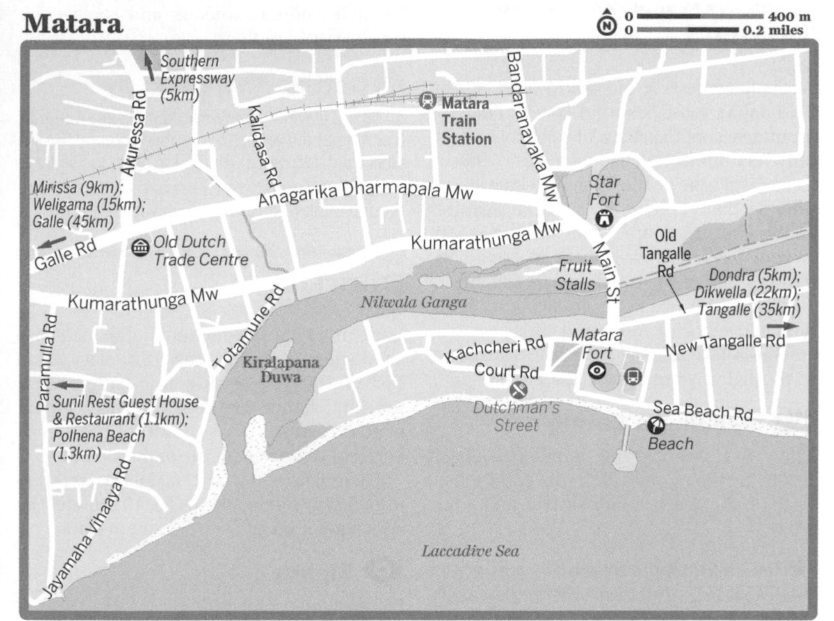

don't pay commission, many three-wheeler drivers will tell you it's closed – it's not.

★**Dutchman's Street** SRI LANKAN **$$**
(☎041-223 6555; www.thedutchmansstreet.com; Court Rd; meals Rs 500-1300; ⏲9am-10pm; 📶) A cool, arty, red-brick cafe-restaurant serving well-priced international dishes (saucy fried chicken wings, battered fried prawns) in the colonial enclave of Matara Fort. It occasionally hosts DJs and live music events and has a lovely sea-facing garden.

ℹ Getting There & Away

BUS

Matara's **bus station** (New Tangalle Rd; ⏲24hr) is a vast multilevel place; look for tiny destination signs over the queuing pens.

As Matara is a regional transport hub, services are frequent in all directions; most buses are not air-conditioned. For Kandy, travel via Colombo.

TRAIN

Matara's **train station** (Railway Station Rd) is the present terminus of the coastal railway. A new railway line between Matara and Kataragama is in the pipeline but while a short section of track has been completed it's going to be quite a few years until the rest of the line is done. Destinations include the following:

Bentota 2nd/3rd class Rs 190/105, two hours, five to six daily

Colombo 2nd/3rd class Rs 280/155, 2¾ to four hours, five to six daily

Galle 2nd/3rd class Rs 90/50, one to 1½ hours, six to eight daily

Kandy (via Colombo) 2nd/3rd class Rs 500/315, seven hours, daily

Dondra

The small town of Dondra was one of Sri Lanka's primary places of worship until its grand Tenavaram temple was destroyed by the Portuguese back in the 16th century. Today it's famous as marking the southernmost point in Sri Lanka. The landmark **Dondra Head Lighthouse** (Lighthouse Rd) provides an exclamation mark to the southernmost point of Sri Lanka. Visitors are not permitted to enter the lighthouse compound or climb up the structure's interior, but the fine oceanside setting is still inspiring and there's a pretty cove beach with a few colourful fishing boats hauled onto the sand just next to it. It's 1.2km south of the centre. Buses from Matara (every 15 minutes) will drop you in the centre of Dondra. From here you can catch a three-wheeler or walk to the lighthouse.

Talalla

☎041

Strongly contesting the award for southern Sri Lanka's most beautiful beach, Talalla is an utterly sublime curve of sand that's been only very lightly touched by tourism. Indeed as you walk the idyllic kilometre-long shoreline, virtually the only artificial features you'll encounter are small fishing boats. Nature feels very close here at the idyllic western end of the beach, where patches of tropical forest are home to swinging monkeys and snoozing monitor lizards.

The eastern side of Talalla is less attractive as the highway runs much closer to the shore.

Sleeping & Eating

There is a slow-growing number of places to stay including several simple guesthouses back off the beach, a villa or two, and a fine hotel.

★Talalla Sunshine Beach GUESTHOUSE $

(☎077-514 1533; www.talalla-sunshine-beach.com; r with fan/air-con from Rs 3800/4700;) The incredibly hospitable owners really make this budget-friendly place, located just behind the beach. All rooms have partial sea views, mosquito nets, optional air-con, and private bathrooms with hot water. Food here is a real highlight: Nisansala's rice and curries and hopper breakfasts are very special indeed; she also offers cooking lessons.

Handun Villas HOTEL $$

(☎077-347 0830; www.handunvillas.com; r incl breakfast from US$60;) With salt-stained wooden doors, white and slate-grey linens and wooden floors, there's a simple, understated elegance to this impressive eight-room hotel. The place is set within large gardens, which are full of garish tropical flowers and big trees, and the food is excellent. Take note though that it's on the inland side of the main road.

★Talalla Retreat RESORT $$$

(☎041-225 9171; www.talallaretreat.com; off Matara-Tangalle Rd; incl breakfast dm US$46, r US$57-124;) One of the island's foremost retreats at a price anyone can afford. The location is inspirational, set back from the shore with views of the ocean from the wonderful restaurant. There's a whole array of accommodation options from classy (though pricey) dorms through to magnificent open-plan and open-sided units (though raiding monkeys and some noise can be issues in these).

Getting There & Away

All buses travelling between Matara and Tangalle (running about every 15 minutes) pass by the access road, located at the 171km post, to Talalla.

There's no public transport to the beach itself, though a tuk-tuk from the highway is Rs 250.

Dikwella

☎041

Little more than a wide spot in the road with a few shops useful to locals, Dikwella – 22km east of Matara – is close to a couple of interesting sights. The area's low-key stretch of coast features some beautiful beaches in perfect little coves off the main road.

Dikwella is connected to Matara (Rs 50, 30 minutes) and Tangalle (Rs 36, 40 minutes) by very regular buses from 5.30am to 7pm.

Sights

Ho-o-maniya Blowhole LANDMARK

(Rs 1000; dawn-dusk) The Ho-o-maniya blowhole is sometimes spectacular and other times a fizzle. During the southwest monsoon (June to August is the best time), high seas can force water 23m up through a natural chimney in the rocks and then up to 18m in the air. At other times, the blowhole will leave you limp. From the parking area, it's a 300m up-and-down walk past numerous vendors and, sadly, lots of rubbish.

Wewurukannala Vihara BUDDHIST SITE

(Wewurukannala Rd; Rs 200; dawn-dusk) A 50m-high seated Buddha figure – the largest in Sri Lanka – is a highlight of this somewhat gaudy temple, which is often thronged with worshippers. Before reaching the Buddha you pass through a hall of horrors full of life-sized models of demons and sinners. The punishments depicted include being dunked in boiling cauldrons, sawn in half and disembowelled.

Be aware that the complex also houses an elephant who appears to be kept chained up almost all of the time.

Sleeping & Eating

Dickwella Beach Hotel HOTEL $$

(☎041-225 5522; www.dickwellabeach.lk; 112 Mahawela Rd; r from US$40;) This family-run place has two blocks, a modern structure with a prime beachfront location where the rooms have dreamy sea views, and budget rooms by the road. The lovely oceanside dining zone is just perfect for sipping a fresh coconut and gazing at the waves. Look for the turn-off from the main road about 1km east of Dikwella.

Hiriketiya

041

In the space of two or three years, this tiny horseshoe-shaped cove, which is fringed by tropical forest and lapped by surging surf, has gone from being a little known, mellow beach retreat with just a stirring of tourist life to full-blown, surf hipster resort that you are either going to love or hate. For the fans, Hiriketiya's appeal is easy to understand: it's tucked well away from the highway traffic that curses many southern Sri Lankan beaches, the waves are good and there's plenty of decent (but pricey) places to eat and stay, plus of course the beach itself is an absolute beauty bomb.

Surfing is a huge draw. Novices and the less-experienced will love the waves close to the central shoreline, while there's a long, left point break on the eastern edge of the bay that's especially good for longboarders. You'll find boards for rent racked up right along the beach (lessons average Rs 3000 for 1½ hours and board hire is around Rs 300 per hour) and most guesthouses can also organise lessons. You may read elsewhere that the waves at Hiriketiya are quiet compared to other parts of southern Sri Lanka. This is no longer the case, and on any given day during the tourist season you can expect huge numbers of surfers in the water and a lot of dropping in on each other. Swimming is usually good close to shore and on the western edge of the bay.

Sleeping & Eating

Dot's Bay House GUESTHOUSE $$

(077-793 5593; www.dotsbayhouse.com; incl breakfast dm US$14, d from US$68;) Small artistically decorated rooms in a guesthouse known for its good vibes and chilled atmosphere; you'll pay extra for air-con. The rooms are a tad pricey and, in the cheaper ones, the bathroom leaves a lot to be desired, but such is Hiriketiya's draw they're often fully booked. It's a good place to meet others and there's a great cafe.

The dorm is actually just six beds with mosquito nets in an open-sided hut. There's zero privacy but it's as cheap as you'll get on this beach. There's a small pool and surfboard rental is included in the rates. There are frequent yoga classes too.

Salt House GUESTHOUSE $$$

(041-225 6819; www.salthousesrilanka.net; Hiriketiya Rd; r US$85;) A stylish, upmarket guesthouse with six rooms (some open-sided, so expect some noise, others enclosed and air-conditioned) and there's a spacious chill-out space on the top deck. Next door there's a lovely garden with a superb forest-facing yoga studio, a small pool and a fine healthy-eating restaurant. It's 100m inland from the shore.

Beach House Hiriketiya GUESTHOUSE $$$

(076-617 6969; www.beachhousehiriketiya.com; r US$80;) There's a row of simple beach-chic rooms here at the back of the restaurant, all thoughtfully designed in creams and whites, with time- and salt-weathered doors and window shutters; the beds have deep, comfortable mattresses and all have outdoor en-suite bathrooms. Book well ahead as it's very popular.

The Grove Lanka BOUTIQUE HOTEL $$$

(www.facebook.com/thegrovelanka; r incl breakfast US$100;) Two-room boutique guesthouse in a standout, modern cube building set in spacious grounds a short way from the beach. Both rooms have floor-to-ceiling windows and a sense of well-planned style though they do pick up a bit of noise from the (very good) downstairs bar and restaurant.

Malu Poke INTERNATIONAL $$$

(meals around Rs 1000; 8am-9.30pm) Popular, beachside health-food restaurant serving smoothie bowls and poke bowls (the Hawaiian version of sushi). Pick your own protein-packed ingredients and power up for a surf while lounging on a bean bag.

Getting There & Away

Hiriketiya is only a kilometre or so from Dikwella. Very regular buses buzz between Matara (Rs 20, 30 minutes) and Tangalle (Rs 36, 40 minutes) from 5.30am until 7pm; all pass through Dikwella.

A tuk-tuk from Dikwella is Rs 250 to 300.

Unakuruwa

047

If you had to design the perfect Sri Lankan hideaway then the deep, horseshoe cove of Unakuruwa, with its ribbon of ivory sand and headlands still cloaked green in coconut

Safari Guide

Sri Lanka is arguably the best safari destination in Asia. With a little advance planning and a lot of luck, you might get to see a leopard hunt. It's important to plan properly: the quality of vehicles, guides and drivers can all make or break a Sri Lankan safari. Here we give a few pointers on how to ensure you have a safari to remember – for all the right reasons.

When to Safari

Most animals – and leopards in particular – are most active around dawn and dusk, so you need to be in the park, binoculars at the ready, as soon as the park opens at 6am. By about 9am it's getting hot and most animals have gone for a siesta. Late afternoon is also a great time. The light is often lovely, there are less other safari vehicles around and the animals are stirring back into action again.

Getting Ready to Go

You've organised a jeep and you're primed for an early morning start, but before you go, ask yourself the following questions.

➡ Are the services of a dedicated guide included? This is normally only included on top-end safaris on dedicated wildlife-watching holidays. Many drivers are also very good at animal spotting, but might not be able to share that much about the creatures. At most parks, a park-provided 'guide' is mandatory and included in the entry fee. However, these guides speak little English and do not always do much animal spotting. They're really there to check that you and your driver respect the park rules.

➡ Does your prospective driver seem in a rush? One common complaint is that

BLUEORANGE STUDIO/SHUTTERSTOCK ©

ROSTISLAV STACH/SHUTTERSTOCK ©

1. Elephant-spotting on safari **2.** Kingfisher, Bundala National Park (p144) **3.** Binoculars

MATT MUNRO/LONELY PLANET ©

drivers zip across the countryside, reducing the tour to a gut-wrenching blur.

➡ Does the driver provide binoculars? These are only likely to be included on top-end safaris. Bring your own, as otherwise a safari can be reduced to squinting at brown blobs in the distance.

➡ The merest hint of a large animal can spark a convoy of jeeps. Do your part to keep things calm by asking your driver to refrain from madcap chases. The resulting quiet is more conducive for spotting anyway.

➡ When at a sighting, ask your diver to switch the vehicle engine off. You'll be amazed at the difference to enjoyment levels this makes.

➡ Don't rush and don't become obsessed with seeing leopards and elephants. The best safaris are taken slowly with plenty of stops to appreciate the scenery, birds and smaller creatures.

VEHICLES

Standards between jeeps vary greatly, although almost all are open-sided, with a high roof for shade. The standard rate at almost any Sri Lankan national park for a half-day vehicle hire is Rs 6000, but there can be a little variation, especially if hiring a vehicle through a budget hotel.

Avoid very old vehicles, which often have inward-facing seats along the sides which is very bad for animal spotting. A good safari vehicle has three rows of two forward-facing seats that are stepped up towards the back so you can see over the heads of those in front of you.

trees, is what your mind would conjure. For the moment at least, this enchanting beach village remains undeveloped and unsullied by over-tourism and the atmosphere is redolent of the Sri Lanka of yesteryear.

Any bus travelling between Matara and Tangalle will drop you at the very discreet Unakuruwa turn-off. A three-wheeler from Tangalle bus station costs Rs 500.

Sleeping & Eating

For the moment, Unakuruwa has been spared the destructive overdevelopment of many other beaches in southern Sri Lanka. Accommodation is limited, but what there is is very good.

ANB Surf View GUESTHOUSE $$
(071-232 1800; r incl breakfast US$30;) Just a quick duck under the coconut trees from the beach, this fantastic value, new guesthouse has smart two-storey villas with two rooms in each villa. The rooms are bright and spotless, and come with balconies or terraces and little kitchenettes. A first-rate breakfast is included.

★Aga Surf View BOUTIQUE HOTEL $$$
(077-920 7322; www.agasurfviewtangalle.com; incl breakfast d US$120-130, f US$160;) This outstanding boutique hotel, just back from the beach, is one of the finest places to stay in Sri Lanka. Tastefully decorated rooms have wooden-tones, quality art and big windows. The family units are especially good as they have sliding doors between the parents and kids rooms. There's a small manicured garden, exemplary service, great food and one of the best pools in the area. And, to round it all out, the owner is a coffee enthusiast who roasts and grinds his own beans.

★Top Surf Bar SEAFOOD $$
(mains Rs 500-1000; 8am-11.30pm) Wonderfully funky beach bar slapped together out of driftwood and bits of timber. The smiling, jiving owners sway to low-key reggae music as they serve up delicious juices, cocktails and a small selection of super-fresh seafood.

Goyambokka

047

There's nothing much to tiny Goyambokka, which consists of some secluded and sublime sandy coves and a small selection of coastal hotels. For the moment this corner of the south coast remains relatively unblemished by the overdevelopment taking place in some other areas, and it retains much of the tropical-beach beauty that attracted people to southern Sri Lanka in the first place.

Look out for the turn-off, Goyambokka Rd, just west of the 194km post.

Sleeping & Eating

It's mainly about hotel restaurants on this stretch, though there are a few shacky beach cafes. Head into nearby Tangalle for more choice.

Goyambokka Guest House GUESTHOUSE $$
(077-790 3091, 047-224 0838; www.goyambokkaguesthouse.com; Goyambokka Rd; r incl breakfast from US$37;) This excellent property has a good choice of accommodation, from fan-cooled rooms to sleek units in two-storey villas and other options for families. All are dotted around a tropical garden with a pool and dancing palm trees, a short walk from the beach.

Sea Breeze Garden Guest House GUESTHOUSE $$
(r incl breakfast with/without air-con Rs 5500/3500;) The three rooms at this guesthouse might be very bare-bones, but the welcome is warm, the food excellent and the magical nearby beach has more seabird footprints than human ones.

★Amanwella LUXURY HOTEL $$$
(047-224 1333, 091-223 4591; www.amanresorts.com; off Matara-Tangalle Rd; ste incl breakfast from US$750;) A true temple of luxury, Amanwella's suites all have plunge pools and tasteful, modish design touches. Indeed the mood is so sybaritic you may need to be bribed to leave. All units have ocean views, but suites 110, 111 and 112 are nearest the beach. And what a stunner of a beach it is (though be careful of undertows)!

The infinity pool is one of Sri Lanka's best, measuring 50m.

★Think Club SEAFOOD, SRI LANKAN $$
(077-364 1739; off Goyambokka Rd; meals Rs 600-1000) Quirky shack on the beach run by a father-and-son team; you climb a rickety ladder to an ocean-facing deck for your meal. The seafood is surf-fresh and delicious and there are cold beers.

It's on a tiny cove with nothing but a couple of colourful fishing boats hauled up onto the beach. It's wildly romantic in the evening, when the sky tinges red and the waves slap the empty sand.

Getting There & Away

Any bus (they pass every 10 minutes) travelling between Matara and Tangalle will drop you at the Goyambokka turn-off. A three-wheeler from Tangalle bus station costs Rs 400.

Tangalle & Around

047 / POP 72,500

Tangalle (pronounced Tan-galla) is the gateway to the wide-open spaces and wide-open beaches of southern Sri Lanka. It's the last town of any size before Hambantota and has some old-world charm. But you're really here to find your perfect beach, and there are several to choose from nearby. Some are busy, buzzy town beaches, some are quiet coves and some stretch toward an uncluttered horizon. Whatever kind of beach bum you are, Tangalle will have a stretch of sand to suit. And the best thing is that compared to many of the beaches west of Matara, these beaches remain relatively unspoiled. Take note though, beaches to the east of town tend to have steep drop-offs, strong currents and heavy shore breaks, which can make them dangerous for swimming.

Sleeping

There are several areas in and around Tangalle in which to stay. The beach places close to town are convenient, but tend to be packed together. As you go east, many hotels are more secluded and lie at the end of rough tracks off the Hambantota Rd.

Medaketiya Beach

Frangipani Beach Villas GUESTHOUSE $$
(071-533 7052, 077-314 8889; Jayawardana Rd; r US$48-90;) Located close to town,

TANGALLE AREA BEACHES

Tangalle marks the dividing line between the picture-perfect tropical coves that dominate much of the south coast and the long, wind- and wave-lashed beaches that dominate the southeast of the island. Amid this long strip of sand are several beach zones, each with a distinct character. The following are listed geographically, from Tangalle east to Rekawa.

Tangalle

The town beaches south of the centre consist of pretty coves lapped by calm turquoise waters, but sadly the busy main road runs very close to the edge of the sand, meaning lots of fascinated bus passengers watching you lounge about in a bikini.

Medaketiya Beach

The long sandy beach here, which extends northeast away from the town, is lined with budget guesthouses and cafes and is by far the busiest and most developed beach in Tangalle (though compared with beaches elsewhere in southern Sri Lanka it's all very low-key). The sand is golden, but dumping waves can make swimming dangerous. At the northeast end, the busy road turns inland and it becomes quieter. Unfortunately, new breakwaters here are messing up the flow of the ocean and causing erosion.

Some places here offer surf lessons for around US$40 per person, but the waves are totally unsuitable for learning to surf and we'd suggest you head further west along the coast for your first board experiences.

Marakolliya Beach

Virtually a continuation of Medaketiya Beach, but much further out of town, the beach here is utterly breathtaking. Unfurling along the coast is a seemingly endless tract of soft sand backed by palms, tropical flowers and mangrove lagoons. However, note that the dramatic surf that pounds the beach here has undertows, and it's frequently too dangerous to swim.

At night, turtles lumber ashore here to lay eggs. Plenty of guesthouses and hotels offer lagoon tours, birdwatching and kayak rental (generally around Rs 1000 per person for a couple of hours).

Rekawa Beach

Around 10km east of Tangalle, this is another corker of a beach. Like Marakolliya, but even less developed, it's an endless stretch of wind- and wave-battered sand that isn't safe for swimming. It's also famous for nesting turtles, of no fewer than five different species. An access road wanders off the Hambantota Road at the 203km post.

Tangalle & Around

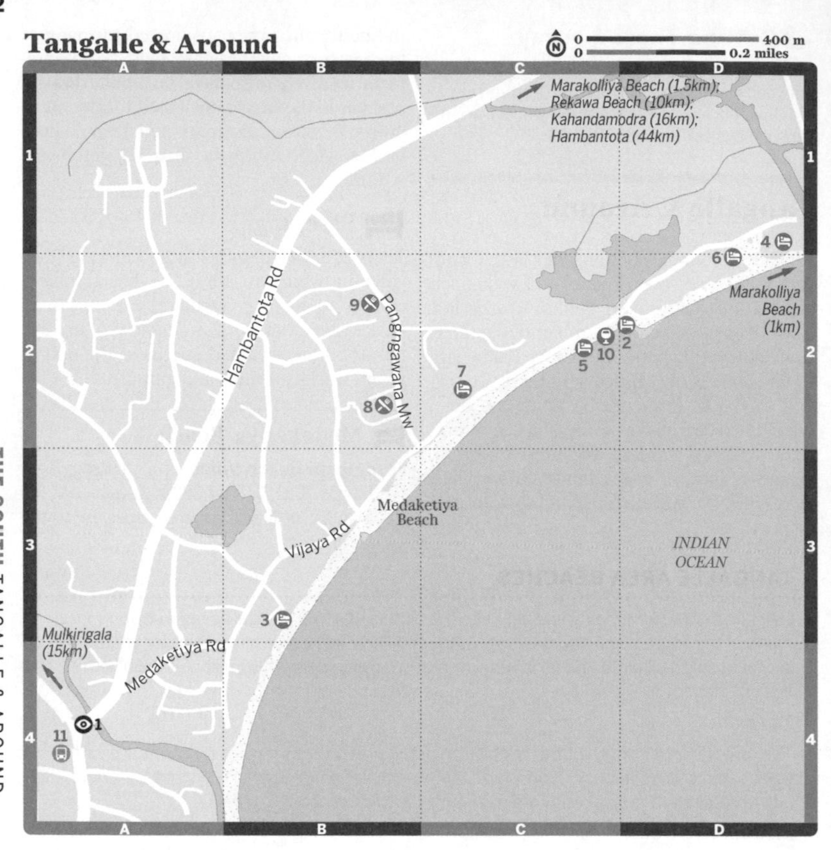

Tangalle & Around

Sights
1 Clock Tower A4

Sleeping
2 Cinnabar Resort D2
3 Frangipani Beach Villas B3
4 Ganesh Garden D1
5 Ibis Guest House C2
6 Serein Beach D2
7 Villa Araliya C2

Eating
8 Dream Family Restaurant B2
9 Mango Shade B2

Drinking & Nightlife
10 Lounge C2

Transport
11 Bus Station A4

this traveller favourite has an internationally themed decoration: Indian textiles, Mexican sombreros and photos of Southeast Asian monuments. The owners are warm and friendly, and there's a very pleasant beachside cafe. Note the pool is located about 300m along the shore where a couple of more upmarket rooms were under construction when we visited.

Villa Araliya GUESTHOUSE $$
(☎047-224 2163; www.villa-araliya.net; Vijaya Rd; r US$35-60, villa US$215;) A German-run beachside place set in luxuriant gardens with bungalows furnished with vintage pieces, including lovely carved wardrobes. The compound has a charm that's lacking nearby, while the villa has three bedrooms and is perfect for friends sharing or a family.

Marakolliya Beach

A tuk-tuk from town to the hotels around here costs in the region of Rs 400 depending on exactly which hotel you're headed for.

★ **Mangrove Beach Cabanas** BUNGALOW $$
(047-2240020,077-7906018; www.beachcabana.lk; off Hambantota Rd; r US$55-100;) On a breathtaking stretch of near-deserted beach, this long-running place is one of Tangalle's best. It has rustic-chic cabanas that feature lots of twisted driftwood furnishings and hammocks slung between the palms. Its rooms either have delightful open-air bathrooms or ones secreted away below ground and accessed via a trapdoor. The open-air bar-cafe has ocean views and good food.

Cinnabar Resort BUNGALOW $$
(077-965 2190, 076-581 3855; www.cinnabarresort.wordpress.com; Madilla Rd; incl breakfast cabana US$55, treehouse US$110;) Everything you need to know about Cinnabar is that half of its rooms are extraordinary treehouses perched 5m above the ground and connected to one another by wobbly wooden footbridges. If you're bored, it wouldn't be much effort to find driftwood on the beach to build another – this really is a rustic experience.

For those who prefer to keep two feet firmly planted in the sand then it also has some fine cabanas. Cinnabar, which is easily one of Tangalle's most original places to stay, also has a social ambience and its atmospheric beach cafe is the perfect spot for a sundowner or meal. The treehouses aren't suitable for younger children.

Ibis Guest House GUESTHOUSE $$
(047-567 4439; www.guesthouse-ibis.de; Vijaya Rd; r Rs 4500-9500;) Despite its chain-hotel name, this rambling place is all local and has a delicious old-fashioned appeal. The rooms are either in a colonial-era villa filled with heavy wooden furnishings, four-poster beds and easy chairs, or in more modern cottages. You'll be happy with either! There's a secluded beach outside (but rocks and currents make the swimming here treacherous even by Tangalle standards).

Serein Beach BOUTIQUE HOTEL $$
(047-224 0005; www.sereinbeach.com; Madilla Rd; r incl breakfast from US$60;) Much more upmarket than most in Tangalle, the Serein Beach is a smart three-storey hotel with attractive rooms featuring stylish furniture; book one on the upper floor for full-frontal sea views. Solar energy is used to heat water, staff are professional and there's a wonderful rooftop deck. The location is sun-drenched, there's a good pool and a better beach.

The Hideaway GUESTHOUSE $$
(071-125 2930; www.srilanka-holiday-tours.com/accommodation; r incl breakfast Rs 7000-8500;) Set just back from a semi-dry lagoon that attracts huge flocks of waterbirds, and a short walk from the beach, this is the place for those who wish to drop out and relax in total peace and tranquillity. The large rooms are spotless and contemporary in design and there's a raised terrace restaurant.

Mangrove Chalets BUNGALOW $$
(077-790 6018, 047-224 0020; www.beachcabana.lk; off Hambantota Rd; r from US$54;) These large bungalows (some sleep up to four) have spacious verandas facing the sea or lagoon. It's a good spot for families, as the mangrove waters are calm for swimming. You can access the site by a very Hollywood-feeling creaky bamboo bridge.

It's the more upmarket sister property to Mangrove Beach Cabanas.

Eating & Drinking

Just about all the places to stay serve meals. Many have cafes with dreamy ocean views, and seafood is always a good choice.

Mango Shade SRI LANKAN $$
(077-720 1859; Pangngawana Mw 141; meals Rs 350-750; 11.30am-10pm;) Down a lane, 300m inland from the beach, this is the place for home cooking, Sri Lankan style, with richly spiced (sometimes a little too spiced!) sauces, fresh seafood and very moderate prices for the area (rice and curry from Rs

OFF THE BEATEN TRACK

Tucked up beside a mangrove-lined lagoon, far, far away from anyone and anything, the blissful rural **Back of Beyond Wellness Retreat Kahandamodara** (047-362 6542; www.backofbeyond.lk; Kahandamodara;) offers terracotta mud-and-thatch, bush-chic bungalows set within 6 hectares of riverside woodlands and scrub. The wild and almost unknown Kahandamodara beach is a short walk (or kayak paddle) away and other activities include yoga, cooking courses and helping out on the farm.

WORTH A TRIP

MULKIRIGALA

Dangling off a rocky crag 16km northwest of Tangalle and nestled away among a green forest of coconut trees are the peaceful **Mulkirigala Rock Temples** (Mulkirigala Rd; Rs 500; 7am-6pm) . Clamber in a sweat up the 500 or so steps and you'll encounter a series of seven cleft-like caves on five different terraced levels. Housed in the caves are a number of large reclining Buddha statues interspersed with smaller sitting and standing figures.

Vying with these for your attention are some fantastical wall paintings depicting sinners pleasuring themselves with forbidden fruit on Earth and then paying for it with an afterlife of eternal torture – apparently it was worth it! Further on up, and perched on top of the rock some 206m from the base, is a small dagoba (stupa) with fine views over the surrounding country.

Temples, in some form or another, have been located here for over 2000 years, but the current incarnations, and their paintings, date from the 18th century. Nearby is a Buddhist school for young monks.

Pali manuscripts found in the monastic library here by a British official in 1826 were used for the first translation of the Mahavamsa (Great Chronicle), which unlocked Sri Lanka's early history to the Europeans. For more detail on the site and a series of photographs, see www.srilankaview.com/mulkirigala_temple.htm.

Mulkirigala can be reached by bus from Tangalle via either Beliatta or Wiraketiya. (Depending on the departures, it might be quicker to go via Wiraketiya than to wait for the Beliatta bus.) A three-wheeler from Tangalle costs about Rs 1800 for a return trip.

500). It's run by a kindly couple and you sit (as the name indicates) under mango trees.

Dream Family Restaurant SRI LANKAN **$$**
(077-502 2575; Pagngnawasa Mawatha 117 mains Rs 500-900; 8am-10pm) This small, wooden hut serves good seafood and Sri Lankan classics in a laid-back atmosphere. It's popular and space is limited so get there early.

Lounge BAR
(077-342 4723; Madilla Rd; 10am-2am;) With tables and seats made from crates, swing chairs by the bar and cool playlists, this hip beach bar has its own individual style. There are fine cocktails, and the food (prepared from an open kitchen) is good, though pricey. The chatty sports-mad Sri Lankan owner lived in London for years.

Getting There & Away

Tangalle is an important bus stop on the main coastal road. You can flag buses anywhere on the coastal road or use the **bus station** (Main Rd) in the centre of town; most buses are not air-conditioned. There are four luxury air-con buses daily via the Southern Expressway to Colombo (Rs 700, three hours). Frequent buses (every 15 minutes or so) to other destinations include the following:

Colombo (via coastal road) Rs 280, six hours
Galle Rs 150, two hours
Kataragama Rs 150, 2½ hours
Matara Rs 73, one hour
Tissamaharama Rs 140, two hours

Bundala National Park

Much less visited than nearby Yala National Park, **Bundala National Park** (adult/child US$10/5, vehicle Rs 250, service charge per group US$8, plus overall tax 17%; 6am-6pm, last entrance 4.30pm) is an excellent choice for birders, and you've a good chance of spotting crocs, wild boar, mongooses, monitor lizards, monkeys and elephants.

Bundala is a fantastic maze of waterways, lagoons and dunes that glitter like gold in the dying evening sun. This wonderland provides a home to thousands of colourful birds ranging from diminutive little bee-eaters to grotesque open-billed stalks. It is a wetland sanctuary of such importance that it has been recognised under the Ramsar Convention on Wetlands. There are also many big mammals present, with between 15 and 60 elephants depending on the season (December is the best month).

The park shelters almost 200 species of birds within its 62-sq-km area, with many journeying from Siberia and the Rann of Kutch salt marsh in India to winter here, arriving between August and April (December to March is the peak time). It's also a winter home to the greater flamingo; up to 2000 have been recorded here at one time.

Bundala also has civets, giant squirrels and lots of crocodiles. Between October and January, four of Sri Lanka's five species of marine turtles (olive ridley, green, leatherback and loggerhead) lay their eggs on the coast.

There's a visitor centre at the main gate that has views over the marshes; check out the skeleton of a fearsomely huge crocodile. Bundala is open year-round, allowing wildlife junkies to get a wet-season fix.

Bundala stretches nearly 20km along a coastal strip between Kirinda and Hambantota. The entrance is west of the 251km post. It is 18km from Tissamaharama or 10km from Hambantota. There's no public transport inside the park. Most people organise tours or hire jeeps from Tissamaharama; exact rates of safari packages depend on numbers, guides and the vehicle.

Sleeping

There's no accommodation in the park itself and most people stay in Tissamaharama. There are a couple of hotels on the highway close to the entrance, but you'll still need to hire jeeps to access the park.

Lagoon Inn GUESTHOUSE $
(☎071-631 0173; lagooninn@yahoo.com; off Tissamaharama Rd; r incl breakfast from Rs 3500; ❄📶) A friendly homestay 2km east of Bundala National Park's northern entrance gate. Rooms are functional; some suffer a little from traffic noise, but those upstairs have a shared balcony overlooking the marshes allowing you to birdwatch from the comfort of a chair. Kamal, the owner, is an experienced guide who organises good park tours at fair rates.

Tissamaharama

☎047 / POP 79,618

In Tissamaharama (usually shortened to Tissa), eyes are automatically drawn upwards and outwards. Upwards to the tip of its huge, snowy-white dagoba and outwards, beyond the town's confines, to nearby wildlife reserves crawling with creatures large and small. With its pretty lakeside location and sense of space, Tissa is an ideal mellow base for the nearby Yala and Bundala National Parks.

Sights

★Tissa Wewa LAKE
The centrepiece of the town and its surrounds is the lovely Tissa Wewa (Tissa Tank), a huge artificial lake. In the evening, check out the flocks of egrets that descend onto the trees around the lake to roost. The road along the southern edge has a wide **Lakeside Walkway** for strolling. Don't be tempted to swim here as crocodiles are sometimes spotted.

Tissa Dagoba BUDDHIST STUPA
(off Rubberwatte Rd) FREE This large much-restored dagoba looming between Tissa town centre and the *wewa* is believed to have been originally built around 200 BCE by Kavantissa, a king of Ruhunu, located in present-day Tissamaharama. The white stupa has a circumference of 165m and stands 55.8m high. It is thought to have held a sacred-tooth relic and forehead-bone relic. It's attractively lit up at night.

Next to the dagoba is a statue of Queen Viharamahadevi. According to legend, Viharamahadevi was sent to sea by her father, King Devanampiya Tissa, as penance after he killed a monk. Unharmed, the daughter landed at Kirinda, about 10km south of Tissa, and subsequently married Kavantissa. Their son, Dutugemunu, was the Sinhalese hero who liberated Anuradhapura from Indian invaders in the 2nd century BCE.

Within the site is the much smaller **Sandagiri Wehera** dagoba and the remains of a monastery complex thought to date back around 2000 years.

JEEP TOURS

Tissamaharama is the most popular starting point for jeep tours to Yala National Park and Bundala National Park, and drivers can be arranged easily at your accommodation. Tour rates to the national parks vary a lot depending on the type of jeep, but the standard rates for a half-day jeep that has been customised for safaris and has forward-facing seating and open sides is Rs 6000. Prices do not include entry fees. It's sometimes possible (normally through budget guesthouses with their own vehicles) to find cheaper vehicle hire from as little as Rs 4500 for a half day, but these vehicles might have inward-facing seats and are totally unsuitable for comfortable safaris.

Ajith Safari Jeep Tours (☎047-223 7557, 077-790 5532; www.yalawild.com; 414 Debarawewa) is a well-established private safari operator specialising in trips to Yala, Uda Walawe and Bundala National Parks. Guides are well-trained and the modern 4WDs are in good shape.

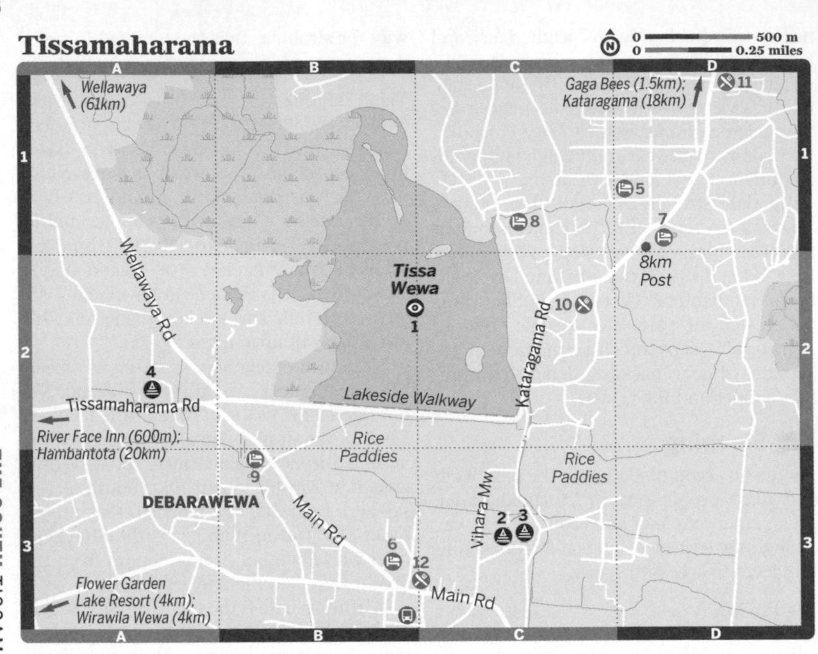

Tissamaharama

Top Sights

1 Tissa Wewa B2

Sights

Museum .... (see 4)
2 Sandagiri Wehera C3
3 Tissa Dagoba C3
4 Yatala Wehera A2

Sleeping

5 Blue Turtle D1
6 Hotel Tissa B3
7 Kithala Resort D1
8 My Village C1
9 Traveller's Home B3

Eating

10 Chef Lady Restaurant C2
11 Flavors D1
12 Hot Spot Restaurant C3

Yatala Wehera BUDDHIST STUPA
(Tissamaharama Rd) Lotus ponds surround this site, which has a wealth of elephant details in the carvings (note the footpads). It was built 2300 years ago by King Mahanaga in thanks both for the birth of his son, Yatala Tissa, and for his safe escape from an assassination attempt in Anuradhapura. It's an easy walk from town.

Don't miss the small neighbouring **museum** (9am-4pm Wed-Mon) FREE which contains an extraordinary range of treasures including an ornate, ancient bidet, which – as well as an elaborate filtration system that limited water pollution – had murals of ugly faces carved into it in order to stop the user thinking about sex! Note that hours vary as the caretaker is not always around.

Sleeping

Prices are lower here than on the coast and there are pleasant hotels and guesthouses scattered all about Tissa. Lakeside ones have obvious appeal; just about every place has a restaurant. Note that for Yala tours, hotels along the park access roads and near the beach in Kirinda are also good options.

Tissa Wewa & Town Centre

Hotel Tissa GUESTHOUSE $
(077-644 9535, 071-711 5744; www.hoteltissa.com; Main Rd; r US$10-13;) Just 100m from the bus station, the functional, good-value budget rooms here are divided between the main building and quieter block out back. All have air-con, while more deluxe units

have fridges and hot water. It's run by a super friendly young couple.

Traveller's Home GUESTHOUSE $
(047-223 7958, 077-601 0208; Main Rd; r Rs 3000-5000;) This traveller-aware guesthouse is just off Main Rd and has a variety of bright, refurbished rooms all with a balcony or patio and private hot-water bathrooms. Cheaper fan-cooled options and a three-bed bungalow are also available. There are free bicycles for guests and a good restaurant.

★ **My Village** GUESTHOUSE $$
(077-350 0090; www.myvillagelk.com; 69 Court Rd; r US$30-60;) They get almost everything right at this beautiful seven-bedroom guesthouse, which is actually the modernist dream creation of a local designer. There's a stylish open-plan cafe and communal area for socialising. The shady grounds are peaceful and have hammocks. Guests can use bicycles for free. Do check out the totally spotless open kitchen where your complimentary breakfast is prepared.

★ **Blue Turtle** BOUTIQUE HOTEL $$
(047-223 8263, 077-548 6836; www.blueturtlehotel.com; 119/2 Tissamaharama Rd; r US$25-65;) Offering exceptional value, this hotel sits in a large, tranquil compound with accommodation facing a shimmering blue 20m pool and elegant lobby-restaurant. Rooms are in attractive two-storey blocks, all with balconies or verandas, and are comfortable and quiet. The restaurant offers fine Sri Lankan and Western food, and there's also a bar.

Gaga Bees BUNGALOW $$
(071-620 5343; www.gagabeesyala.com; off Sandagirigama Rd; r incl breakfast Rs 7000-10,000;) This compound of nine rustic-chic bungalows is in a serene setting surrounded by rice fields. All have been built from natural materials – mud bricks, palm thatch and local wood – and have two beds, air-con and verandas. There's a small on-site cafe and pool, some lily-filled ponds and the birdlife is prolific.

Kithala Resort HOTEL $$$
(047-223 7206; www.themeresorts.com/kithala resort; Kataragama Rd; r/ste incl breakfast from US$120/170;) Rooms at this good-value resort have high, wooden ceilings, dashes of style, hardwood furnishings, hip bathrooms, and balconies with views over the pool, rice fields and a lake full of birds, terrapins and – the thing that swings it for us – a couple of resident crocodiles (so don't annoy the staff or you may become dinner for a toothy reptile!).

Deberawewa

West of Tissa, there are some good choices amid lush rivers and wide lakes.

River Face Inn GUESTHOUSE $
(077-389 0229; www.yalariverfaceinn.com; off Hambantota Rd; r with/without air-con Rs 2500/1500;) This family-run riverside guesthouse is blessed with a huge covered terrace where an array of tables with chairs, comfy loungers and hammocks await the weary big-game-spotter. Whether you choose a fan-cooled or an air-con room, all guests get to enjoy the idyllic rural setting and total peace and quiet. There's also tasty food available at night. It's 2.5km west of Tissa.

Flower Garden Lake Resort HOTEL $$
(077-791 0575; off Wewa Rd; r incl breakfast Rs 5500-10,500;) In a quiet and remote location about 3km west of central Tissa, this small and very good hotel has a grand lakeside setting on Wirawila Wewa. There's nothing other than the song of birds to interrupt the silence. Rooms have satellite TVs and there is a small pool. The cafe is good, and wine and beer are served.

Eating

Chef Lady Restaurant SRI LANKAN $$
(077-109 9588; mains Rs 900-1300; 6-10pm) Surrounded by coconut palms, this is a cute, garden restaurant with a thatch awning and a menu bursting with deliciously well-prepared barbeued and devilled seafood, as well as rice, curry and pasta dishes.

Flavors SRI LANKAN, INTERNATIONAL $$
(077-760 4190; www.facebook.com/flavors.tissamaharama; Kataragama Rd; meals Rs 700-900; 8am-10pm;) Flavors' owner-chef has honed his cooking skills overseas and prepares good Italian and Chinese food, as well as excellent local devilled dishes and curries (from Rs 840). It's a small and quiet roadside place with nice wooden seating.

Getting There & Away

Tissa's centrally located **bus station** (off Main St) has very regular services along the coast. There are very few buses up to the Hill Country, but very regular services from the Wirawila junction (Rs 28, 15 minutes) west of town, most via Wellawaya (Rs 84). For Arugam Bay change at Wellawaya. There are no buses to Yala National Park. There are four luxury air-con buses daily via the Southern Expressway to Colombo (Rs 900, 5½ hours).

Other major bus destinations from Tissa (departing every 15 to 30 minutes) include the following:

Colombo (via coastal road) Rs 550, eight hours
Kataragama Rs 44, 30 minutes
Kirinda Rs 32, 20 minutes
Tangalle Rs 120, two hours

Three-wheelers around town will cost Rs 150 to 250.

Kirinda

047

Oceanside Kirinda, 12km south of Tissa, is a place on the edge. On one side its sandy streets and ramshackle buildings give way to a series of magnificently bleak and empty beaches (heavy undertows make swimming here treacherous) that are perfect for long evening walks. In the other direction tangled woodlands and sweeps of parched grasslands merge into the national parks.

The village itself centres on a Buddhist shrine dramatically perched on top of huge round rocks right at the shore. Not all that many people stay in Kirinda but it's actually closer to Yala National Park than Tissamaharama, and it's just as simple to organise a safari from here (jeep rental prices are the same). Throw in the seaside setting, and the silent at noon atmosphere, and you get an inviting alternative to Tissamaharama.

Sights & Activities

Visible offshore are the wave-smashed **Great Basses reefs** with their lonely lighthouse.

The diving out on these reefs is ranked as about the best in the country, but it's not for inexperienced divers as conditions are often rough. The best time is only between mid-March and mid-April. There are no dive operators in the area, so you'd need to organise an expedition with dive operators further west.

Kirinda Temple BUDDHIST SHRINE

Kirinda centres on this imposing hilltop Buddhist shrine, which includes a stupa and huge standing Buddha. It's dedicated to Queen Viharamahadevi, who lived in the 2nd century BCE and is at the heart of a local legend: when raging waters threatened Ceylon, King Kelanitissa ordered his youngest daughter, then a princess, into a boat as a sacrifice. The waters were calmed and the princess was washed safely ashore here. Some 2000 years later, the temple was a place of refuge during the 2004 tsunami.

Sleeping & Eating

Suduweli Beauties of Nature GUESTHOUSE $

(072-263 1059; Yala Junction; r US$25-50;) Accommodation at this rural idyll consists of basic but clean rooms in the main house and a handful of comfortable, vaguely alpine-style cottages in the gardens. There's a small lake on the grounds and wildlife abounds, including iguanas and peacocks. The owners are a welcoming Swiss–Sri Lankan couple. Book ahead in order to ensure that there's someone here when you arrive.

Kirinda Beach Resort HOTEL $$

(077-020 0897; www.kirindabeachresort.com; r/f incl breakfast Rs 6000/7500;) Right next to a wild, oceanic, boulder-strewn beach, this quirky compound is perfect for long days exploring the coast and for those who enjoy nature. Gaze upon the pounding surf from the uniquely elevated swimming pool, then enjoy a meal in the large, airy cafe before retiring to a rustic wood chalet or earthy mud hut. It's 1km southwest of the Kirinda temple.

Elephant Reach RESORT $$$

(047-721 2640; www.elephantreach.com; Yala Junction; r/chalet incl breakfast from US$100/120;) Rooms and chalets at this pleasant lodge have an attractive, natural feel thanks to the stone floors, hemp curtains, coir rugs, and walls decorated with wildlife photography and art. Outside, the large pool curls like a water snake around the gardens.

Getting There & Away

There is a bus from Tissa to Kirinda every half-hour or so (Rs 32, 20 minutes); a three-wheeler is Rs 500.

Yala National Park

With trumpeting elephants, monkeys crashing through the trees, peacocks in their finery and cunning leopards sliding like shadows through the undergrowth, **Yala National Park** (www.yalasrilanka.lk; adult/child Rs 4900/2600, jeep & tracker Rs 250, service charge per group US$8, plus overall tax 17%; 5.30am-6pm mid-Oct–Aug) is *The Jungle Book* brought to glorious life.

Rightly, Sri Lanka's most famous national park, Yala splays across 979 sq km of megafauna-filled scrub, light forest, grassy plains and brackish lagoons. It's very rich in wildlife and you're virtually certain to encounter elephants, crocodiles, buffaloes and monkeys. Plan your trip carefully, however – such is Yala's appeal that the main tracks and viewing spots can be crowded.

Yala National Park is divided into five blocks, with the most visited being Block I (141 sq km). Also known as Yala West, this zone was originally a reserve for hunters, but was given over to conservation in 1938. It's the closest to Tissa. The entrance fees are payable at the main office, which is near the west entrance. Recently, two other gates have opened to visitors as has the huge wilderness zone of Block III. These new park entry gates are the Katagamuwa entrance, a short way southeast of Kataragama and the Galge entrance, which is in the northern part of the park and handy for those coming from Ella. The Katagamuwa entrance gives access to the quieter northern part of Block I and also to Block III. The Galge entrance gives access to the still undeveloped and little-visited northern half of the wild Block III. The only practical way to visit the park is on a safari tour – for Block III, you will need a serious 4WD and a guide with some knowledge of the area.

With over 20 leopards thought to be present in Block I alone, Yala is considered one of the world's best parks for spotting these big cats. *Panthera pardus kotiya,* the subspecies you may well see, is unique to Sri Lanka.

The park's estimated 300 elephants can be more elusive, although some regularly appear in the most visited areas. Other animals of note include the shaggy-coated sloth bear and fox-like jackals. Sambars, spotted deer, boars, buffaloes, mongooses and monkeys are also here, along with startlingly large crocodiles.

Over 200 species of bird have been recorded at Yala, many of which are doing the same as you and escaping the northern winter, such as white-winged black terns, curlews and pintails. Locals include jungle fowl, hornbills, orioles and peacocks by the bucketload.

Despite the large quantity of wildlife, the light forest can make spotting animals quite hard; however, small grassy clearings and lots of waterholes offer good opportunities. The end of the dry season (March and April) is the best time to visit because during and shortly after the rains, the animals disperse over a wide area.

The wildlife in Block I is generally pretty blasé about safari vehicles, but the animals in Block III can be a little more skittish. If you want a quick and easy half-day safari where you can tick off most of the key animals then head to Block I. If you're a more passionate safari-goer willing to endure a little more discomfort (rough roads) and less guaranteed wildlife sightings as well as being willing to trailblaze a new area of the park, then Block III is for you.

As well as herds of wildlife, Yala contains the remains of a once-thriving human community. A monastic settlement, **Situlpahuwa**, appears to have housed 12,000 inhabitants. Now restored, it's an important pilgrimage site. A 1st-century BCE *vihara* (Buddhist complex), **Magul Maha Vihara**, and a 2nd-century BCE *chetiya* (Buddhist shrine), **Akasa Chetiya**, point to a well-established community, believed to have been part of the ancient Ruhunu kingdom.

Block I is very popular. At times jeeps can mimic a pack of jackals in their pursuit of wildlife. It's a good idea to discuss with your driver and/or guide where you can go to get away from the human herd (or head to Block III). Be sure, however, to make time for the park's **visitor centre** (6am-6pm) at the western entrance of Block I. It has excellent displays about Yala and a good bookshop.

Most people visit Yala and Bundala National Parks on jeep tours from Tissamaharama. Half-day tours start with a Tissa hotel pick-up at around 4.30am followed by a one-hour drive to the park for a dawn start. You are usually back by noon. Dusk tours run about 3pm to 7pm. Full day tours run 4.30am to 5pm and include stops at beaches and other sights.

Sleeping & Eating

The national park manages four simple lodges inside the park. These are mainly geared to Sri Lankan groups of 10 or more, but you can book online in advance via the Yala National Park website (www.yalasrilanka.lk). You can also sleep inside the park on an organised camping trip; these are best set up in Tissa.

Several top-end resorts are located off the 12km road that runs into the park from Yala Junction.

★Back of Beyond Dune Camp TENTED CAMP **$$$**
(077-395 1527; www.backofbeyond.lk/locations/yala-dune-camp.html; Palatupana; full board s/d US$250/310) This bewitching and secluded (no phone signal, no mains electricity, no proper road access) tented camp has four well-equipped safari tents burrowed away

among towering sun-tinged sand dunes halfway between Kirinda and Yala. Tents have beds, desks and open-air bathrooms. It won't be to everyone's taste, but if you want a genuine bush safari experience, this is the place.

Quality safaris can be organised and afterward you can spend hours strolling alone along an especially wild and woolly bit of coastline. It's great for adventurous kids. Advance bookings essential.

Jetwing Yala RESORT **$$$**
(047-471 0710; www.jetwinghotels.com; r incl breakfast from US$320;) Only 4km from the park entrance, this posh resort is set amid the dunes near the beach. Its modish rooms boast stunning views from their balconies, or book a luxury tented villa for a more intimate experience. Staff can arrange sunset picnics on the beach and there's a 50m pool and spa, too.

Cinnamon Wild Yala LODGE **$$$**
(047-223 9449; www.cinnamonhotels.com; r half-board from US$220;) This large lodge offers bush-chic accommodation in individual luxe bungalows. The hotel runs on solar power, some of the waste water is recycled and there's a tree-planting scheme. At night elephants often wander through the grounds. There are two bars and a fine restaurant.

Getting There & Away

There's no public transport to the park. The drive to Yala takes about one hour due to road conditions whether you take the 22km route via Yala Junction from Tissa, or a somewhat shorter road past some remote and pretty lakes.

Katearagama

047 / POP 12,600

This most holy of towns is a compelling mix of pomp and procession, piety and religious extravagance. Along with Sri Pada (Adam's Peak; p175), Kataragama is the most important pilgrimage site in Sri Lanka; a holy place for Buddhists, Muslims, Hindus and Veddah people.

It is one of those wonderful destinations where the most outlandish of legends becomes solid fact and magic floats in clouds of incense. Many believe that King Dutugemunu built a shrine to Kataragama Deviyo (the resident god) here in the 2nd century BCE, but the site is thought to have been significant for even longer.

In July and August, the Kataragama Festival draws thousands of pilgrims. Apart from festival time, the town is busiest at weekends and on *poya* (full moon) days. It's easily visited from Tissa and very few foreigners stay the night here. However, it does make an alternative base for Yala National Park.

THE LONG WALK TO KATARAGAMA

Forty-five days before the annual Kataragama Festival starts on the Esala *poya* in July, a group of Kataragama devotees start walking the length of Sri Lanka for the Pada Yatra pilgrimage. Seeking spiritual development, the pilgrims believe they are walking in the steps of the god Kataragama (also known as Murugan) and the Veddahs, who made the first group pilgrimage on this route.

The route follows the east coast from the Jaffna peninsula, via Trincomalee and Batticaloa to Okanda, then through Yala National Park to Kataragama. It's an arduous trip, and the pilgrims rely on the hospitality of the communities and temples they pass for their food and lodging. Although often interrupted during the war years, the walk is again hugely popular.

Pilgrims arrive in Kataragama just before the festival's feverish activity. Elephants parade, drummers drum. Vows are made and favours sought by devotees, who demonstrate their sincerity by performing extraordinary acts of penance and self-mortification on one particular night: some swing from hooks that pierce their skin, others roll half-naked over the hot sands near the temple. A few perform the act of walking on beds of red-hot cinders – treading the flowers, as it's called. The fire-walkers fast, meditate and pray, bathe in Menik Ganga (Menik River) and then worship at Maha Devale before facing their ordeal. Then, fortified by their faith, they step out onto the glowing path while the audience cries out encouragement.

The festival officially ends with a water-cutting ceremony (said to bring rain for the harvest) in Menik Ganga.

Kataragama

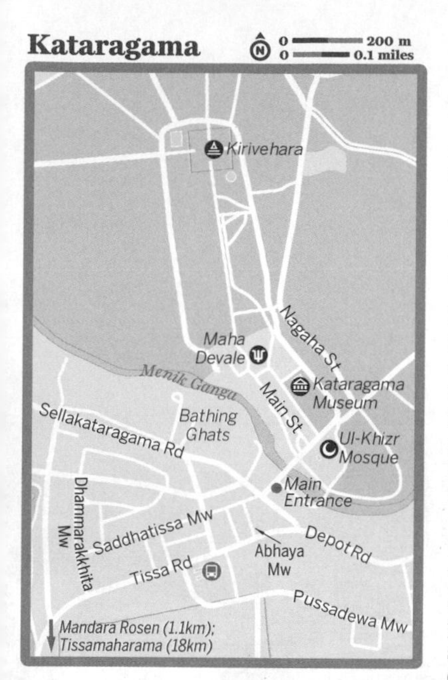

Sights

The sacred precinct is set on the other side of Menik Ganga, a chocolate-coloured river in which pilgrims wash before continuing towards the shrines. The site's wide promenades are lined with grey monkeys always on the lookout for a handout – or a dropped personal item. Watch your stuff!

★Maha Devale HINDU SHRINE

This is Kataragama's most important shrine. It contains the lance of the six-faced, 12-armed Hindu war god, Murugan (Skanda), who is seen as identical to the Kataragama Deviyo. Followers make offerings at daily *puja* at 4.30am, 10.30am and 6.30pm (no 4.30am offering on Saturday). Outside this shrine are two large boulders, against which pilgrims smash burning coconuts while saying a prayer.

Kirivehara BUDDHIST STUPA

This impressive 29m white dagoba in the north of the sacred compound is thought to have been built during the reign of King Mahasena (276–303 CE) who also constructed the Jetavanarama Dagoba in Anuradhapura and many large tanks (lakes).

Ul-Khizr Mosque MOSQUE

The second holy site you see as you pass through the compound. This beautiful mosque contains the tombs of two holy men (who originated from Central Asia and India). In a corner of the compound is a small building containing what is touted as a 'miraculous healing stone'. Place both hands on it and it will suck bad spirits out of you.

It's a fine example of the kind of non-orthodox forms of Islam that flourish in South Asia but would never be tolerated in parts of Arabia.

Kataragama Museum MUSEUM

(Rs 910; ⏲8am-5pm Wed-Mon) This archaeological museum inside the complex has a collection of Hindu and Buddhist religious items, as well as huge fibreglass replicas of statues from around Sri Lanka. The labelling, however, is woeful and it's often closed when it's supposed to be open.

Festivals & Events

★Kataragama Festival RELIGIOUS

(www.kataragama.org) In July and August this predominantly Hindu festival draws thousands of devotees who make the pilgrimage (the Long Walk to Kataragama) over a two-week period.

Sleeping & Eating

Kataragama's accommodations are limited. Book well ahead during the festival or find a bed in neighbouring Tissa and visit as a day trip.

Mandara Rosen HOTEL **$$$**

(☎047-223 6030; www.mandararesorts.com; Tissa Rd; r incl breakfast from US$150; ❄📶🏊) The smartest address in the area is the Rosen, which is surrounded by woodlands 2km south of the centre. The rooms are good, but the hotel's most unusual asset is the pool, which has an underwater music system (ask them to play the *Jaws* theme tune!). There's also a spa and a good, shaded cafe open to all.

Getting There & Away

There are frequent buses to Tissamaharama and Colombo. The **bus station** (Tissa Rd) is centrally placed and has connections, including the following:

Colombo (via coastal road) Rs 600, 8½ hours, every 30 minutes

Colombo (via expressway) luxury air-con Rs 1000, six hours, four daily

Tissamaharama regular Rs 44, 30 minutes, every 20 minutes

AT A GLANCE

POPULATION
Kandy: 125,000

GATEWAY CITY
Kandy (p155)

BEST TEA PLANTATION RETREAT
Tea Trails (p176)

BEST BUFFET SPREAD
Sharon Inn (p164)

BEST BUDDHIST ARTISTRY
Buduruwagala (p198)

WHEN TO GO

Jan Perfect for clear days, crisp nights and the pilgrimage up Adam's Peak.

Apr The Sinhalese New Year means horse racing and a hectic social calendar in Nuwara Eliya.

Nov The rains have finally cleared away, leaving the hills radiantly gorgeous.

Kandy (p155)
YAKOV OSKANOV/SHUTTERSTOCK ©

The Hill Country

Sri Lanka's Hill Country is the island at its most scenic, a mist-wrapped tumble of emerald peaks and stupendous views, of hillsides carpeted with tea plantations and graced by astonishing waterfalls. This is a place where you can wear a fleece in the daytime and cuddle up beside a log fire in the evening. Where you can enjoy a fabulous meal in a posh Kandy eatery or at a humble roadside shack in lovely Ella. A region where you can walk to the end of the world, stand in the footsteps of the Buddha and be surrounded by a hundred wild elephants. Or ride a train, utterly bewitched by the vistas, paddle a raft down a raging river, and enjoy the drumbeat of traditional Sri Lankan dance, before savouring the silence on a lonely mountaintop.

INCLUDES

The Hill Country Highlights

❶ **Horton Plains** (p190) Hiking across a plateau to the lofty viewpoint of World's End.

❷ **Nuwara Eliya** (p180) Sipping a G&T in an atmospheric colonial-era hotel.

❸ **Adam's Peak (Sri Pada)** (p175) Ascending the sacred mountain Sri Pada by torchlight.

❹ **Hills Railway** (p196) Rattling through the scenic journey from Haputale to Ella.

❺ **Sinharaja Forest Reserve** (p201) Discovering your inner birdwatcher.

❻ **Ella** (p192) Savouring this small town's big vistas.

❼ **Knuckles Range** (p173) Trekking through montane forests, well off the beaten path.

❽ **Uda Walawe National Park** (p199) Counting elephants by the dozen in this wildlife-rich reserve.

❾ **Haputale** (p188) Watching the morning mists part to reveal an artist's palette of green tea bushes.

Colombo to Kandy

The uphill journey from Colombo to Kandy passes through the lush foothills of Sri Lanka's central mountains. Dotted along the route are several attractions worth visiting.

The first place of interest is the **Henerathgoda Botanic Gardens** (Gampaha Botanical Garden; ☎033-222 2316; Gampaha; adult/child Rs 2000/1000; ⏲8.30am-5pm), about 30km northwest of Colombo, where the first rubber trees in Asia were planted (in 1876, after being brought here from Brazil). These lush tropical gardens cover 17 hectares and are home to over 400 plant species, including towering palms and a good orchid collection.

About 50km from Kandy is **Cadjugama**, famous for its cashew nuts. At the 48km post is **Radawaduwa**, notable for woven cane items. Roadside shops in both villages sell the local products.

Kegalle, 77km from Colombo, is surrounded by several spice farms and is the nearest town to the Pinnewala Elephant Orphanage.

Initially created to protect abandoned or orphaned elephants, the **Pinnewala Elephant Orphanage** (☎035-226 6116; http://nationalzoo.gov.lk/elephantorphanage; adult/child Rs 3000/1500; ⏲8.30am-5.30pm) is one of Sri Lanka's most popular attractions. It's a highly commercialised experience, with hefty entrance fees for foreigners (25 times the local price) and mahouts demanding extortionate tips for photos. Sure, you get up close to elephants and see them bathing, but the orphanage's conservation value is questionable and organisations including Born Free (www.bornfree.org.uk) have published negative critiques of the centre. Overall, national parks are the best places to see Sri Lankan elephants.

Two kilometres from Pinnewala on the Karandupona–Kandy road is the **Millennium Elephant Foundation** (☎035-226 3377; www.facebook.com/millenniumelephantfoundation; adult/child Rs 1000/500; ⏲8.30am-4.30pm; 📶), which houses elephants rescued from aggressive mahouts, and elephants retired from working in temples. Be aware that though elephants are well cared for here, they are chained for quite long periods and elephant rides are offered; we recommend against these because of the harm they can cause to the elephants. Volunteers are welcome at the foundation.

Kandy

☎081 / POP 125,000 / ELEV 500M

The cultural heart of the island, the royal city of Kandy spreads around the city's beautiful centrepiece lake and is backed by a forested halo of misty hills. All spiritual and cultural life here focuses on the impressive Temple of the Sacred Tooth Relic. It's one of Buddhism's most sacred shrines and constantly buzzes with pilgrims.

And when you're done paying your respects to the Buddha, Kandy entertains with dance shows and cultural performances, interesting museums, intriguing cave temples, a growing foodie scene and, a short way out of town, one of Asia's finest botanical gardens. Kandy is also starting to attract hiking tourists keen to sample the varied trails that spin through the hills not far from the city.

Too many tourists rush through Kandy in a day, but this is a city that rewards those who linger.

History

Kandy served as the capital of the last Sinhalese kingdom, which fell to the British in 1815 after defying the Portuguese and Dutch for three centuries. It took the British another 16 tough years to finally build a road linking Kandy with Colombo. As it's the self-proclaimed cultural capital of the island, the locals still proudly see themselves as a little different from – and perhaps a tad superior to – Sri Lankans from the island's lower reaches.

Sights

Kandy Lake LAKE

Dominating the town is Kandy Lake. A leisurely stroll around it, with a few stops on the lakeside seats, is a pleasant way to spend a few hours, although diesel-spurting buses careening around the southern edge of the lake can mar the peace somewhat. The nicest part to walk along is the area around the Temple of the Sacred Tooth Relic (p156). Due to some past cases of harassment, women are advised not to walk here alone after dark.

The lake was created in 1807 by Sri Wickrama Rajasinha, the last ruler of the kingdom of Kandy. Several minor local chiefs protested because their people objected to labouring on the project. In order to stop the protests they were put to death on stakes in the lake bed. The central island was used as Sri Wickrama Rajasinha's personal harem. Later the

TOP SIGHT
TEMPLE OF THE SACRED TOOTH RELIC

This golden-roofed temple houses Sri Lanka's most important Buddhist relic: a tooth of the Buddha. The tooth (which you don't actually get to see) is kept within a stunning central shrine. The entire complex is rich in atmosphere, and though it can get very busy, there's always a calm corner to sit and soak up the powerful spirituality.

The Main Shrine

After passing through several rounds of security and removing your shoes (leave them at the ticket office), you enter the main temple building. The lower levels of this three-storey shrine have some exquisite woodcarvings and paintings around them. The most important part of the shrine, though, is upstairs on the second level. The central room of the shrine is flanked by elephant tusks and draped in red and gold material. Pilgrims leave piles of flowers and other offerings here. The tooth itself is kept in a gold casket shaped like a dagoba (stupa), which contains a series of six dagoba caskets of diminishing size.

DON'T MISS

- Main Shrine
- World Buddhism Museum
- Alut Maligawa

PRACTICALITIES

- Sri Dalada Maligawa
- www.sridaladamaligawa.lk
- adult/Saarc/child Rs 1500/1000/free
- temple 5.30am-7.30pm, puja 5.30-7am, 9.30-11am & 6.30-7pm

Alut Maligawa

The **Alut Maligawa** (entrance included in temple ticket; 5.30am-8pm) is a large hall behind the main temple displaying dozens of sitting Buddhas donated by devotees from Thailand. Its design resembles a Thai Buddhist temple, reflecting the fact that Thai monks re-established Sri Lanka's ordination lineage during the reign of King Kirti Sri Rajasinha.

Set on the upper two floors, the **Sri Dalada Museum** (entrance included in temple ticket; 7.30am-6pm) displays a stunning array of gifts donated to the temple by several presidents and Buddhist leaders from across the world. Letters and diary entries from the British era reveal the colonisers' surprisingly respectful attitude to the relic. More recent photographs reveal the significant damage caused to the temple complex by a truck bomb detonated by the Liberation Tigers of Tamil Eelam (LTTE) in 1998.

Audience Hall

To the north of the Temple of the Sacred Tooth Relic, but still within the compound, is the 19th-century **Audience Hall** (entrance included in temple ticket; 5.30am-8pm), an open-air pavilion with stone columns carved to look like wooden pillars. Adjacent in the Rajah Tusker Hall are the stuffed remains of Rajah, a Maligawa tusker who died in 1988.

World Buddhism Museum

Housed inside the former High Court buildings, the **World Buddhism Museum** (Rs 500; 7am-7pm) contains lots of photographs, models and displays illustrating Buddhism around the world. Note that a large number of the statues and other exhibits are actually reproductions.

History of the Tooth

The sacred tooth of the Buddha is said to have been snatched from his funeral pyre in 483 BCE and smuggled into Sri Lanka during the 4th century, hidden in the hair of a princess. At first it was taken to Anuradhapura, then it moved through the country on the waves of Sri Lankan history before ending up at Kandy. In 1283 it was carried back to India by an invading army, but it was retrieved by Parakramabahu III.

The tooth grew in importance as a symbol of sovereignty, and it was believed that whoever had custody of it had the right to rule the island. In the 16th century the Portuguese apparently seized the tooth and burnt it with Catholic fervour in Goa. Not so, say the Sinhalese: the Portuguese had actually stolen a replica tooth, while the real incisor remained safe. There are still rumours that the real tooth is hidden somewhere secure and that the tooth kept here in Kandy is a replica.

The temple was constructed mainly under Kandyan kings from 1687 to 1707 and from 1747 to 1782, and the complex was part of the Kandyan royal palace. The imposing pinky-white structure is surrounded by a moat. The moat's octagonal tower was built by Sri Wickrama Rajasinha to house an important collection of *ola* (talipot-palm leaf) manuscripts. This section of the temple was heavily damaged in the 1998 bombing.

The main shrine occupies the centre of a paved courtyard. The 1998 bomb exposed part of the front wall to reveal at least three layers of 18th- to 20th-century paintings depicting the *perahera* (procession) and various Jataka tales (stories of the Buddha's previous lives).

Sri Lankan Buddhists believe they must complete at least one pilgrimage to the temple, as worshipping here improves one's karmic lot immeasurably.

GUIDES

Freelance guides will offer their services around the entire temple complex for around Rs 600, and free audio guides are available at the ticket office. An elevator facilitates access for travellers with disabilities.

TAKE A BREAK

There's nowhere to eat within the complex, but just next to the main entrance is the superb Empire Cafe (p164); it's the ideal place to have a cold drink and delicious lunch while digesting all that you saw.

Kandy

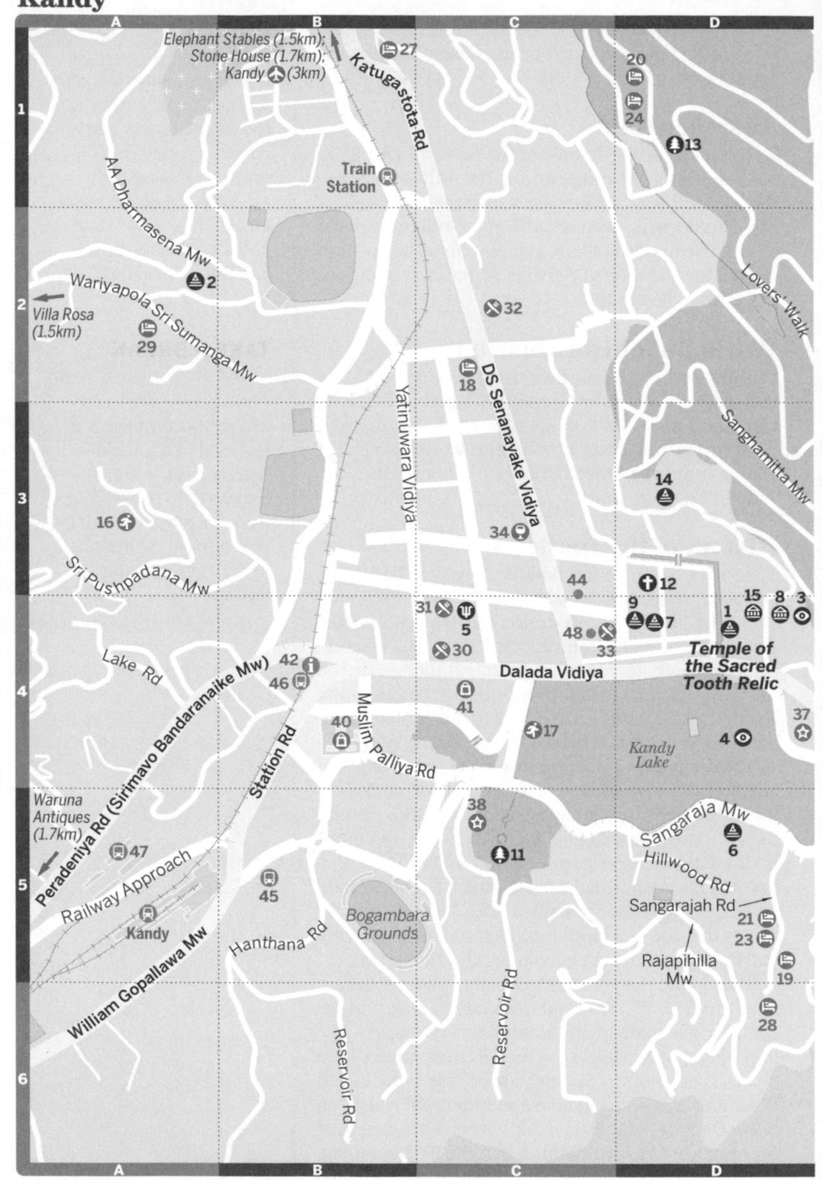

British used it as an ammunition store and added the fortress-style parapet around the perimeter. On the south shore, in front of the Malwatte Maha Vihara (p160), the circular enclosure is the monks' bathhouse.

At the western end you can rent small motorboats for a putter about.

National Museum MUSEUM

(☎081-222 3867; www.museum.gov.lk; adult/child Rs 600/400; ⏲9am-5pm Tue-Sat) This museum once housed Kandyan royal concubines and now features royal regalia and reminders of pre-European Sinhalese life. One of the most impressive exhibits is Rajasinha II's golden

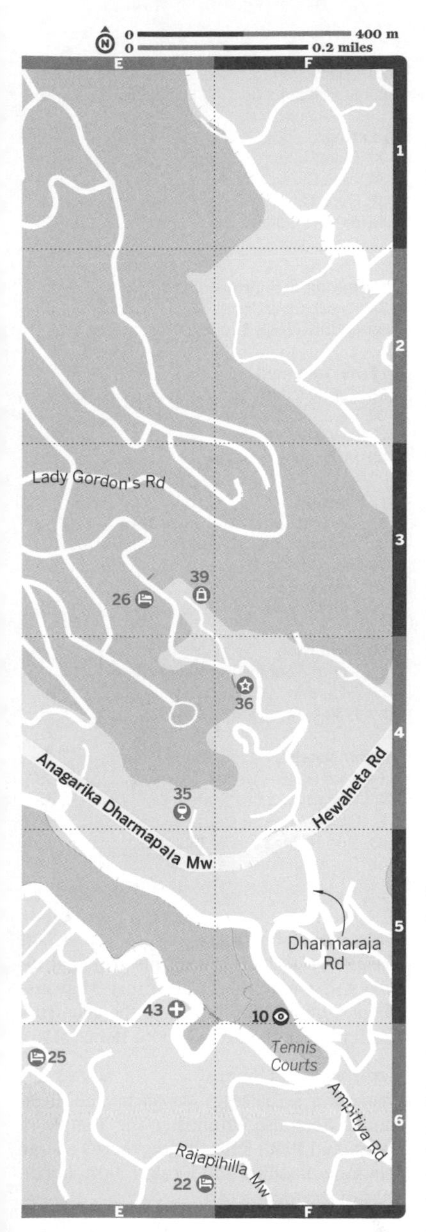

crown, but for visitors the museum is let down by poor lighting, labelling and general layout. The tall-pillared audience hall hosted the convention of Kandyan chiefs that ceded the kingdom to Britain in 1815. Last entry is 30 minutes before closing.

Kandy Garrison Cemetery CEMETERY

(8am-1pm & 2-6pm) FREE This well-maintained cemetery contains 163 graves from colonial times. Perhaps the most striking aspect of a visit here is learning just how young most people were when they died – if you made it to 40 you were of a very ripe old age. Some of the deaths were due to sunstroke, elephants or 'jungle fevers'. You'll probably be shown around by the highly informed caretaker, who once guided the UK's Prince Charles here, and who seems to have a tale for every tomb.

St Paul's Church CHURCH

(Deva Veediya) Construction of this impressive red-brick colonial-era church began in 1843 and was completed five years later. Built in neo-Gothic style, it originally served as a garrison church for British troops based nearby.

Udawattakelle Sanctuary FOREST

(adult/child Rs 864/432; 6am-5.30pm) This forest on the north side of Kandy Lake has soaring hardwood trees and giant bamboo, good birding and loads of cheeky monkeys. There are two main paths you can follow: one of around 1.5km and the other of 5km.

Be careful if you're visiting alone. Muggers are rare, but not unknown; solo women should take extra care.

Enter by turning right after the post office on DS Senanayake Vidiya. Last tickets issued at 5pm.

Devales

There are four Kandyan *devales* (special temples) to the gods who are followers of Buddha and protect Sri Lanka.

Natha Devale BUDDHIST TEMPLE

(24hr) FREE The 14th-century Natha Devale is the oldest of Kandy's *devales*. It perches on a stone terrace with a fine *vahalkada* (solid panel of sculpture) gateway. Bodhi trees and dagobas stand in the *devale* grounds. Natha means, no shape or form, and so it's commonly believed that the temple is dedicated to Lord Maitreya, or the coming Buddha.

Vishnu Devale BUDDHIST TEMPLE

(24hr) The Vishnu Devale is reached by carved steps and features a drumming hall. The great Hindu god Vishnu is the guardian of Sri Lanka, demonstrating the intermingling of Hinduism and Buddhism.

Kandy

Top Sights
1 Temple of the Sacred Tooth Relic ... D4

Sights
Alut Maligawa ... (see 15)
2 Asgiriya Maha Vihara ... A2
Audience Hall ... (see 15)
3 Kandy Garrison Cemetery ... D4
4 Kandy Lake ... D4
5 Kataragama Devale ... C4
6 Malwatte Maha Vihara ... D5
7 Natha Devale ... D4
8 National Museum ... D4
9 Pattini Devale ... D4
10 Playground ... F5
11 Royal Palace Park ... C5
Sri Dalada Museum ... (see 15)
12 St Paul's Church ... D3
13 Udawattakelle Sanctuary ... D1
14 Vishnu Devale ... D3
15 World Buddhism Museum ... D4

Activities, Courses & Tours
16 Best Kandy Kitchen ... A3
17 Joy Motorboat Service ... C4
Trekking Expeditor ... (see 19)

Sleeping
18 Clock Inn Kandy ... C2
19 Expeditor Guest House ... D5
20 Forest Glen ... D1
21 Freedom Lodge ... D5
22 Helga's Folly ... E6
23 Hotel Mango Garden ... D5
24 Kandy Cottage ... D1
25 McLeod Inn ... E6
26 Nature Walk Resort ... E3
27 Secret Kandy ... B1
28 Sharon Inn ... D6
29 St Bridget's Country Bungalow ... A2

Eating
30 Bake House ... C4
31 Cafe Divine Street ... C4
32 Cafe The Vibe ... C2
33 Empire Café ... C4
Sharon Inn ... (see 28)

Drinking & Nightlife
34 Royal Bar & Hotel ... C3
35 Slightly Chilled Lounge Bar ... E4

Entertainment
36 Kandy Lake Club ... F4
37 Kandyan Art Association & Cultural Centre ... D4
38 Mahanuwara YMBA ... C5

Shopping
39 EW Balasuriya & Co Jewelers ... E3
Jayamali Batiks Studio ... (see 40)
40 Main Market ... B4
41 Odel Luv SL ... C4
Selyn ... (see 33)

Information
42 Kandy Tourist Information Center ... B4
43 Lakeside Adventist Hospital ... E5

Transport
44 Blue Haven Tours & Travels ... C3
45 Bogambara Bus Station ... B5
46 Clock Tower Bus Stop ... B4
47 Goods Shed Bus Station ... A5
48 SriLankan Airlines ... C4

Pattini Devale BUDDHIST TEMPLE
(Temple St; ⏲24hr) The very popular, simple-looking Pattini Devale is dedicated to the goddess of chastity. It's frequented by pregnant women and those seeking a cure to disease.

Kataragama Devale HINDU TEMPLE
(Kotugodelle Vidiya; ⏲24hr) The brightly painted tower gateway of the Kataragama Devale demands attention amid the bustle on Kotugodelle Vidiya. Murugan, the god of war, has six heads, and 12 hands wielding weapons.

Viharas
The principal *viharas* (Buddhist complexes) in Kandy have considerable importance – the high priests of the two best known, Malwatte and Asgiriya, are the most important in Sri Lanka. These *viharas* are the headquarters of two of the main *nikayas* (orders of monks).

Malwatte Maha Vihara BUDDHIST SITE
(Sangaraja Mawatha) One of the principal *viharas* in Kandy, the 15th-century Malwatte Maha Vihara is located across the lake from the Temple of the Sacred Tooth Relic (p156).

Asgiriya Maha Vihara BUDDHIST SITE
(Wariyapola Sri Sumanga Mawatha) The head monks here also administer the Temple of the Sacred Tooth Relic. Inside, there's a large reclining Buddha. It's located 1km northwest of the town centre.

Activities
There are many walks around Kandy, including through the **Royal Palace Park** (Rs 200; ⏲8.30am-5pm), constructed by Sri Wickrama Rajasinha and overlooking the lake. The Peradeniya Botanic Gardens (p167) are also perfect for a leisurely stroll. Up on Rajapihilla Mawatha there are lovely views

over the lake, the town and the surrounding hills. For longer walks, there are paths branching out from Rajapihilla Mawatha.

Best Kandy Kitchen COOKING
(☎071-210 8210; www.facebook.com/Bestkandykitchen; 42/11 Sri Pushpadana Mawatha; classes from US$25) Twice-daily two- to three-hour cooking courses take place in a home environment. Participants will learn to make 10 vegetable curries plus your choice of a chicken or fish curry. They also throw in a bottle of beer!

Sri Lanka Trekking HIKING
(☎075-799 7667, 071-499 7666; www.srilankatrekking.com) These professionals can arrange trekking around Kandy, and camping and trekking (and birdwatching) expeditions to the rugged Knuckles Range. They also offer safaris to Wasgamuwa National Park (and many other reserves), plus mountain-biking and rafting trips.

For a standard overnight trek in the Knuckles, expect to pay €75. The per-person price decreases with group size.

Trekking Expeditor WALKING
(☎081-223 8316, 076-541 9079; www.trekkingexpeditor.com; 41 Saranankara Rd) Based out of the Expeditor Guest House, this highly experienced trekking company offers treks in the Knuckles mountains as well as birdwatching trips led by an expert birder. Treks cost €75 per person per day for a single person and €55 for two people. Birdwatching trips cost €11 for a day's birding around Kandy and €65 for trips further afield.

Joy Motorboat Service BOATING
(20min Rs 2000; ⏲9am-6pm) Put on an eye patch and set sail like a pirate into the great blue...lake. Little puttering boats can be hired from this place on the jetty at the western end of the lake.

Sleeping

Kandy has many good guesthouses, and the more comfortable hotels often occupy spectacular hilltop or riverside locations.

In the city centre, the highest concentration of accommodation is along or just off Anagarika Dharmapala Mawatha and Saranankara Rd (buses 654, 655 and 698 will get you there, or just ask for 'Sanghamitta Mawatha' at the clock-tower bus stop).

Most places have in-house restaurants.

Expeditor Guest House GUESTHOUSE $
(☎081-223 8316, 076-541 9079; 41 Saranankara Rd; r Rs 2500-5500; ❄📶) Lots of potted plants, balconies with views, a warm welcome, spotless rooms (some have shared bathrooms) and the opportunity to mix with the hospitable proprietors give Expeditor a cosy bed-and-breakfast feel. Speak to the owners about treks in the Knuckles mountains and other regions.

Hotel Mango Garden GUESTHOUSE $
(☎081-223 5135; www.mangogarden.lk; 32A Saranankara Rd; r Rs 3000-4000, with shared bathroom Rs2500; ❄📶) Manager Malik and his French wife run a tight ship here. Rooms are plain, and some are showing their age a bit, but the bedding is good and there's a lovely terrace restaurant for drinks and excellent meals (open to all). Call them for free pickup from the bus or train station.

Clock Inn Kandy HOSTEL $
(☎081-223 5311; www.clockinnkandy.lk; 11 Hill St; dm/d from Rs 1800/6300; ❄📶) This well-set-up hostel right in the city centre has a buzzing reception area and knowledgable staff who organise an array of day trips. The plain white rooms and air-con dorms (all with lockers, comfy bunks and reading lights) are a bit overpriced, though, and road noise can be an issue.

It also offers some totally wacky rooftop capsule-style tube-beds (Rs 1800) that are definitely not for the claustrophobic!

KANDY FOR CHILDREN

Kandy isn't as obviously child-friendly as Sri Lanka's beaches and national parks, but there are a few sights and activities that'll keep little ones – and therefore you as well – happy and sane.

Renting a boat from Joy Motorboat Service for a putter about the lake and then hiring a tuk-tuk to buzz around the city streets is sure to delight. Children can burn off energy in the Udawattakelle Sanctuary (p159) and Peradeniya Botanic Gardens (p167), and, with their elaborate costumes and fire eaters, Kandy's various **dance shows** will surely meet with approval. The Temple of the Sacred Tooth Relic (p156) has enough exotica to capture the imagination of most children, and there's a surprisingly good **play park** (Sangaraja Rd; ⏲7am-6pm Tue-Sun) at the eastern end of the lake.

Freedom Lodge HOMESTAY $$

(☎7173-83171, 081-222 3506; https://freedom-lodge-kandy-lk.book.direct/en-gb; 30 Saranankara Rd; r incl breakfast from Rs 6500;) This popular, well-established guesthouse is surrounded by towering palm trees. It's owned by a friendly family, one member of whom worked in hospitality for years. The rooms have a pleasingly chintzy old-fashioned style, but the hot-water bathrooms are modern. Home-cooked meals can be requested; you eat communally, so you can mix with other guests.

St Bridget's Country Bungalow HOMESTAY $$

(☎081-221 5806; www.stbridgets-kandy.com; 125 Wariyapola Sri Sumangala Mawatha, Asgiriya; r in old villa Rs 4000, d in new building US$45;) What was once a humble homestay has now morphed into a slick guesthouse with impressive rooms and an inviting pool. However, for those who prefer a taste of how things used to be, the original rooms in the antique villa are still available. Breakfast (Rs 600) is a feast of homemade jams and bread, and good dinners are also on offer.

It's a 20-minute uphill walk from town, or about Rs 250 in a three-wheeler.

Sharon Inn HOTEL $$

(☎077-780 4900, 081-222 2416; www.sharoninnhotel.com; 59 Saranankara Rd; d/tr/f incl breakfast Rs 5000/6500/10,000;) This small hilltop place is one of Kandy's longest-running hotels, and it has excellent views and scrupulously clean rooms decorated with Sri Lankan arts and crafts. Staff are genuinely welcoming and fully switched on to travel information and tours. Excellent family rooms are available. Don't miss the dinner buffet (p164), which is one of the best dining experiences in Kandy.

McLeod Inn GUESTHOUSE $$

(☎081-222 2832; www.mcleodinnkandy.com; 65A Rajapihilla Mawatha; r Rs 4000-5000;) A fine family-run guesthouse with astounding lake views from some of its 10 comfortable, clean and well-presented rooms. You'll enjoy the dining area and its valley views. Breakfast costs an extra Rs 600.

Kandy Cottage GUESTHOUSE $$

(☎081-220 4742; www.kandycottage.com; 160 Lady Gordon's Rd, Sri Dalada Thapowana Mawatha; d from US$30;) Run by Thomas and Mani, a very welcoming couple, this slightly bohemian place is a great escape from the city: a Sri Lankan cottage tucked away in a forested valley on the fringes of the Udawattakelle Sanctuary. There are three rooms with chunky wooden furniture and polished-concrete floors, though no air-con.

Nature Walk Resort GUESTHOUSE $$

(☎077-771 7482; www.naturewalkhr.net; 9 Sanghamitta Mawatha; d/f incl breakfast Rs 5500/6500;) Terracotta tiles and French doors lead to bougainvillea-draped balconies with, from some rooms, excellent forest views. The rooms are spacious and airy, and you can look forward to troops of monkeys in the morning and squadrons of bats at dusk. All this makes it a great base for wildlife lovers.

Forest Glen GUESTHOUSE $$

(☎077-732 5228; 150/6 Lady Gordon's Rd, Sri Dalada Thapowana Mawatha; s/d incl breakfast Rs 4000/5500;) This wonderfully secluded, though slightly faded, four-room family guesthouse on the edge of Udawattakelle Sanctuary has fine forest views from its terrace and makes for an atmospheric and peaceful retreat from the bustle of downtown Kandy. Indra is a welcoming host and prepares tasty breakfasts. It's 1.5km north of central Kandy.

Clove Villa BOUTIQUE HOTEL $$$

(☎081-221 2999; www.clovevilla.com; 48 PBA Weerakoon Mawatha; r US$170-205;) A superb converted villa with seven gorgeous rooms, all with plush, tasteful furnishings and a dash of art, and kitted out with every mod con you could want. There's fine in-house dining, a billiards table and a library. It's 5km north of the centre, located on a bend in the river.

Prices can drop by almost 50% at quiet times.

★**Villa Rosa** BOUTIQUE HOTEL $$$

(☎081-221 5556; www.villarosa-kandy.com; Asgiriya; s/d/f incl breakfast from US$75/140/265;) Dotted with antiques, and offering stunning views over a secluded arc of the Mahaweli Ganga, Villa Rosa is an inspiring place to stay. Spacious wooden-floored rooms in cool, neutral tones share the limelight with relaxing lounges and a lovely reading room. A separate pavilion houses yoga and meditation centres. Two-night minimum stay.

★**Stone House** BOUTIQUE HOTEL $$$

(☎081-757 5747; www.stonehousekandy.com; 42 Nittawela Rd; d incl breakfast US$350;) The five rooms at this stunning boutique hotel are filled with original sculptures made from wrought iron and old farming implements. Some rooms have free-standing bathtubs. The service is polished and discreet, and there's a pool with views over milky-blue hills, but how anyone keeps the lush, jungly gardens under control is a mystery.

Elephant Stables BOUTIQUE HOTEL **$$$**
(072-899 1456; www.elephantstables.com; 46 Nittawela Rd; d/f incl breakfast US$200/250;) This stunning villa was once the home of Sir Cudah Ratwatte, the first elected mayor of Kandy. Today, it's been lovingly converted into a beautiful hotel, with excellent service, earthy tones, polished concrete and gnarled wood. Two rooms have balconies overlooking an inviting pool and the not-so-distant mountains; the family rooms are especially good.

There's a fab bar, and a reading room well stocked with Sri Lanka–related titles.

True to its name, elephants used to be stabled here.

Secret Kandy BOUTIQUE HOTEL **$$$**
(077-599 5999; www.thesecrethotels.com; 25 Lady Gordon's Dr; s/d incl breakfast US$125/140;) This 125-year-old colonial villa was once the home of esteemed national philosopher Siddi Lebbe. Today it's a beautifully restored and good-value boutique hotel. Its five elegant and airy rooms blend tropical wood furnishings with eye-catching statues, and rather than engage in philosophical debate you can concentrate on more important things like sipping cocktails by the courtyard pool.

Eating

For many years Kandy, like so many other Sir Lankan hill towns, didn't have much of a dining scene, and most travellers ate in their hotel. In the last year or two, though, things have slowly started to improve and there is now a small but growing number of interesting cafes and restaurants in and around the town centre.

Bake House SRI LANKAN **$**
(081-494 0801; www.bakehousekandy.com; 36 Dalada Vidiya; meals from Rs 280; 7.30am-8pm) Old-timer Bake House now has a smart (air-conditioned) dining room as well as the ground-floor cafe. On the dependable, but not wildly exciting, menu you'll find baked goodies, curries, sandwiches, and Chinese and Indian dishes. Pop in just after 3pm, when the second bake of the day comes out and the short eats are still warm.

KANDY ESALA PERAHERA

This *perahera* (procession) is held in Kandy to honour the sacred tooth enshrined in the Temple of the Sacred Tooth Relic (p156). It runs for 10 days in the month of Esala (July/August), ending on the Nikini *poya* (full moon).

The first six nights are relatively low-key. On the seventh night, proceedings escalate as the route lengthens and the procession becomes more splendid. (Accommodation prices increase accordingly.) The procession is led by thousands of Kandyan dancers and drummers beating drums, cracking whips and waving colourful banners. Then come long processions of up to 50 elephants. The Maligawa tusker is decorated from trunk to toe. On the last two nights of the *perahera* it carries a huge canopy sheltering the empty casket of the sacred relic cask. A trail of pristine white linen is laid before the elephant.

The Kandy Esala Perahera has been performed annually for many centuries and is described by Robert Knox in his 1681 book *An Historical Relation of Ceylon*. There is also a smaller procession on the *poya* day in June, and special *peraheras* may be put on for important occasions.

The ceremony is certainly one of South Asia's most spectacular. But before you go ahead and book tickets you may want to consider the elephants' welfare. Sri Lankan campaigners point out that the cacophonous *perahera* noise can deeply affect the mammals, which have very sensitive hearing, and that the constant prodding by mahouts and their *ankus* (hooks) is painful. Chains and buckles are used to control elephants and constrain their mobility. Their long journey to Kandy is made either on the back of a truck (in the scorching sun) or on foot, treading on sizzling tarmac.

If you do decide to attend it's essential to book roadside seats for the main *perahera* at least a week in advance. Prices range from Rs 6000 up to Rs 15,000. Once the festival starts, seats about halfway back in the stands are more affordable.

WORTH A TRIP

HELGA'S FOLLY

'If expecting a regular hotel experience best look elsewhere', says the marketing blurb, and that's 100% accurate, for **Helga's Folly** (081-223 4571; www.helgasfolly.com; r US$100-130, nonguest admission US$3;) could have been dreamt up as a joint project between Gaudí and Dalí. This hotel/art gallery/surrealist dream off Rajapihilla Mawatha has to be the most extraordinary hotel in Sri Lanka. Indeed, the Stereophonics famously wrote the song 'Madame Helga' about the owner.

It's run and designed by the outlandish Helga da Silva, who grew up in a world of 1950s Hollywood celebrities, artists, writers, politicians and general intrigue, and she has to be one of the only hotel owners who prefer their properties not to be full! As for spending a night here, well, yes, in truth once you've peeled through all the decorations you'll see that the place is looking a little tatty, but even so, it's the most memorable place to stay in Sri Lanka, and with rates as low as US$100 a night, this is one Hollywood fantasy we can all afford to partake in. The alternative to staying here is popping past for a poke about and a drink – for many people it's one of the most interesting sights in Kandy – or sign up for dinner (US$20; 7.30pm; advance bookings required) at one of the long tables lit up with spooky candle chandeliers.

Cafe Divine Street INTERNATIONAL $$
(077-699 2799; www.facebook.com/cafedivinestreet; 139 Colombo St; meals from Rs 350; 10am-9pm Wed-Sun) Run by an industrious local, this tiny, inexpensive cafe offers great burgers, kebabs and fried-rice dishes; all are well seasoned and attractively presented. There are more tables upstairs, with good street views.

Cafe The Vibe INTERNATIONAL $$
(077-730 4530; www.cafethevibe.com; 258 Senanayake St; mains Rs 350-600; 9am-10.30pm) Head up the stairs to this cool 1st-floor cafe, which has a loyal following among young locals, and within its wood-panelled and blackboard-lined walls you can enjoy well-prepared fried rice, creative *kottu* (chopped *rotti* with veg, chicken or eggs), good burgers and passable pasta.

★**Sharon Inn** SRI LANKAN $$$
(081-222 2416; 59 Saranankara Rd; dinner buffet Rs 1450; 7-9pm;) The nightly buffet dinner at this hotel (p162), served from 7pm in the starlit rooftop restaurant, is a tasty short cut to falling in love with Sri Lankan cuisine. It's a true feast of veggie curry – jackfruit, banana leaf, aubergine and others are all lovingly prepared. Plus there's one meat curry.

★**Empire Café** INTERNATIONAL $$$
(081-223 9870; www.facebook.com/EmpireCafeKandy; 21 Temple St; meals Rs 700-1000; 8.30am-8.30pm;) This flamboyantly styled, very inviting restaurant, in colonial-era premises, has a selection of vibrantly painted (pink and turquoise) dining rooms that make for a great place to take a break from sightseeing. Tuck into tasty breakfasts, rice and curries, pastas, wraps, salads, juices and milkshakes.

Shopping

Central Kandy has shops selling antique jewellery and silver belts, and you can buy crafts in the colourful **main market** (Station Rd; 8am-7pm).

Selyn FASHION & ACCESSORIES
(081-223 7735; www.selyn.lk; 7/1/1 Temple St; 9.30am-6pm) Fair-trade textiles, clothing (including saris, sarongs and shirts) and jewellery made of recycled fabric, paper and other materials.

Odel Luv SL CLOTHES
(www.odel.lk; shop no L3-3, Kandy City Centre Mall; 10am-9pm) Wacky T-shirts, flashy flip-flops and glitzy women's clothing. It's on the 3rd floor of the Kandy City Centre Mall.

★**Jayamali Batiks Studio** CLOTHING
(077-783 3938; www.jayamalibatiks.com; 1st fl, 194 Main Market; 10am-6pm) Breathtakingly beautiful fine batik clothing and homewares (bedspreads and wall hangings) in modern, artistic styles created by designer Upali Jayakody. Expect to pay around US$250 for a smaller wall hanging. It's on the upper floor of the main market.

Information

MEDICAL SERVICES

Lakeside Adventist Hospital (☎081-222 3466; http://lakesideadventisthospital.blogspot.co.uk; 40 Sangarajah Mawatha) Has English-speaking staff.

SAFE TRAVEL

➡ The back alleys of the town centre are worth avoiding after dark as they are the natural habitat of drunks and shady characters.

➡ Solo women are sometimes hassled around the lakeside at dusk and after dark. Get a three-wheeler back to your guesthouse to keep safe.

TOURIST INFORMATION

Kandy Tourist Information Center (☎081-312 2143; Dalada Vidiya; ⊙8.30am-7pm) The main tourist office is right by the clock-tower bus stop. Staff have a few leaflets to dispense and can help with train and dance-performance schedules.

Getting There & Away

AIR

Cinnamon Air (p326) Runs scheduled flights once or twice daily to and from Colombo and daily to Hambantota, Koggala and Dickwella.

SriLankan Airlines (☎019-733 3101; 19 Temple St; ⊙8.15am-5pm Mon-Fri, to 1.15pm Sat) Ticket reservations can be made here.

BUS

At the time of research, the brand-new **Bogambara Bus Station** (Station Rd) had just opened and the exact departure point for many buses was in flux. Eventually, all intercity services will move to this new station, while services to villages around Kandy will use the current Goods Shed bus station and the series of bus stops near the clock tower. Check with guesthouses where your bus leaves from.

At research time the Goods Shed station had long-distance buses, while regular local buses, such as those to Peradeniya (Rs 20), Ampitiya (Rs 18), Matale (Rs 48) and Kegalle (Rs 65), left from near the clock tower.

For Sigiriya, you must change in Polonnaruwa and for Dalhousie you normally have to go to

DANCERS & DRUMMERS

With elaborate costumes, gyrating dance moves and show-stopping, fire-breathing stunts, a Kandyan dance performance is one of the defining experiences of a stay in Kandy. Calling it a traditional Kandyan dance performance is something of a misnomer as the shows are very much aimed at audience entertainment and contain dance routines and costumes from across the country, including the famous 'devil' dances of the west coast (which are very hard to see in their home region).

There are three main venues. All have nightly performances that last an hour (arrive 30 minutes in advance to get a better seat). None of the venues have air-con, and all can get hot. Tickets for all venues can be bought at the door and as long as you turn up at least half an hour before a performance you should be able to get a ticket. If you want to be certain of a seat, pop by earlier in the day to reserve. Some guesthouses also sell tickets.

Kandy Lake Club (☎077-226 0666; www.facebook.com/kandylakeclub; 7 Sanghamitta Mawatha; Rs 1250; ⊙show starts 5pm) Located 300m up Sanghamitta Mawatha, this place has arguably the best costumes of any of the venues staging traditional Sri Lankan dance shows. Performances often conclude with a 'fire walking' (stepping on burning coals) finale. Arrive early for good seats.

Kandyan Art Association & Cultural Centre (www.facebook.com/KandyanArtAssociation; 72 Sangarajah Mawatha; Rs 1000; ⊙show starts 5pm) This is the busiest dance-show venue, and in high season it can be overwhelmingly crammed with tour groups. However, the auditorium makes it easier to take photographs here than at other venues. It's on the northern lake shore. Be sure to arrive well ahead of time to secure seats.

Mahanuwara YMBA (☎081-223 3444; 5 Rajapihilla Mawatha; Rs 1000; ⊙show starts 5.30pm) Southwest of the lake, the YMBA guesthouse is a low-key venue for Sri Lankan dance; the performances here are entertaining and the crowds somewhat thinner.

You can also hear Kandyan drummers every day at the Temple of the Sacred Tooth Relic (p156) and the other temples surrounding it – their drumming signals the start and finish of the daily *puja* (offering or prayers).

DIGGING FOR TREASURE

The upmarket gem retailer **EW Balasuriya & Co Jewelers** (081-223 4369; www.ewbjewel.com; 7/2 Sanghamitta Mawatha; 8.30am-5.30pm) contains a small museum where a fascinating, free guided tour explains the background and processes of Sri Lanka's important gem industry. A visit begins with an informative short film, and you'll then see an artisan gem mine (complete with endlessly hammering and chiselling mannequins) before making a quick stop at the workshops, where you can see stones being examined, polished and turned from grubby rock to lush jewel. The tour finishes in the gem shop. There's no real hard sell, but if you're in the market for a gem then this is the place to come. Only certified, highest-quality stones are sold here, but be warned that prices are not displayed – if you have to ask, you probably can't afford it!

Hatton and change there. Heading to Ella, you'll have to change in Badulla.

TAXI

Cars can generally be hired, with a driver and petrol, for approximately Rs 6000 per day if you're not straying too far from the area around Kandy. Many long-distance taxi drivers hang around the Temple of the Sacred Tooth Relic, or ask at your guesthouse or hotel.

Some guesthouses advertise day trips to all three cultural-triangle destinations (Sigiriya, Anuradhapura and Polonnaruwa), but this is an exhausting itinerary for both driver and passengers, and one that encourages manic driving. An overnight stay in Anuradhapura, Sigiriya or Polonnaruwa is a saner and safer option.

Blue Haven Tours & Travels (077-737 2066; www.bluehaventours.com; 1st fl, 34 Colombo St) A recommended car-hire company, charging around US$50 per day.

Nishantha Maldeniya (077-084 9137; nishantha.maldeniya71@gmail.com) Offers fair rates for local and long-distance trips.

TRAIN

Kandy is a major railway station, and trains to and from here are well patronised by visitors. Seats in the 1st-class observation saloon on the Badulla-bound train are very popular. Trains heading from Kandy deeper into the hills stop in Hatton (near Adam's Peak), Nanu Oya (for Nuwara Eliya), Haputale, Ella and a number of other Hill Country stations. Observation-class tickets cost a set Rs 800 for anywhere between Kandy and Nanu Oya and Rs 1200 for any of the stations east of there. Note that delays are common on the line to Hatton. The observation-class train doesn't actually leave from Kandy but from Peradeniya Junction, a short way southwest of the city. At weekends a special tourist-class train (train 27) leaves Kandy for Badulla at 7.40am. Tickets on this train cost Rs 2000 to Nanu Oya and Rs 3000 to Ella.

There are several ordinary trains each day from Kandy to both Colombo and Badulla (and stops in between). The table below lists prices of unreserved tickets bought moments before departure. On all these trains you can also reserve tickets in advance; these are generally around twice the price of the fares listed below. Most of these trains also have a 1st-class carriage, for which tickets must be reserved in advance. A reserved 1st-class ticket to Colombo, Nanu Oya and stops up to Nanu Oya costs Rs 1000 and to points east of Nanu Oya Rs 1200. The train through the Hill Country is very popular with tourists and, between Nanu Oya and Ella, in particular, don't be at all surprised if there are hardly any Sri Lankans on the train and that all passengers are other foreign tourists. Be warned that, despite the number of tourists buying train tickets, the process can be a little confusing, with various sales desks quoting different prices depending on what train the seller thinks you might want. Also note that the price boards on display in the station are not always correct.

BUSES FROM KANDY

DESTINATION	BUS STATION	FARE (RS) LUXURY	FARE (RS) NORMAL	DURATION (HR)	FREQUENCY
Anuradhapura	Goods Shed/clock tower	400	206	3½	every 30min
Badulla	Goods Shed/clock tower	215	160	3	hourly
Colombo	Bogambara	350	181	3-4	every 15min
Negombo	Bogambara	–	185	3-4	hourly
Nuwara Eliya	Bogambara	270	135	3½	every 30min
Jaffna	Goods Shed/clock tower	450	–	6	hourly

Trains run to the following (prices are for unreserved tickets):

Destination	Fare 2nd/3rd class (Rs)	Duration (hr)	Frequency (per day)
Badulla	350/195	7-8	5
Colombo	250/140	2½-3½	7-9
Ella	310/175	6-7	5
Haputale	280/155	5-6	5
Hatton	150/85	2½-3	5
Nanu Oya (for Nuwara Eliya)	210/120	3½-4	5

Getting Around

BUS

Buses to outlying parts of Kandy and nearby towns such as Peradeniya, Ampitiya, Matale and Kegalle leave from near the clock tower.

THREE-WHEELER

Expect to pay around Rs 300 for a three-wheeler from the train station to the southeast end of the lake.

Around Kandy

For many people the sights in the countryside around Kandy are more interesting than most of those in the city itself. Although all of the following can be visited by a combination of public transport and walking, it's far easier to hire a three-wheeler or taxi for the day. The Three Temples Loop (including the Lankatilake, Gadaladeniya and Embekka Devale temples) is a worthwhile excursion. You might then choose to hit the botanic gardens for the afternoon to make it a full day out.

Sights

★Peradeniya Botanic Gardens GARDENS
(www.botanicgardens.gov.lk; adult/child Rs 2000/1000, 7.30am-6pm) These stunning gardens, 6km from Kandy, were once reserved exclusively for Kandyan royalty. Today, everyone is allowed in to enjoy the most impressive and largest (60 hectares) botanic gardens in Sri Lanka.

Highlights include a fine collection of orchids, a stately avenue of royal palms, the extraordinary, aptly named cannonball fruit tree and 40m-high Burma bamboo. Another big hit is the giant Javan fig tree on the great lawn, with its colossal central trunk and umbrella-like canopy of branches.

You'll share the gardens with thousands of wing-flapping fruit bats, hundreds of monkeys and dozens of canoodling courting couples.

Inside the grounds are an overpriced cafeteria (mains Rs 550 to Rs 1000), serving Western and Sri Lankan food, and a small cafe by the exit gate. A better option is to stock up on picnic items before you come.

Bus 644 (Rs 16) from Kandy's clock-tower bus stop goes to the gardens. A three-wheeler from Kandy is about Rs 500 one way. Many taxi drivers incorporate a visit to the gardens with the Kandy Three Temples Loop.

Last entry to the gardens is 5pm.

★Lankatilake Temple RELIGIOUS SITE
(Rs 300; 8am-6pm) This impressive 14th-century temple, mounted on a rocky bluff, is the most imposing in the region. It's divided into two halves – one half Buddhist and one half Hindu – and features a seated Buddha image, Kandy-period paintings, rock-face inscriptions and stone elephant figures. A caretaker or monk will unlock the shrine if it's not already open. A *perahera* takes place here in August.

The setting is as memorable as the temple. It's located 15km southwest of Kandy.

From Kandy, you can go directly to the temple on bus 644 heading towards Pilimatalawa. Get off at Dawulagala Rd, from where it's a 750m walk to the temple. You can also reach Lankatilake from the neighbouring temple of Embekka Devale via a 3km stroll beside rice paddies.

Embekka Devale HINDU TEMPLE
(Rs 300; 8am-6pm) Dedicated to the worship of the Hindu deity Mahasen, this beautiful temple, with its finely carved wooden pillars depicting swans, eagles, wrestling men and dancing women, was constructed in the 14th century. The best carvings are in the drummers' hall.

To get here by public transport, catch the frequent bus 643 (to Vatadeniya via Embekka) from near the clock-tower bus stop in Kandy for Rs 40. The village of Embekka is about 7km beyond the Peradeniya Botanic Gardens (about 45 minutes from Kandy). From the village, it's a pleasant rural stroll of about 1km to the temple.

Around Kandy

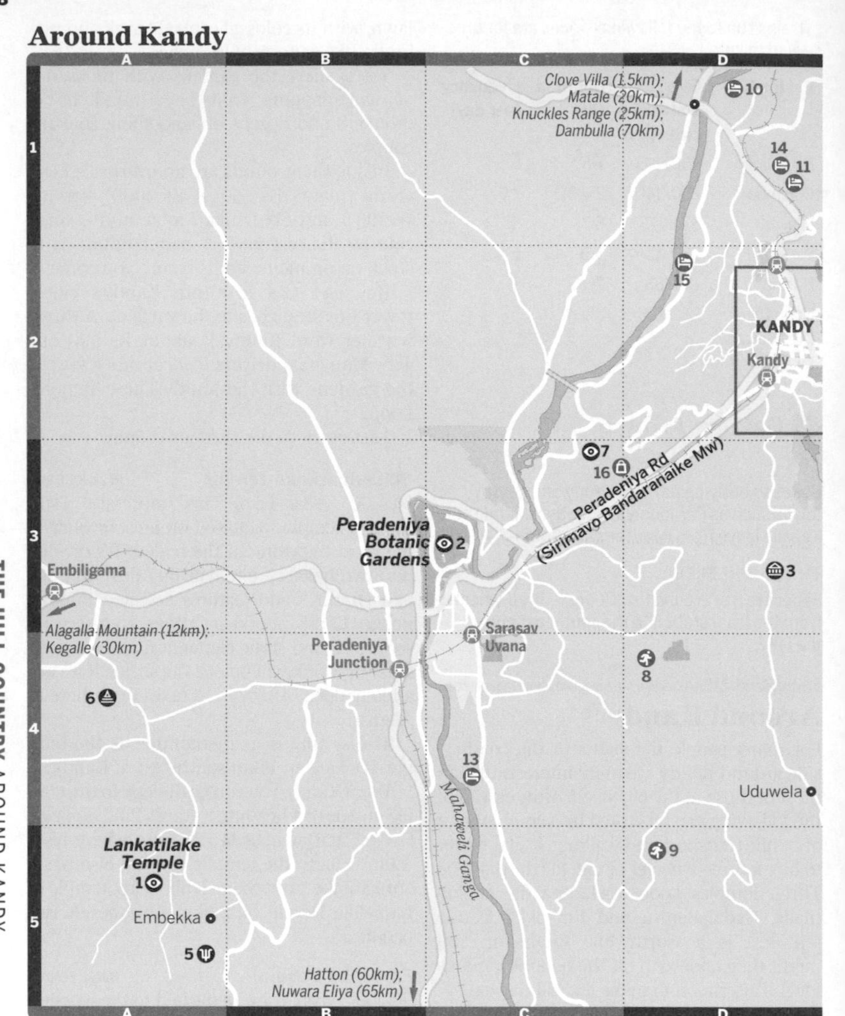

Gadaladeniya Temple BUDDHIST, HINDU TEMPLE

(Rs 300; ⏲8am-6pm) This Buddhist temple with a Hindu annexe dates from the 14th century, and the main shrine room contains a stunningly beautiful, gilded seated Buddha. Built on a rocky outcrop and covered with small pools, the temple is reached by a series of steps cut into the rock.

You may encounter it protected by scaffolding and a tin roof to prevent further rain-induced erosion. It's 13km southwest of central Kandy.

From Kandy, bus 644 (Rs 30), among others, will take you to the temple. The turn-off from the A1 Hwy is close to the 105km post, from where it's 1km to Gadaladeniya.

Ceylon Tea Museum MUSEUM

(☎081-494 6737; www.facebook.com/CEYLONTEAMUSEUM; Hantane; adult/child Rs 800/400; ⏲8.30am-3.45pm Tue-Sat, to 3pm Sun) This museum occupies the 1925-vintage Hantane Tea Factory, 4km south of Kandy on the Hantane road. Abandoned for more than a decade, it was recently refurbished and has good exhibits on tea pioneers James Taylor and Thomas Lipton, and lots of vintage tea-processing paraphernalia. A quick tour (all guides are knowledgable, but you feel

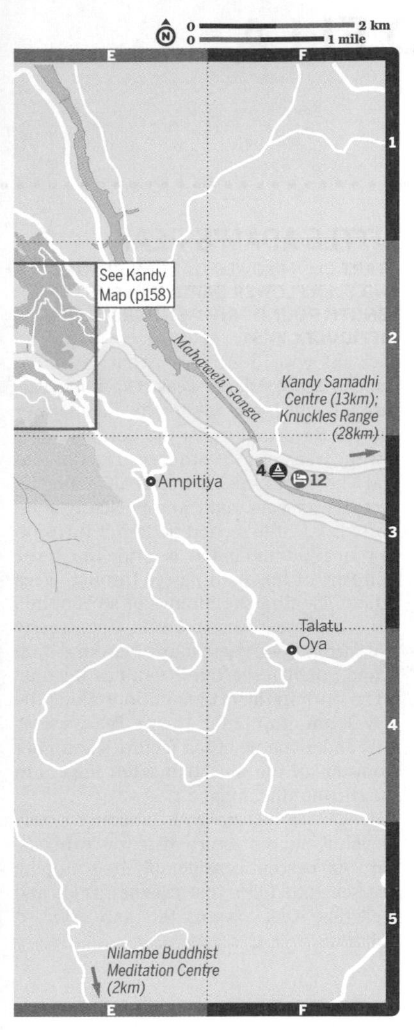

Around Kandy

Top Sights

1 Lankatilake Temple.......A5
2 Peradeniya Botanic Gardens.......C3

Sights

3 Ceylon Tea Museum.......D3
4 Degal Doruwa Raja Maha Vihara.......F3
5 Embekka Devale.......A5
6 Gadaladeniya Temple.......A4
7 Kandy War Cemetery.......C3

Activities, Courses & Tours

8 Amaya Hills.......D4
9 Dhamma Kuta Vipassana Meditation Centre.......D5

Sleeping

10 Clove Villa.......D1
11 Elephant Stables.......D1
12 Kandy House.......F3
13 Nisha Tourist Home.......C4
14 Stone House.......D1
15 Villa Rosa.......D2

Shopping

16 Waruna Antiques.......C3

that some just go through the motions) is included and there's a free cuppa afterwards in the top-floor tearoom.

Degal Doruwa Raja Maha Vihara BUDDHIST TEMPLE
(Lewella; by donation; 8am-6pm) Hidden away in Kandy's leafy outskirts is the little-visited but fascinating Degal Doruwa Raja Maha Vihara cave temple, constructed (with the help of some obliging boulders) in the 18th century. The interior of the cave is covered top to bottom with slightly faded but captivating murals. These fine Kandyan-era paintings depict scenes from the Jataka stories (tales). Among these are some out-of-place paintings depicting men with guns. These are likely to have been inspired by the first firearms to have arrived in Sri Lanka. Alongside the paintings is a large reclining Buddha.

Visitors are likely to be shown around by one of the seven resident monks. After visiting the temple, scramble above the boulders to a small clearing with a stately old prayer-flag-draped bodhi tree.

Kandy War Cemetery CEMETERY
(www.cwgc.org; Deveni Rajasinghe; by donation; 10am-noon & 1-6pm) This small and beautifully melancholic cemetery is maintained by the Commonwealth War Graves Commission. It is the final resting place for those who died defending Sri Lanka during WWII.

Activities

There are several well-regarded meditation centres close to Kandy.

Nilambe Buddhist Meditation Centre MEDITATION
(www.nilambe.net; donation requested) Offers serious meditation (mainly silent and sitting meditation) courses lasting from five to 11 days. Basic accommodation with no electricity is available. Days start with a 4.45am wake-up gong and end with group chanting,

HIKES AROUND ELLA

GET PREPARED

Most of the walks around Ella are fairly simple and none takes more than half a day. Most of them can be done with children (the only exception to this might be the Ella Rock hike, but even this can be completed by most children above the age of about seven). For all the walks covered here there are enough other people on the trail to mean that a guide isn't strictly needed, and most accommodation can give you a hand-drawn map of local paths. However, for Ella Rock, in particular, a guide isn't a bad idea for single travellers, those who haven't done much walking, or if the weather isn't looking great. Most guesthouses can organise a guide for Rs 1800 per group. Guide or not, make sure you wear proper shoes or, better, hiking boots and bring something to snack on as well as plenty of liquid refreshment (Ella is notably hotter than most other parts of the Hill Country and the heat and humidity are the hardest part of most walks).

LITTLE ADAM'S PEAK

START ELLA FLOWER GARDEN RESORT
END ELLA FLOWER GARDEN RESORT
LENGTH ROUND TRIP 1½ HOURS, 4.5KM
DIFFICULTY EASY

Kick off with a stroll to what is locally dubbed Little Adam's Peak. Go down Passara Rd until you get to the Ella Flower Garden Resort, just past the 1km post. Follow the track past guesthouses The Chillout and The One; Little Adam's Peak is the biggest hill on your right and is clearly signposted. Take the second path that turns off to your right and follow it to the top of the hill. Part of this path passes through a tea estate. The final 20 minutes or so is uphill, but otherwise it's an easy walk. Get an early start from your guesthouse – around 7am – and you'll meet Tamil families heading off to work in the tea plantations along the way. From atop Little Adam's Peak, waterfalls and a couple of tea factories shimmer from out of the mist that often lingers in the surrounding hills.

If you get fed up with plodding slowly downhill on the return trip you can hasten your descent considerably by strapping yourself into Ella's first **zip-line** (p193) and rocketing back towards the start point at 80km/h!

The hills that rise around Ella make for some superb hikes. Walks here will take you weaving through tea fields, through the spray of waterfalls and up to lofty viewpoints.

ELLA ROCK

START ELLA TOWN
END ELLA TOWN
LENGTH ROUND TRIP THREE TO FOUR HOURS, 9KM
DIFFICULTY MODERATE

Walking to Ella Rock is more demanding than the Little Adam's Peak hike, but it's also more rewarding. Most mornings there's a constant stream of people walking the trail and a guide isn't strictly necessary. The views from the top are extraordinary. From the town centre, walk up the steep hill (Waterfall View Rd) and past the Zion View guesthouse. Keep going to where this road meets the train tracks and follow the tracks in the direction of Bandarawela. You'll quickly pass a small shrine at the foot of a big old banyan tree. Keep going along the train tracks for another 40 minutes or so. Just after the black bridge there's a small shrine on the left. Turn left a metre or so after this, down a short embankment and past a house where the owners sell coconuts and soft drinks. Cross a concrete bridge over the small Rawana Falls and then go right up the dirt track immediately after the bridge. Now start climbing uphill. From here on it's easy to get lost, especially on misty or cloudy days. Watch for the occasional faded blue waymarker. An alternative is to continue along the railway tracks for an extra couple of minutes until you get to the Kithaella station. Continue for a further 10 minutes until you see an obvious trail descending to the left. Take this, go past the houses and then head straight uphill until you meet up with the standard route. This is a slightly easier trail. You can even shorten your hike by taking a three-wheeler from Ella to Kithaella station (15 to 20 minutes, Rs 600 to Rs 700). Once at the summit you'll find a couple of people selling overpriced drinks and a whole bunch of monkeys keen to relieve you of any snacks you brought.

For an easier walk (2.5km from town), follow the route to Ella Rock but only go as far as Rawana Falls.

OFF THE BEATEN TRACK

ALAGALLA MOUNTAIN HIKE

Kandy is hemmed in by mountains and some of these offer excellent walking. The Alagalla range lies immediately to the west of the city and its steep slopes make for one of the most exciting day hikes in Sri Lanka. The Alagalla hike is an airy walk along the spine of an exposed granite ridge. With huge vertical drops on either side, it's an exhilarating experience, but be warned: this is not a hike for casual walkers. The low altitude compared to other parts of the Hill Country means that it's very hot and the walk across darkened granite in full sunlight makes it even hotter than normal. The ascents and descents are at times almost vertical and there are fixed ropes to help ease you up and down some especially steep short sections (these ropes aren't strictly needed unless it's been raining, when the rock becomes ice-rink slippery, but most people use them anyway). A guide is a very good idea for this walk (inquire with trekking agencies in Kandy), and children and those with vertigo are advised to give it a miss. If you found the Adam's Peak walk tough, don't attempt this one.

The walk begins from the **Alagalla Tea Factory** (Polaththapitiya) – the nearest train station is **Kadugannawa** – and starts with a gentle amble through tea estates. The path then veers off uphill and makes its way through a secondary forest full of monkeys. After half an hour of this, the trail emerges onto open grassland and things suddenly get much tougher. The trail climbs very sharply and the sun beats down without mercy. At times it's so steep you'll need to use your hands as well as your feet to climb upwards. Eventually, you'll reach the foot of the granite outcrop. A small gap in the rock face can be accessed via a short (5m) fixed rope that hangs out over a now near-vertical drop (there are tremendous views if you're brave enough to turn and look!). Once you're on the **summit**, there's a little more room to breathe and admire the wonderful views of the land falling away all around. From the summit, you stroll along the granite ridge for a few hundred metres before reaching another short, steep drop-off of about 25m. There's another fixed rope here, but it's really not needed unless the rock is wet and slippery. Then you can just amble through cool, shady forest for 20 minutes until you come to another rock outcrop topped by a modern temple. To descend either, retrace your footsteps or, for a longer, harder hike, take the narrow path that veers west down the rock face from just before the temple. This descent is extremely steep and jarring on the legs and is in direct sunlight the entire way. It feels like you're walking in an oven. After 1½ hours of descent, you'll reach a few houses and then the **Gangoda train station**, from where you can get a train back to Kandy (2nd/3rd class Rs 70/35) at 12.40pm, 2.42pm or 6.30pm. In total, allow five hours for this walk and start as early in the day as you can.

Sri Lanka Trekking (p161) in Kandy charges Rs 9000 for a guide, picnic lunch and transport for this walk.

and different kinds of meditation take place throughout the rest of the day. Reservations should be made through the website at least two weeks in advance.

The centre is 24km south of Kandy. It can be reached by bus 633 (catch a Delthota bus via Galaha and get off at Office Junction). From Office Junction, you can walk a steep 3km through tea plantations or take a three-wheeler for Rs 350 to the centre. A three-wheeler or taxi from Kandy costs about Rs 1400 one way.

Amaya Hills AYURVEDA

(☎081-447 4022; www.amayaresorts.com; Heerassagala; facials from US$30, oil massages & steam baths from US$48) The nicest Ayurveda centre in the Kandy area, with professional staff and wonderful massages and treatments – the Udvarthana body scrub is recommended. Try to make a day of it: have lunch and spend a few hours around the stunning pool. Amaya is high in the hills on a winding road. A three-wheeler here from Kandy costs around Rs 600.

Dhamma Kuta Vipassana Meditation Centre MEDITATION

(☎081-238 5774; www.kuta.dhamma.org; Mowbray, Hindagala; donation requested) This centre offers courses from one to 10 days following the SN Goenka system of meditation. Booking ahead is mandatory. There's dorm accommodation with separate male and female quarters.

Take a Mahakanda-bound bus from the clock-tower bus stop in Kandy and get off at the last stop. It's a steep 2km walk.

Sleeping & Eating

As Kandy becomes increasingly congested, the verdant rolling hills around town gain in appeal as a base. There's a growing number of hotels and guesthouses in this highly scenic region.

Restaurants are limited, but most hotels and guesthouses offer meals.

Nisha Tourist Home HOMESTAY **$$**
(☎077-084 9137; nishantha.maldeniya71@gmail.com; 47/9A Riverside, Galaha Rd, Peradeniya; r US$25;) Maintained by a kind family, the rooms in this home are kept clean and have hot-water en suites. The location is very quiet, though quite isolated, so make use of the bikes for rent. Pickups can be arranged from Peradeniya Junction station (3.5km away), cooking lessons are offered, and Nisha is an excellent driver and guide.

★**Kandy House** BOUTIQUE HOTEL **$$$**
(Amunugama Walauwa; ☎081-492 1394; www.thekandyhouse.com; Amunugama Walauwa, Gunnepana; r incl breakfast from US$345; @) Thanks to masses of exotic tropical flora, the air at this divine hotel, once home to a Kandyan chief, literally tastes perfumed. Now fully restored, its nine rooms are furnished with colonial antiques, and service is courtesy of a butler who is assigned to you on arrival. An infinity pool segues to emerald-green rice paddies, and eating here is a real highlight.

Note that no children under 12 are allowed.

Kandy Samadhi Centre BOUTIQUE HOTEL **$$$**
(☎071-454 8279; www.thekandysamadhicentre.com; Kukul Oya Rd, Kandy; s/d from US$145/200;) At this bohemian Ayurvedic and yoga centre 23km from Kandy, mud huts, rooms and pavilions – each furnished with Asian textiles and four-poster beds – are dotted around a forested hillside. Various packages that include treatments and yoga sessions are offered. Food is both organic and vegetarian (dinner US$15), and no alcohol is served.

Getting There & Away

Many people rent a three-wheeler for the day to get around this area; expect to pay around Rs 3000 from central Kandy. A car will be around Rs 6000. Ask at your guesthouse.

Buses operate along the main highways. If you're combining public transport with walking, you'll need to ask the way occasionally, and note: there's a fair amount of walking involved and it does get hot!

Knuckles Range

Parts of Sri Lanka's central mountains are inscribed on Unesco's World Heritage list (where they are known as the Peak Wilderness Protected Area), and the craggy, biodiverse Knuckles Range forms a key part of that recognition. This **massif** is home to pockets of rare montane and cloud forest, and offers fine hiking and birdwatching possibilities. The name 'Knuckles' derives from the mountains' profile, which looks like a closed fist. This rugged highland region remains relatively unknown to foreign visitors and is one of the best areas in the Hill Country to get off the beaten tourist path.

If you are coming here in order to hike, you'll need to be well prepared. A knowledgeable guide is virtually essential.

Hotels in the Knuckles Range can organise short guided hiking trips. In Kandy, contact Sri Lanka Trekking (p161) or Trekking Expeditor (p161). A guide for the high peaks is compulsory, and some serious wet-weather gear and leech protection are vital. For anything more ambitious than a couple of hours' stroll around the foothills, you will need to be totally self-sufficient, with camping equipment and food.

The foothills of the Knuckles are covered in small villages and there are no restrictions on walking here. The high massif, though, is a protected zone and entrance is Rs 750. Tickets cannot be purchased at the gate itself, but they will normally be obtained by your guide from a forestry-department office and the cost included in the overall trekking-package price. The standard trekking package is a two-day tour. On day one you walk around 21km from the eastern boundary of the park and camp overnight; on the following day you walk a further 14km to the western boundary of the park. The standard packages cost €75 per person for one person and €55 per person for two or more people. This includes all food, transport, guiding fees and camping equipment. Bring wet-weather gear no matter what time of year you visit.

Sleeping & Eating

There are some excellent mountain lodges and boutique hotels in this highland area. You'll find several places around the village of Elkaduwa, which is a good base for the Knuckles Range.

Virtually all hotels and guesthouses provide meals; otherwise, eating options are very limited.

Green View HOTEL **$$**
(☎077-781 1881; bluehavtravels@gmail.com; Karagahinna, Elkaduwa; s/d incl breakfast from Rs 2800/3600;) A well-managed lodge, this cheery hillside place has spectacular views of a forested mountain valley. Rooms are clean and plain but showing their age a little. Staff will happily lead you on easy, low-level strolls or much tougher hikes around the edge of the Knuckles Range. Book ahead and they'll pick you up from Kandy.

★**Rangala House** BOUTIQUE HOTEL **$$$**
(☎081-240 0294; www.rangalahouse.com; 92B Bobebila Rd, Makuldeniya, Teldeniya; half-board s/d from US$199/235, studios from US$276;) Located at around 1000m, this gorgeous former tea planter's bungalow enjoys a temperate, sometimes coolish climate on a steep forested hillside surrounded by spice trees. It has three double rooms and a studio for families. You'll love the large living and dining room (with fireplace) and views down to the distant bright lights of Kandy.

Madulkelle Tea & Ecolodge BOUTIQUE HOTEL **$$$**
(☎081-380 1052; www.madulkelle.com; Madulkelle Village; d incl breakfast from US$410;) Definitely glamping not camping, this upmarket lodge's luxe tents are scattered around a verdant hillside, and feature commodious beds, fully equipped bathrooms and wooden writing desks. Stroll around the Madulkelle estate, then relax in the infinity pool, gazing over mountain creases and the deep greens of the surrounding tea plantations.

The main building, containing the grand dining room, is filled with polished antiques and leather armchairs set beside a roaring log fire. Note: the access road is very rough and a high-clearance car is usually necessary.

Getting There & Away

Hiking trips to the Knuckles from Kandy usually include return transport. Otherwise, a tuk-tuk or taxi from Kandy to Elkaduwa should cost Rs 1000 one way. Alternatively, take a bus to Wattegama (from near the clock tower in Kandy), and then catch another to Elkaduwa.

Kitulgala

☎036

West of the road from Kandy to Nuwara Eliya, amid thickly forested hills, Kitulgala has long been a popular adventure-sports centre, as well as a pleasant place to kick back riverside. Most visitors are the young and energetic of Colombo, but foreign visitors are also starting to discover the region's white-water rafting, jungle trekking, birdwatching and cave exploration. Unfortunately, a major new hydroelectric project, scheduled to be completed by 2021, is already having a major impact on river patterns and has been negatively affecting rafting.

The town's other main claim to fame is that David Lean filmed his 1957 Oscar-winning epic *Bridge on the River Kwai* here on the banks of the Kelaniya Ganga.

A few kilometres from Kitulgala is a large **cave system** where 28,500-year-old remains of early humans have been discovered. Many hotels in the area can arrange a guide to the caves.

Sights

Only the concrete foundations of the 'Bridge on the River Kwai' remain. To reach the site, follow the signs from the main road, about 1km from the Plantation Hotel in the direction of Adam's Peak. Wannabe guides will attempt to show you the way but are not necessary. Apparently the actual railway carriages used in the movie now lie at the bottom of the river, after being sunk in an explosive conclusion. You'll have to bring your own scuba gear if you want a look.

Activities

Birdwatching

The area is famous for birdwatching – 23 of Sri Lanka's 27 endemic bird species inhabit the surrounding forest. Rafter's Retreat has the best ornithological guides. A half day of birdwatching is around Rs 7000. Birdwatching generally takes place in the Makandawa Forest, which is the protected forest zone on the opposite side of the river from the village. Entry to the area costs Rs 800 and a boat across the river is Rs 200 (park entry and boat fees are generally included in activity package costs).

White-water Rafting

At the time of research, the Kelaniya Ganga, the river that runs through Kitulgala, offered the best white-water rafting in Sri Lanka. However, the construction of two new dams upstream (scheduled to be finished by 2021) will disrupt the river and impact future rafting trips. Contact Rafter's Retreat or **Borderlands** (☎077-789 9836; www.discoverborderlands.com; per person incl full board US$65; 📶) for the latest situation.

For now, the typical rafting excursion takes in seven Class II to III rapids in 7km for US$25 per person, including transport and lunch. You'll be on the water for around two hours. Some operators also combine river canyoning with a rafting trip.

Almost every hotel can organise rafting trips with over a dozen local operators. All offer pretty similar packages, but not all have insurance – ask to see their papers before you sign up.

Trekking

The sheer hills surrounding Kitulgala are covered in rainforest and the area makes for some decent, but quite strenuous, jungle hikes. You will need a guide, good footwear, waterproofs and leech repellent. Most hotels can arrange a guide and suggest a suitable route; Channa Perera at Rafter's Retreat is the most experienced 'jungle man' in the area and is knowledgable about the local flora and fauna. A half-day trek costs around US$25.

Zip-lining

A small zip-line (US$20) runs from the Rafter's Retreat out over the river and across a small bit of forest.

Sleeping & Eating

There's a good range of accommodation in Kitulgala, but prices are high (perhaps because of its popularity with visitors from Colombo).

Royal River Resort BOUTIQUE HOTEL **$$$**
(☎011-273 2755; www.trioresorts.com; Eduru Ella; s/d incl half board Rs 11,500/13,900; ❄📶🏊) In a remote rainforest location, 6km north of Kitulgala via a rough road, this hotel is fantastically secluded. It has four timber cottages built around, onto and into a series of boulders and waterfalls. The rooms are pleasantly decorated in colonial shades. There's a good restaurant and a sublime river-fed pool.

Rafter's Retreat CABIN **$$$**
(☎031-228 7598; www.raftersretreat.com; s/d incl half board US$75/90; 📶) This old colonial-era bungalow serves as the hub for a rafting and birdwatching outfit that sprawls along the riverbank. The 10 quirky riverside cottages are basic and fan-cooled. You just pull up a blind to see the gushing river. There's a natural river swimming hole right in front of the property.

The breezy riverside restaurant is a great place for a few beers, and jovial owner Channa can organise all manner of tours and activities.

Getting There & Away

It's easy to stop at Kitulgala even if you're travelling by bus. Coming from Colombo, catch the bus to Hatton and get off at Kitulgala (Rs 160). When you're over Kitulgala, flag a bus on to Hatton from the main road (Rs 80). For Nuwara Eliya and Kandy, change in Hatton.

Adam's Peak (Sri Pada)

☎051 / ELEV 2243M

Located in a beautiful area of the southern Hill Country, this lofty peak has sparked the imagination for centuries and been a focus for pilgrimage for more than 1000 years.

It's variously known as Adam's Peak (the place where Adam first set foot on earth after being cast out of heaven), Sri Pada (Sacred Footprint, left by the Buddha as he headed towards paradise), or perhaps most poetically as Samanalakande (Butterfly Mountain; where butterflies go to die). Legends attribute the huge 'footprint' crowning the peak to St Thomas, the early apostle of India, or even Lord Shiva.

The pilgrimage season begins on *poya* day in December and runs until the **Vesak festival** in May. In season, pilgrims and tourists alike make the climb up the countless steps to the top. At other times, the summit's temple can be unused, and is often obscured by clouds.

The peak is accessed from the nearby tourist village of Dalhousie.

Activities

Walking

Perhaps not surprisingly, the only walking most people do around here is the taxing hike up Adam's Peak (p178). But the rolling hills, coloured in the rich green sheen of tea bushes and patches of forest, make for some wonderful short walks (and don't worry: none of these will punish your legs like Adam's Peak!) that amply repay an extra night's stay. The most worthwhile walk from Dalhousie is the 8km circular walk to the **Laxapana Tea Factory** (051-351 9520; www.laxapanatea.com; 6am-4pm Mon-Sat) in the hills just to the north of the town. You can visit the roadside **Mohini waterfalls** on the way. A guide isn't really needed for this walk, as many guesthouses can provide maps and easy-to-follow route descriptions.

A longer trip is to the **Moray waterfalls**, tucked into a pretty, forest-lined gorge, and some nearby tea factories. It's a 24km round trip from Dalhousie, and most people take a three-wheeler at least one way (Rs 1500) and then walk back through the exquisite countryside. There's good swimming in the natural pool at the base of the falls.

Sleeping & Eating

Dalhousie is the best place to start the climb, but accommodation standards are pretty average overall and not great value for money.

Most guesthouses are on your left as you reach Dalhousie.

Dalhousie has simple restaurants, and stores selling snacks. Most guesthouses and hotels offer meals.

PILGRIMAGE ON A POYA DAY

Thinking of climbing Adam's Peak on a *poya* (full moon; p28) day or weekend? Go for it! It'll likely turn out to be one of the most memorable things you do in Sri Lanka. But take note: the last time we climbed the mountain on such a night we got within 800m of the summit and then stood in a queue for nearly three hours. We advanced forward by around only 100m before giving up (as did most other tourists there who were not so spiritually enlightened). We've heard of some travellers taking more than nine hours to reach the summit on a *poya* day. This doesn't mean you should avoid climbing on such days; there's a real carnival-like atmosphere on the mountain, the tea shops are packed, and there's plenty of colour and noise – some Hindu pilgrims even dress up as Shiva himself! Just don't expect to have a silent moment of reflection as the sun rises above the mountains.

Dalhousie

White House HUT **$**

(077-791 2009; Dalhousie; r incl half board Rs 3200-4800;) This place has helpful staff and a pretty riverside location next to a swimming hole with lots of hammocks and easy chairs. Accommodation, ranging from basic to fairly smart rooms, could be better maintained, but all rooms have en suites (with hot water) and are fine for a night or two. Guided walks through tea estates can be organised.

★Hugging Clouds Guesthouse GUESTHOUSE **$$**

(077-686 5392; d incl breakfast Rs 6000;) Creative new five-room guesthouse. The funky art and twisted wooden furnishings make this a memorable place to stay and the chatty staff are very helpful and can organise walks to waterfalls and other nearby attractions. It's close to the trailhead.

Slightly Chilled GUESTHOUSE **$$**

(071-909 8710, 052-205 5502; www.slightly-chilled.tv; r incl half board US$30-55;) One of Dalhousie's best options is Slightly Chilled in name and very chilled in nature. You'll find spacious, comfortable and colourful rooms with polished wooden floors, many with great views of Sri Pada, and there's an airy restaurant. Staff have lots of information on other trails in the area.

Around Adam's Peak

Chances are that after ascending – and, more to the point, descending – Adam's Peak your leg muscles are going to be screaming at you to take them straight off for a well-deserved rest, and what better place to do so than in one of the delightful, luxury tea-estate bungalows that can be found dotted about the beautiful countryside near Adam's Peak? Yes, it's going to cost you a bit, but your legs will love you forever if you splash out on a night or two at one of the following. And once you've let your muscles recover you can force them into some pleasing strolls through the tea estates that carpet the countryside here. Hotels can supply guides and suggest routes.

★Tea Trails HISTORIC HOTEL **$$$**

(Colombo 011-774 5700; www.resplendentceylon.com/teatrails; Dikoya; d incl full board from US$765;) Tea Trails comprises five stunning colonial-style residences built for British

DON'T MISS

CHRIST CHURCH WARLEIGH

If you have a car and driver and are travelling around the edge of the Castlereigh Reservoir, it's well worth making a quick stop at the tiny colonial-era **Christ Church Warleigh** (Dikoya), which is beautifully set among terraced tea fields. Dating back to 1878, the cemetery surrounding the stone church is full of the graves of colonial tea planters, almost all of whom met their maker at a very young age. The church itself is notable for its stained-glass windows that were transported here from the UK and a Bible that dates back to 1879. The most unusual feature, though, is the unique miniature organ with keys made from elephant rib bones. The church is still in use today and services are held every Sunday.

tea-plantation managers. Completely refurbished, the bungalows each have four to six large bedrooms, spacious dining areas, and verandas and gardens with views over rolling tea estates. 'Summerville' is very special indeed, as it's located on a spit of land that juts into the Castlereigh Reservoir.

Rates are all-inclusive (even of laundry). Western and Sri Lankan meals are prepared by a resident chef, along with complimentary drinks (yes, that means alcohol, and single-estate teas). There are self-guided walks through the region's tea-carpeted hills. All bungalows are well stocked with fine books to browse. And after a gourmet dinner, sipping a single-malt whisky by your bungalow's log fire is one of Sri Lanka's unique experiences.

★**Farm Resorts** HISTORIC HOTEL **$$$**
(☎077-695 6520, 051-222 3607; www.thefarmresorts.com; Norton Rd, Dikoya; cottages incl breakfast Rs 22,000-25,000; 📶) These beautifully presented, and very good-value, cottages with attractive furnishings and a stylish touch are in a lovely spot under eucalyptus trees on the edge of the Castlereigh Reservoir. Staff can arrange a boatman for tours on the lake as well as guided tea-estate visits.

The attractive restaurant, also open to non-guests (mains Rs 1500 to Rs 3500), serves excellent Western and Sri Lankan meals.

ℹ Getting There & Away

A taxi from Hatton to Dalhousie costs Rs 2600 and a three-wheeler is Rs 1800. On busy pilgrimage nights the roads to Dalhousie can get clogged with traffic in the early evenings, and it can take hours to cover the final kilometres into town, so try to set off for Dalhousie as early as you can in the day.

BUS

Buses run to Dalhousie from Kandy, Nuwara Eliya and Colombo in the pilgrimage season. Otherwise, you need first to get to Hatton or to Maskeliya, about 20km along the Hatton–Dalhousie road.

Throughout the year there are services to Hatton from Colombo (Rs 270), Kandy (Rs 121) or Nuwara Eliya (Rs 90). There are also limited direct buses from Nuwara Eliya and Colombo to Maskeliya.

There are buses from Hatton to Dalhousie via Maskeliya every 30 minutes in the pilgrimage season (Rs 100, two hours). Otherwise, you have to take a bus from Hatton to Maskeliya (Rs 42, last departure about 6pm) and then another to Dalhousie (Rs 38, last departure about 7pm).

Out-of-pilgrimage-season buses may drop you off in Dalhousie's main square, but during the season buses stop wherever they can find a space.

TRAIN

Hatton is the nearest station to Dalhousie. There are five daily trains between Colombo and Nanu Oya, all via Kandy and Hatton. From Kandy, trains cost Rs 150/85 (2nd/3rd class) and take 2½ to three hours. However, note that delays are common on this line, particularly on pilgrimage-season weekends.

From Nanu Oya, it costs Rs 60/45 (2nd/3rd class) and the journey time is between 1½ and two hours. Advance reservations in either of these classes is Rs 700 and an observation-class seat in either direction is Rs 1000.

Kandy to Nuwara Eliya

The road from Kandy to Nuwara Eliya climbs nearly 1400m as it winds through jade-green tea plantations and reservoirs. The 92km of asphalt allows for plenty of stops at waterfalls and tea outlets. The tea estates and factories along this route are well set up for visitors, but at the same time most of them are aiming more for big tour groups and the experience of visiting them can be less personal than at estates east of Nuwara Eliya.

Kothmale Reservoir (also known as Puna Oya Reservoir) can be seen on the way. It's part of the Mahaweli Development Project and blamed by some locals for

CLIMBING ADAM'S PEAK

The moderately tough, steep hike to the sacred summit of Adam's Peak is a challenge undertaken by many Sri Lankans and travellers from Dalhousie.

During the pilgrimage season the route is illuminated by a sparkling ribbon of lights that is visible from kilometres around and from afar looks like a trail of stars leading into the heavens. Out of season you will need a torch.

The Climb

You can start the 7km climb from Dalhousie soon after dark, as most Sri Lankans do. This will allow you to plod up very slowly and take lots of tea breaks on the way. Alternatively, you can blast to the top and then settle down for a few hours' kip in one of the many pilgrim huts near the summit (there's no charge for staying in these), but do bring a good sleeping bag to keep you warm. The other option is to start at about 2am; if you walk steadily you should be at the summit about an hour before dawn. The climb is up steps most of the way (about 5200 of them, and by the end you'll be cursing each and every one), and on a quiet day you'll reach the top in 2½ to four hours. Start on a *poya* day or a weekend, though, and the throng of pilgrims will add hours and hours to your climb.

From the car park, the slope is gradual for the first half hour, passing under an entrance arch and then by the Japan–Sri Lanka Friendship Dagoba. The pathway gets steeper until it becomes a continuous flight of stairs. There are teahouses all the way to the top, which stay open throughout the night in season, as well as a number of small shrines and temples. The authorities have banned litter, alcohol, tobacco, meat and recorded music, so the atmosphere remains reverential. The last part of the walk is very steep indeed and crowds can often be quite dense on this narrow flight of steps, even on quieter nights.

Some pilgrims prefer to make the longer, more tiring – but equally well-marked and -lit – seven-hour climb from Ratnapura via the Carney Estate because of the greater merit thus gained.

Between June and November, when the pathway isn't illuminated and there aren't many people around, travellers are urged to do the hike at least in pairs. Expect to pay around Rs 1500 for a guide at this time. In season a guide is not needed.

climatic quirks in recent years. **Ramboda Falls** (108m), about 1.5km from the road, is a spectacular double waterfall.

Nearing Nuwara Eliya, the road gains elevation abruptly, passing several tea estates, then roadside stalls overflow with all sorts of veggies and flowers.

Sights

Ambuluwaw Temple TOWER

(Gampola; adult/child Rs 300/150; 8.30am-5pm) Atop a hill high above the scrappy little town of Gampola, the Ambuluwaw Temple is an unusual lighthouse-like tower that spirals towards the heavens. It's become a firm favourite with selfie-obsessed tourists who like to photograph themselves tiptoeing higher and higher up the vertiginous tower.

Despite the tower's relative youth (it opened in 2006), the place has more than a passing resemblance to a decaying multistorey car park, and it feels worryingly as if the merest puff of wind could send the whole thing tumbling to the ground. The views from the top are impressive, though.

A tuk-tuk from Gampola town to the summit costs Rs 1400 return. Otherwise you can drive two-thirds of the way up the mountain and then walk the rest of the way. Tuk-tuks are also available from the car park to the top, but they'll try to charge Rs 1500 return, which is more than you'd pay taking one all the way from town!

Blue Field Tea Estate FACTORY

(https://bluefieldteagarden.com; 8am-4pm Mon-Sat) FREE This large tea estate is 20km north of Nuwara Eliya. Short tours are offered, and there's a decent restaurant too.

Glenloch Tea Estate FACTORY

(052-225 9646; A5 Hwy, Katukithula; 8am-5.30pm) FREE Around 27km north of Nuwara Eliya, this factory offers informative tours explaining cultivation, types of tea, and the drying and packing processes. There's some fine old machinery from the UK still in use. Unlike in many tea factories, photography is allowed here. There's a large cafe and gift shop selling everything and anything tea related as well as Ayurveda items.

The Summit

The summit can be cold, so it's not worth getting there too long before dawn and then sitting around shivering. It's wise to bring a fleece and a thermal top with you.

As dawn illuminates the holy mountain, the diffuse morning light uncovers the Hill Country rising in the east and the land sloping to the coast to the west. Colombo, 65km away, is easily visible on a clear day.

Adam's Peak saves its most breathtaking moment for just after dawn. The sun casts a perfect shadow of the peak onto the misty clouds down towards the coast. As the sun rises higher, this eerie triangular shadow races back towards the peak, eventually disappearing into its base.

Some pilgrims wait for the priests to make a morning offering before they descend. As well as the main shrine containing the rock footprint there are a number of smaller shrines on the summit, so it's worth making time to savour the atmosphere at each.

The Descent

Many people find that the hardest part is coming down. The endless steps can shake the strongest knees, and if your shoes don't fit well, you can add blisters and crushed toes. Walking poles or even just a sturdy stick will make the descent much less jarring on your legs. Take a hat, as the morning sun intensifies quickly. Remember to stretch your legs when you finish; booking a massage is highly recommended too.

Equipment

Definitely wear hiking shoes if you have them or, at a push, good-quality sports shoes. Bring warm clothes and pack plenty of water. If you're in Dalhousie in the pilgrimage season, you'll find stalls at the market selling warm jackets and headgear (although on busy nights the crush of humanity can be so intense that you'll be kept warm simply by the close proximity of so many other people).

Damro Labookellie Tea Factory FACTORY
(http://damrotea.com; A5 Hwy; ⏲8am-5.15pm) FREE On the A5, 11km northwest of Nuwara Eliya, this is a convenient factory to visit as it's right on the roadside. Its tours are very brief, but they do include a free cup of tea. Be warned that many hundreds of visitors stop here in high season and the place can be rammed.

Sleeping & Eating

There are a few hotels along the route, but there's far more choice in Kandy or Nuwara Eliya.

Ecolanka LODGE $$
(☎051-223 3133; www.ecolanka.com; Maussawa Estate, Pundaluoya; incl breakfast s/d from €50/72, cottages from €116; 📶) In a remote location 28km north of Nuwara Eliya, this rustic lodge is just the place to get all off-grid and don your walking boots – you'll find several good trails nearby. Some rooms have shared bathrooms, or book the deluxe cottage for more comfort. There are gorgeous views of central Lanka's rolling hills, and fine nutritious food is prepared.

★**Weir House** BOUTIQUE HOTEL $$$
(☎081-384 5420; www.backofbeyond.lk; Ulapane; incl breakfast r US$110-140, f US$200) Tucked away in a secret valley thick with jungle trees, this boutique guesthouse has four luxuriously appointed rooms with statement art and floor-to-ceiling windows with forest views. Staff can organise tea-estate, spice-farm and village visits, and cooking classes are available. It's an ideal place in which to hide away from the world for a while.

It's a few kilometres south of the town of Gampola near the village of Ulapane and a short detour off the main Kandy–Nuwara Eliya road.

Shopping

Tea Bush TEA
(⏲9am-6pm) This is a veritable shopping mall of all things tea related, and although there's no tea factory or tours here it's a good place to buy a range of brews. There's also a cafe, a small (free) tea museum and views to

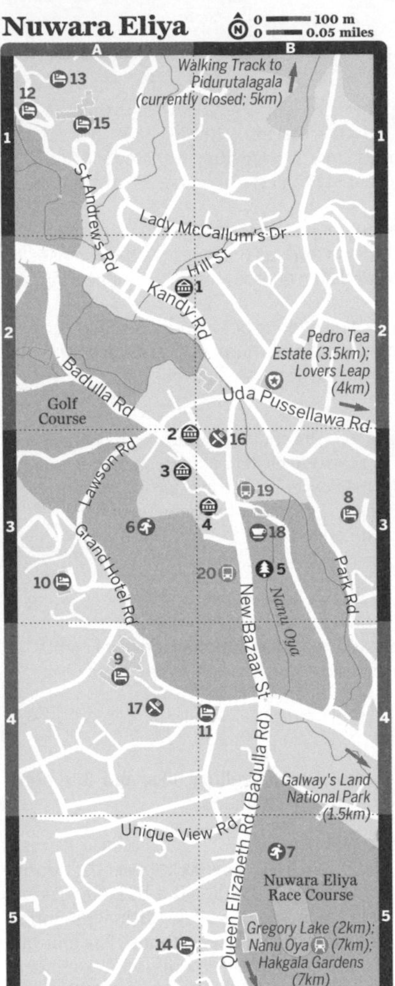

Nuwara Eliya

Sights

1 Cargills Supermarket A2
2 Mackwoods Museum A3
3 Police Superintendent's Office A3
4 Post Office B3
5 Victoria Park B3

Activities, Courses & Tours

6 Nuwara Eliya Golf Club A3
7 Royal Turf Club B5

Sleeping

8 Ferncliff B3
9 Grand Hotel A4
10 Hill Club A3
11 Hotel Glendower B4
12 King Fern Cottage A1
13 Oatlands A1
14 Single Tree Hotel A5
15 St Andrew's Hotel A1

Eating

16 De Silva Food Centre B3
17 Grand Indian A4
Hill Club (see 10)
Nuwara Eliya Golf Club Dining Room (see 6)

Drinking & Nightlife

High Tea at St Andrew's (see 15)
High Tea at the Grand (see 9)
High tea at the Hill Club (see 10)
18 Themparadu B3

Transport

19 CTB Bus Station B3
20 Private Bus Station B3

the Ramboda waterfalls, which you can walk to in five minutes from the other side of the road tunnel.

Getting There & Away

Buses (regular/express Rs 135/270, 3½ hours) connect Kandy and Nuwara Eliya every 45 minutes or so.

Nuwara Eliya

052 / POP 27,500 / ELEV 1889M

Sri Lankans often refer to Nuwara Eliya as 'Little England', and it's true that in places this genteel highland community does have a rose-tinted, vaguely British-country-village feel to it, with its colonial-era bungalows, Tudor-style hotels, well-tended hedgerows and pretty gardens. Indeed, Nuwara Eliya was once *the* favoured cool-climate escape for the hard-working and hard-drinking English and Scottish pioneers of Sri Lanka's tea industry.

A recent construction boom has blighted the scene to a degree, and the dusty and bustling centre is a thoroughly Sri Lankan urban tangle, but Nuwara Eliya still makes a fine base for a few days' relaxation. The verdant surrounding countryside of tea plantations, carefully tended vegetable plots and craggy hills is highly scenic and the town has a lot more character than some popular tourist towns in the Hill Country. To get the most out of a visit to

Nuwara Eliya you should treat yourself to a night in one of the town's colonial hotels, play a round of golf or a few frames of billiards, make time each afternoon for 'high tea' and generally just soak up the town's unique bygone heritage.

A rainy-day, misty-mountain atmosphere blankets the town from November to February, so don't come expecting tropical climes (you'll need a thick jumper in the evenings). But during April's spring release the town is crowded with domestic holidaymakers enjoying horse racing and sports-car hill climbs, and celebrating the Sri Lankan New Year. The cost of accommodation escalates wildly, transport into and out of town can be booked solid, and Nuwara Eliya becomes a busy, busy party town.

History

Originally an uninhabited system of forests and meadows in the shadow of Pidurutalagala (aka Mt Pedro; 2524m), Nuwara Eliya became a singularly British creation, having been 'discovered' by colonial officer John Davy in 1819 and chosen as the site for a sanatorium a decade later.

Later the district became known as a spot where 'English' vegetables and fruits, such as lettuce and strawberries, could be successfully grown for consumption by the colonists. Coffee was one of the first crops grown here, but after the island's coffee plantations failed due to disease, the colonists switched to tea. The first tea leaves harvested in Sri Lanka were planted at Loolecondera Estate, in the mountains between Nuwara Eliya and Kandy. As tea experiments proved successful, the town quickly found itself becoming the Hill Country's 'tea capital', a title that endures.

As elsewhere in the Hill Country, most of the labourers on the tea plantations were Tamils, brought from southern India by the British. Although the descendants of these 'Plantation Tamils' (as they are called to distinguish them from Tamils in northern Sri Lanka) have usually stayed out of the ethnic strife that has rocked Jaffna and the North, there have been occasional outbreaks of tension between the local Sinhalese and Tamils. The town was partly ransacked during the 1983 riots.

At nearby Hakgala there is a significant Muslim population, but internecine strife is not a problem.

Sights

Victoria Park PARK

(adult/child Rs 300/150; ⏲7am-6pm) This is one of the country's most attractive, and best-maintained, town parks. A stroll around its paths, past manicured lawns, is a pleasure. The park comes alive with flowers around March to May, and August and September. It's also home to quite a number of Hill Country bird species, including the Kashmir flycatcher, Indian pitta and grey tit.

Look out for the plaques erected beneath some of the trees commemorating events in the life of George V.

At the far end of the park are a small playground and a miniature train.

Galway's Land National Park NATIONAL PARK

(Hawaeliya; adult/child Rs 1800/972; ⏲6am-6pm) One of Sri Lanka's newest (2007) and smallest (29 hectares) national parks, Galway's Land is a dense patch of montane forest a couple of kilometres east of town. It is renowned for its birdlife, including seven Sri Lankan endemic species, as well as giant squirrels, wild boars, barking deer and other mammals. There's very little on-site information, but there's a 2km-long walking trail from the ticket office. Add 8% VAT to ticket prices.

Lake Gregory LAKE

(entry Rs 300; ⏲8am-6pm) This lake is popular with domestic tourists, who enjoy strolling the 5km-long circular footpath and taking out a swan-shaped **pedal boat** (Rs 2500 for 30 minutes). However, be warned that jet skis and motorboats (Rs 4000 for 30 minutes) disturb the peace on weekends, and during holiday times expect big crowds and funfairs. There are picnic tables, a small restaurant and a snack bar.

Mackwoods Museum MUSEUM

(☎052-222 4965; 3rd fl, Queen Elizabeth Plaza, Badulla Rd; ⏲9am-6pm) FREE This small town-centre museum, owned by the Mackwoods Estate, is a good place to start a Nuwara Eliya tea tour. Among the displays of old tea-processing equipment is a miniature 'tea factory' where visitors can have a go at drying and sorting their own leaves. There's also a shop and a lovely tea room.

Around Nuwara Eliya

Hakgala Gardens GARDENS

(adult/child Rs 2000/1000; ⏲7am-6pm) These attractive gardens, 10km southeast of Nuwara

DON'T MISS

COLONIAL BUILDINGS

Nuwara Eliya has a number of colonial-era buildings that are worth checking out.

The pink-brick, Tudor-style **post office** (Badulla Rd) stands in the town centre. It was built in 1894 and is notable for its distinctive clock tower. Nuwara Eliya's branch of the nationwide **Cargills Supermarket** (90 Kandy Rd; ⏲8am-9pm) still occupies the same 1898 building it's always been in. The signs outside still advertise gramophones and suiting services (good luck finding them inside, though!). The **police superintendent's office** (Badulla Rd; no photos) is housed within another impressive late-19th-century building.

Eliya, are a peaceful retreat. Highlights include a fine rose garden, a Japanese garden, an orchid collection, cedars and giant cypresses. Planting season is between January and late March, and at these times the gardens don't really look their best.

To get here, take a Welimada-bound bus (Rs 24, 20 minutes).

Seetha Amman Temple HINDU TEMPLE
(A5 Hwy, Sita Eliya) FREE This colourful Hindu temple, 7km southeast of Nuwara Eliya, is said to mark the spot where Sita was held captive by the demon king Rawana, and where she prayed daily for Rama to come and rescue her. On the rock face across the stream are circular depressions said to be the footprints of Rawana's elephant.

Lovers Leap VIEWPOINT
From the Pedro Tea Estate, take a very enjoyable 5km (round-trip) walk to Lovers Leap, an impressive waterfall.

From the tea factory, cross the main road and follow the signs to the tea manager's bungalow along the dirt road. At the first crossroads go left and at the three-way junction take the middle path until, after about 15 minutes, you hit a dirt parking area. A foot-only track heads left through the tea gardens towards the forest and a rock face. Follow this trail and, just beyond the small Shiva shrine, you'll see the spluttering waterfalls.

Activities

The Grand Hotel, St Andrew's Hotel, Hill Club and Hotel Glendower all have snooker rooms (see p184). The Hill Club also has four clay tennis courts.

Nuwara Eliya Golf Club GOLF
(☎052-223 2835; www.nuwaraeliyagolfclub.com; green fees Rs 6800-8300, club & shoe hire Rs 3750; ⏲6am-6pm) It didn't take the tea planters long to lay out land for drives and putts in their holiday town: this golf club was founded in 1889. The course is beautifully kept and has a retinue of languid dogs guarding more than a few of the greens. Watch out for thieving crows, which pinch golf balls!

As with most golf clubs, a certain standard of dress applies (shirts and trousers or shorts of a 'respectable' length). The club has a convivial wood-lined bar and a billiard room (open to all) that absolutely shouldn't be missed.

Royal Turf Club HORSE RIDING
(www.royalturfclub.com; Nuwara Eliya Race Course) The Royal Turf Club hosts horse racing at the 1875-vintage Nuwara Eliya Race Course. The most important event every year is the Governor's Cup, held over the April Sinhala and Tamil New Year season.

Cycling

There are steep dirt trails radiating into the hills from the outskirts of town. Ask at the Single Tree Hotel about mountain-bike rental (Rs 1250 to Rs 1500). A relatively challenging but undeniably spectacular day trip is through the verdant blanket of tea plantations to the Damro Labookellie Tea Factory (p179). There are a few hills to climb, but the reward of swooping downhill makes it worthwhile.

Hiking

Sri Lanka's highest mountain, **Pidurutalagala** (2524m), also known as Mt Pedro, rises behind the town. Since the April 2019 terrorist attacks in Sri Lanka the mountain has been out of bounds (there's a high-security communications centre on the summit). However, at the time of research rumours were circulating that the walking trail and road up the mountain may reopen to the public.

An alternative walk is up **Single Tree Hill** (2100m), which is a two-hour return hike. Walk south on Queen Elizabeth Rd, go up Haddon Hill Rd as far as the communications tower and then take the left-hand path. Guesthouses can supply you with a rudimentary map. For a longer variation walk first to Single Tree Hill and then cross through the forest to **Santhipura village**, the highest village in the country. There's a viewpoint just above the village (Rs 40), but you won't see anything more from there than from anywhere else on the way up. Allow at least three hours. A guide (Rs 8000) is a good idea.

For longer hikes, ask at the Single Tree Hotel.

Sleeping

Staying in a colonial-style hotel, revelling in the heritage ambience, is one of Sri Lanka's unique experiences, and even if you normally stick religiously to budget hotels it's worth trying to build a night or two in such a place into your travel budget. It really will make the Nuwara Eliya experience worthwhile. That said, don't expect great value for money and note that around Sri Lankan New Year (April) room rates rocket in price.

You'll need blankets at almost any time of year. Some hotels light log fires on chilly nights – you won't find a toastier way to keep warm.

There aren't many backpacker-oriented guesthouses.

King Fern Cottage GUESTHOUSE **$**
(077-358 6284; 203/1A St Andrews Rd; r Rs 3200-6500;) A quirky place to stay, King Fern is a minimalist's nightmare with its clashing colours, garish bedspreads, huge handmade beds and logwood tables. However, for those of an artistic persuasion, somehow it all works. The setting is good, in a timber pavilion beside a bubbling stream. Call for free pickup from Nanu Oya station.

The owner is a musician and there's live music most nights.

★ **Heidi's Home** GUESTHOUSE **$$**
(077-769 9042; 12A Glen Field; d incl breakfast US$50-70;) You won't forget this place in a hurry! It's a tie-dye, psychedelic hippy fantasy festooned in art, colour and flowers – the curtains in the reception area are made from peacock feathers and the gardens are a veritable botanic maze. Each of the highly individual rooms is kept spotlessly clean and high-quality furnishings are used throughout.

It's run by a friendly family and dinner is available on request. It's at the far end of Gregory Lake, off Badulla Rd. Book ahead.

Villa Tea Fields HERITAGE HOTEL **$$**
(071-315 3186; www.villateafields.com; 13/111 Badulla Rd; d incl breakfast Rs 10,000;) Two colonial-style tea planters bungalows set delightfully among fields of tea. Some of the rooms are wood lined and feel like alpine ski chalets, while others have free-standing bathtubs. All are spotless. There's an attractive dining room. It's a couple of kilometres beyond the end of Gregory Lake and a short drive from town.

Single Tree Hotel GUESTHOUSE **$$**
(052-222 3009; singletreehtl@sltnet.lk; 178 Haddon Hill Rd; s/d/tr US$30/35/40;) This popular travellers' guesthouse is spread over two neighbouring buildings, with a sociable vibe and helpful staff. Rooms, some with lots of wood trim, are a shade pricey and pretty functional, but the bed linen is fresh and the place is clean. The switched-on owners offer lots of good tours of the region, and rent bikes (Rs 1250/1500 per half day/day).

★ **Ferncliff** BOUTIQUE HOTEL **$$$**
(072-231 9443; www.ferncliff.lk; 7/10 Wedderburn Rd; r incl breakfast US$182;) Set in spacious lawned grounds, this colonial-era bungalow is straight out of a period drama – even the sprucely turned-out staff hovering in the background play their parts perfectly. There are just six spacious rooms, each with modish en suites, and you'll love the guests' lounge complete with log fire. Dining here is excellent, with delicious, filling meals.

WORTH A TRIP

PEDRO TEA ESTATE

To see where your morning cuppa originates, head to the **Pedro Tea Estate** (Rs 250; 8am-5pm Mon-Sat, to 4.30pm Sun), about 3.5km east of Nuwara Eliya on the way to Kandapola. You can take a 20-minute guided tour of the factory, originally built in 1885 and still packed with 19th-century engineering. However, due to the type of tea produced here (a very light tea), processing only takes place at night, when it's colder, so you're unlikely to see much action.

A three-wheeler from Nuwara Eliya should cost Rs 430 return, including waiting time. Alternatively, you could hop on a Ragalla-bound bus (Rs 15) from the main bus station in Nuwara Eliya.

★Hill Club HERITAGE HOTEL $$$
(052-222 2653; www.hillclubsrilanka.lk; 29 Grand Hotel Rd; r incl breakfast from US$130;) Established in 1876 (though the current building dates to the 1930s) as a British gentlemen's club, the Hill Club is heavily redolent of King and Empire. Rooms have recently been given a long-overdue makeover, but they retain many original features. This all adds up to make the Hill Club the most authentic colonial experience in town.

Oatlands BOUTIQUE HOTEL $$$
(052-222 2445; www.jetwinghotels.com/oatlands; d incl breakfast from US$120;) This colonial-era bungalow has been immaculately restored and is one of the best heritage properties in town. The four guest rooms have polished-wood furnishings, floral curtains, and walls decorated with oil paintings of the local birdlife. There's a formal dining room and a lounge with an open fire. It all comes across like an upmarket English B&B.

It's run by the Jetwing group and guests can use all the facilities of neighbouring big-sister property St Andrew's.

St Andrew's Hotel HERITAGE HOTEL $$$
(052-222 2441, 052-222 3031; www.jetwinghotels.com; 10 St Andrews Rd; s/d incl breakfast from US$205/235;) North of town, on a beautifully groomed rise overlooking the golf course, this striking colonial residence was once a planters' club. Today it's a luxurious, carefully renovated heritage hotel, well managed by the Jetwing group. Highlights include a 1920s-style cocktail bar, a library filled with dusty books and a roaring log fire, a billiards room and a decent restaurant.

Grand Hotel HERITAGE HOTEL $$$
(052-222 2881; https://thegrandhotelnuwaraeliya.com; Grand Hotel Rd; r/ste incl breakfast from US$220/277;) This huge mock-Tudor edifice has immaculate lawns, a reading lounge and an impressive, partly open dining terrace. Rooms are comfortable and well equipped, but they lack the character of other heritage accommodation in Nuwara Eliya – that's because much of the hotel is actually an extension. Facilities are good, including a gym and a wood-panelled snooker room.

Hotel Glendower HISTORIC HOTEL $$$
(052-222 2501; www.hotelglendower.com; 5 Grand Hotel Rd; r incl breakfast from Rs 6500;) This rambling colonial building has bundles of South Asian–style olde-worlde English charm, thanks to its terrific bar, lounge, billiard rooms and garden (complete with croquet set). Recent, ongoing upgrades to the rooms make it a very good-value option for those searching for a little nostalgia combined with comfort.

Around Nuwara Eliya

Stashed away among the tea estates around Nuwara Eliya are some fabulous places to stay. Ideally, you'll have your own transport if you stay at one of these.

Highest Village Bungalow GUESTHOUSE $
(077-617 1208, 052-205 1938; highestvillagebungalow@yahoo.com; 222 School Rd, Shanthipura; r Rs 3000;) Run by a very hospitable family, this charming little guesthouse is located up in the hills, 4km northwest of town, in a mountain village said to be the highest in Sri Lanka. There are fine views, good local walks, excellent food and clean rooms. Call for free pickup from the town centre.

★Heritance Tea Factory BOUTIQUE HOTEL $$$
(052-555 5000; www.heritancehotels.com; Kandapola; r incl breakfast from US$170;) High in mist-wrapped hills 13km northeast of Nuwara Eliya, this unique place has been built into and around a century-old tea factory. Blurring the line between museum and luxury hotel, much of the factory machinery is still in situ and has been incorporated into the design. Rooms are stately and plush and have heating. Service is first rate.

There are two restaurants (one inside an old steam-train carriage) serving some of the best meals in the hills. Note: there's a pretty strict dress code for dinner.

Langdale HOMESTAY $$$
(052-492 4959; www.amayaresorts.com; Radetta, Nanu Oya; d incl breakfast US$200;) For the ultimate luxury 'homestay', try this offering from the Amaya chain. It's a converted old colonial building set, of course, in a tea estate, around 11km west of Nuwara Eliya on the road to Hatton. It all feels like a very posh homestay and the service is excellent. You'll love the grass tennis court and croquet lawn.

Eating

Dining options are surprisingly limited. You'll find cheap options in the town centre, but for dinner you'll probably want to eat at your guesthouse or at one of the ritzier hotel eateries.

DON'T MISS

HIGH TEA

The clink of teacups, plates of dainty cakes and sandwiches, and a view over expansive parkland – nobody should miss high tea in Nuwara Eliya. All the main colonial-style hotels serve high tea, though in each the ceremony is a little different. The most popular place is the tea room at the **Grand Hotel** (☎052-222 2881; www.tangerinehotels.com; Grand Hotel Rd; high tea Rs 1800; ⏲3.30-6pm). At 3.30pm sharp, waiters in white livery unveil bulging plates of perfectly groomed sandwiches and cakes, which are washed down with a vast selection of teas. Cheaper and quieter is high tea at **St Andrew's Hotel** (☎052-222 2441, 052-222 3031; www.jetwinghotels.com; 10 St Andrew's Rd; Rs 1200; ⏲3-6pm). If the weather's fine you can enjoy your tea and scones on the large lawns. However, as good as these two places are, perhaps the most authentically colonial place to have high tea is the grande dame of Nuwara Eliya hotels: the **Hill Club** (☎052-222 2653; www.hillclubsrilanka.lk; 29 Grand Hotel Rd; US$25; ⏲3-6pm). High tea here requires 45 minutes' notice and costs more than at the other two hotels, but the setting simply can't be beaten.

★ Nuwara Eliya Golf Club Dining Room INTERNATIONAL $$$
(☎052-222 2835; www.nuwaraeliyagolfclub.com; Nuwara Eliya Golf Club; menu from Rs 1050; ⏲12.30-3pm & 6.30-11pm) One of the finest – and most authentic – colonial experiences in Nuwara Eliya is a visit to the town's golf club (p182) for a drink at the dusty wood-panelled bar or a meal of classic bland English cuisine, such as lamb chops with mint sauce (though a few Asian dishes are sneaking in) in the similarly atmospheric restaurant.

★ Hill Club INTERNATIONAL $$$
(☎052-222 2653; 29 Grand Hotel Rd; set menu US$25; ⏲7-10.30pm) Dinner at the Hill Club is an event in itself. The menu focuses on traditional English dishes such as roast beef with all the trimmings and rich puddings – in cuisine terms it's far from sophisticated, but it'll be familiar (to homesick Brits at least). The whole thing is carried off with faded colonial panache. All diners must wear formal attire.

Grand Indian INDIAN $$$
(https://thegrandhotelnuwaraeliya.com/culinary-dining; Grand Hotel Rd; mains Rs 800-1300; ⏲noon-3.30pm & 6.30-10pm; 📶) This is far and away the town's favourite restaurant, so much so that in the evenings you often have to wait for a table. The food here is the rich, delicious fare of northern India; try the *palek paneer* (puréed spinach with fresh cheese) or the tandoori chicken.

Indian Summer INDIAN $$$
(☎052-222 4511; www.indiansummerlk.com; Badulla Rd; meals from Rs 1000; ⏲9am-9.45pm; 📶) The sign says 'fusion cuisine', but this smart restaurant with views over Lake Gregory is best for authentic North Indian curries. Prices are quite high, but service is efficient, flavours are authentic and the attractive premises are comfortable. No alcohol is served.

🍷 Drinking & Nightlife

Several colonial hotels have fine bars that are perfect for an evening G&T, including the Hill Club, St Andrew's and Glendower. The bar of the Nuwara Eliya Golf Club is also a wildly atmospheric place for a drink.

Themparadu CAFE
(☎077-883 1777; Victoria Park; mains Rs 300-500; ⏲9.30am-8.30pm) This colourful place festooned in dream catchers and with a lovely parkside setting is immensely popular with foreigners. Even so, the simple meals (noodles, curries and burgers) are only average, so we'd recommend it more as a place to get a juice or tea. Off New Bazaar St.

ℹ Information

Police (Jayathilaka Mawatha) Centrally located.

ℹ Getting There & Away

Over the Sri Lankan New Year holiday period in April, half the population of the island seems to decamp for Nuwara Eliya. Public transport into and out of the town can be booked solid and the approach roads can become clogged with traffic. Our advice? Avoid Nuwara Eliya at this time.

BUS

The government CTB bus station is by the main roundabout in the town centre, off New Bazaar St. The **private bus station** (New Bazaar St) is just up the road. There are buses to/from the following destinations:

TEA ESTATES ROAD TRIP

If you have a car and driver, an enjoyable 100km half-day driving tour can be made through the beautiful countryside to the west of Nuwara Eliya. Along the way you can marvel at waterfalls, coo over hillsides carpeted in tea bushes and stop at a couple of tea factories.

1 Talawakelle

From Nuwara Eliya drive west downhill to the train station at Nanu Oya and then continue on to the small, predominately Hindu town of Talawakelle. The scenery on this road is a nonstop montage of tightly terraced tea fields splayed across the hills.

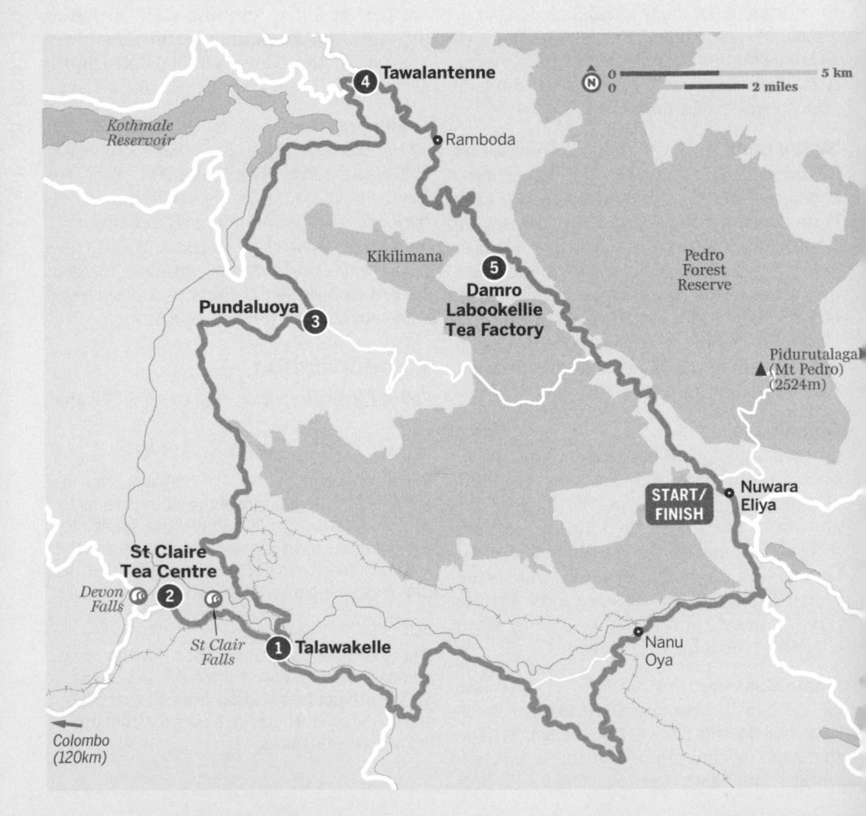

Duration/Distance Half-day 100km / 62 miles

Great for... Food & Drink, Outdoors

Best Time to Go November to December for clear views.

DRINKING TEA

Although black tea is fairly forgiving, there are still right and wrong ways to prepare a brew.

- Use fresh water and boil it (water that's been boiling for a while or that was previously boiled gives a flat-tasting cup of tea).
- Too accustomed to tea bags? With loose tea, it's one teaspoon per average-size cup, plus one extra spoonful if you're making a pot.
- Let the tea brew. It takes three to five minutes for the tea to fully release its flavour.
- Conversely, once the tea is brewed, toss the tea leaves, whether they were loose or in a tea bag. Tea leaves quickly become bitter once brewed.
- For milk tea, pour the milk into the cup and then add the tea: the flavours mix better.

2 St Clair Tea Centre

From Talawakelle continue west a short way to the **St Clair Tea Centre** (☎077-344 2160; http://stclairstea.com; Hatton-Nuwara Eliya Rd; ⏲8am-6pm) and the nearby **St Clair Falls** and **Devon Falls.** You can enjoy a cuppa in the gardens of the tea centre while admiring the Devon Falls.

3 Pundaluoya

Return to Talawakelle and take the minor road that twists and turns north to the small town of Pundaluoya. Scenically this is by far the most impressive part of the drive. The road twists and turns like a drunken serpent and at one point is merely a notch high up on a cliff face.

4 Blue Field Tea Estate

Continue north to **Tawalantenne** on the main Kandy–Nuwara Eliya road and follow the road back to Nuwara Eliya, stopping off at the Blue Field Tea Estate (p178).

5 Damro Labookellie Tea Factory

It's only a short drive eastward along the Kandy–Nuwara Eliya road to another major tea factory (and yes, another excuse for a cup of tea), the Damro Labookellie Tea Factory (p179). Afterwards, continue back into Nuwara Eliya.

Destination	Price	Duration	Frequency
Colombo	normal Rs 272, intercity express Rs 600	6hr	every 45min
Bandarawela	Rs 110	3hr	4 daily
Hatton	normal Rs 95, intercity express Rs 130	2hr	7 daily
Kandy	normal Rs 135, intercity express Rs 270	3½hr	every 30min
Welimada	Rs 73	1hr	every 30min

TRAIN

Nuwara Eliya is served by the Nanu Oya train station, 9km along the road towards Hatton and Colombo. Most Nuwara Eliya accommodation will pick you up – often for free – if you have already booked. A taxi from the station is around Rs 800 and a three-wheeler is Rs 400 to Rs 500.

A 1st-class observation-carriage seat is Rs 1000 to Rs 1500 depending on the exact train you catch. The limited number of seats in this class are in high demand, so try to book ahead. Not all trains have a 1st-class carriage. A 2nd-class reserved seat is Rs 700 to anywhere between Kandy and Badulla.

Destination	Price (2nd/3rd class)	Duration (hr)	Frequency (per day)
Badulla	Rs 190/105	3¼-5	5
Bandarawela	Rs 90/50	2-3	5
Colombo	Rs 380/215	6-7½	4
Ella	Rs 150/80	2½-3	5
Haputale	Rs 100/55	1½	5
Hatton	Rs 80/45	1½	6
Kandy	Rs 160/90	4-5	4

Haputale

057 / POP 5496 / ELEV 1580M

Perched at the southern edge of the Hill Country, the largely Tamil town of Haputale clings to a long, narrow mountain ridge with the land falling away steeply on both sides. On a clear day you can view the south coast from this ridge, and at night the Hambantota lighthouse pulses in the distance. On a not-so-clear day, great swaths of mist cling magnetically to the hillsides. Either way, Haputale is perhaps the most impressively situated town in the country.

The scruffy town centre is a dusty ribbon of traffic, three-wheelers and small-scale commerce. But take a short walk and you'll be rewarded with extraordinary views as the land cascades downward on either side of the ridge and quiet country roads or walking trails lead to tea estates, viewpoints, forests and monasteries.

Haputale is also a useful base for trips to Horton Plains; guesthouses arrange vans for Rs 4500 per person.

Haputale today mainly reflects the influence of Sinhalese and Tamil cultures, but the legacy of the British tea planters also lives on. Tea estates blanket the hillsides, punctuated by graceful planters' bungalows, all enveloped in a damp and heavy climate that must have made the British settlers feel right at home. The pretty Anglican church (St Andrew's) on the Bandarawela road has a graveyard filled with poignant memories of earlier times.

Sights & Activities

★Lipton's Seat VIEWPOINT

(person/vehicle Rs 100/100; 5.30am-5.30pm) The Lipton's Seat lookout is one of Sri Lanka's most impressive viewpoints. However, you must get there early in the morning (before 9am), otherwise the cloud will almost certainly have risen off the coastal plains and there'll be nothing at all to see. The Scottish tea baron Sir Thomas Lipton used to survey his burgeoning empire from here, and today it's said you can see across emerald hills and tea estates to no fewer than seven provinces.

Although you can hike to the lookout from the Dambatenne Tea Factory, a climb of about 8km through lush tea plantations, most people drive up and stroll leisurely back down through the tea estates. Look forward to the company of Tamil tea pickers going off to work as you walk. Driving up and walking back also ensures you'll be there early enough to see the view. Tuk-tuks charge around Rs 2000 return from Haputale or Rs 1000 return from the Dambatenne Tea Factory. At the viewpoint are an overpriced cafe and a statue of Sir Thomas.

★Dambatenne Tea Factory FACTORY

(Rs 250; 8am-6pm) This popular tea factory was built in 1890 by Sir Thomas Lipton, one

Haputale

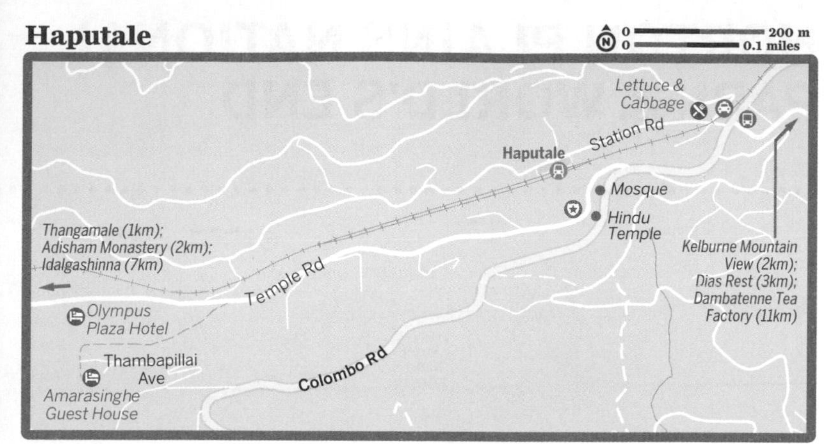

of the most famous figures in tea history. The 20-minute tour through the works is an education on the processes involved in the fermentation, rolling, drying, cutting, sieving and grading of tea. On Sunday no picking takes place, which means that on Monday there's often no processing and thus little to see.

Dambatenne is 9km northeast of Haputale. Buses (Rs 28, 20 minutes) from Haputale pass the factory every 30 minutes. A three-wheeler one way/return costs Rs 600/1000 from Haputale.

Adisham Monastery MONASTERY
(057-226 8030; www.adisham.org; adult/child Rs 150/50; 9am-4.30pm Sat & Sun, poya days & school holidays) This beautiful Benedictine monastery once belonged to tea planter Sir Thomas Lester Villiers. To recreate his English lifestyle, he developed some country-cottage gardens, which are still enchanting visitors today. Inside, you can see the living room and the library, which is filled from floor to ceiling with dusty tomes. If you like the monastery so much you want to stay, well, you can: there's a small **guesthouse** (r incl full board adult/child Rs 3000/1500). No photography is permitted inside the building.

Thangamale NATURE RESERVE
This woodland west of town is called a bird sanctuary, but it's more of a highland forest with a pleasant ridgetop walking trail. You can access the reserve from the Adisham Monastery, from where a path leads west through the reserve to Idalgashinna, 4.3km away.

Hiking

Aside from the popular walk from Lipton's Seat to the Dambatenne Tea Factory there are a number of other walking trails in the area. One simple one that offers spectacular views involves taking the train to **Idalgashinna**, 8km west of Haputale. Walk back beside the train tracks, enjoying a view of the terrain falling away on both sides.

Some visitors hike along the train lines from Haputale to **Pattipola** (14km, an all-day hike), the highest train station in Sri Lanka. From Pattipola you can continue on foot or via tuk-tuk to Ohiya train station, and from there to the Horton Plains.

Sleeping & Eating

For many years Haputale played second fiddle as a tourist destination to nearby Ella and that was reflected in the town's fairly poor crop of guesthouses and few dining options. But, as Ella has become increasingly overdeveloped, more and more visitors are discovering the delights of Haputale. This increase in tourist traffic has led to most of the guesthouses getting a much-needed makeover, and now there's even a good place to eat – Haputale is on the up!

★**Amarasinghe Guest House** HOMESTAY $
(057-226 8175; agh777@sltnet.lk; Thambapillai Ave; r Rs 2500-3500;) This orderly, well-run family guesthouse in a tranquil location (with no views) has been in business for decades. There are five superb-value new rooms with a contemporary finish, plus three older units, all well presented and clean. The kindly owner will pick you up from the train

HORTON PLAINS NATIONAL PARK & WORLD'S END

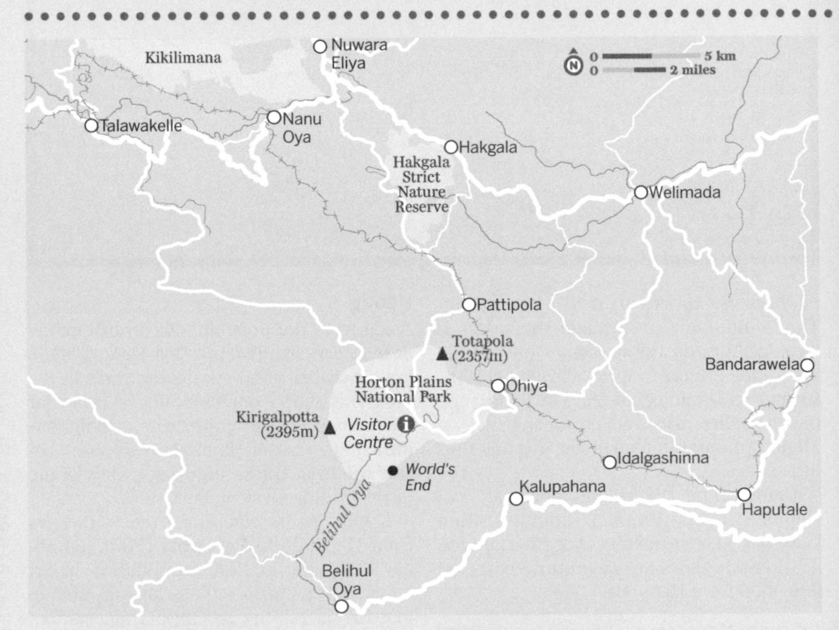

HORTON PLAINS NATIONAL PARK

The 'plains' form an undulating plateau over 2000m high, covered by wild grasslands and interspersed with patches of thick forest, rocky outcrops, waterfalls and lakes. The surprising diversity of the landscape is matched by the wide variety of wildlife, although many of the larger animals are very elusive. Birdwatchers will be well rewarded.

This stunning national park is one of the few in Sri Lanka where visitors can walk on their own (on designated trails). Although the main focus of the park is on World's End, don't underestimate the joy of the walk across the grassland plains. Longer and more challenging walks up Mt Kirigalpotta and Mt Totapola are also possible.

Almost every guesthouse in Nuwara Eliya and Haputale operates trips to Horton Plains and World's End; expect to pay Rs 4000 or 4500 respectively. Park fees are not included and must be paid at the **National Park Office** (6am-6pm) a couple of kilometres before **Farr Inn**. The last tickets are sold at 4pm.

WORLD'S END

The Horton Plains plateau comes to a sudden stop at World's End, a stunning escarpment that plunges 880m and offers incredible views of the lowlands far below. The walk here from the car park and visitor centre at Farr Inn is 4km, but the trail then loops back to Baker's Falls (2km) and continues round to the entrance (another 3.5km). The 9.5km round trip takes a leisurely three hours.

Unless you get there early, the view from World's End is often obscured by mist, particularly during the rainy season from April to September.

Guides at the national park office expect about Rs 2000. A guide isn't really needed if you're just walking to World's End because the route is so obvious, but a good guide can explain a lot about the plants and animals found in the park. Solo women may also want to consider hiring one for safety. Two guides who are genuinely enthusiastic about the park and unusually knowledgable about the area's fauna and flora are **Mr Nimal Herath** (077-618 9842; hrthnimal@gmail.com) and **Mr**

Horton Plains National Park is an eerie, cold and bleak but starkly beautiful highland plateau with excellent hikes in the shadows of Sri Lanka's second- and third-highest mountains, Kirigalpotta (2395m) and Totapola (2357m).

Kaneel Rajanayeka (☎077-215 9583; nuwaraeliyatrekkingclub@hotmail.com). They tend to sell whole packages including transport to and from the park and a picnic lunch.

Wear strong and comfortable walking shoes, a hat and sunglasses. Bring sunscreen, food and water. Ask your guesthouse to prepare a breakfast package for you, and reward yourself with an alfresco breakfast once you reach World's End. The weather can change very quickly on the plains – one minute it can be sunny and clear, the next chilly and misty. Bring a few extra layers of warm clothing.

It is forbidden to leave the paths, which can be slippy and tough to negotiate in places. There are no safety rails around World's End and there have been accidents where people have fallen to their deaths. If you have young children with you, keep a very firm grip on them as you approach the cliff edge.

Do be aware that in season this is a very popular walk. It's not uncommon to have several hundred people walk to World's End each morning! Try to avoid Sundays and public holidays, when it can get even more crowded.

FARR INN

A local landmark, Farr Inn was a hunting lodge for high-ranking British colonial officials, but it's now a visitor centre with displays on the flora, fauna and geology of the park. A small souvenir stand nearby has books about Horton for sale.

GETTING THERE & AWAY

Note that even if you want to just drive through the park you'll have to pay the hefty entrance fees.

Nuwara Eliya Most people come from Nuwara Eliya, a trip that takes about an hour one way (around Rs 4000 return by van). If taking a tour from Nuwara Eliya, you can ask to be dropped afterwards at Pattipola train station to catch the afternoon train to Haputale and Ella.

Ohiya The village of Ohiya is 10km east of Horton Plains and has a train station served by five daily trains to Haputale and Nanu Oya. From here you can hire a tuk-tuk (around Rs 1800) to the park's Farr Inn. The road rises in twists and turns through forest before emerging on the open plains. Keep your eyes peeled for monkeys.

Haputale You can also get to Farr Inn from Haputale. It takes about 1½ hours by road (Rs 4500 return).

CLIMBING KIRIGALPOTTA & TOTAPOLA

Almost every visitor to Horton Plains focuses on walking to World's End, but there's far more to the park than this (admittedly stunning) viewpoint.

An interesting alternative is to climb **Mt Kirigalpotta** (2395m), Sri Lanka's second-highest peak. Note that this is a much harder walk than the one to World's End, although it's still within easy reach of almost anyone of reasonable fitness. The four- to five-hour return hike begins from Farr Inn, but rather than following the masses along the main trail to World's End, take the minor trail westward behind the visitor centre. For the most part, the walk heads gently upward and passes through a landscape of high grasses, twisted dwarf forests festooned in lichens and through squelchy bogs. The last part of the walk, though, climbs much more steeply to the summit and rewards with impressive views over the park and down to the coastal lowlands. Very, very few people climb this mountain. And be aware that the 'trail' is very indistinct and criss-crossed by numerous animal trails. It's easy to get lost – especially if it's cloudy – and a guide who knows the route is essential. Unfortunately, not many guides do know the way. **Mr Nimal Herath** is one who does. He charges Rs 7000 including transport from Nuwara Eliya.

Another equally interesting but much shorter hike is to the summit of Sri Lanka's third-highest mountain, **Mt Totapola** (2357m). The trail starts from a short way past the ticket office and takes about two hours return. Again a guide is needed because the trail is indistinct and rarely walked.

TRAINS FROM HAPUTALE

Haputale is on the Colombo–Badulla line, so you can travel by train directly to and from Kandy or Nanu Oya (for Nuwara Eliya). A 1st-class observation ticket is Rs 1000 for anywhere between Badulla and Nanu Oya and Rs 1250 from Nanu Oya to Kandy. A 2nd-class reservation is Rs 700 to any of the following locations:

DESTINATION	PRICE (2ND/3RD CLASS)	DURATION	FREQUENCY (PER DAY)
Bandarawela	Rs 30/20	30min	5
Colombo	Rs 440/245	8½-9hr	4
Ella	Rs 60/35	1hr	5
Kandy (incl Peradeniya Junction)	Rs 280/155	5½hr	5
Nanu Oya	Rs 100/55	1½-2hr	5
Ohiya	Rs 40/25	30-45min	5

station or bus stand for no charge and good meals are available.

Dias Rest GUESTHOUSE **$**
(White Monkey; 057-568 1027; http://diasrest.blogspot.com; Thotulagala; r from Rs 1800;) Run by a welcoming crew (the owner is an experienced guide and can advise on local treks) and popular with backpackers, this place has simply astonishing views. Yes, rooms are fairly basic (and a tad chilly), but they are kept tidy, and the Sri Lankan food is excellent and very affordable. It's 3km east of the town centre.

Room rates vary wildly and seem to depend on what you appear to be willing to pay!

Kelburne Mountain View BOUTIQUE HOTEL **$$$**
(011-257 3382, 070-288 8111; www.facebook.com/kelburnecottages; Kelburne Tea Estate; bungalows Rs 19,600-22,000;) Kelburne is a simply sublime spot to relax for a few days, with cosy accommodation in immaculately renovated former tea-planters' bungalows and dapper white-suited staff attending to your needs. What really makes the property stand out, though, are the beautiful flower gardens, the surrounding tea estates and the stupendous views.

★ **Lettuce & Cabbage** INTERNATIONAL **$$**
(057-312 8000; Station Rd; meals from Rs 275; 9.30am-9pm;) Above a row of shops, this fancy-looking cafe has modern white seating, big views and a good menu featuring Western food like bacon and avocado salad as well as local dishes full of spice and all things nice. It's run by the owner of the Amarasinghe Guest House, and reliable independent travel info is available.

Getting There & Away

BUS

Buses depart from stops close to the main junction on the east side of the town centre. There are regular services to Badulla (Rs 90, two hours), Bandarawela (Rs 42, 30 minutes) and Wellawaya (Rs 120, 2½ hours). For Ella and Nuwara Eliya, change in Bandarawela. To get to Tangalla or Embilipitiya, change in Wellawaya.

TAXI

Guesthouses can arrange shared minibus 'taxis' to take you to Horton Plains (Rs 4500 return, including waiting time).

Ella

057 / POP 428 / ELEV 1041M

Welcome to everyone's favourite Hill Country village, and the place to ease off the travel accelerator with a few leisurely days resting in your choice of some of the country's best guesthouses. The views through Ella Gap are stunning, and on a clear night you can even spy the subtle glow of the Great Basses lighthouse on Sri Lanka's south coast. Don't be too laid-back, though: definitely make time for easygoing walks through tea plantations to temples, waterfalls and viewpoints. After building up a hiking-inspired appetite, look forward to some of Sri Lanka's best home-cooked food and a reviving cuppa.

In recent years, Ella's popularity has soared and the town's attractiveness has been somewhat compromised by some multistorey concrete eyesores, but take a room in a guesthouse just a few minutes' walk away from the town centre and Ella still captivates in the way it always has.

Ella

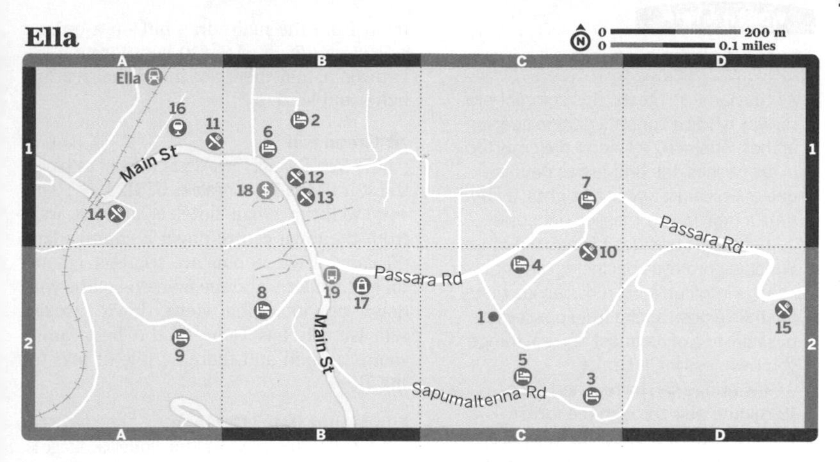

Ella

Activities, Courses & Tours
1 Lanka's Restaurant & Cooking Classes ... C2
Matey Hut Cooking Classes ... (see 14)

Sleeping
2 Eeshani Guest Inn ... B1
3 Ella Mount Relax Cottage ... C2
4 Freedom Guest Inn ... C2
5 Green Hill ... C2
6 Hangover Hostel ... B1
7 Little Folly ... C1
8 Okreech Cottages ... B2
9 Zion View ... A2

Eating
10 AK Ristoro ... C2
11 Cafe C Ella ... A1
12 Cafe Chill ... B1
13 Dream Café ... B1
Little Folly Restaurant ... (see 7)
14 Matey Hut ... A1
15 Umbrella Art Cafe ... D2

Drinking & Nightlife
16 Cafe One Love ... A1

Shopping
17 T-Sips ... B2

Information
18 Bank of Ceylon ... B1

Transport
19 Bus Stop ... B2

Activities & Courses

Most people are in town to hike, or just chill, but when it's time to rest your boots, you'll find cooking and yoga classes too.

Cooking Classes

Matey Hut Cooking Classes COOKING
(077-258 3450; Main St; Rs 2000; 11am & 4.30pm) These cooking classes have become so popular that chef-owner Madu now offers them twice daily. You'll learn the ropes and prepare up to seven veggie dishes. The morning class lasts two hours and the afternoon one is 2½ hours. Advance bookings are essential.

★ Lanka's Restaurant & Cooking Classes COOKING
(077-695 7495; tuktuklanka79@gmail.com; Rs 2000; noon & 5pm) The best-regarded cooking class in Ella, these two-hour classes are held in a delightful forest setting where you'll cook on traditional clay and wood burners. The course includes lots of explanations on how to feel and smell the correct ingredients.

Adventure Sports

Flying Ravana Zipline & Abseil ADVENTURE SPORTS
(057-493 000; www.flyingravana.com; 9am-5pm) A popular new destination in Ella is this activity centre that offers zip-lining (adult/child US$20/15), abseiling (US$15), quad biking (Rs 2700), archery (Rs 1800) and more. It's halfway up the trail to Little Adam's Peak, and riders on the 550m-long zip-line will flash past the scenery at speeds of up to 80km/h.

WORTH A TRIP

NINE ARCHES BRIDGE

As the name suggests, this colonial-era railway **bridge** consists of nine soaring arches. Spanning a steep valley matted in tea bushes, the bridge has become one of Sri Lanka's clichéd sights: every time a train is due, masses of people gather on the hillsides to snap a picture. Watching professional Instagrammers change into fluttering red dresses ready to strike a pose as the train passes is possibly one of the most surreal things you'll witness in Sri Lanka!

The bridge can be reached via a 15-minute walk through the forest. The trail starts almost opposite the start of the trail to Little Adam's Peak. Alternatively, you can drive most of the way there by continuing another kilometre from the turn-off for Little Adam's Peak.

Trains are scheduled to pass at 6.15am, 6.30am, 9.20am, 11.50am, 12.40pm, 1.15pm, 2.40pm, 3.30pm, 5.30pm and 7.15pm, but they're often running late.

Sleeping

Ella has a very high standard of accommodation, though there are few real cheapies. During the peak Christmas–New Year period, prices can double from those listed here, though at quiet times discounts can come thick and fast.

Expect some attention on the train from touts telling tall tales about the hotel of your choice being closed down, rat-infested or the like. These guys are just fishing for a commission and hope you'll go with them to a place that pays one.

Eeshani Guest Inn HOMESTAY $
(☎057-222 8703; eeshaniguestinn@yahoo.com; r incl breakfast Rs 3000-6000;) This five-room homestay is run by an endearing old couple who'll bustle you in and sit you down for a nice cuppa and a chat. The house is filled with sepia photos of their family, and there's a pretty, flower-filled garden and great local-style breakfasts.

Hangover Hostel HOSTEL $
(☎077-313 9797; www.hangoverhostels.com; dm US$13;) Part of a small, island-wide chain of hostels, Ella's version has a large, attractive garden and a good location just a moment from the main drag but on a quieter side street. Each of the 10-bed dorms has a bathroom, and there are individual reading lights and lockers.

★**Green Hill** HOTEL $$
(☎077-919 2937; incl breakfast r without bathroom US$30, r US$35-90, bungalows US$120;) This very well-run small hotel is a short walk from the town centre down a country lane off Passara Rd. Rooms are spotless, colourful and modern, and the floor-to-ceiling windows give incredible views down through Ella Gap. It has some of the best family rooms around and there's a pile of toys for the kids.

Ella Mount Relax Cottage GUESTHOUSE $$
(☎077-507 7066; www.ellamountrelaxcottage.lk; Sapumaltenna Rd; r incl breakfast from US$50;) Beautifully secluded guesthouse set among tea fields and pine trees but still only a few minutes' walk to the main street. The five wooden cottages here are well equipped and spacious, and they have balconies from which to admire the valley views. Staff can arrange yoga classes.

Little Folly CHALET $$
(☎057-222 8817; www.facebook.com/LittleFollyInElla; Passara Rd; cottages incl breakfast Rs 4500-6000;) Quaint Little Red Riding Hood wooden cottages squirrelled away in a forest that, if not the home of a big bad wolf, is probably home to a monkey or two. The cottages are airy, bright and clean, and everything is made of logs and bamboo. There's a great roadside **tea and cake shop** (Passara Rd; cakes Rs 200; 8am-8pm;), too.

Okreech Cottages COTTAGE $$
(☎077-779 4007, 077-238 1638; www.ellaokreechcottages.com; r from US$35;) An artistic touch is evident at this place, which has a collection of attractive, slightly quirky two-storey cottages scattered around a hillside garden. All are quite plain inside but attractive, with great balconies and modern hot-water private bathrooms.

★**Zion View** GUESTHOUSE $$$
(☎077-381 0313; http://zionviewella.com; incl breakfast s/d US$110/130, apt from US$190;) A wonderful guesthouse where the rooms have enormous glass-panel windows and terraces strewn with hammocks and chairs. Eating breakfast on the sunny terrace with views down through the Ella Gap is what Sri Lankan dreams are made of. The owners go

out of their way to help; call for free pickup from the train station or bus stop.

It's very well set up for travelling families (most rooms are suitable for families), not least because it has a pool and a big play area for smaller kids. Grown-ups will appreciate the Ayurveda centre and daily yoga classes (Rs 2000).

The in-house restaurant (open to outside guests) serves a mighty fine rice and curry. Booking directly with the hotel brings an automatic 18% discount.

Eating & Drinking

There's a wide choice of cafes and restaurants on Ella's main drag. However, you'll find some of the best food in the simplest guesthouses – just be sure to order in advance. Some places offer rice- and curry-making classes, too.

Curd (made with buffalo milk) and treacle (syrup from the *kitul* palm; sometimes misnamed 'honey') is a much-touted local speciality, as is *lamprais*, a delicious mess of rice, meat and curry cooked in a banana leaf.

★Cafe C Ella SRI LANKAN $

(071-814 1746; Main St; mains Rs 250-600; 8.30am-9.30pm) A small, unassuming roadside restaurant with graffiti-stained walls and arguably the tastiest rice and curry (from Rs 450) in town, as well as delicious juices, noodles, *kotthu* (*rotti* chopped up and mixed with vegetables) and more. There are only a couple of tables, so best get there early.

Umbrella Art Cafe INTERNATIONAL $

(072-814 9595; Passara Rd; mains Rs 250-350; 9am-9pm) You can't miss the psychedelic wall mural of an umbrella (or perhaps it's a jellyfish?) at this cute roadside cafe. The juices, lassis, flavoursome *kotthus* and big breakfasts make for a rewarding treat after tackling nearby Little Adam's Peak.

AK Ristoro INTERNATIONAL $$

(057-2050 676; mains Rs 700-900; noon-10pm) An Italian-Japanese restaurant in Sri Lanka – can it get any more international than that? Well, yes, as it happens it can. Step inside this large, popular and consistently reliable restaurant and you'll discover a menu that also contains Spanish tapas and British fish and chips. The cocktails score high marks from everyone. It's off Passara Rd.

Matey Hut CAFE $$

(Main St; rice & curry from Rs 480; 11am-9pm) Run by a jovial, talented chef, this simple wooden cabin always has a huge queue of hungry travellers waiting for a space at one of the eight tables. The reason they wait? Delicious, authentic home-cooked rice and curry (which might take in mango, pumpkin and okra dishes and a dash of coconut sambal) and tasty *kotthu*.

It also offers excellent cooking classes.

★Cafe Chill INTERNATIONAL $$

(Main St; mains Rs 600-900; 10am-10pm;) Run by an engaging local team, this huge, stylish roadside cafe-bar-restaurant continues to set the standard in Ella. The food coming out of the large open-plan kitchen is excellent, with flavoursome local and Western dishes and espresso coffee. Try the *lamprais* or one of the 10 curries.

Cafe One Love BAR

(Station Rd; 24hr) Festooned in tribal and hippy-inspired art, One Love is the most happening nightspot in Ella. Sit on the bean bags under a giant thatched awning and enjoy the daily beer and cocktail specials.

Shopping

Main St is lined with stores selling travel essentials, clothing and souvenirs.

T-Sips TEA

(077-788 3434; Passara Rd; 9am-7.30pm) This fair-trade tea shop (selling leaves rather than cups of tea) helps local tea-estate children. It donates 5% of all money made to community projects. Also sells an array of local teas and infusions as well as a few spices.

Information

Every guesthouse and most bigger restaurants have wi-fi.

Bank of Ceylon (Main St; 8.30am-5pm Mon-Fri, to 1pm Sat) Has an ATM.

Getting There & Away

BUS

Buses leave from Main St, from stops just south of the Passara Rd turn-off. No buses originate in Ella and many are full (standing room only) by the time they pass through.

➡ Regular buses go to Badulla (Rs 36, 45 minutes), Bandarawela (Rs 50, 30 minutes) and Wellawaya (Rs 72, one hour).

➡ For Kandy you must change in Badulla, and for destinations on the south coast as well as Arugam Bay, change in Wellawaya.

TRAIN

Ella is an hour or so from Haputale and Badulla on the Colombo–Badulla line. The stretch from Haputale (through Bandarawela) has particularly lovely scenery. Roughly 10km north of Ella, at Demodara, the line performs a complete loop around a hillside and tunnels under itself at a level 30m lower.

Ella's pretty train station is so quaint it has won the 'Best-Kept Station' award. It's like *Thomas the Tank Engine* come to life. Station manager Mr Ashendria Disanayake deserves mention for winning the 'Most Helpful Station Manager' award.

Fares and timetables are well posted. Observation class is Rs 1000 for anywhere between Nanu Oya and Badulla, and Rs 1200 to Kandy and Colombo. A 2nd-class advance reservation is Rs 500 for anywhere between Nanu Oya and Badulla, and Rs 600 to Kandy and Colombo.

There are sometimes one-off 'special' trains running between Ella and Nanu Oya. Every once in a while this might even be pulled by a restored steam engine.

Destination	Fare (2nd/3rd class)	Duration	Frequency (per day)
Badulla	Rs 50/30	1hr	5
Bandarawela	Rs 30/20	35min	5
Colombo	Rs 470/260	9hr	4
Haputale	Rs 60/35	1-1½hr	5
Kandy	Rs 310/175	6-10hr	5
Nanu Oya (for Nuwara Eliya)	Rs 150/80	2½-3hr	5
Ohiya	Rs 100/55	2hr	5

TAXI

Private minibus taxis gather on the roadside close to the Dream Café and charge the following rates:

Destination	Price
Colombo	Rs 16,000
Galle	Rs 15,000
Horton Plains	Rs 9000
Mirissa	Rs 13,000
Nuwara Eliya	Rs 8000
Tangalla	Rs 10,500
Tissamaharama	Rs 7500

Around Ella

There are a number of interesting sights in the vicinity of Ella. Some can be reached by public transport or, for more convenience, on a half-day tour by tuk-tuk or taxi.

Sights

★Uva Halpewaththa Tea Factory FACTORY

(☎057-493 3282; www.halpetea.com; adult Rs 540; ⏲tours 8am-4pm) The Uva Halpewaththa Tea Factory, 5km north of Ella, runs some of the better tea-plantation tours in Sri Lanka. After you've enriched yourself with knowledge, treat your taste buds by trying samples of the estate's different teas. There's also a small shop selling leaves and tea-related paraphernalia. Tours take place throughout the day, but the frequency of tours varies slightly depending on the kind of tea being processed. To be safe, visit in the morning. No production on Sunday.

To get here, catch a bus towards Bandarawela, get off at **Kumbawela junction** and flag a bus going towards Badulla. Get off just after the 27km post, near the **Halpe Temple**. From here you have a very steep 2km walk to the factory. A three-wheeler from Ella will charge Rs 1200 to Rs 1500 return.

Rakkhiththakanda Len Viharaya Cave Temple BUDDHIST TEMPLE

The rock face around this remote and little-visited cave temple, which is signed off the road to Wellawaya, is covered in faded Kandyan-era paintings, including one of the British royal coat of arms. Inside, the paintings are in far better condition and completely cover the walls. There's also a reclining Buddha. It's 21km south of Ella.

Sleeping & Eating

Bunk Station Hostel HOSTEL $

(☎071-928 0799; dm incl breakfast US$12; 📶) Cool, urban-style hostel off Passara Rd, right by the walking routes to both Nine Arches Bridge (p194) and Little Adam's Peak. There's a buzzing backpacker atmosphere, a vast, minimalist lounge area filled with bean bags and cushions, and four dorms, each of which has eight to 10 beds, lockers and a bathroom. One of the dorms is female only.

★Waterfall Homestay GUESTHOUSE $$

(☎057-567 6933, 077-695 7496; www.waterfalls-guesthouse-ella.com; incl breakfast s/d from Rs 6500/7500, f Rs 11,000; 📶) A delightfully

Around Ella

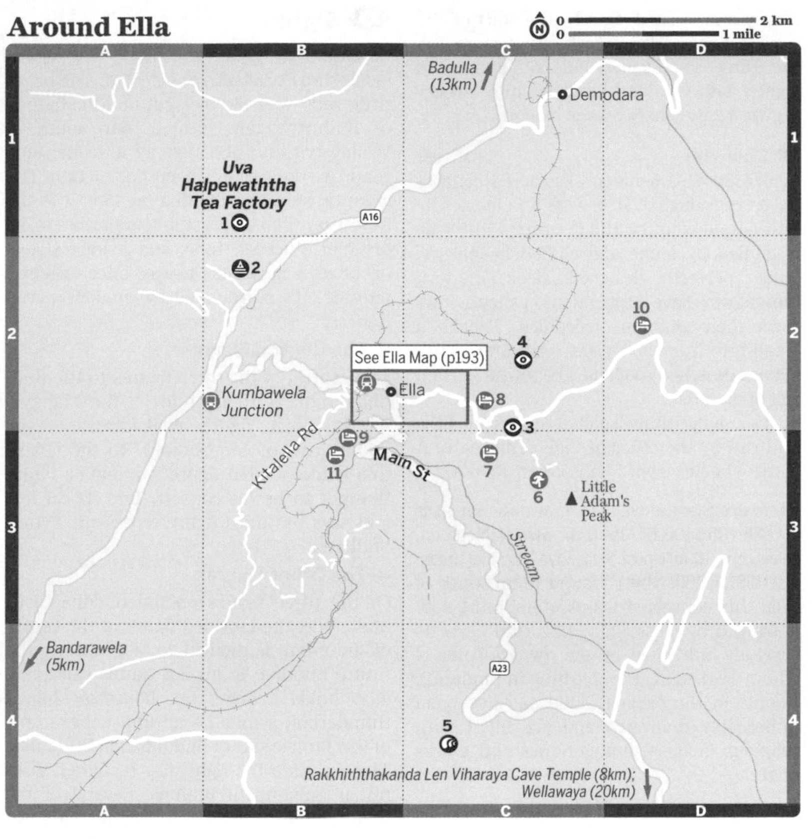

Around Ella

Top Sights
1 Uva Halpewaththa Tea Factory B1

Sights
2 Halpe Temple B2
3 Newburgh Green Tea Factory C2
4 Nine Arches Bridge C2
5 Rawana Ella Falls C4

Activities, Courses & Tours
6 Flying Ravana Zipline & Abseil C3

Sleeping
7 98 Acres Resort C3
8 Bunk Station Hostel C2
9 Chamodya Homestay B3
10 Chill Ville D2
Chillout .... (see 7)
11 Waterfall Homestay B3

secluded homestay run by an Australian couple with a flair for art and design. The building melds into the hillside and offers views over the Rawana Falls. Expect some original art or a statue in each individually decorated room. Memorable breakfasts are served communal style on the terrace. It's 1.5km from town.

Chamodya Homestay HOMESTAY $$
(078-535 4726; r incl breakfast Rs 6000;) One of the best homestays in the Ella region, Chamodya is run by a lovely couple who take very good care of their guests. Guests get to enjoy a glorious outlook over a forested valley, and the five rooms are very well presented, all with hot-water bathrooms. Do eat here.

It's 2km west of the centre, via a track; a three-wheeler costs Rs 250.

Chillout GUESTHOUSE $$
(077-404 9777; dhanushka4049@gmail.com; r incl breakfast US$50;) Run by a welcoming

family and located right by the start of the trail to Little Adam's Peak, off Passara Rd, the three good-value and well-appointed rooms with fans and minibar enjoy sweeping views and share a large balcony.

★Chill Ville COTTAGE **$$$**

(077-180 4020; 6-mile post, Passara Rd; cottages incl breakfast from US$130;) One of the best bargains in the Hill Country, Chill Ville is chilled by name and chilled by nature. Huge, perfectly designed, sleek, modern bungalows have stupendous valley views from their generous balconies. There's a small infinity pool, a classy restaurant with a giant thatched roof and a beautiful garden full of orchids.

It's a delightfully isolated 8km from Ella, and run by the efficient Cafe Chill team. A three-wheeler from Ella is about Rs 600.

Planters Bungalow HISTORIC HOTEL **$$$**

(055-205 5600, 077-154 0737; www.plantersbungalow.com; 10-mile post, Wellawaya Rd; r incl breakfast US$100-160;) Around 16km south of Ella, this converted tea-planters' bungalow is fringed by blossoming, beautiful gardens carefully cultivated by the owners (one of whom worked in art publishing in England). Rooms in the original building have been impeccably renovated and are filled with religious imagery, fine antiques and works of art.

Getting There & Away

From Ella you can hop on buses heading to towns including Wellawaya, Bandarawela and Badulla to access the sights in this region. However, hiring a tuk-tuk is more convenient; expect to pay around Rs 2500 for a half-day trip.

Wellawaya

055 / POP 58,000

Wellawaya is a small crossroads town sitting at the very foot of the southern Hill Country. It's notably hotter than anywhere else in the Hill Country and, apart from the considerable allure of the nearby Buduruwagala carvings, there's no great reason to stay. It's surrounded by dry plains that were once home to the ancient Sinhalese kingdom of Ruhunu.

Roads run north through the spectacular Ella Gap to the Hill Country, south to Tissamaharama and the coast, east to the coast and west to Colombo.

Sights

★Buduruwagala MONUMENT

(adult/child Rs 364/182; 7am-6pm) The beautiful, 1000-year-old rock-cut Buddha figures of Buduruwagala, located 9km south of Wellawaya and accessed by a scenic side road, are the region's biggest attraction. The gigantic standing Buddha (at 15m, it is the tallest on the island) still bears traces of its original stuccoed robe, and a long streak of orange suggests it was once brightly painted. It's surrounded by smaller carved figures.

➡ The Central Figures

The central of the three figures to the Buddha's right is thought to be the Mahayana Buddhist figure Avalokitesvara (the bodhisattva of compassion). To the left of this white-painted figure is a female figure thought to be his consort, Tara. Local legend says the third figure represents Prince Sudhana.

➡ The Other Figures

Of the three figures on the Buddha's left-hand side, the crowned figure at the centre of the group is thought to be Maitreya, the future Buddha. To his left stands Vajrapani, who holds a *vajra* (an hourglass-shaped thunderbolt symbol) – an unusual example of the Tantric side of Buddhism in Sri Lanka. The figure to the right may be either Vishnu or Sahampath Brahma. Several of the figures hold up their right hands with two fingers bent down to the palm – a beckoning gesture.

The name Buduruwagala is derived from the words for Buddha (Budu), images *(ruva)* and stone *(gala)*. The figures are thought to date from around the 10th century and belong to the Mahayana Buddhist school, which enjoyed a brief heyday in Sri Lanka during this time.

An ancient stupa has recently been uncovered halfway along the road from the junction to the carvings.

➡ Museum

A small **museum** (A2 Hwy; 8am-4.30pm Wed-Mon) FREE, located next to the junction from the main road to the statues, houses a few artefacts from the site, including a beautiful ancient Buddha statue made of moonstone.

➡ Practical Tips

You may be joined by a guide, who will expect a tip. A three-wheeler from Wellawaya costs about Rs 800 return. Some people walk (or cycle) from the junction of the main road, which is very pleasant but can also be very hot. The 4km track crosses a series of delicate lakes. Keep an eye out for local birdlife, including many egrets and herons. These wetlands and surrounding forest are a proposed forest reserve.

Sleeping & Eating

Jetwing Kaduruketha HOTEL **$$$**
(055-471 0710; www.jetwinghotels.com; s/d incl breakfast US$367/394;) In a rural location 2km north of Wellawaya, this peaceful boutique hideaway has plush rooms in which the sides lift up to give each unit the feel of a chic safari tent. Views stretch out over rice fields and across towards the bulk of the central highlands. The only things that might disturb the peace here are songbirds and peacocks.

There are free bikes for guests, an eye-catching swimming pool and wonderful organic meals. It's a perfect spot to just sit back and enjoy the magic of rural Sri Lanka. During quiet times, rates can be slashed by 50%.

Living Heritage Koslanda BOUTIQUE HOTEL **$$$**
(077-935 5785; www.koslanda.com; Koslanda; r incl breakfast US$235-445;) Set within 32 hectares of grounds, which include tangled forest and even a waterfall, the planters-style bungalows here are cool, calm and impeccably decorated. They were constructed by local craftspeople using traditional techniques, but gorgeous open-air bathrooms and private jacuzzis have also been incorporated, and there's a glorious infinity pool.

Getting There & Away

Wellawaya is a common staging post between the Hill Country and the south and east coasts. You can usually find a connection here until mid-afternoon. For Tissamaharama, change at Pannegamanuwa Junction (Rs 92). Buses leave from the large station when full.

Destination	Price (Rs)	Duration (hr)	Frequency
Badulla	110	1½	every 30min
Ella	72	1	every 30-40min
Embilipitiya	180	2½	5 daily
Monaragala	83	1	every 20min
Tangalla	300	3½	every 30min

WORTH A TRIP

DIYALUMA FALLS

The 171m-high Diyaluma Falls is Sri Lanka's third-highest waterfall. Cascading down an escarpment of the Koslanda Plateau, the falls leap over a cliff face and plunge (in one clear drop) to a pool below. It's more impressive in the rainy season. Diyaluma Falls is 13km west of Wellawaya; any bus heading to Haputale passes by.

A path to the upper part of the falls leaves from close to the 207.5km post on the A4 Hwy. It's a steep 45-minute hike to the top.

Uda Walawe National Park

Framed by soaring highlands on its northern boundary, **Uda Walawe National Park** (adult/child US$15/8, service charge per group US$8, vehicle charge per group Rs 250; 6am-6pm) is one of Asia's best places to see wild elephants as well as wild buffaloes, sambars and spotted deer, crocodiles, monitors and a huge variety of colourful birds. Largely comprising grasslands and scrubby bush forest dotted with giant water pans and lakes, it's also one of the most beautiful parks in Sri Lanka and the best organised for game-spotting.

Elephants are Uda Walawe's key attraction, with around 600 in the park in herds of up to 50. There's an elephant-proof fence around the perimeter of much of the park, (supposedly) preventing elephants from getting out into areas with a higher human population and cattle from getting in. Elephants can and do migrate in and out of the park along unfenced borders. The best time to observe herds is from 6.30am to 10am and again from 4pm to 6.30pm.

The park, which centres on the 308.2-sq-km Uda Walawe Reservoir, is lightly vegetated, but it has a stark beauty and the lack of dense vegetation makes game watching easy.

The entrance to the park is 12km from the Ratnapura–Hambantota road turn-off and 21km from Embilipitiya. Visitors buy tickets in a building a further 2km on. Most people take a tour organised by their guesthouse or hotel, but a trip with one of the 4WDs waiting outside the gate should be around Rs 3500 for a half day for up to eight people. Last tickets are usually sold at 5pm.

A park guide is included in the cost of admission. These guys, who all seem to have hawk-like wildlife-spotting eyes, are normally very knowledgable about the park and its animals. However, unless you specifically request otherwise, the whole safari can be a rush between one elephant herd and the next, with no time to pause and enjoy the myriad other, equally interesting creatures who reside here. To get the best out of a safari, explain to your driver and guide beforehand that you're interested in seeing things other than just elephants. When you stop at a sighting, ask your driver to switch off the engine so that you can hear the chatter of birds rather than the roar of the 4WD. Also be aware that, as in all of Sri Lanka's more popular parks, there are serious issues with drivers crowding and disturbing the flagship animals. As a rule of thumb – and for the benefit of the animals and the enjoyment of all concerned – there shouldn't be more than five vehicles at a sighting at any one time. If there are too many vehicles, ask your driver to pull back and wait, or better still, go and find something else to look at. Guides and drivers expect a tip.

The park is also home to mongooses, jackals, water monitor lizards, lots of crocodiles, sloth bears and the occasional leopard. There are 30 varieties of snake and a wealth of birdlife – 210 species at last count; northern migrants join the residents between November and April.

Sights

Elephant Transit Home ZOO

(CP de Silva Rd; adult/child Rs 500/250; feedings 9am, noon, 3pm & 6pm) This complex is a halfway house for orphaned elephants. After rehabilitation, the elephants are released back into the wild, many into Uda Walawe National Park. Although you can't get too close to the elephants, seeing them at feeding time (from a viewing platform) is still a lot of fun. It's on the main lakeside road, about 5km west of the park entrance. It can be very busy. Get there early to secure a prime spot.

Sleeping & Eating

There's a wide choice of places to stay on the fringes of the park. Rates are high, though – expect to pay more than you would on the coast or up in the highlands.

All the hotels around the park have restaurants.

★**Nature House** GUESTHOUSE $

(077-704 3482; r Rs 4000;) One of the best guesthouses in southern Sri Lanka, Nature House does almost everything right. It's superb value and very well run, and its immaculate small rooms are tastefully furnished. There's also an attractive open-air restaurant where a delicious rice-and-curry buffet is served each night. Demand for rooms is heavy, so book ahead. It's off Thanamalwila Rd.

Silent Bungalow GUESTHOUSE $

(071-271 8941; Uda Walawe; r incl breakfast Rs 1500-3000;) A welcoming place offering good budget accommodation in simple, quite spacious fan-cooled rooms with private bathrooms. Breakfasts, indeed all meals, are excellent. Owner Sudath organises good safaris from here at fair rates and you've a chance to share costs with others as it's a popular base for independent travellers. Book ahead. It's behind the army camp, off Dakunu Ala Rd.

Countryside HOTEL $$

(076-839 6086; www.tcsudawalawe.com; Thanamalwila Rd; r incl breakfast Rs 6000;) Good-quality cottages with high ceilings, balconies and polished-cement floors. Unusually, they also provide enough sheets on the bed to actually keep you warm at night (after a while in Sri Lanka you'll know what we mean)! It's set in an attractive grassy compound.

Athgira River Camping CAMPGROUND $$$

(077-037 5857; www.athgirarivercamp.com; Mudunmankada Rd; d incl half board Rs 12,500;) This safari camp has comfortable canvas tents strung along the riverbank with attached (cold-water) bathrooms and proper beds (with mozzie nets), although the tents are a bit too close together to offer true privacy. It's a social place and the friendly staff organise frequent riverside barbecue nights. There are bikes for hire, too, and a large pool.

Getting There & Away

Day tours of the park are offered from Ella, Ratnapura, Tissa and many south-coast resorts. However, taking in a tour from these places means you'll be visiting the park in the heat of the day when all the animals are having a siesta. It's far better to spend at least one night here, which will allow you to do an early-morning and an evening safari.

Buses from Embilipitiya (Rs 50, every 45 minutes) pass the park entrance, where 4WDs for safaris can be hired.

Most of the cheaper accommodation is in or close to the village of Uda Walawe. More upmarket places can be found strung along the road between the park entrance and Uda Walawe village. Bus drivers will usually drop you off outside your hotel of choice, though note that many places are located down dusty side tracks.

BUSES FROM EMBILIPITIYA

Embilipitiya is sometimes used as a base for tours to Uda Walawe National Park, as it's only 23km south of the park's ticket office. However, with the increasing range of accommodation around the park itself, there's much less reason to stay in this otherwise busy and dusty agricultural town.

Buses leave from the central **bus station** (A18 Hwy, Embilipitiya) frequently for the following destinations:

Destination	Price	Duration	Frequency
Matara	Rs 142	2½hr	every 20min
Ratnapura	Rs 144	3hr	every 30min
Tangalla	Rs 70-90	2hr	every 30min
Uda Walawe	Rs 50	45min	every 30min

Sinharaja Forest Reserve

The largest lowland rainforest in Sri Lanka, **Sinharaja Forest Reserve** (adult/child Rs 756/378; 6am-6pm, ticket office to 4.30pm) is an abundant, biodiverse habitat, bordered by rivers and rich in forest wildlife, including rare mammals and many endemic birds. Unlike most Sri Lankan national parks, access to the forest is only on foot, accompanied by a ranger or guide. Most visitors base themselves in the nearby settlements of Deniyaya or Kudawa, where entrance tickets are sold at the main Forest Department offices.

Because the forest is so dense, wildlife-spotting isn't as easy here as it is in many other Sri Lankan reserves and parks. A good guide certainly helps. On most days, the jungle is shrouded by copious rain clouds, which replenish its deep soils and balance water resources for much of southwestern Sri Lanka. Recognising its importance to the island's ecosystem, Unesco declared the Sinharaja Forest Reserve a World Heritage Site in 1989 and in 2019 the government announced a fourfold expansion (bringing it to 360 sq km) of the size of the reserve.

There are many villages around the forest, and locals are permitted to enter the area (on motorbikes) to tap palms to make jaggery (a hard brown sweet) and treacle, and to collect dead wood and leaves for fuel and construction. Medicinal plants are collected during specific seasons. Rattan collection is of more concern, as the demand for cane is high. Sinharaja attracts illegal gem miners, too, and abandoned open pits pose a danger to humans and animals, and cause erosion. There is also some poaching of wild animals.

Activities

The only access to the Sinharaja forest is via a guided walk, either using freelance guides (based at the park entrances) or as part of a tour.

Tours are possible from Deniyaya and Kudawa, and as day trips with operators in several south-coast resorts, including Unawatuna and Galle. It's best to avoid these day tours from the coast, though: you'll spend a lot of time in a vehicle and be in the reserve in the middle of the day, when the wildlife is less active.

Exact guiding rates depend on how many are in your group, but you can expect to pay around Rs 3000 for a half-day guided walk for two people.

As it can rain in the reserve at any time of year, waterproofs are advisable, and leech gear is essential after rain.

Sleeping & Eating

There are several possible bases from which to explore the reserve, including Kudawa on the north side and Deniyaya on the south side.

All guesthouses and hotels provide meals.

Kudawa

This village is the settlement of choice for many visitors with their own transport. The forest is a little less disturbed on this side of the park.

Rock View Motel HOTEL $$
(045-567 7990; www.rockviewmotel.com; Rakwana Rd, Weddagala; d/tr incl breakfast Rs 5250/7500;) Rock View offers functional and airy rooms with balconies that have views over rolling hills of forest and tea bushes. It's 2km east of Weddagala and about the best-value deal in these parts. However, expect noise at weekends, when it often hosts wedding parties.

Deniyaya & Around

If you don't have your own wheels, the small town of Deniyaya is a convenient base. Accommodation also tends to be better value here. There is a growing number of places to stay right by the park entrance, and with convenient park access and all the excitement of staying in the forest and listening to the sounds of the jungle at night, this is by far the choicest area to stay.

★ **360 Rainforest** LODGE $$
(071-801 0700; www.facebook.com/360rainforest; incl breakfast cottages/safari tents Rs 6000/6500;) This is a delightful small safari camp just 100m from the park entrance. Choose between slickly turned-out hillside cottages or a row of high-quality, en-suite safari tents raised on stilts and overlooking the river. Staff members bend over backwards to help.

The only downside is that the restaurant of the neighbouring property backs right onto the safari tents.

Sinharaja Forest Edge HOTEL $$
(077-297 8233; www.sinharajaforestedge.com; r incl breakfast from Rs 4000;) Right next to the park entrance, this is the most upmarket place to stay in these parts. The glass-fronted rooms with stylish jungle-leaf sculptures on the walls look out over a turquoise-blue swimming pool set among a series of lily-fringed ponds filled with frogs and fish. The restaurant, which is raised on stilts, overlooks the river.

SINHARAJA WILDLIFE

The largest carnivore here is the leopard. Its presence can usually be gauged only by droppings and tracks, and it's seldom seen. Even rarer are rusty spotted cats and fishing cats. Sambars, barking deer and wild boars can be found on the forest floor. Groups of 10 to 14 purple-faced langurs are fairly common. There are three kinds of squirrel: the flame-striped jungle squirrel, the dusky-striped jungle squirrel and the western giant squirrel. Porcupines and pangolins waddle around the forest floor, mostly unseen. Civets and mongooses are nocturnal, though you may glimpse the occasional mongoose darting through the foliage during the day. Six species of bat have been recorded here.

Plant Life

Sinharaja has a wild profusion of flora. The canopy trees reach heights of 45m, with the next layer down topping 30m. Nearly all the subcanopy trees found here are rare or endangered. More than 65% of the 217 types of tree and woody climber endemic to Sri Lanka's rainforest are found in Sinharaja.

Birdlife

There's a wealth of birdlife: 147 species have been recorded, with 19 of Sri Lanka's 20 endemic species seen here. The forest is renowned for its mixed 'bird wave'. This is when several species of bird move in a feeding flock together. It's commonly seen in many parts of the world, but in Sinharaja it's worth noting for the length of time a flock can be viewed and the number of species (up to a dozen). It sometimes even contains mammals (such as ground squirrels).

Reptiles

Sinharaja has 71 species of reptile, around half of them endemic. Venomous snakes include the green pit viper (which inhabits trees), the hump-nosed viper and the krait, which lives on the forest floor. One of the most frequently found amphibians is the wrinkled frog, whose croaking is often heard at night.

Sinharaja Rest GUESTHOUSE **$$**
(☎041-227 3368, 077-341 9061; https://sinharajarest.net; Temple Rd, Deniyaya; r incl breakfast Rs 5000; 📶) Brothers Palitha and Bandula Rathnayaka are both certified forest guides and have more wilderness experience than most other guides in the region. The rooms at their home are fairly basic, but there's good home cooking and a lovely private garden. They can organise superb day trips to the forest. Trips are also open to nonguests.

Rainforest BOUTIQUE HOTEL **$$$**
(☎076-690 0900; www.rainforest-ecolodge.com; r incl breakfast from US$185; 📶) 🍃 At the edge of the Sinharaja reserve (where very rare purple-faced langurs are regularly seen), this is one of the most remote hotels in Sri Lanka. Highly original rooms with stupendous views have been created out of metal shipping containers. The staff are trained from the local community, water comes from nearby springs and there's an impressive recycling scheme.

It's 18 rather tortuous kilometres north of Deniyaya.

ℹ Getting There & Away

There are several park access points, but the most relevant to travellers are those via Kudawa in the northwest and via Mederapitiya (reached from Deniyaya) in the southeast. The Mederapitiya entrance is the easiest to reach by public transport.

BUS

- From Ratnapura to Deniyaya there are four daily buses (Rs 213, five hours) from 6.30am to 2.30pm. There are also three daily buses to and from Galle (Rs 140, three hours).
- Heading to Kudawa can be complicated and slow going. From Ratnapura, regular buses go to Kalawana (Rs 70, 1½ hours) and from there to Weddagala (4km before Kudawa; Rs 32, 20 minutes), and then, finally, you hop on one to Kudawa (Rs 20, 15 minutes).

CAR

The road through Hayes Tea Estate, north of Deniyaya en route to Madampe and Balangoda (for Belihul Oya, Haputale or Ratnapura), is very scenic. Trying to loop from the north to the south entrances of the park is also a fine drive, but slow and painful, as the roads are rough.

AT A GLANCE

POPULATION
Anuradhapura: 64,000

GATEWAY CITY
Anuradhapura (p230)

BEST SACRED SITE
Sri Maha Bodhi (p236)

BEST OFF-THE-BEATEN-TRACK SITE
Yapahuwa Rock Fortress (p243)

BEST BUDGET ESCAPE
Roy's Villa (p213)

WHEN TO GO

Jun A great festival, the Poson Poya, is held at Mihintale on the full-moon night.

May–Sep Elephants gather in the central and easily visited Minneriya National Park.

Nov Ceremonies are held in Anuradhapura for Unduvap Poya, marking the sacred bodhi tree's arrival.

Abhayagiri Dagoba (p236), Anuradhapura
EFESENKO/SHUTTERSTOCK ©

The Ancient Cities

Crumbling temples, lost cities and sacred Buddhist sites draw travellers in their droves to the cultural heartland of Sri Lanka. It was here on the central plains that ancient Sinhalese dynasties set up their first capitals and supported massive artistic and architectural movements. Eventually these kingdoms fell, slowly to be reclaimed by the forest and jungles.

For more than a century archaeologists have been slowly stripping away the greenery to reveal the region's many layers of history. The rock fortress at Sigiriya, the monumental dagobas (stupas) of Anuradhapura and the refined carvings of Polonnaruwa are but a few of the sites now ranking as national treasures. With four Unesco World Heritage Sites, this 'Cultural Triangle' is seventh heaven for amateur archaeologists and historians.

INCLUDES

Ancient Cities Highlights

1 Abhayagiri Dagoba (p237) Feeling humbled by the epic scale of the former capital of Anuradhapura.

2 Sigiriya (p211) Scaling the rock for epic views, outstanding murals and intriguing ruins.

3 Polonnaruwa (p219) Admiring the exquisite carved temples and Buddhas at this World Heritage Site.

4 Minneriya (p229) Spotting elephants, crocodiles and birdlife on the lake shores of this popular national park.

5 Dambulla Cave Temples (p208) Peering at some of Sri Lanka's most stunning Buddhist murals.

6 Ridi Vihara (p244) Getting off the beaten track at this little-visited Buddhist temple, with its beautiful murals.

7 Mihintale (p241) Climbing monumental stairways to the stupas and viewpoints where Buddhism first took root in Sri Lanka.

Getting Around

The towns and cities of the Cultural Triangle are well connected by frequent buses, and in rare cases by train. Distances are not great and most roads are good, so getting around the main destinations by public transport is relatively straightforward.

The easiest way to tour, as always, is with a car and driver, and this is particularly useful for visiting sights off the main routes, and if you are staying in top-end places outside the main towns. You can reach the area by train or bus and then arrange for a car and driver on a daily basis through your accommodation.

For a reliable car and driver (around Rs 6000 per day) to cover the sites around the Cultural Triangle, and beyond, **Let's Go Lanka** (077-630 2070; www.letsgolanka.com; Giritale) and **Nadee Lanka Tours** (077-999 8859; www.nadeelankatours.com; 21st Mile Post, Jayanthipura) are recommended.

Three-wheelers are readily available in every small town and at most road junctions. Some negotiation is necessary.

Matale

066 / POP 46,000

The midsize, regional city of Matale is a featureless urban sprawl with a congested one-way system, so you're unlikely to want to linger. However, the road north of town has several visitor-friendly spice plantations, as well as the historically important Buddhist site of Aluvihara, making for an interesting stop between Kandy and Dambulla. The area is also famous for its *kohila* (a type of watercress) and small, mild chillies.

Sights

Aluvihara BUDDHIST MONASTERY

(A9 Hwy; adult Rs 300; 7am-6pm) Set in foothills 3km north of Matale, surrounded by giant boulders, this monastery is a low-key, but intriguing, site. There's a charming series of Buddhist caves, religious wall paintings, and a stupa or two. It's easily accessible just off the main highway.

It was in Aluvihara that the Buddhist canon known as the *Tipitaka* was first transcribed from oral and Sinhalese sources into Pali text by 500 resident monks, during the Fourth Buddhist Council of the 1st century BCE.

Sri Muthumariamman Thevasthanam HINDU TEMPLE

(exterior/interior Rs 150/350; 7am-noon & 4.30-7.30pm) Just north of the bus stand for Kandy (at the north end of town) is this large South Indian–style Hindu temple. A couple of garages to the side house five enormous, colourful ceremonial chariots pulled along by crowds during the dramatic Theru festival in February/March.

Eating

A&C Restaurant SRI LANKAN $$$

(072-367 4501; 3/5 Sir Richard Aluvihara Mawatha; meal Rs 990; 11am-3pm) For a step up in class from your standard-issue rice and curry, this unlikely and unsigned family-run location offers a delicious Sri Lankan set meal of eight varied and flavourful curries.

It's popular with guides and drivers but hard to find by yourself: take the side road to the right of the Pearl Chamin Restaurant (on the main A9 highway, 1km south of Aluvihara) and then follow the first immediate left lane to the end.

Shopping

Baba Batik ARTS & CRAFTS

(066-222 4053; www.bababatiks.com; 793/5 Trincomalee St; 8am-5pm Mon-Fri, to 4pm Sat & Sun) This batik factory and showroom is a great place to see the batik-making process, from the drawing of the designs and multi-stage dyeing of cloth to the boiling away of the wax. The tasteful and excellent-quality batiks are then made into dresses, sarongs, scarves and children's clothes. Discounts of 40% on the marked prices are common.

The factory and lovely century-old residence is on the main A9 highway 1.5km south of Aluvihara.

Getting There & Away

Buses 593 and 636 run from Kandy's clock tower to Matale (bus/air-con-minibus Rs 50/100, one hour) every 10 minutes.

Buses to Dambulla (Rs 80, 90 minutes), Anuradhapura (Rs 180, three hours) or Kawatayamuna can drop you at Aluvihara (Rs 14) or the spice gardens.

Air-conditioned minibuses to Kandy and Colombo (Rs 420, four hours) leave from just outside the Sri Muthumariamman temple.

There are six trains daily on the pretty spur line between Matale and Kandy (3rd class Rs 40, 1½ hours). On weekdays there is a direct train to Colombo (1st/2nd/3rd class Rs 700/290/160, 4½ hours) departing at 6.30am. The station is on the eastern edge of the town centre.

Nalanda Gedige

The venerable **Nalanda Gedige** (7am-5pm) FREE enjoys a wonderfully peaceful location next to the Bowatenna Reservoir on a site that is considered the geographical centre of the island. It's worth a brief stop between Dambulla and Kandy if you have your own transport. This South Indian–style temple consists of an entrance hall connected to a taller *shikara* (holy image sanctuary), with a courtyard for circumambulations. It's one of the earliest stone buildings in Sri Lanka.

The temple's richly decorated stone-block walls, reassembled from ruins in 1975, are thought to have been fashioned during the 8th to 11th centuries. The plinth bears some faint Tantric carvings with sexual poses – the only such sculptures in Sri Lanka.

Nalanda Gedige is 25km north of Matale and 20km south of Dambulla, 1km east of the main road; look out for the sign near the Km 49 post. Anuradhapura buses from Kandy or Matale will drop you at the turn-off.

Dambulla

066 / POP 72,500

Dambulla's famed rock cave temple is an iconic Sri Lankan image – you'll be familiar with its spectacular Buddha-filled interior long before you arrive in town. The Buddhist cave murals are some of the most beautiful in Sri Lanka and should not be missed.

The town of Dambulla has heavy traffic heading for one of Sri Lanka's biggest wholesale markets. Consider visiting the site as a day trip from the more relaxing environs of Kandy or Sigiriya.

Sights & Activities

In recent years, two rival monastic groups have been fighting over legal control of the Dambulla caves, with the result that the **ticket office** (6am-6pm) is now in an inconvenient location 1km west of the main highway, on the south side of the hillside leading up to the temples. The easiest thing to do is take a three-wheeler to the ticket office to buy your ticket, climb 20 minutes up steps to the cave temples from here and then descend down the main stairway to the Golden Temple on the main road.

★Dambulla Cave Temples BUDDHIST TEMPLE
(adult/child Rs 1500/750; 6am-7pm) The beautiful Royal Rock Temple complex sits about 160m above the road in the southern part of Dambulla. Five separate caves contain about 150 absolutely stunning Buddha statues and paintings, some of Sri Lanka's most important and evocative religious art. Buddha images were first created here more than 2000 years ago, and over the centuries subsequent kings added to and embellished the cave art.

From the caves there are superb views over the surrounding countryside; Sigiriya is clearly visible some 20km distant.

Dambulla is thought to have been a place of worship since the 1st century BCE, when King Valagamba (also known as Vattagamini Abhaya), driven out of Anuradhapura, took refuge here. When he regained his throne, he had the interior of the caves carved into magnificent rock temples. Further paintings were commissioned by later kings, including King Nissanka Malla, who had the caves' interiors gilded, earning the place the name Ran Giri (Golden Rock).

This process of retouching original and creating new artwork continued into the 20th century. Remarkably, the overall impact is breathtakingly coherent.

You'll need to cover your arms and legs to enter the site. Sarongs can be rented at the entrance for Rs 100. A guided tour costs Rs 750.

Cave I (Devaraja Viharaya) BUDDHIST TEMPLE
The first cave, the Temple of the King of the Gods, has a 15m-long reclining Buddha. The so-called 'sleeping' position actually depicts Buddha attaining *parinirvana* (entering nirvana) upon his death. Ananda, the Buddha's loyal disciple, and a seated Buddha are depicted nearby.

Cave II (Maharaja Viharaya) BUDDHIST TEMPLE
The Temple of the Great King is arguably the most spectacular of the caves. It measures 52m from east to west and 23m from the entrance to the back wall; the highest point of the ceiling is 7m. This cave is named after the two statues it contains. There is a painted wooden statue of King Valagamba on the left as you enter, and another statue further inside of Nissanka Malla.

The cave's main Buddha statue, which appears to have once been covered in gold leaf, is situated under a *makara torana* (archway decorated with mythological crocodile-elephants), with the right hand raised in *abhaya mudra* (pose conveying protection). Hindu deities are also represented. The vessel inside the cave collects water that constantly

Dambulla

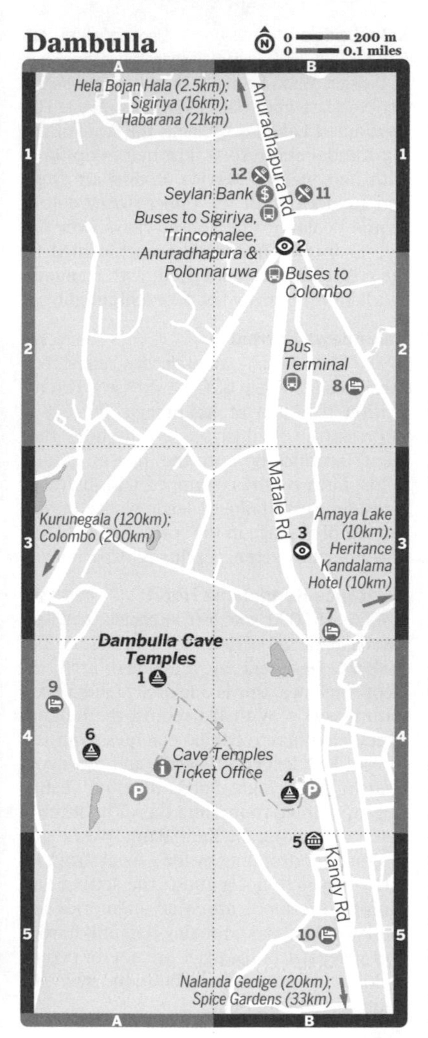

drips from the ceiling of the temple – even during droughts – which is used for sacred rituals.

Cave III (Maha Alut Viharaya) BUDDHIST TEMPLE
This well-lit cave, the New Great Temple, was said to have been converted from a storeroom in the 18th century by King Kirti Sri Rajasinghe of Kandy, one of the last Kandyan monarchs. A statue of him stands to the right of the doorway as you enter. It is filled with Buddha statues, including a beautiful reclining Buddha, and is separated from Cave II by only a masonry wall.

Dambulla

Top Sights
1 Dambulla Cave Temples A4

Sights
Cave I (Devaraja Viharaya) ....(see 1)
Cave II (Maharaja Viharaya) ....(see 1)
Cave III (Maha Alut Viharaya)......(see 1)
Cave IV (Pachima Viharaya)........(see 1)
Cave V (Devana Alut Viharaya) ...(see 1)
2 Clock Tower B1
3 Dambulla Produce Market................. B3
4 Golden Temple...................................... B4
5 Museum of Wall Paintings.................. B5
6 Somawathiya Stupa A4

Sleeping
7 Dambulla Heritage Resthouse........... B3
8 Freedom Village B2
9 Rock View Homestay.......................... A4
10 Sundaras B5

Eating
11 Bentota Bake House............................ B1
Dambulla Heritage Resthouse Restaurant..................................(see 7)
12 Mango Mango B1

Cave IV (Pachima Viharaya) BUDDHIST TEMPLE
The relatively small Western Cave is actually not the most westerly cave – that position belongs to Cave V. The central Buddha figure is seated under a *makara torana,* with its hands in *dhyana mudra* (a meditative pose in which the hands are cupped). The small dagoba in the centre was broken into by thieves who believed that it contained jewellery belonging to Queen Somawathiya.

Cave V (Devana Alut Viharaya) BUDDHIST TEMPLE
This newer cave was once used as a storehouse, but it's now called the Second New Temple. It features a reclining Buddha; Hindu deities, including Kataragama (Murugan) and Vishnu, are also present.

Somawathiya Stupa BUDDHIST SITE
Just 100m from the Dambulla Cave Temples ticket office is this little-visited ancient stupa and monastery complex, with the foundations of a chapter house and *bodhigara* (building to house a bodhi tree).

Museum of Wall Paintings MUSEUM
(adult/child Rs 370/180; ⌚7.30am-4.30pm) The English-language displays here are a good primer on Sri Lankan wall art – from cave paintings to 18th-century frescoes – but the

poor reproductions fail to inspire the enthusiasm the subject deserves. The building is 500m south of the Golden Temple.

Dambulla Produce Market MARKET
(Matale Rd; ⌚noon-3am) Even if you're not looking to buy a truckload of bananas, this huge wholesale market south of the town centre offers a fascinating look at the vast range of produce grown in Sri Lanka. What you see being carted about with manic energy (be careful and stay out of everybody's way) will be sold in Colombo tomorrow.

Golden Temple BUDDHIST TEMPLE
(www.goldentemple.lk; ⌚dawn-dusk) FREE At the foot of the cave temples hill stands this kitschy modern temple, atop which sits a huge golden Buddha image in the *dhammachakka mudra* (wheel-turning pose). Give the dull museum a miss.

Sleeping

Trucks on Hwy A9, which cuts across the heart of Dambulla, thunder through town night and day, so bear this in mind when choosing a room.

Rock View Homestay GUESTHOUSE $
(☎071-914 0755, WhatsApp 071-399 3521; Pirivena Rd; s/d Rs 2000/2700;) This good-value, family-run guesthouse has just four rooms of varying sizes but all are spotless with modern bathrooms and a relaxing balcony terrace. English-speaking hosts Upal and Wattsala are very helpful. It's in a quiet, rural location, with the caves' ticket office just a 700m walk away, but you'll need a three-wheeler (Rs 200) to get into town.

Freedom Village HOTEL $$
(☎077-997 0602; www.freedomvillagedambulla.com; Economic Center Rd, 8th Canal; s/d incl breakfast from Rs 5500/7150;) This quiet and laid-back mini-resort, a couple of blocks east of the bus station, is a relaxing and useful central sightseeing base. The clean, modern rooms overlook a pool and the suite-like superior rooms are particularly spacious. Staff offer free transport to the caves and a three-wheeler day trip to Sigiriya (Rs 2000).

Around Dambulla

The best top-end resorts are way out in the lush countryside by the Kandalama lake; for these you'll need your own transport or a three-wheeler.

Lake Lodge BOUTIQUE HOTEL $$$
(☎066-205 2500; www.lakelodgekandalama.com; 16 Division, Wewa Rd, Kandalama; superior/deluxe incl breakfast from US$105/125;) The 12-roomed Lake Lodge lacks the scale of the big Kandalama resorts, but makes up for it with personalised service. Rooms are fresh and modern, with the upper-storey deluxe rooms boasting fine sunset views over the forest canopy. The hotel is French-owned, so the coffee and food are good, with romantic candlelit dinners by the pool a highlight.

Kalundewa Retreat HOTEL $$$
(☎077-520 5475; www.kalundewaretreat.com; Kalundewa Rd; r from US$270;) The attention to detail at Kalundewa Retreat is impressive, with just six stylish suites that blend seamlessly into the nearby paddy fields. Each room is equipped with bicycles, a resident ornithologist leads walks, or you can simply lounge in the spring-fed pool. It's a wonderfully serene, exclusive experience.

Heritance Kandalama Hotel RESORT $$$
(☎066-555 5000; www.heritancehotels.com; Kandalama Wewa; s/d incl breakfast from US$313/370;) Designed by renowned architect Geoffrey Bawa, this is one of Sri Lanka's signature hotels. With 124 rooms, the hulking brutalist concrete edifice emerges from the forest like a lost city, its walls and roofs covered in vines. Light floods into the beautifully appointed rooms and there's an infinity pool overlooking the Kandalama Wewa.

Consider dropping by for a meal (from Rs 2000) if you're not a guest; the setting and dining experience are what memories are made of. That said, the day-tripping hordes and sheer size of the place are not for people looking for an intimate boutique stay. It's 11km east of Dambulla.

Eating

★**Hela Bojan Hala** SRI LANKAN $
(A6 Hwy; snacks Rs 20-100; ⌚7am-7pm) This government-run stand exists to preserve traditional local foods, offering travellers an excellent opportunity for some culinary exploration. Try a portion of *pittu* (mixture of rice flour and coconut steamed in a bamboo mould) followed by a *narang kewum* (fried coconut and honey ball), washed down with a belimal flower tea, all for sale for pennies.

It's out of town, by the roadside 3.5km northeast of Dambulla, on the road to the Inamaluwa junction.

WORTH A TRIP

AUKANA BUDDHA

According to legend, the magnificent 12m-high standing **Aukana Buddha** (adult/child Rs 1000/500; ⌚24hr) was sculpted during the reign of Dhatusena in the 5th century, though some sources date it to the 12th or 13th century. Aukana means 'sun-eating', and dawn – when the first of the sun's rays light up the huge statue's finely carved features – is the best time to see it.

Note that although the statue is still narrowly joined at the back to the rock face it is cut from, the lotus plinth on which it stands is a separate piece. The Buddha's pose, *ashiva mudra,* signifies blessings, while the burst of fire above his head represents the power of total enlightenment. Don't miss the lily-filled rock-cut pond behind the white stupa at the edge of the site.

You'll need long trousers or a sarong to visit the statue; the ticket office is at the top of the first set of steep steps. A couple of vendors sell drinks near the parking area.

The statue is 800m from the village of Aukana. Frequent buses between Dambulla and Anuradhapura stop at the junction town of Kekirawa, from where there are local buses every 30 minutes for the 19km to Aukana (Rs 40, No 548). A return three-wheeler from Kekirawa to Aukana is Rs 1000 with waiting time.

Aukana (Awkana) is on the Colombo to Trincomalee rail line, but only four daily trains stop here: the station is 1km from the statue.

Sasseruva Buddha

A convoluted 16km west of Aukana is the 12m-tall standing rock-carved **Sasseruva Buddha** (Res Vehara; adult/child Rs 1000/500), a smaller version of the Aukana Buddha. In fact the two are believed to have been created by a *guru-gola* (master and understudy) team in the 12th or 13th century. Sesuruwa means 'similar'.

The attached monastery remains of Res Vihara (Temple of Light) date back to the 3rd century BCE. A monk from the modern temple can lead you past a 2000-year-old bodhi tree to several cave temples with some excellent Kandy-style murals. The last cave features an 11.5m-long reclining Buddha.

Bentota Bake House SRI LANKAN $$
(☎060-228 3144; Anuradhapura Rd; mains Rs 200-370, upstairs Rs 625-900; ⌚6am-10pm) This budget local chain offers cheap and tasty string hoppers or rice and curry downstairs, and a wider choice of dishes such as grilled fish (Rs 875) in the pricier air-conditioned upstairs (until 4pm).

Dambulla Heritage Resthouse Restaurant INTERNATIONAL $$
(Kandy Rd; mains Rs 300-800; ⌚7am-10pm; 📶) This classy cafe-restaurant, all monochrome photographs and period furniture, is atmospheric for a drink (beer Rs 450) or meals such as pot-roasted chicken and lake fish. There's a good wine selection and pleasant terrace seating, despite the thunderous traffic.

ℹ Getting There & Away

Dambulla is 72km north of Kandy on the road to Anuradhapura. The junction with the Colombo–Trincomalee road (A6) forms the centre of town.

The closest train station is in Habarana, 23km north.

Local buses run frequently from the bus terminal to Kurunegala (Rs 100), Matale (Rs 78) and Sigiriya (Rs 40, 45 minutes, every 45 minutes).

For other places you'll have to jump on a through bus and hope there's a seat. Buses to Kandy stop just outside the bus terminal. Buses to Anuradhapura (Rs 180, two hours), Habarana, Sigiriya and Polonnaruwa (Kaduruwela) stop just north of the clock tower, while buses to Colombo stop southwest of the clock tower.

Colombo Rs 320, five hours, every 30 minutes
Kandy Rs 120, two hours, every 30 minutes
Polonnaruwa (Kaduruwela) Rs 80, 1¾ hours, every 45 minutes

Three-wheelers cost Rs 100 to 150 in town.

Sigiriya

☎066 / POP 1800

Rising dramatically from the central plains, the enigmatic rocky outcrop of Sigiriya is perhaps Sri Lanka's single most dramatic sight. Near-vertical walls soar to a flat-topped summit that contains the ruins of an ancient palace, thought to have been the epicentre of the short-lived kingdom of Kassapa. The

Sigiriya

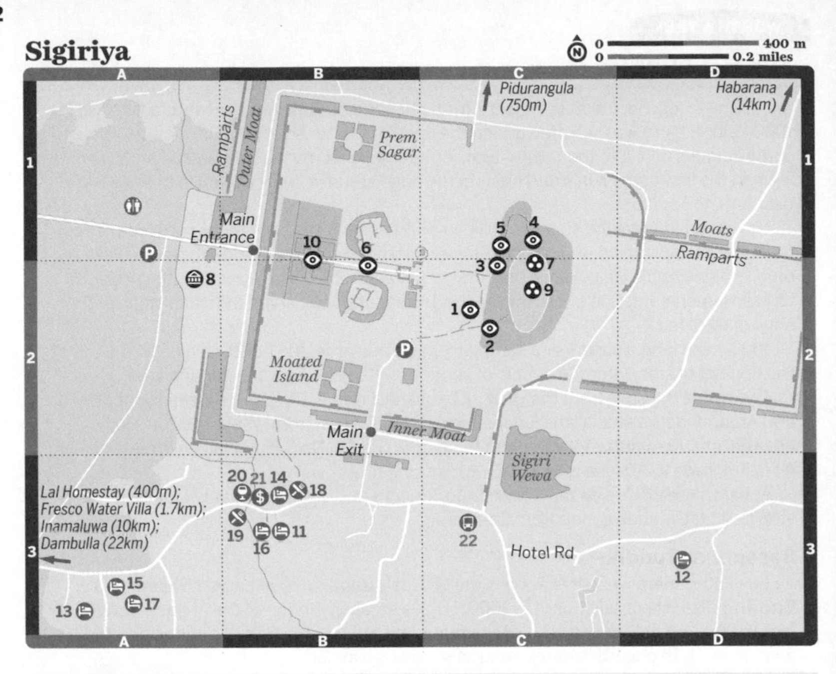

Sigiriya

Sights
1 Boulder Gardens ... C2
2 Cobra Hood Cave ... C2
3 Frescoes ... C2
4 Lion's Paws ... C1
5 Mirror Wall ... C1
6 Royal Gardens ... B2
7 Sigiriya ... C2
8 Sigiriya Museum ... A2
9 Summit ... C2
10 Water Gardens ... B2

Sleeping
11 Flower Inn ... B3
12 Hotel Sigiriya ... D3
13 Il Frangipane ... A3
14 Nilmini Lodge ... B3
15 Rainbow Lodge ... A3
16 River Retreat Homestay ... B3
17 Sigiri Lion Lodge ... A3

Eating
18 Chooti ... B3
19 Sam's Burgers ... B3

Drinking & Nightlife
20 Rasta Rant ... B3

Information
21 Commercial Bank ATM ... B3
Ticket Office ... (see 8)

Transport
22 Bus Stop ... C3

early morning vistas across mist-wrapped forests are spellbinding.

Lots of great accommodation for all budgets and proximity to Minneriya National Park and the Dambulla caves make Sigiriya an ideal base for regional trips.

Sleeping

New hotels and homestays are opening all the time around Sigiriya. It's easy to understand the appeal: the village is a mellow little place, off the main highway, and a far more preferable base than Dambulla town.

See Dambulla for rural hotels between Dambulla and Sigiriya that can also serve as a base for visiting the rock.

★ **Sigiri Lion Lodge** GUESTHOUSE $
(☎071-479 3131; www.sigirilionlodge.com; 186 Main Rd; r incl breakfast Rs 2500-5000; ❄☜) An outstanding place to stay, thanks to the genuine welcome and attention paid to guests by Ajith and Ramya, the owners. Rooms are immaculate and spacious and breakfast is

served on private tables outside the rooms. It's up a little lane about 500m west of the village. Add on Rs 1000 for air-con.

★Roy's Villa HOSTEL $
(077-039 4468; Rangirigama; dm US$12, d US$30-40;) The dorm rooms at Roy's are famously upmarket, with full-sized beds, air-con and attached bathrooms. But the reason people really love this place is Roy himself, who creates an inclusive, social but still laid-back atmosphere. Roy offers free cooking demonstrations and trips to a nearby swimming hole, plus good-value excursions to Pidurangula and shared 4X4 safaris to nearby national parks.

The rural location is wonderfully peaceful, surrounded by paddy fields. Get off the Dambulla–Sigiriya bus at the signed turn-off to Jetwing Vil Uyana and staff will pick you up for the last 1km.

Lal Homestay GUESTHOUSE $
(066-228 6510; lalhomestay@gmail.com; 209 Ehelagala; s/d Rs 1500/2000;) For a family experience that maintains your privacy, Lal's is perfect. Your host family could not be more welcoming or friendly, offering home-cooked meals (try the delicious jackfruit curry) and useful travel info. The five rooms, each with veranda and hot-water bathroom, are spotless. The two back rooms have less road noise. It's 1km west of the centre. Add Rs 800 for air-con.

Rainbow Lodge GUESTHOUSE $
(071-290 8181; 185 Kayamwala Rd; s/d Rs 2500/3000;) Set back off the main road down a private driveway, this spacious, two-storey house feels quite classy, with large sitting areas surrounded by palm trees. Upstairs rooms are best, featuring big, modern bathrooms and high ceilings, but currently only ground-floor rooms have air-con. It's within walking distance of the centre.

★Il Frangipane BOUTIQUE HOTEL $$
(077-190 0807; raveenf@gmail.com; 91/1 Kayamwala Rd; s/d/tr incl breakfast Rs 5000/6500/7500, ste Rs 10,000;) A lovely boutique place, with just four spacious rooms overlooking an enticing pool, and located within walking distance of both Sigiriya Rock and the village centre. The modern, Italian-influenced design boasts exposed brick walls, stylish wooden furniture and a breezy thatched restaurant. Book this one early.

The Hideout Sigiriya LODGE $$
(077-771 6088; www.sigiriyahideout.com; Palatawa Rd, Rangirigama; dm US$15, s/d incl breakfast US$58/78, treehouse $90-166;) The aptly named Hideout is indeed a real escape, surrounded by paddy fields and with viewing platforms for spotting eagles and peacocks. The treehouse rooms with private deck are particularly magical, the pool is a delight and the rural setting is pulse-lowering. It's 7km west of Sigiriya, 1km south of the main road. Discounts of 25% are common.

Fresco Water Villa HOTEL $$
(066-228 6161; www.frescowatervilla.com; Kimbissa; s/d incl breakfast US$70/75;) Groups like the villa-style rooms, fine balconies and stylish modern design at this well-tended resort surrounded by *araliya* (frangipani) trees. The 25m pool is heaven after a hard day tackling the rock. It's 5km west of Sigiriya.

Here's a secret: book a budget room at the Fresco Garden wing across the road (from US$40 online) and you'll be upgraded when business is quiet.

DON'T MISS

EXPLORING AROUND SIGIRIYA

With a bike or scooter you can explore several lesser-visited spots around Sigiriya.

One place not to miss is Pidurangula (p218) rock, the temples of which actually predate Sigiriya. If you explore the dirt roads north then west of here you'll find several water tanks, such as the Halmilla Wewa, which offers lovely reflected views of both Sigiriya and Pidurangula rocks.

Another good longer bike or scooter ride follows backroads for 25km to Dambulla via the **Kandalama Wewa** reservoir.

En route you can stop at the **Kaludiya Pokuna** (Dakinigiriya Vihara) FREE, 3km off the main road down a dirt track left just past the Paradise Resort. Forest trails take you past a stupa, the standing monolithic stones of a prayer hall, several rock inscriptions and caves, a small tank and many fabulous buttressed trees. It'll likely be only you and the monkeys here. Road erosion means you may have to walk the final 500m to the site.

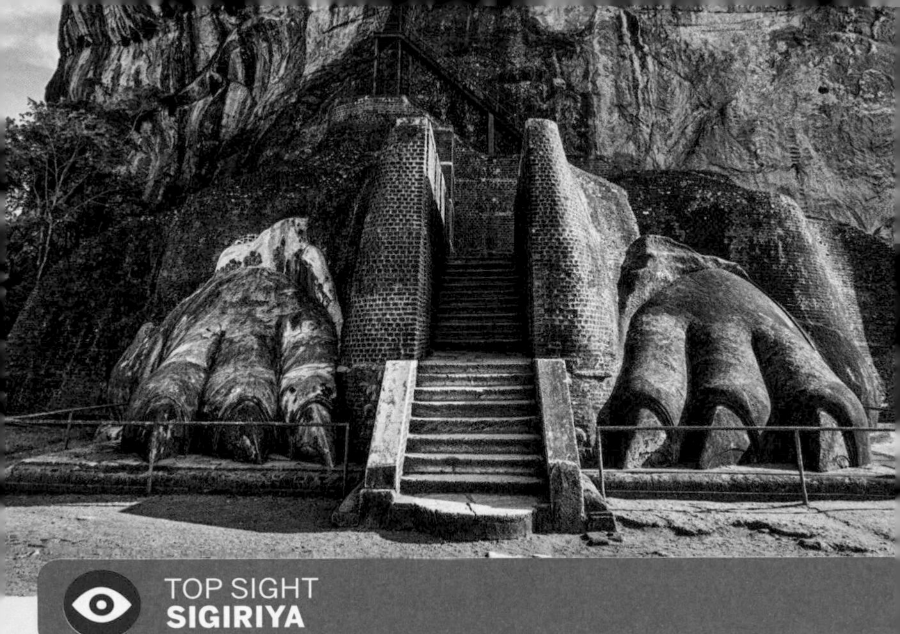

TOP SIGHT
SIGIRIYA

The World Heritage Site of Sigiriya refuses to reveal its secrets easily, and you'll have to climb a series of vertiginous staircases attached to sheer walls to reach the top. On the way you'll pass a number of quite remarkable frescoes and a pair of colossal lion's paws carved into the bedrock. The surrounding landscape – lily-pad-covered moats, water gardens and cave shrines – only add to Sigiriya's rock-star appeal.

DON'T MISS

- Royal Gardens
- Frescoes
- Lion's Paws
- Summit
- Pidurangala

PRACTICALITIES

- www.ccf.gov.lk/sigiriya.htm
- adult/child US$30/15
- tickets 6.30am-5pm

History

Peppered with natural cave shelters and rock overhangs – supplemented over the centuries by numerous hand-hewn additions and modifications – Sigiriya may have been inhabited in prehistoric times. The rock itself is an ancient magma plug from a long-ago-eroded volcano.

The established historical theory is that the rock formation served royal and military functions during the reign of King Kasyapa (r 477–495), who built a garden and palace on the summit. According to this theory, King Kasyapa sought out an unassailable new residence after overthrowing and murdering his own father, King Dhatusena of Anuradhapura. After 16 years on the throne Kasyapa eventually took his own life on the battlefield, following the return of his vengeful half-brother.

After the 14th century the complex was abandoned. British archaeologist HCP Bell rediscovered the ruins in 1898, and they were further excavated by British explorer John Still in 1907.

Royal Gardens

The base of the Sigiriya rock is a beautifully landscaped **garden area** dotted with formal water features, terraced gardens and natural boulders that were once home to numerous Buddhist shrines. It's a beautiful place to explore away from the crowds.

From the main entrance you pass a series of symmetrical **water gardens**, which extend to the foot of the rock and include bathing pools, little islands with pavilions that were used as dry-season palaces, and landscaped borders.

A series of steps continues up through terraced gardens to the western face of the rock, and then ascends it steeply.

The charming **boulder gardens**, closer to the rock itself and best seen on the descent from the rock, feature boulders that once formed the bases of monastery buildings. The step-like depressions in the sides of the boulders were the foundations of brick walls and timber columns. The cistern and audience-hall rocks are impressive, and the entire area is fun to explore.

The rocky projection known as the **Cobra Hood Cave** earned its name because the overhang resembles a fully opened cobra's hood. The plastered interior of the cave was once embellished with floral and animal paintings; a couple of faint traces remain. Below the drip ledge is an inscription from the 2nd century BC that indicates it belonged to Chief Naguli, who donated it to a monk. Because this cave lies off the route leading up to the rock, you generally pass by this cave after descending from the summit on your way to the south gate and the car park.

Climbing the Rock

Halfway up the Sigiriya rock an open-air spiral stairway leads to a long, sheltered gallery of **frescoes** decorating the sheer rock face. The paintings of the buxom, wasp-waisted women are popularly believed to represent either apsaras (celestial nymphs) or King Kasyapa's concubines. Protected from the sun in the sheltered gallery, the frescoes remain in remarkably good condition, their colours still glowing.

Modern theory suggests the female forms represent aspects of Tara – a bodhisattva and one of the most important figures in Tantric Buddhism. They are similar in style to the rock paintings at Ajanta in India, but have a specific character in their classical realist style. No one knows the exact dates of the impressive frescoes, though it's unlikely they date as far back as the 5th century (when King Kasyapa reigned).

TIPS FOR VISITING SIGIRIYA

- Sigiriya is an archaeological site, not a sacred one, so shorts are fine and a sarong is not necessary.
- To avoid the fiercest heat and the thickest crowds, get as early a start as possible; the ticket office inside the museum opens at 6.30am.
- Expect a visit to last half a day.
- Most people enter the site from the west and exit to the south.
- A good strategy is to head straight for the rock itself so that you're climbing Sigiriya in the relative cool of the early morning. Then later in the morning you can amble around the gardens and tour the museum.
- The narrow staircases in particular get clogged with visitors after about 9.30am.
- The ascent involves steep climbs, so if you're not fit it may be tough.
- There's no shade on the exposed summit, so bring a hat and water.
- Wasps build their nests on the rock face and can be a nuisance in July and August, so take care if you are sensitive to stings.

The paintings are at their best in the late-afternoon light. Photos are not allowed.

Beyond the Sigiriya frescoes, the path inches along the sheer side of the rock and is protected on the outside by a 3m-high wall. This so-called **mirror wall** (not the actual rock face) was coated with a smooth glaze upon which visitors felt impelled to note their impressions of the women in the gallery above – or so says local legend. The graffiti was inscribed between the 6th and 14th centuries.

You'll have to look hard beyond the modern mess to see the ancient messages. The graffiti is of great interest to scholars because they show the development of the Sinhala language and script, and because they demonstrate an age-old appreciation of art and beauty.

The Lion's Paws

At the northern end of the rock, a narrow pathway emerges on to the large platform from which the site derives its name – Sigiriya (from *sinha-giri*) means 'Lion Rock'. HCP Bell, the British archaeologist responsible for an enormous amount of archaeology in Sri Lanka, found the two enormous **lion paws** when excavating here in 1898 (pictured on previous page).

At one time a gigantic brick lion sat at this end of the rock, and the final ascent to the top commenced with a stairway that led between the lion's paws and into its mouth. The lion symbolism serves as a reminder to devotees ascending the rock that Buddha was Sakya-Sinha (Lion of the Sakya Clan) and that the truths he spoke of were as powerful as the sound of a lion's roar.

The 5th-century lion has since disappeared, apart from the first steps and the paws. Reaching the top means clambering up across a series of metal stairs, but you can still see the original grooves and steps cut into the rock.

The Summit

The spectacular terraced **summit** of the rock covers 1.6 hectares. This is thought to be the site chosen by King Kasyapa for his fortified capital. Today only the low foundations of structures exist, and the remains are visually unimpressive. Still, it's hard not to be captivated by the astonishing views from this lofty perch, which extend for kilometres across an emerald ocean of forest.

A smooth stone slab (the so-called king's throne, possibly a meditation spot) sits 30m away from the ruins of a dagoba. The 27m-by-21m tank, hewn out of the rock, looks for all the world like a modern swimming pool, although it was doubtless used for water storage.

Sigiriya Museum

This decent **museum** (⏲7.30am-5pm) has a fine diorama of the site, providing an excellent overview and explaining Sigiriya's cultural importance beyond the obvious natural beauty. Trade routes are explained, showing Sigiriya's connections with the Gulf, China, India and the Roman Empire.

Look for the wonderful black-and-white photos of British archaeologist HCP Bell and his somewhat reluctant family exploring the site soon after its rediscovery.

The museum is near the eastern entrance to the site. If you are visiting Sigiriya in the morning, visit the museum after ascending the rock to avoid the heat of midday. If visiting the afternoon, visit the museum before ascending in the cool of the late afternoon.

giriya Summit

Detour to Pidurangula

This prominent rock (p111), about 1km north of the Sigiriya site, offers amazing views of Sigiriya from its wide summit. It's a 20-minute hike up to the top, past several small temples, a 12.5m brick reclining Buddha and a final tricky scramble over boulders. Most people come at sunset but a sunrise visit is equally beautiful (bring a torch for both). The first section can be hard to find in the dark; veer right at the second modern temple instead of taking the staircase.

A return three-wheeler costs around Rs 700, including waiting time. A small archaeological site 100m further along the road contains a stupa, bodhigara and monk residences.A return three-wheeler costs around Rs 700, including waiting time. A small archaeological site 100m further along the road contains a stupa, *bodhigara* (building to house a bodhi tree) and monk residences.

PALACE OR MONASTERY?

Though the established view is that Sigiriya's summit was the site of Kasyapa's palace, some (including Dr Raja de Silva, Sri Lanka's former archaeological commissioner) are not convinced. In particular, the absence of stone bases, post holes, visible foundations for cross walls or window sashes, and a lack of lavatory facilities has caused doubt and provoked heated academic debate as to the purpose of the structures.

For de Silva, this site was a vast Buddhist monastery, embracing both Theravada and Mahayana practices, and existing for many centuries before and after Kasyapa's rule. The summit was a sanctuary for meditation, containing *kutis* (cells) for monks and paved paths for Buddhist perambulation.

DON'T MISS

THE SLENDER LORIS

The forests around Sigiriya are some of the best places in the world to spot the grey slender loris. These lovely, bizarre-looking primates are about eight inches long, with sad-looking, giant disc-like eyes, no tail, pencil-thin limbs and five frog-like fingers.

Unexpectedly, around a dozen loris live on the property of the luxury Jetwing Vil Uyana (which recently halted construction of new rooms to preserve their habitat) and the resident nature guide leads evening spotting tours (US$35 per person; 6.30pm) that are open to nonguests. Despite being silent and slow moving, the loris are actually fairly easy to spot with a guide – one reason both the BBC and National Geographic have filmed documentaries on the property.

The moment you spot a loris' eyes reflecting your torchlight back at you through the darkness is one you won't forget. Their nocturnal eyes are very sensitive to light, though, so use a red light filter on torches and don't take flash photos.

★Jetwing Vil Uyana LUXURY HOTEL **$$$**
(☎066-228 6000; www.jetwinghotels.com; Kimbissa; r from US$340;) For natural-world immersion – crocodiles in the pond and slender loris in the trees – the Jetwing is a great choice. The huge, individual chalets ('water' or 'forest' rooms have the best views) blend in with the environment but are also equipped with all mod cons (most have a private plunge pool) and butler service.

Hotel Sigiriya HOTEL **$$$**
(☎066-493 0500; www.serendibleisure.com; Hotel Rd; s/d incl breakfast US$75/85;) There are truly remarkable views of the rock from the pool area at this hotel. The 40-year-old breeze block exteriors are dated, but the fresh rooms have been renovated with polished concrete, bright colours and a beach-house feel. The resident naturalist leads much-lauded birdwatching trips (US$25).

Eating & Drinking

There is a line of somewhat disappointing traveller-geared cafe-restaurants in Sigiriya village. Most guesthouses located outside of town offer meals. For a special occasion consider dining at Jetwing Vil Uyana for its blowout five-/seven-course set lunch/dinner (US$25/35) or à la carte dishes such as Ceylon tea and cinnamon smoked tiger prawns.

Sam's Burgers BURGERS **$$**
(meals Rs 790; 8am-10pm;) If you are tiring of rice and curry, head to this pleasant creekside joint for a range of decent burgers and fries, including an Aussie special with egg and beetroot, alongside good desserts and cold beer. Bring mosquito repellent.

Rasta Rant BEER GARDEN
(☎077-794 2095; mains Rs 350-500; 11am-11pm) A young backpacker crowd frequent this chilled creek-side hang-out. Bob Marley is on heavy musical rotation, and there are plenty of hammocks and riverside loungers made out of shipping pallets.

Getting There & Away

Sigiriya is about 10km east of the Inamaluwa junction on the main road between Dambulla and Habarana. Buses to Dambulla run every 30 minutes from 6.30am to 6pm (Rs 40, 45 minutes) from a small stop southeast of the site exit and pass through the village centre. A three-wheeler between Dambulla and Sigiriya is around Rs 900/1500 one way/return.

To get to Polonnaruwa either take the Dambulla bus to the Inamaluwa junction to catch a northbound bus there or, for a shorter option, take a three-wheeler (Rs 900) north to the Moragasawewa junction with the Habanara–Polonnaruwa Rd and catch an eastbound bus from there.

Cinnamon Air (p326) operates daily flights to/from Colombo (US$215) from the airport 5km west of town.

Guesthouses can organise day trips with a private car to Anuradhapura or Polonnaruwa for around Rs 8000 return, to Dambulla for around Rs 3000 return, or a one-way drop at Colombo airport for Rs 9000.

Sigiriya and its surrounds are ideally explored by bike (Rs 350 per day) or scooter (Rs 1500); most guesthouses can organise rentals.

Habarana

☎066 / POP 8700

This small town isn't a destination in itself, but it serves as a potential base for Sigiriya, Dambulla and safaris to Minneriya and

Kaudulla National Parks, if you have your own transport.

Sleeping

In the last few years many new upmarket places have opened around Habarana but budget places are still limited.

Cinnamon Lodge LUXURY HOTEL $$$
(066-227 0012; www.cinnamonhotels.com; r US$230-330;) A classy and professionally run resort, Cinnamon blends Portuguese colonial design with traditional Sri Lankan stone architecture. A nature trail leads through 11 hectares of peaceful lake-shore landscaping to a tree-house platform for viewing birds (155 species), deer and monkeys. Rooms are tastefully presented with tropical decor and are very comfortable.

The elegant main restaurant area overlooks the lovely pool and is renowned for its buffet (with an entire room devoted solely to desserts!) and the rooms even come with soap menus. The excursions desk offers yoga, nature walks and bicycle tours. The hotel entrance is just south of the main Habarana junction. Discounted online rates often hover around US$100.

Galkadawala Forest Lodge LODGE $$$
(077-373 2855; www.galkadawala.com; Galkadawala, Palugaswewa; s/d incl breakfast from US$75/90;) Harmoniously built in a forest setting from recycled materials, this serene ecolodge is perfect for wildlife enthusiasts, with nature (outstanding birdlife and the odd elephant) very much on your doorstep. Maulie, your amiable and well-informed host, is very knowledgeable about the area and the vegetarian (only) food is a real highlight.

The Other Corner LODGE $$$
(077-332 7995; www.tocsrilanka.com; Laksirigama; s/d incl breakfast US$110/130;) Cross the rope bridge into this ecolodge and you quickly feel a million miles from anywhere, even though it's just 1.5km from Habarana centre. The 11 mudbrick and wood cabanas are set in extensive, shady grounds, and food is prepared freshly to order from the organic garden. The resident naturalist leads excellent birdwatching walks and can arrange night safaris. Walk-in rates drop by 40%.

Getting There & Away

Transport links are excellent: Habarana has the nearest train station to both Dambulla and Sigiriya and sits on a busy crossroads.

BUS

Buses stop at the crossroads outside the Heritage Habarana hotel. Frequent services include to Anuradhapura (Rs 150, two hours), Dambulla (Rs 25, 30 minutes) and Polonnaruwa (Rs 150, one hour).

TRAIN

The tiny train station is 2km north of town on the Trincomalee road. Trains from Colombo (departing at 6.05am and 3.05pm) are a popular way to get to the region.

The infrequent train services include the following:

Batticaloa 2nd/3rd class Rs 280/155, 3½ hours, two daily, at 11.18am and 8.15am

Colombo 1st/2nd/3rd class Rs 620/390/220, five hours, two daily, 4.45am and 9.40am

Polonnaruwa 3rd class Rs 65, one to two hours, three daily at 8.15am, 11.18am and 6.42pm (express)

Polonnaruwa

027 / POP 15,800

Kings ruled the central plains of Sri Lanka from Polonnaruwa 800 years ago, when it was a thriving commercial and religious centre. Though the kingdom only lasted around 200 years, the glories of that age can be seen in the archaeological treasures that still give a pretty good idea of how the city looked in its heyday.

That Polonnaruwa is close to elephant-packed national parks only adds to its popularity. And with good accommodation and plenty of bikes for hire, the town itself makes a pleasant base for a day or two, fringed by a huge, beautiful tank with a relaxed ambience.

The nearby town of Kaduruwela, 4km east of Polonnaruwa, has the lion's share of banks, shops and transport facilities.

Sleeping

Most hotels in town maintain a rural vibe despite recent road construction. Nearby Giritale is a good alternative accommodation base if you have transport.

★**Thisara Guest House** GUESTHOUSE $
(027-222 2654; www.thisaraguesthouse.com; New Town Rd; s/d/tr Rs 3000/3500/4000;) About 100m off the main road south of the Old Town, this family-run place has clean, spacious rooms with terrace seating in two blocks; the two new upper-floor rooms or the rear-block rooms with rice-paddy views from a private terrace are the ones to request. The

Polonnaruwa

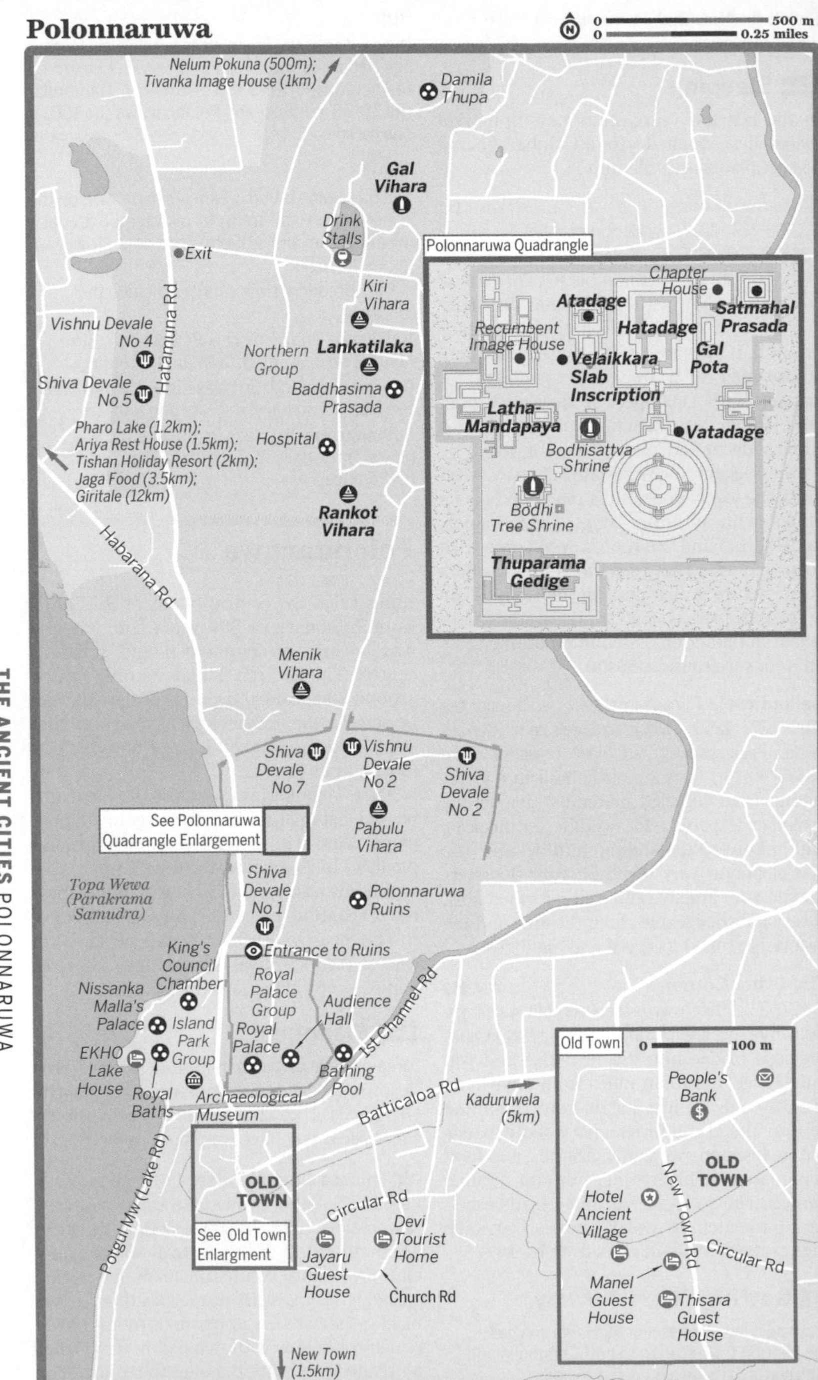

small restaurant has charming paddy views. Subtract Rs 1000 if you don't need air-con.

Devi Tourist Home HOMESTAY **$**
(027-222 3181; www.facebook.com/devitourist home; Church Rd; r Rs 2000-4500;) Down a quiet, leafy suburban lane, this well-run, inviting and orderly homestay owned by a Malay-Muslim couple since 1981 is a good choice, with five rooms (the cheapest are fan-only, with no hot water) arranged around a pretty garden. Cooking classes (Rs 1500, including dinner) and bicycles are available (Rs 300 per day).

Hotel Ancient Village HOTEL **$$**
(072-212 3063; www.hotelancientvillage.com; Sri Sudarshana Rd, Thopawewa; s/d incl breakfast Rs 3800/4400;) At the end of a side road and surrounded on three sides by rice paddies, this modern eight-room hotel is close to the centre but feels relaxingly rural. The rooms are fresh and tiled, with balconies or terrace, and there's a peaceful thatched, cabana-style restaurant.

Tishan Holiday Resort GUESTHOUSE **$$**
(027-222 4072; www.facebook.com/Tishan-HolidayResort; Habarana Rd, Bendiwewa; s/d/tr Rs 2500/3000/4000, deluxe Rs 4000/4500;) A good-value place (especially considering there's a nice pool with loungers) that straddles budget and midrange with plain but comfortable rooms. Deluxe poolside rooms have a small terrace. It's 4.5km west of the centre of town, but they rent bicycles and scooters, and there's a good restaurant.

EKHO Lake House HISTORIC HOTEL **$$$**
(027-570 01550; www.ekhohotels.com; r incl breakfast US$107-140;) With 14 luxurious rooms, this former British circuit bungalow has a superb location on a peninsula beside the Topa Wewa, right next to the Heritage ruins. The highlights are the unbeatable lake views (wonderful at sunset), an excellent restaurant with bar and a classy mix of historic heritage and modern design.

Queen Elizabeth II stayed in the suite room (Rs 65,000) during her 1954 stopover and guests can soak in her golden bathtub.

Pharo Lake RESORT **$$$**
(42 Deewara Mawatha, Bendiwewa; s/d incl breakfast US$80/100;) The amazing lakeside location is the real draw here, with fabulous sunset views, dawn boat trips with local fishermen and the occasional wild elephant visiting in July and August. The family rooms are worth the extra few dollars for the added space and privacy. Discounts of 50% are common. It's 4km from the centre.

The in-house travel agent can arrange country-wide trips – visit www.unseenceylon.com.

Eating

There are surprisingly few eating options in central Polonnaruwa. Most people head out of town for lunch and have dinner in their hotel.

Ariya Rest House SRI LANKAN **$$**
(077-358 8060, WhatsApp 077-876 2528; Bendiwewa; buffet Rs 600-900; 11.30am-4.30pm) This large and well-run restaurant is set up for tourist groups, but it's a convenient place to take a break between sightseeing. The lunch buffet is available all afternoon and the good range of dishes normally stretches to banana flower and wild mango curries. Coffee and beer are available.

Come for lunch or dinner and staff will let you use the swimming pool for free. It's 4km northwest of the centre, but easily reached by bicycle or three-wheeler (Rs 250).

★ **Jaga Food** SRI LANKAN **$$$**
(077-742 1042; 22 Junction, Jayanthipura; buffet Rs 1000; 11.30am-4pm & 6.30-9pm;) This family-run garden restaurant is halfway between Polonnaruwa (6km) and Giritale (7km), so you need transport, but it's worth the detour for the buffet of 10 curries that are slow cooked on traditional firewood stoves. Wander the lush garden to see the organic vegetables and herbs that go into your meal, then spot water monitors in the nearby pond.

Information

People's Bank (8.30am-3.30pm Mon-Fri) Changes foreign currency and has a 24-hour ATM.

Tourist police (027-222 3099; Batticaloa Rd) In the Old Town at the main traffic circle.

Getting There & Away

BUS

Polonnaruwa's main bus station is in Kaduruwela, 4km east of Old Town on Batticaloa Rd. Buses to and from the west pass through Polonnaruwa, but to make sure you get a seat, start at Kaduruwela.

Buses run every 30 minutes or so until about 4pm on main routes, which include the following:

Anuradhapura Rs 177, three hours

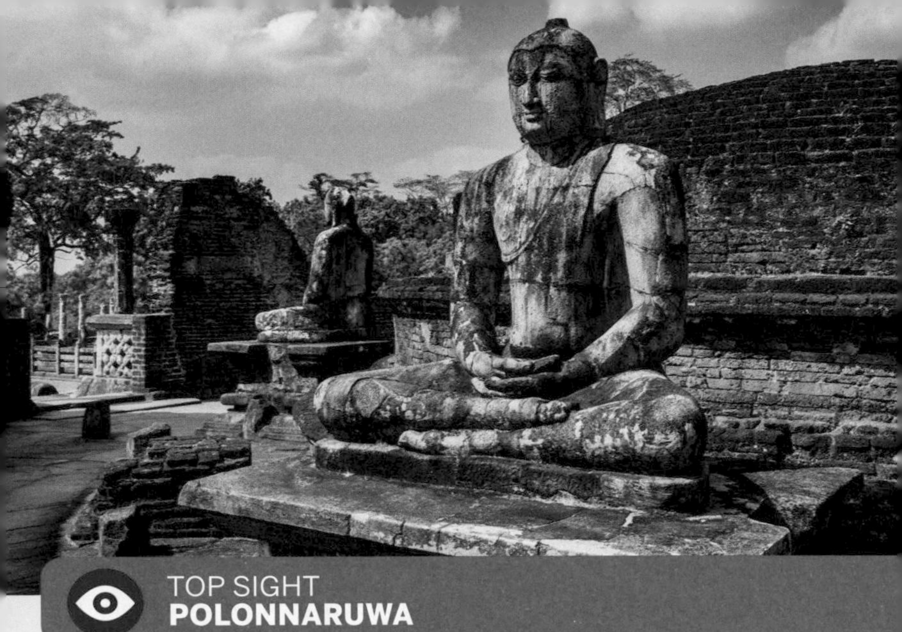

TOP SIGHT
POLONNARUWA

The sprawling one-time capital of Polonnaruwa is a delight to explore, with hundreds of ancient tombs, temples, statues and dagobas (stupas) spread over several distinct zones. At times it is breathakingly epic, at others intimately detailed, and there is enough at this World Heritage Site to keep you entertained for a full day.

Royal Palace Group

This group of buildings dates from the 12th-century reign of Parakramabahu I, the city's greatest king. The walled enclosure is the logical place to start a tour of Polonnaruwa, before continuing north to see the other principal monuments.

Royal Palace

The **Royal Palace** constructed by Parakramabahu I was a magnificent structure measuring 31m by 13m, and is said to have had seven storeys. Today its crumbling remains look like giant cavity-ravaged molars.

The 3m-thick walls have holes to receive the floor beams for two higher floors; however, if there were another four levels, these must have been made of wood. The roof in this main hall, which had 50 rooms in all, was supported by 30 columns.

Audience Hall

Just east of the palace, Parakramabahu I's **Audience Hall** (Council Chamber) is notable for the frieze of elephants, each of which is in a different pose. There are fine lions at the top of the steps.

DON'T MISS

- The Quadrangle
- Rankot Vihara
- Lankatilaka
- Gal Vihara
- Archaeological Museum

PRACTICALITIES

- 027-222 4850
- www.ccf.gov.lk/polonnaruwa.htm
- adult/child US$25/12.50
- 7.30am-6pm

From here, continue outside the southeast corner of the palace grounds to the **Bathing Pool** (Kumara Pokuna), which has a central lotus island and two of its crocodile-mouth spouts remaining. The foundations to the right were a changing room.

Quadrangle

Only a short stroll north of the Royal Palace ruins, the area known as the **Quadrangle** is literally that – a compact group of fascinating ruins in a raised-up area bounded by a wall. It's the most concentrated collection of buildings you'll find in the Ancient Cities – an archaeologist's playpen.

Over time, the Atadage, the Vatadage and the Hatadage all likely housed the Buddha tooth relic on their upper floors, each one built by a successive king to show his personal devotion.

As well as the major ruins here, also look for the **recumbent image house**, **chapter house**, **Bodhisattva shrine** and **bodhi tree shrine**.

Remove your hat and shoes when entering the buildings.

In the northeast corner of the Quadrangle stands the unusual ziggurat-style **Satmahal Prasada**, which consists of six diminishing storeys (there used to be seven), shaped like a stepped pyramid. Check out the figurines set above the four side niches.

Vatadage

In the southeast of the Quadrangle, the **Vatadage** (circular relic house) is typical of its kind. Its outermost terrace is 18m in diameter, and the second terrace has four entrances flanked by particularly fine guardstones. The moonstone at the northern entrance is reckoned to be the finest in Polonnaruwa. Four separate entrances lead to the central dagoba with its four Buddhas. The flower-patterned stone screen is thought to be a later addition, probably by Nissanka Malla.

Thuparame Gedige

At the southern end of the Quadrangle, the Thuparama Gedige is the smallest *gedige* (hollow Buddhist temple with thick walls) in Polonnaruwa, but is also one of the best: it's the only one with its roof intact, supported by corbel arch-style supports. The inner chamber is delightfully cool and contains four beautifully executed standing Bodhisattva statues, though the main Buddha statue is missing.

The building's exterior shows a marked Hindu influence and is thought to date from the reign of Parakramabahu I.

HISTORY

The South Indian Chola dynasty made its capital at Polonnaruwa after conquering Anuradhapura in the late 10th century, as Polonnaruwa was a strategically better place to guard against any rebellion from the Ruhunu Sinhalese kingdom in the southeast. When the Sinhalese King Vijayabahu I (r 1055–1110) drove the Cholas off the island in 1070, he kept Polonnaruwa as his capital, replacing Anuradhapura.

Under King Parakramabahu I (r 1153–86), Polonnaruwa reached its zenith. The king erected huge buildings, planned beautiful parks and, as a crowning achievement, created a 25-sq-km tank, which was so large that it was named the Parakrama Samudra (Sea of Parakrama).

Parakramabahu I was followed by Nissanka Malla (r 1187–96), who virtually bankrupted the kingdom through his attempts to match his predecessors' achievements. By the early 13th century, Polonnaruwa was beginning to prove as susceptible to Indian invasion as Anuradhapura had been, and eventually it, too, was abandoned and the centre of Sinhalese power shifted to the western side of the island.

Latha-Mandapaya

The industrious Nissanka Malla was responsible for this unique **structure**, which consists of a latticed stone fence – a curious imitation of a wooden fence with posts and railings – surrounding a very small dagoba. The dagoba is encircled by sinuous stone pillars shaped like lotus stalks, topped by unopened buds. It is said that Nissanka Malla sat within this enclosure to listen to chanted Buddhist texts.

Tooth Relics & Inscriptions

The **Atadage** shrine was built for the tooth relic when it was transferred from Anuradhapura and is the only surviving structure in Polonnaruwa dating from the reign of Vijayabahu I.

The attached 12th-century **Velaikkara Slab Inscription** records the oath taken by the Velaikkara royal guards to protect the Buddha tooth relic after an earlier rebellion was quashed.

The next-door **Hatadage** monument probably also once housed the Buddha tooth relic at one stage. Originally a two-storey building, it is said to have been built in 60 (*hata*) hours. Three standing Buddha statues mark the inner sanctum.

The nearby **Gal Pota** (Stone Book) is a colossal stone representation of an *ola* (palm leaf) manuscript. It is nearly 9m long by 1.5m wide, and 40cm to 66cm thick. The inscription on it – the longest such stone inscription in Sri Lanka – indicates that it was a work ordered by Nissanka Malla. Much of it extols his virtues as a king, but it also includes the footnote that the slab, weighing 25 tonnes, was dragged from Mihintale, an astonishing 100km away.

Satmahal Prasada

In the northeast corner of the Quadrangle stands the unusual ziggurat-style Satmahal Prasada (p223), which consists of six diminishing storeys (there used to be seven), shaped like a stepped pyramid. Check out the figurines set above the four side niches.

Around the Quadrangle

Dotted around the fringes of the Quadrangle are a number of structures, including several Shiva *devales* (Hindu temples), relics from the South Indian invasion of the 10th century.

Just south of the Quadrangle, the 13th-century **Shiva Devale No 1** is particularly notable for the superb quality of its stonework.

For a little-visited site that is fun to explore en route to the Northern Group try the **Menik Vihara**, a minor 9th-century monastic complex that consists of a stupa, relic house, image house, monks' cells, refectory and dispensary.

Pablu Vihara

Also known as the Parakramabahu Vihara, **Pabulu Vihara** is a typical dagoba from the period of Parakramabahu I. This brick stupa is the third-largest dagoba in Polonnaruwa, and is located down a side road. It was built on the orders of Queen Rupavali, the wife of Parakramabahu I and gets its name from the beads (*pabulu*) found nearby.

Just next door, the **Shiva Devale No 2** is the oldest structure in Polonnaruwa and dates from the brief Chola period, when the Indian invaders established the city. It was built entirely of stone, so the structure today is much as it was when built. Look for the statue of Shiva's mount, Nandi the bull.

nkot Vihara

Northern Group

These ruins, all north of the city wall, start about 1.5km north of the Quadrangle. They include the impressive **Alahana Pirivena group** (consisting of the Rankot Vihara, Lankatilaka, Kiri Vihara, Buddha Seema Prasada and the other structures around them). The name of the monastery means 'crematory college' – it stood in the royal cremation grounds established by Parakramabahu I.

Further north is Gal Vihara, probably the most famous group of Buddha images in Sri Lanka.

A bike makes exploration of the Northern Group a lot easier.

Rankot Vihara

The 54m tall **Rankot Vihara** dagoba, the largest in Polonnaruwa and the fourth largest on the island, has been ascribed to the reign of King Nissanka Malla. Like the other major dagobas in Anuradhapura and Polonnaruwa, the bubble-shaped dome consists of earth fill covered by a brick mantle and plaster, while the base is ringed with shrines. The construction clearly imitates the Anuradhapura style.

Encircling the stupa base are four *ayaka* (front pieces) and image halls. One has the brick remains of a reclining Buddha.

Just to the north of the dagoba is a ruined 12th-century **hospital**, whose excavated surgical instruments are surprisingly similar to those used today; see examples in the Archaeological Museum.

TOP TIPS

- Most visitors will find a day enough time to explore the ruins.
- The main entrance to the central archaeological site is from Habarana Rd, about 500m north of the museum; buy your ticket at the museum first.
- Although tickets technically allow you only one entrance, you can ask a ticket collector to sign and date your ticket so you can return after lunch.
- Tickets are not needed to visit the Island Park or Southern Groups.
- A bike is an ideal way to explore the area. Most hotels will rent you one, or you can hire one at stands opposite the main entrance.
- Start early as it gets hot here. Vendors sell cold drinks (including chilled king coconuts) at the major sights.
- The 'Heritage Lanka' smart phone app allows you to scan QR codes at several sites to get additional background information.

Also found here was a stone trough for therapeutic herbal baths and scales for weighing medicines.

Continuing north, you'll pass the **Baddhasima Prasada**, Polunnaruwa's largest *uposathaghara* (convocation hall), where monks met fortnightly.

Lankatilaka

One of the most evocative structures in Polonnaruwa, the **Lankatilaka** temple was built by Parakramabahu I and later restored by Vijayabahu IV. This massive *gedige* (stone Buddhist temple with corbelled roof and thick walls) has 17m-high walls, although the roof has collapsed. The cathedral-like aisle leads to a huge standing (headless) brick and plaster Buddha. Offerings of incense, and the structure's columns and arches, add to the devotional atmosphere.

Kiri Vihara

Construction of the dagoba **Kiri Vihara** is credited to Subhadra, King Parakramabahu I's queen. Originally known as the Rupavati Chetiya, the present name means 'milk white' because when the overgrown jungle was cleared away recently after 700 years of neglect, the original lime plaster was found to be in perfect condition. It is still the best-preserved unrestored dagoba at Polonnaruwa.

Far Northern Sights

Several unusual sights on Polonnaruwa's northernmost road are worth the detour.

The main site at the end of the road is the **Tivanka Image House**. Tivanka means 'thrice bent', and refers to the fact that the Buddha image within is in a three-curve position normally reserved for female statues. The building is notable for its fine Jataka frescoes depicting Buddha in his past lives – the only Polonnaruwa murals to have survived (photos not allowed).

As you return back south along the road, a track to the west leads to unusual **Nelum Pokuna** (Lotus Pond), nearly 8m in diameter, which has five concentric, descending rings of eight petals each. The pool was probably used by monks.

Also on this northern road is the half-hidden **Damila Thupa**. King Parakramabahu I planned this 12th-century stupa to be the world's largest Buddhist monument, but even with the enforced assistance of Tamil prisoners it was never completed. The enormous 600m circumference base is under excavation and slowly emerging from the forested hillside.

Island Park Group

Concentrated just north of the Archaeological Museum are the ruins of **Nissanka Malla's Palace**, which have almost been reclaimed by the earth. On the way there, you'll pass the **Royal Baths**, still fed via a sluice from the main tank. Entry to this group of ruins is free.

King's Council Chamber

This pillared **hall** at the heart of the palace area is where the King Nissanka Malla's council would have met. Inscribed into each of the 48 columns in the chamber is the name of the minister whose seat was once beside it, while the royal throne, in the shape of a stone lion, dominates the head of the hall. Just offshore is a tiny island on which are the ruins of a small summer house used by the king.

Archaeological Museum

This excellent **museum** (⏲7.30am-5.30pm) has rooms dedicated to the citadel, the outer city and the monastery area, with models showing how the ruins would have looked with a roof and wooden walls. The last room contains a wonderful selection of Hindu bronzes. Photos are not allowed.

Southern Group

The small Southern Group is close to several top-end hotels. By bicycle, it's a pleasant ride on Potgul Mawatha (Lake Rd) alongside the shores of the Topa Wewa (Parakrama Samudra) tank. It's particularly lovely at sunset.

Potgul Vihara

Also known as the library dagoba, the **Potgul Vihara** in the heart of the Southern Group is an unusual structure. A thick-walled, hollow, dagoba-like building, it is thought to have been used to store sacred books. It's effectively a circular *gedige*, and four smaller solid dagobas arranged around this central dome to form the popular Sinhalese quincunx arrangement of five objects in the shape of a rectangle (one at each corner and one in the middle).

Just to the north, and standing nearly 4m high, is an enigmatic **statue** that displays an unusually lifelike human representation (in contrast to the normally idealised or stylised Buddha figures). Exactly whom it represents is a subject of some debate. One theory is that it's the Indian Vedic teacher Agastya, holding a manuscript. Alternatively, it could be that the bearded, stately figure is Parakramabahu I clasping the 'yoke of kingship'. Others say that the king is simply holding a piece of papaya.

DON'T MISS: GAL VIHARA

This group of four beautiful Buddha images, cut from one long slab of granite, probably marks the high point of Sinhalese rock carving. At one time, each Buddha was enshrined within a separate enclosure.

The **standing Buddha** is 7m tall and is said to be the finest of the series. The unusual crossed position of the arm and sorrowful facial expression led to the theory that it portrayed the Buddha's disciple Ananda, grieving for his master's departure for nirvana, but it is now accepted as an image of the Buddha. Notice how the figure's weight seems delicately shifted onto the right foot.

The **reclining Buddha** depicted entering *parinirvana* (nirvana-after-death) is 14m long. Notice the subtle depression in the pillow under the head and the lotus symbols on the pillow end and on the soles of Buddha's feet.

The **seated Buddha** on the far left has four further Buddhas depicted in the *torana* above, making this a probable depiction of the Five Dhyani Buddhas. The carvings make superb use of the natural marbling in the rock.

Colombo Rs 330, six hours

Dambulla Rs 110, 1½ hours; take a Kandy, Kurunegala or Colombo bus

Kandy Rs 200, three hours

TRAIN

Polonnaruwa is on the Colombo–Batticaloa railway line and is about 30km southeast of Gal Oya, where the line splits from the Colombo–Trincomalee line. The train station is in Kaduruwela.

Trains include the following:

Batticaloa 2nd/3rd class Rs 190/110, 2½ hours, three daily, notably at 10.20am

Colombo 2nd/3rd class Rs 450/250, five to seven hours, four daily, including a morning train at 8.30am and one sleeper (1st/2nd/3rd class Rs 1500/750/600) at 10.25pm

Getting Around

Frequent buses (Rs 20) link Polonnaruwa and Kaduruwela. Three-wheeler drivers ask for Rs 250.

Bicycles are great for getting around Polonnaruwa's monuments, which are surrounded by shady woodland. Most guesthouses rent bikes for Rs 350 per day, and a few can find you a scooter for Rs 1500.

Giritale

027 / POP 8200

Northwest of Polonnaruwa on the Habarana road, Giritale is a sleepy, spread-out settlement alongside the impressive 7th-century Giritale Wewa. There's little to see here but the few places to stay (all 7km to 15km from Polonnaruwa) make a good base for visiting Polonnaruwa and Minneriya National Park, and also the outlying ruins of the Mandalagiri Vihara.

Sleeping

★Rice Villa Retreat GUESTHOUSE **$$**

(077-630 2070; www.ricevillaretreat.com; 21st Mile Post, Polonnaruwa Rd, Jayanthipura; s/d Rs 5000/6000;) A memorable place to stay, this beautifully located guesthouse enjoys an idyllic position overlooking an expanse of rice paddies, replete with the sounds of peacocks and bullfrogs. The five bungalows are well appointed, with modern bathrooms, terrace seating and contemporary design touches. Best of all, the hospitality from the family owners is warm and genuine.

Subtract Rs 1000 if you don't need air-con. The meals are excellent and cooking classes are offered for guests. The owners (p207) are expert at arranging local transport to Polonnaruwa (Rs 500) and beyond.

Giritale Hotel HOTEL **$$**

(027-224 6311; www.giritalehotel.com; r Rs 12,000-15,000;) Rooms at this recently renovated hotel are spacious and pleasant (deluxe rooms are better value), but the real draw is the unmatched sunset view from the bar terrace – come for a drink (Rs 700) if you have your own transport. It's behind the Deer Park hotel, 1.5km south of the Giritale junction.

Deer Park RESORT **$$$**

(027-777 7777; www.deerparksrilanka.com; r from US$180;) A large resort-style property made up of 80 rooms in dozens of cottages. The pool, bar area and restaurant are all excellent. Some rooms have outdoor showers, and the priciest rooms have a private deck with views of Giritale Wewa. Borrow some binoculars and you might spot elephants on the far side of the tank. It's south of the Giritale junction.

WORTH A TRIP

MANDALAGIRI VIHARA

For a fun half-day excursion from Polonnaruwa, head out to **Mandalagiri Vihara** (Medirigiriya; dawn-dusk), an uncrowded rural complex centred around an impressive *vatadage* (circular relic house) atop a low hill. An original structure may have been built here around the 2nd century, but the one that stands today was constructed in the 7th century by Aggabodhi IV.

A granite flight of steps leads up to the *vatadage*, which has concentric circles of 16, 20 and 32 pillars around the dagoba and is noted for its fine stone screens. Four large Buddhas face the four cardinal directions. There was once a hospital next to the *vatadage*, and you can still see one temple with three standing Buddhas.

At 3.5km past Medirigiriya, itself about 30km north of Polonnaruwa, Mandalagiri Vihara is best visited as a half-day trip from Giritale. A return three-wheeler costs around Rs 2800 from Polonnaruwa or Giritale. By scooter, make your way to Hingurakgoda, then 14km to Medirigiriya, then take the left branch at the clock-tower roundabout.

There was no-one selling tickets at the time of research, but this could change.

DON'T MISS

THE GATHERING

One of Asia's great wildlife spectacles occurs at Minneriya National Park in August and September. Some 200 or more elephants congregate for several weeks in one concentrated area, in what is known as 'the Gathering'.

The elephants surround the Minneriya Wewa, the huge reservoir first built in the 3rd century C. It was assumed that they were there for the water, as it remains wet even when smaller waterholes dry up. However, biologists have discovered that the water's retreat from the land is what really lures the elephants. As the reservoir shrinks, it leaves behind vast swaths of muddy earth that are soon covered in rich, tender grass. It's a tasty feast for the elephants and they come in droves.

Getting There & Away

Frequent buses on the road between Polonnaruwa and Habarana (and other towns to the west) stop in Giritale village. None of the places to stay are especially near the stop, so arrange for pickup.

Minneriya & Kaudulla National Parks

With their proximity to Polonnaruwa and Habarana, the Minneriya and Kaudulla National Parks offer an excellent chance of seeing elephants and other animals without the crowds of Yala National Park. On some days, you won't even need to enter the parks to view elephants, as they freely roam the countryside and even the main Habarana–Giritale Rd.

Be sure to keep a safe distance; in 2016 a tourist on a motorbike was killed while taking photos of a wild elephant from a road between Minneriya and Sigiriya.

Before visiting, first speak to locals (guesthouse staff, tour companies or guides) as they'll know which of the parks has the greatest concentration of elephants at any one time, depending on water levels and the growth of seasonal grass.

The parks are well served by tours: during busy times you'll find guides in jeeps waiting at the park gates. Typically, however, you'll arrange a trip with your guesthouse or hotel. With guide fees – and the many park fees – two people can expect to pay around US$80 for a private four-hour safari. **Ceylon Rides** (www.ceylonrides.com) at Roy's Villa (p213) can arrange group safaris for as low as Rs 4000 per person.

Groups normally tip their driver (and guide if you have one) around 10%.

Sights

Minneriya National Park NATIONAL PARK
(☎027-327 9243; adult/child US$15/8, service charge per group US$8, charge per vehicle Rs 250, plus 8% tax; ⊙6am-6pm) This national park is one of the best places in the country to see wild elephants, which are often present in huge numbers. Dominated by the ancient Minneriya Wewa, the park has plenty of scrub, forest and wetlands in its 89 sq km to also provide shelter for toque macaques, sambar deer, buffalo, crocodiles and leopards (the latter are very rarely seen, however).

The dry season, from April to October, is reckoned to be the best time to visit. Elephants can number 200 or more and flocks of birds, such as little cormorants, painted storks, herons and large pelicans all fish in the shallow waters. However, it's also possible to see large numbers of elephants here at other times of year, too; we saw over 100 in February when we visited.

The park entrance is on the Habarana–Polonnaruwa Rd. A visitor centre near the entrance sells tickets and has a few exhibits about the park's natural history. A park service guide from here costs Rs 1000. The initial 40-minute drive (along a poor dirt road) into the heart of the park is through dense forest, where wildlife sightings are rare. But then the landscape opens up dramatically, and the views across the tank are superb. Early mornings are generally best for birds and late afternoon is the best time to see elephants.

Kaudulla National Park NATIONAL PARK
(☎027-327 9735; adult/child US$10/5, service charge per group US$8, charge per vehicle Rs 250, plus tax 8%; ⊙6am-6pm) Like Minneriya, Kaudulla offers a good chance to view elephants. In October, there are up to 250 elephants in the park, including herds of juvenile males. There are also leopards, fishing cats, sam-

bar deer, endangered rusty spotted cats and sloth bears. The best time to visit is from January to March and, less reliable in terms of wildlife-spotting, May to June.

This park stands on the fringe of the ancient Kaudulla Wewa, 6km off the Habarana–Trincomalee Rd at Gal Oya junction. It is part of a 66.6-sq-km elephant corridor between Somawathiya National Park and Minneriya National Park.

Hurulu Eco Park NATURE RESERVE
(adult/child Rs 1296/648, vehicle Rs 350, service charge Rs 750-1500; ⌚6am-5pm) Tour companies often run safaris to this forestry reserve during the dry season months of December, January and February, when elephants head to the park's dry higher ground. There are normally a couple of tour jeeps waiting outside the park entrance, which is next to Habarana train station.

Getting There & Away

Everyone visits the parks as part of a jeep safari. It's possible to arrange your jeep at the park gates, but most people take the jeep from where they are overnighting. Figure on Rs 3000 to 4500 for the jeep costs alone for a three-hour tour.

Ritigala

Deep inside the Ritigala Strict Nature Reserve are the sprawling, jungle-covered **ruins** (adult/child Rs 1000/500; ⌚8am-4pm) of this extensive forest monastery.

Ritigala was probably a place of refuge as long ago as the 4th century BCE and claims a mythological significance. It's said to be the spot from which Hanuman (the monkey god) leapt to India to tell Rama that he had discovered where Sita was being held by the demon king of Lanka.

Monks found Ritigala's caves ideal for an ascetic existence, and more than 70 have been discovered. Royals proved generous patrons, especially King Sena I, who in the 9th century CE made an endowment of a monastery to the *pamsukulika* (rag robes) monks.

Ritigala was abandoned following the Chola invasions in the 10th and 11th centuries, after which it lay deserted and largely forgotten until it was rediscovered and excavated by British surveyors in the late 19th century.

Sights

The ruins of Ritigala forest monastery complex consist of two main groups, with dozens of smaller buildings and residences hidden among the boulders. Plan on a couple of hours for a visit.

Paths lead from the ticket office past an Archaeology Department bungalow to the huge *banda pokuna* (artificial pond), which still fills with water during the rainy season. From here, you cross the inlet over a stone bridge and follow the ceremonial staircase past the first of three round junctions.

The first main ruin is a large reception building. A path to the right leads to the *janthagara* (monastery bathhouse), with a central sunken bath surrounded by a roofed colonnade. You can still see the grinding stones used to prepare herbs for baths.

Further up the flagstone staircase is the main roundabout, with two paths to the left. The first leads back past half-hidden ruins to a monolithic bridge and raised library. There are several other buildings here to explore.

Further up the main staircase you finally get to Building No 16, a *padhanaghara* (double-platformed building) set in a moat-like depression, used for meditation, teaching and ceremony. Look for the ornate latrine stone in the right corner.

Getting There & Away

The turn-off for Ritigala is 15km northwest of Habarana on the road to Anuradhapura. It's then 5.5km on a good paved road followed by a dirt track for 2km. The latter may be impassable after heavy rains.

You might get lucky and find a three-wheeler (Rs 1000 return) waiting at the junction on the main road; otherwise, you need your own transport.

You could combine Ritigala and Aukana (p211) to make an interesting day's drive between Sigiriya and Anuradhapura.

Anuradhapura

☎025 / POP 64,000

The sprawling archaeological ruins, massive stupas and huge water tanks of Anuradhapura (pronounced *AnuRAdha-pura*) are one of South Asia's most evocative sights. Several of the buildings remain in use as sacred Buddhist shrines and pilgrimage sites, giving Anuradhapura a relevancy and vibrancy that's in contrast to the museum-like ambience at Polonnaruwa or other Ancient Cities sites.

Current-day Anuradhapura is a pleasant albeit sprawling city; a small town that feels more like a large village. It offers loads of good-value accommodation, easy bike hire and a relaxed pace, making it a good place to spend an extra day.

Each December, thousands of pilgrims flock to Anuradhapura for **Unduvap Poya**, a festival that commemorates the arrival of the sacred bodhi tree from India.

History

Anuradhapura became Sri Lanka's first capital in 380 BCE under King Pandukabhaya, but it was under Devanampiya Tissa (r 307–267 BCE) – during whose reign Buddhism reached Sri Lanka – that it first rose to great importance. Soon Anuradhapura became a great and glittering Buddhist complex, the importance of which was reinforced when the relic of Buddha's tooth was enshrined in the city in the 4th century CE.

In 204 BCE the city was captured for the first time by the South Indian Chola dynasty – a fate that was to befall it repeatedly for more than 1000 years. It was almost a half-century until the Sinhalese hero Dutugemunu led an army from a refuge in the far south to recapture Anuradhapura. The 'Dutu' part of his name, incidentally, means 'undutiful' because his father, fearing for his son's safety, forbade him to attempt to recapture Anuradhapura. Dutugemunu disobeyed him, and later sent his father a woman's ornament to indicate what he thought of his courage.

Dutugemunu (r 161–137 BCE) set in motion a vast building programme that included some of the most impressive monuments in Anuradhapura today. Other important kings who followed him included Valagamba (r 103 BCE and 89–76 BCE), who lost his throne in another Indian invasion but later regained it, and Mahasena (r 276–303 CE), the last 'great' king of Anuradhapura, who was the builder of the colossal Jetavanarama Dagoba. He also held the record for water-tank construction, building 16 of them in all, plus a major canal.

Anuradhapura was to survive until the early 11th century before finally being replaced as the capital by Polonnaruwa. The Anuradhapura site was sacked by the Cholas in 1017 and never retained its earlier heights, though a handful of monks continued to live here for another 200 years.

Sleeping

Anuradhapura has some of the best-value budget accommodation in Sri Lanka, with dozens of excellent family-run guesthouses scattered around the pleasant leafy neighbourhoods southeast of Main St.

Balcony Rest GUESTHOUSE **$**
(071-614 1590; balconyrestanuradhapura@gmail.com; 1160/B Nagasena Mawatha; s/d Rs 2000/2500;) There are just two rooms at this stylish family home, so two couples could have the entire upper floor to themselves. Rooms are excellent value, with a spotless bathroom and a fine wooden balcony. The residential location is a bit out of the centre and hard to find, so call ahead. English teacher Nimali and her husband Jayantha are excellent hosts.

★ **Milano Tourist Rest** HOTEL **$**
(025-222 2364; www.milanotouristrest.com; 596/40 Bandaranayake Mawatha; s/d Rs 3000/3500;) Hidden in a quiet residential street, Milano is a professionally run place in an elegant late-1950s house. The eight rooms are somewhat old-fashioned, but with a touch of class, and all rooms have thick mattresses, fridges and modern bathrooms. The restaurant does an excellent rice and curry (Rs 850) and there's a lovely garden for alfresco dining.

Milano also runs several other guesthouses, including the nearby and equally good **Melbourne Tourist Rest** (025-223 7843; www.melrest.com; 388/28 Rest House Rd, Stage 1; s/d Rs 3000/3500;), so if Milano is full you may be directed to one of these.

London Palace GUESTHOUSE **$**
(025-223 5070; www.londonpalacesl.com; 119/29/1 Mailagas Junction; s/d Rs 3000/3500;) An impressive two-storey place ('palace' is a little ambitious!) with 10 lovely, clean, bright and airy rooms with TV, fridge and a communal sitting area. The six front rooms with balcony/terrace are easily the best; back rooms are smaller and cheaper. The residential location is a hike from the centre, but bicycles are available and bus/train station pickups are free.

★ **Aryana Boutique Hotel** BOUTIQUE HOTEL **$$**
(025-205 7520; www.aryanahotel.com; 395/14 Bandaranayake Mawatha; r US$55-70, ste US$108;) There are just eight rooms in this stylish and hip place, so book in advance. An interior courtyard and an outdoor restaurant frame the central plunge pool and the lush greenery pops against the cream walls. Rooms are on the small side but are contemporary and fresh and the suite can sleep four.

★ **Ulagalla** BOUTIQUE HOTEL **$$$**
(025-205 0280, Colombo 011-232 8832; www.ugaescapes.com; Ulagalla Walawwa, Thirappane; r from US$400;) Exclusive and stylish, the 20 villas in this remote rural retreat,

Anuradhapura

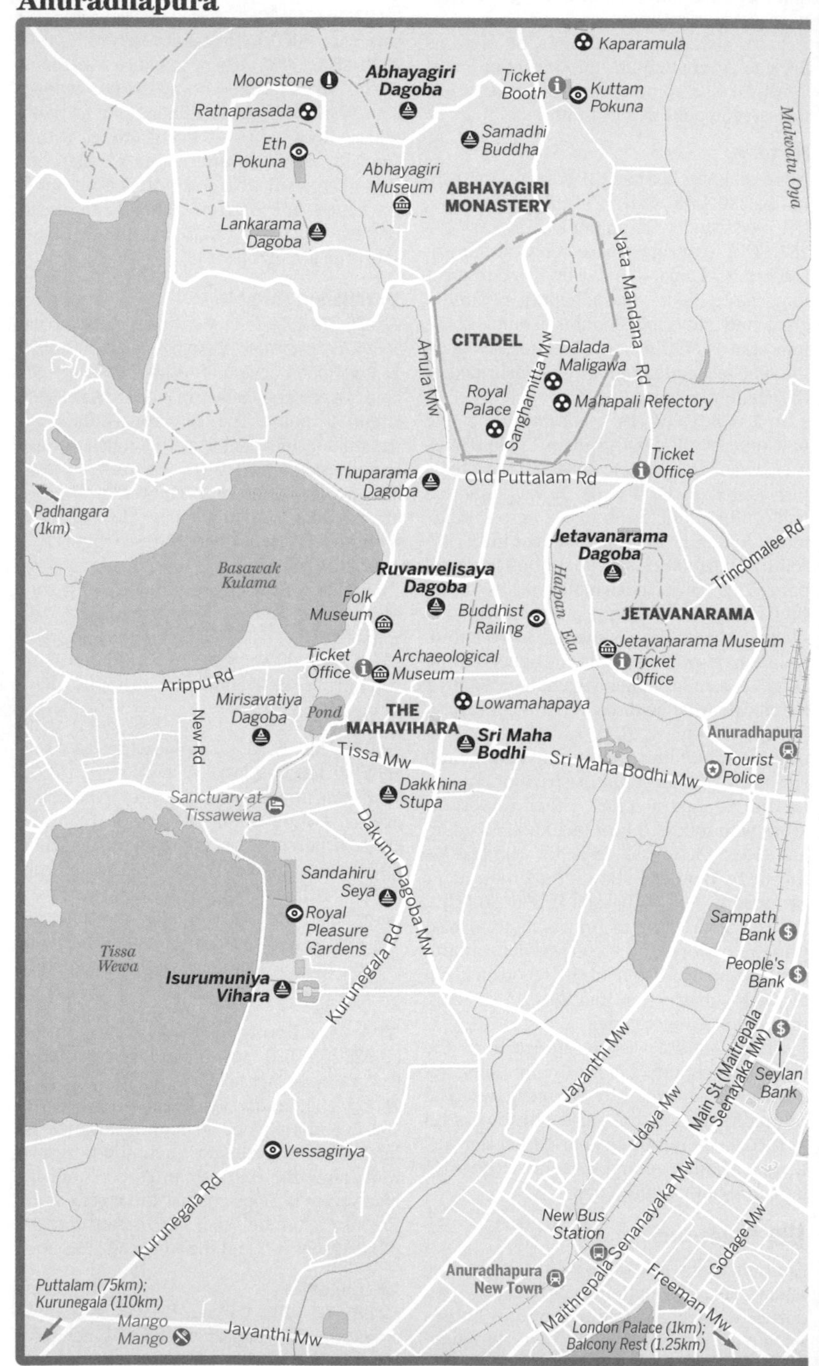

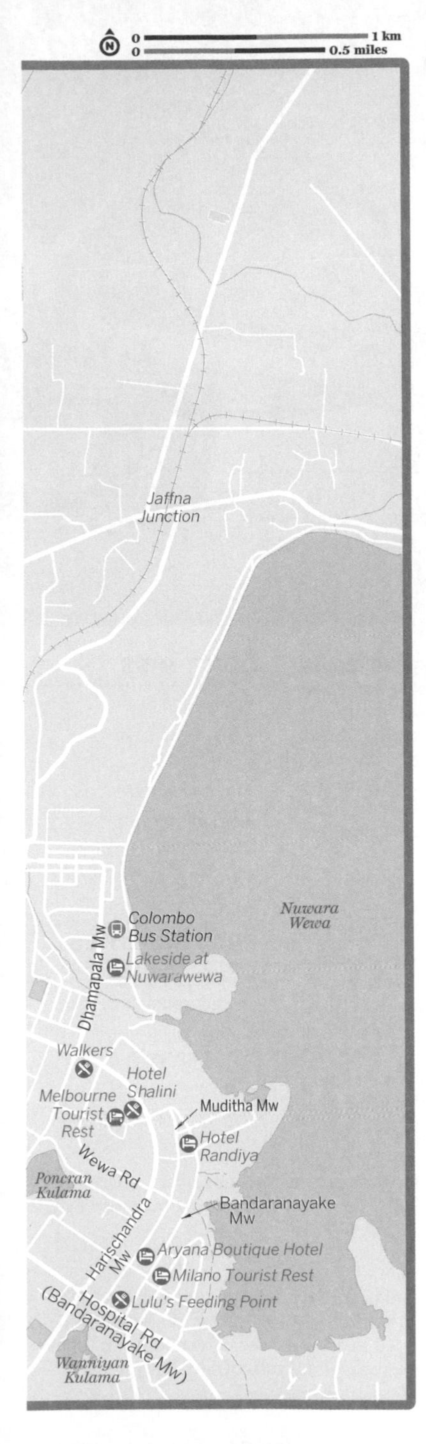

40km from Anuradhapura, are top of the line, with private plunge pools and relaxing decks, in addition to a lovely central pool. The century-old main building lends a classy colonial air, making it a superb place to unwind.

The real highlight is the sense of privacy and space, but the luxury also comes with eco credentials; rain water is harvested and 50% of the electricity comes from solar power. Online rates can drop to US$200.

★Lakeside at Nuwarawewa HOTEL **$$$**
(☎025-222 1414; www.nuwarawewa.com; Dhamapala Mawatha; s/d incl breakfast from US$87/107; ❄📶🏊) Renovated from top to tail, this modern hotel has a fine location near the lovely Nuwara Wewa tank. Rooms are stylish and fresh and come with a balcony or veranda; Avoid the musty 'superior' rooms but save a few dollars by ditching the deluxe pool view for an equally pleasant semi-deluxe garden view.

The restaurant (meals Rs 900) is excellent, with pleasant outdoor seating and a bar. Nonguests can use the pool for Rs 850.

Sanctuary at Tissawewa HISTORIC HOTEL **$$$**
(☎025-222 2299; www.tissawewa.com; off Old Puttalam Rd; deluxe s/d incl breakfast US$130/140; ❄📶) For colonial class this Raj-era relic (formerly a British governor's residence) can't be matched. It's been respectfully restored, the stylish rooms boast all mod cons and the verandas are a delightful place to enjoy a peaceful afternoon. The spacious, upper-floor deluxe rooms offer the best value. Guests are free to use the pool at the sister property Lakeside at Nuwarawewa.

Eating

Dining choices are surprisingly limited in Anuradhapura. Several hotels have good restaurants, including the Sanctuary at Tissawewa.

Lulu's Feeding Point SRI LANKAN **$**
(Hospital Rd; meals Rs 180-240) This self-service corner-shop joint is perfect for shoestringers staying at one of the many nearby budget guesthouses. The rice and curry, string hoppers, *kotthu* (*rotti* chopped up and mixed with vegetables) and quasi-Chinese dishes are all good, plus there's airy roadside seating and the staff are friendly and helpful.

★Hotel Shalini SRI LANKAN **$$**
(☎071-807 3335, 025-222 2425; www.hotelshalini.lk; 41/388 Harischandra Mw; set meals Rs 850; ⌚noon-2pm & 6-11pm) With its airy,

TOP SIGHT
ANURADHAPURA

The huge ruined Buddhist complex of Anuradhapura contains a rich collection of archaeological and architectural wonders: enormous dagobas (stupas), ancient water tanks and crumbling temples, built during Anuradhapura's thousand years of rule over Sri Lanka. The epic scale of the ruins point to the high water mark of Buddhism in Sri Lanka and rank as some of the world's greatest and oldest Buddhist monuments.

Orientation

Anuradhapura has four main zones. The Mahavihara was the spiritual centre of Anuradhapura, home to Sri Maha Bodhi – the sacred bodhi tree. Nearby are the Citadel, a compact collection of structures about 1000 years old, and Jetavanarama, with a huge dagoba and important museum. Further north is the Abhayagiri Monastery, arguably the most evocative part of the entire site, with several temples and dagobas dating back more than 2000 years, spread over a large, forested area.

DON'T MISS

- Sri Maha Bodhi
- Ruvanvelisaya Dagoba
- Abhayagiri Dagoba
- Jetavanarama Dagoba
- Isurumuniya Vihara

PRACTICALITIES

- www.ccf.gov.lk/anuradhapura.htm
- adult/child US$25/12.50
- 24hr

Mahavihara

This is the heart of ancient Anuradhapura and the focus of religious observances, which draw masses of people dressed in their finest. Relics here date from the 3rd century BCE to the 11th century CE.

Sri Maha Bodhi

The sacred bodhi tree (6am-noon & 2-9pm; pictured) FREE is central to Anuradhapura in both a spiritual and physical sense. It was grown from a cutting brought from Bodhgaya in India and is said to be the oldest historically authenticated tree in the world, tended by an uninterrupted succession of guardians for over 2000 years. Today thousands of devotees come to make offerings, particularly on *poya* (full moon) days and weekends. Sunset is a magical time to visit and stroll down to the spot-lit Ruvanvelisaya Dagoba.

The faithful believe it was Princess Sangamitta, daughter of the Indian Emperor Ashoka and sister of Mahinda (who introduced Buddhism to Sri Lanka), who brought the cutting from India. These days there is not one but many bodhi trees here; the oldest and holiest stands on the top platform. Railing and other structures around the trees are festooned with prayer flags.

In 1985, during the civil war, Tamil Tigers opened fire in the enclosure, killing several worshippers as part of a larger attack that took the lives of almost 150 civilians.

April and December are particularly busy months as pilgrims converge on the site for *snana puja* (offerings or prayers).

Ruvanvelisaya Dagoba

This magnificent white **dagoba** is guarded by a wall with a frieze of 344 elephants standing shoulder to shoulder, most modern replacements of originals from 140 BCE. Today, after incurring much damage from invading Indian forces, it rises 55m, considerably less than its original height; nor is its form the same as the earlier 'bubble' shape.

During the dagoba's consecration, a portion of Buddha's ashes were allegedly enshrined here, in a grand ceremony attended by monks from Rajagriha, Vaishali, Patna, Kashmir and Afghanistan. At the time, it was the biggest stupa in the world, with a 7m-deep foundation made of limestone broken with hammers and then crushed by elephants.

Ruvanvelisaya was commissioned by King Dutugemunu, but he didn't live to see its completion. However, as he lay on his deathbed, a false bamboo-and-cloth finish was placed around the dagoba so that Dutugemunu's final sight could be of his 'completed' masterpiece. A limestone statue in a small pavilion south of the great dagoba is popularly thought to be of Dutugemunu.

The land around the dagoba is dotted with the remains of ponds and pools, and collections of columns and pillars, all picturesquely leaning in different directions. Slightly southeast of the dagoba, en route to the Sri Maha Bodhi Temple, you can see one of Anuradhapura's many monks' refectories.

Lowamahapaya

So called because it once had a bronze-tiled roof, the ruins of **Lowamahapaya** (Brazen Palace) stand close to the bodhi tree. The remains of 1600 columns are all that is left of this huge pavilion, said to have had nine storeys and accommodation for 1000 monks and attendants.

TOP TIPS

- You'll need at least one full day, preferably two, to properly explore Anuradhapura.
- You can buy the Anuradhapura ticket at the Jetavanarama Museum, near the Archaeological Museum, at a ticket office just east of the Citadel and sometimes at a ticket booth near the Abhayagiri site. All are open from 7.30am-6.30pm.
- The scale of the ruins is huge. You can appreciate individual areas on foot, but a bicycle is an ideal way to get around the car-free trails and red-earthed walkways that link the main sites.
- The Anuradhapura ticket is pricey and valid for only one day. To avoid having to buy more than one, you'll need to be strategic.
- Tickets are most closely inspected in the Abhayagiri and Jetavanarama collections of sites and museums. You could squeeze your touring of these important sites into one day and then use a second day for sites with their own entrance fees such as Sri Maha Bodhi and Isurumuniya Vihara.

It was originally built by King Dutugemunu more than 2000 years ago, but what you see today dates from a 12th-century rebuild.

Thuparama Dagoba

In a beautiful woodland setting north of the Ruvanvelisaya Dagoba, the **Thuparama Dagoba** is the oldest dagoba in Sri Lanka – indeed, probably the oldest visible dagoba in the world. It was constructed by King Devanampiya Tissa in the 3rd century BCE and is said to enshrine the right collarbone of the Buddha. Its 'heap-of-paddy-rice' shape was restored in 1862 to a more conventional bell shape and to a height of 19m.

The slender, capital-topped pillars of the surrounding *vatadage* (circular relic house), perhaps the dagoba's most unique feature, enclose the structure in four concentric circles. Impressions on the dagoba pediments indicate the pillars originally numbered 176, of which 41 still stand. Sri Lankan scholars believe these once supported a conical wooden roof.

Archaeological Museum

An old British colonial administration building to the east of the main Mahavihara site houses this **museum** (⏲9am-4pm Wed-Mon) FREE, with an interesting collection of artwork, carvings and everyday items from Anuradhapura. Exhibits include relic caskets and photos of Anuradhapura's massive stupas before renovation, covered in vines and foliage.

Abhayagiri Monastery

For the sheer delight of exploring an ancient city, much of it still enveloped in tropical forest, the 2000-year-old Abhayagiri Monastery area can't be beaten. Head off the main trails and your only companions will be strutting egrets and the occasional dog-sized monitor lizard.

A map at the entrance shows how the forest surrounding the main dagoba was home to four main *mula* (colleges or faculties), each with its own residences, refectories, meditation centres and bodhi-tree shrines. An estimated 5000 monks lived here at its peak.

Abhayagiri Dagoba

Dating back to the 1st century BCE, this colossal **dagoba** was the ceremonial focus of the 5000-strong Abhayagiri Monastery. Originally over 100m high, it was one of the greatest structures in the ancient world, its scale only matched by the pyramids of Giza (and nearby Jetavanarama). Today, after several reconstructions, Abhayagiri Dagoba soars 75m above the forest floor. Visually, it's stunning, and your first glimpse of this brick monument through a gap in the surrounding forest is breathtaking.

The name means 'Hill of Protection' or 'Fearless Hill'. The Saddarma Rathnawaliya scripture records that a statue of a golden bull containing relics of the Buddha was buried in the core of the stupa.

Abhayagiri Dagoba has some interesting bas-reliefs, including one near the western stairway of an elephant pulling up a tree. A large slab with a Buddha footprint can be seen on the northern side, and the eastern and western steps have unusual moonstones made from concentric stone slabs (the word 'moonstone' relates to the shape of the stone, not the type of stone itself). As you walk around the northern side of the stupa, look for the octagonal yupa (spire) and shaft that originally topped the dagoba before the current square top was added.

The **Abhayagiri Museum** (⏲10am-5pm), south of the dagoba, is arguably the most interesting in Anuradhapura and contains a collection of squatting plates, jewellery, pottery and religious sculpture from the site. The Chinese-funded building commemorates the visit of Chinese Buddhist monk Fa Xian to Anuradhapura.

Fa Xian spent two years (412–13 AD) living at Abhayagiri, translating Buddhist texts that he later carried back to China along the Silk Route.

West of the Dagoba

Sitting northwest of the Abhayagiri Dagoba is a ruined 9th-century residential complex for monks that is notable for having the finest carved **moonstone** in Sri Lanka; look for the fine steps held up by jovial *gana* (dwarfs).

Just a few steps to the southwest is the 8th-century **Ratnaprasada** or 'Jewel Palace'. Most of it lies in ruins today, though it was originally seven storeys high with a graceful, tiered roof. The entrance is marked by a beautifully carved *muragala* (guardstone), which depicts the Cobra King holding a vase of abundance and a flowering branch, with a dwarf attendant at his feet and his head framed by a cobra hood.

Further south and surrounded by forest is a huge body of water known as the **Eth Pokuna** (Elephant Pond), thought to have acted as an ancient water storage tank for the Abhayagiri monastery, rather than as a pool for pachyderms. Such is the scale of the tank – 159m long, 53m wide and 10m deep – that six Olympic-sized swimming pools could comfortably fit inside it.

Explorers can continue south to the whitewashed 1st-century-BCE **Lankarama Dagoba**.

East of the Dagoba

Walk east of the Abhayagiri Dagoba and you'll come across a prominent 4th-century **Buddha statue**, seated in the *samadhi* (meditation) pose. It is regarded as one of the finest Buddha statues in Sri Lanka. When constructed, it was likely one of four statues placed at the cardinal directions. Jawaharlal Nehru, a prominent leader in India's independence movement and its first prime minister, is said to have maintained his composure while imprisoned by the British by regular contemplation of a photo of this statue.

Further east are the two swimming-pool-like ponds of the **Kuttam Pokuna** (Twin Ponds), most likely used by monks from nearby Kaparamula residence hall. Water entered the larger pond through the mouth of a *makara* (a mythical hybrid beast featuring the body of a fish, the mouth of a crocodile and the trunk of an elephant) and then flowed to the smaller pond through an underground pipe. Note the five-headed cobra guard stone figure close to the *makara* and the nearby water-filter system, both at the northwestern end of the ponds.

One interesting off-beat site just to the north is **Kaparamula** This *mula*, or college, housed the bulk of Anuradhapura's many foreign monks and it was

TEMPLE ETIQUETTE

➡ Because so many of Anuradhapura's major sites are still considered sacred, it is important to be prepared to don modest dress.

➡ Remove your shoes and hat, cover your upper arms and wear a sarong if you are wearing shorts.

➡ It's a good idea to bring a pair of socks for the hot and rocky ground.

➡ Sri Lankan pilgrims wear white, which is considered a holy colour, a mode you might choose to copy out of respect (and also as it reflects strong sunlight).

TOURS

Most places to stay can arrange for licensed guides if you'd like – useful if you want a deep understanding of Anuradhapura and its rich history. Rates start at about Rs 2000 for a half day with you providing the transport.

probably here that Chinese pilgrim Fa Xian spent two years studying Buddhist Sanskrit texts. Archaeological digs are still under way, allowing you to see the brick foundations emerge from the forest soil.

Citadel

Despite dating from a later period than most of the Buddhist constructions, time has not been kind to the Citadel. Its once-great walls have almost entirely been reabsorbed by the earth, offering a fine Buddhist lesson in the nature of impermanence.

Royal Palace And Other Ruins

Built in 1070 (some 12 centuries after Anuradhapura's heyday), the **Royal Palace** FREE was an attempt by King Vijayabahu I to link his reign with the glories of the ancient Sinhalese capital. Little remains today except two fine, but surprisingly modest, guardstones.

The nearby **Mahapali refectory**, or alms hall, is notable mainly for its immense trough (nearly 3m long and 2m wide) that the lay followers filled with rice for the monks.

Also in this area is the **Dalada Maligawa**. The central relic chamber of this ruined temple may have been the first Temple of the Tooth in the 4th century CE. Other sources claim the tooth resided in the Abhayagiri Dagoba.

Jetavanarama

The huge Jetavanarama Dagoba dominates the eastern part of Anuradhapura. This area was once part of an ancient pleasure park called Nandana Uyana, said to be the site of the first sermons on Buddhism preached by Mahinda in the 3rd century BCE.

Jetavanarama Dagoba

The massive dome of the **Jetavanarama Dagoba** rises above the entire eastern part of Anuradhapura. Built in the 3rd century CE by King Mahasena, it may have originally topped 120m, but today is about 70m – similar to the Abhayagiri. When it was built it was almost certainly the third-tallest monument in the world, the first two being Egyptian pyramids.

Its vast, bulbous form is unplastered and said to consist of more than 90 million bricks. A British guidebook from the early 1900s calculated that this was enough bricks to make a 3m-high wall stretching from London to Edinburgh.

Around it stand the ruins of a monastery that housed 3000 monks. One building has door jambs over 8m high still standing, with another 3m still buried underground.

Jetavanarama Museum

A 1937 British colonial building provides a suitably regal venue for some of the treasures found at Jetavanarama. The objects displayed in the **museum** (8am-5.30pm) range from the sublime (finely carved ivory finials) to the ridiculous (ancient toilet pipes). Highlights include the elaborately carved urinal in Room 1 and the tiny 8mm-long gold decoration featuring eight exquisite flowers in Room 2.

Other Sites

South and West of the main historic and sacred areas are several important and enigmatic sights. You can link the Mirisavatiya Dagoba, Isurumuniya Vihara and Royal Pleasure Gardens in a stroll or bike ride along the banks of the Tissa Wewa.

Mirisavatiya Dagoba

This huge **dagoba** FREE was the first built by King Dutugemunu after he recaptured the city in the 2nd century BCE. The story goes that Dutugemunu went to bathe in the tank, leaving his ornate sceptre implanted in the bank. When he emerged he found his sceptre, which contained a relic of the Buddha, impossible to pull out. Taking this as an auspicious sign, he had the dagoba built.

Sandahiru Seya

Two thousand years after the first of Anuradhapura's great dagobas was constructed, this huge new **stupa** (Moon-Sun Temple) is slowly rising on the south side of Anuradhapura, commissioned by President Mahinda Rajapaksa in 2010. Designed to reach 85m in height, with a circumference of 244m, it is being constructed from over 30 million bricks and will be plastered and then whitewashed when finished.

Royal Pleasure Gardens

Known as the Park of the Goldfish, these extensive 2000-year-old royal pleasure **gardens** (Ranmasu Uyana) FREE cover 14 hectares and contain two ponds artfully designed to fit around the huge boulders in the park. Look out for the fine elephant carvings at the second pool.

Carved onto the back side of a rock face in the southwest corner of the park is an intriguing geometric mandala design of circles, crosses and sea creatures that some have suggested is one of the earliest ever depictions of a world map (others suggest it was a meditation aid or a star chart).

Isurumuniya Vihara

This charming rock **temple** (Rs 200; ⏲6am-8.30pm), dating from the reign of Devanampiya Tissa (r 307–267 BCE), is set around a lovely lotus pond, the corner of which is carved with images of elephants playfully splashing water. The central temple has some particularly fine murals. Climb around the back to the rock summit to see the bell-shaped stupa and a pair of Buddha footprints etched into the rock.

The small museum features the famous Gupta-style 'lovers' sculpture, which dates from around the 5th century AD and depicts Prince Saliya (the son of King Dutugemunu), who gave up his right to the throne in order to marry his low-caste love Asokamala.

Vessagiriya

South of the Isurumuniya Vihara are the faint remains of the **Vessagiriya** FREE cave monastery, a series of evocative, gravity-defying boulder overhangs etched with inscriptions and water channels. You can easily picture monks meditating in their cave retreats here.

WATER TANKS

Anuradhapura has three great artificial water tanks *(wewa)*, commissioned by the city's kings to provide water for irrigation and to raise tax revenue for the Buddhist community. All are good for quiet bike rides and walks along the shorelines.

Nuwara Wewa, on the east side of the city, is the largest, covering about 12 sq km. It was built around 20 BCE and is well away from most of the old city. The dirt road tracing the northwestern corner offers fine sunset views of the old city's skyline of stupas.

The 160-hectare **Tissa Wewa** is the southern tank in the old city and is encircled by a dirt road. It's easily accessed from behind the Isurumuniya Vihara or Royal Pleasure Gardens.

The oldest tank, probably dating from around the 4th century BCE, is the 120-hectare **Basawak Kulama** to the north.

THE WORLD'S MOST ORNATE TOILETS

In the 8th century, a new order of *tapovana* (ascetic) monks settled in the western fringes of Anuradhapura. Living among the lowest castes and dressed in scraps of clothing taken from the surrounding graveyards, they renounced the luxury of the main monastery and lived, it is said, on nothing more than rice.

To show their contempt for the effete, luxury-loving monks, the monks of the western monasteries carved beautiful stone squat-style toilets, with their brother monks' monasteries represented on the bottom. Their urinals illustrated the god of wealth showering handfuls of coins down the hole.

Ironically, these squatting plates remain some of the most beautifully ornate objects left in Anuradhapura; you can see fine examples at the Archaeological Museum, Abhayagiri Museum and the Padhanagara site in the western suburbs of Anuradhapura, as well as in Ridi Vihara (p244).

upper-storey pavilion and dripping eaves, this *haveli* (town house)-style building has a charming setting, but it's the food that really stands out. The menu changes daily, but the family recipes normally include the excellent lotus root salad, string hopper biryani and two delicious types of aubergine, along with unusual medicinal dishes such as tuber-like *kohila*. Bring mosquito repellent.

Mango Mango INDIAN **$$**
(☎025-222 7501; Jayanthi Mawatha; curries Rs 350-450; ⏲7-10am, noon-3.30pm & 6-10pm) The location in the southern outskirts of town is not the most convenient, but this bright and hip restaurant is worth the trip if you are in the mood for an Indian curry (dinner offers the widest choice). The tandoori dishes are good, as is the chicken *chettinad* (cubes of chicken in a peppery, yogurty tomato sauce).

★**Sanctuary at Tissawewa** INTERNATIONAL **$$$**
(www.tissawewa.com; mains Rs 800-1600; ⏲7.30-9.30am, noon-3pm & 7.30-9.30pm; 📶) There is no more atmospheric place for a leisurely meal or pot of tea than the veranda or dining room of this beautiful colonial hotel. Try the chilli-marinated grilled pork chops, the lake fish or the four-course set dinner (Rs 1500), followed by coffee served in white embossed china cups. No alcohol is served.

ℹ Information

Main St and Dhamapala Mawatha in the centre have banks and ATMs.

People's Bank (Main St; ⏲9am-5pm Mon-Fri)

Sampath Bank (Main St; ⏲8am-8pm) Long opening hours, no commission and fast service at this bank and ATM.

Seylan Bank (Main St; ⏲9am-5pm Mon-Fri)

Tourist Police (☎011-313 3686; Sri Maha Bodhi Mawatha; ⏲24hr) The place to come if you have an emergency.

ℹ Getting There & Away

BUS

Unless noted otherwise, daytime service in all directions is frequent (every 30 minutes or so).

Colombo Bus Station

For Colombo and destinations en route head to the small Colombo Bus Station in the northern part of the new town.

Buses to Colombo run via Dambulla and Kurunegala (bus No 15) or faster via Puttalam and Negombo (bus No 4).

Services include the following:

Colombo Rs 420 to 460, six hours

Dambulla Rs 200, 1½ hours; take a Kandy- or Kurunegala-bound bus

Kandy Rs 400, 3½ hours, No 43; air-con minibuses are the fastest

New (Main) Bus Station

Buses heading to points east and north start from the New (Main) Bus Station. Services include the following:

Jaffna Rs 400, four hours, eight daily; en route from Colombo, stopping outside the bus station

Mihintale Rs 40, 30 minutes; take the No 835 towards Horowupotana

Polonnaruwa Rs 177, three hours, No 75; bus is labelled 'Kaduruwela'; also for Habarana (Rs 120)

Trincomalee Rs 180, three hours, two daily, 7.50am and 11.30am; or change in Horowupotana

Vavuniya Rs 90, one hour, No 857

TRAIN

Anuradhapura's main train station is an art deco gem. Some services stop also at the new train station further south. Train services include the following:

Colombo 1st/2nd/3rd class Rs 1200/600/400, five hours, five daily, including fast Intercity trains at 6.40am and 9.15am

Jaffna 1st/2nd/3rd class Rs 1200/550/400, 3½ hours, four daily; trains continue to Kankesanturai

Getting Around

The city's commercial district is quite compact, but the rest of the town is too spread out to investigate on foot. A three-hour taxi/three-wheeler tour costs about Rs 1500/1200. Bicycles are the best local means of transport and can be rented at most hotels and guesthouses (Rs 400 to 500 per day).

Mihintale

This sleepy village and **temple complex** (adult Rs 1000; 24hr), 13km east of Anuradhapura, holds a special place in the annals of Sri Lankan lore. In 247 BCE, King Devanampiya Tissa of Anuradhapura was hunting a stag on Mihintale Hill when he was approached by Mahinda, son of the great Indian Buddhist emperor, Ashoka. Mahinda tested the king's wisdom and, considering him to be a worthy disciple, promptly converted the king on the spot. Mihintale has since been associated with the earliest introduction of Buddhism to Sri Lanka and draws a lot of local pilgrims.

As the climb takes 25 minutes, consider visiting early in the morning to avoid the midday heat or late in the afternoon for sunset views. If coming by bus, walk past the museum to the stairway at the base of the hill. You can cut the uphill walk in half by driving up the side Old Rd and starting near the Monks' Refectory.

Guides charge Rs 1500 for a two-hour tour. Tickets are sold at the second landing.

Sights

Monks' Refectory & Relic House — RUINS

Just above the ticket office is the monks' refectory with huge stone troughs that the lay followers kept filled with rice for the monks.

Nearby, on a raised platform identified as the monastery's relic house, are two inscribed stone slabs erected during the reign of King Mahinda IV (r 975–91). The inscriptions laid down the rules relating to the relic house and the conduct of those responsible for it.

Assembly Hall — RUINS

To the side of and just below the relic house, this hall, also known as the convocation hall, is where monks met to discuss matters of common interest. The raised dais in the middle of the hall was where the most senior monk would have presided over the discussions. Sixty-four stone pillars once supported the roof. The main stairway to the Ambasthale Dagoba leads up from here.

★Sinha Pokuna — MONUMENT

Just below the monks' refectory on the second landing, and near the entrance if you are coming via Old Rd, is a small pool decorated with a 2m-high rampant stone lion, reckoned to be one of the best pieces of animal carving in the country. Anyone placing one hand on each paw would be right in line for the stream of water from the lion's mouth. There are some fine friezes around this pool.

★Ambasthale Dagoba — BUDDHIST STUPA

The main ceremonial stairway, lined with frangipani trees, leads to the Ambasthale Dagoba, built over the spot where Mahinda converted Devanampiya Tissa to Buddhism. Just before you arrive you should take off your shoes.

A nearby **statue of the king** wearing traditional dress marks the spot where he met Mahinda. The name Ambasthale means 'Mango Tree' and refers to a riddle that Mahinda used to test the king's intelligence.

To the side, up a flight of rock-carved steps, is a large white **Buddha statue**.

The **bodhi tree** to the left of the steps leading to the Mahaseya Dagoba is said to be one of the oldest surviving trees in Sri Lanka. The tree is surrounded by a railing festooned with prayer flags left by pilgrims.

Aradhana Gala — VIEWPOINT

To the east of Ambasthale Dagoba is a steep path over sun-heated rock-carved steps leading up to a point with great views of the surrounding valley. A railing goes up all the way. Aradhana Gala means 'Meditation Rock'.

Relic House — BUDDHIST TEMPLE

This modern building houses an ornate golden relic casket flanked by elephant tusks, inside which are bones and relics from Mahinda's tomb.

Mahinda's Cave — CAVE

A path leads downhill from the back of the relic house courtyard, northeast of the Ambasthale Dagoba, for 10 minutes to a cave where there is a large flat stone where Mahinda lived. The track to the cave is hard on tender, bare feet.

Mahaseya Dagoba — BUDDHIST STUPA

This dagoba (the largest at Mihintale) is thought to have been built to house relics of Mahinda, though some sources claim it enshrines a hair of the Buddha.

To the side you'll find the original, smaller brick **Sela Chaitya**, one of the oldest

Mihintale

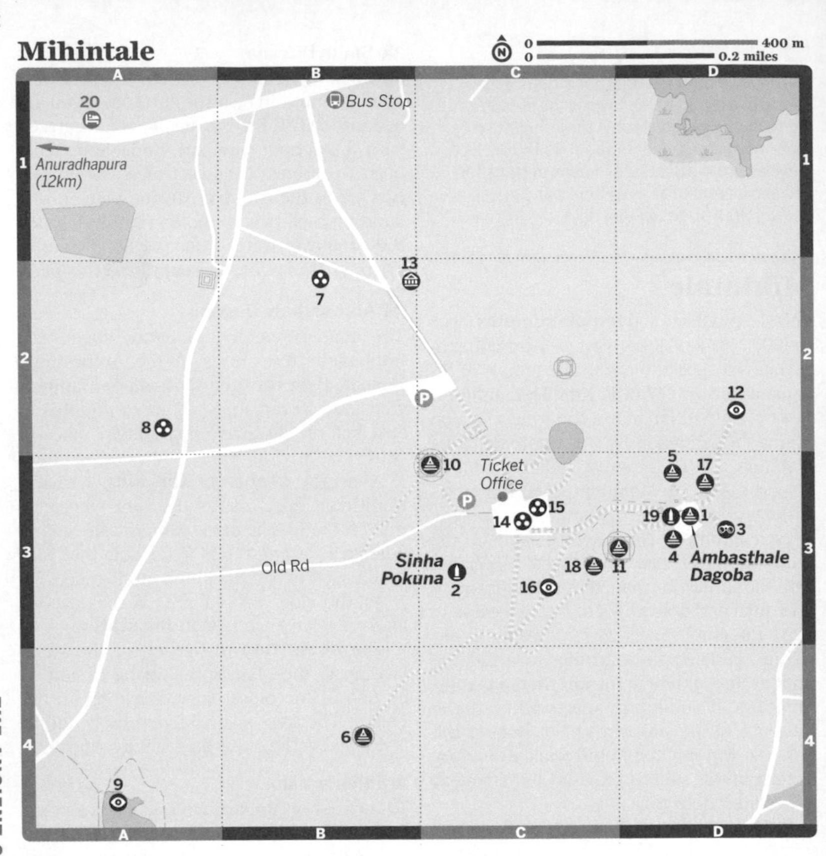

stupas in Sri Lanka and said to mark a meditation site of the Buddha. From here, there are views over the lakes and trees to Anuradhapura.

Naga Pokuna POND

Follow the steps behind the Sela Chaitya and you'll drop down to a junction. The right branch here takes you to the Naga Pokuna (Snake Pool), so called because of a five-headed cobra carved in low relief on the rock face of the pool. Its tail is said to reach down to the bottom of the pool. Water from here fed the Sinha Pokuna below.

From here you can descend to the stairway and the second landing. Alternatively, return to the junction and take the path up to Et Vihara.

Et Vihara BUDDHIST STUPA

At an even higher elevation (309m) than the Mahaseya Dagoba is the little-visited and modest 5m-high Et Vihara (literally, 'Elephant Monastery') stupa, which offers excellent views over the valley. It's a fine place to watch the sun set.

Kantaka Chetiya BUDDHIST STUPA

At the first landing, a side flight of 100 steps branches right to this partly ruined dagoba, one of the oldest at Mihintale. It's 12m high (originally more than 30m) and 130m around its base. A Brahmi inscription decrees that funding for the dagoba came from taxes on a nearby water tank. Four stone flower altars backed by *vahalkada* (solid panels of sculpture) stand at the cardinal points, and surrounding these are sculptures of dwarfs, geese and other figures.

Mihintale Museum MUSEUM

(⌚8.30am-4.30pm) FREE This small museum on the road leading to the stairway base is worth a short visit for its modest collection of artefacts collected from Mihintale.

Hospital RUINS

The remains of a 9th-century hospital sit a stone's throw from the site museum. The

Mihintale

Top Sights
1 Ambasthale Dagoba ... D3
2 Sinha Pokuna ... C3

Sights
3 Aradhana Gala ... D3
Assembly Hall ... (see 15)
4 Bodhi Tree ... D3
5 Buddha Statue ... D3
6 Et Vihara ... B4
7 Hospital ... B2
8 Indikatu Seya Complex ... A2
9 Kaludiya Pokuna ... A4
10 Kantaka Chetiya ... C3
11 Mahaseya Dagoba ... D3
12 Mahinda's Cave ... D2
13 Mihintale Museum ... B2
14 Mihintale Ruins ... C3
15 Monks' Refectory & Relic House ... C3
16 Naga Pokuna ... C3
17 Relic House ... D3
18 Sela Chaitya ... C3
19 Statue of the King ... D3

Sleeping
20 Mihintale Rest House ... A1

hospital consisted of a number of patients' cells. A *bat oruwa* (large stone trough) sits near the entrance. The interior of the trough is carved in the shape of a human form, and the patient would climb into this to be immersed in healing oils.

Inscriptions have revealed that the hospital had its specialists – there is reference to a *mandova,* a bone and muscle specialist, and to a *puhunda vedek,* a leech doctor. There was also a steam room and a pharmacy onsite. Surgical instruments from the hospital are in the site museum.

Indikatu Seya Complex RUINS
On the road leading to Old Rd, west of the site proper, are the remains of a monastery enclosed in the ruins of a stone wall. Visible here are two dagobas, the larger known as Indikatu Seya (Dagoba of the Needle).

Kaludiya Pokuna LAKE
(Dark Water Pond) On the southwest outskirts of Mihintale is the lovely Kaludiya Pokuna, an artificial pool that features a rock-carved bathhouse and the ruins of a small monastery. It's a charming spot for a quiet picnic.

Festivals

Poson Poya RELIGIOUS
This large annual festival is held on the Poson full-moon night (usually in June) to commemorate the conversion of Devanampiya Tissa to Buddhism.

Getting There & Away

Mihintale is 13km east of Anuradhapura. Buses run frequently (Rs 40, 30 minutes) from Anuradhapura's New (Main) Bus Station, with the last bus returning from a bus stop just north of the Mihintale site around 6.30pm.

A return taxi from Anuradhapura, with two hours to visit the site, costs about Rs 2500; a three-wheeler is about Rs 1500.

Yapahuwa Rock Fortress

Rising 100m from the surrounding plain like a mini Sigiriya, the impressive granite outcrop of **Yapahuwa** (Fire Rock; 037-227 5245; adult/child Rs1000/500; 7am-6pm), pronounced yaa-pow-a, is off the beaten track, but it's a fascinating place with an important history. Try to visit early in the morning to avoid the day's heat, or come for the fine sunsets from the summit.

There has been a Buddhist monastery at Yapahuwa since the 3rd century BCE, but the site hit its zenith between 1272 and 1284, when King Bhuvanekabahu I used the rock fortress as his capital and housed Sri Lanka's sacred Buddha tooth relic here. Indians from the Pandavan dynasty captured Yapahuwa in 1284 and carried the tooth relic to South India, only for it to be recovered four years later by King Parakramabahu III. From this point onwards the capital shifted to Kurunegala.

The small **museum** is off a parking area about 300m before the entrance to the steps. On display are stone sculptures of Vishnu and Kali and coins showing trade connections as far away as China.

Past the museum you wander through the south gate and the inner and outer ramparts and moats protecting the ancient fortress, which once housed the royal palace.

From the ticket office next to a huge split boulder you climb up the **ornamental staircase**, Yapahuwa's single finest feature, which leads to a platform that once housed the Temple of the Tooth. The porches on the stairway had extraordinarily beautiful pierced-stone windows, one of which is in the site museum. One of the lions near the top of the staircase appears on the Rs 10 note.

Eventually you reach the rock summit and its wonderfully breezy 360-degree views. There are faint traces of the stupa and bodhi tree shrine that once stood here.

Back on ground level, to the side of the main monastery buildings, a **cave temple** contains some lovely 13th-century frescoes. You may have to ask the monk to unlock the temple with its giant key.

Sleeping

Hotel Yapahuwa Paradise HOTEL $$
(037-227 5826; www.hotelyapahuwaparadise.com; Yapahuwa, Maho; s/d/tr US$65/75/90;) This spacious and comfortable resort is useful for visiting Yapahuwa, 1.5km away. The relaxing grounds include a pool, beer garden and several ponds teeming with herons, turtles and kingfishers. The spacious, modern luxury rooms are worth the extra US$40. Discounts of 40% are standard.

Getting There & Away

Yapahuwa is 9km east of the Anuradhapura–Kurunegala highway at Daladagama, which is well served by buses. Three-wheelers charge Rs 1000 return (including waiting time) to the site from Daladagama.

Alternatively, slow bus No 57/5 runs from Kurunegala to Maho (Rs 80, two hours) every 15 minutes, from which it's a shorter 4km three-wheeler ride to the site.

Maho (Mahawa) also has a railway station, where the Trincomalee line splits from the Colombo–Anuradhapura line.

Panduwasnuwara

Almost abandoned, the **ruins** (Kottambapitiya; dawn-dusk) of the short-lived, 12th-century capital of Parakramabahu I are spread across the countryside, about 36km northwest of Kurunegala. They are worth a stop if you have a particular interest in Buddhist ruins or are travelling between Negombo and the Ancient Cities.

The archaeological site is spread over a wide area. Just south of the tiny **archaeological museum** (037-119 1065; B79; donation expected; 8am-4pm Wed-Mon) is a moat, a massive citadel wall and the remains of a royal palace. Further on are the image houses, brick dagobas and living quarters of three monasteries.

Follow the road as it branches left, and you'll eventually come to the pillars of a restored Temple of the Tooth (Dalada Maligawa) next to a bodhi tree, a reclining Buddha temple with colourful Kandy-style murals and, behind that, the remains of a fascinating round tower (apparently once multistoreyed) enclosed in a circular moat.

Legend has it that the tower kept Parakramabahu I's daughter Unmada Chithra (the 'Beauty Who Overwhelms All with Maddening Desire') in chaste isolation after it was prophesied that if she bore a son, he would eventually kill all his uncles to claim the throne. Which, of course, is exactly what happened.

Getting There & Away

Panduwasnuwara is about 20km southwest of Padeniya on the road between Wariyapola and Chilaw.

Frequent buses (No 525) between Kurunegala and Chilaw pass Panduwasnuwara (Rs 60, one hour), from which you could walk or hire a three-wheeler to take you around the ruins, the furthest of which are around 2km from the road.

Ridi Vihara

Literally the 'Silver Temple', **Ridi Vihara** (www.rideeviharaya.lk; 7am-8pm) FREE was named for the silver ore that was discovered here in the 2nd century BCE and that helped King Dutugemunu finance the construction of the huge Ruvanvelisaya Dagoba in Anuradhapura. The main attractions are the wonderful frescoes painted in two Buddhist cave temples but the entire monastery complex is charming and feels well off the beaten track. Remove your shoes before entering the monastery gate.

The primary attraction for pilgrims is the golden standing Buddha statue in the main cave called the **Pahala Vihara** (Lower Temple), which also houses a 9m recumbent Buddha resting on a platform decorated with a series of blue-and-white tiles. The tiles were a gift from the Dutch consul and depict scenes from the Bible, including animals entering Noah's ark two by two. As you exit the room past a giant Buddha statue, look for the beautiful ivory inserts in the old wooden door.

The next-door **Uda Vihara** (Upper Temple) was built by Kandyan King Kirti Sri Rajasinghe in the 18th century and features stunningly vibrant murals and carvings painted in yellows, reds and black. Some clever visual tricks were used by the fresco artists; in one case, above the exterior doorway to the right, what appears to be an elephant reveals itself on closer inspection to be a formation of nine maidens.

Outside the temple complex you can walk past the Indian-style stone temple (currently under restoration) up the ceremonial pathway, past several ancient rock inscriptions, to a renovated **stupa**. From here paths lead through the forest (bring your shoes) for 800m up to good views from Pahangala rock.

Those with a special interest in Buddhism can overnight in the comfortable and modern **Pilgrim's Rest** (☎077-505 0670; rideeviharaymba@gmail.com; Ridi Vihara Monastery; by donation; ❄📶) monastery guesthouse; otherwise, most people visit on a day trip from Kurunegala or en route between Dambulla and Kandy.

Getting There & Away

Ridi Vihara is situated east of the Kurunegala–Dambulla Rd, 2km southeast of Ridigama village.

From Kurunegala take the No 564 Keppitigala bus to Ridigama (Rs 45, one hour). Alternatively, take a No 556 Matale-bound bus, get off at the junction 2.5km north of Ridigama and take a three-wheeler from there to Ridigama (Rs 150).

From Ridigama, a three-wheeler to Ridi Vihara costs Rs 120 each way.

MONARAGALA VIHARIYA BUDDHA

This 20m-tall sitting **Buddha** (Rambadagalla village) FREE, 4km southeast of Ridigama, was unveiled in 2015 as the largest (though not exactly the loveliest) granite statue in the world. Set on a plinth of carved peacocks, elephants and lotus buds, the Buddha is in *samadhi* (meditation) pose. It's worth a quick visit if you have your own transport, otherwise Keppitigala-bound buses pass by the entrance.

Kurunegala

☎037 / POP 34,500

Kurunegala is a bustling market town and transport hub between Colombo and Anuradhapura, and Kandy and Puttalam. The town is not a destination in itself, but it's a useful base for nearby excursions if you are using public transport.

Sights

The large, smooth rocky outcrops that loom over the town are the most striking feature of this city. Named for the animals they appear to resemble (Tortoise Rock, Elephant Rock etc), the outcrops are, unsurprisingly, endowed with mythological status. It's said they were formed when animals that were endangering the free supply of water to the town were turned into stone.

Athagala BUDDHIST SITE

(Elephant Rock) An atmospheric rock-cut staircase winds up Athagala, a large black rock outcrop on the eastern side of the city, to offer fine views from a 22m-tall white Buddha statue. A road also winds up to the same spot. On the way up you pass a small monastery, the **Ibbagala Vihara**. A three-wheeler to the top costs Rs 700 return. Come for sunset.

Sleeping & Eating

Mangala Lodge GUESTHOUSE $$

(☎071-814 9087; mangala.lodge12@gmail.com; 12 Sama Mw, Wilgoda Rd; r economy/standard Rs 4000/4500; ❄📶) A charming, relaxed place in the west of town run by the ever-helpful Mr Mangala. Opt for the better standard rooms, which surround a courtyard lined with local antiques. Rooms are simple but clean, with comfortable beds, and the dinners (Rs 600) are excellent.

A three-wheeler to or from the bus station costs Rs 150, and the stop for buses to Panduwasnuwara and Maho is just a five-minute walk away. The residential house is tricky to find, so call ahead.

Hotel Viveka HOTEL $$

(☎037-222 2897; www.hotelviveka.com; 64 North Lake Rd; s/d Rs 4000/4500; ❄📶) An elegant, if somewhat threadbare, colonial villa with a veranda overlooking the lake in a leafy part of town. Its five rooms have been renovated and have modern bathrooms. Take a sunset stroll around the lake. Viveka doubles as Kurunegala's most convivial bar and restaurant (meals Rs 800), so it can be busy on weekends. Subtract Rs 1000 if you don't want air-con.

Getting There & Away

Buses depart from a chaotic, fume-filled bus station in the very centre of town. Frequent services (every 20 minutes) include the following:

Anuradhapura Rs 170, three hours

Colombo normal/express air-con Rs 120/280, 3½ hours

Dambulla Rs 100, two hours

Kandy normal/express air-con Rs 76/150, one hour

Negombo Rs 130 to Rs 250, three hours

Trains depart from a station 2km southwest of the town centre.

AT A GLANCE

POPULATION
Trincomalee: 102,563

GATEWAY CITY
Trincomalee (p267)

BEST BEACHFRONT RESTAURANT
Galaxy Lounge (p255)

BEST TEMPLE
Kandasamy Kovil (p267)

BEST HISTORIC SITE
Kudumbigala Forest Hermitage (p258)

WHEN TO GO

Jan–Feb Low season with few visitors and up to 50% discount on some accommodation rates.

Mar–Apr The most reliable months for spotting blue whales off Trincomalee.

Jun–Jul Nesting season in Kumana; surfing from Nilaveli to Arugam Bay is at its prime.

Kandasamy Kovil (p267), Trincomalee
OSCAR ESPINOSA/SHUTTERSTOCK ©

The East

With palm-fringed beaches, lush paddy fields and ancient riverine forest, the East Coast has a distinct and tranquil charm. Add fascinating cultural diversity to its verdant beauty and it's surprising that the area receives so few visitors. Most of those who do stray East, tend to do so during the reliable surfing season (April to September). For the rest of the year, the region returns to more traditional seasonal rhythms.

Arab traders settled in this part of Sri Lanka in the eighth century, bringing Islam with them, and vibrant Muslim communities remain here to this day. While cultural gems include mosques, Buddhist monuments, colonial-era churches and magnificent Hindu temples, the region's lagoons make this a birdwatcher's paradise.

INCLUDES

Monaragala

055 / POP 10,550

Nestled beneath Peacock Rock, a forested mountain on the edge of the coastal plains, the bustling town of Monaragala acts as a gateway to the East Coast from the Hill Country. With its Hindu temple complexes, large Sunday market, tropical landscape and hot, sultry climate, it makes a good introduction to the region. Few travellers break their journey in Monaragala these days, but nearby hiking options invite a stay of a day or two for those looking for a distinctly local experience.

Sights & Activities

An easy but beautiful hike begins near the bus station. Heading towards an ageing rubber factory, the route passes by the colourful **Ganesh Temple**. At a yellow road sign marked 'Asst Superintendent's Bungalow' it veers to the left onto a rock-paved footpath. This climbs between attractive boulder fields and threads through Monaragala's famous rubber plantations.

A much more demanding trek is the full-day hike to the summit of the densely forested **Maragala Rock**. There is no specific trail up the mountainside so a guide is necessary. This can be organised through Kanda Land Villa guesthouse for around Rs 1500.

For something less strenuous, a walk around the sprawling **Sunday Market** (6am-6pm Sun) is fun. Colourful textiles, mounds of spices and pungent pyramids of stacked dried fish compete with the displays of tropical fruit, plastic goods and sandals.

Sleeping

Kanda Land Villa GUESTHOUSE $

(055-227 6925; raxawa@yahoo.com; Analiya Uyana Rd, off Wellawaya Rd; r with fan/air-con Rs 2200/4400;) Tucked into a garden of bamboo and hibiscus, this friendly-family establishment (housed in the former YMCA building) has five spacious rooms. The owner has a fascinating story to tell of his local, planter's heritage and can advise on visits to the family spice garden on nearby Maragala Rock. Home-cooked meals and yoga are other appealing features at this favourite among travellers.

Kanvel Hotel HOTEL $$

(077-316 6711; kanvelhotel@gmail.com; 190/6 Wellawaya Rd; r without breakfast Rs 4400;) Around 2km from the town centre, this bright hotel is newer than many options in town. With wood and slate interior design, the chic lobby isn't entirely matched by the rooms but nonetheless these are large, clean and come with a balcony and big bathrooms. The takeaway section of the hotel's popular restaurant is ideal for picnic supplies.

Eating & Drinking

★ **Key Ceylon** SRI LANKAN $

(071-235 5355; Wellawaya Rd; breakfast/lunch or dinner buffet Rs 250/300; 7am-10pm) This delightful new restaurant is housed in a tiny renovated colonial cottage on the main road, near the heart of town. Set in a small garden, it offers buffets with a local theme and some Western snacks.

Pavilion and Bakery SRI LANKAN $$

(055-227 6127; 1 Pottuvil Rd; mains Rs 400-850; 6am-9pm) By the roundabout in the heart of town, the Pavilion has a wide variety of Sri Lankan dishes while the on-site bakery produces short eats – sweet and savoury snacks handy for a long onward journey. The buffet lunch (Rs 450 with dessert) is a local favourite.

Victory Inn BAR

(055-227 6100; www.victoryinnmonaragala.com; 65 Wellawaya Rd; 6-10pm;) Around 100m from the bus station, this old workhorse of a hotel, with its smoked-glass facade, is a hangover from the 1970s. While there are better places to stay, this is a convivial spot for a beer or the local toddy.

Getting There & Away

Monaragala is a convenient junction town between the east, the south and the hills. Some handy bus routes include the following, but note that there is no direct bus to Ella – passengers are dropped nearby with onward connections using a local bus or three-wheeler.

Ampara Rs 130, 2½ hours, hourly

Colombo regular/air-con Rs 385/780, seven hours, hourly

Ella Rs 150, two hours, six daily

Kandy Rs 260, five hours, five daily

Nuwara Eliya Rs 260, four hours, one daily

Pottuvil (for Arugam Bay) Rs 120, 2½ hours, seven daily

Wellawaya (via Buttala; for the Hill Country and south coast) Rs 60, one hour, frequent

The East Highlights

1 Uppuveli (p270) Enjoying the chilled-out beach vibe at this strip of sand.

2 Kumana National Park (p259) Spotting black-necked storks, elephants and leopards in the varied terrain of Yala's eastern neighbour.

3 Pigeon Island National Park (p272) Snorkelling or diving with reef sharks around this gem of an island off Nilaveli.

4 Arugam Bay (p251) Hanging ten on the endless rights of this chilled-out surfers' paradise.

5 Driving North from Trinco (p270) Venturing along the empty B424 Hwy passing idyllic beaches, lagoons and ancient cultural sites.

6 Lagoon (p256) Watching waders from a catamaran in one of Pottuvil's mangrove swamps.

7 Batticaloa (p260) Cycling around the old town, pausing for a cookery lesson or a visit to the Heritage Museum.

8 Trincomalee Enjoying seafood and vegetarian short eats in this historic port.

WORTH A TRIP

SLEEPING UNDER THE TREES

Couched in the magnificent Weliara Forest, a short three-wheeler ride from Buttala, **Tree Tops Jungle Lodge** (077-703 6554; www.treetopsjunglelodge.com; Illukpitiya; per person all-inclusive 1st night US$150, less each additional night) offers a genuine wilderness experience. Elephants melt into the surrounding forest shadows, but the real draw here (besides the beauty of the location) is the prolific birdlife. Accommodation is in three spacious, furnished tents with private bathrooms. Hearty meals (mostly vegetarian) are included. Sit on the lodge deck with a fruit juice (or something stronger) and watch paradise flycatchers by day and fireflies by night to enjoy the best of this blissfully peaceful, solar-powered eco-retreat.

Free guided walks with expert local naturalists offer opportunities to spot several endemic bird species, including jungle fowl (Sri Lanka's national bird) and the tiny emerald green hanging parrot. Ninety-two bird species have been photographed in and around the lodge, with sightings of more than 150. Two nearby tanks straddling farmland and the forest reserve attract a wealth of waders and raptors, while exotic butterflies, including crimson and lemon immigrant, float along the water's edge.

Call ahead to reserve accommodation and to arrange a transfer from Buttala bus station (around 9km, mostly along a narrow bumpy track). Tree Tops also organises half-day guided safari trips ($78 per person; minimum of two required) to the less visited parts of Yala nature reserve (Blocks 3 to 5), a 40-minute drive away.

Yudaganawa

In a forest clearing near the village of Buttala, the ancient site of Yudaganawa is an enigmatic site, worth a detour on the route between the East Coast and the Hill Country if transiting through Buttala.

★**Yudaganawa Dagoba** RUINS
(off A4; Rs 300; 6am-6pm) Although interesting scraps of masonry are scattered across the large Yudaganawa archaeological site, the most striking construction is the ruined dagoba (stupa) that looms large in a clearing between majestic hardwood trees. The stupa is thought to have been built some 2300 years ago, though various alterations over the years – including an ongoing renovation that began in the 1970s – have somewhat obscured its history. Offerings of blue waterlilies still garland a small adjacent shrine with finely carved wooden doors.

Dating back to the 7th century, the shrine is protected by a pair of carved wooden doors depicting leopards, while the interior is adorned with sensitive wall paintings of three-eyed elephants among other striking imagery. Three-hundred-year-old Buddha statues complete the tiny but engaging ensemble. It's a short walk, often in the company of monkeys, to the minimal ruins of **Chulangani Vihara**.

Getting There & Away

Buses from Monaragala to Buttala (Rs 50, 25 minutes) run every 30 minutes. From Buttala it is a 3km three-wheeler ride to Yudaganawa (Rs 500 return including an hour's waiting time). A three-wheeler from Monaragala costs Rs 1300 return, or around Rs 3000 for both the Yudaganawa sites and Maligawila.

The turning for Yudaganawa lies 1.5km west of Buttala on the A4, at the 232km marker. From the main road the site is a further 1.5km along a paved road.

Maligawila

The village of Maligawila is so diffuse it virtually dissolves into the surrounding forest. Only ribbons of corn seed, spread and raked along the road to dry, give hints of the local community. Visitors make the detour here from Buttala, however, not for the village's bucolic charms, but for the Buddhist site of **Patha Vihara**, buried in the surrounding forest. The route from Buttala to Maligawila is another reason to visit. Threading through a beautiful sequence of green paddy fields, edged with mature hardwoods, the B522 passes the entrance of picturesque Dematamal Vihara.

Pathma Vihara BUDDHIST SITE
(dawn-dusk) FREE Among the trees of verdant Maligawila lie the extensive remains of a 7th-century Buddhist monastery, noted for

two, well-preserved giant statues. Linked by a shady avenue of magnificent banyan trees with multiple aerial roots, the statues stand serenely in forest clearings 500m apart.

Standing atop five flights of crumbling steps, the 10m-high Maitreya Bodhisattva (Avalokitesvara) was rebuilt between 1989 and 1991 from over 100 fragments unearthed in the 1950s. Its 11m-tall companion is among the tallest free-standing ancient Buddha statues in Sri Lanka. Both are protected by modern steel canopies but these do not detract unduly from the beauty of the forest setting.

Dematamal Vihara BUDDHIST TEMPLE

Gracing the B522, around 7km from Buttala, the whitewashed, red-tiled buildings of Dematamal Vihara are striking against the vivid green landscape of rice fields that surround this frequented complex. Pride of place is a spreading bodhi tree that shades the temple grounds.

Getting There & Away

Maligawila is 17km east of Buttala along winding, paved roads, made narrow in the harvest by drying crops spread along the tarmac. A three-wheeler from Monaragala costs Rs 2000 return, or Rs 2500 for a Monaragala–Maligawila–Yudaganawa–Monaragala loop. Frequent buses connect Maligawila with Monaragala (Rs 60, 40 minutes) and Buttala (Rs 45, 25 minutes).

Arugam Bay

063

Lovely Arugam Bay, a moon-shaped curl of golden sand, is home to a famed point break that many regard as the best place to surf in the country. With a population of only a few hundred, the town mainly comprises a single road that parallels the coast, flanked by salt-water lagoons. The northern half of the bay is where most of the guesthouses and traveller haunts are located, while the southern half is trimmed with fishing boats and the shacks of hard-working crews. It's a popular local gathering spot at dusk for a bathe in the calmer water.

The town has two distinct characters. During the surfing season from April to September, Arugam Bay has a party vibe with seasonal shops and eateries bursting into life to cater for the influx of visitors. For the rest of the year, the town slides into a delightfully mellow hibernation. Some enterprises close in the low season, but those that remain open offer generous discounts.

Arugam Bay is the perfect base for adventures into the surrounding hinterland, including safaris in Kumana National Park (p259) and boat rides on surrounding lagoons.

Activities

While **surfing** (p252) is without a doubt the key activity in Arugam Bay, promoting a high season all of its own when the swell is at its best (April to October), it is not the only activity. Swimming and wildlife-watching can be enjoyed year-round.

Swimming

The sea tends to be rough along the main crescent of Arugam Bay, even in low season, but swimming is possible for confident swimmers; those who prefer a more gentle dip should head for the shallow water at the southern end of the bay. This is really a fishing beach, so it's worth walking towards the point for a quieter place to lounge. Beyond the point, the wild beach is lovely, but essentially without shade. Beware of plunging into the sea without some local advice first, as strong currents visit the whole East Coast at different times of the year.

Wildlife-Watching

Arugam Bay makes the perfect base for wildlife excursions. Near to town on nearby Urani lagoon, the Eco Tourism Center (p257) offers small boat trips into the heart of the shrubby mangrove landscape. There is a small reception centre on the edge of a channel through the mangroves where trips can be arranged. Dawn has the best birdsong, but dusk offers the best photography, with iridescent bee-eaters and kingfishers posing near to the water's edge.

Further afield, tours to Kumana National Park, the habitat of leopards, elephants, wild buffalo, crocodiles and exceptional birdlife, are easily arranged through Arugam Bay guesthouses and hotels.

Sleeping

Most local hotels and guesthouses are located virtually on the high tide line. Many of these family-owned enterprises have a homespun charm and what they may lack in terms of polished exteriors, they make up for in the warmth of their welcome. A few small hotels compete for guests, offering air-con and hot-water showers, but given the cool night breezes and the tropically hot daytime temperatures, these conveniences are not wholly necessary.

SURFING ARUGAM BAY

A-BAY SURF

The famous, long right point break at the southern end of Arugam Bay offers consistent surf from April to September, with some good (and much quieter) days until November. Other local points get going around May or June.

If not entirely world-class, Arugam Bay does consistently produce long and fairly fat slow-breaking waves that are ideal for intermediate surfers. Surf averages 1m to 1.5m, with a few rare 2m days. On small days the surf can be very shallow and broken, while boils and bumps are to be expected on any day. In season, it can get dangerously busy; the more southerly **Surf Point** is quieter, and learners should stick to nearby **Baby Point**.

A **championship** organised by the World Surf League (www.worldsurfleague.com) takes place each August or September.

NORTH OF ARUGAM BAY

To the immediate north of Arugam Bay (around a 20-minute three-wheeler journey from town) are many breaks of good quality, most of which need a decent-sized swell.

☆ Pottuvil Point

Beautiful Pottuvil Point sits at the end of a scenic peninsula-like stretch of sand, north of the centre and east of the lagoon. It's a slow right-hander ideal for learners.

☆ Whiskey Point

Whiskey Point is a good surfing point for beginners, and the waves are consistent here from late April until October. Although just a five-minute walk north along the beach from Pottuvil Point (if the spit of sand between the two is intact), it takes around 30 minutes along rutted rural lanes to travel between the two points by road.

☆ Lighthouse Point

Lighthouse Point, another beginner/medium right-hander, is 20km north of Pottuvil. It's a lovely, remote spot and its fine sandy beach is little visited. The surf season is May to October. **Green House**, another point further north, is a 15-minute walk along the beach. The area makes a tranquil and beautiful retreat off-season, if somewhat isolated.

SOUTH OF ARUGAM BAY

Close-by surf points, reached via the coast road from Arugam Bay, include **Crocodile Rock** (Rs 800 return by three-wheeler), **Elephant Rock** (Rs 1000) and **Peanut Farm** (around Rs 1000).

At the northern end of Panama's beach, close to the jellyfish-processing plant (jellyfish are sent to East Asia for use in cooking), is a fairly lame right-point break that is good for novice surfers. Nearby **Okanda** has possibly the best right point break in and around Arugam Bay.

GEARING UP

Several surf shops rent out boards and offer lessons with certified instructors (beware of unqualified teachers posing as surfing instructors). They can also arrange camping trips to some of the further points. Convenient camping tours allow the focus to remain on the surfing, but it's also possible to arrange a DIY trip with a packed lunch and transport organised through a guesthouse.

The well-organised **Safa Surf School** (☎077-955 2268; www.safaarugambay.com; Panama Rd; short & long board/body board rental per day Rs 1000/750, lessons from US$30), run by local surfer Fawas Lafeer, offers lessons from certified instructors and has good-quality board hire. It also carries out repairs. In high season, the school offers simple accommodation in a large beachside camp, shaded by tamarisk trees.

Arugam Bay, a crescent of golden sand, is famed for a point break that many regard as the best place to surf in Sri Lanka.

Reliable **Dylan's Surf Company** (☎063-224 8801; www.dylanssurfcompany.com; Panama Rd; surfboard rental per day from Rs1000, lessons from Rs2500; ⌚shop 8am-10pm, surf school 6am-10pm Apr-Sep) is primarily a surf shop with all types of gear. The rental boards are of high quality and Dylan runs a friendly service. He has plans to open all year.

Another outfit, **A-Bay Surf Shop** (Panama Rd; bodyboard & surfboard rental per day from Rs 1000, lessons from Rs 2500; ⌚8am-8pm), has a good selection of old boards suitable for learners. It also has expert ding-repair service, wax and sunscreen.

SLEEPING AT SURF POINT

A couple of sleeping options in Arugam Bay are so close to the surf, they virtually use the waves as pillows.

Located on a gorgeous part of the beach, the enchanting, spacious **Upali Beach Surf Resort** (☎077-112 8866; Main Point; cabanas US$110; 📶) has built on its success as a cafe. The fan-only 'glam cabannas' are good value, although cheaper options are available. A buffalo cart in high season brings guests from the road; for the rest of the year it's accessed by walking around the bay. Lessons with qualified instructors are on offer.

The surfer favourite, **Mambo's** (☎077-782 2524; www.mambos.lk; s/d from US$45/60, bungalows US$85-140; ⌚Apr to Oct only; ❄📶), right next to Main Point, allows guests to tumble out of bed straight into the line-up. The cosy bungalows feature earthy, simple decor and little porches in a delightful garden of palms and desert roses. There's a bar-restaurant with hammocks and Saturday-night parties. Access is via a beach full of fishing boats – not easy with luggage.

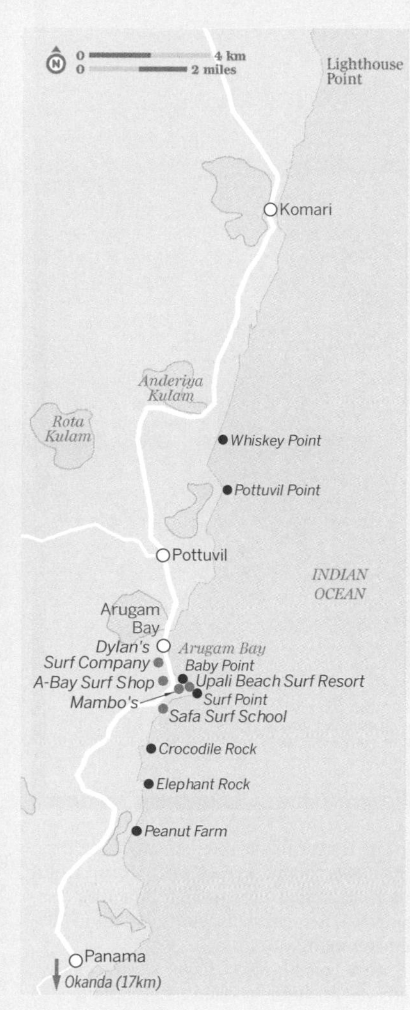

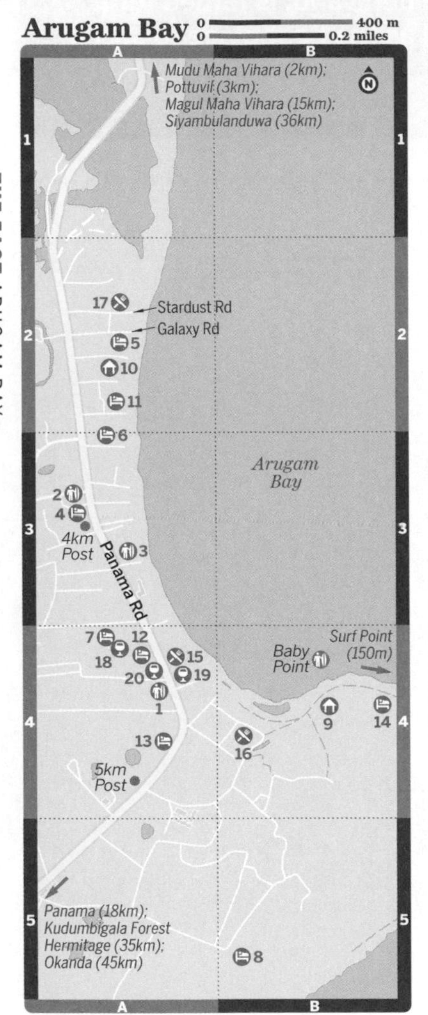

Arugam Bay

Activities, Courses & Tours

1 A-Bay Surf Shop A4
2 Dylan's Surf Company A3
3 Safa Surf School A3

Sleeping

4 Danish Villa A3
5 Galaxy Lounge Beachfront Cabanas A2
6 Happy Panda A3
7 Hideaway A4
8 Hotel Stay Golden B5
9 Mambo's B4
10 Ranga's Beach Hut A2
11 Sandy Beach Hotel A2
12 Spice Trail A4
13 The Long Hostel A4
14 Upali Beach Surf Café and Resort B4

Eating

Galaxy Lounge .... (see 5)
Hideaway Restaurant .... (see 7)
15 Perera Restaurant A4
16 Samanthi's Restaurant B4
17 Stardust Restaurant A2

Drinking & Nightlife

18 Hide & Chill Bar A4
Local Bar .... (see 12)
Main Bites .... (see 12)
19 Siam View Hotel A4
20 Surf N Sun A4

The term 'cabana' refers to anything from ultra basic plank or *cadjan* (coconut-frond matting) huts to luxurious full-facility bungalows. Low-season discounts of 20% to 50% are common.

Most guesthouses have shared shady terraces for home-cooked meals; many also offer a laundry service as well as information on transport and local tours, including boat trips on the lagoon and longer trips to Kumana.

★ **Ranga's Beach Hut** HUT $
(☎ 077-160 6203; www.arugambaybeachhut.com; off Panama Rd; huts Rs 600-700, cabanas Rs 1000-1500; 📶) Catering to backpackers and surfers for around 35 years, this is one of the original guesthouses in Arugam Bay. Delightfully quirky, locally owned and with four cabanas right on the beach, this travellers' favourite has a convivial atmosphere and is lively with guests, even in low season. There's a choice of 22 digs built of wood and thatch, including huts on stilts under the trees.

The Long Hostel HOSTEL $
(☎ 077-394 3199; www.thelonghostel.com; Panama Rd; bunk bed in r of 4 Rs 1800; ⏲ Mar-Oct; ❄ 📶) With solar panels, a ban on plastic and a 'no music after 11pm' rule, this single-storey hostel takes community responsibility seriously. There are four bunks to a room with private shower and air-con and there's dedicated storage space for backpacks. With a bright, garden aspect and an easy walk to the beach, it books up quickly.

★ **Galaxy Lounge Beachfront Cabanas** GUESTHOUSE $$
(☎ 063-224 8415; www.galaxysrilanka.com; Galaxy Rd, off Panama Rd; cabanas Rs 5000-10,000;

budget huts Rs 3000; ❄📶) The garrulous management at this deservedly popular guesthouse provides a wealth of regional information, including tales of the 2004 tsunami that swept through the guesthouse garden. The 13 cabanas vary in quality, but the beach-side, sunrise-watching location is superb and the Sri Lankan food excellent. Help is also available for exploring East Coast attractions.

Hotel Stay Golden INN $$
(☎077-490 9609; www.staygoldenarugam.com; off Panama Rd; r US$20-65; ❄📶) On a bluff, a short three-wheeler drive from town, this small enterprise sits behind a fine stretch of beach at the southern end of the bay. It has seven attractive, well-furnished cabanas with red-tiled roofs and porches. While the sea is only a short stroll away, it's not readily visible, except from raised decks attached to some of the cabanas.

Sandy Beach Hotel HOTEL $$
(☎063-224 8403; abktaf@gmail.com; off Panama Rd; r US$20-50; seaview r with breakfast US$90; ❄📶) This fine beachside two-storey hotel has 15 rooms – all beautifully presented and most with minibars. Some of the rooms have ocean views. There's also a set of new one-storey cabanas with porches in the attractive garden plot. The owner, Badur Khan, is a well-travelled host who goes the extra mile for his guests.

Hideaway INN $$$
(☎063-224 8259; www.hideawayarugambay.com; Panama Rd; r US$70-200; ❄📶🏊) This inland guesthouse is a cut above the rest in terms of architecture, fixtures and fittings. Artfully designed cabanas emerge from a beautiful, landscaped garden and feature porches with cane loungers for enjoying the shady views. A colonial-style villa draped in bougainvillea and watched over by a gentle ridge-back (dog) forms the hub of this elegant complex.

Spice Trail HOTEL $$$
(☎063-224 8008; www.thespicetrail.com; Panama Rd, 69th Mile Post; r US$169; ❄📶🏊) Each of the 12 villas in this attractive new hotel on the inland side of the main road has a secret walled garden shaded by bamboo. Rooms are spacious, minimally furnished and chic in design with polished concrete floors and stylish linens. The popular hotel bar and poolside restaurant are open year-round.

Eating & Drinking

Perera Restaurant SRI LANKAN $
(☎063-205 0840; Panama Rd; mains Rs 250-500; ⏰8am-10pm) This simple roadside venue, with its laid-back owner and distinctive red cook pots, attracts local residents – a good indication that the rice and curry is up to scratch. Also serves some Western food, including generous breakfasts.

Samanthi's Restaurant SRI LANKAN $
(☎077-068 8311; Freedom Beach Cabanas, off Panama Rd; mains Rs 250-700; ⏰7.30am-10pm Apr-Oct; 📶) 🌿 Samanthi's is run by a family of cheerful women. Order ahead for rice and curry (around Rs 400); other dishes are the standard A-Bay mix of Western and modified (meaning less spicy) Sri Lankan fare. The buffalo curd is a regional speciality, usually served with honey. Watch out for thieving monkeys!

★**Galaxy Lounge** SRI LANKAN $$
(☎063-224 8415; Galaxy Rd, off Panama Rd; meals Rs 400-1000; ⏰7am-9pm) The cook at this beachfront guesthouse prepares excellent Sri Lankan fare. His rice and curry even tempted the Sri Lankan cricket team to make a repeat visit. Steamed catch of the day with ginger and prawn curry (or crab curry when it's in season) are highlights. Order the day before to sample a full Sri Lankan breakfast.

★**Hideaway Restaurant** INTERNATIONAL $$$
(☎063-224 8259; www.hideawayarugambay.com; Panama Rd; mains Rs 900-1600; ⏰7.30-9.30pm; 📶) This romantic restaurant, surrounded by tropical shrubs, features a menu built around fresh, locally sourced ingredients and a Mediterranean theme. There are also several vegetarian, vegan and gluten-free choices. In high season, coffee, paninis, juices and smoothies are served in the adjoining Blue Cafe.

Stardust Restaurant INTERNATIONAL $$$
(☎063-224 8191; https://arugambay.com; off Panama Rd; meals Rs 800-2000; ⏰breakfast 7.45-11am, lunch noon-3pm, dinner 6-9pm; 📶) For a quiet meal off the main drag, this beachfront hotel restaurant offers the catch of the day as well as European and Asian dishes. There are also tasty juices, lassis and fresh coffee. Set in a pretty garden, the elegant open-sided dining area catches the ocean breeze.

★**Local Bar** BAR
(☎063-224 8008; Spice Trail Hotel, Panama Bay, 69 Mile Post; ⊙5.30-10pm) One of the few bars in town open throughout the year, this attractive venue offers a signature cocktail each night featuring farm-to-table organic flourishes (basil, mint, cucumber). Outside the popular happy hour, there are DJ parties and it's only a short stumble to the restaurant for tasty pan-Asian fare and in-season barbecues. There's a popular happy hour from 6pm to 7.30pm.

★**Main Bites** COFFEE
(☎063-224 8008; Panama Rd, 69 Mile Post; biscuits and cakes Rs 300-500;) The Scandinavian owner of Arugam Bay's most stylish coffee shop has created a northern European aesthetic and caters to a sweet tooth. The on-site bakery makes delicious 'brookies' (combination of brownies and cookies) and fresh cheesecakes – the perfect accompaniment to the 100% Arabica coffee, brewed up the Italian way.

Surf N Sun BAR
(☎077-606 5099, 063-224 8600; www.thesurfnsun.com; Panama Rd; beers Rs 3000; ⊙11am-10pm Apr-Oct;) With A-Bay's most beautiful tropical garden, illuminated with candles and lanterns, this delightful hotel has a well-stocked bar. Slide from bar stool to restaurant table for a classy seafood supper and buy a cotton shirt in the boutique on the way out.

Siam View Hotel BAR
(www.arugam.com; Panama Rd; ⊙high season 11am-late, low season 11am-5pm;) This ungainly looking, rickety roadside party HQ creaks with action almost around the clock. In high season, it hosts party nights, with everything from tech-house DJs to local reggae bands rocking the dance floor. In low season, the cracks in the floor become all too obvious!

Information

As Arugam Bay is a conservative Muslim community, a T-shirt worn over a swimsuit is appreciated on the beach and helps avoid unwanted attention. Off the beach, both men and women should dress modestly, covering shoulders and thighs.

There have been cases of attempted sexual assault in secluded areas, particularly south behind the surf point. Matters for the police should be reported through guesthouses or hotels.

There are a couple of ATMs along Panama Rd and many in nearby Pottuvil.

Getting There & Away

Pottuvil is the gateway to Arugam Bay, but direct buses to Pottuvil from other parts of the country are uncommon. Siyambulanduwa (a market town 37km to the west) and Monaragala are much better connected and there are frequent buses from either of these destinations to Pottuvil (Rs 40 and Rs 120 respectively).

Guesthouses and hotels can arrange private air-con cars to/from Colombo (around Rs 20,000, five to eight hours) and taxi shares for other destinations. Some also arrange rental of bicycles (about Rs 500) and scooters (Rs 1000 to 1500). A three-wheeler from Pottuvil to Arugam Bay costs Rs 250. With an excellent knowledge of travellers' haunts in and around Arugam Bay, call **Dhammika** (☎071-175 7588) for trips by three-wheeler to the various surfing points nearby.

Pottuvil & Around

☎063

For those who have the time and inclination to inch around the area's traditional rural lanes, Pottuvil and its beachside neighbourhoods have spectacular lagoons to explore, some intriguing ancient ruins and a number of picturesque, if somewhat isolated places to stay.

Pottuvil Point, Whiskey Point and Lighthouse Point are three popular **surfing** (p252) spots that spring into life during the surf season and retreat into tranquil rural backwaters between October and March. At this time of year, sleeping and eating options are considerably reduced, with travellers usually visiting the area by three-wheeler on a day trip from Arugam Bay.

Sights

Magul Maha Vihara RUINS
About 12km west of Pottuvil lies the evocative 5th-century ruin of Magul Maha Vihara. Set in a peaceful forested location, and probably built by King Dhatusena (r 459–77), the site was most likely part of a royal compound. The main point of interest is the beautiful and well-preserved moonstone at the foot of a former shrine; it's unusual for depicting mahout astride some of the elephant images. The site is 800m south of the A4 on a road just west of the 307km post.

Mudu Maha Vihara RUINS
This moody little site, partly submerged in the encroaching sand dunes, features a fine 3m-high standing Buddha statue flanked by

two bodhisattva figures. The **beach** just behind is wide, beautiful and undeveloped, but not safe for swimming. A good road leads here from the south.

Activities & Tours

Eco Tourism Center Urani BIRDWATCHING
(☎077-122 7503; A4, 325km post; 2hr tour per person Rs 2200, minimum 2 people, discount for groups) Birdwatching by the side of any of the many lagoons surrounding Pottuvil is rewarding, but entering the swampy habitats by catamaran offers a unique dimension. Members of the Urani Rural Fisheries Organization offer trips into the lagoon throughout the year. It's best to call ahead to book a tour or turn up at the dedicated office. Life jackets are provided.

Sleeping & Eating

Most visitors to the area stay 5km south in Arugam Bay, but there are recommended sleeping options near the surf break in Pottuvil, around Whiskey Point a tad further north and in the rural hinterland of Lighthouse Point, some 20km from Pottuvil town centre. All of the guesthouses and hotels recommended can prepare meals for guests (with a little advance warning).

Paper Moon Kudils INN **$$**
(☎071-810 9999, 071-997 9797; www.papermoonkudils.lk; Whiskey Point; r US$70-90; ❄🛜🏊) This pleasant establishment is right on the beach and boasts a big pool. Rooms are in spotless, bungalow-style units with tiled roofs and are minimally but adequately furnished. There's a restaurant and pool-side bar that make for lazy, relaxed low-season evenings. In high season, there are inescapable late-night parties in the neighbouring bar – if you can't beat 'em, join 'em!

Lighthouse Beach Hut HUT **$$**
(☎077-317 9594; www.lighthousebeachhut.com; Lighthouse Point; cabanas from Rs 3500) Eight rustic cabanas are tucked into the shadows of cassia trees by the surf break of this rural plot. The tree-house huts are fun, but perhaps less so if you need to use the downstairs bathroom in the night!

★**Kottukal Beach House** BOUTIQUE HOTEL **$$$**
(☎077-534 8807; www.jetwinghotels.com; Pottuvil Point; r US$190-225; ❄🛜🏊) This luxurious beachfront hotel, 5km north of Arugam Bay, has a magnificent (if difficult to find) location on a private headland, shaded by

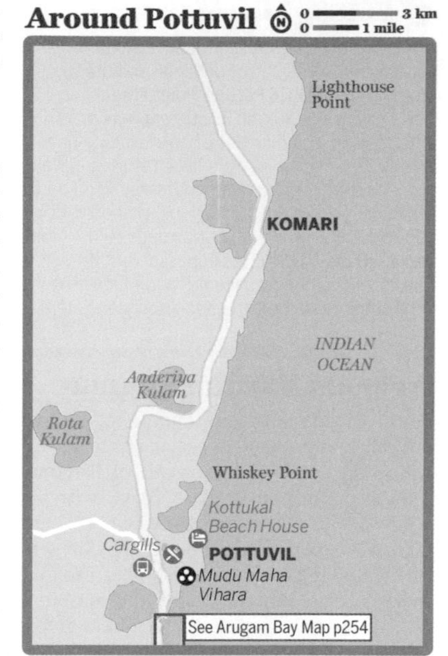

giant coconut trees. Four rooms are in the traditional-style red-tiled villa, while two new chalets sport fashionable open-to-sky bathrooms. There's an extensive menu in the hotel's fine dining restaurant, which has sweeping views of Pottuvil Point.

SaBaBa Surf Café CAFE **$$**
(☎077-711 8132; Whiskey Point; mains Rs 350-1000; ⏲7am-10pm Apr-Oct) During the surfing season, this popular driftwood venue is the centre of life at Whiskey Point. With cushioned seating around a huge wooden deck, good food, beds on the beach and regular parties (usually Wednesdays and Fridays), it attracts crowds of ravers from Arugam Bay. DJs play full-volume house and electronica till dawn (and beyond).

Getting There & Away

Direct buses to Pottuvil are limited. It's possible, however, to transit through Siyambulanduwa or Monaragala (Rs 120). Useful private and Central Transport Board (CTB) bus services from the **bus terminal** (Panama Rd) include:

Batticaloa Rs 160, three to four hours, hourly

Colombo Regular/air-con Rs 485/1200, eight hours, three each night

Monaragala (for connections to Wellawaya and the south coast) Rs 190, 2½ hours, seven daily

Getting Around

Pottuvil is the gateway to Arugam Bay via three-wheeler (Rs 250). For the 30-minute trip from Arugam Bay to Pottuvil Point, three-wheelers charge around Rs 300 one way or Rs 1600 return, including three hours' waiting time. It costs Rs 750 one-way (Rs 1800 return and waiting time) from Arugam Bay to Whiskey Point and it's Rs 1500 from Arugam Bay to Lighthouse Point (Rs 3500 return). Note that the roads on the 4km trek from the A4 are often impassable in the rainy season (November to January) and rough at any time of the year; the signage is also inconsistent.

Arugam Bay to Panama

South of Arugam Bay, one long, almost entirely uninterrupted beach stretches towards the sleepy fishing town of Panama. This is quintessential East Coast, with its empty white sands interrupted only where lagoons are periodically breached by the sea. The whole region is a birder's paradise and there is something magical in the combination of sparsely populated farmland interspersed with open grasslands edged with tropical woodland.

The B374 from Arugam Bay to Panama takes a mostly inland course, but intersects with lagoons frequented by waterfowl, wading birds and water buffalo. The occasional elephant, crocodile or water monitor wander into this rural landscape, while the thatched, raised huts of farmers are a reminder that not everyone is as pleased at the prospect of marauding wildlife as the passing visitor.

Getting There & Away

Panama is 13km south of Arugam Bay on the smooth B374, which is ideal for cyclists. A three-wheeler costs around Rs 2000 return. Buses connect Panama with Pottuvil (Rs 80, one hour, every two hours).

Panama to Okanda

The paved road from Arugam Bay ends in Panama. Continuing south towards the seasonal fishing settlement of Okanda, the grandly designated B355 is in reality a rough dirt track. At around 16km along the track, the route branches to the left for Okanda or continues straight ahead for another kilometre for the entrance to Kumana National Park.

The scenery here is a verdant combination of wetlands and savanna, interspersed with a few fields of rice paddy, which are either livid green after the rains or a burnt umber after the harvest. Wildlife, including elephants, deer and crocodiles, often stray beyond the park boundary and sightings of large birdlife such as painted storks, peafowl and Brahminy kites are possible from the roadside.

Okanda is interesting in its own right, with seasonal fishing huts and a beige-coloured **beach** with an excellent right point break popular with surfers fleeing the crowds at Arugam Bay. Large deer often sit in the shade of parked buses and monkeys make mischief in the trees. If making a day of it, it's worth taking a detour to the nearby hermitage of Kudumbigala, if only to explore the surrounding tropical forest.

★Kudumbigala Forest Hermitage RELIGIOUS SITE

(off B355; 9am-5pm) FREE The 47-sq-km site of Kudumbigala Forest Hermitage is a magical jumble of Sigiriya-style outcrops nudging their way through dense tropical canopy. Over 200 shrines and hermits' lodgings are sequestered in caves or tucked under overhanging rocks here, with a communal area carved out of a hilltop clearing. Modestly dressed visitors may follow pilgrims as they carry sacks of rice up the steps towards this point, but it's forbidden to enter the prayer hall or stray off the main paths.

While today's hermitage only dates back to 1954, the site, which was retrieved from the encroaching forest, was originally founded by the first Buddhist king of Sri Lanka in 2 BCE.

It's possible to climb the Sigiriya-style rock summit of **Belum Gala** via ancient steps that may date back to the site's 1 BCE heyday. The hike is accessed via a small track off to the right, around 500m from the car park, just before a large overhanging rock bearing ancient inscriptions and decorated with prayer flags. While not as steep as Sigiriya, this is a much more isolated spot, so those with vertigo may want to be sure of managing the descent before scrambling up to the top, as there's only a rough attempt at a safety rail. Crowned by a dagoba, the sacred summit offers magnificent views of the forest canopy, Helawa Lagoon and the sandbars that straddle Panama beach. The approach must be made without hat, shoes, sunglasses or camera – bring a bag to avoid langurs or macaques making off with them.

Kudumbigala, which is around 15km inland from the B355, is usually visited on a combined taxi or three-wheeler tour from

DON'T MISS

KUMANA NATIONAL PARK & KUMANA RESERVE

With beautiful wetland landscapes and an abundance of wildlife, **Kumana National Park** (063-363 5867; off B355; adult/child US$10/5, vehicle Rs 250, service charge per group US$8, plus overall VAT 8%; ticket office 6am-4pm), formerly Yala East National Park, is a top East Coast destination. Few visitors recognise this fact, so the park is blissfully quiet, providing the perfect opportunity for intimate wildlife encounters without the irritation of competing jeeps. The park is a particular joy for bird enthusiasts, with several endemic species regularly sighted and opportunities to spot the very rare black-necked stork.

In fact, the 357-sq-km park is contiguous with neighbouring Yala National Park. While its busy neighbour has a higher density of animals, much less frequented Kumana still supports about a dozen bears and sightings of elusive leopard, elephant, wild buffalo and crocodiles are reasonably common. The main draw of the park, however, is the 200-hectare bird reserve; from May to June, thousands of birds congregate along the edge of the lagoons to nest.

It's possible to organise a camping trip within the park. This is best arranged in advance through a guesthouse in Arugam Bay for around US$300 for two people including camping equipment, meals and a dusk and dawn safari.

Birdwatching Highlights

Common species of bird spread across the park's varied terrain of lagoons, ponds, villu grassland and riverine forest include the Malabar pied hornbill, which may be seen hopping along the ground in unison (they mate for life), large numbers of lesser whistling-duck, crested serpent eagle, chestnut-headed bee-eater, coppersmith barbet and the beautiful orange-breasted green pigeon. Endemics include the gorgeous Sri Lanka junglefowl, while there are also large numbers of other crowd-pleasers, such as peacocks, painted storks and pelicans. A pair of binoculars and a field guide to birds greatly enhances the experience.

Getting There & Away

Enter the park through the main gate near Okanda, 22km southwest of Arugam Bay. It's possible to make half-day jeep trips from Arugam Bay (around Rs 10,000 per vehicle for a half-day tour including park fees). These leave before sunrise to catch the dawn chorus or at 2pm to make the most of the golden dusk. This is when the landscape is at its most photogenic and nocturnal animals start to pace out from their daytime lairs.

It's also possible to arrange a jeep from the park office, just inside the entrance (Rs 6000 for around 3½ hours). Entry fees are additional; these include a mandatory guide (usually an expert spotter), and cover service and VAT. A discretionary tip for both guide and driver for good sighting is customary. In high season, jeep availability may not be guaranteed.

Arugam Bay. Tours generally include the gateway to (but not safari within) Kumana National Park and a trip to the seasonal fishing village of Okanda.

Okanda Sri Murugan Kovil HINDU TEMPLE
(off B355, Okanda) Though relatively small, the main temple here has a colourful *gopuram* (gateway tower) and is a major destination on the Pada Yatra pilgrimage to Kataragama. Thousands of pilgrims gather here during the two weeks before the July *poya* (full moon) before attempting the last, and most challenging, five-day leg of the 45-day trek from Jaffna. Some 25,000 pilgrims attempt the journey each year.

Getting There & Away

It can take up to an hour by car or three-wheeler to travel the 16km along the unpaved B355 from Panama to Okanda. It is 90 minutes from Arugam Bay. Day trips on three-wheelers from Arugam Bay can usually be arranged for about Rs 4000. These may include a visit to the Kudumbigala Forest Hermitage, but will not include entry to Kumana National Park, other than a brief stop to watch birds from a hide on the lagoon at the park entrance.

Ampara

063 / POP 44,941

The busy rural town of Ampara sits in the midst of glorious countryside, studded with paddy fields, lakes and palm groves. Though the town has only a few sights, it does offer opportunities to stock up on supplies, top up on phone credit, enjoy an utterly spicy rice and curry – not modified for Western tastes – and to drop by the seldom-visited national park of Gal Oya, 20km to the southwest.

Sights

Gal Oya National Park NATIONAL PARK
Lying southwest of Ampara, this large park encompasses a semi-evergreen forest reserve, savanna and a large tank. The birdwatching here is good at any time of the year and it is home to elephants, among other wildlife. Yellow-footed pigeon, plum-headed parakeet and Layard's parakeet are among many of the colourful birds possible to spot here and it's a good place for cuckoos, nightjars, owls and woodpeckers.

As this is a seldom-visited park, it's worth making arrangements through the eco-friendly **Gal Oya Lodge** (076-842 4612; www.galoyalodge.com/lodge; r in bungalow with full board for 2 people US$252).

Buddangala Rajamaha Viharaya BUDDHIST SITE
(Buddangala Rock Hermitage; off Buddangala Rd; donations accepted; 6am-8pm) Rising above the forest north of Ampara, this 150m-high hill offers panoramic views from its rocky summit (including, occasionally, of wild elephants at dusk). Buddangala is said to be 1800 years old, and when the old temple, the remains of which are to the left of the main shrine, was excavated in 1964, a gold casket containing a tooth of the Buddha was discovered. This is now housed inside the dagoba and is on view every June for three days around *poya* day.

Sleeping & Eating

Terrel Residencies GUESTHOUSE $
(063-222 2215; terrelb@gmail.com; 153 Stores (Gabada) Rd; s/d with fan Rs 1500/1850, with air-con Rs 2750/3000; restaurant 11am-10pm;) This bustling, attractive guesthouse is set around a central garden with multiple stands of bamboo. There are 11 large, comfortable rooms available in a two-storey block. The popular restaurant offers tasty Chinese-style mains (Rs 300 to 600) among the Sri Lankan fare.

The genial Mr Terrel can arrange three-hour boat safaris (from Rs 6000 for two people) plus three-wheeler transport to nearby lagoons and lakes (Rs 2500).

Ambhasewana Guest House GUESTHOUSE $
(063-222 3865; cnr 1st & 4th Aves; r with fan/air-con from Rs 1000/3000;) Run by a welcoming family, this family home doubles as a guesthouse and occupies a shady plot on a quiet side street, two blocks from the town centre. The 13 airy rooms fit the bill for a short stopover.

Monty Hotel HOTEL $$
(063-222 2169; www.montyhotel.lk; 1st Ave; r Rs 6200-9200, ste Rs 12,200, incl breakfast;) In a leafy neighbourhood 1km south of the centre, the likeable Monty is a surprisingly urban chic hotel, given the rural location. Fan rooms are functional and a tad dark, but air-con options are bright and modern and there's an attractive terraced restaurant.

Keells New City SRI LANKAN $
(DS Senanayke Rd; meals Rs 150-300; 7am-10pm) A good bet for a lunchtime rice and curry, *kotthu* (*rotti* chopped up and mixed with vegies etc) in the evening or short eats (deep-fried snacks and other small bites) for the times in between. There is an adjoining bakery producing delicious coconut sweets and a supermarket. It's just east of the 1980 clock tower in the heart of town.

Getting There & Away

Ampara's new bus terminal is just south of the main clock tower and has CTB and private services. Services include the following:

Batticaloa Rs 150, three hours, four daily
Kandy regular/air-con Rs 400/500, 5½ hours, hourly
Pottuvil (for Arugam Bay) Rs 200, three hours, twice daily or more frequently via Kalmunai

Batticaloa

065 / POP 94,954

Historic Batticaloa, Batti for short, enjoys a spectacular position surrounded by lagoons with palm-filtered sunlight glancing off the water. The compact centre, with its huge fortress and many churches, is well worth a half-day's exploration on foot. To the east of Batti's centre, lies Kallady – a small suburb on a long, sandy isthmus. There are some fine beaches here and one or two places to stay, although these are mostly open only in the high season. Exploring the entire region by bike is a delight.

Sights

There are several distinct areas of interest in Batti, each divided by the waters of the Batticaloa lagoon. Despite the Muslim influence prevailing in much of the region, the road (A4) between Ampara and Batticaloa has many fine Hindu temples with elaborate gateway towers.

Puliyanthivu

Home to the fort, the atmospheric old quarter of Batti is on an island graced with several colonial-era buildings – in particular **St Mary's Cathedral** (St Mary's St), the **Methodist Church** (Post Office Rd; 8am-5pm) and **St Michael's College** (Central Rd).

★Dutch Fort FORT

(Fort Rd; 8.30am-4.30pm) FREE This once-mighty fort is now home to administrative offices, and though large sections of the structure are crumbling, it's still an atmospheric place to wander around. It was built by the Portuguese in 1628, but the Dutch took over after just 10 years, followed by the British. Inside the courtyard are some dishevelled, yet colonnaded, old colonial buildings. Look for English cannons, surviving watchtowers and a ruined bell tower.

There are fine lagoon views from the ramparts, which can be accessed via a crumbling ladder to the left of the entrance.

Anaipanthi Srishithivigneshwara Alayar HINDU SITE

(Hospital Rd) Of the many Hindu temples, the expanding Anaipanthi Srishithivigneshwara Alayar is visually the finest, with a magnificent *gopuram* that's decorated with a riotous festival of intertwined figures.

Mahatma Gandhi Park PARK

(Bazaar St) This small but orderly park along Old Batti's waterfront is popular with strolling couples and includes features such as the Batticaloa Gate – a 19th-century welcoming arch to the harbour.

New Town

Across the lagoon to the north of Puliyanthivu is New Town. This is the commercial hub, with broad streets lined with shops and banks.

Imperial Salon BARBERSHOP

(077-248 7815; Trinco Rd; 8.30am-8.30pm Mon-Sat, to 1pm Sun) Consider a haircut and head massage (Rs 500) at this tiny salon, a delightful monument to kitsch. Every centimetre of the walls is covered in decorative painting, fake flowers, sequins, filigree, stained glass or tinsel garlands, and at the back of the salon, up towards the trompe l'oeil ceiling, is an interfaith shrine, from where Durga, Mary and the Buddha keep a watchful eye over the razor-wheeling barbers. There's even a verse or two of Quranic script to ward off the evil eye.

Batticaloa Lighthouse LIGHTHOUSE

(off B46, Palameenmadu; boat trips Rs 400-3000; boat trips 8am-7pm) At the end of a sandbar, surrounded by lagoons and mangroves, this 28m-tall lighthouse dates from 1913. For a small donation, the site keeper gives the intrepid climber access to the tower via a rickety vertical ladder. Perhaps a safer way to enjoy the sheltered coastline is to enjoy a swim in the calm water to take a one-hour motorboat cruise (Rs 4000). Three-wheelers charge around Rs 500 from Batticaloa. It's 5km northwest from New Town via the B46.

Auliya Mosque MOSQUE

(Lady Manning Dr) The tiny Auliya Mosque sports a prominent green minaret. It not only offers a good vantage point for the Dutch Fort across the water, it is also in the heart of an attractive suburb of traditional Sri Lankan bungalows that make an interesting focus for a local wander.

RETURN TO MULTI-ETHNIC CALM

While the tragic events of the Easter suicide bombing of 2019 rocked the city of Batticaloa, they did not succeed in destroying the city's ethnic cohesion. An attack on the protestant Zion church took place on the morning of 21 April 2019, killing 26 and wounding over 100. In the immediate aftermath, faith leaders sent strong messages of solidarity, with the Christian community and Muslim shops closed in a sign of respect for victims' families.

In contrast to the Sinhalese majority in the rest of Sri Lanka, the Eastern Province is home to an equal number of Sinhalese, Tamils and Muslims and while tensions develop from time to time, a desire for peace has prevailed. Visitors do not need to be on heightened alert in Batti, or indeed anywhere along Sri Lanka's ethnically diverse East Coast.

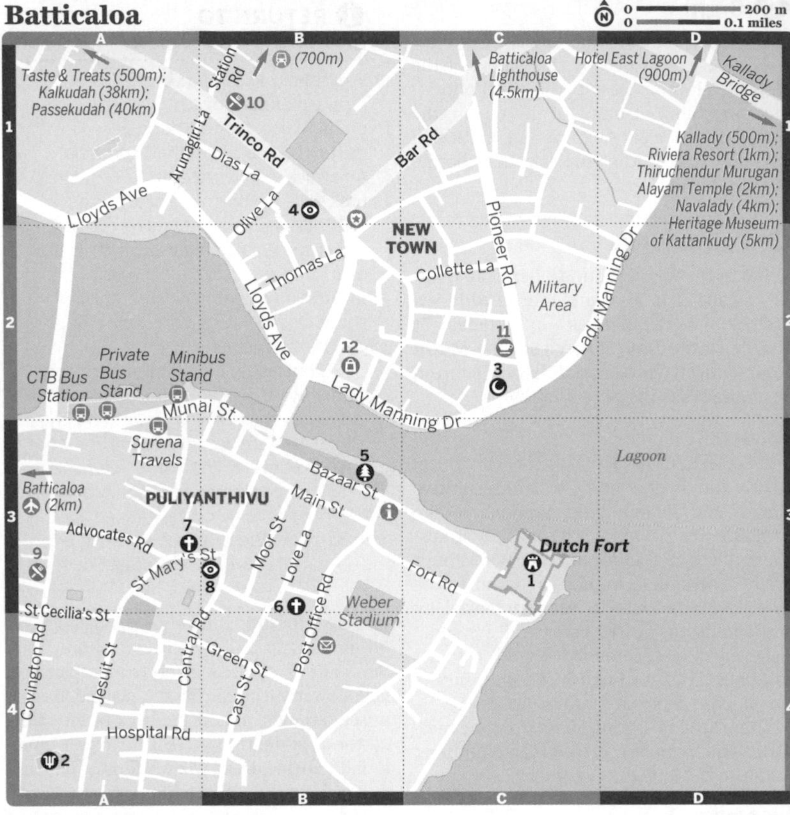

Batticaloa

Top Sights

1 Dutch Fort C3

Sights

2 Anaipanthi Srishithivigneshwara Alayar A4
3 Auliya Mosque C2
4 Imperial Salon B1
5 Mahatma Gandhi Park B3
6 Methodist Church B3
7 St Mary's Cathedral A3
8 St Michael's College B3

Eating

9 RN Take Away & Buffet A3
10 Sun Shine Cafe B1

Drinking & Nightlife

11 Café Chill C2

Shopping

12 Batticaloa Market B2

Kallady

Kallady lies on the east side of Batti and is reached on foot or by bike via the picturesque 1924 bridge (cars use a modern alternative). It has a busy commercial strip, leafy older quarters and large expanses of beach. You can see the effects of the 2004 tsunami in places, where the land still looks scrubbed bare.

★ Heritage Museum MUSEUM
(☎065-224 8311; A4, Kattankudy; adult/child Rs 250/100; ⏲9am-6pm Sat-Thu) This fine museum explores the history of Arab traders and their impact on the local and national culture. Spread over four floors, there are good collections of brass and copper coffeepots, ceramic dishes evidencing trade with the Far East, jewellery and practical items such as cooking pots and fishing tackle. Each floor has a diorama of life-sized models depicting traditional scenes, from the marketplace to a honeymoon room. The English-speaking

staff give a helpful introduction to the museum and can act as guides if desired.

The top floor documents the Arab influence in the region through large posters, taking a chronological sweep starting from the first Arab settlement (in Kattankudy, 3km south of Batti) in pre-Islamic times. The story goes that an Arab crew sailing from the Malabar Coast in the 5th century were shipwrecked nearby and found the verdant coast too good to leave. In the 8th century, they were joined by Arab traders who brought Islam to the region. From these small incursions, Batti grew into one of the most densely populated areas of Arab and Islamic heritage in the country.

Thiruchendur Murugan Alayam Temple HINDU SITE
(Navalady Rd) Built in 1984 as a stopping point on the Pada Yatra pilgrimage to Kataragama, the temple's Murugan image is said to have opened its own eyes before the painter completed the task. The structure was rammed by the tsunami, leaving the *gopuram* leaning at an alarming angle. It's located between 3rd and 4th Cross Sts.

Kallady & Navalady Peninsula Beach BEACH
This long beach extends along the entire length of the isthmus offering reasonable, if mostly unshaded, swimming. Access to the beach is possible via bike at numerous places from Navalady Rd.

Activities & Tours

Exploring the area by bike is a top activity in Batti. Rentals can be organised through guesthouses and hotels. The Kallady roads in particular are bike-friendly.

Don't miss Batti's legendary singing fish – they can be heard on a night-time tour of the lagoon. Guests of the Riviera Resort can rent kayaks to explore the lagoon, while the East N' West On Board initiative can help organise fishing and cooking sessions with local residents.

Sri Lanka Diving Tours DIVING
(077-764 8459; www.srilanka-divingtours.com; Deep Sea Resort, off Navalady Rd, Kallady; 2-tank dive boat trips from US$70; 8am-6pm Mar-Sep) This professional dive school specialises in wrecks, and Batticaloa has a world-class one: the HMS *Hermes*, a British aircraft carrier that was sunk by Japanese bombers in 1942. This dive is for tech divers only (the five-day certification course, for very advanced divers, is also offered here), but there are several other dives in the area for those less advanced.

There are also rooms you can stay in as part of packages.

★ **East N' West On Board** CYCLING
(065-222 6079; www.eastnwestonboard.com; 65 Thiruchentoor Beach Rd, Kallady; bike rentals per day Rs 500, bike tours for 2 people from Rs 7900, incl lunch; 9.30am-5.30pm Mon-Fri) A helpful resource, this Sri Lankan-French initiative promotes tourism in the Batti region through bike rentals, free maps and advice. A range of local tours by bike and three-wheeler are also on offer, including visits to villages and households to promote local culture. Cooking lessons and fishing are also arranged.

Sleeping

The Kallady area is attractive, with the lagoon on one side and the beach on the other, but the far tip can feel somewhat isolated in the low season. East N' West On Board can arrange for homestays at six local Kallady homesteads or three in the more remote countryside. These are highly recommended and cost Rs 7400 for two people half-board.

Naval Beach Villa GUESTHOUSE $
(077-469 2121; School Rd, Kallady; s/d/tr with fan Rs 1100/1430/1870, with 12/24hr air-con from Rs 2800/3500;) A green-walled compound some 100m from the beach, this guesthouse is a convivial spot with shared kitchen and barbecue facilities and the opportunity to dial in a takeaway. Rooms are basic but large and, with hammocks swinging in the delightful garden and friendly hosts, some guests never make it to the beach.

★ **Riviera Resort** HOTEL $$
(065-222 2164, 065-222 2165; www.riviera-online.com; New Dutch Bar Rd, Kallady; r with fan/air-con from Rs 3600/5800;) Perched at the water's edge beside Kallady Bridge and with serene views of the lagoon, the Riviera is an enchanting place to stay. Celebrating 30 years of family-run business, the resort accommodation has old-fashioned charm, especially the units with large patios, while the clearly beloved plot (replanted after the 1977 cyclone) is managed as a biogas and solar-energy project.

Kayaks are available to hire (single/double Rs 500/800) for exploring the lagoon during the day and there's a range of bikes too (Rs 400). Model railway enthusiasts will be intrigued to see the host's private project in one of the outbuildings.

Hotel East Lagoon HOTEL $$
(☎065-222 9222; www.hoteleastlagoon.lk; Munai Lane, Uppodai Lake Rd, New Town; r incl breakfast US$55-77;) This modern four-storey hotel enjoys a peaceful lagoon-side setting 1km northeast of the centre, with fine views over the water to Kallady from its spacious rooms. Staff are very accommodating and there's a bar for sampling the local arrack (liquor distilled from toddy) and a popular restaurant for excellent local food, including lots of vegetarian choices.

Eating & Drinking

Sun Shine Cafe SRI LANKAN $
(☎065-227 528; 136 Trinco Rd, New Town; meals Rs 200-450; 10am-10pm) This modern, clean and welcoming restaurant is popular for its biryanis, mutton curries and pilau rice. It also serves burgers and snacks (samosas for Rs 25), juices and lassis and the bakery sells tasty cupcakes.

RN Take Away & Buffet SRI LANKAN $
(☎077-582 2987; 42 Covington Rd, Puliyanthivu; meals Rs 150-650; 6am-9pm) This busy little outlet, run by an industrious couple, is locally famed for its excellent takeaways (vegie/meat meals Rs 150/200) that are popular with office workers. They're hoping to expand into a restaurant on the same site soon.

★**Taste & Treats** BAKERY $
(362/1 Trinco Rd, New Town; wrapped cake portions from Rs 200; 9.30am-7.30pm Mon-Sat) This Christian, family-run bakery produces consistently delicious fruitcake, pound cake with pineapple, and rich cake with a hint of local spices – the kind of cakes that might be commonly served up after church on a Sunday. It's opposite Batti's Pizza Hut outlet.

★**Riviera Resort** SRI LANKAN $$
(☎065-222 2164; www.riviera-online.com; New Dutch Bar Rd, Kallady; meals Rs 350-1000; noon-3pm & 5-10pm;) Dining here evokes memories of bygone times, as waiters fix pre-supper drinks (ideally a gin and tonic) on the veranda before taking an order for supper in the dining room or on the terrace. Excellent crab curries and seafood are available in season. Ask about the after-dinner singers for a fishy treat.

★**Café Chill** CAFE
(☎077-777 9598; www.facebook.com/cafeinbatticaloa; 9 Pioneer Rd, New Town; 10am-9pm;) A meeting point for Batti's in-crowd, romantic couples and film crews, this tiny rustic cafe with its oxcart decorations and thatched roof is picturesque enough to feature in local television dramas. When it's not having its picture taken, it serves good coffee, tea (including herbal varieties), juices, lassis and snacks in a tiny shaded garden close to the lagoon.

LOCAL KNOWLEDGE

BATTI'S CROONER FISH

While in Batti, don't miss the opportunity to be serenaded by the crooners of the deep. The town is famous for this after-dinner entertainment, which wheezes to the strain of a G-string. If all this sounds a bit fishy, that's because it is. Since the 18th century, fishermen have been navigating the waterways around town with the aid of singing fish, using their oars to 'amplify' the sound.

The Riviera Resort can arrange one-hour tours to experience this fascinating phenomenon at around 9.45pm each evening (it only occurs at night) with a 95% chance of hearing the fish. According to some, the sound is resembles a guitar string being plucked – but Eric Clapton it's not!

Shopping

Main St in the heart of Puliyanthivu is a fun place to wander, but for something a little different, head for the main strip in Kallady. Here, browsing the wares of traders, some of whom can trace their roots to Arabia, there's a distinctly Middle Eastern character to the goods for sale, including gold jewellery, textiles and woven basketry. Arab script is in evidence on some of the shop signs, Arabesque columns decorate the pavement and the middle of the road is planted with date palms instead of coconut trees. For a full history of the Arab influence on local commerce and culture, the Heritage Museum of Kattankudy (p262) is highly recommended.

Handloom Village TEXTILES
(☎065-205 4407; 440A New Kalmunai Rd, Kattankudy; 9am-7pm Mon-Sat) Shopping here causes sensory overload. In an area of Middle Eastern influence, the bright primary colours of the typically Sri Lankan textiles sold here jump out in contrast. Handloomed in characteristic grids of bright colour, the cotton textiles are mostly sold as saris and sarongs, but a few other goods, such as bags and shawls, are also on sale.

WORTH A TRIP

DRIVING SOUTH FROM TRINCO

It's possible to cover the 110km on Hwy A15 between Trincomalee and Kalkudah in two hours, but a number of attractions along the way tempt travellers to make a day of it. Heading out of Trinco, the A15 loops around the fringes of Trincomalee Bay, passing the airport. After 17km there's a turn-off on the left for **Marble Beach** (026-302 1000; www.marblebeach.lk; off A15; per person Rs 20, parking Rs 50; dawn-dusk). This glorious cove, bookended by wooded headlands, is home to a resort and a popular beach ideal for swimming.

The road passes through the Muslim town of **Mutur**, which is a good place to stop for a milk tea or a king coconut. Just south of the 101km post, following the partially paved road for 7.5km leads to **Seruwawila Rajamaha Viharaya** (Seruwawila). This is one of the holiest Buddhist monuments in Sri Lanka, founded in the 2nd century BCE, but it was only rediscovered and reconstructed in the 1920s. The stupa, renovated in 2009, looms above the landscape and attracts a steady stream of devotees.

Continuing south, the A15 crosses a fertile plain of rice paddies before the farmland gives way to a sparsely populated region of small fishing communities. At the 58km post, just after the town of Vakarai and the Panichchankeni bridge, a track meanders through wooded plots towards the sea and after 2.5km arrives at a remote and picturesque **beach**. The surprise find here is **Sallitivu Guesthouse** (077-910 5304; Panichchankeni, Vakarai; d with breakfast Rs 5500;), the labour of love of its Sri Lankan owner, who bought the house in memory of childhood excursions. Off limits in the civil war, and then obliterated by the tsunami (evacuation route signs flank the path), the original Coral Cottage has been lovingly rebuilt, but with sophisticated refinements such as a polished deck, luxurious bathrooms and seafront pavilion. Nautilus wash up on the beach here.

Back on the A15, at the 45km post, there's a **coffee shop** close to the sea. Alternatively, it's only 20km south to the twin beaches of Kalkudah and Passekudah and the promise of a cold beer and sociable nightlife in the grand hotels of the resort strip.

Batticaloa Market MARKET
(Lloyds Ave, New Town; 7am-2pm Mon-Sat) This is the place to shop for tropical fruit as well as gifts for back home, such as spoons made from coconut shells and palmyra palm jaggery (raw sugar).

Information

There are numerous ATMs in all commercial areas.

Police station (Bar Rd; 24hr)

Getting There & Away

AIR

The commuter carrier Cinnamon Air (p326) links Colombo with Batticaloa once daily. Flights take one hour and fares start at Rs 45,000. Flights use Batticaloa Airport, which is 2km west of Puliyanthivu.

BUS

CTB buses, private buses and minibuses have adjacent bus stations on Munai St. Combined CTB and private departures include the following:

Ampara Rs 110, three hours, three daily, from 6.40am

Badulla Rs 330, six hours, five daily

Colombo Rs 365, nine hours, three daily

Jaffna (via Vavuniya) Rs 427, eight hours, four daily

Polonnaruwa Rs 150, two hours, every 30 minutes

Pottuvil (for Arugam Bay) Rs 180, three hours, 12 daily

Trincomalee Rs 240, four hours, every 30 minutes

Valaichchenai (for Passekudah and Kalkudah) Rs 64, 90 minutes, every 20 minutes

Most people prefer taking a private bus to Colombo, although these services travel at night:

Surena Travels (065-222 6152; Munai St, Puliyanthivu; 4.30-8.30pm) Ordinary/air-con Rs 700/1200, eight to nine hours, two daily (at 8.30pm and 9pm)

TRAIN

Book ahead at the **railway station** (065-222 4471; Station Rd, New Town; ticket office 8.30am-6pm) for trains to Colombo (1st/2nd/3rd class Rs 1250/630/480, nine hours, twice daily); these currently leave at 7.15am and 8.15pm. Book the night train at least one week in advance.

Kalkudah & Passekudah

065

These spectacular back-to-back beaches, 34km north of Batticaloa, offer two contrasting experiences. At the northern tip of the peninsula on a tightly enclosed bay, the breathtaking white sands of sickle-shaped **Passekudah beach** have been developed as part of a 'Special Economic Zone', with luxury hotels spread discretely around the bay ending in a public beach with shallow waters. As resorts go, the development has been carefully executed with mostly attractive properties arranged in well-landscaped gardens.

In contrast, **Kalkudah beach**, 2km southeast, is barely developed and the rougher, ocean-side beach mostly deserted – save for the odd fisherman and his boat. A few guesthouses have returned here after the 2004 tsunami, but it remains a tranquil spot. Watch out for sharp coral mixed in the sand.

Anchoring these two areas is the nondescript inland town of Valaichchenai. Located near the junction of the A11 and A15 highways, it acts as the area's transport hub.

Sights

Coconut Cultural Park PARK

(071-817 5996, 065-365 9028; Coconut Board Rd, Passekudah; Rs 1300; 7.30am-4.30pm Mon-Sat) Just behind the resorts, this attraction is dedicated to the coconut, surely the world's most remarkable plant and inexorably linked with Sri Lanka (its cultivation is mentioned in the Mahavamsa). Visitors wander under coconut groves and learn about the coconut palm's many uses – timber for housing and shelter, coir rugs and rope, cooking oil and toddy. Coconut ice creams are on sale and other useful plants are showcased.

Sleeping & Eating

Luxury resorts are dotted along Coconut Board Rd and strung out along the extensive Passekudah shoreline, making it unfeasible to wander from one resort to another. Budget and midrange places are concentrated inland along the Valaichchenai–Kalkudah Rd and along the sandy lanes inland from Passekudah beach.

★ New Land Guesthouse GUESTHOUSE $

(077-293 1403, 065-568 0440; 283 Valaichchenai-Kalkudah Rd, Passekudah; r with fan from Rs 1500, d/family r with air-con Rs 2500/5000;) A welcoming family-run place with a selection of rooms featuring mosquito nets and wooden furnishings; rooms in the new block are a tad smaller. The locally famous seafood restaurant is a major draw at lunchtime (noon to 2.30pm); book the spectacular lobster dinners (if in season) one day in advance.

Nandawanam Guesthouse GUESTHOUSE $$

(065-225 7258; www.nandawanam.blogspot.com; off Valaichchenai-Kalkudah Rd, Passekudah; r Rs 3300-7000;) This large, traditional villa, painted lime green and sporting matching roof tiles, is set well back from the road in beautiful gardens. Rooms vary and most could do with a makeover to replace the dated furniture, but there are good thick mattresses and cable TV. Meals are available and the beach is about a 1km walk away.

★ Anantaya Resort RESORT $$$

(065-223 3200; www.anantaya.lk/passikudah; Coconut Board Rd, Passekudah; r from US$140;) At the northern end of the strip and tucked exquisitely into landscaped gardens, this hotel has 55 rooms scattered across the beautiful beachside plot, mostly in artfully designed two- and three-storey buildings. The free-form pool winding between the units and crossed by wooden bridges is one of the area's largest and kept sparklingly blue by the excellent staff.

Anilana Pasikuda RESORT $$$

(065-203 0900; www.anilana.com; 14 Hotel Development Rd, Passekudah; r US$90-200; @) Around the bluff from the main strip, this tasteful beachfront resort has an enormous atrium and attractive decking around the infinity pool. All rooms (in the main building or by the shore) feature modish lighting and bathrooms and there's a well-regarded spa.

The Crab & Lobster SEAFOOD $$$

(065-492 9679; Main St, Valaichchenai; meals Rs 900-1500; 11am-9.30pm) On a sharp bend in the road, right by the harbour, this attractively renovated old colonial building serves up 'the ultimate seafood in town' according to its English menu. The catch of the day is landed within walking distance of the kitchen, so freshness is pretty much guaranteed.

Getting There & Away

The town of Valaichchenai is the gateway to the twin beaches. Trains stop at the **Valaichchenai Railway Station** (Railway Rd; ticket office 8am-6pm), which is just north of the A15. Services:

Batticaloa 1st/2nd/3rd class Rs 110/60/30, 45 minutes, four times daily (departing just past 3pm, 6pm, midnight and 2am)

Colombo 1st/2nd/3rd class Rs 1230/630/380, eight hours, three times daily (departing at 7am, 5.30pm and 9pm)

There's no bus terminal, but buses stop on the main road near the train station. Three-wheelers charge Rs 300 for the short hop between Valaichchenai and Passekudah or Kalkudah. Buses include the following:

Batticaloa Rs 62, 90 minutes, frequent

Polonnaruwa Rs 97, 90 minutes, every 30 minutes

Trincomalee Rs 160, three hours, every 30 minutes

Trincomalee

☎026 / POP 102,563

Trincomalee (Trinco) sits on one of the world's finest natural harbours. This deep-water asset has made it a target for all manner of attacks over the centuries; by the time of the British takeover in 1795, the city had changed colonial hands seven times. In fact, the city can trace a far more ancient lineage as the possible site of Gokana in the Mahavamsa (Great Chronicle), with Trinco's Shiva temple the site of Trikuta Hill in the Hindu text Vayu Purana.

Today the town has chugged into quieter waters, with the future of the port a topic of political discussion as part of a metropolis development scheme. Most visitors, meanwhile, just pass through the city on their way to the nearby beaches of Uppuveli and Nilaveli. Those willing to spend time walking or cycling around the old quarter, however, will find a town of authentic charm.

Sights & Activities

Picturesque **Dutch Bay** makes a pleasant place for a stroll, while **Manayaweli Cove** is good for a dip. Note that Inner Harbour and Back Bay are too polluted for swimming. Three-wheeler drivers offer a one-hour Trinco city tour (Rs 3000 for two people).

For those with their own transport, there are two rewarding full-day excursions from Trinco. One involves a drive south (p265) along the A15 towards Passekudah. The other is a drive north (p270), past Nilaveli and along the almost deserted B424. There are accommodation options along both routes for those wanting to make a longer trip.

★Kandasamy Kovil HINDU SITE

(Koneswaram Kovil; Fort Frederick) This revered temple at the summit of a rocky outcrop is one of Sri Lanka's *pancha ishwaram,* five historical Hindu temples dedicated to Shiva and established to protect the island from natural disaster. It houses the *lingam* (Hindu phallic symbol) known as the Swayambhu Lingam. It's an ancient place of worship, but the current structure dates from 1952. Pilgrims from across the nation flock here; its *puja* (prayers) at 6.30am, 11.30am and 4.30pm are always well attended.

★Fort Frederick FORTRESS

(Konesar Rd) FREE Occupying the neck of a narrow peninsula, Fort Frederick has been a defensively important site for centuries. A fortress was initially constructed here by the Portuguese in 1623 and later rebuilt by the Dutch. The British assumed control in 1782 (look out for royal insignia crowning the elongated gateway tunnelled into the battlements). The fort is used today by the Sri Lankan military, but it's possible to explore on foot or by car.

Among the colonnaded colonial-era buildings is **Wellesley House**, named after a Duke of Wellington and dating from the late 1700s (not open to visitors). Note too the standing Buddha statue at **Gokana Temple**. Assorted cannons and artillery are dotted around the enclave, used as scratching posts for spotted deer and shade for peacocks.

★Kali Kovil HINDU TEMPLE

(Dockyard Rd) This superbly painted temple with its remarkable *gopuram* features a riot of coloured plasterwork, but it's not so much the plump deities that attract the eye as the delightful details that are wedged in between: hands of bright yellow bananas, the smiling lion with his woolly mane, a peacock proudly wearing a medal, a lavish bow resting on big pot belly – all signs of the artists' sense of humour.

Devotees pour in and out of the inner sanctum at all times of the day, pausing at the entrance to waft purifying incense and dash coconuts as an offering before prayers.

Maritime & Naval History Museum MUSEUM

(Dockyard Rd; ⏲9am-4pm Wed-Mon) FREE This worthy museum, which will appeal mostly to history buffs, is housed within a fine 18th-century Dutch colonial building that is worth a visit in its own right. Displays on the ground floor cover Sri Lankan naval history since Marco Polo's time. Those interested in

Trincomalee

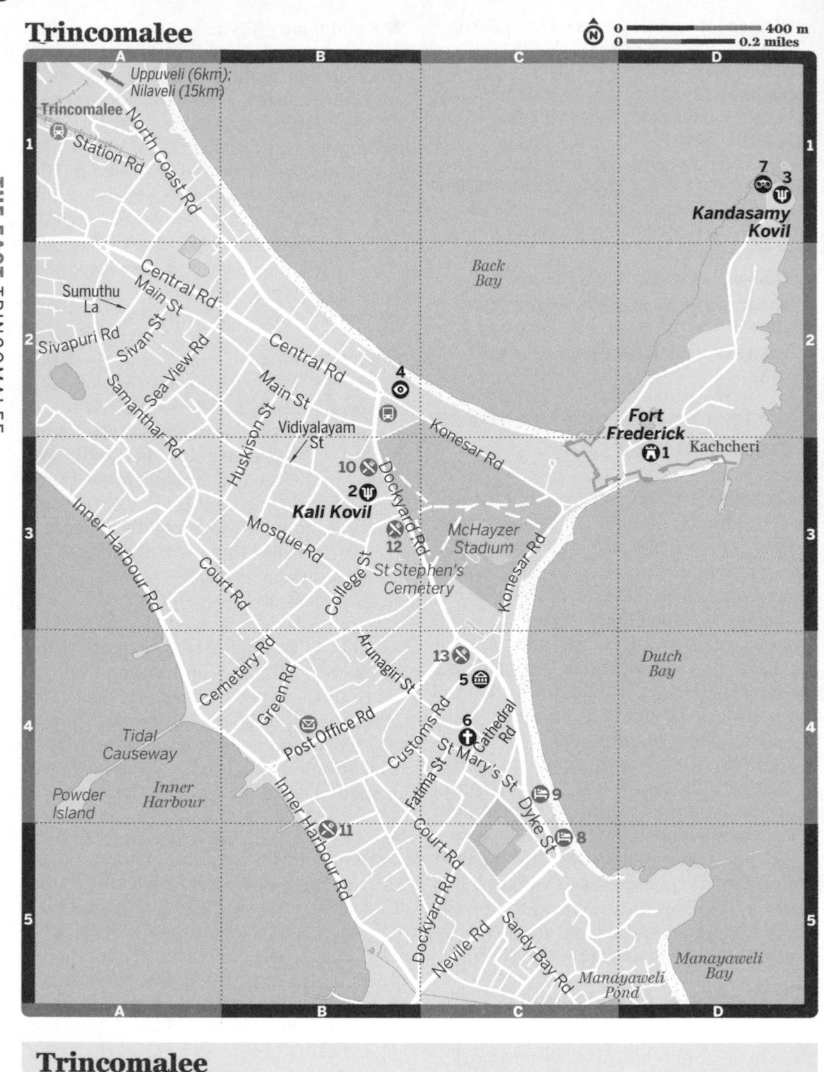

Trincomalee

Top Sights

1 Fort Frederick D3
2 Kali Kovil B3
3 Kandasamy Kovil D1

Sights

4 Fish Market B2
5 Maritime & Naval History Museum C4
6 St Mary's Cathedral C4
7 Swami Rock D1

Sleeping

8 Dyke Rest C5
9 Hotel Blue Ocean C4

Eating

10 Anna Pooram Vegetarian Restaurant B3
11 Dutch Bank Cafe B5
12 Meendum Nes Cafe B3
13 Trinco Rest House C4

natural history should make the effort to climb to the upper floor, where there are fine views of whale-frequented Dutch Bay and helpful displays on regional flora and fauna.

St Mary's Cathedral CHURCH

(St Mary's St; ⏲8am-5pm) Of the city's many churches, St Mary's Cathedral is particularly attractive. Built in 1852, this Catholic place of worship is graced with a white, neo-baroque facade and a striking set of half cloisters with red roof tiles. Visitors are welcome to step inside the bright, cool interior if there is no mass (or wedding) in progress.

Fish Market MARKET

(Konesar Rd; ⏲5-11am) For those interested in what lies under the famous east coast surf but don't want to get wet in finding out, then a trip to the raucous daily fish market (near the bus station) may just solve the mystery. Early in the morning, dozens of customers jostle to snap up various tropical sensations that rarely make it onto a tourist menu.

Sleeping

★Dyke Rest INN $

(☎026-222 5313; www.facebook.com/DykeRest; 228 Dyke St; r with fan and shared bathroom Rs 1500-2500, with air-con from Rs 4400; ❄📶) The friendly management here is incentive enough to spend a night or two in Trinco at this two-storey, beachside gem. There's a porch and an upper deck decorated with fun murals, from which to enjoy lovely views of the cove and its fishing boats. Rooms are small but attractive and the comment walls throughout the communal areas contribute to the traveller vibe.

Hotel Blue Ocean GUESTHOUSE $

(☎026-222 5578; 290 Dyke St; r with fan from Rs 1500, with air-con from Rs 3500; ❄📶) Right on Dutch Bay Beach, this simple guesthouse has a narrow front on the sand. The basic rooms, spread across three storeys within the labyrinthine interior, are a bit dark but well-maintained. In whale season (March to November) the guesthouse can arrange two-hour whale-watching trips (Rs 3500). Breakfast costs Rs 600.

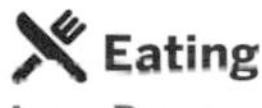

Eating

Anna Pooram Vegetarian Restaurant SOUTH INDIAN $

(415 Dockyard Rd; mains Rs 150-400; ⏲6.30am-9.30pm) This bustling vegetarian eatery excels at Tamil dishes and is particularly popular at lunchtime. Famous for its *sambar* (soupy lentil dish with veg) and rice and curry, it only has a couple of tables, but it mostly caters for takeaways and delicious short eats (samosas, mushroom cutlets and *dal vadai*).

Trinco Rest House SEAFOOD $$

(☎026-222 4440; Post Office Rd; dishes around Rs 500; ⏲7am-10pm) Usefully located next to the Maritime & Naval History Museum at Dutch Bay, the grounds of this smart, modern restaurant are shaded by an enormous banyan tree. A large menu of seafood dishes is interspersed with traveller favourites.

★Dutch Bank Cafe INTERNATIONAL $$$

(☎077-269 0600; 88 Inner Harbour Rd; meals Rs 600-1600; ⏲8am-10pm; 📶) Central Trinco's most polished restaurant is housed in a historic building that combines exposed stone arches with contemporary design. Simple international favourites (pizza, burgers and noodle dishes) are on offer, together with Sri Lankan specials. The best venue in town for an espresso or cappuccino, juices and shakes, it has a view of the Inner Harbour from the terrace.

Getting There & Away

AIR

The commuter carrier Cinnamon Air (p326) links Colombo with Trinco once daily. Flights take one hour and fares start at Rs 45,000. The airport is a 12km drive west of town.

BUS

CTB and private bus departures all use the same **bus terminal** (Dockyard Rd). Services include the following:

Anuradhapura Rs 200, four hours, six daily

Batticaloa Rs 300, four hours, every 30 minutes

Colombo regular Rs 450, seven hours, hourly

Colombo (air-con; book in advance) express/luxury Rs 600/950, six hours, six daily

DON'T MISS

WHALE WATCHTOWER

Jutting into the ocean on the east side of the city of Trincomalee, **Swami Rock** (Fort Frederick) has been declared by oceanographers as the world's greatest vantage point for blue-whale spotting. These gentle giants are present in the seas off Trinco all year round, though sightings are most frequent between February and November. Sperm whales also regularly cruise by. If exploring Kandasamy Kovil, bring some binoculars and cast an eye over the big blue offshore for spouting cetaceans.

Jaffna (via Vavuniya) Rs 320, seven hours, nine daily

Kandy Rs 250, 5½ hours, seven daily

TRAIN

There are two trains daily (one departing in the morning and one in the evening) between Trincomalee and Colombo Fort; the evening service is a direct overnight sleeper service. Reserve at **Trincomalee Station** (☎ 026-222 2271; Station Rd; ⏰ bookings 8am-4pm). You can also travel to Polonnaruwa and Batticaloa via a change in Gal Oya.

Colombo sleeper 1st-/2nd-/3rd-class sleeper Rs 1250/550/350, eight hours; this service currently leaves at 7.30pm. Reserve at least one week ahead.

Colombo unreserved (transfer in Gal Oya) 2nd/3rd class Rs 480/305, nine hours. This service currently leaves at 7am.

Uppuveli

☎ 026

Uppuveli, just 6km north from Trincomalee, is a fun little coastal enclave consisting of a fine beach of golden sand, lots of attractive places to stay and eat, and easy access to both historic Trinco and the wildlife haven of Pigeon Island. With an intimate feel and some good-value accommodation, it's easy to see why many travellers call it their favourite spot in the East.

Sights & Activities

Commonwealth War Cemetery CEMETERY
(300 Nilaveli Rd (B424); ⏰ dawn-dusk) This beautifully kept cemetery is the last resting place for 364 Commonwealth servicemen who died at Trinco during WWII, most of them during a 1942 Japanese raid that sank over a dozen vessels. The amiable caretaker, whose

WORTH A TRIP

DRIVING NORTH FROM TRINCO

From Trinco, the East Coast is comprised of a string of beautiful beaches, from the coconut-shaded resorts of sociable Uppuveli to the forest-edged sands of more tranquil Nilaveli. It is at this point that the rural B424 leaves the tourist enclaves behind and heads into remote countryside. With the ocean on one side and lagoons on the other, the drive makes for a great day out by car or, for those with some stamina, on a bicycle. Peacocks, monkeys and herds of water buffalo are commonly sighted.

Some 9km north of Nilaveli, the Uga Jungle Beach Resort (p273) offers the first opportunity for refreshment; set-menu breakfasts (call ahead) are served in a beautiful woodland glade. Thereafter, the B424 crosses a river estuary at Kumpurupiddi before running very close to the beach – a perfect opportunity to check for sundials, spiny murex and other Indian Ocean seashells. The shallow lagoon to the west is sectioned to form **salt pans** from which salt is harvested in the dry season.

Continuing north, the signposted archaeological site of **Kuchchaveli** lies off the 34km post on the B424. Occupying a rocky promontory, the stupa's elevated position (reached via 50 steps, strewn with sleeping dogs) has spectacular views over the flanking twin beaches, which are perfect for swimming.

Around the 40km post, the shoreline is dotted with colourful fishing boats. The sands around here are often naturally streaked black with traces of valuable **heavy minerals** such as gakone, ilmenite, serkone and magnetite, washed down to the sea through the river. Thereafter, the terrain changes markedly with dense mangroves, home to monitor lizards and prolific birdlife, before reaching an army checkpoint.

At the 45km post, a small road heads west for 4km towards **Girihandu Seya**, thought to be the site of the first Buddhist temple built in Sri Lanka and dating back to the 3rd century BCE. There are remnants of complex carvings near the parking lot, but the best of the site is the magnificent view from the hilltop.

Back on the B424, there's a tea stop at a small cafe run by the army by a big banyan tree near the 46km post. From here, it's a short trip through fields graced with thickly clustered sugar palms to the isolated village of **Pulmoddai** at Km 54, which sits just inland from the **Kokkilai Lagoon**, an important bird sanctuary.

Buses (Rs 90, 1½ hours, hourly) connect Pulmoddai with Trincomalee, passing through Nilaveli and Uppuveli en route. Services also head to Mullaittivu (Rs 100, two hours, hourly), offering a coastal route to northern Sri Lanka and Jaffna.

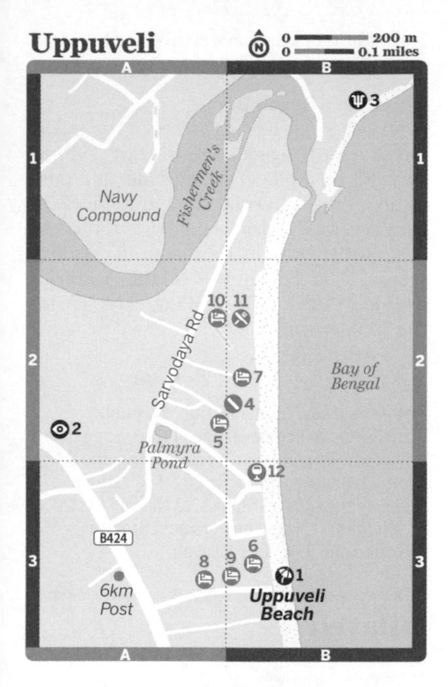

Uppuveli

Top Sights
1 Uppuveli Beach ... B3

Sights
2 Commonwealth War Cemetery ... A2
3 Salli Muthumariamunam Kovil ... B1

Activities, Courses & Tours
4 Angel Diving ... B2

Sleeping
5 Anantamaa ... A2
6 Coconut Beach Lodge ... B3
7 Golden Beach Cottages ... B2
8 Orion Beach Way ... A3
9 Palm Beach Resort ... B3
10 Trinco Blu by Cinnamon ... A2

Eating
Coconut Beach Lodge ... (see 6)
11 Crab ... B2
Palm Beach ... (see 9)
Tonic's ... (see 7)

Drinking & Nightlife
12 Fernando's Beach Bar ... B3

knowledge of the cemetery is encyclopedic, offers a guided tour of specific graves, pointing out the 13 nationalities buried here.

Salli Muthumariamunam Kovil HINDU SITE
One of the distintinctive features of this temple is that it is located right on the beach. While it is 4km by road from Uppuveli, it's only a short wade (or hop by boat if the tide is high) from the northern end of Uppuveli beach, masked by the rocks near Fishermen's Creek.

★**Angel Diving** DIVING
(077-865 8431; www.facebook.com/angeldivingsrilanka; Uppuveli Beach; 2-tank boat dives from US$80; 7am-10pm Mar-Sep) A very popular dive shop, praised for its customer service. Located along the beach next to the Golden Beach Cottage, it organises trips to Pigeon Island and the fabled HMS *Hermes*, among others.

Sleeping

Orion Beach Way CABANAS $
(076-169 0936; http://orionbeachway.com; 178/15 Alles Garden, off Nilaveli Rd; r Rs 2700;) The fan-only rooms at this little assembly of huts and cabanas represent good value, as evidenced by the comments written on the whitewashed walls by happy customers. Managed by someone with green fingers, the gorgeous tropical shrubs, hanging baskets and giant creepers have artfully been used to turn this little inland plot into an eye-catching delight. Diving information is available.

★**Golden Beach Cottages** GUESTHOUSE $$
(026-493 1210, 077-134 4620; www.goldenbeachcottages.com; 24 Alles Garden, off Nilaveli Rd; r Rs 4000-11,000;) This delightful guesthouse is situated on the beach, graced by two young coconut trees and a shady garden of tropical almonds and frangipani. The 12 generous-sized rooms are simple, but each features artistic flourishes, spotless bathrooms and a porch. There's also an open cafe, perfectly located to make the best of the views. Airport transfers from Colombo (Rs 16,000) are available.

Coconut Beach Lodge GUESTHOUSE $$
(026-222 4888; coconutbeachlodge@gmail.com; 178 Alles Garden, off Nilaveli Rd; r Rs 5000-12,000;) With a prime beachfront location and a large attractive restaurant sitting on the high tide line, there's much to commend about this friendly, well-looked-after guesthouse. The garden compound, with its ornamental palms, is a secluded plot. There's an elegant villa in the middle of the garden providing a traditional-style shady lounge area. Thoughtful touches include artwork in the bathrooms.

Anantamaa HOTEL $$$
(☎026-205 0250; www.anantamaa.com; 7/42 Alles Garden, off Nilaveli Rd; r from US$120; ❄ 📶 🏊) Set back from the beach, but with its own private path to the sand, this professionally managed hotel has clean and comfortable rooms in two-storey blocks around a large pool. One of the best features of the property is the pretty garden; the tamarisk trees, colourful shrubs, frangipani and lily ponds make it a tranquil retreat.

Eating & Drinking

★**Coconut Beach Lodge** SRI LANKAN $$
(☎026-222 4888; 178 Alles Garden, off Nilaveli Rd; meals Rs 350-700; 📶) Coconut Beach is considered by some to be the best place in town for Sri Lankan–style home cooking. Rice and curry, grilled seer fish and giant prawns, plus vegetarian delights, are served on a pretty candlelit patio. Reserve by 3.30pm. A good place to try a full Sri Lankan breakfast (Rs 400).

Tonic's SEAFOOD $$
(☎026-493 1210; Golden Beach Cottages, 24 Alles Garden, off Nilaveli Rd; meals Rs 500-1200; ⏲11am-10pm) Named after the owner's aged, globe-trotting cat, Tonic's is likely to delight any traveller (four legs or two). At the top of the tide line, it has just the kind of relaxed atmosphere that makes Uppuveli Beach so appealing. Call in for an early breakfast before snorkelling at Pigeon Island, or drop by at dusk for a seafood platter of fresh-off-the-boat specials.

Palm Beach ITALIAN $$
(☎026-222 1250; Ward 2, 14km post, Alles Garden, off Nilaveli Rd; meals Rs 550-900; ⏲6.30-9pm Feb-Nov; 📶) Italian food, including fine pasta and seafood, is rustled up by the chef here; with 25 years of experience preparing this cuisine, his creations (given the location) are surprisingly authentic. The menu changes daily, but always includes a special or two. A Sri Lankan chef is on hand for those who are reluctant to forgo the daily rice and curry.

★**Crab** INTERNATIONAL $$$
(☎026-222 2307; Trinco Blu by Cinnamon, off Sarvodaya Rd; meals Rs 1000-2800; ⏲5-11pm) In a breezy spot near the beach, this stylish hotel restaurant offers a romantic evening out. There's a wide selection of dishes with Asian favourites, including Indonesian *nasi goreng* and Thai satay. The star of the show, however, is the local crab curry. With a full bar and first-class service, this is the obvious choice for a special occasion.

Fernando's Beach Bar BAR
(Aqua Inn; ⏲7am-10pm) *The* beach bar in Uppuveli. Many nights seem to start and end here. Sit on a pillow on the sand, at a table or up on the driftwood-covered terrace. The beer is cold, the drinks potent and the vibe fun, particularly on DJ nights in the high season. The Fernando Cocktail, featuring the local arrack with rum, lime and banana (Rs 700), is worth a try.

Getting There & Away

The easiest way to reach Trinco by public transport is to flag down one of the frequent Irakkandy–Trincomalee buses that ply the B424 every 20 minutes or so (Rs 20). The same bus stops, in the other direction, at Nilaveli (Rs 20, 10 minutes). Three-wheelers cost around Rs 550 to Trinco and Rs 650 to Nilaveli.

Nilaveli

☎026

Nilaveli is the more northerly of Trinco's two beach resort areas and is more remote than its sociable neighbour, Uppuveli. Hotels are widely scattered along the 4km of extensive and largely unfrequented beach, accessible only via unpaved tracks off the coastal highway (B424). Offshore, **Pigeon Island** offers excellent diving and snorkelling through dive schools such as **Poseidon Diving Station** (☎077-881 0766; www.divingsrilanka.com; off B424, near 9km post; 2-tank boat dives from around €100; ⏲Apr-Nov).

Sights & Activities

★**Pigeon Island National Park** DIVING, SNORKELLING
(☎071-322 7050; child/adult US$5/10) With its powdery white sands and glittering coral gardens, and lying just 1km offshore, Pigeon Island is a gem of the Indian Ocean. A nesting area for rock pigeons, the island has its own attractions with pools and paths running through thickets, but most people choose to explore the underwater landscape. The reef here is shallow, making snorkelling almost as satisfying as diving, and it's home to dozens of corals, reef fish (including blacktip reef sharks) and turtles.

Irresponsible tourism has somewhat damaged the reef. As such, it's important to avoid contributing to the problem – refrain from standing on corals, remove litter and be sure to pay national park fees for the protection of this special site.

The **Pigeon Island National Park Ticket Office** (☎026-320 3850; ⏲6am-5.30pm) is on the beach in front of the Anilana hotel. The park is busy between May and September.

Nilaveli Private Boat Service BOAT TRIP, SNORKELLING
(☎071-593 6919, 077-886 9285; Ward 4, Irakkakandi; fishing trips 1-4 people Rs 6000, whale-watching trips per 2/4 people Rs 14,000/16,000; ⏲8am-5pm) The local boat owners' association, near the park ticket office, ferries passengers to Pigeon Island for a set price (Rs 2000 per boat excluding park fees, plus Rs 600 for snorkelling gear). Book a day ahead in July and August.

★**Faith Travel & Tours** TOURS
(☎031-223 0339, 072-539 3871; shalindew@gmail.com) Manjula Fernando offers tours of Nilaveli, Uppaveli, Trinco and the whole east coast of Sri Lanka. An excellent driver, Mr Manju is not just a safe pair of hands, but also knowledgeable about the location of sights and places to stay, in and around the towns and beach areas of the region.

Sleeping & Eating

★**That's Why** HUT $
(☎077-175 6290; off B424; r Rs 3500-10,000; 📶) The convivial ringmaster Sameera runs this delightful beachfront assembly of huts within touching distance of the surf. There are eight well-appointed, cone-shaped cabanas (some with air-con), and the friendly little beach bar (11am to late) is a relaxed place to lounge and chat with the amiable staff. All in all, it's a classic travellers' haven.

★**Uga Jungle Beach Resort** RESORT $$$
(☎026-567 1000; www.ugaescapes.com/junglebeach; B424, 27km post, Kuchchaveli; cabins US$100-300; ❄📶🏊) 🍃 This eclectic resort (and spa) is magical to arrive in at night as the gantry to reception disappears into the tree canopy. In fact, trees are the main theme of this resort, with even the spectacular beach accessed via tunnels through the woodland. The luxurious rooms have private forest glades and woodland birds flit through the restaurant, attracted by tasteful water features.

Nilaveli

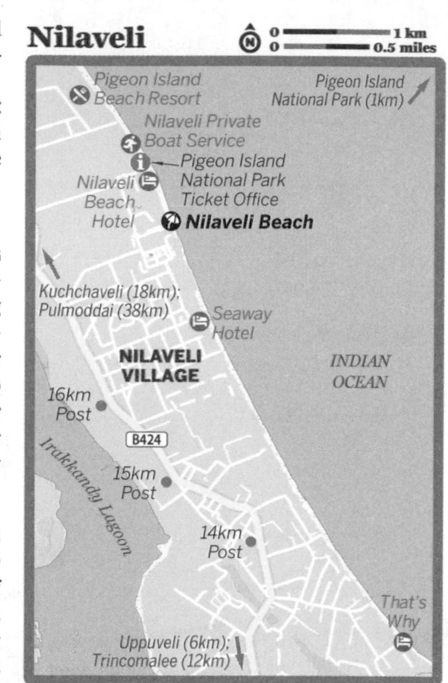

Nilaveli Beach Hotel RESORT $$$
(☎026-223 2293; www.nilaveli.tangerinehotels.com; off B424; r US$90-200; ❄📶🏊) With shady hammock groves and a gorgeous pool area, this well-run hotel also encompasses a beautiful stretch of beach with views across to Pigeon Island. Rooms are simple, comfortable bungalows with porches, while the communal areas are a tastefully eclectic mix of contemporary and rustic chic.

Pigeon Island Beach Resort INTERNATIONAL $$$
(☎026-738 8388; off B424; mains from Rs 1000; ⏲7-9.30pm) For a break from the seashore and the opportunity for more international-style cuisine, this resort restaurant has an old-world charm about it, decked out with antique furniture and surrounded by a mature garden of trees. The daily specials, available even in low season, make the most of local ingredients.

Getting There & Away

Flag down any passing bus along the B424 for Trincomalee (Rs 40, 30 minutes, every 20 minutes). A three-wheeler costs around Rs 900 to Trincomalee or Rs 600 to Uppuveli.

AT A GLANCE

POPULATION
Jaffna: 169,000

GATEWAY CITY
Jaffna (p277)

BEST HINDU TEMPLE
Nallur Kandaswamy Kovil (p280)

BEST JAFFNA CURRY
Mangos (p283)

BEST HISTORICAL RUIN
Mannar's Dutch Fort (p294)

WHEN TO GO

Feb The best month to view greater flamingos, present in their hundreds on Mannar Island.

Jun–Jul High season sees sunshine, moderate heat and delicious mangoes.

Jul–Aug Jaffna's extraordinary 25-day Nallur festival has parades, ice cream and ritual self-mutilation.

Dutch Fort (p294), Mannar Island
SAIKO3P/SHUTTERSTOCK ©

Jaffna & the North

With towering, rainbow-coloured Hindu temples and a spectacular coastline fringed with palmyra and coconut palms, the North is a different world. Here the climate is arid for most of the year and the fields are sun-baked. The light is stronger: surreal and white-hot on salt flats in the central Vanni, bright and lucid on coral islands and northern beaches, and soft and speckled in Jaffna's leafy suburbs and busy centre. Look for the shimmer of colours from the wild peacocks that seem to wander everywhere.

Then there are the cultural differences. From the language to the cuisine and religion, Tamil culture has its own rhythms, and people here are proud of their Hindu heritage. Inevitably, given the region's recent history, there's a noticeable military presence. But the ambience is relaxed as locals focus on building for the future and reviving the rich traditions of northern life.

INCLUDES

Jaffna & the North Highlights

1 Jaffna's Islands (p290) Marvelling at the spectacular seascapes and surreal light while exploring offshore treasures such as Nainativu.

2 Mannar Island (p294) Discovering ancient baobab trees, a historic fort, remote bays, fishing villages and a view almost to India.

3 Scenic Rides (p288) Riding along the spectacular coastal roads of the Jaffna peninsula, notably from Valvettiturai to Point Pedro.

4 Northeast Shore (p288) Finding your own perfect palm-fringed ribbon of sand, such as isolated Manalkadu Beach.

5 Jaffna (p277) Attending a *puja* (prayers) at Nallur Kandaswamy Kovil, Jaffna's sprawling and historic main temple, before appreciating the city's history among the old walls of Jaffna Fort.

History

The North has always existed a bit apart from the rest of the island; even under colonial regimes the region remained highly autonomous. Jaffna, especially, has always been an important city, and one of the defining moments on the path to war came in 1981 when a group of Sinhalese burnt down Jaffna's library, seen as a violent affront to the Tamils' long and rich intellectual tradition.

The war began two years later, and for two decades the North was synonymous with death and destruction as the Liberation Tigers of Tamil Eelam (LTTE) and Sri Lankan military contested control. Since the war ended on the shores of Mullaittivu in 2009 a sense of calm and stability has returned to the North.

Harassment, detentions and occasional disappearances continue. Most people are looking to the future and are relieved to put the war behind them, but old tensions remain under the surface.

Jaffna

021 / POP 169,000

A bastion of Hindu tradition, art and creative culture, Jaffna welcomes visitors warmly. It's intriguing, unimposing, slightly off the beaten path and a thoroughly rewarding place to learn about Sri Lankan Tamil culture.

The city is surprisingly green and leafy, with attractive palm-shaded suburbs and beautiful temples and churches. New building projects and upgraded transport connections show that Jaffna's days of isolation are long behind it.

The city rewards a couple of days to tour the South Indian-style temples and Dutch fort, and to taste northern Sri Lankan cuisine, including the town's signature Jaffna-style crab curry.

It's also an ideal base for day trips to the idyllic islands just to the west, and jaunts along the coastline and lagoons of the surrounding peninsula.

History

For centuries Jaffna has been Sri Lanka's Hindu-Tamil cultural and religious centre – especially during the Jaffna Kingdom, the powerful Tamil dynasty that ruled from Nallur for 400 years beginning in the 13th century. But the Portuguese tried hard to change that. In 1620 they captured Cankili II, the last king (his horseback statue stands on Point Pedro Rd, near the Royal Palace ruins), then set about systematically demolishing the city's Hindu temples. A wave of mass Christian conversions followed.

Following a bitter three-month siege, the Portuguese surrendered their 'Jaffnapattao' to the more tolerant Dutch a few decades later, and Dutch Jaffna, which lasted for almost 140 years, became a major trade centre. Jaffna continued to prosper under the British, who took over in 1795 and sowed the seeds of future inter-ethnic unrest by 'favouring' the Jaffna Tamils.

The city played a crucial role in the lead-up to the civil war and by the early 1980s escalating tensions overwhelmed Jaffna; for two decades the city was a no-go war zone. Variously besieged by Tamil guerrillas, Sri Lanka Army (SLA) troops and a so-called peacekeeping force, the city lost almost half of its population to emigration. In 1990 the LTTE forced Jaffna's few remaining Sinhalese and all Muslim residents to leave. Jaffna suffered through endless bombings, a crippling blockade (goods, including fuel, once retailed here for 20 times the market price) and military rule after the SLA's 1995 recapture of the town.

Then, in the peace created by the 2002 accords, the sense of occupation was relaxed and Jaffna sprang back to life: domestic flights began; refugees, internally displaced persons (IDPs) and long-absent émigrés returned; and new businesses opened and building projects commenced. Hostilities recommenced in 2006 and tension continued through to the end of the war in 2009.

Today a renewed focus on the future is palpable across Jaffna. New building projects are being launched and the last scars of the war have been erased – at least the physical ones.

Sights

Jaffna is dotted with Hindu temples, easily identified by their red-and-white-striped walls. They range from tiny shrines to sprawling complexes featuring *mandapaya* (raised platforms with decorated pillars), ornate ponds and towering *gopuram* (gateway towers).

The city also has its landmark fort and an abundance of churches, many located on shady streets east of the centre. Commercial activity is crammed into the colourful hurly-burly of Hospital, Kasturiya and Kankesanturai (KKS) Rds.

Jaffna

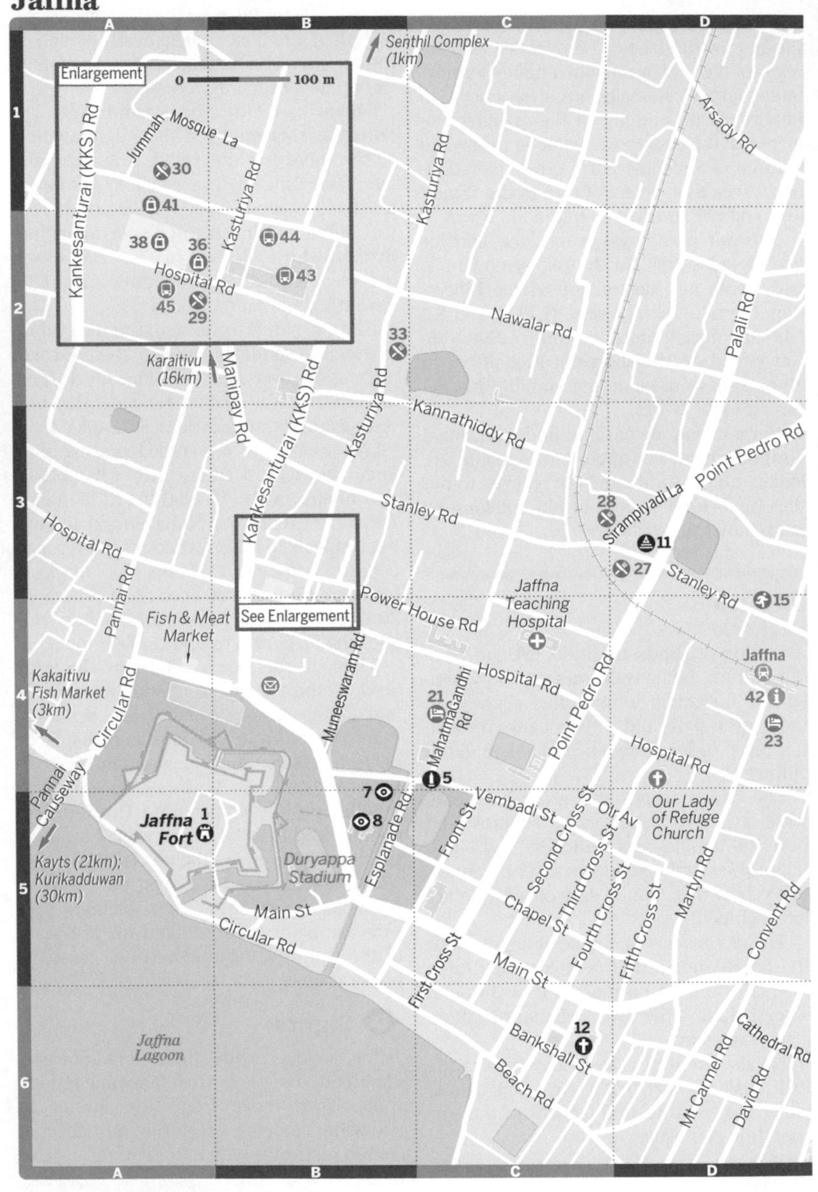

Central Jaffna

★Jaffna Fort FORT

(Main St; child/adult US$2/4; 7.30am-6pm) Once one of the greatest Dutch forts in Asia, this vast complex overlooking the Jaffna lagoon was built in 1658 over an earlier Portuguese original (1619). Defensive triangles were added in 1792 to produce the classic Vaubanesque star form.

Long the gatehouse of the city, Jaffna's fort has been fought over for centuries. Today you can wander its walls, gateways and

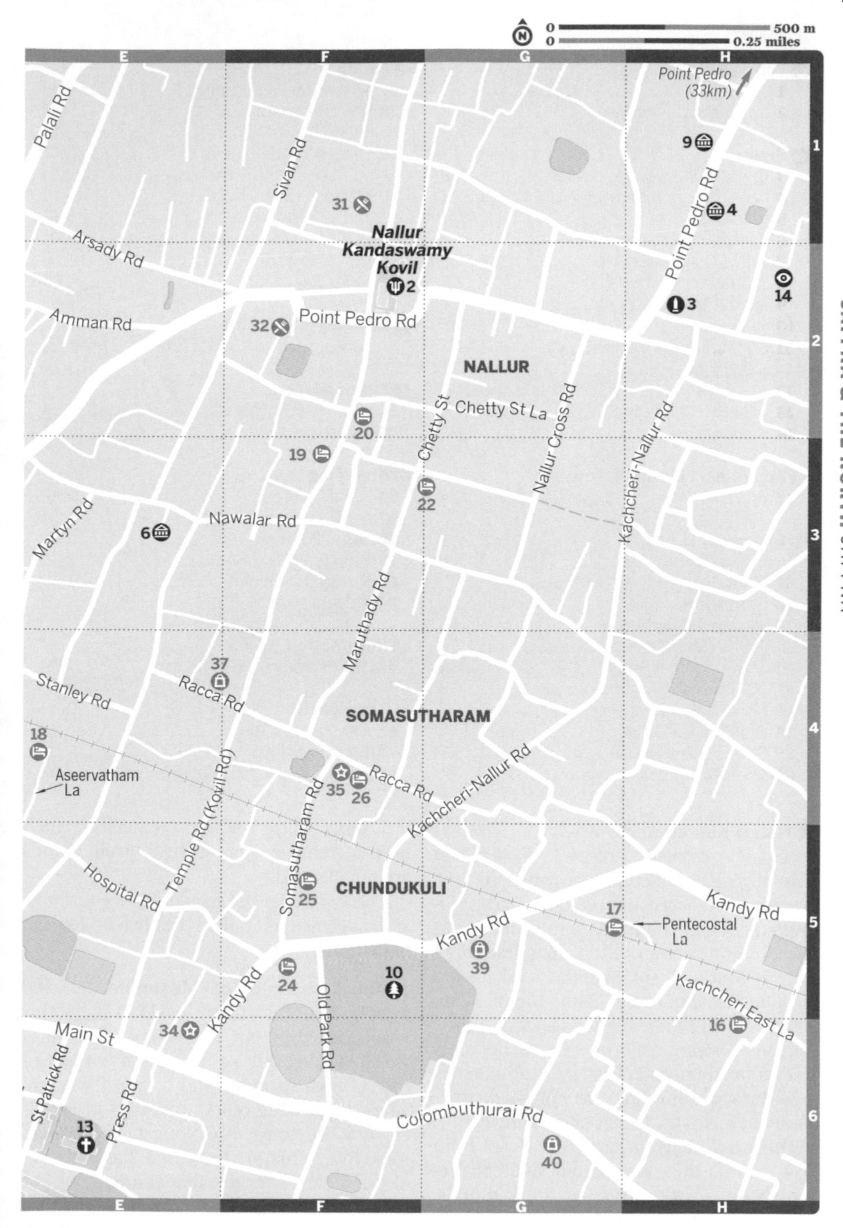

moats, see the barracks that once housed thousands of troops and civilians, and view the city from its ramparts.

During the war government forces used it as an encampment, and in 1990 the LTTE – at the time in control of the rest of Jaffna – forced out government troops after a grisly 107-day siege.

Today a room inside the main portal has exhibits on the archaeological history of the fort. Restoration of the coral, stone, brick and mortar walls continues.

Jaffna

Top Sights
1 Jaffna Fort ... A5
2 Nallur Kandaswamy Kovil ... F2

Sights
3 Cankili II Statue ... H2
4 Cankili Thoppu Archway ... H1
5 Clock Tower ... C4
6 Jaffna Archaeological Museum ... E3
7 Jaffna Cultural Centre ... B5
8 Jaffna Public Library ... B5
9 Mantiri Manai ... H1
10 Old Park ... F5
11 Sri Nagavihara International Buddhist Centre ... D3
12 St James' Church ... C6
13 St Mary's Cathedral ... E6
14 Yamuna Eri ... H2

Activities, Courses & Tours
15 Sri Lanka Click ... D4

Sleeping
16 D'Villa Garden House ... H6
17 D'Villa Guest House ... G5
18 Green Grass Hotel ... E4
19 Jaffna Heritage Hotel ... F3
20 Jaffna Heritage Villa ... F2
21 Jetwing Jaffna Hotel ... C4
22 Lux Etoiles ... G3
23 North Gate by Jetwing ... D4
24 Old Park Villa ... F5
25 Sarras Guest House ... F5
26 Theresa Inn ... F4

Eating
27 Akshathai Restaurant ... D3
28 Cosy Restaurant ... C3
Green Grass ... (see 18)
29 Hotel Rolex ... A2
Jaffna Heritage Hotel ... (see 19)
30 Malayan Café ... A1
31 Mangos ... F1
Peninsula Restaurant ... (see 21)
32 Rio Ice Cream ... F2
33 Rolex Bake Mart ... B2

Drinking & Nightlife
Jetwing Jaffna Rooftop Bar ... (see 21)

Entertainment
34 Alliance Française ... E6
35 British Council ... F4

Shopping
36 Anna Coffee ... A2
37 Art Gallery ... E4
38 Jaffna Market ... A2
39 Kathier Wine City ... G5
40 Rosarian Convent ... G6
41 Zahra Tailors ... A1

Information
42 Tourist Information Centre ... D4

Transport
43 Central Bus Stand ... B2
44 Minibus Stand ... B2
45 Private Buses to Colombo ... A2

★ **Nallur Kandaswamy Kovil** HINDU SITE
(Temple Rd; donations accepted; ⏲4am-7pm) This huge Hindu temple, crowned by two towering god-encrusted, golden-ochre *gopuram,* is one of the most significant Hindu religious complexes in Sri Lanka. Its sacred deity is Murugan (or Skanda), and during cacophonous *puja* – at 5am, 10am, noon, 4.15pm (small *puja*), 4.30pm ('special' *puja*), 5pm and 6.45pm – offerings are made to his brass-framed image and other Hindu deities in shrines surrounding the inner sanctum. It's about 1.5km northeast of the centre.

The *kovil*'s current structure dates from 1734, and its huge compound shelters decorative brasswork, larger-than-life murals, pillared halls and a colonnaded, stepped holy pool.

You can say a prayer at the sacred tree in the temple's southern courtyard anytime: get a piece of gold-threaded cloth from outside the temple, wrap some coins in it, and tie it to the tree along with a prayer. Afterwards, ring the big brass bell.

Visitors must remove their shoes; men need to remove their shirts as well. Photos are not allowed.

The temple is the focus of the enormous and spectacular Nallur Festival (p282) in midsummer.

Jaffna Archaeological Museum MUSEUM
(Nawalar Rd; ⏲8am-4.45pm Wed-Mon) FREE This small, unkempt but interesting museum is worth seeking out. At the door are a pair of rusty Dutch cannons and a set of piled-up whale bones. The quirky treasures inside include a lice comb, a dugong tusk necklace, some fine miniature ivory Buddhas and a set of brass sieves for grading pearls. Look for the terrifying hooks and nail sandals used for self-mortification during bloody *kavadai* rituals. No photos allowed.

Jaffna Public Library LIBRARY
(☎021-222 6028; Esplanade Rd; ⏲4.30-6pm Tue-Sun) Jaffna residents have long considered their city to be one of Asia's finest intellectual capitals, and this library is an important Ta-

mil cultural centre and historic institution. Inaugurated in 1841, it was burnt down by pro-government mobs in July 1981 – few acts were more significant in the build-up to civil war. It was one of the first major buildings to be rebuilt after the 2002 ceasefire. In its reconstruction architects kept true to the elegant original neo-Mughal design from 1959.

The original world-renowned collection destroyed in the fire included more than 90,000 volumes, including irreplaceable Tamil documents, such as the one surviving copy of *Yalpanam Vaipavama,* a history of Jaffna.

Jaffna Cultural Centre CULTURAL CENTRE
(Esplanade Rd) Jaffna's renaissance is symbolised by this huge new cultural centre, gifted by India and due for completion by 2021. The multistorey building will include a large theatre, museum and art galleries and will revolutionise Jaffna's cultural scene.

Clock Tower MONUMENT
(Vembadi St) An architectural curiosity, the spindly Clock Tower has an oddly Moorish domed top. It was erected in 1875 to honour a visit by the Prince of Wales. In 2000 the current prince, Charles, donated the working clocks you see today to replace those damaged by fighting.

St Mary's Cathedral CHURCH
(021-222 2457; Cathedral Rd; 8am-5pm) Built by the Dutch along classical lines in the 1790s, St Mary's Cathedral is astonishingly large. It's jarring to see corrugated-iron roofing held up by such a masterpiece of wooden vaulting. It's the main church for Roman Catholics.

St James' Church CHURCH
(021-222 5189; Main St; 8am-5pm) This is the grandest church in Jaffna, a classical Italianate edifice used by Anglicans that dates to 1827.

Sri Nagavihara International Buddhist Centre BUDDHIST SITE
(071-808 9457; Stanley Rd) This solitary Buddhist site was quickly rebuilt after government forces retook Jaffna in 1995. The white stupa is particularly eye-catching.

Old Park PARK
(Kandy Rd) This grand expanse of park, first laid out by the British in 1829, features the surprisingly impressive ruins of the former British Residency, also known as the old *kachcheri* (district secretariat), with its notable semicircular walls.

Kakaitivu Fish Market MARKET
(Kaakai Theevu; 6-9am) It's well worth heading out early in the morning to this bustling fish market, 6km outside Jaffna, to watch the fishing boats unload their catch in incandescent dawn light. The bigger fish get packed on ice and shipped by wholesalers to Colombo, Dubai and beyond, while the less valuable fish and cuttlefish are sold on the spot. It's a photogenic place and easily visited en route to Karaitivu.

Jaffna Kingdom

Nallur was the capital of the Jaffna Kingdom for 400 years, beginning in the 13th century, until the Portuguese took over. A few weathered structures of the royal palace remain in the northeast of the city; there's not much to see but it's a pleasant excursion on a bicycle.

Cankili Thoppu Archway HISTORIC BUILDING
(Sangili Thoppu; Point Pedro Rd) This dislocated archway is thought to have been one of the royal palace's original entrances. Among its weathered yet intricate carvings is an inscription to King Cankili (Sangili) I on his accession to the throne in 1519.

Mantiri Manai HISTORIC BUILDING
(Minister's House; Point Pedro Rd) Set back from the road, this once beautiful building is now completely derelict. Most sources date it back to the Jaffna Kingdom, when it would have been used by visiting ministers. Others place the portico in the Dutch or Portuguese colonial era, or even as late as the 1890s.

Yamuna Eri HISTORIC SITE
(Chemmani Rd, off Point Pedro Rd) This U-shaped pool made of carved stones is neglected but still intact – it's thought to have been the women's bathing pool of the royal family. The tank is up a lane and then right, north of St James' Church, which is on Chemmani Rd (and not to be confused with the church of the same name on Main St). There's not much to see but it's an intriguing site.

Cankili II Statue MONUMENT
(Point Pedro Rd) Glistening in the sun, this gold-hued statue was first erected in 1974. It portrays Cankili (Sangili) II, the last king of the Jaffna Kingdom, who was deposed by the Portuguese in 1619. During the war the original statue was removed. It was restored in 2011 but not without the kind of controversy that is common in the North. Some Tamils

contend that the current version lacks some of the heroic features of the original.

Activities

★Sri Lanka Click CYCLING
(077-848 8800; www.srilankaclick.com; 447 Stanley Rd; bike/scooter rental per day from Rs 500/1750; 8am-6pm) Great shop with a range of rental bikes and scooters. Price includes helmet and lock. It can offer lots of good touring advice and arrange a variety of tours of the region by bike or vehicle.

Festivals & Events

Nallur Festival RELIGIOUS
Spread over a period of 25 days in July and/or August, this Hindu festival climaxes on day 24 with parades of juggernaut floats and gruesome displays of self-mutilation by entranced devotees.

Jaffna International Cinema Festival FILM
(www.jaffnaicf.lk; Sep) This weeklong celebration of international independent film is an important part of Jaffna's cultural resurgence. Screenings take place over several days at Jaffna University, the British Council and other locations.

Sleeping

Jaffna has an excellent selection of good-value places to stay, with more options arriving every month.

★D'Villa Garden House GUESTHOUSE $
(077-155 3060, 021-221 3060; www.dvillajaffna.lk; 148 Kachcheri East Lane; s/d/tr Rs 2500/3000/3500;) Probably the most popular budget place in town, this collection of eight large rooms set in a garden with a sociable breakfast area is in a quiet residential neighbourhood. The concrete floors feel a bit unfinished but it's a pleasant place to be based. It's a three-wheeler ride from anywhere (tell the driver to take you to Punkankulam), or rent a bicycle/scooter for Rs 500/1500.

Discounts of 20% are common when things are quiet.

D'Villa Guest House GUESTHOUSE $
(021-221 4131; www.dvillajaffna.lk; 6 Pentecostal Lane, Kandy Rd; s/d/tr Rs 2000/2500/3000;) Budget travellers like the prices at this converted upper-floor house. Rooms come with hot-water bathrooms and air-con, plus a sociable common balcony and dining area, but it's literally 10m from the railway tracks, so expect your bed to shake five times a day when the trains pass by. Owner Dilan is very helpful.

Theresa Inn GUESTHOUSE $
(071-856 5375, 021-222 8615; calistusjoseph89@gmail.com; 72 Racca Rd; s/d with air-con from Rs 2000/2500;) A good-value choice on a leafy plot on a quiet street, with eight spartan, white rooms behind the main family house. The owners are helpful, offer tasty meals and can organise bicycle/scooter hire (Rs 350/1500 per day), or a car and driver (from Rs 5500). More rooms are under construction. Subtract Rs 500 if you don't want air-con.

Senthil Complex GUESTHOUSE $$
(021-222 5226; senthilcomplexjaffna@gmail.com; 88 Sivapragasam Rd; s/d/tr incl breakfast Rs 3500/4500/6500;) An excellent place that straddles budget and midrange. Six of the rooms boast a private balcony but there's also a pleasant patio sitting area. Canadian filter coffee is available and there's a library of English books. It's in the northwest of town, a three-wheeler ride from the centre. Bike and scooter hire is available.

Sarras Guest House GUESTHOUSE $$
(021-567 4040; 20 Somasutharam Rd; old house r Rs 3000-4000, new block s/d Rs 5000/5500;) An ageing colonial mansion with some (faded) character, set around a jackfruit tree. The plain but spacious top-floor main house rooms with wooden balconies are atmospheric. Much more comfortable are the four fresh, modern duplex rooms that come with a private balcony/terrace. The pleasant, breezy upper-floor restaurant specialises in seafood, so order your crab and seafood curries in advance.

Ask about the wonderful boat excursions that combine fishing with a hidden white sand beach (Rs 9000 per boat).

Jaffna Heritage Hotel BOUTIQUE HOTEL $$
(021-222 2424; www.jaffnaheritage.com; 195 Temple Rd; r Rs 7500;) A fine modern hotel where the seven rooms tick all the contemporary design boxes, with modern accents, high ceilings and stylish fittings; the hotel grounds are fringed by coconut palms and there is a pleasant, upstairs terrace. Staff are very welcoming and the (all vegetarian) meals are excellent. The two rooms off the ground floor lobby can be noisier than the others.

It also runs the nearby **Jaffna Heritage Villa** (021-222 2411; 240 Temple Rd; s/d Rs 5000/6500;), with seven darker and more old-fashioned rooms in an old villa.

Guests staying here can use the main hotel restaurant and pool.

★North Gate by Jetwing HOTEL **$$$**
(☎021-203 0500; www.jetwinghotels.com; 136 Martin/Station Rd; s/d US$110/125; ❄📶🏊) The second of Jaffna's two Jetwing properties is probably the one best suited to tourists, with spacious, modern rooms, balconies, a pool and bar area, a gym and a useful location just 50m from Jaffna train station. Choose between a pool or railway view. Here's a secret: the 2nd floor railway-facing rooms boast a large terrace with table and chairs.

On Sundays nonguests can splash out on pool access and a Jaffna-style lunch buffet for Rs 1400. Room discounts of 50% are common.

Jetwing Jaffna Hotel HOTEL **$$$**
(☎021-221 5571; www.jetwinghotels.com; 37 Mahatma Gandhi Rd; r US$100; ❄📶) Jetwing's first hotel is in a central location with upper-floor rooms offering sweeping views (request a lagoon-facing room). The 55 rooms are compact and the hotel suffers in general from a lack of space but the decor is modern, service is good and the restaurant and rooftop bar are both excellent. Room discounts of 50% are common.

Eating & Drinking

Jaffna is a good place to try South Indian-style cuisine. Red-hued *pittu* (rice flour and coconut, steamed in bamboo), *idiyappa* (string hoppers or steamed noodles) and *vadai* (deep-fried doughnut-shaped snacks made from lentil flour and spices) are local favourites. Don't leave without trying Jaffna's famous spicy *nandu culambu* (crab curry).

★Rio Ice Cream ICE CREAM **$**
(☎021-222 7224; 448A Point Pedro Rd; ice creams & sundaes Rs 60-250; ⏲9am-10pm) For a typical Jaffna treat head to this popular ice-cream parlour near the landmark Nallur Kandaswamy Kovil. Rio is a local favourite; join the families enjoying the air-conditioned interior or pout on the terrace. It is the best of the small cluster of ice-cream places here.

Just outside is a monument to Theepam Thileepan, the LTTE political wing leader who died in 1987 after a hunger strike in support of Tamil political demands.

Malayan Café SRI LANKAN **$**
(☎021-222 2373; 36 Power House Rd; meals Rs 60-150; ⏲7am-9pm) A highly authentic and atmospheric old-school eatery in the market district with marble-topped tables, swirling fans and photos of holy men illuminated by bright fluorescent bulbs and peering down on diners. The cheap, tasty vegetarian fare – masala dosas, rice and curry for lunch and light meals – is spooned out of buckets onto banana leaves and eaten by hand.

The easiest way to order is with the English-speaking cashier.

Akshathai Restaurant SOUTH INDIAN **$**
(www.akshathai.lk; 60 Stanley Rd; meals Rs 200-300; ⏲8am-10pm) This unassuming vegetarian place doesn't look like much at first but the 'ghee paper masala roast' is easily the best dosa in town, if not Sri Lanka. Top things off with a cup of milk tea and piece of nutty fudge from the sweets cabinet. We miss it already.

Hotel Rolex SRI LANKAN **$**
(☎021-222 2808; 340 Hospital Rd; meals Rs 100-300; ⏲8am-9pm) In the heart of the bustling centre, this local spot is always busy and has friendly English-speaking management, an interior air-conditioned hall and a good range of food options. The brownies are surprisingly delicious.

★Mangos SOUTH INDIAN **$$**
(☎021-222 8294; www.facebook.com/mangosjaffna/; off 359 Temple Rd; meals Rs 400-900; ⏲8am-10pm) With an open kitchen, lots of space and outdoor seating, Mangos is wildly popular with extended Tamil families and Westerners. The vegetarian-only South Indian food is exceptional with around 20 dosas, great chilli *parotta* (Keralan-style flat bread) and *idiyappa kotthu*. Lunch (11.30am to 3.30pm) offers the best value with a range of unbeatable thalis (Rs 300 to 620).

It's down a small lane, close to Nallur Kandaswamy Kovil.

Green Grass SRI LANKAN **$$**
(☎021-222 4385; www.jaffnagreengrass.com; 33 Aseervatham Lane, Hospital Rd; meals Rs 600-900; ⏲11am-11pm; 📶) The restaurant at this hotel, with tables under a mango tree, is a good spot for either a meal or an evening beer. Try the Jaffna-style curries or wide range of Indian dishes, but avoid the stodgy indoor dining room.

Cosy Restaurant NORTH INDIAN **$$$**
(☎021-222 5899; 15 Sirampiyadi Lane, Stanley Rd; meals Rs 700-1100; ⏲11am-11pm; 📶) The pleasant open courtyard seating is popular here but the big attraction is the tandoori oven, which fires up at 6pm daily and pumps out

delicious, but surprisingly pricey, Indian-style naan bread, tikkas and tandoori chicken.

★Peninsula Restaurant SRI LANKAN $$$
(Jetwing Jaffna Hotel; meals from Rs 1500; ⌚noon-2.30pm & 7-10.30pm; 📶) One of the best places to try spice-laden Jaffna cuisine in a classy atmosphere. You can order à la carte (check out the separate menu of regional Sri Lankan specials) or come for the Wednesday night Jaffna buffet (Rs 1980), with crab and cuttlefish curries.

Order the signature Jaffna speciality *odiyul khool* (a seafood stew thickened with palmyrah root flour) half a day before; it's enough for two.

Shopping

Jaffna Market MARKET
(Grand Bazaar, Modern Market; Hospital Rd; ⌚7am-6pm Mon-Sat) Jaffna's colourful fruit and vegetable market is west of the bus stand, but the greater market area encompasses several bustling blocks beyond that, including Power House Rd, where there is a collection of tailors. You can spend an interesting hour wandering around.

Anna Coffee COFFEE
(No 4, Jaffna Market; ⌚8.30am-6pm Mon-Sat) Sri Lankan coffee and tea from a venerable old shop in the market district. It also produces its own line of spices and even tooth powder.

Rosarian Convent DRINKS
(Thoma Monastery; 48 Colombuthurai Rd; ⌚9am-1pm & 2-5pm Mon-Sat) The convent makes Rosetto 'wine' (from Rs 450 per bottle). Sweet and laced with cinnamon and cloves, it tastes like German *Gluhwein*. There's also startlingly coloured grape and *nelli* (Indian gooseberry) fruit cordials, the latter used in Ayurvedic treatments.

TRAVEL RESTRICTIONS IN THE NORTH

Foreigners visiting the north will typically see only a few vestiges of the high security that once dominated the area. You might find that you have to get off your bus at road checkpoints and pass through a bag and passport check.

Note that a few roads in the north are closed around the many military and naval camps and it's best not to take photos anywhere near these camps.

Politically active locals (and foreigners) can face state intimidation. For this and other reasons locals may not want to speak openly about politics or the war; use sensitivity and tact.

Information

You're never far from an ATM in central Jaffna.

Jaffna Teaching Hospital (☎021-222 3348; Hospital Rd; ⌚24hr) A large government hospital. The main facility in the North.

Tourist Information Centre (☎021-205 7132; www.tourismnorth.lk; Jaffna Train Station; ⌚9am-7pm) A particularly helpful place run by enthusiastic and switched-on staff. It's just across the railway station courtyard.

Getting There & Away

AIR

Jaffna International Airport (Palali Airport) is 17km north of town at Palali.

FitzAir (www.fitsair.com) operates three flights a week to Colombo's domestic Ratmalana airport (Rs 7500). The frequency is expected to rise to daily.

The Air India subsidiary Alliance Air flies thrice weekly to Chennai.

A taxi to the airport costs Rs 1500.

BUS

Long-distance

The **Central Bus Stand** (☎021-222 2281; off Power House Rd) has frequent long-distance services:

Anuradhapura Rs 400, four hours, take a Colombo bus (Nos 87 and 15)

Kandy Rs 450 to 540, eight hours, nine daily, No 43

Mannar Rs 200, three hours, 10 daily, No 812

Mullaittivu Rs 250, three hours, nine daily, No 89

Trincomalee Rs 350, seven hours, five daily, No 88

Vavuniya Rs 215, three hours, every 30 minutes, Nos 87 and 86

Colombo

Numerous private bus companies offer air-con luxury overnight coaches to Colombo. Around a dozen offices are all grouped together on Hospital Rd.

Cheaper buses go from the Central Bus Stand. Bus No 87 routes via Puttalam and Negombo; No 15 via Dambullah.

Rates are Rs 850/900/1300 for an ordinary/semi-luxury/luxury bus; the journey time is eight hours.

Jaffna Peninsula

Destinations around the peninsula (including the islands) are served by both government buses from the eastern part of the Central Bus Stand and private minibuses from a **stop** (Power House Rd) just north of the stand. Be warned that local buses are slow and can be infrequent; check return times before you head out. Services include the following:

Kairanagar via Vaddukkodai (782,785, 786) Rs 70, 1½ hours, every 30 minutes

Kayts (777) Rs 50, one hour, every 30 to 60 minutes (bus 780 also goes here but takes longer)

Keerimalai Spring (minibuses 82, 87, 89, bus 778) Rs 55, one hour, every 20 minutes

Kurikadduwan (KKD; 776) Rs 70, 1½ hours, hourly

Point Pedro via Nelliady (750) Rs 80, 1½ hours, every 30 minutes

Point Pedro via Valvettiturai (VVT; 751) Rs 80, 1½ hours, every 30 to 60 minutes

Tellippalai via Chunnakam (for Thurkkai Amman Kovil, Kantarodai, Keerimalai Spring; 769) Rs 35, every 30 minutes

CAR & MOTORCYCLE

Many travellers prefer the freedom of renting a motorbike or car to explore the peninsula and islands. Traffic is light and roads are in good condition. Scooters cost about Rs 1500 per day (excluding petrol), a car with driver around Rs 6500 per day. Most places to stay can arrange either.

TRAIN

Trains on the Jaffna–Colombo line use the art-deco **Jaffna Railway Station** (Station Rd). It has a small cafe offering drinks and food you can take on the train. There is an ATM.

Trains include a slow night mail train (no sleeping berths) and three daily express Intercity trains departing at 6.10am, 9.45am and 1.45pm (the latter 1st class only). Fares for the Intercity services include the following:

Anuradhapura 3rd/2nd/1st class Rs 500/600/1200, three hours

Colombo 3rd/2nd/1st class Rs 600/1000/1700, seven hours

Vavuniya 3rd/2nd/1st class Rs 350/550/1000, two hours

Getting Around

Jaffna is not a large city and the central area is easily explored on foot or by bicycle.

Many guesthouses rent bicycles (Rs 350 to 500 per day). An excellent rental source is Sri Lanka Click (p282).

Three-wheelers are very common and cost around Rs 50 per kilometre. At night, locals recommend having someone call one for you for security reasons. Most places to stay can recommend local drivers.

Jaffna Peninsula

021

Once you get beyond Jaffna's already rustic outer boroughs, you're plunged into fields of palmyra palms, Technicolor temples, holy springs and kilometres of coastline. Few of the sights are individually outstanding but together they make for interesting day trips, especially if you have your own transport.

Make a few areas your focus: the sacred oceanside Keerimalai spring, the stunning coastal road between Valvettiturai and Point Pedro, and the northeast shore with its beautiful beaches.

Road conditions are good across the peninsula. There are some bus services (to Keerimalai spring and Point Pedro), but to really explore you'll want your own wheels. Riding bikes here is rewarding, especially along the lonely shore roads.

The North Coast & Keerimalai Spring

There are several important religious and ancient sites on the road to Kankesanturai (KKS). The town itself is right on the ocean in a pretty, tree-shaded setting. It is surrounded by military bases, but only the direct coast road to Keerimalai spring is actually off limits to civilians.

Sights

Keerimalai Spring HISTORIC SITE

(B277) This spring is an interesting little spot: the men's side has a picturesque stepped pool of aquamarine water set right against the ocean, while the women have a smaller pool surrounded by tall walls. The waters are supposed to be healing. There are changing rooms on-site; women should bathe in something modest. Frequent Jaffna minibuses run to the spring, or get a three-wheeler from the Tellippalai junction (Rs 400/700 one way/return).

Kantarodai Ruins RUINS

(Kadurugoda; off B380, Chunnakam; 8.30am-5pm) Some 1km via a squiggle of lanes south of the B380 is the enigmatic former monastery of Kantarodai – two dozen or so dagobas (stupas), 1m to 2m in height, in a palm-fringed field. A flourishing Buddhist monastery existed here during the Anuradhapura and Polonnaruwa periods. The original 60 stupas commemorated 60 monks who are said to have died here from food poisoning.

Jaffna Peninsula

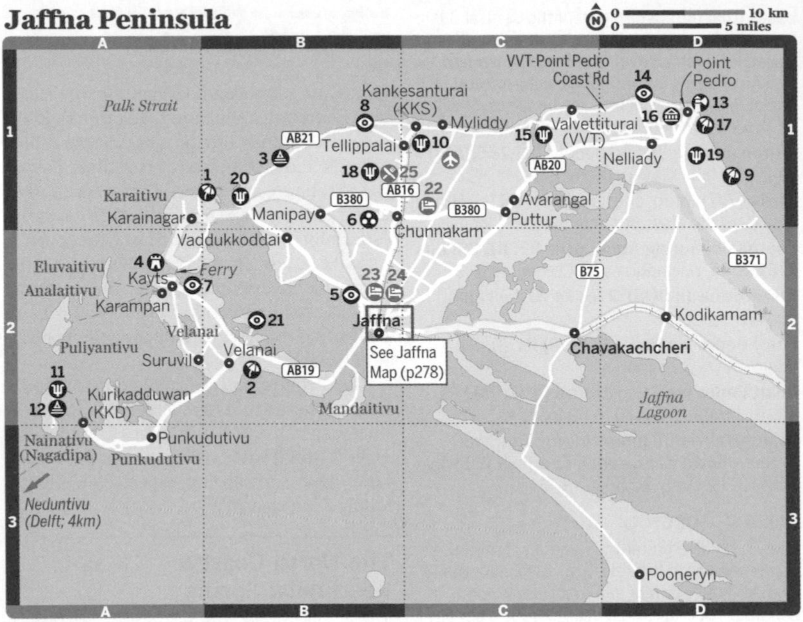

Jaffna Peninsula

Sights

1 Casuarina Beach B1
2 Chaatty Beach B2
3 Dambakola Patuna B1
4 Fort Hammenhiel A2
5 Kakaitivu Fish Market B2
6 Kantarodai Ruins B1
7 Kayts A2
8 Keerimalai Spring B1
9 Manalkadu Beach D1
10 Maviddapuram Kanthaswamy Kovil C1
11 Naga Pooshani Amman Kovil A2
12 Nagadipa Temple A2
Naguleswaram Shiva Kovil .... (see 8)
13 Point Pedro Lighthouse D1
14 Sakkotei Cape D1
15 Selvachannithy Murugan Kovil C1
St Anthony's Church .... (see 7)
16 Theru Moodi Madam D1
17 Thumpulai East Beach D1
18 Thurkkai Amman Kovil B1
19 Vallipura Aalvar Kovil D1
20 Varatharaja Perumal Kovil B1
21 War Memorial B2

Sleeping

Fort Hammenhiel Resort .... (see 4)
22 Margosa Green C1
23 Senthil Complex B2
24 Thinnai B2

Eating

Fort Hammenhiel Resort .... (see 4)
25 Jaffna Kitchen B1

Naguleswaram Shiva Kovil HINDU SITE
(B277, Keerimalai) Just before Keerimalai spring is the 6th-century-BCE Naguleswaram Shiva Kovil, one of the *pancha ishwaram,* five temples dedicated to Lord Shiva in Sri Lanka. Before the civil war, this was a thriving Hindu pilgrimage site with several temples and six *madham* (rest homes for pilgrims) and *samadhi* (shrines for holy men). Much has been rebuilt since the temple was bombed by the army in 1990.

Maviddapuram Kanthaswamy Kovil HINDU SITE
(AB16, Tellippalai) Maviddapuram Kanthaswamy Kovil is now flourishing again after the war. The unpainted *gopuram* is right by the road junction to Keerimalai and is surrounded by lush banana trees.

Thurkkai Amman Kovil HINDU SITE
(Durgai Amman Kovil; AB16, Tellippalai; 5.30am-7pm, closed 1-3pm some days) Beside the KKS road at the 13km marker, south of the village of Tellippalai, the Thurkkai Amman Kovil is

set behind a deep, stepped pool. The temple celebrates the goddess Durga and draws crowds of women on Tuesdays and Fridays, when devotees pray for a good spouse. Look for the carving of elephants pulling a train.

Dambakola Patuna BUDDHIST STUPA
(AB21; ⌚dawn-dusk) Drive the lonely coastal road between Keerimalai spring and the causeway to Karaitivu Island and you'll pass this small but important Buddhist temple, marking the spot where Sanghamitta, the daughter of Indian Emperor Ashoka, landed in Sri Lanka bearing the sapling of the bodhi tree that now grows in Anuradhapura. There's a modern stupa, a small temple and a superbly peaceful stretch of beach.

Eating

Jaffna Kitchen SRI LANKAN $
(☎021-222 5999; 573 KKS Rd, Tellippalai; buffet Rs 200; ⌚10.30am-1pm) The hotel restaurant at the Jaffna Heritage Bungalow, near the Thurkkai Amman Kovil, has a daily lunch rice and curry buffet, making it a useful option if sightseeing north of Jaffna.

Getting There & Away

With the lifting of military restrictions it is now possible to drive the coast all the way from Kankesanturai (KKS) east to Valvettiturai (VVT) and on to Point Pedro. No public transport runs this route.

The direct coastal road between Keerimalai and Kankesanthurai remains off-limits.

Frequent buses run from Jaffna to Keerimalai and Kankesanturai (KKS). Technically the rail line runs to KKS from Jaffna, but the trains are not frequent enough to make it a useful option.

According to optimistic news reports, an international ferry is planned between Kankesanturai port and Karaikal in the Indian territory of Puducherry. If it materialises the passage is expected to take three hours and cost Rs 6000 to 7500 per person.

Point Pedro & the Northeastern Coast

Workaday Point Pedro (Paruthithurai) is the Jaffna peninsula's second town. Some sources say it was named after the Dutch sailor who declared it the island's northernmost point; others say it comes from the Portuguese name Ponta de Pedras (Rocky Point).

It has a few faint hints of colonial architecture but was hit hard by the 2004 tsunami: locals say fishing boats were found 1km inland. A busy commercial centre today, the town has good beaches nearby and is connected to Valvettiturai (VVT) by a beautiful coastal drive.

Point Pedro has regular buses from Jaffna (Rs 80, 90 minutes, every 30 minutes).

Sights

Point Pedro town is centred around its market. The namesake geographic landmark – with lighthouse and the first of a long stretch of beach – is 1.5km northeast.

Theru Moodi Madam HISTORIC BUILDING
(Thumpulai Rd) These mysterious and elaborately carved ruins of a gate over the road are thought to have served as an *ambalam*, or resting place for travellers. It's about 100m east of the heart of Point Pedro, from a turn-off 100m south of the bus station.

Point Pedro Lighthouse LIGHTHOUSE
Occupies a prominent spot with sweeping views at the east end of the spectacular VVT–Point Pedro Coast Rd. Although the lighthouse is fenced off and photos are forbidden, there is a small beach right beside it where you can have a dip or a picnic.

Thumpulai East Beach BEACH
(off B370, Point Pedro) Simply a very fine beach, 1.5km southeast of the Point Pedro Lighthouse. It's often good for swimming when

TAMIL TIGER BURIAL GROUNDS

Although bodies of the deceased are generally cremated in Hindu tradition, the bodies of fighters for the Liberation Tigers of Tamil Eelam (LTTE) were buried instead, beneath neatly lined rows of identical stones. The fallen Tigers were called *maaveerar* – 'martyrs' or 'heroes' – and their cemeteries called Maaveerar Thuyilum Illam (Martyrs' Sleeping Houses).

When the Sri Lanka Army (SLA) took control of the Jaffna peninsula in 1995 it destroyed many of the cemeteries, only to have the LTTE build them up again after the 2002 ceasefire. But when the SLA conquered areas in the East in 2006 and 2007, and then again after the war's end in 2009, all cemeteries (and other LTTE monuments) across the North and East were bulldozed anew – to the distress of many Tamils, especially family members of the deceased.

Today, as the military builds monuments celebrating its victory in the war, many Tamils honour Maveerar Naal, Heroes Day each year on 27 November.

DON'T MISS

THE AB21 COASTAL ROUTE

The coast road that runs 9km east from Valvettiturai (VVT) to the Point Pedro Lighthouse (p287) is easily one of the most beautiful drives in the north. It hugs the shore, with aquamarine waves breaking on rocks right alongside the road. At some points there are reefs right offshore.

Valvettiturai is famous as the birthplace of LTTE leader Vellupillai Prabhakaran. From here you'll pass a succession of tiny fishing hamlets, with fish sun-drying in neat rows by the road and fishing boats beached on protected, sandy coves.

Stop en route at **Sakkotei Cape**, where a plaque marks Sri Lanka's most northerly point.

If you fancy a longer drive the coastal road from Kakesanturai to Valvettiturai is now open to tourists, despite passing a huge army base. It's not quite as scenic as the section further east but it does pass the eye-catching shipwreck of the **SS Hind** at Myliddy Harbour, and ends near the charming waterfront temple of **Selvachannithy Murugan Kovil** (Thondaimanaru), 4km west of VVT.

the water is calm. A nearby shop sells cold drinks, ice cream and snacks.

Vallipura Aalvar Kovil HINDU SITE
The much-revered Vallipura Aalvar Kovil is 5km south from central Point Pedro. Its *gopuram* is painted in an unusually restrained colour palette. It's famous for the boisterous, recently revived water-cutting festival in October, which attracts thousands of pilgrims. *Puja* is at 7am, 9.30am, noon, 4.15pm and, on Sunday, 6pm.

Manalkadu Beach BEACH
(off B371) A small dirt road runs for 3km off the B371 to this lovely beach, 11km southeast of Point Pedro. There are a few fishing boats, some palm trees and not much else on the sand. The views extend up and down the beach as far as you can see. There are no vendors or services.

As you approach the beach look for the ruins of a **Dutch church**, dramatically half-buried in the shifting sand. Just before the beach you'll see the new **St Anthony's Church** with its 6m-tall statue of Jesus.

Chempiyanpattu Beach BEACH
(off B402) There's a stunning beach here – a classic tropical picture of white sand, azure ocean and swaying coconut palms – and absolutely no facilities. Perfect if you want to get away from it all. Note the huge old baobab tree.

Chempiyanpattu is 30km southeast of Point Pedro, off the lonely B371. It's a further 17km southwest to Elephant Pass via the B402.

Elephant Pass

Some 52km southeast of Jaffna via the A9 highway is Elephant Pass, a narrow causeway that connects Jaffna peninsula to the rest of Sri Lanka. The pass gets its name from the hundreds of elephants that were herded through here en route to India between 300 BCE and the 19th century.

For most Sri Lankans the name is inexorably linked with the civil war; for decades the government and Tamil Tigers contested control of this strategic spot – the gateway to Jaffna – with particularly bloody battles waged in 1991, 2000 and 2009.

Bulldozer Memorial MEMORIAL
(A9) About 1km south of the causeway's southern end there is a large memorial to Gamini Kularatne, a Sri Lanka Army soldier who single-handedly disabled an armoured LTTE bulldozer. The repainted vehicle – complete with a large hole from an explosion in its side – is mounted on a plinth. Nearby is a display about Kularatne's life, complete with letters to his mother, a pay stub and more.

Elephant Pass War Memorial MONUMENT
(A9) This grandiose, vaguely stupa-like monument glorifies the role of the Sri Lankan armed forces in defeating the LTTE and lauds the role of then President (and current Prime Minister) Mahinda Rajapaksa. Huge bronze hands hold aloft a model of the country and are surrounded by bandoleer-wearing lions. It's at the north end of the causeway, 2.5km north of the Bulldozer Memorial.

Getting There & Away

Both memorials are right beside the A9, so you'll pass them on any bus or train headed to Jaffna.

Jaffna's Islands

A highlight of the region, Jaffna's low-lying islands are a blissful vision of the tropics.

The main pleasure is not any specific sight, but the hypnotic quality of the waterscapes and the escapist feeling of boat rides to end-of-the-earth villages.

As the sea here is very shallow (only a metre or so deep in places) the light is very special indeed, with sunlight bouncing off the sandy seafloor. The islands are all dotted with spikey palmyra palms; the salt flats are often brightened by colonies of pink flamingos.

Causeways and boat connections link the islands, making a number of idyllic day trips possible. The islands' beaches may not be as beautiful as those on the south coast, but they do offer pleasant swimming in balmy water. Women should swim in T-shirts and shorts.

You can assemble several adventuresome itineraries to explore Jaffna's islands. One option is to head from Jaffna city to Velanai and then to the island of Punkudutivu, ferry-hopping from here across to the temples of Nainativu and then returning by Kayts and Karaitivu island to the mainland. The second option is an excursion to the remote idyll of Neduntivu (Delft); if you start early and time your ferry rides right you could visit Neduntivu and Nainativu in one day.

Getting Around

Bus connections to the islands from Jaffna are not that frequent. The ideal way to explore these islands is with your own wheels (ideally only two), giving you the freedom to pull over when and where you want. The terrain is very flat so it's perfect for covering while astride a bicycle or scooter. Traffic is light, so riding is relaxed.

Kurikadduwan (KKD) on Punkudutivu is the jumping-off point for navy-run boats to Neduntivu and Nainativu. Punkudutivu is linked to Velanai Island by several causeways, and frequent bus 776 links Jaffna to the ferry dock at Kurikadduwan (KKD; Rs 70, 1½ hours, hourly). If driving, budget 45 minutes and set off at dawn for stunning skies and birdlife.

Velanai

Velanai island, connected by causeway to Jaffna, is sometimes referred to as Leiden, its Dutch name, or Kayts, after the village on its northeast coast. One of the highlights of a trip here is a dawn drive along the causeway and the thousands of birds feeding in the island's bays and lagoons.

Kayts VILLAGE

Kayts is a moody little village with a few scuttled fishing boats down by the ferry dock and some big old banyan trees. This was the port from which elephants were shipped to India, and you can still see traces of its colonial past. The waterfront has views of evocative Fort Hammenhiel (p291) across the shallow waters.

St Anthony's Church CHURCH

(AB19, Kayts) Built in 1820, this large colonnaded church is dishevelled, but the faithful have strung colourful garlands from the soaring rafters. Immediately west ponder the ruins of **St Anthony's Villa**, which still has some elaborate carvings set amid numerous grazing goats.

War Memorial MEMORIAL

(off AB19) About 2km north of the AB19 along a dirt track near Arali Point is a sombre memorial to Lieutenant General Denzil Lakshman Kobbekaduwa and nine other Sri Lankan army officers, who were killed in 1992 by a roadside bomb. It was a major victory for the LTTE. The remains of the motorcade's mangled vehicles mark the lonely and solemn site.

Chaatty Beach BEACH

(Chaddy Beach; Velanai) The thin strip of Chaatty Beach is no white-sand wonder, but it's passable for swimming and has changing rooms, picnic gazebos and snack vendors. It's the closest beach to Jaffna, 11km away.

THE PALMYRA PALM

Symbolising the north of the nation, the towering, fan-leafed palm tree known as the palmyra is abundant across the region, its graceful crown of leaves defining many a horizon at sunset. Of the estimated 11 million or so palmyra trees in Sri Lanka, 90% are found in the three provinces of Jaffna, Mannar and Kilinochchi.

An essential part of Tamil culture, palmyra has many uses: timber for construction; leaves for fencing, roofing and woven handicrafts; fibre for rope; and sap for drinking. If left to ferment for a few hours the sap becomes a mildly alcoholic, fragrant toddy. Young palmyra roots are high in calcium and eaten as a snack and also ground to make flour for a porridge called *khool*. In markets across the North you'll find great blocks of jaggery (delicious golden-coloured unrefined palm sugar) made from unfermented palmyra toddy.

ℹ Getting There & Away

Bus 777 (Rs 55, one hour, every 30 to 60 minutes) runs to Kayts from Jaffna.

At Kayts, the free Velanai to Karaitivu ferry runs every 30 minutes from 6am to 6pm and takes 10 minutes to cross the narrow channel. Scooters and bicycles can board the ferry.

Note that many mapping apps show a road across the water to the mainland from Arali Point north of Velanai village. This does not exist, though there is a little-used ferry crossing here. The AB19 is the only road link to the island.

Nainativu (Nagadipa)

Known as Nainativu in Tamil and Nagadipa in Sinhalese, this 6km-long lozenge of palmyra groves is holy to both Buddhist and Hindu pilgrims. It's a quiet place, with barely 2500 inhabitants. *Poya* (full-moon) days are observed by both Hindus and Buddhists on the island; expect crowds.

Navy-run ferries (Rs 40, 20 minutes) depart Kurikadduwan (KKD) on Punkudutivu island for Nainativu every 30 minutes or so from 7.30am to 5.30pm. You don't need transport to see the two sights. During festival times the wait for ferry passage can last hours.

Nagadipa Temple BUDDHIST SITE
(US$5 donation requested; ⌚dawn-dusk) This is the North's only major Buddhist pilgrimage site. According to legend, the Buddha came to the island in the sixth century BCE to prevent war between a local king and his nephew over ownership of a gem-studded throne. Buddha's solution: give it to the temple instead. The precious chair and original two-millennia-old temple disappeared long ago, but today there is an attractive silver-painted dagoba.

The temple is right at the southern dock, the first stop when coming from Kurikadduwan.

Naga Pooshani Amman Kovil HINDU TEMPLE
(⌚dawn-dusk) This lovely complex is an airy Hindu temple set amid mature neem (Indian lilac) trees, a 10-minute walk north from the Nagadipa Temple. The main temple deity is Parvati in the form of the *naga* (serpent) goddess Meenakshi, a consort of Shiva. Women wishing to conceive come here seeking blessings, delivered during the trance-inducing midday *puja*.

The site is one of the Indian Subcontinent's 51 Shakti Peethas – locations where pieces of the goddess Shakti's body (in this case her ankle) fell to earth after she self-immolated.

An impressive festival is held in June/July every year and attracts over 100,000 people.

It's directly in front of the northern ferry jetty, from where boats depart for Kurikadduwan.

Neduntivu (Delft)

The intriguing, windswept island of Neduntivu (Delft) is 10km southwest of KKD on Punkudutivu island. Around 6000 people live here, but it feels deserted. Dirt roads run through coconut-palm groves, and aquamarine water and white sand fringe the shore. Hundreds of field-dividing walls are hewn from chunks of brain and fan corals.

Of the various islands in the Jaffna region, this is the one to aim for if you simply want to leave the world behind, and with the most actual things to see. Unlike Nainativu it has no important religious shrines.

ELEPHANT QUAY

Elephants were once indispensable to South Asian armies: they could transport troops through difficult terrain and waterways, carry heavy supplies, knock down the doors of forts and, when lined up with steel balls swinging from their trunks, scare the fight out of any enemy. Sri Lanka's elephants were known to be exceptionally strong, intelligent and large, and so the island became a major supplier to India – a practice that began around 300 BCE and continued to the early 19th century.

Most elephants were caught in the Vanni, then marched through the Jaffna peninsula and shipped out from Elephant Quay in Kayts. (Elephant Pass, linking the Jaffna peninsula to the rest of Sri Lanka, really was an elephant pass.) They were shipped in custom-made wooden elephant boats constructed in Kayts, and the town was renowned as an elephant port. As powerful as the elephants were, however, they were frightened and confused by loud noises, so the arrival of firearms put an end to their war prowess and the Kayts elephant trade.

Sights

Three-wheelers (Rs 1500 to 2000 for two hours) and even some pickups wait at the ferry to take visitors on a tour of the island's half dozen sights.

Closest to the dock (1.5km) is a restored Dutch hospital, a **pigeon tower** (used to send messenger birds) and a **courthouse** used by the British. The Meekaman **Dutch fort**, 100m further west, has impressively thick walls built from great chunks of coral limestone.

Further away in the far west of the island are an 800m long Dutch-era horse **stables**, a curious rock depression in the shape of a **giant footprint** and a second Dutch fort.

Back in the southeast corner of the island is a calcified **'growing rock'** with sacred importance and a large **banyan tree**. Most tours also stop to catch a look at some of the island's 2000 or so wild horses, descended from Dutch mounts.

In the extreme southeastern tip is the intact **Quindah (or Queen's) Tower**, actually a Dutch fire-fuelled lighthouse. You'll have to add on Rs 500 to your three-wheeler fee to make it this far.

Sleeping

Delft Samudra HOTEL **$$**

(021-221 5282; https://delft-samudra.business.site/; Maveli Periyathurai Rd; d Rs 5000-6000;) Delft's best hotel (there are two) has 16 simple villa-style rooms set around a weedy courtyard, with mountain bikes for hire (Rs 500 per half-day) and a classic Austin Cambridge rusting in the parking lot. It is poorly run and you'll have to haggle to get value for money, but it's your best option if you want to explore the island at a slower pace.

Getting There & Away

A rusty Sri Lanka Navy–operated ferry (free or Rs 80 depending on the sailing, one hour) departs KKD at 8am, 9am, 1.30pm and 4.30pm. Double-check timings if you are coming on a Sunday, where there are often only two sailings. The vessels get crowded so arrive early and prepare to jam aboard for the uncomfortable, if memorable, trip.

If you're travelling by bus from Jaffna you'll need to catch the 6.40am departure to KKD to make a ferry connection.

Bring your passport for registration on arrival at Neduntivu dock.

Karaitivu

Karaitivu has several appeals: ferry access to Kayts; the crossing from the mainland across a long, water-skimming causeway, with views of wading fishermen and shrimp traps; a good public beach; and an atmospheric old fort.

Sights

Casuarina Beach BEACH

(New Rd; per person Rs 20, plus motorbike Rs 20, car Rs 50; ticket office 7am-6pm) An attractive stretch of sand with good swimming and, as the name indicates, a shoreline backed by mature casuarina trees. It's popular with folks from Jaffna on weekends, and has a couple of fried rice vendors and an ice cream shop disguised as an aeroplane. Buses from Jaffna to Karainagar pass within 2km of the beach, from where you can hire a three-wheeler.

Fort Hammenhiel FORT

(021-381 8216) A tiny fairy-tale islet in the bay is home to the pocket-sized Fort Hammenhiel, a small Portuguese-built bastion that passed on to the Dutch in the 1650s. It feels like the kind of place that would house the Count of Monte Cristo. The thick coral walls are over 4m high and are now home to a Navy-run hotel. Boats (Rs 3300) make the five-minute trip out here from the restaurant dock.

Sleeping & Eating

Fort Hammenhiel Resort MULTICUISINE **$$$**

(021-750 8072; www.forthammenhielresort.lk; meals Rs 550-1100; 10am-9.30pm;) The navy-run restaurant is right on the waterfront, with great views of the fort from its terrace seating. It's a good stop for lunch, with seafood dishes and fish curries, or just for a cold beer (Rs 330). It's open to the public and is 1km west of the ferry jetty to Kayts, reached through the Navy base.

There are four **hotel rooms** (r incl breakfast US$132;) out in the fort itself, offering a memorable stay with fine sunset and sunrise views and a superbly romantic location.

Getting There & Away

Buses from Jaffna run to Kairanagar via Vaddukkodai (782, 786; Rs 70, 1½ hours, every 30 minutes).

On the south end of the island, the free Karaitivu to Velanai ferry runs every 30 minutes from 6am to 6pm and takes 10 minutes to cross the narrow channel. The ferry takes motorbikes.

Mullaittivu

021

The northeastern region around Mullaittivu today looks broadly pastoral and green; in 2009 it was anything but. This is where the decades-long civil war came to an end as the Sri Lankan military waged an all-out assault on the LTTE.

Alleged human-rights abuses in the region, including the shelling of civilians, have yet to be investigated despite urging from the UN and the international community.

For now it is a region in transition, with new hotels and white beaches in stark contrast to towns such as Puthukkudiyiruppu that are still filled with shell-marked buildings.

There's not a great deal to actually do in Mullaittivu but it has a certain quirky off-the-beaten-track appeal.

Sights

The **beach** at Mullaittivu is long, white and beautiful, though unsafe for swimming for much of the year. About 3km north on the A35 is the **Vaddu Vakal Bridge** (A35), often lined with people casting nets. This single-lane concrete veteran still bears war scars. The Nanthi Kadal Lagoon here is a haven for birds.

About 6km north of town, just off A35, was the so-called **Sea Tiger Shipyard**, a former base for the LTTE navy who launched suicide attacks on government ships and ports using bizarre experimental submarines and fast boats that were assembled here. Visitors used to be able to poke around a dozen or so craft but the Sri Lankan Navy recently closed the site.

Back on the A35, 10km from Mullaittivu, is the army's **Monument of Victory**. Set in a pond, a huge gold-coloured torso of a soldier juts up from the ground. It's bombastic to say the least. Nearby map displays show the final months of the military campaign but are incomprehensible without an English-speaking guide.

Sleeping & Eating

The beachside restaurant at the Ocean Park Resort serves tasty rice and curry and some seafood (meals Rs 600 to 1000) and offers particularly good-value lunchtime takeaway deals.

Pub Admin Rest BUSINESS HOTEL $
(021-229 0339; milankavshalnnn@gmail.com; r with fan/air-con Rs 2500/4500, deluxe Rs 6500;) This government-run 'Public Administration Resthouse' welcomes tourists and offers compact but comfortable rooms right on the beach, next to the Mullai Cafe. Upper-floor rooms are best. There's no food here so head to the nearby Ammachchi Restaurant for breakfast.

Ocean Park Resort RESORT $$
(021-229 0444; Kovilkudiyirippu; r Rs 7200-13,500;) It's not perfect but this low-key resort has a lot going for it; a lovely beachfront location, a breezy restaurant, lush grounds, the only bar in town and a decent swimming pool. The cheapest rooms are small, with a 'private' bathroom that is outside the room, but deluxe rooms are more spacious. The wi-fi is in public areas only.

Sun & Sand GUESTHOUSE $$
(071-034 5047, 021-206 1919; sunandsand.mullaitivu@yahoo.com; Kovilkudiyiruppu, Selvapuram; r incl breakfast Rs 4950;) This family-run, three-roomed villa is somewhat overpriced, but the spacious air-con rooms are clean, the terrace seating has peaceful garden views and the beach and bus station are a five- and 10-minute walk away respectively.

Mullai Cafe FAST FOOD $
(meals Rs 150-250; 7.30am-9.30pm) This functional, canteen-style spot beside the beach is run by a military officer and serves up decent rice and curry for lunch, and *kotthu* or fried rice for dinner.

Getting There & Away

Buses run hourly to Vavuniya (Rs 150, two hours) and Jaffna (Rs 200, three hours) from the bus station, the latter passing the roadside Monument of Victory.

Vavuniya

024 / POP 79,000

These days few travellers stop in the bustling transport hub of Vavuniya (*vow*-nya), but you might need to break here if travelling on public transport to Mannar or Mullaittivu.

Sights

The town arcs around an attractive **tank** that's best observed from the waterside **Kudiyiruppu Pillaiyar Kovil** (Pandaravanniyan Rd), a ramshackle Ganesh temple. The **market area** surrounding the **Grand Jummah Mosque** (Horowapatana Rd) is the most interesting part of town for a wander.

Vavuniya

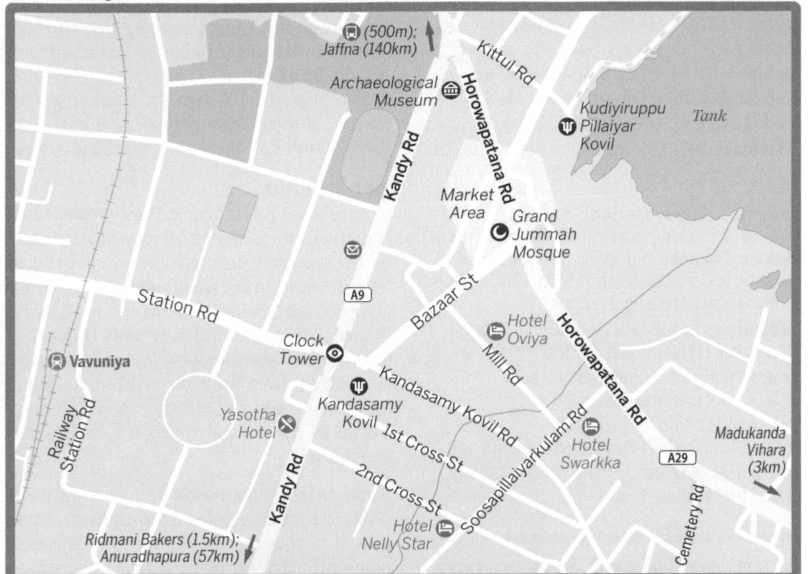

Madukanda Vihara BUDDHIST SITE

(Horowapatana Rd/A29) The quietly charming Madukanda Vihara is a Rs 400 return three-wheeler ride from central Vavuniya, 4km southeast on the A29. It was reputedly the fourth resting point in the journey of the sacred Buddha tooth relic from Mullaittivu to Anuradhapura during the 4th-century reign of King Mahsen. The modest archaeological remains of two buildings sit alongside a functioning monastic school.

Kandasamy Kovil HINDU SITE

(Kandasamy Kovil Rd) This photogenic Murugan (Skanda) temple has a very ornate, if faded, *gopuram*. Walk back through the surrounding buildings to appreciate it, as it's somewhat obscured.

Archaeological Museum MUSEUM

(024-222 4805; Horowapatana Rd; 8.30am-4.30pm Wed-Mon) FREE This museum is unlikely to impress if you're arriving from the ancient cities, but the pinched-faced terracotta figures from Kilinochchi (4th to 5th century) are delightful and the central hexagonal chamber has some fine 5th-to-8th-century Buddha statues carved from Mannar limestone.

Sleeping & Eating

Hotel Oviya HOTEL $

(024-222 7959; hoteloviya@gmail.com; 47 Mill Rd; s/d standard Rs 2750/3300, deluxe Rs 3740/5170;) Welcoming reception staff, spacious rooms and clean, modern bathrooms make this a good choice. The restaurant is probably the best in town, serving hoppers for breakfast and tasty chicken biryani for lunch.

Hotel Nelly Star HOTEL $

(024-222 4477; www.hotelnelly.com; 84 2nd Cross St; s/d/tr Rs 3500/4000/4500;) Rooms here are workaday but decent value and some come with a balcony (back-facing rooms are brighter). It boasts an Indian restaurant (meals Rs 600), a dingy bar and is the only place in town with a swimming pool. Subtract Rs 800 if you don't want air-con. Staff can arrange a car to Jaffna for Rs 4000 to 5000.

Getting There & Around

Many of Vavuniya's three-wheelers are equipped with meters, so figure on Rs 50 per km.

BUS

Vavuniya's bus station is 1km north of town on the Kandy Rd.

Anuradhapura Rs 90, one hour, every 20 minutes

Colombo normal/express luxury Rs 330/550, 6½ hours, every 30 minutes, No 15

Jaffna Rs 215, three hours, every 30 minutes, No 87/3

Kandy Rs 220, five hours, 12 daily, No 43

Mannar Rs 130, two hours, hourly, No 83

Mullaittivu Rs 150, two hours, hourly, No 87/3

Trincomalee Rs 130, 3½ hours, hourly, No 88

TRAIN

Vavuniya's **railway station** (☎024-222 2271; Railway Station Rd) is a major stop on all trains between Colombo and Jaffna. The most useful services to Colombo leave at 8am, 12.25pm and 3.30pm (the latter only 1st class).

Fast trains to Jaffna leave around 8.20am, 10am (only 1st class) and 4.20pm.

Anuradhapura 1st/2nd/3rd class Rs 160/90/50, one hour, six daily

Colombo 1st/2nd/3rd class Rs 1500/800/500, five to seven hours, six daily

Jaffna 1st/2nd/3rd class Rs 1200/600/400, two to three hours, four daily

Mannar Island & Around

☎023 / POP 51,000

Sun-blasted Mannar Island is a dry near-peninsula with lots of white sand and palm trees, wild donkeys and fishing boats. Culturally, it's an intriguing place: it's dotted with ancient baobab trees (native to Africa and said to have been planted by Arab merchants many centuries ago) and crumbling colonial edifices built by the Portuguese, Dutch and Brits.

The island still feels like a world apart, with a slightly forlorn air but some intriguing sights to track down. For birders, the island is one of the best places in Sri Lanka to spot migratory waders and shore birds from Europe and Asia who winter here from November to March.

Once a prosperous pearling centre, today Mannar is one of the poorest corners of Sri Lanka. The island was once a major exit and entry point to India, just 30km away, but those services are now a distant memory. The civil war saw a mass exodus of people from the island. Today the inhabitants are 60% Tamil Catholics (a legacy of the Portuguese) and 25% Muslim.

Sights

Mannar Town

Reached via a 3km-long causeway from the mainland, Mannar town is a somewhat scruffy transport hub. The port here has historically been of great importance, as all westbound shipping was funnelled through here to avoid the treacherous sandbanks of Adam's Bridge.

Excepting the fort there's not that much for tourists, but as the only town of any size on the island this is where most travellers pause.

★Dutch Fort FORT

(Mannar Town) An imposing Portuguese-Dutch construction, this fortress is situated right by the causeway to the island and is ringed by a moat. It's a bit shambolic, but the walls are atmospheric and contain the roofless remains of a chapel, dungeon and Dutch bell tower. Climb the ramparts for an impressive perspective over the Gulf of Mannar. Don't miss the carved Dutch headstone at the entrance to the central courtyard (where you can park).

Baobab Tree Pallimunai LANDMARK

(Pallimunai Rd, Mannar Town) An offbeat attraction, this ancient baobab tree was allegedly planted by Arab traders. It has a circumference of 20m and is believed to be over 700 years old. In Africa the baobab is sometimes called the upside-down tree (because its branches look like roots); locals in Mannar refer to it as the *ali gaha* (elephant tree) since its tough, gnarled bark resembles the skin of an elephant. It's 1.2km northeast of the town centre.

Around the Island

The island is not endowed with beautiful stretches of sand, but **Keeri Beach** has good swimming, though no shade. Expect some trash. It's located 5km west of Mannar Town.

Heading northwest from Mannar Town you pass a cluster of **baobab trees** after about 3km. Around the 8km marker is **Our Lady of the Martyrs**, a church and huge prayer hall. Continuing on you pass a vast lagoon; look out for flamingos in February, and white and blue herons at most times.

Near the Palmyrah House, animal lovers can pop into the **Donkey Clinic & Education Centre** (☎071-263 5444; https://donkey-clinic-education-centre.business.site; Thailankudiyiruppu; Rs 1000; ⏲9am-4.30pm), set up to care for the hundreds of donkeys that wander wild on Mannar Island. Admission includes a tour and a chance to feed and groom the tame donkeys; kids will love it. It's 1km off the main road, next to the railway line.

WORTH A TRIP

CHURCH OF MIRACLES

This **Our Lady of Madhu Church** (Madhu; ⊙church 5.30am-7.30pm, information office 7.30am-5.30pm) is Sri Lanka's most hallowed Christian monument (though it's thought to have been constructed over an ancient Hindu shrine). Its walls shelter Our Lady of Madhu, a diminutive but revered Madonna-and-child statue brought here in 1670 by Catholics fleeing Protestant Dutch persecution in Mannar.

The statue rapidly developed a reputation for miracles – it was particularly revered as offering protection from snake bites – and Madhu has been a place of pilgrimage ever since. The vast Madhu compound served as a refugee camp during the civil war.

The present church dates from 1872 and is notable for its portico painted cream and duck-egg blue. The church attracts huge crowds of pilgrims to its 10 annual festivals, especially the one on 15 August. The grounds boast huge golden statues representing the stations of the cross.

Our Lady is 12km along Madhu Rd, which branches off the A14 at Madhu Junction on the 47km marker. Vavuniya–Mannar buses stop at Madhu Junction. From here three-wheelers cost Rs 900 return, including waiting time. A partially paved road runs east from the church to join the A30, giving a shortcut to Vavuniya.

Nearby is the small fishing centre and beach of **Pesalai**, which has an impressive number of boats bobbing away offshore.

Soon you reach Talaimannar, 38km from Mannar.

Talaimannar

This was once the passage to India. From 1914 until 1990 ferries departed regularly to India, first to Dhanushkodi and then later to Rameswaram in Tamil Nadu, from this tiny port on the island's western extreme. But those days are long gone – the last ferry departed in 1994, with refugees fleeing the violence.

Today you feel at the end of the world here. A lonely **lighthouse** (off A14, Talaimannar) stands near the **old rusty ferry pier**, both off limits and guarded by soldiers. A sign describes the history, and the views over the turquoise water are alluring.

The narrow beach around the old pier is OK for swimming but it's better 1km to the east. Boats line the beach, but there are empty sands a short walk away.

For a remoter beach with whitesand bars continue 3.5km to Western Talaimannar and deserted **Urumale Beach**.

Just before the bus stand at Western Talaimannar a junction marked by a statue of Jesus leads west to Vayu Resort and Adam's Bridge (p296).

Sleeping & Eating

Mannar Guest House GUESTHOUSE $
(☎077-316 8202; www.mannarguesthouse.com; 60 Uppukulam, Mannar Town; s/d with fan Rs 2000/3000, with air-con Rs 3000/3500; ❄📶) In a mixed Hindu/Muslim residential neighbourhood, a short walk from the bus station, this architecturally eclectic guesthouse has 21 rooms of various size, all with private bathrooms (but no hot water) and offering access to shared balconies. Good-value meals (Rs 350) and scooter hire (Rs 1000) are a bonus.

El Shadai GUESTHOUSE $
(☎076-898 3739; vimal76kumatha@gmail.com; 81 Eluthoor Rd; s/d Rs 1800/2800, with air-con Rs 3500/4800; 📶) Vimal and Rosemary are welcoming hosts at this homestay at the far northern end of Mannar. The one room next to their house is fan only but leads onto a pleasant breakfast area; air-con rooms are in a villa out front. Rosemary's rice and curry dinner (Rs 900) is delicious.

Vimal rents bicycles (Rs 500) and a somewhat unreliable scooter (Rs 1250). A three-wheeler from Mannar centre (3km) costs Rs 200.

Baobab Guest House GUESTHOUSE $
(☎077-525 7641, 023-222 2306; 83 Field St, Mannar Town; s/d with shared bathroom Rs 1500/2000, with private bathroom Rs 2000/3000; ❄📶) A simple, centrally located homestay run by Jerome, Baobab has a quiet location, a net-enclosed porch for relaxing, and good-value breakfasts (Rs 300). There are only four simple rooms, two with shared bathroom (cold water only). Take off 20% if you don't want air-con.

Four Tees Rest Inn LODGE $$
(☎071-044 4066, 023-205 0210; 4teessrestinn@gmail.com; Station Rd, Thoddaveli; ⊙s/d Rs 2200/3300; ❄📶) This likeable albeit isolated budget lodge, 9km northwest of Mannar

OFF THE BEATEN TRACK

ADAM'S BRIDGE

Offshore Mannar Island's western tip is Adam's Bridge – a remarkable chain of reefs, sandbanks, shoals and islets that also nearly connects Sri Lanka to the Indian subcontinent, a mere 32km away across the Palk Strait. In the Ramayana these islands ('Rama's Bridge') were the stepping stones that the monkey king Hanuman used in his bid to help rescue Rama's wife Sita from Ravana, the demon king of Lanka.

The chain is also called the 'Dancing Isles', because of the tendency of the sandbanks to shift size and even location during strong tides and storms. Until recently it used to be possible to walk out to the first island over a sandbank (13km return), but a 50m section of the ever-shifting sands was recently washed away.

The Indian government has long entertained a proposal, known as the Sethu Samundran (Bridge the Ocean) project, to dredge a channel through the shallows and open up the strait to international shipping, but religious and environmental objections have currently mothballed the project. The Sri Lankan side of the strait is now designated a marine national park

Today the only way to catch sight of the beginning of Adam's Bridge is to book lunch (Rs 1000) at the Vayu Resort and walk 30 minutes out to the beginning of the spit. Alternatively, follow public access paths there from outside the resort's perimeter fence. En route you pass Adam's Grave, a 40ft long grave built for a burial casket carved with Arabic inscriptions that washed up nearby. You'll need a three-wheeler or scooter to get here.

Town, offers a quiet, rural base in a three-acre garden of mature trees. Manager Mr Lawrence is a great source of information and can organise birding excursions and scooter hire. Good meals are available. It's 100m from the Thoddaveli train stop. Add on Rs 1000 for air-conditioning.

Vayu Resort RESORT **$$**
(☎077-377 0744; www.kitesurfingmannar.com; per person tent/garden/deluxe d US$43/64/75 full board; ❄📶) This kitesurfing resort has a dreamy location near the beginning of Adam's Bridge, 30 minutes' walk from the ocean. Accommodation ranges from hot tents with a shared bathroom block to stylish but sunblasted wooden or concrete chalets with private bathrooms, some of which offer air-con (d US$86 per person full board). Head to the upper-floor deck for fine sunset views.

Kitesurfing gear rental costs US$75 per day and a three-hour block of group/private tuition costs US$107/166 per person. The season is May to mid-September for beginners (in the sheltered lagoon), or January to February for more experienced offshore surfers.

★**Palmyrah House** HOTEL **$$$**
(☎011-259 4467; www.palmyrahhouse.com; off A14, Karisal; s/d incl breakfast from US$99/102; ❄📶🏊) This top-notch and well-run resort has spacious, stylish rooms, excellent staff and an understated class. It's set in 37 acres of peaceful grounds, 12km northwest of Mannar Town. The resident ornithologist and rentable Nikon binoculars make it particularly popular with birders. The full board option is recommended.

ℹ Getting There & Away

The A14 to Mannar Town is in excellent condition. From here west to Talaimannar, it's potholed. There are petrol stations at Mannar, Talaimannar and Pesalai.

BUS

Government (A14, Mannar Town) and **private buses** (A14) run from separate stands 100m apart in central Mannar. Buses include the following:

Colombo Rs 600, eight hours, seven daily

Jaffna Rs 180, three hours, 10 daily

Mullaittivu Rs 250, two daily at 5.30am and 7.30am

Tallaimannar Rs 65, 30 minutes, hourly until 7.30pm.

Vavuniya Rs 130, two hours, hourly until noon

TRAIN

Trains run from Colombo via the junction at Medawachchiya to Mannar, where the **railway station** (S Bar Rd) is 2.3km west of town (Rs 250 in a three-wheeler).

Trains from Colombo continue on to Talaimannar at 4.30pm, making numerous whistle stops across the island.

Trains from Mannar include the following:

Colombo 2nd/3rd class Rs 520/285, eight hours, two daily, at 7.30am and 9pm.

Talaimannar 3rd/2nd Rs 35/70, 45 minutes.

Understand Sri Lanka

History

Sri Lanka's location at the southern tip of India, lying on hundreds of ancient trade routes, has made it attractive to immigrants, invaders, missionaries, traders and travellers from across the globe for millennia. Many stayed on, and over generations, assimilated and intermarried, converting back and forth between faiths and adding their own flavours to Sri Lanka's melting pot. Although debates still rage over who was here first – and can therefore claim Sri Lanka as their homeland – the island's history is one of shifting dominance and constant flux.

Prehistory & Early Arrivals

Sri Lanka's history is a source of pride for both the Sinhalese and Tamils, the country's two largest ethnic groups. Unfortunately, the two communities have completely different stories about what happened. Every historical site, religious structure, even village name seems to have conflicting stories about its origin, blended over time with religious myths and local legends. The end results are often used as evidence that the island is one group's exclusive homeland.

Did the Buddha leave his footprint on Adam's Peak (Sri Pada) while visiting the island that lay halfway to paradise? Or was it Adam who left his footprint embedded in the rock as he stepped onto the earth from the Garden of Eden? Was the chain of islands linking Sri Lanka to India the same chain that Rama crossed to rescue his wife Sita from the clutches of Ravana, demon king of Lanka, in the epic *Ramayana*?

Whatever the legends, Sri Lanka's original inhabitants, the Veddah people (or, as they refer to themselves, Wanniyala-aetto: 'forest dwellers'), were hunter-gatherers who subsisted on the island's abundant natural resources. Their origins are unclear, but most anthropologists believe they are descended from people who migrated from India, and possibly Southeast Asia, perhaps as early as 32,000 BCE. It's also likely that rising waters submerged a land bridge between India and Sri Lanka in around 5000 BCE, cutting off their migration route.

A megalithic culture later emerged in Sri Lanka around 900 BCE, with striking similarities to the South Indian cultures of that time. Objects

TIMELINE

Pre-6th century BCE

The island is inhabited by the Veddah people (Wanniyala-aetto), a hunter-gatherer society who anthropologists believe existed here as early as 32,000 BCE.

6th century BCE

Vijaya, a shamed North Indian prince, is cast adrift from India, making landfall on Sri Lanka's west coast. He establishes the island's first recorded kingdom at Anuradhapura.

4th century BCE

India's first poet pens the Hindu epic the *Ramayana*, in which the god Rama conquers Lanka and its demon-god Ravana.

inscribed with Brahmi (an ancient 'parent' script to most South Asian scripts) have been found from the 3rd century BCE. Sri Lankans still dispute which is the original, 'true' culture of Sri Lanka, but rather than there being two distinct ethnic histories, it is more likely that multiple migrations from West, East and South India happened during this time and that new arrivals mixed with the indigenous population.

Anuradhapura

The 5th-century CE Pali epic, the Mahavamsa (Great Chronicle), is the country's primary historical source. Although a fairly accurate record of kingdoms and Sinhalese political power from around the 3rdcentury BCE, its historical accuracy is shakier – and indeed full of beautiful myths – before this time. Many Sinhalese claim they're descended from Vijaya, a 6th-century BCE North Indian prince who, according to the epic, had a lion for a grandfather and a father with lion paws who married his own sister. Vijaya was banished from India for bad behaviour, with a contingent of 700 men, landing near present-day Mannar, supposedly on the exact day that the Buddha attained enlightenment.

Vijaya and his crew settled around Anuradhapura, and soon encountered Kuveni, described as a vicious queen and a seductress, who allegedly assumed the form of a 16-year-old maiden to snag Vijaya. She handed Vijaya the crown, joined him in slaying her own people and had two children with him before he kicked her out and ordered a princess – and wives for his men – from South India's Tamil Pandya kingdom. By this account, the forefathers of the Sinhalese race all married Tamils, something overlooked by Sinhalese nationalists! Vijaya's rule formed the basis of the Anuradhapura kingdom, which developed from the 4th century BCE.

The Anuradhapura kingdom covered large parts of the island by the 2nd century BCE, but it frequently coexisted with, and fought, other dynasties over the centuries, especially the Tamil Cholas from the north. The boundaries between Anuradhapura and various South Indian kingdoms were frequently shifting. A number of Sinhalese warriors arose to repel advances by South Indian kingdoms, including Vijayabahu I, who finally abandoned Anuradhapura and made Polonnaruwa his capital in the 11th century.

For centuries, the kingdom was able to rebuild after its battles through *rajakariya*, a system of free labour for the king (enforced for his subjects, though they obtained land for their efforts). This provided the resources to restore buildings, tanks and irrigation systems and to develop agriculture. The system was only ended on the island in 1832, when the British passed laws banning slavery.

The indigenous Veddah people were called Yakshas, or nature spirits, by the island's early arrivals. No one knows if this is because they were so at home in nature or because they prayed to their departed ancestors – spirits known as *nae yaku*.

Veddah Place Names

Gal Oya National Park

Nanu Oya

Kelaniya Ganga

Vedi-Kanda

3rd century BCE

The Indian emperor Ashoka sends his son and daughter to spread the Buddha's teachings. King Devanampiya Tissa converts, making Buddhism the official religion of Anuradhapura.

205–161 BCE

Reign of Chola King Elara, described in the Mahavamsa as a just leader. A Tamil Hindu, he offers alms to Buddhist monks and employs both Sinhalese and Tamils.

103–89 BCE

Five Tamil kings from India invade Anuradhapura and rule for 14 years. King Valagamba is forced to flee and shelters in the caves around Dambulla.

1st century BCE

The Fourth Buddhist council is held in Aluvihara. The Buddha's teachings, previously preserved by oral tradition, are written down for the first time.

TANK-BUILDING

The science of building water tanks is the key to early Sri Lankan civilisation. The tanks, which dot the plains of the ancient dominions of Rajarata (in the north-central part of the country) and Ruhunu (in the southeast), started as modest reservoirs for water supplies and religious rituals, but by the 5th century BCE they reached such dimensions that local legends say they were built with supernatural help. It is claimed that giants helped scoop out the Giant's Tank near Mannar Island, while other tanks were said to have been constructed by a mixed workforce of humans and demons.

The irrigation system expanded rapidly during the millennium before the Common Era, ranking with the ancient *qanats* (underground channels) of Iran and the canals of Pharaonic Egypt in sophistication. These dry-zone reservoirs sustained and shaped Sri Lanka's civilisation for more than 2500 years, until war and discord overtook the island in the 12th to 14th centuries CE.

The Buddha's Teaching Arrives

Buddhism arrived from India in the 3rd century BCE, transforming Anuradhapura and sowing the seeds for what is now known as Sinhalese culture. The mountain at Mihintale marks the spot where the local King Devanampiya Tissa is said to have first received the Buddha's teaching from the Indian Buddhist monk Mahinda, son of the empire-building Indian emperor Ashoka.

Mahinda's sister Sanghamitta joined the mission, bringing with her a cutting from the bodhi tree under which the Buddha attained enlightenment, at Bodhgaya in India. Tended by generations of devotees, the tree still survives in Anuradhapura, garlanded with prayer flags and thronged by pilgrims. Strong ties grew between Sri Lankan royalty and Buddhist religious orders. In exchange for monastic support, the monarchy bolstered the monasteries, and a symbiotic political economy between religion and state was established – a powerful contract that still endures.

Sri Maha Bodhi, the bodhi tree in Anuradhapura, has been tended by generations of devotees for over 2000 years, making this the oldest-known human-planted tree in the world.

Buddhism was further entrenched when its original oral teachings were documented in writing in the 1st century BCE. Early Sri Lankan monks went on to write a vast body of commentaries on the teachings of the Buddha in the Pali language, the sacred language of Theravada (doctrine of the elders) Buddhism. This pool of classical literature continues to be referenced by Theravada Buddhists around the world. The arrival of the Buddha's tooth relic at Anuradhapura in 371 CE reinforced the authority of Buddhism in Sinhalese society, inspiring a Buddhist national identity.

4th century CE

Buddhism is further popularised with the arrival in Anuradhapura of the sacred tooth relic of the Buddha.

5th century

After engineering his father's death and expelling his older brother Mugalan, King Kasyapa constructs the rock fortress at Sigiriya before Mugalan retakes the throne.

5th century

The Mahavamsa (Great Chronicle) epic poem is written by Buddhist monks, telling the Buddhist and royal history of the island, interwoven with supernatural tales.

5th century

Indian scholar-monk Buddhaghosa arrives in Sri Lanka and writes the *Visuddhimagga*, a manual for the Buddha's teachings.

Polonnaruwa

Sri Lanka's next capital, at Polonnaruwa, survived for over two centuries and produced two more notable rulers. Parakramabahu I (r 1153–86), nephew of Vijayabahu I, expelled the South Indian Tamil Chola empire from Sri Lanka, and carried the fight to South India, even making a raid as far north as Myanmar. He also constructed many new tanks and lavished public money to make Polonnaruwa a mighty capital to rival Anuradhapura.

His benevolent successor, Nissanka Malla (r 1187–96), was the last great king of Polonnaruwa. He was followed by a series of weak, decadent rulers, and with the decay of the irrigation system, disease spread and Polonnaruwa was abandoned. The lush jungle reclaimed the second Sinhalese capital in just a few decades.

After Polonnaruwa, Sinhalese power shifted to the southwest of the island, and between 1253 and 1400 there were five further capitals, none of them as powerful as Anuradhapura or Polonnaruwa. Meanwhile, the powerful Hindu kingdom of Jaffna expanded to cover northern parts of Sri Lanka. When Arab traveller Ibn Batuta visited Ceylon in 1344, he reported that its territories extended south as far as Puttalam.

With the decline of the Sinhalese northern capitals and ensuing Sinhalese migration south, a wide jungle buffer separated the northern, mostly coastal Tamil settlements and the southern, interior Sinhalese settlements. For centuries, this jungle barrier kept Sinhalese and Tamils largely apart, reducing community clashes.

Enter the Portuguese

With its strategic location midway between Southeast Asia and the Middle East, Sri Lanka was already a thriving trading hub by the time Arab traders arrived in the 7th century CE in search of gemstones, cinnamon and ivory, introducing a new faith to the island. Early Muslim settlements grew up in Jaffna and Galle, but the arrival of a European colonial power, focused as much on domination as trade, pushed these early converts inland.

When the Portuguese reached the island in 1505, Sri Lanka had three main kingdoms: the Tamil kingdom of Jaffna and two powerful Sinhalese kingdoms centred on Kandy and Kotte (near Colombo). Lourenço de Almeida, the son of the Portuguese Viceroy of India, established friendly relations with the Kotte kingdom and gained a monopoly on the valuable spice trade, dominated by the island's famous cinnamon. The Portuguese eventually gained control of the Kotte kingdom, while Kandy remained fiercely independent.

Mozambican enslaved people were brought to Sri Lanka by the Portuguese, but this population was almost totally assimilated. Their most obvious contributions to Sri Lankan culture are *bailas*, love songs with Latin melodies and African rhythms.

7th–15th centuries

Arab traders settle in Sri Lanka, marrying locally and establishing Islam on the island, founding Muslim settlements along the coast at Jaffna and Galle.

11th century

King Vijayabahu I defeats the Cholas and moves the Sinhalese capital southeast to Polonnaruwa; a brief golden age follows.

1216

As Polonnaruwa declines, the Tamil kingdom of Jaffna is established and briefly becomes a feudatory of South India's Pandya kingdom before gaining independence.

1505

Sinhalese power shifts to Kandy and Kotte in the southwest. The Portuguese arrive and conquer the entire west coast, but Kandy resists their advances.

Tamil–Portuguese relations were less cordial, and Jaffna successfully resisted two Portuguese expeditions before falling in 1619, at which point the Portuguese destroyed Jaffna's many beautiful Hindu temples and its royal library. Portugal eventually took over the entire west coast, then the east, but the Kandyan kingdom steadfastly resisted domination.

The Portuguese brought with them missionaries, including Dominicans and Jesuits. Many coastal communities converted voluntarily, but resistance to Christianity was met with massacres and the destruction of temples. Buddhists fled to Kandy and the city assumed the role of protector of the Buddhist faith.

The Dutch

In 1602 the Dutch arrived, casting a greedy eye over the lucrative traffic in Indian Ocean spices. In exchange for Sri Lankan autonomy, and the forcible removal of the resented Portuguese, the Kandyan king, Rajasinha II, gave the Dutch a monopoly on the spice trade. Despite cordial beginnings, however, the Dutch later made a series of unsuccessful attempts to subjugate Kandy during their 140-year rule.

The Dutch were more industrious than the Portuguese, and left more of a mark on the nation. Canals were built along the west coast to transport cinnamon and other crops (some can be seen around Negombo today) and civic buildings were erected around the country, including the island's first formal hospital in Colombo (though older religious hospitals had existed for centuries in Sri Lanka's ancient cities). The legal system of the Dutch era still forms part of Sri Lanka's legal canon. Dutch colonial power, however, was curtailed by the arrival of the British in the dying years of the 18th century.

The British

The British viewed Sri Lanka in strategic terms, and considered the eastern harbour of Trincomalee as a counter to French influence in South India, then centred on Pondicherry (Puducherry). After the French took over the Netherlands in 1794, pragmatic Dutch settlers ceded Sri Lanka to the British in exchange for 'protection' in 1796. The British moved quickly, making the island a formal colony in 1802 and finally seizing Kandy in 1815. Three years later, the first unified administration of the island by a European colonial power was established.

The British conquest unsettled many Sinhalese, who believed that only the custodians of the tooth relic had the right to rule the island. Their apprehension was somewhat allayed when a senior monk spirited away the relic from the Temple of the Sacred Tooth Relic, thereby securing it (and the island's symbolic sovereignty) for the Sinhalese people.

1658

Following a treaty with the Kandyan kingdom, the Dutch establish a monopoly on the spice market and wrest control of coastal Sri Lanka from the Portuguese.

1796

The Netherlands comes under French control, and Sri Lanka's Dutch rulers surrender to the British in exchange for protection. The British administer the island from Madras, India.

1802

Sri Lanka becomes a British colony. The island is viewed as a strategic bulwark against French expansion, but its commercial potential for tea, coffee and rubber production is soon recognised.

1815

Determined to rule the entire island, the British finally conquer the Kandyan kingdom. It's the first (and only) time all of Sri Lanka is ruled by a European colonial power.

Sinhalese anger grew when British settlers began arriving in the 1830s. Colonial crops of coffee and rubber were replaced by tea from the 1870s, and the island's demographic mix was profoundly altered with a new influx of Tamil labourers – so called 'Plantation Tamils' – from South India. At the same time, Tamil settlers from the North made their way to Colombo, while Sinhalese headed north to Jaffna, mixing together communities who had hitherto lived separately.

Growing Nationalism

The dawn of the 20th century was an important time for the grassroots Sri Lankan nationalist movement. Buddhist and Hindu campaigns were established with the dual aim of making the faiths more contemporary in the wake of European colonialism and defending traditional Sri Lankan culture against the impact of Christian missionaries. The logical progression was for these groups to demand greater Sri Lankan participation in government, and by 1910 they had secured the concession of Sri Lankans being permitted to elect one lonely member to the Legislative Council.

By 1919 the nationalist mission was formalised as the Ceylon National Congress. The Sinhalese-nationalist activist Anagarika Dharmapala was forced to leave the country, and the mantle for further change was taken up by a variety of youth leagues. In 1927 Mahatma Gandhi visited Tamil youth activists in Jaffna, providing extra momentum to the cause.

Further reform came in 1924, when a revision to the constitution allowed for representative government, and again in 1931, when a new constitution finally included the island's leaders in the parliamentary decision-making process and granted universal suffrage. Under the constitution no one ethnic community could dominate the political process, and a series of checks and balances were imposed to ensure the involvement of all ethnic groups.

Running in the Family is a fascinating, fictionalised memoir by *English Patient* author Michael Ondaatje, exploring the lifestyle of Dutch-Ceylonese families in later Sri Lankan society.

From Ceylon to Sri Lanka

Following India's independence in 1947, the island that the British called Ceylon became fully independent on 4 February 1948. Despite featuring members from all of the island's ethnic groups, the ruling United National Party (UNP) primarily represented the interests of an English-speaking Sri Lankan elite. The UNP's decision to try to deny the 'Plantation Tamils' citizenship and repatriate them to India was indicative of a rising tide of Sinhalese nationalism.

In 1956 this divide increased when the Sri Lankan Freedom Party (SLFP) came to power with an agenda based on socialism, Sinhalese nationalism and government support for Buddhism. One of the first tasks of SLFP leader SWRD Bandaranaike was to fulfil a campaign promise to make Sinhala the country's sole official language, a response to the

1832

Sweeping changes in property laws open the door to British settlers. English becomes the official language, state monopolies are abolished and capital flows in, funding the establishment of many plantations.

1843–59

Unable to persuade the Sinhalese to labour on plantations, the British bring in almost one million Tamil labourers from South India. Today 'Plantation Tamils' are 4% of the population.

1870s

The coffee industry drives the development of roads, ports and railways, but leaf blight forces a shift to growing tea and rubber.

1919

Following the British arrest in 1915 of Sinhalese leaders for minor offences, the Ceylon National Congress unifies Sinhalese and Tamil groups behind an ethos of pro-independence.

large number of educated, English-speaking Tamils in universities and public-service jobs. Post election, however, Bandaranaike alienated many of his nationalist backers, prompting his assassination by a militant Buddhist monk in 1959.

As the main political parties played on Sinhalese fears that their religion, language and culture could be swamped by Indians, Sri Lanka's Tamils, whose Hindu identity had become more pronounced in the lead-up to independence, found themselves a threatened minority. The Sinhala-only bill effectively disenfranchised Sri Lanka's Hindu and Muslim Tamil-speaking population: almost 30% of the country suddenly lost access to government jobs and services. Although tensions had been simmering since the end of colonial rule, this decision marked the beginning of Sri Lanka's ethnic conflict.

Fuel was added to the fire in 1970, when a new law was passed favouring Sinhalese for admission to universities, reducing numbers of Tamil students. Then, following an armed insurrection against the government by the hardline anti-Tamil, student-led People's Liberation Front (Janatha Vimukthi Peramuna or JVP), a new constitution, which changed Ceylon's name to Sri Lanka, gave Buddhism 'foremost place' and made it the state's duty to 'protect and foster' the Buddhist faith.

Unrest grew among northern Tamils, and a state of emergency was imposed on their home regions for several years from 1971. The police and army that enforced the state of emergency included few Tamils (partly because of the 'Sinhala only' law), creating, for Tamils, an acute sense of 'us' and 'them'.

Birth of the Tigers

In the mid-1970s several groups of young Tamils, some of them militant, began campaigning for an independent Tamil state called Eelam (Precious Land). They included Vellupillai Prabhakaran, a founder of the Liberation Tigers of Tamil Eelam (LTTE), widely referred to as the Tamil Tigers.

Not an easy read but an important one, *When Memory Dies*, by A Sivanandan, is a tale of Sri Lanka's ethnic crisis and its impact on one family over three generations.

Clashes between Tamils and security forces developed into a cycle of reprisals, all too often with civilians caught in the crossfire. A pivotal moment came in 1981, when a group of Sinhalese rioters (some say government forces) burnt down Jaffna's library, which contained, among other things, various histories of the Tamil people, some on ancient palm-leaf manuscripts.

Small-scale reprisals followed, but the world only took notice two years later, in 1983, when full-scale anti-Tamil massacres erupted in Colombo in response to the Tigers' killing of 13 soldiers in the Jaffna region. In a riot now known as Black July, up to 3000 Tamils were murdered, and Tamil property was looted and destroyed.

1931

A new constitution introduces power sharing with a Sinhalese-run government. Universal suffrage is introduced and the country becomes the first Asian colony to give women the right to vote.

1948

Ceylon becomes an independent nation in the Commonwealth, six months after neighbouring India. The United National Party (UNP) consolidates power by depriving Plantation Tamils of citizenship.

1956

The Sri Lankan Freedom Party (SLFP) defeats the UNP on a socialist and nationalist platform. Protests and ethnic riots break out after a 'Sinhala only' language law is passed.

1958

The country sees its first island-wide anti-Tamil riot, leaving more than 200 people dead in violent attacks and displacing thousands of Tamils.

WHAT'S IN A NAME?

Changing the country's name from Ceylon to Sri Lanka in 1972 caused considerable confusion for foreigners. However, for the Sinhalese the country had always been known as Lanka and for the Tamils as Ilankai. The *Ramayana*, written perhaps as early as 500 BCE, describes the abduction of Sita by the king of Lanka. Outsiders, however, came up with their own names. The Romans knew the island as Taprobane and Muslim traders talked of Serendib, meaning 'Island of Jewels' in Arabic. The word Serendib became the root of the word 'serendipity' – making happy and unexpected discoveries. The Portuguese somehow twisted the name Sinhala-dvipa (Island of the Sinhalese) into Ceilão, and in turn, the Dutch altered this to Ceylan and the British took it one step further to Ceylon. The rebranding of the island as Sri Lanka was, in many ways, a wiping clean of the years of colonial influence, with the addition of 'Sri', a title of respect.

The government, the police and the army were either unable or unwilling to stop the violence; some officials even assisted. Hundreds of thousands of Tamils left the country or fled to Tamil-majority areas in the North or East – and many joined the militants – while many Sinhalese fled south. The horror of Black July prompted a groundswell of sympathy and funding from fellow Tamils in southern India, as well as from the government of Indira Gandhi.

Revenge and counter-revenge attacks continued, and grew into atrocities and massacres – on both sides. The government was widely condemned for acts of torture and disappearances, but it in turn pointed to brutal violence against civilians, including both Hindus and Muslims, by the Tamil fighters, who turned to suicide bombings to maximise civilian casualties. Implementation of a 1987 accord – offering limited Tamil autonomy and formalising Tamil as a national language – failed to materialise, and the conflict escalated into a 25-year civil war that eventually claimed upwards of 100,000 lives.

Enemy Lines: Warfare, Childhood, and Play in Batticaloa, by Margaret Trawick, describes living and working in eastern Sri Lanka and witnessing the recruitment of teenagers as child soldiers for the Liberation Tigers of Tamil Eelam (LTTE).

Indian Peacekeeping

In 1987 government forces pushed the LTTE back into Jaffna as part of a major offensive. An anxious India pressed the Sri Lankan government to withdraw, and the two heads of state, JR Jayawardene and Rajiv Gandhi, negotiated an accord: the Sri Lankan government would call off the offensive, Tamil rebels would disarm and an Indian Peace Keeping Force (IPKF) would protect the truce. Tamil regions would also have substantial autonomy, as Colombo devolved power to the provinces.

It soon became clear the deal suited no one. The LTTE paid lip service to the treaty, but ended up fighting the IPKF after refusing to disarm. Opposition also came from the Sinhalese, a revived JVP and sections of the sangha (the Buddhist clergy), leading to violent demonstrations.

1959

Despite coming to power with a Sinhalese-nationalist manifesto, SWRD Bandaranaike begins negotiating with Tamil leaders for a federation, resulting in his assassination by a Buddhist monk.

1959

Widow Sirimavo Bandaranaike assumes her late husband's SLFP post, becoming the world's first female prime minister. She is appointed prime minister several more times before her death in 2000.

1972

A new constitution is created. It changes Ceylon's name to Sri Lanka, enshrines Sinhalese as the official state language and gives Buddhism 'foremost place' among the island's religions.

1970s

Young Tamils begin fighting for an independent Tamil state called Eelam (Precious Land) in Sri Lanka's north. The Liberation Tigers of Tamil Eelam (LTTE) emerge as the strongest group.

In 1987 the JVP launched a second attempted revolution with political murders and strikes, and by late 1988 the economy was crippled and the government paralysed. The authorities struck back with a ruthless counter-insurgency campaign, killing tens of thousands.

By the time the Indian peacekeepers withdrew, in March 1990, they had lost more than 1000 soldiers in just three years. But no sooner had they left than the war between the LTTE and the Sri Lankan government resumed. By the end of 1990 the LTTE held Jaffna and much of the North, while the East remained under government control. In May 1991 former Indian prime minister Rajiv Gandhi was assassinated in Chennai (Madras) by a 17-year-old female suicide bomber affiliated with the LTTE, presumably in retaliation for consenting to the IPKF arrangement.

The 2002 Ceasefire

After years of conflict, most Tamils and Sinhalese had grown weary of violence, but extremists on both sides pressed on with war. President Ranasinghe Premadasa was assassinated at a May Day rally in 1993; the LTTE was suspected but never claimed responsibility. The following year, the People's Alliance (PA) won the parliamentary elections; its leader, Chandrika Bandaranaike Kumaratunga, the daughter of former leader Sirimavo Bandaranaike, won the presidential election, promising to end the civil war, but the conflict continued.

William McGowan's *Only Man Is Vile* is an incisive, unrelenting account of ethnic violence in Sri Lanka, penetrating deeply into its complexities.

In 2000 a Norwegian peace mission brought the LTTE and the government to the negotiating table, but a ceasefire had to wait until after the December 2001 elections, which handed power back to the UNP. Ranil Wickremasinghe became prime minister, bringing strong economic growth while peace talks appeared to progress. Wickremasinghe and President Kumaratunga, however, were from different parties, and circled each other warily until 2003, when Kumaratunga dissolved parliament and essentially ousted Wickremasinghe and the UNP.

In 2002, following the Norway-brokered ceasefire agreement, a careful optimism spread. In the North, refugees and displaced persons began to return, bringing an economic boost to devastated Jaffna. Nongovernmental organisations started work to remove an estimated two million land mines, and vast amounts of undetonated ordnance.

But peace talks stumbled. In October 2003 the US listed the LTTE as a Foreign Terrorist Organisation in response to its systematic targeting of civilians. In early 2004 a split in LTTE ranks added a new dynamic, and a new wave of killings, leading to abandonment of the Norwegian peace mission. At that stage almost all of Sri Lanka, including most of the Jaffna peninsula, was controlled by the Sri Lankan government, while the LTTE controlled a small area south of the Jaffna peninsula and pockets in the East.

1981

Jaffna Public Library, home to many ancient Tamil works and a symbol of Tamil culture and learning, is burnt down by Sinhalese mobs, galvanising the Tamil separatist movement.

1983

The ambush of an army patrol near Jaffna ignites widespread ethnic violence. Up to 3000 Tamils are killed by Sinhalese rioters in what is now known as Black July.

July 1987

An accord is signed, with India's involvement, granting Tamils an autonomous province in the country's north, but disagreements over its implementation prevent it from going into effect.

1987

Government forces push the LTTE back into Jaffna. An Indian Peace Keeping Force (IPKF) attempts to establish stability, but is also dragged into conflict with the LTTE.

After the Tsunami

An event beyond all predictions struck on 26 December 2004, affecting not only the peace process but also the entire social fabric of Sri Lanka. As people celebrated the monthly *poya* (full moon) festivities, a tsunami triggered by an earthquake in Indonesia surged towards the country, killing 30,000 people and leaving many more injured, homeless and orphaned. Initial optimism that the nation would come together in the face of catastrophe collapsed as communal arguments erupted over aid distribution, reconstruction and land ownership.

Meanwhile, President Kumaratunga attempted to alter the constitution to extend her term. Thwarted by a Supreme Court ruling, she set presidential elections for 2005, with former prime minister, Mahinda Rajapaksa, defeating opposition leader, Ranil Wickremasinghe, in part due to a boycott on voting by the LTTE.

President Rajapaksa pledged to bring in peace negotiators from the UN and India, renegotiate a ceasefire with the LTTE, reject Tamil autonomy and bar the LTTE from obtaining tsunami aid. Such policies didn't auger well for future peace. Meanwhile, LTTE leader Prabhakaran insisted on a political settlement in 2006, and threatened to 'intensify' action if this didn't occur, placing Sri Lanka on a precipice.

The 2004 Indian Ocean tsunami killed more than 225,000 people in 14 countries. The waves, which were in some places more than 30m tall, travelled as far as the East African coast from the epicentre in Indonesia.

An Elusive Ceasefire

The final route to peace was marked by some of the worst violence of the entire civil war. Another ceasefire was signed in early 2006, and collapsed quickly. Major military operations by both sides resumed in the North and East, and a wave of disappearances and killings in 2006 and 2007 prompted human rights groups and the international community to strongly criticise all belligerents. By August the fighting in the northeast was the most intense since the 2002 ceasefire, and new peace talks in Geneva also failed to change hearts and minds.

In January 2008 the Sri Lankan government officially pulled out of the ceasefire agreement, signalling its dedication to ending the 25-year-old civil conflict by military means. Later in the year, the LTTE offered a unilateral 10-day ceasefire in support of the South Asian Association for Regional Cooperation (SAARC) summit being held in August in Colombo. The government, suspicious that the LTTE planned to use the ceasefire to shore up its strength, responded with an emphatic no, drawing the lines for a brutal end game.

At least one million land mines were laid during the civil war in the 1990s. The Halo Trust (www.halotrust.org) is one of several organisations still working to remove the landmines that continue to blight lives in Sri Lanka.

Cornering the LTTE

A change in military strategy saw the Sri Lankan security forces fight fire with fire using guerrilla-style attacks, and by August 2008 the Sri Lankan Army (SLA) had entered the LTTE's final stronghold, the jungle area of

1987–89

The Janatha Vimukthi Peramuna (JVP) launches a second Marxist insurrection, and attempts a Khmer Rouge–style peasant rebellion in the countryside. Up to 35,000 die in the resulting fighting.

1991

A teenaged, female Black Tiger (an LTTE fighter trained in suicide missions) kills former Indian prime minister Rajiv Gandhi, in protest against IPKF involvement in Sri Lanka.

1994

President Chandrika Kumaratunga comes to power pledging to end the war with the LTTE. Peace talks are opened, but hostilities continue. In 1999 she survives a suicide-bomb attack.

1998

Hostilities between the Sri Lanka military and the LTTE intensify; following more failed attempts at negotiation, the LTTE bombs Kandy's Temple of the Sacred Tooth Relic.

the Vanni. The Sri Lankan government stated that the army was on track to capture the LTTE capital Kilinochchi by the end of 2008. Faced with a series of battleground defeats, the LTTE struck back with yet another suicide bomb in Anuradhapura, killing 27 people.

In September 2008 the Sri Lankan government ordered UN agencies and NGOs to leave the Vanni region, saying it could no longer guarantee their safety. The departure of the NGOs and the barring of independent journalists from the site of the conflict made (and continues to make) it impossible to verify claims made by either side about the final battles of the war. What is certain is that by February 1990, the LTTE had lost 99% of the territory it had controlled just 12 months earlier.

Government advances pushed remaining LTTE forces and the 300,000 Tamil civilians they brought with them to an increasingly tiny area near Mullaittivu. The UN called for an immediate ceasefire in February 2009; the government responded by opening escape routes for those fleeing the fighting to move to no-fire zones. However, escaping civilians were then shelled by government forces after claims of LTTE attacks from within safe zones. The UN High Commissioner for Human Rights Navi Pillay accused both sides of war crimes, but the international community remained largely silent.

The Bitter End

By April 2009, tens of thousands of Tamil civilians and LTTE fighters were confined to a single stretch of beach. The LTTE offered the Sri Lankan government a unilateral ceasefire, but given that the Sri Lankan military's objectives were so close to being fulfilled, it was dismissed as 'a joke' by the Sri Lankan Defence Secretary. Government forces finally penetrated LTTE lines and ordered trapped war refugees to move to safe areas. According to UN investigations, the Tigers blocked many from leaving and killed others; refugees reported that government forces raped and executed many who surrendered.

The end finally came in May when the Sri Lankan military captured the last sliver of coast and surrounded the few hundred remaining LTTE fighters. The LTTE responded by announcing they had 'silenced their weapons' and that the 'battle had reached its bitter end'. Several senior LTTE figures were killed, including leader Vellupillai Prabhakaran, and the war that terrorised the country for 26 years was finally over.

Rapid Change

The end of war was quickly followed by an inrush of money and tourists to Sri Lanka. Foreign investment from China and India manifested itself in huge loans for development schemes in Colombo and elsewhere that included expanding ports and commercial areas. The largest of these, near

2002

After two years of negotiation, a Norwegian peace mission secures a ceasefire. Sri Lankans from overseas, and the North and East, return, anticipating peace.

2004

A tsunami devastates coastal Sri Lanka, leaving 30,000 people dead. It's thought the disaster will bring unity, but the government and LTTE fight over aid distribution and funds for reconstruction.

2005

Sinhalese nationalist Mahinda Rajapaksa wins presidential elections. Before the election Rajapaksa signs a deal with the Marxist JVP party, rejects Tamil autonomy outright and denies tsunami aid to the LTTE.

2008

The government pulls out of the 2002 ceasefire agreement to focus on a military solution. The Sri Lankan civil war enters its end game.

A FLAG FOR COMPASSION

Sri Lanka's flag was created in 1948 and took on many changes over the years. The core element was the lion on a crimson background, a symbol used on flags throughout Sri Lankan history, beginning with Prince Vijaya, who is believed to have brought a lion flag with him from India. On this first version of the national flag, the lion represented the Sinhalese people, and gold represented Buddhism, but as Sri Lanka settled into independence, the flag evolved. In 1951 green and orange stripes were added to signify Sri Lanka's Muslims and Hindus, respectively, and in 1972 four bodhi-tree leaves were added to represent *metta* (loving-kindness), *karuna* (compassion), *upekkha* (equanimity) and *muditha* (happiness).

the president's home town of Hambantota was immediately condemned for handing control over a national asset to the government of China.

Around the country a building programme produced new toll roads and repaired infrastructure in the East and North that had been damaged during the war. And tourists poured in, with visitor totals increasing by 20% each year. This provided much-needed investment across the nation, as new hotels, guesthouses, cafes, tour companies and more materialised to serve the new demand.

Another Political Tug-of-War

Until 2015, the grinning face of President Mahinda Rajapaksa was everywhere in Sri Lanka. Then a funny thing happened on the way to the next election, which Rajapaksa called early, expecting the process to be a rubber stamp. Instead, former allies rallied around his rival, former Minister for Health, Maithripala Sirisena, who led the Sri Lankan Freedom Party (SLFP) to victory by a vote of 51 to 48 percent.

However, early signs of reconciliation and progress faltered. Sirisena established a commission to investigate graft, and promised to combat human rights abuses, but resisted UN calls for investigations into abuses during the civil war. A string of officials were arrested and prosecuted for corruption, but low-level Tamil resentment continued to simmer, and a number of LTTE cadres were arrested with explosives.

Things turned sour for the Sirisena administration in 2018. First came violent clashes between Muslims and Buddhists, allegedly triggered by attacks on Buddhists but fanned by hardline Buddhist leaders. Then came a constitutional crisis, as Sirisena summarily fired Prime Minister Ranil Wickremasinghe, replacing him with former president Mahinda Rajapaksa. After public demonstrations, the courts intervened, eventually forcing the reinstatement of Wickremasinghe.

2008–2009

In the war's final months, up to 40,000 civilians are killed, according to a later report by a UN special panel. The Sri Lankan government denies any civilian deaths.

May 2009

After almost 30 years, Asia's longest-running war ends in May when the LTTE concedes defeat after a bloody last battle at Mullaittivu.

2013

The Commonwealth Heads of Government Meeting triggers protests against the the rule of President Mahinda Rajapaksa over human rights abuses. Three nations refuse to attend.

2015

In a shock result, Mahinda Rajapaksa loses his bid for reelection after his own party abandons him to protest his autocratic rule. His former lieutenant Maithripala Sirisena is elected president.

Violence from an Unexpected Quarter

The start of 2019 revealed a country on an upward trajectory, despite more political upsets, including the reintroduction of the death penalty and a national electricity crisis. But on Easter Sunday, 21 April, peace was shattered once again, as suicide bombers detonated devices in tourist hotels and churches full of Easter worshippers in Colombo, Negombo and Batticaloa.

A state of emergency was declared immediately as police combed the country for conspirators, but initial accusations against Tamils quickly evaporated as it emerged that the bombers were Islamist extremists allied to the Islamic State group, some from wealthy Sri Lankan Muslim families. The government soon found itself on the defensive, as evidence emerged that it had ignored warnings from foreign intelligence agencies about impending attacks.

At the same time, a backlash against Muslims gathered pace, with anti-Muslim riots in May 2019, and the resignation of all Muslim ministers from the government that June following protests by hardline Buddhist groups. The November 2019 election saw Sirisena dumped by voters in favour of former military officer Gotabaya Rajapaksa, brother of Mahinda Rajapaksa. The SLPP-led government promptly installed Mahinda Rajapaksa as prime minister, putting the two brothers in charge of the highest levers of state authority.

After the elections, Sri Lanka returned to a state of uneasy peace, reeling from the economic effects of plummeting visitor numbers. In the months after the attacks, tourist arrivals fell by as much as 30%, before slowly starting to recover at the end of the year. The country entered the new decade traumatised by the return of violence, and unsure how to process a new front in a previously two-sided history of communal conflict.

Hopes for an easier 2020 were quickly dashed. The global pandemic of Covid-19 saw the country close its borders, bringing tourism to an abrupt halt, and the 2020 parliamentary election concentrated even more power in the hands of allies of the Rajapaksa family. On the plus side, however, the lockdown was remarkably effective; the country has seen only a tiny fraction of the cases that have plagued neighbouring India, boding well for plans to reopen to visitors. Sri Lanka eased its borders to travellers in early 2021, with the requirement for a negative Covid test before travel, further tests on arrival, and a quarantine period at an approved hotel, except for those who are fully vaccinated.

2016

The UN releases a report detailing continued human rights abuses of the Tamil population. It cites murky quasi-military groups that continue to settle scores dating back to the war.

2018

Scattered acts of violence against Buddhists lead to anti-Muslim riots. The sudden replacement of Prime Minister Ranil Wickremasinghe by Mahinda Rajapaksa triggers a constitutional crisis.

21 April 2019

Suicide bombers linked to the Islamic State group attack churches and hotels in Colombo, Negombo and Batticaloa on Easter Sunday, killing 259 people.

16 November 2019

Gotabaya Rajapaksa – the brother of the prime minister – wins the 2019 presidential election, placing the two most important roles in Sri Lankan politics in the hands of one family.

Environmental Issues

At first glance, Sri Lanka looks like a verdant Garden of Eden (indeed, legend has the island as the first place visited by Adam after leaving the Biblical garden). But its rainforests, mangroves, beaches, waterways and plains are under threat due to a combination of rapid development, pollution, deforestation and human-wildlife conflict.

Pear-Shaped Treasure

Looking a little like a plump pear, the island of Sri Lanka floats in the Indian Ocean off the southern tip of India, to which it was joined by a land bridge until around 5000 BCE. At roughly 66,000 sq km, Sri Lanka is slightly smaller than Ireland, but home to 4.5 times as many people, squeezed into a space stretching 433km from north to south and only 244km at its widest point.

Soaring above the encircling coastal plains, the centre of the island is dominated by mountains and tea-plantation-covered hills, flattening out into broad plains to the north. The highest point is broad-backed Mt Pidurutalagala (Mt Pedro; 2524m), rising above the former colonial settlement of Nuwara Eliya. However, the pyramid profile of 2243m-high Adam's Peak (Sri Pada) is far more recognisable.

Hundreds of waterways channel abundant rain from the central wet zone down through terraced farmland, orchards and gardens to the paddy-rich plains below. The Mahaweli Ganga, Sri Lanka's longest river, has its source close to Adam's Peak and runs 335km to Koddiyar Bay, the deep-sea harbour of Trincomalee.

North of Kandy, the highlands change from high, rolling hills – and the dramatic landscapes of the Knuckles Range – to flat plains, comprising the so-called dry zone, where most of Sri Lanka's ancient cities are located.

Sri Lanka's coastline consists of hundreds of mangrove-fringed lagoons and marshes, interspersed with fine white-sand beaches, the most picturesque of which line the southwest, south and east coasts. A group of low, flat islands lies off the Jaffna peninsula in the north, off-limits during the civil war, but now opening up again to tourism.

Largest Surviving Tracts of Rainforest

Sri Pada Peak Wilderness Reserve (224 sq km)

Knuckles Range (175 sq km)

Sinharaja Forest Reserve (360 sq km)

Flora

The southwestern wet zone is home to the country's largest areas of surviving tropical rainforest, characterised by dense undergrowth and a tall canopy of hardwood trees, including ebony, teak and silkwood. The central hills are dominated by cloud forests and some unusual zones of hardy grassland and elfin (stunted) woodland.

Common trees across the country include banyan and bodhi trees (also known as *bo* or *peepu*, of religious significance to Hindus and Buddhists), and flame, rain, Ceylon ironwood and neem trees, each with easily recognisable leaves and flowers. In the Hill Country, towering eucalyptuses provide shade in tea estates. There are traditional medicinal or culinary uses for many Sri Lankan trees, including cinnamon, indigenous to the island and a major source of Sri Lanka's wealth in medieval times.

What Tree Is That? by Sriyanie Miththapala and PA Miththapala contains handy sketches of common trees and shrubs in Sri Lanka, and includes English, Sinhala and botanical names.

BIOLOGICAL HOT SPOT

Conservation International (www.conservation.org) has identified Sri Lanka as one of the planet's 25 biodiversity hot spots, which means the island is characterised by a very high level of 'endemism' (species unique to the area). Endemism is found in 23% of Sri Lankan flowering plants and 16% of mammals, but as with other hot spots around the world, habitats are seriously at risk due to human expansion and over-exploitation of resources.

Native fruit trees such as mangoes, tamarinds, wood apples and bananas grow widely, supplemented by introduced species like papayas and guavas. The jackfruit and its smaller relative, the *del* (breadfruit), will certainly catch your eye. The jackfruit tree produces the world's largest fruit, which can weigh up to 30kg and hangs close to the trunk rather than dangling from the branches.

Fauna

When it comes to animals, elephants are just one of a zoological garden's worth of exotic creatures in Sri Lanka. The island has a huge range of animals for such a small area. Where Africa has its famous 'Big Five' (lion, leopard, elephant, rhino and Cape buffalo), Sri Lanka has a 'Big Four' (leopard, elephant, sloth bear and wild Asiatic water buffalo), plus the ginormous blue whale found offshore. Then there are the island's birds – more than 500 species at the latest count. It all adds up to a wildlife spotter's paradise.

Save the Elephants

Never ride elephants; this can cause debilitating spinal injuries for the animals.

Avoid commercial centres where elephants are kept in chains.

Don't feed elephants in the wild or encourage drivers to crowd groups of wild elephants.

Do observe elephants from a safe distance in national parks to support conservation efforts.

Sri Lanka's Elephants

Elephants occupy a special place in Sri Lankan culture. In ancient times they were Crown property and killing one was a terrible offence. Legend has it that elephants stamped down the foundations of the dagobas (stupas) at Anuradhapura, and elephant iconography is a reoccuring theme in Sri Lankan temple art.

Even today elephants are the subject of great ritual devotion. Of those in captivity, the Maligawa tusker, which carries the sacred tooth relic for the Kandy Esala Perahera (p163), is perhaps the most venerated of all, though there is growing concern over the welfare of elephants used in religious rituals in Sri Lanka.

Although wild elephants are easily spotted in the island's national parks – particularly during 'the Gathering' from July to September in Minneriya National Park – Sri Lanka's elephant population has declined significantly, down to around 6000 animals today. The island has become known for its elephant orphanages, but some centres have been accused of exploiting elephants for commercial gain.

In recent years, animal welfare campaigners have also turned an unflattering spotlight on the treatment of the elephants used as temple guardians and in religious parades, after one elephant collapsed from exhaustion and another charged the crowds during the 2019 Kandy Esala Perahera.

Sri Lanka's strong conservation lobby has also firmly opposed the export of elephants as gifts to other nations. Nandi, a young elephant from Pinnewala (p155), was donated as a gift to Auckland Zoo by President Maithripala Sirisena, but protestors stopped the export in April 2017.

Dwindling Numbers

At the end of the 18th century an estimated 10,000 to 20,000 elephants roamed freely across Sri Lanka. By the mid-20th century human action had reduced the population to as few as 1000, clustered in the low-country dry zone. The British played a particularly brutal role through the expansion of big-game hunting. Experts disagree about whether the modern population is increasing or diminishing, but the present population is believed to consist of around 6000 wild elephants, half of which live on protected land, plus about 300 domesticated animals.

Human-Elephant Conflict

The origins of human-elephant conflict in Sri Lanka are easy to understand. Farmers in elephant country face an ever-present threat from elephants that eat and trample their crops, destroy their buildings and even take their lives. During the cultivation season, farmers maintain round-the-clock vigils for up to three months to scare off unwelcome raiders. For farmers on the breadline, close encounters with wild elephants are a luxury they can't afford.

Meanwhile, elephants, which need about 5 sq km of land each to support their 200kg-per-day appetites, are compelled to roam outside of protected areas to find food, forcing them into conflict with local farmers. It's a vicious cycle that leads to human lives being lost, and elephants being killed in revenge.

Attempts to keep the two sides apart have had mixed results. Electric fences installed around national parks to contain elephants prevent the animals seeking out neighbouring grasslands (their preferred diet) for grazing and disrupt natural migration patterns. This leads to elephants going hungry, and sometimes starving, according to the Born Free Foundation (www.bornfree.org.uk).

While the establishment of national parks and reserves has reduced the killing of wild elephants, in parks such as Uda Walawe, vendors have

RESPONSIBLE TRAVEL IN SRI LANKA

The best way to visit Sri Lanka responsibly is to be as minimally invasive as possible. This is, of course, easier than it sounds, but consider the following tips:

Demand green Sri Lanka's hotel and guesthouse owners are especially accommodating and, as visitor numbers soar, most are keen to give customers what they want. Share your environmental concerns and tell your hosts that their green practices – or lack thereof – are very important to you.

Watch your use of water Travel in the Hill Country of Sri Lanka and you'll think the island is coursing with water, but demand outstrips supply. Take up your hotel on its offer to save both money and water use by not having your sheets and towels changed every day.

Don't hit the bottle Those pre-filled bottles of purified water are convenient but the plastic rubbish they create mounts up and is a major blight. Many hotels have their own water treatment facilities or purified supplies, and can provide guests with refills if you bring your own water bottle.

Conserve power While loved by sun-blasted tourists, using air-con strains an already overloaded system. Try to save as much energy as possible; act as if you are paying your own electricity bill and turn off air-con, lights and fans whenever you leave your room.

Don't drive yourself crazy Can you take a bus or train, or even walk or cycle, instead of using a hired car? Using shared mass transport, walking or cycling will cut down your carbon footprint; many guesthouses offer bikes for guests.

Bag the bags Just say no to plastic bags (and plastic straws, too). If you see plastic rubbish in natural areas, pick it up, carry it out, and dispose of it where it can be properly handled in an urban area.

Elephant tourism Sri Lanka has several elephant camps of dubious conservational merit. Avoid anywhere that offers elephants walks using howdah. These magnificent mammals are definitely best seen in a national park.

ENDANGERED SPECIES

The International Union for Conservation of Nature's Red List of Threatened Species counts some 60 species in Sri Lanka as endangered or critically endangered. They include the Asian elephant, purple-faced langur, red slender loris and toque macaque. All five of Sri Lanka's marine turtle species are threatened, as are the estuarine crocodile and the mild-mannered dugong, all of which are killed for their meat.

While leopards and sloth bears can be spotted quite easily in Sri Lanka, their numbers are also declining. Also under threat are dozens of species of birds, fish and insects. Do your bit while in Sri Lanka by minimising your use of water and other resources, collecting litter for proper disposal, and encouraging tourism operators to try to reduce their impact on the natural environment.

set up fruit stands where the park borders the highway, so tourists can feed elephants. An increasing number of elephants now hang out all day by the roadside waiting for their tasty handouts, losing the inclination and ability to forage for their normal diet.

Possible Solutions

Some people are looking for long-term solutions to the conflict. One approach involves fencing humans in, rather fencing elephants out of human areas. This approach has been proven effective by the **Sri Lanka Wildlife Conservation Society** (SLWCS; ☎072 999 9520; www.slwcs.org; Udahamulla, Nugegoda), an award-winning wildlife conservation group.

The Nature of Sri Lanka, with stunning photographs by L Nadaraja, is a collection of essays about Sri Lanka by eminent writers and conservationists.

Other groups aim to provide farmers with alternative livelihoods and change land practices to accommodate wild elephant behaviour – for example, collecting elephant dung for the production of paper. Encouraging the cultivation of crops which elephants find unpalatable like chillies, citrus fruits and *thibbatu* (baby aubergines) has also proved a successful way to counter human-elephant conflict.

Deforestation & Overdevelopment

Sri Lanka's biggest environmental threat is almost certainly deforestation and human expansion, leading to serious habitat loss. At the beginning of the 20th century about 70% of the island was covered by natural forest. By 2005 this had shrunk to about 20%. In recent years Sri Lanka has had one of the highest recorded rates of primary-forest destruction in the world: an 18% reduction in forest cover and 35% loss of old-growth tracts.

Chena (shifting cultivation) is blamed for a good part of this deforestation, but irrigation schemes, clearance for cultivation and building, armed conflict and illegal logging have all been contributing factors. Along the coastline, beaches and mangroves are being polluted by waste water and sewerage from hotels and resorts, and in some cases destroyed to provide space and construction sand for resorts.

The boom in Sri Lanka's economy brought about by peace is bound to put even more pressure on the environment. With tourism increasing rapidly, new construction projects are proliferating, many ignoring rules put in place after the 2004 tsunami to prevent the construction of hotels and restaurants within 100m of the high-tide line.

The People of Sri Lanka

Sri Lanka is an amalgamation of different peoples, sharing one physical space. Buddhist families bring flowers to white-domed dagobas (stupas), Hindu women in bright saris take offerings to rainbow-coloured temples, Christians head to Sunday services and whitewashed mosques call the faithful to prayer. Despite Sri Lanka's decades of war and violence, for the most part people manage to peacefully coexist in daily life, a testament to the positive attitude of Sri Lankans from all communities.

Tradition & Ethnicity

Traditionally, Sri Lankan life was centred on the *gamma* (village), a highly organised hub of activity, where each member of the community fulfilled specific roles. Before the arrival of Buddhism and Hinduism, every village had its own protector deities associated with aspects of nature.

Veddahs

The Veddahs (Hunters), or Wanniyala-aetto (People of the Forest), are Sri Lanka's original inhabitants. Today their descendants are so few in number that they don't even make the census, and only a tiny percentage of those retain any semblance of their original hunter-gatherer lifestyle. The remaining Kele Weddo (jungle-dwelling Veddahs) and Can Weddo (village-dwelling Veddahs) live mainly in the area between Badulla, Batticaloa and Polonnaruwa.

To learn more about historical and contemporary Veddah life and customs, see www.vedda.org.

Sinhalese

The predominantly Buddhist Sinhalese, the majority on the island, sometimes divide themselves into 'low country' and 'high country' (ie Kandyan) communities. The Kandyan Sinhalese take fierce pride in the time when Kandy was the primary repository of Sinhalese Buddhist culture. Although the Buddha taught universalism, the Sinhalese have their own caste system, with everyone falling somewhere along the spectrum between aristocrat and itinerant entertainer.

Tamils

Most Tamils are Hindu and have cultural and religious connections with South Indian Tamils across the water, though they generally see themselves as a distinct group.

In fact, there are two Tamil communities in Sri Lanka. 'Jaffna Tamils' live mostly in the North and East and have been settled in Sri Lanka for many centuries. 'Plantation Tamils' on the other hand were brought by the British from India in the 19th century to work on tea farms.

As Hindus, Tamils regard caste as an important cultural characteristic. Jaffna Tamils are mainly of the Vellala caste (landlords and blue bloods), while Plantation Tamils mainly come from lower castes, which may explain a certain distance between the two groups. Though caste

In Hindu mythology elephants are seen as symbols of water, life and fortune. They also signify nobility and gentleness. In Sri Lanka, only the elephant is permitted to parade with sacred Buddhist relics and Hindu statues.

distinctions are gradually eroding, intermarriage between castes can be controversial and is often opposed in rural areas.

Moors

The island's Muslims – known locally as Sri Lankan Moors – are descendants of Arab or Indian traders who arrived around 1000 years ago. To escape Portuguese persecution, many moved into the Hill Country and the east coast, and you'll still see predominantly Muslim towns like Hakgala near Nuwara Eliya. Most Moors speak Tamil and follow the Sunni branch of Islam.

Multifaith Pilgrimages

- *Adam's Peak (Sri Pada)*
- *Kataragama*
- *Nainativu*

Burghers

The Burghers are mixed-race descendants of the Portuguese, Dutch and British. Even after independence, Burghers had a disproportionate influence over political and business life, and this small community still punches above its weight today. Look out for Dutch surnames containing double vowels, or the *tussenvoegsel* (prefix) van or de. Portuguese heritage or influence in Sri Lanka is evident through surnames such as Fernando, de Silva and Perera.

Religion

Religion has been the cause of much division in Sri Lanka, but Sri Lanka's many religions mix openly and amicably in day-to-day life. Buddhists, Hindus, Muslims and Christians visit many of the same pilgrimage sites, a Catholic may pay respect to a Hindu god, and Sri Lankan Buddhism has Hindu influences and vice versa.

Buddhism

Buddhism is the primary belief system of the Sinhalese and it plays a significant role in the country, spiritually, culturally and politically. Sri Lanka's literature, art and architecture are all strongly influenced by Buddhist precepts, though scriptures arguing for tolerance and the avoidance of violence have not always been followed.

In *Buddhism: Beliefs and Practices in Sri Lanka,* Lynn de Silva combines lucid writing, fascinating information and a scholarly (but accessible) approach to shed light on the island's Buddhist tradition.

Strictly speaking, Buddhism is not a religion but a practice and a moral code espoused by the Buddha. The Buddha taught meditation to people of various religions, and emphasised that no conversion was necessary (or even recommended) to benefit from his teachings, also known as the Dhamma.

Born Prince Siddhartha Gautama in what is today Nepal around 563 BCE, the Buddha abandoned his throne aged 29 after seeing human suffering for the first time, and pursued a life of severe austerity and inner reflection. After years of wandering, the Buddha discovered the Four Noble Truths: existence itself is suffering; suffering is caused by craving for sensual and material pleasures; the way out of suffering is through eliminating craving; and craving can be eliminated by following a path of morality and cultivating wisdom through meditation. After many states of spiritual development, nirvana (enlightenment, or *nibbana* in Pali) is achieved, bringing freedom from the cycle of birth and death.

Historical Buddhism

King Devanampiya Tissa's acceptance of the Buddha's teaching – brought to the island in the 3rd century BCE by the son of the proselytising Indian emperor Ashoka – firmly implanted Buddhism in Sri Lanka, and a strong relationship developed between Sri Lanka's kings and the Buddhist clergy, something mirrored in secular government today.

Worldwide there are two major schools of Buddhism: Theravada and Mahayana. Theravada (way of the elders) scriptures are in Pali, one of the languages spoken in North India in the Buddha's time, while Mahaya-

POYA DAYS

Poya (or *uposatha*) days fall on each full moon and are observed by both monks and laypeople as an occasion to strengthen personal Buddhist practice. Devout Buddhists visit a temple, fast after noon and abstain from entertainment and indulgences. *Poya* days are public holidays in Sri Lanka and each is associated with a particular ritual. Key dates to note are:

Duruthu (January) Marks the Buddha's first supposed visit to the island.

Vesak (May) Celebrates the Buddha's birth, enlightenment and *parinibbana* (final passing away).

Poson (June) Commemorates Buddhism's arrival in Sri Lanka.

Esala (July/August) Observes, among other things, the Buddha's first sermon, with a huge ceremonial procession in Kandy.

Unduvap (December) Celebrates the visit of Sangamitta, who brought the bodhi tree sapling to Anuradhapura.

na (greater vehicle) scriptures are in Sanskrit. Theravada is regarded as more orthodox, and Mahayana more inclusive.

Most Sri Lankan Buddhists are Sinhalese and follow the Theravada tradition, attaching vital meaning to the words of the Mahavamsa (Great Chronicle; one of their sacred texts), in which the Buddha designates them protectors of the Buddhist teachings. This commitment was fuelled by centuries of conflict between the Sinhalese (mainly Buddhist) and Tamils (mainly Hindu).

Many Buddhist sites in southern and central India were destroyed when Hinduism underwent a great resurgence in the 10th century CE and Hindu writers attempted to woo back Buddhists by declaring the Buddha an incarnation of Vishnu, adding to the sense amongst Sri Lankan Buddhists that their faith was under siege.

Buddhist Nationalism

Since the late 19th century an influential strand of 'militant' Buddhism has developed in Sri Lanka, centred on the belief that the Buddha charged the Sinhalese people with making the island a citadel of Buddhism. It sees threats to Sinhalese Buddhist culture in Christianity, Hinduism and, more recently, Islam. Sri Lankan Buddhism is historically intertwined with politics, and it was a Buddhist monk who assassinated Prime Minister SWRD Bandaranaike in 1959, in response to a perceived political 'drift' from a Sinhala-Buddhist focus.

Subsequent years have seen many incidents of violence against Tamil Hindus and Muslims, fanned by hardline clerics. In recent years, hardline attitudes have led to tourists being deported for having tattoos or wearing clothing depicting the Buddha. However, it's worth considering that the Sinhalese insistence that visitors respect their Buddhist beliefs is not so different from the codes of conduct expected of travellers in Muslim countries. No matter what the religion, respecting local values is the best way to ensure a trouble-free trip.

While Hinduism's myriad deities can be seen as different aspects of a smaller pool of divine entities, the faith is said to venerate some 330 million gods.

Hinduism

Tamil kings and their followers from South India brought Hinduism to northern Sri Lanka, although the religion may have existed on the island well before the arrival of Buddhism. Hindu communities are most concentrated in the north, the east and tea-plantation areas, where indentured workers were brought over from India by the British.

Hinduism is a complex mix of beliefs and gods. All Hindus believe in Brahman: the myriad deities are manifestations of this formless being, through which believers can understand all facets of life. Key tenets include belief in ahimsa (nonviolence) – often overlooked in a similar way to Buddhist teachings on violence – and samsara (the cycle of death and rebirth), as well as karma (the law of cause and effect) and Dhamma (moral code of behaviour or social duty).

Hindus believe that living life according to Dhamma improves the chance of being born into better circumstances. Humans can be reborn in animal form, but it's only as a human that one may gain sufficient self-knowledge to escape the cycle of reincarnation and achieve *moksha* (liberation).

For a deeper understanding of Hinduism, see www.bbc.co.uk/religion/religions/hinduism.

The Hindu pantheon is prolific: some estimates put the number of deities at 330 million. The main figures are Brahma, who created the universe, and his consort Saraswati, the goddess of wisdom and music; Vishnu, who sustains the universe and is lawful and devout, and his consort Lakshmi, the goddess of beauty and fortune; and Shiva, the destroyer of ignorance and evil, and his consort Parvati.

In the modern age Shiva, Vishnu and their associated consorts are the most revered deities, while Brahma – once the most important deity in Hinduism – has been demoted to a minor figure.

Islam

Sri Lanka is home to almost two million Muslims – many of whom are descendants of Arab traders who settled on the island from the 7th century, not long after Islam was founded in present-day Saudi Arabia by the Prophet Mohammed. Islam is monotheistic, and avows that everything has been created by Allah. The Quran is taken to be the literal word of God, as imparted to Mohammed by Allah.

After Mohammed's death the movement split into two main branches, the Sunnis and the Shiites. Sunnis emphasise following and imitating the words and acts of the Prophet. They look to tradition and the majority views of the community. Shiites believe that only imams (exemplary leaders) can reveal the meaning of the Quran. Most of Sri Lanka's Muslims are Sunnis, although small communities of Shiites have migrated from India.

All Muslims believe in the five pillars of Islam: the shahada (declaration of faith: 'there is no God but Allah; Mohammed is his prophet'); prayer (ideally five times a day); the zakat (tax, usually a donation to charity); fasting during the month of Ramadan; and the hajj (pilgrimage) to Mecca.

Most Sacred Sites

- *Nallur Kandaswamy Kovil, Jaffna*
- *Temple of the Sacred Tooth Relic, Kandy*
- *Kechimalai Mosque, Beruwela*
- *Our Lady of Madhu Church, Madhu*
- *City of Anuradhapura*

Christianity

Christianity in Sri Lanka potentially goes back to the time of the Apostle Thomas, who is said to have sailed to South India in the 1st century CE. It's certain that in the early centuries CE small numbers of Christians established settlements along the coast.

With the arrival of the Portuguese in the 16th century, Roman Catholicism arrived in force, and many fishing families converted. Today, Catholicism remains strong among western coastal communities, in areas such as Negombo.

The Dutch brought Protestantism and the Dutch Reformed Church, mainly present in Colombo, while the British left their own stone churches across the Hill Country. Often marginalised by Buddhists, Hindus and Muslims alike, Sri Lanka's Christian community was the main target for the Easter bombings in 2019.

Sri Lankan Tea

The Dutch may have come to Sri Lanka in search of its native cinnamon, but the country is best known for an imported plant – tea, introduced by the British. Today, Sri Lanka is among the world's top tea-producing nations and Ceylon tea is perhaps the country's most powerful, internationally recognised brand.

Shaping the Nation

Tea was introduced into Sri Lanka after leaf blight decimated the island's coffee plantations in the 19th century. The very first Sri Lanka–grown tea was produced in 1867 at the Loolecondera Estate, southeast of Kandy, but rival tea estates soon sprung up across the central highlands.

Shipments of Ceylon tea started flowing into London warehouses in the 1870s, and fortunes were made by the early growers, which included a name still famous worldwide today: Thomas Lipton. By the 1890s, Lipton's tea plantations were exporting around 30,000 tonnes of tea annually.

Today Sri Lanka is the world's fourth-biggest tea-producing nation, with 304 million kg yielded in 2018. Sri Lankan tea (branded internationally as 'Ceylon' tea) enjoys a premium positioning and income from tea exports topped US$1.43 billion in 2018.

Tea plantations cover about 1900 sq km of Sri Lanka's land surface, primarily in the southern part of the Hill Country.

Quality

The many varieties of tea are graded by size (from cheap 'dust' through small pieces known as fannings and broken grades to premium 'leaf' teas) and by quality. Whole leaves are best and the tips (the youngest and most delicate tea leaves) are the very top tier.

The name pekoe is given to superior grades of black tea, with the top grades designated as 'orange pekoe' for reasons that are lost to history, but may relate to the Dutch house of Orange-Nassau, who popularised tea across Europe. However, the white tea known as Ceylon silver tips is the most expensive Sri Lankan tea, selling for as much as US$1500 per kilo.

Altitude is another strong indicator of tea quality. Udawatte (high-grown tea, cultivated near Dimbula, Nuwara Eliya and Uva) is considered the finest quality, while Medawatte (mid-grown tea) from around Kandy is less refined. Yatawatte (low-grown tea) is grown in the foothills around Ratnapura and Galle, and often used to make sweetened milk tea.

When Thomas Lipton took his tea company public in 1898, he raised the equivalent of US$3 billion in today's money, earning himself US$1.2 billion in the process.

Cultivation

Tea bushes are typically planted a metre or so apart on contoured terraces to help irrigation, interspersed with taller trees to provide limited shade. Tea bushes are regularly pruned to encourage new shoots, prevent flowering and fruit formation and maximise leaf production.

Tea leaves are plucked by hand every seven to 14 days, a task traditionally carried out by women from Sri Lanka's so-called 'Plantation Tamil' community for very low wages, as little as Rs 700 per day. After plucking, the tea leaves are taken to a factory where they are left to wither (demoisturised by blowing air at a fixed temperature through them).

Colombo is the world's largest auction centre for tea, shifting 5.5 million kilos per week.

STAYING ON A TEA PLANTATION

Many tea planters' and estate managers' cottages have been turned into guesthouses or villas for rent, offering an atmospheric taste of those times. Pull up a planters' chair (a rattan recliner with two fold-out supports for your feet) at one of the following:

Heritance Tea Factory (p184), Nuwara Eliya

St Andrew's Hotel (p184), Nuwara Eliya

Bandarawela Hotel (☎057-222 2501; www.aitkenspencehotels.com; 14 Welimada Rd; s/d/ste incl breakfast US$71/84/101;), Bandarawela

Tea Trails (p176), Adam's Peak

Madulkelle Tea & Ecolodge (p174), near Kandy

98 Acres Resort (Map p197; ☎057-205 0050; www.resort98acres.com; Uva Greenland Tea Estate; s/d incl breakfast from US$195/205;), Ella

Kelburne Mountain View (p192), Haputale

The partly dried leaves are then crushed, starting a fermentation process, which is stopped at the right moment by 'firing' the tea at an even higher heat to produce a dry, stable leaf. Finally the tea is separated and graded. It takes only 24 hours from picking until tea is loaded into bags for shipment.

Visiting a Tea Plantation

Tea factories and plantations throughout the Hill Country offer tours to explain the process, usually using machinery and technology that have largely remained unchanged since the 19th century. Most places also offer a chance to taste and buy the estate tea. See if the estate will let you take a walk amongst the tea bushes to see the picking process close up.

Recommended Tea Plantations & Factories

There are plantations across the Hill Country. Some of our favourite places to get up close and smell the tea include the following:

Ceylon Tea Museum (p168) Near Kandy. An informative early stop in your tea tour.

Handunugoda Tea Estate (p127) Near Koggala. Produces over 25 varieties of tea, including many rare varieties.

Pedro Tea Estate (p183) Near Nuwara Eliya. Has tours of the factory, which was originally built in 1885.

Dambatenne Tea Factory (p189) Near Haputale. Built by Sir Thomas Lipton in 1890 and offers good tours.

Damro Labookellie Tea Factory (p179) A factory well positioned by the Nuwara Eliya road; handy if you're in a hurry.

Buying Tea

The tea factories and plantations in the Hill Country have a bewildering array of teas on offer. Specialist tea stores, including the state-run Sri Lanka Tea Board Shop (p86) in Colombo, carry an incredible range of teas, many beautifully packaged in ornamental tins ready for transport. You'll find tea sold almost anywhere tourists gather.

Ceylon black tea is the best known and is famous for its citrusy taste, but it's worth paying extra for leaf grades rather than broken, fannings or dust teas. As well as black teas, look out for green teas, and expensive silver tips, produced from very young buds that are silvery white.

Survival Guide

Directory A–Z

PRACTICALITIES

Digital For news, try www.hirunews.lk; for features and eating listings, try www.yamu.lk.

Newspapers *Daily Mirror* (www.dailymirror.lk) has regularly updated news online and in print.

TV Government-run stations dominate, most in Sinhala or Tamil. More expensive hotels have satellite TV.

Smoking Smoking is banned on buses, trains and in public places.

Weights & Measures The metric system is used, but distances are sometimes in miles. The term *lakh* is often used in place of '100,000', while *koatiya* or *koti* is 10 million.

Accessible Travel

Rough roads and pavements can be difficult for those in a wheelchair and for the visually impaired. Few hotels have rooms specifically set up for wheelchair users, but many have ground-floor rooms. Buses and trains don't have facilities for wheelchairs, but hiring a car and driver may be an option.

Accessible travel specialists such as Disabled Holidays (www.disabledholidays.com) offer supported trips to Sri Lanka. Download Lonely Planet's free Accessible Travel guide from https://shop.lonelyplanet.com/products/accessible-travel-online-resources-2019.

Accommodation

Sri Lanka has a wide range of accommodation, from simple rooms in family homes to lavish five-star resorts. Rates are very seasonal, particularly at beach resorts; inquire about discounts in the low season. The high season is December to April on the west and south coasts, and April to September on the east coast.

Most hotels, guesthouses and hostels accept bookings through sites like www.agoda.com and www.booking.com, however there are reports of some hotels refusing to honor prepaid reservations; it may be better to book directly with hotels.

Some midrange and top-end hotels quote room prices in US dollars or euros, but accept the current rupee equivalent. Note that a service charge of 10% will usually be added to the rate you're quoted; some places add VAT and other local taxes of up to 15%.

BOOK YOUR STAY ONLINE

For more accommodation reviews by Lonely Planet authors, check out www.lonelyplanet.com. You'll find independent reviews, as well as recommendations on the best places to stay.

Customs Regulations

Sri Lanka Customs (www.customs.gov.lk) has the usual list of prohibited imports, including drugs, weapons, fresh fruit and anything remotely pornographic. Note that possession of drugs can carry a life sentence in Sri Lanka.

Items allowed:

- 0.25L of perfume
- 2.5L of alcohol.

Electricity

The electric current is 230V, 50 Hz. Local sockets are similar to Indian sockets, taking plugs with two small round pins and one large round pin; you may also find US-, EU- and British-style plugs in your room. Adaptors are readily available.

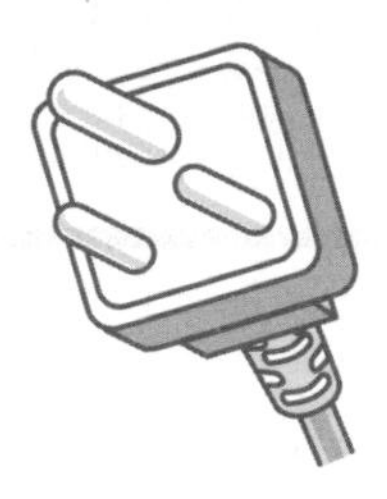

Type D
230V/50Hz

Embassies & Consulates

Your embassy can't help if you break the law, other than put you in touch with a lawyer, but may be of help in a political crisis or natural disaster. The following embassies are in Colombo:

Australian High Commission (Map p70; 011-246 3200; www.srilanka.embassy.gov.au; 21 RG Senanayake Mw/Gregory's Rd, Col 7; 9.30am-4pm Mon-Fri)

Canadian High Commission (Map p70; 011-522 6232; www.canadainternational.gc.ca/sri_lanka; 33A 5th Lane, Col 3; 8.30am-noon & 1-4pm Mon-Thu, 8.30am-noon Fri)

French Embassy (Map p70; 011-263 9400; www.lk.ambafrance.org; 89 Rosmead Pl, Col 7; 8.30am-1pm & 2.30-6pm Mon-Thu, 8.30am-1pm Fri)

German Embassy (Map p70; 011-258 0431; www.colombo.diplo.de; 40 Alfred House Ave, Col 3; Mon-Fri by appointment only)

India Visa Office (Map p70; 011-255 9435; www.ivsvisalanka.com; 129 Phillip Gunawardena Mw, Col 4; 9am-1pm Mon-Fri)

Indian High Commission (Map p70; 011-232 7587; www.hcicolombo.gov.in; 36-38 Galle Rd, Col 3; 9am-5.30pm Mon-Fri)

Netherlands Embassy (Map p70; 011-251 0200; www.nederlandwereldwijd.nl/landen/sri-lanka; 25 Torrington Ave, Col 7; 8.30am-5pm Mon-Thu, 8.30am-2pm Fri)

UK High Commission (Map p70; 011-539 0639; www.gov.uk/government/world/organisations/british-high-commission-colombo; 389 Bauddhaloka Mw; 8am-4.30pm Mon-Thu, 8am-1pm Fri)

US Embassy (Map p70; 011-249 8500; https://lk.usembassy.gov; 210 Galle Rd, Col 3; 8am-4.30pm Mon-Thu, 8am-noon Fri)

EATING PRICE RANGES

The following price ranges refer to a standard main course.

$ less than Rs 350

$$ Rs 350–800

$$$ more than Rs 800

Food & Drink

Sri Lanka has a glorious cuisine and wide range of places to eat. Book in advance for high-end restaurants.

Restaurants Found in larger towns and beach resorts, and usually offer alcohol.

Hotels Actually basic local eateries, serving no-nonsense local grub at affordable prices.

Cafes Found in cities and beach resorts; serve sandwiches and snacks.

Bakeries Offer 'short eats': local meat- and fish-filled pastries etc.

See Eat & Drink Like a Local (p35) for more information.

Gay & Lesbian Travellers

Same-sex sexual activity is illegal in Sri Lanka, though no one has been convicted for over 60 years. It pays to be discreet considering increasing conservatism on the island. Colombo has a small, very low-key gay scene.

Equal Ground (011-280 6184; www.equal-ground.org) is a Colombo-based organisation that supports gay and lesbian rights and has useful online resources.

Insurance

Travel insurance is a must for Sri Lanka – keep emergency numbers handy. Worldwide travel insurance is available at www.lonelyplanet.com/travel-insurance. You can buy, extend and claim online anytime – even if you're already on the road.

Internet Access

Wi-fi is the norm in hotels, guesthouses, hostels, cafes and restaurants and few travellers make use of internet cafes. Mobile data is reasonably quick (at least 3G speeds) in larger towns and all cities; you may get no signal in rural areas.

Legal Matters

Sri Lanka's legal system is a complex, almost arcane mix of British, Roman-Dutch and local laws and regulations. The tourist police in major towns and tourist hot spots can help with minor matters such as theft. Stay away from drugs; the penalties, even for possession, are severe.

Note that travellers have been deported from Sri Lanka for having tattoos or wearing clothes depicting the Buddha, regarded as disrespectful to Sri Lankan culture.

Money

ATMs and foreign exchange facilities are found in most settlements.

ATMs

ATMs are easily found in towns and cities of any size but issue large bills; break large notes down quickly. Bank of Ceylon ATMs do not charge a fee for foreign cards.

Cash

Any bank or exchange bureau will change major currencies in cash, including US dollars, Euros and British pounds. Change rupees back into hard currency at the airport before security; they're rarely accepted outside Sri Lanka. Travellers cheques are not widely accepted.

Credit & Debit Cards

MasterCard and Visa are commonly accepted at midrange and top-end hotels and some tourist shops.

Currency

The Sri Lankan currency is the rupee (Rs), which is divided into 100 cents. Rupee coins come in denominations of one, two, five and 10 rupees. Notes come in denominations of 10, 20, 50, 100, 200, 500, 1000, 2000 and 5000 rupees.

Money Changers

Money changers can be found in Colombo and all major tourist centres. Their rates are competitive, but be wary of scams. Banks are safer and more reliable.

Taxes & Refunds

The VAT (value added tax) in Sri Lanka was cut from 15% to 8% in December 2019. Most places quote prices including VAT where it applies. There is no tourist refund scheme for VAT.

Opening Hours

Apart from in tourist areas, many businesses are closed on Sunday.

Bars Usually close by midnight; last call is often 11pm

Restaurants and cafes 8am to 9pm daily, later in areas popular with travellers

Shops 10am to 7pm Monday to Friday, 10am to 3pm Saturday

Shops and services catering to visitors 9am to 8pm

Photography

- Ask permission before taking photos of local people, and never photograph dams, airports or anything associated with the police or military.
- Never pose beside or in front of a statue of the Buddha (ie with your back to it).
- Flash photography can damage frescoes and murals; observe the restrictions at historic sites.

LOCAL & TOURIST PRICES

Sri Lanka operates a system of different entry prices to sights and attractions for visitors and locals. Tourists tend to pay much higher rates for entry than Sri Lankans, while the fees paid by travellers from SAARC countries fall somewhere in the middle.

Post

Sri Lanka Post (www.slpost.gov.lk) has offices in most towns and cities. Service to the outside world is inexpensive but slow; see the website for rules and regulations.

Public Holidays

With four major religions, Sri Lanka has a lot of public holidays, many moving from year to year with the Lunar calendar. See Month by Month (p26) for more information. Also, all *poya* (full moon) days are public holidays and many businesses close. Key public holidays include the following:

New Year's Day 1 January

Tamil Thai Pongal Day 15 January (depending on the moon)

Independence Day 4 February

Good Friday March/April

Sinhala and Tamil New Year 13 April (but can vary by a few days)

Labour Day 1 May

Id ul-Fitr Marks the end of Ramadan. Date varies with the lunar calendar.

Christmas Day 25 December

Safe Travel

Despite the end of civil war, communal riots and terrorism are ongoing risks; monitor government warnings and the local press. In the event of a natural disaster or political unrest, stay away from crowds and avoid affected areas.

Telephone

There is good mobile phone (and 4G data) coverage all over Sri Lanka.

Mobile Phone Companies

Mobile coverage is good across Sri Lanka and phone companies have desks in the arrivals hall at Colombo airport offering tourist SIMs with a one-month duration. Data and voice packages start from Rs 500. Major providers include the following:

Dialog (www.dialog.lk)

Hutch (www.hutch.lk)

Mobitel (www.mobitel.lk)

Time

Sri Lanka Standard Time (GMT/UTC + 5½ hours) is the same as India Standard Time. There is no summer/daylight savings time. Sri Lanka is 4½ hours behind Australian EST and 10½ hours ahead of American EST.

Toilets

- All top-end and midrange hotels and guesthouses have sit-down flush toilets. Squat toilets are only found in the cheapest places.
- Public toilets are scarce (and are usually grim); use facilities in restaurants, hotel lobbies and at tourist attractions (carry your own paper).

Tourist Information

Sri Lanka Tourist Board (SLTB; Map p70; ☎011-242 8600; www.srilanka.travel; 80 Galle Rd, Col 3; ⏲8am-9pm) The Colombo main office has useful glossy brochures and maps, and its website has useful country-wide information.

Visas

Most tourists travel with an Electronic Travel Authorisation (ETA), obtained online before visiting at www.eta.gov.lk. It costs US$35 to US$40 for a 30-day visit, depending on your nationality. Two-day transit visas are free. Sri Lankan missions overseas offer visas for longer stays.

GOVERNMENT TRAVEL ADVICE

Government travel warnings may have implications for your travel insurance, so monitor the following sites:

Australia (www.smartraveller.gov.au)

Canada (www.travel.gc.ca)

Japan (www.mofa.go.jp/region/index.html)

New Zealand (www.safetravel.govt.nz)

UK (www.gov.uk/foreign-travel-advice)

US (www.travel.state.gov)

Obtaining a Visa

Before visiting Sri Lanka, do the following to get a 30-day visa:

- Visit the Sri Lanka electronic visa website (www.eta.gov.lk) around a week before arriving.
- Follow the online application process and pay with a credit or debit card.
- Once approved, print out the visa confirmation to show immigration officials on arrival.

You can also obtain visas at Sri Lankan embassies abroad and there is a counter at Bandaranaike International Airport offering visas on arrival for a higher fee of US$40.

Visa Extensions

You can renew a 30-day tourist visa twice, for 30 days each time, to a total of 90 days (providing your passport is valid for at least two months after the end of the 90 days). Contact the **Department of Immigration and Emigration** (☎011-532 9000; www.immigration.gov.lk; Sri Subuthipura Dr, Battaramulla; ⏲8.30am-4.15pm). The process involves jumping through some bureaucratic hoops, paying a fee, and downloading some forms; to complete the process in one day, arrive at the office by 10am and expect it to take at least four hours.

Women Travellers

Sri Lanka has quite conservative attitudes and women travelling alone may experience uncomfortable levels of male attention. Outside Colombo, it is a good idea to cover your legs and shoulders. Away from the popular tourist beaches of the South and West, or in smaller, less touristy places, consider swimming in a T-shirt and shorts.

Women travelling alone can experience being followed day and night. Physical harassment (grabbing and groping) is not uncommon, particularly in crowds, and solo women have been attacked by guides and drivers. The best policy is to travel with at least one other companion.

Most medical products needed by women are easy to find, but stock up on tampons as they can be very hard to find.

Work

The only foreigners who normally work in the country are hired for specific roles by companies ready to deal with the significant bureaucratic hurdles in place when hiring a foreign national.

Transport

GETTING THERE & AWAY

Air links to Sri Lanka become more extensive each year, but despite regular discussions between India and Sri Lanka, there are currently no sea routes to the island.

Flights, cars and tours can be booked online at lonelyplanet.com/bookings.

Entering the Country

Immigration at Bandaranaike International Airport is straightforward, particularly if you have arranged your Electronic Travel Authorisation (ETA) before arrival.

Passport

You must have your passport with you at all times in Sri Lanka. Before leaving home, check that it will be valid for at least six months after you plan to leave Sri Lanka, and apply for an ETA at least a week before travel at www.eta.gov.lk.

Air

Almost all visitors to Sri Lanka arrive by air.

Airports

On paper, Sri Lanka has three international airports, but in practice, almost all airlines fly into Bandaranaike International Airport, a few domestic flights serve Colombo International Airport Ratmalana and almost no one uses Mattala Rajapaksa International Airport.

INTERNATIONAL AIRPORTS

Sri Lanka's main international airport is **Bandaranaike International Airport** (CMB; ☎011-226 4444; www.airport.lk), at Katunayake, 30km north of Colombo. There are 24-hour money-changing facilities in the arrivals and departures halls as well as ATMs, mobile-phone SIM card vendors, taxi services and more. Arriving is fairly hassle-free as touts are mostly kept away from the arrivals area.

The airport is the hub for the national carrier, **SriLankan Airlines** (☎011-777 1979; www.srilankan.com; World Trade Centre, Bank of Ceylon Mw, Col 1; ⌚8.30am-5pm), which operates an extensive network to Asia and the Middle East. It has a safety record on par with other international carriers. Local connections are provided by seaplane and turboprop on **Cinnamon Air** (Map p64; ☎011-247 5475; www.cinnamonair.com; 2nd fl, 11 York St, Col 1; ⌚8.30am-5pm Mon-Fri) and a few other small carriers.

Airlines Flying to/from Sri Lanka

Bandaranaike International Airport is a busy air hub. National carrier SriLankan Air-

CLIMATE CHANGE & TRAVEL

Every form of transport that relies on carbon-based fuel generates CO_2, the main cause of human-induced climate change. Modern travel is dependent on aeroplanes, which might use less fuel per kilometre per person than most cars but travel much greater distances. The altitude at which aircraft emit gases (including CO_2) and particles also contributes to their climate change impact. Many websites offer 'carbon calculators' that allow people to estimate the carbon emissions generated by their journey and, for those who wish to do so, to offset the impact of the greenhouse gases emitted with contributions to portfolios of climate-friendly initiatives throughout the world. Lonely Planet offsets the carbon footprint of all staff and author travel.

lines has regular direct flights from destinations across South and Southeast Asia, and long-haul routes to London and Melbourne. Flights from other destinations usually involve a change in the Middle East, China, India or Southeast Asia.

Budget carrier **Air Asia** (www.airasia.com) flies into Sri Lanka from Kuala Lumpur, offering one potential cheap route in if coming from Australia. Several Gulf state airlines serve Sri Lanka and the Maldives on the same flight route, making it easy to combine the two destinations on one trip.

MATTALA RAJAPAKSA INTERNATIONAL AIRPORT

Mattala Rajapaksa International Airport (www.airport.lk/mria) is 15km north of Hambantota near the south coast. A notorious white elephant, it is used by occasional charter flights and the odd domestic service, but at the present time there are no scheduled international flights. The large terminal is shiny, but there are few services or amenities. If you are flying in, be sure to have transportation arranged in advance.

Sea

It is not currently possible to travel to Sri Lanka by sea, but plans are afoot for a sea link between Kankasanthurai near Jaffna and either Karaikal or Sidambaranagar in India's Tamil Nadu. A second stage may see a resumed service between between Talaimannar (on Mannar Island) and Rameswaram in Tamil Nadu.

GETTING AROUND

Some useful points to consider when getting around Sri Lanka:

- There are limited domestic flights, but distances by road are not vast and new expressways are shrinking travel times.
- Travelling on public transport is a choice between buses and trains: both are cheap. Trains can be crowded, but it's nothing compared with the huge number of passengers that squash into ordinary buses. Standing on a train is better than standing on a bus.
- On the main roads from Colombo to Kandy, Negombo and Galle, buses cover around 40km to 50km per hour. On highways across the plains and to the North, it can be 60km or 70km an hour. In the Hill Country, this can slow to just 20km an hour.
- All public transport gets crowded around *poya* (full moon) holidays and their nearest weekends, so try to avoid travelling then.

Air

Bandaranaike International Airport (CMB; ☎011-226 4444; www.airport.lk; Katunayake) has connecting domestic flights provided by **Cinnamon Air** (Map p64; ☎011-247 5475; www.cinnamonair.com; 2nd fl, 11 York St, Col 1; ⏲8.30am-5pm Mon-Fri), which operates a second hub in Kandy. Expensive flights by turboprop and seaplane serve destinations such as Batticaloa, Dikwella, Sigiriya and Trincomalee. It also offers charter flights to points around the country at fares starting from US$1800.

A handful of charter airlines operate out of tiny **Colombo International Airport Ratmalana** (☎011-262 3030; www.airport.lk/rma; Ratmalana), set on an airforce base 15km south of Colombo. Tiny **FitsAir** (☎011-255 5158; www.fitsair.com) flies from Colombo to Jaffna and Batticaloa.

Bicycle

With the heavy traffic on roads in Sri Lanka, long-distance cycling is best in the North and East, where roads are quieter. Cycling around historic areas such as Anuradhapura and Sigiriya is the best way to see these important sites; guesthouses rent out bikes to guests.

Hire

Cheap, Chinese and Indian-made mountain bikes make up most of the rentals you'll find in guesthouses and hotels. Rates average about Rs 500 per day.

- If your accommodation doesn't hire bikes, it can usually put you in touch with with someone who does.
- Bikes available for day use typically are not suitable for long-distance riding.
- Bike-rental shops offering quality long-distance machines are rare. Consider bringing your bike from home if you plan on serious cycle touring.

Bike Tours

Tour and outfitting companies organise cycling tours of Sri Lanka and may also help you get organised for independent travel. Some operators are:

Eco Team (Map p70; ☎070-222 8222; www.srilankaecotourism.com; 20/63 Fairfield Gardens; ⏲8.30am-5.30pm)

SpiceRoads Cycle Tours (☎in Thailand +66 89 895 5680; www.spiceroads.com)

Srilanka Bicycle Trips (☎071-419 1187; www.srilankabicycletrips.com)

DEPARTURE TAX

Departure tax is included in the ticket price for international flights to and from Sri Lanka.

Long-Distance Cycling

➡ Long-distance cyclists will find easy conditions on the coastal plain, once they escape the traffic chaos of Colombo. When heading out of Colombo in any direction, take a train to the edge of the city before you start cycling.

➡ Start early in the day to avoid the heat, and carry water and sunscreen. Daily distances will be limited by the roads and driving conditions; be prepared for lots of prudent 'eyes down' cycling as you negotiate a flurry of obstacles from potholes to chickens. Speeding buses, trucks and cars use all parts of the roadway and shoulder, so be cautious and wear visible clothing, and pull over to let large vehicles pass.

➡ If you bring your own bicycle, also pack a supply of spare tyres and tubes, as replacement parts for foreign bikes can be hard to obtain, though a few shops in Colombo carry imported parts. The normal bicycle tyre size in Sri Lanka is 28in by 1.5in. Keep an eye on your bicycle at all times and use a good lock.

➡ When taking a bicycle on a train, there are forms to fill out, so arrive early, at least an hour before departure (more in Colombo). Bikes are transported as cargo and not every train will take bikes, so check in advance. It costs about twice the 2nd-class fare to take a bicycle on a train.

Boat

With the exception of small ferries used to reach the islands southwest of Jaffna, there are no regular ferry services of note in Sri Lanka.

Bus

Bus routes cover about 80% of the nation's 90,000km of roads. There are two kinds of bus in Sri Lanka:

Sri Lanka Transport Board (SLTB) buses These red-painted, government-run rattletraps are the default buses and usually lack air-con. However, inexpensive and frequent services run through the day on most long-distance and local routes.

Private buses Independent bus companies have vehicles ranging from modern air-conditioned coaches to ancient minibuses used for short hops between towns and villages. Private air-con intercity routes often use smaller buses that can zip through traffic, so are faster and more comfortable than standard private and government buses.

General Tips

Bus travel in Sri Lanka provides some rewarding opportunities to interact with locals. Many Sri Lankans speak some English, so you may have some enjoyable conversations. Vendors board to sell snacks and gifts on long-distance routes.

Important considerations for bus travel:

➡ Buses on major routes run several times an hour during daylight hours.

➡ Finding the right bus at the chaotic bus stations of major cities and towns can be challenging, although almost all buses now have part of their destination sign in English.

➡ Many buses operate on fixed routes with a route number, which makes it easier to locate the correct bus. However not all buses run the length of the route, so check the destination.

➡ There is usually no central ticket office; you must locate the right parking area and buy your bus ticket either from a small booth or on board the bus.

➡ You may be able to reserve a seat on a bus in advance; check at the station to see if there's a reservation desk.

➡ 'Semi-comfortable' (or 'semi-luxe') buses are run by private companies and have larger seats and window curtains, but lack the air-con of the best intercity buses.

➡ Luggage space is limited or nonexistent; you may have to buy a ticket for your bag.

➡ The first two seats on government buses are reserved for clergy (Buddhist monks).

➡ To guarantee a seat, board the bus at the beginning of its journey.

➡ When you arrive at your destination, confirm the departure details for the next stage of your journey.

Costs

In most cases, private bus companies run similar ordinary (non-air-con) bus services to the government bus company, for similarly low fares. Air-conditioned express buses cost around twice as much as SLTB buses, but are more than twice as comfortable and usually faster. There are also some large air-conditioned buses plying long-distance routes, with such luxuries as reclining seats.

Car & Motorcycle

Self-drive car hire is possible in Sri Lanka, though it is far more common (and almost certainly safer) to hire a car and driver. If you're on a relatively short visit to Sri Lanka on a midrange budget, the costs of hiring a car and driver can be quite reasonable. If you do want to drive yourself, hire companies are based at Bandaranaike International Airport.

Motorcycling is an alternative for intrepid travellers. Distances are relatively short and some of the roads are a motorcyclist's delight; the trick is to stay off the main highways. The quieter Hill Country roads offer some glorious views, and secondary roads along the coast and the plains are reasonably quick. Motorcycle and moped rental is nowhere near as commonplace as in countries such as India and Thailand, but it's easy to arrange at most resorts on the coast, with rates starting from Rs 1000 per day.

Hiring a Car & Driver

Hiring a car and a driver guarantees maximum flexibility in your travels, and while the driver deals with the chaotic roads, you can look out the window and relax, or at least try to! When planning your itinerary, you can count on covering about 35km/h in the Hill Country and 55km/h in most of the rest of the country.

You can find taxi drivers who will happily become your chauffeur for a day or more in all the main tourist centres, either through local travel agencies, or through guesthouses and hotels.

Recommended companies with drivers include the following, or ask for recommendations on the Lonely Planet Thorn Tree forum.

Ancient Lanka (☎077-727 2780; www.ancientlanka.com)

Let's Go Lanka (☎077-630 2070; www.letsgolanka.com; Giritale)

COSTS

Various formulas exist for setting costs. Some companies offer rates per kilometre plus a lunch and dinner (and accommodation if necessary) allowance for the driver and separate fuel payments. Some companies expect drivers to stay in the cheap driver accommodation provided by some hotels, but the quality varies widely and this can lead to drivers making accommodation plans on your behalf based on what works best for them (often involving a commission, which will be added to your room rate).

The simplest policy is to agree on an all-inclusive flat fee with no extras, giving you more control over the process. Expect to pay US$65 to US$75 per day, or more for a newer air-con vehicle. Other considerations:

- Most drivers will expect a tip of about 10%.
- Meet the driver first as you may sense bad chemistry.
- Consider hiring a driver for only two or three days at first to see if you fit.
- You are the boss. It's great to get recommendations from a driver, but don't be bullied. Drivers are known to dissuade travellers from visiting temples and other sights where there are no commissions.
- Unless the driver speaks absolutely no English, a guide in addition to the driver is unnecessary.

Self-Drive Hire

Colombo-based company **Shineway Rent a Car** (☎071 278 9323; www.rentalcarsri-lanka.com; 45/15 Nawala Rd, Narahenpita, Col 5) offers self-drive car hire, or there are big international operators based at Bandaranaike International Airport. You'll find local firms in most tourist towns. You can usually hire a car for about US$30 per day with 100km of included kilometres, but it's rare to see visitors driving themselves in Sri Lanka.

Working with local three-wheeler owners, **Tuk-tuk Rental** (☎077-292 8618; www.tuktukrental.com) and Negombo-based **Ceylon**

SRI LANKA'S NEW HIGHWAYS

Various new expressways have opened up in recent years, with more on the way. Most will be toll roads, with relatively cheap tolls.

Colombo–Katunayake Expressway Greatly reducing travel time between Bandaranaike International Airport and the city. Starting 4km northeast of Fort at Kelani Bridge, the expressway will get you to the airport in 30 minutes. Unfortunately, during the day the city streets remain as congested as ever between Fort and Kelani Bridge.

Outer Circular Expressway Completed in 2017, this belt road runs through the far eastern suburbs of Colombo. It links the Southern Expressway to the Katunayake Expressway, which means you can drive from the airport to Galle in well under three hours.

Southern Expressway The first new expressway completed. It is 161km long and runs from Colombo's southern suburb of Kottawa, near Maharagama, to Matara via an exit near Galle. However, it can take as long to get from Fort to the expressway entrance as it does from there to Galle. Plans call for the road to eventually be extended to reach Hambantota.

Colombo–Kandy Expressway Approved in 2012, this road is expected to reduce travel time to close to an hour, but as yet there is no confirmed opening date.

Adventure Tours (☎077-717 3007; www.ceylonadventuretours.com; 117 Lewis Pl) offer self-drive rental of three-wheelers, for a novel way to drive yourself around Sri Lanka. Rates start from US$14 per day.

Motorbike and moped rental is widely available in established resorts on the coast; rentals start at about about Rs 1000 per day.

DRIVING LICENCE

An International Driving Permit (IDP) is required to drive in Sri Lanka and this must be locally endorsed by the **Automobile Association of Ceylon** (Map p70; ☎011-242 1528; www.aaceylon.lk; 40 Sir Mohamed Macan Markar Mawatha, Col 3). Most rental firms can do this on your behalf.

Road Conditions

Driving in Sri Lanka requires constant attention to the road. Country roads are often narrow and potholed, with constant pedestrian, bicycle and animal traffic to navigate. Punctures are a part of life here, so every village has a repair expert. Note, however, that Sri Lanka's massive road-building program is improving long-distance travel across the nation, especially in the North and East.

Road rules are routinely flouted. It's common for a bus, car or truck to overtake in the face of oncoming smaller road users. Three-wheelers, cyclists, and smaller cars and vans simply have to move over or risk getting hit. To announce they are overtaking, or want to overtake, drivers sound a shrill melody on their horns. If you're walking or cycling along any kind of busy main road, be very alert.

Road signs are in English, Sinhala and Tamil. Throughout Sri Lanka, Mw is an abbreviation for Mawatha, meaning 'Avenue'.

Road Rules

- Speed limit 50km/h in towns, 70km/h in rural areas and 100km/h on the new expressways.
- Driving is on the left-hand side of the road, as in the UK and Australia.
- Parking is offered by many hotels, and is free by the roadside in rural areas, but in short supply in cities, though most have paying parking lots downtown.

Hitching

Hitching is never entirely safe, and Sri Lanka's cheap fares make it an unnecessary option. We don't recommend it, and travellers who do choose to hitch should understand that they are taking a small but potentially serious risk.

Local Transport

Many Sri Lankan towns are small enough to walk around. In larger towns, you can get around by bus, taxi or three-wheeler.

Bus

Local buses go to most places, including villages outside main towns, for fares from Rs 10 to 50.

Taxi

Three-wheelers provide the bulk of the taxi service in Sri Lanka. Car taxis in Sri Lanka tend to be operated by radio-taxi firms, travel agencies or local drivers and you won't see many recognisable taxis to flag down in the street. You can however call for a pick-up from firms such as **Kangaroo Cabs** (☎011-258 8588; www.kangaroocabs.com) and **Ace Cabs** (☎011-281 8818; www.acecabs.lk) in Colombo and other large cities. Elsewhere, make arrangements for a taxi with your hotel or a local travel agency.

In Colombo and other large town and cities, you can count on taxis dispatched via apps such as **Uber**, and Sri Lankan ride-share apps **PickMe** and **TaxiYak**, though the vehicle that arrives may be a three wheeler instead of a car.

Three-Wheeler

Three-wheelers, known in other parts of Asia as tuk-tuks, *bajajs* or autorickshaws, are waiting on every corner and can be flagged down in the street. Increasingly, drivers in Colombo are willing to use the meter (which may be in the cab or on the driver's mobile phone), but elsewhere, use your best bargaining skills and agree on the fare before you get in. As a rule of thumb, a 1kmthree-wheeler ride will cost less than Rs 100 on the meter, but drivers may be reluctant to take less than Rs 200 (and may ask for significantly more) if you have to bargain.

Some drivers will offer extensive detours to commission-paying shops, restaurants and hotels; insist on going where you want to go. Three-wheelers and taxis waiting outside hotels and tourist sights expect higher-than-usual fares. Walk a few hundred metres down the road and flag down a moving three-wheeler and you should get a better deal.

Train

Sri Lanka Railways (☎011-460 0111; www.railway.gov.lk) runs the nation's railways, and trains are a great way to explore the country, particularly since the introduction of the comfortable blue train carriages. Although train journeys can be slow, with the distances involved, there are few overnight or all-day ordeals to contend with, and there is rarely the same kind of crush seen on Indian trains, except on rush hour trains into and out of Colombo, or on *poya* days.

A train ride is almost always more relaxed than a bus ride, and costs are in line with buses; even 1st class rarely exceeds Rs 1000.

Most stations have helpful information windows where English is spoken. Note that trains are often late, and delays of an hour or more are not uncommon.

In the past, the private companies *Rajadhani Express* and *Expo Rail* were permitted to hitch their own air-con train cars onto regular trains for specific routes, but this relationship was suspended at the time of writing.

One private train operating presently is the *Viceroy Special*, a luxury steam train operated on a charter basis by **JF Tours & Travels** (Map p70; ☎011-258 7996; www.jftours.com; 189 Bauddhaloka Mw, Col 4; ⏰9am-5pm Mon-Sat, 9am-1pm Sun) in Colombo. The same company runs the *Viceroy II*, which is also run on a charter basis, but individual seats for tours between Colombo, Kandy and Badulla can be booked through the website https://12go.asia/en/operator/viceroy-ii-by-12go.

There are three main rail lines in Sri Lanka.

South from Colombo A scenic delight. Recently renovated, runs past Aluthgama and Hikkaduwa to Galle and Matara.

East from Colombo To the Hill Country, through Kandy, Nanu Oya (for Nuwara Eliya) and Ella to Badulla. A beautiful route, the stretch from Haputale to Ella is one of the world's most scenic train rides.

North from Colombo Through Anuradhapura to Mannar and also to Jaffna. One branch reaches Trincomalee on the east coast, while another serves Polonnaruwa and Batticaloa.

Other Lines The Puttalam line runs along the coast north from Colombo, via Negombo and Chilaw, and peters out just north of Puttalam, although buses sometimes serve sections of the route. The Kelani Valley line winds 60km from Colombo to Avissawella.

Two good independent references for Sri Lanka trains:

www.seat61.com/SriLanka An excellent overview.

http://slr.malindaprasad.com Schedules and some fares.

Classes

There are three classes on Sri Lankan trains (although many have no 1st class). Often, the best place to sit is at the open doorway of the carriage, buffeted by the breeze.

1st class Comes in three varieties: coaches, sleeping berths and observation saloons (with large windows). The latter are used on some trains inland from Colombo and are the preferred means of travelling these scenic lines. Some have large rear-facing windows and vintage interiors. Seats on the comfortable 'blue trains' from Colombo to Kandy and Badulla often book out weeks before travel.

2nd class Seats have padding and there are fans. On some trains (but not to Galle) these seats can be reserved in advance, but on many services you'll have to board and hope for a seat.

3rd class Seats have little padding and there are no reservations. The cars accommodate as many as can squeeze in and conditions can be grim.

Reservations

- Reservations for 1st-class and 2nd-class carriages (where available) can be made at train stations up to 30 days before departure, often at a designated reservation counter.
- Alternatively, bookings can be made through websites such as https://12go.asia and agencies such as UK-based **Visit Sri Lanka Tours** (☎in UK 01273-306049; www.visitsrilankatours.co.uk).
- Always make a booking for the hugely popular 1st-class observation saloons. Sleeping cars also book up far in advance.
- If travelling more than 80km, you can break your journey at any intermediate station for 24 hours without penalty. You'll need to make fresh reservations for seats on the next leg.

Health

Before You Go

Insurance

Even if you're fit and healthy, don't travel without health insurance: accidents happen and illness isn't always avoidable. You may require extra cover for adventure activities, such as scuba diving. If you're uninsured, emergency evacuation can be cripplingly expensive.

Recommended Vaccinations

Proof of vaccination for yellow fever is required if, in the six days before entering Sri Lanka, you have visited a country in the yellow-fever zone.

The US Centers for Disease Control (CDC) recommends that travellers to Sri Lanka consider the following vaccinations (as well as being up to date with measles, mumps and rubella vaccinations):

Adult diphtheria and tetanus Single booster recommended if none in the previous 10 years.

Hepatitis A Provides almost 100% protection for up to a year.

Hepatitis B Now considered routine for most travellers.

Japanese encephalitis Recommended for rural travel or stays longer than 30 days.

Polio No incidence has been reported in Sri Lanka for several years but the disease must be assumed to be present.

Rabies Vaccination is recommended for long and rural stays and those working with animals.

Typhoid Recommended for all travellers to Sri Lanka, even if you only visit urban areas.

Varicella If you haven't had chickenpox, discuss this vaccination with your doctor.

In Sri Lanka

Availability & Cost of Health Care

Medical care, and its cost, is hugely variable in Sri Lanka. Colombo has some good clinics aimed at expats; the city's **Nawaloka Hospital** (Map p70; ☎1514, 011-557 7111; www.nawaloka.com; 23 Deshamanya HK Dharmadasa Mw, Col 2) also has a good reputation and English-speaking doctors. Embassies and consulates can recommend medical providers. Elsewhere in Sri Lanka, hotels and guesthouses can usually steer you to a local doctor for at least initial treatment. For severe illness, you might be better evacuating to Mumbai.

Before buying medication over the counter, always check the use-by date and ensure the packet is sealed. Colombo and larger towns all have good pharmacies; most medications can be purchased without a prescription.

Sri Lanka also has its own system of holistic traditional medicine known as Ayurveda, but this is best reserved for wellness rather than treatment for serious illnesses.

Infectious Diseases

Dengue fever This mosquito-borne disease is becomingly increasingly problematic; there's no vaccine so avoid mosquito bites at all times. Symptoms include high fever, severe headache and body ache and sometimes a rash and diarrhoea. Treatment is rest and paracetamol – avoid aspirin or ibuprofen and see a doctor to be diagnosed and monitored.

Hepatitis A This food- and water-borne virus infects the liver, causing jaundice (yellow skin and eyes), nausea and lethargy. There is no specific treatment so all travellers to Sri Lanka should be vaccinated.

FOOD SAFETY

Dining out brings the possibility of contracting intestinal bugs. Ways to help avoid food-related illness:

- eat only freshly cooked food
- avoid shellfish and buffets
- peel fruit and avoid uncooked vegetables
- eat in busy restaurants with a high customer turnover.

Hepatitis B This sexually transmitted disease is spread by body fluids and can be prevented by vaccination. The long-term consequences can include liver cancer and cirrhosis.

Hepatitis E Transmitted through contaminated food and water, hepatitis E has similar symptoms to hepatitis A, and can be fatal to mother and baby in pregnant women. There is no commercially available vaccine, so follow safe eating and drinking guidelines.

HIV Spread via contaminated body fluids and present in Sri Lanka. Avoid unsafe sex, unsterilised needles (including in medical facilities) and procedures such as tattoos.

Influenza Present year-round in the tropics, influenza (flu) symptoms include fever, muscle aches, a runny nose, cough and sore throat. It can be severe in people over the age of 65 or in those with medical conditions such as heart disease or diabetes – vaccination is recommended for these individuals. There is no specific treatment, just rest and paracetamol.

Coronavirus The 2019 strain of coronavirus is present in Sri Lanka, though the country has seen just a handful of fatalities. As the nation reopens to tourism, visitors may be required to have tests before and after arrival, and potentially during their stay. Follow local advice and bring disposable face masks and hand sanitiser.

Japanese B encephalitis This viral disease is transmitted by mosquitoes and is rare in travellers. Vaccination is only recommended for travellers spending more than one month outside cities. There is no treatment, and it may result in permanent brain damage or death.

Malaria Malaria was formerly a serious problem, but the World Health Organization declared Sri Lanka malaria-free in 2016. Doctors presently advise that anti-malarial drugs are not necessary.

Rabies Fatal if untreated, this disease is spread by the saliva of an infected animal – most commonly a dog or monkey. You should seek medical advice immediately after any animal bite and commence postexposure treatment with rabies immunoglobulin immediately. Being vaccinated means the postbite treatment is greatly simplified.

Tuberculosis Vaccination is usually only given to children under the age of five, but adults at risk are recommended to have pre- and post-travel TB testing. The main symptoms are fever, cough, weight loss, night sweats and fatigue.

Typhoid This serious bacterial infection is also spread via food and water. It gives a high and slowly progressive fever and headache, and may be accompanied by a dry cough and stomach pain. It is diagnosed by blood tests and treated with antibiotics. Vaccination is recommended for all travellers who are spending more than a week in Sri Lanka. Be aware that vaccination is not 100% effective, so you must still be careful with what you eat and drink.

Traveller's Diarrhoea

This is by far the most common problem affecting travellers in Sri Lanka. It's usually caused by a bacteria, and often clears up on its own, though severe cases may require treatment with antibiotics.

Traveller's diarrhoea is defined as the passage of more than three watery bowel actions within 24 hours, plus at least one other symptom, such as fever, cramps, nausea, vomiting or feeling generally unwell.

Treatment consists of staying well hydrated; rehydration solutions like Gastrolyte are the best for this. Antibiotics such as ciprofloxacin or azithromycin should kill the bacteria quickly. Seek medical attention quickly if you do not respond to an appropriate antibiotic.

Loperamide is just a 'stopper' and doesn't get to the cause of the problem. It can be helpful, though (eg if you have to go on a long bus ride). Don't take loperamide if you have a fever or blood in your stools.

Amoebic dysentery Amoebic dysentery is very rare in travellers but is quite often misdiagnosed. Symptoms include fever, bloody diarrhoea and generally feeling unwell. You should always seek reliable medical care if you have blood in your stool. Tinidazole or metronidazole is used to kill the parasite in your gut and a second drug is used to kill the cysts. If left untreated, complications such as liver or gut abscesses can occur.

Giardiasis Giardia is a parasite that is relatively common in travellers. Symptoms include nausea, bloating, excess gas, fatigue and intermittent diarrhoea, and sometimes, eggy, sulphur-smelling burps. The parasite will eventually go away without treatment, but it's best to seek medical treatment. The treatment of choice is tinidazole.

Women's Health

For gynaecological health issues, seek out a female doctor.

Birth control Bring adequate supplies of your own form of contraception; local products are often low quality.

Sanitary products Pads, but rarely tampons, are readily available.

Thrush Heat, humidity and antibiotics can all contribute to thrush. Treatment is with

WATER

Tap water is not safe to drink. Use filtered water, ideally refilling your own bottle. If you buy bottled water, look for the small round 'SLSI' logo, which shows the water has been tested by the government's Sri Lanka Standards Institution.

antifungal creams and pessaries such as clotrimazole, or fluconazole (Diflucan) tablets.

Urinary-tract infections These can be precipitated by dehydration or long bus journeys without toilet stops; bring suitable antibiotics.

Environmental Hazards

AIR POLLUTION

Air pollution, particularly vehicle pollution, is an increasing problem in most urban areas. If you have severe respiratory problems, speak with your doctor before travelling. It's worth carrying a disposable face mask if you are affected by air quality.

HEAT

Swelling of the feet and ankles is common for those unused to the heat, as are muscle cramps caused by excessive sweating. Prevent these by avoiding dehydration and excessive activity in the heat. Drinking rehydration solution or eating salty food helps. Treat cramps by resting, rehydrating and gently stretching.

Dehydration is the main contributor to heat exhaustion and recovery is usually rapid. Symptoms include the following:

- feeling weak
- headache and irritability
- nausea or vomiting
- sweaty skin and a fast, weak pulse
- normal or slightly elevated body temperature.

Treatment:

- get out of the heat
- fan the sufferer
- apply cool, wet cloths to the skin
- lay the sufferer flat with their legs raised
- rehydrate with water containing one-quarter teaspoon of salt per litre.

Heatstroke is a serious medical emergency that can be fatal. Symptoms include the following:

- weakness and nausea
- a hot, dry body
- temperature of over 41°C
- dizziness and confusion
- loss of coordination
- seizures and eventual collapse.

Treatment:

- get out of the heat
- fan the sufferer
- apply cool, wet cloths to the skin or ice to the body.

Prickly heat is a common skin rash in the tropics, caused by sweat trapped under the skin. Treat it by moving somewhere cool and taking cold showers. Locally bought prickly-heat powder can be helpful.

INSECT BITES & STINGS

Bedbugs Don't carry disease, but their bites can be itchy. You can treat the itch with an antihistamine.

Lice Most commonly appear on the head and pubic areas. You may need numerous applications of an antilice shampoo such as pyrethrin.

Ticks Contracted while walking in rural areas and can carry diseases. Ticks are commonly found behind the ears, on the belly and in armpits. If you have had a tick bite and have a rash at the site of the bite or elsewhere, fever or muscle aches, see a doctor. Doxycycline prevents tick-borne diseases.

Leeches Found in humid rainforest areas. They do not transmit any disease, but their bites are often itchy for weeks and can easily become infected. Apply an iodine-based antiseptic to any leech bite to help prevent infection. Don't pull leeches off; gently remove them by pushing sideways at the point of attachment.

Bee and wasp stings Anyone with a serious bee or wasp allergy should carry an injection of adrenalin (eg an Epipen).

SKIN PROBLEMS

Fungal rashes Fungal rashes can occur in moist areas, such as the groin, armpits and between the toes. Infection starts as a red patch and is usually itchy. Treat with an antifungal cream such as clotrimazole or Lamisil. A second fungus, Tinea versicolor, causes light-coloured patches, most commonly on the back, chest and shoulders; consult a doctor.

Cuts and scratches These become easily infected in humid climates. Immediately wash all wounds in clean water and apply antiseptic. If you develop signs of infection (increasing pain and redness), see a doctor.

SUNBURN

Even on a cloudy day sunburn can occur rapidly.

- Use a strong sunscreen (factor 30) and reapply after a swim.
- Wear a wide-brimmed hat and sunglasses.
- Avoid lying in the sun during the hottest part of the day (10am to 2pm).

If you become sunburnt, stay out of the sun until you have recovered, apply cool compresses and, if necessary, take painkillers for the discomfort. One percent hydrocortisone cream applied twice daily is also helpful.

DIVING & SURFING

Divers and surfers should have a dive medical and seek specialised advice before they travel. Bring a medical kit with treatments for coral cuts and tropical ear infections, and make sure your insurance covers decompression treatment – if not, get specialised dive insurance through an organisation such as Divers Alert Network (www.danasiapacific.org).

Language

Sinhala and Tamil are national languages in Sri Lanka, with English commonly described as a lingua franca. It's easy to get by with English, and the Sri Lankan variety has its own unique characteristics – 'You are having a problem, isn't it, no?' is one example. However, while English may be widely spoken in the main centres, off the beaten track its spread thins. In any case, even a few words of Sinhala or Tamil will go a long way.

SINHALA

Sinhala is officially written using a cursive script. If you read our coloured pronunciation guides as if they were English, you shouldn't have problems being understood. When consonants are doubled they are pronounced very distinctly, almost as separate sounds. The symbols t and d are pronounced less forcefully than in English, th as in 'thin', dh as the 'th' in 'that', g as in 'go', and r is more like a flap of the tongue against the roof of the mouth – it's not pronounced as an American 'r'. As for the vowels, a is pronounced as the 'u' in 'cup', aa as the 'a' in 'father', ai as in 'aisle', au as the 'ow' in 'how', e as in 'met', i as in 'bit', o as in 'hot', and u as in 'put'.

Basics

Hello.	aayu-bowan
Goodbye.	aayu-bowan
Yes.	owu
No.	naha
Please.	karuna kara
Thank you.	istuh-tee
Excuse me.	samah venna
Sorry.	kana gaatui
Do you speak English?	oyaa in-ghirisih kata karenawa da?
What's your name?	oyaaghe nama mokka'da?
My name is ...	maaghe nama ...

WANT MORE?

For in-depth language information and handy phrases, check out Lonely Planet's *Sinhala Phrasebook*. You'll find it at **shop.lonelyplanet.com**, or you can buy Lonely Planet's iPhone phrasebooks at the Apple App Store.

Accommodation

Do you have any rooms available?	kaamara thiyanawada?
How much is it per night?	ek ra-yakata kiyada
How much is it per person?	ek kenek-kuta kiyada
Is breakfast included?	udeh keh-emath ekkada?
for one night	ek rayak pamanai
for two nights	raya dekak pamanai
for one person	ek-kenek pamanai
for two people	den-nek pamanai
campsite	kamping ground eka
guesthouse	gesthaus eka
hotel	hotel eka
youth hostel	yut-hostel eka

Eating & Drinking

Can we see the menu?	menoo eka balanna puluvandha?
What's the local speciality?	mehe visheshayen hadhana dhe monavaadha?

I'd like rice and curry, please.	bahth denna
I'm a vegetarian.	mama elavalu vitharai kanne
I'm allergic to (peanuts).	mata (ratakaju) apathyayi
No ice in my drink, please.	karunaakarala maghe beema ekata ais dhamanna epaa
That was delicious!	eka harima rasai!

Please bring a/the...	... karunaakarala gennah
bill	bila
fork	gaarappuvak
glass of water	vathura veedhuruvak
knife	pihiyak
plate	pingaanak

bowl	vendhuwa
coffee	koh-pi
fruit	palathuru
glass	co-ppuwa
milk	kiri
salt	lunu
spoon	han-duh
sugar	seeni
tea	thay
water	vathura

NUMBERS – SINHALA

0	binduwa
1	eka
2	deka
3	thuna
4	hathara
5	paha
6	haya
7	hatha
8	atta
9	navaya
10	dahaya
100	seeya
200	deh seeya
1000	daaha
2000	deh daaha
100,000	lakshaya
1,000,000	daseh lakshaya
10,000,000	kotiya

Emergencies

Help!	aaney!/aaeeyoh!/ammoh!
Call a doctor!	dostara gen-nanna!
Call the police!	polisiyata kiyanna!
Go away!	methanin yanna!
I'm lost.	maa-meh nativelaa

Shopping & Services

What time does it open/close?	ehika kiyatada arinneh/vahanneh?
How much is it?	ehekka keeyada?
big	loku
medicine	behe-yat
small	podi/punchi
bank	bankuwa
chemist/pharmacy	faahmisiya
... embassy	... embasiya
market	maakat eka
my hotel	mang inna hotalaya
newsagency	pattara ejensiya
post office	tepal kantohruwa
public telephone	podu dura katanayak
tourist office	sanchaaraka toraturu karyaalayak

Time & Dates

What time is it?	velaave keeyada?

morning	udai
afternoon	havasa
day	davasa
night	raah
week	sumaanayak
month	maasayak
year	avuurudeh
yesterday	ee-yeh
today	ada (uther)
tomorrow	heta

Monday	sandu-da
Tuesday	angaharuwaa-da
Wednesday	badaa-da
Thursday	braha-spetin-da
Friday	sikuraa-da
Saturday	senasuraa-da
Sunday	iri-da

SIGNS – SINHALA

ඇතුල්වීම	**Entrance**
පිටවීම	**Exit**
විවෘතව ඇත.	**Open**
වසා ඇත.	**Closed**
තොරතුරු දැන්වුම	**Information**
තහනම් වේ.	**Prohibited**
පොලිස් ස්ථානය	**Police Station**
කාමර ඇත.	**Rooms Available**
කාමර නැත.	**No Vacancy**
වැසිකිළ	**Toilets**
පුරුෂ	**Men**
ස්ත්‍රී	**Women**

Transport & Directions

When does the next ... leave/arrive?	meelanga ... pitaht venne/paminenne?
boat	bohtuwa
bus (city)	bus eka
bus (intercity)	bus eka nagaraantara
train	koh-chiya

I want to get off.	mama methana bahinawa
I'd like a one-way ticket.	mata tani gaman tikat ekak ganna ohna
I'd like a return ticket.	mata yaam-eem tikat ekak ganna ohna

1st class	palamu veni paantiya
2nd class	deveni paantiya
3rd class	tunveni paantiya
bus stop	bus nevathuma
ferry terminal	totu pala
timetable	kaala satahana
train station	dumriya pala

I'd like to hire a ...	mata ... ekak bad dhata ganna ohna
bicycle	baisikeleya
car	kar (eka)

Where is a/the ...?	... koheda?
Go straight ahead.	kelinma issarahata yaanna
Turn left.	wamata harenna
Turn right.	dakunata harenna
near	lan-ghai
far	durai

TAMIL

The vocabulary of Sri Lankan Tamil is much the same as that of South India – the written form is identical, using the traditional cursive script – but there are marked differences in pronunciation between speakers from the two regions. In this section we've used the same pronunciation guides as for Sinhala.

Basics

Hello.	vanakkam
Goodbye.	poytu varukirehn
Yes.	aam
No.	il-lay
Please.	tayavu saydhu
Thank you.	nandri
Excuse me.	mannikavum
Sorry.	mannikavum
Do you speak English?	nin-gal aangilam paysu-virhalaa?
What's your name?	ungal peyr en-na?
My name is ...	en peyr ...

Accommodation

Do you have any rooms available?	ingu room kideikkumaa?
How much is it per night/person?	oru iravukku/aalukku evvalavur?
Is breakfast included?	kaalei unavum sehrtha?
for one/two nights	oru/irandu iravukku
for one/two people	oruvarukku/iruvarukku

SIGNS – TAMIL

வழி உள்ளே	**Entrance**
வழி வெளியே	**Exit**
திறந்துள்ளது	**Open**
அடைக்கப்பட்டுள்ளது	**Closed**
தகவல்	**Information**
அனுமதி இல்லை	**Prohibited**
காவல் நிலையம்	**Police Station**
அறைகள் உண்டு	**Rooms Available**
காலி இல்லை	**No Vacancy**
மலசலகூடம்	**Toilets**
ஆண்	**Men**
பெண	**Women**

NUMBERS – TAMIL

0	saifer
1	ondru
2	iranduh
3	muundruh
4	naan-guh
5	ainduh
6	aaruh
7	ealluh
8	ettu
9	onbaduh
10	pat-tuh
100	nooruh
1000	aayirem
2000	irandaayirem
100,000	oru latcham
1,000,000	pattuh lat-chem
10,000,000	kohdee

campsite	mukhaamidum idahm
guesthouse	virun-dhinar vidhudheh
hotel	hotehl
youth hostel	ilainar vidhudheh

Eating & Drinking

Can we see the menu?	unavu pattiyalai paarppomaa?
What's the local speciality?	ingu kidaikkak koodiya visheida unavu enna?
I'd like rice and curry, please.	sorum kariyum tharungal
I'm a vegetarian.	naan shaiva unavu shaappidupavan
I'm allergic to (peanuts).	(nilak kadalai) enakku alejee
No ice in my drink, please.	enadu paanaththil ais poda vendaam
That was delicious!	adhu nalla rushi!

Please bring a/the...	... konda varungal
bill	bill
fork	mul karandi
glass of water	thanni oru glass
knife	kaththi
plate	oru plate

bowl	kooppai
coffee	kahpee
fruit	paadham
glass	glass
milk	paal
salt	uppu
spoon	karandi
sugar	seeree
tea	te-neer/plan-tea
water	than-neer

Emergencies

Help!	udavi!
Call a doctor!	daktarai kuppidunga!
Call the police!	polisai kuppidunga!
Go away!	pohn-goh!/poi-vidu!
I'm lost.	naan vali tavari-vittehn

Shopping & Services

What time does it open/close?	et-thana manikka tirakhum/mudhum?
How much is it?	adhu evvalavu?
big	periyeh
medicine	marunduh
small	siriyeh
bank	vanghee
chemist/pharmacy	marunduh kadhai
... embassy	... tudharalayem
market	maarket
my hotel	enadu hotehl
newsagency	niyuz paper vitku-midam
post office	tafaal nilayem
public telephone	podhu tolai-pessee
tourist office	toorist nilayem

Time & Dates

What time is it?	mani eth-tanai?
morning	kaalai
afternoon	pit-pahel
day	pahel
night	iravu
week	vaarem
month	maadhem
year	varudem
yesterday	neh-truh
today	indru
tomorrow	naalay

Monday	tin-gal
Tuesday	sevvaay
Wednesday	budahn
Thursday	viyaalin
Friday	vellee
Saturday	san-nee
Sunday	naayiru

Transport & Directions

When does the next ... leave/arrive?	eththanai manikku aduththa ... sellum/varum?
boat	padakhu
bus (city)	baas naharam/ul-loor
bus (intercity)	baas veliyoor
train	rayill

I want to get off.	naan iranga vendum
I'd like a one-way ticket.	enakku oru vahly tikket veynum
I'd like a return ticket.	enakku iru vahlay tikket veynum
1st class	mudalahaam vahuppu
2nd class	irandaam vahuppu
bus/trolley stop	baas nilayem
luggage lockers	porul vaikku-midam
timetable	haala attavanay
train station	rayill nilayem

I'd like to hire a ...	enakku ... vaadakhaikku vaynum
bicycle	sai-kul
car	car

Where is it?	adhu en-ghe irukkaradhu?
Where is a/the ...?	... en-ghe?
Go straight ahead.	neraha sellavum
Turn left.	valadhur pakkam tirumbavum
Turn right.	itadhu pakkam thirumbavum
near	aruhil
far	tu-rahm

SRI LANKAN ENGLISH

Greetings & Conversation

Go and come. – farewell greeting, similar to 'See you later' (not taken literally)
How? – How are you?
Nothing to do. – Can't do anything.
What to do? – What can be done about it? (more of a rhetorical question)
What country? – Where are you from?
paining – hurting
to gift – to give a gift

People

baby/bubba – term used for any child up to about adolescence
batchmate – university classmate
peon – office helper
uncle/auntie – term of respect for elder

Getting Around

backside – part of the building away from the street
bajaj – three-wheeler
bus halt – bus stop
coloured lights – traffic lights
down south – the areas south of Colombo, especially coastal areas
dropping – being dropped off at a place by a car
get down – to alight (from bus/train/three-wheeler)
normal bus – not a private bus
outstation – place beyond a person's home area
petrol shed – petrol/gas station
pick-up – 4WD utility vehicle
seaside/landside – indicates locations, usually in relation to Galle Rd
two-wheeler – motorcycle
up and down – return trip
up country/Hill Country – Kandy and beyond, tea plantation areas
vehicle – car

Food

bite – snack, usually with alcoholic drinks
boutique – a little, hole-in-the-wall shop, usually selling small, inexpensive items
cool spot – traditional, small shop that sells cool drinks and snacks
hotel – a small, cheap restaurant that doesn't offer accommodation
lunch packet/rice packet – rice/curry meal wrapped in plastic and newspaper and taken to office or school for lunch
short eats – snack food

Money

buck – rupee
last price – final price when bargaining
purse – wallet

GLOSSARY

ambalama – wayside shelter for pilgrims

Aurudu – Sinhalese and Tamil New Year, celebrated on 14 April

Avalokitesvara – the *bodhisattva* of compassion

Ayurveda – traditional system of medicine that uses herbs and oils to heal and rejuvenate

bailas – folk tunes based on Portuguese, African and local music styles

baobab – water-storing tree *(Adansonia digitata)*, probably introduced to Mannar Island and the Vanni in northern Sri Lanka by Arab traders

bodhi tree – large spreading tree *(Ficus religiosa);* the tree under which the Buddha sat when he attained enlightenment, and the many descendants grown from cuttings of this tree

bodhisattva – divine being who, although capable of attaining *nirvana*, chooses to reside on the human plane to help ordinary people attain salvation

Brahmi – early Indian script used from the 5th century BC

bund – built-up bank or dyke surrounding a *tank*

Burgher – Sri Lankan Eurasian, generally descended from Portuguese-Sinhalese or Dutch-Sinhalese intermarriage

cadjan – coconut fronds woven into mats and used as building material

Ceylon – British-colonial name for Sri Lanka

chetiya – Buddhist shrine

Chola – powerful ancient South Indian kingdom that invaded Sri Lanka on several occasions

CTB – Central Transport Board, the state bus network

dagoba – Buddhist monument composed of a solid hemisphere containing relics of the Buddha or a Buddhist saint; a *stupa*

devale – complex designed for worshipping a Hindu or Sri Lankan deity

dharma – the word used by both Hindus and Buddhists to refer to their respective moral codes of behaviour

eelam – Tamil word for precious land

gala – rock

ganga – river

gedige – hollow temple with thick walls and a corbelled roof

gopuram – gateway tower

guardstones – carved stones that flank doorways or entrances to temples

Hanuman – the monkey king from the *Ramayana*

Jataka tales – stories of the previous lives of the Buddha

juggernaut – decorated temple cart dragged through the streets during Hindu festivals (sometimes called a 'car')

kachcheri – administrative office

kadé – Sinhalese name for a streetside hut (also called boutiques); called *unavakam* by Tamils

Karava – fisherfolk of Indian descent

karma – Hindu-Buddhist principle of retributive justice for past deeds

Kataragama – see *Murugan*

kiri bath – dessert of rice cooked in coconut milk

kolam – meaning costume or guise, it refers to masked dance-drama; also the rice-flour designs that adorn buildings in Tamil areas

kovil – Hindu temple dedicated to the worship of Shiva

kulam – Tamil word for water tank

lakh – 100,000; unit of measurement in Sri Lanka and India

lingam – phallic symbol; symbol of Shiva

LTTE – Liberation Tigers of Tamil Eelam, also known as the Tamil Tigers; separatist group fighting for an independent Tamil Eelam in the North and the East

Maha – northeast monsoon season

Mahaweli Ganga – Sri Lanka's longest river, starting near Adam's Peak and reaching the sea near Trincomalee

Mahayana – later form of Buddhism prevalent in Korea, Japan and China; literally means 'greater vehicle'

Mahinda – son of the Indian Buddhist emperor Ashoka, credited with introducing Buddhism to Sri Lanka

mahout – elephant master

Maitreya – future Buddha

makara – mythical beast combining a lion, a pig and an elephant, often carved into temple staircases

makara torana – ornamental archway

mandapaya – a raised platform with decorative pillars

masala – mix (often spices)

moonstone – semiprecious stone; also a carved 'doorstep' at temple entrances

mudra – symbolic hand position of a Buddha image

Murugan – Hindu god of war; also known as *Skanda* and *Kataragama*

naga – snake; also applies to snake deities and spirits

nirvana – ultimate aim of Buddhists, final release from the cycle of existence

nuwara – city

ola – leaves of the talipot palm; used in manuscripts and traditional books

oruva – outrigger canoe

oya – stream or small river

Pali – the language in which the Buddhist scriptures were originally recorded

palmyra – tall palm tree found in the dry northern region

perahera – procession, usually with dancers, drummers and elephants

pirivena – centre of learning attached to monastery

poya – full-moon day; always a holiday

puja – 'respect', offering or prayers

rajakariya – 'workers for the king', the tradition of feudal service

Ramayana – ancient story of Rama and Sita and their conflict with *Rawana*

Rawana – 'demon king of Lanka' who abducts Rama's beautiful wife Sita in the Hindu epic the *Ramayana*

relic chamber – chamber in a *dagoba* housing a relic of the Buddha or a saint and representing the Buddhist concept of the cosmos

Ruhunu – ancient southern centre of Sinhalese power near Tissamaharama that survived even when Anuradhapura and Polonnaruwa fell to Indian invaders

samudra – large *tank* or inland sea

Sangamitta – sister of *Mahinda;* she brought the sacred *bodhi tree* sapling from Bodhgaya in India

sangha – the community of Buddhist monks and nuns; in Sri Lanka, an influential group divided into several nikayas (orders)

Sanskrit – ancient Indian language, the oldest known member of the family of Indo-European languages

sari – traditional garment worn by women

Sinhala – language of the Sinhalese people

Sinhalese – majority population of Sri Lanka; principally Sinhala-speaking Buddhists

Skanda – see *Murugan*

stupa – see *dagoba*

Tamils – a people of South Indian origin, comprising the largest minority population in Sri Lanka; principally Tamil-speaking Hindus

tank – artificial water-storage lake or reservoir; many of the tanks in Sri Lanka are very large and ancient

Theravada – orthodox form of Buddhism practised in Sri Lanka and Southeast Asia, which is characterised by its adherence to the *Pali* canon

unavakam – Tamil name for a streetside hut; called kadé or boutiques by the Sinhalese

vahalkada – solid panel of sculpture

vatadage – circular relic house consisting of a small central *dagoba* flanked by Buddha images and encircled by columns

Veddahs – original inhabitants of Sri Lanka prior to the arrival of the Sinhalese from India; also called the *Wanniyala-aetto*

vel – trident; the god *Murugan* is often depicted carrying a *vel*

vihara, **viharaya** – Buddhist complex, including a shrine containing a statue of the Buddha, a congregational hall and a monks' house

Wanniyala-aetto – see *Veddahs*

wewa – see *tank*

Yala – southwest monsoon season

Behind the Scenes

SEND US YOUR FEEDBACK

We love to hear from travellers – your comments keep us on our toes and help make our books better. Our well-travelled team reads every word on what you loved or loathed about this book. Although we cannot reply individually to your submissions, we always guarantee that your feedback goes straight to the appropriate authors, in time for the next edition. Each person who sends us information is thanked in the next edition – the most useful submissions are rewarded with a selection of digital PDF chapters.

Visit **lonelyplanet.com/contact** to submit your updates and suggestions or to ask for help. Our award-winning website also features inspirational travel stories, news and discussions.

Note: We may edit, reproduce and incorporate your comments in Lonely Planet products such as guidebooks, websites and digital products, so let us know if you don't want your comments reproduced or your name acknowledged. For a copy of our privacy policy visit lonelyplanet.com/privacy.

OUR READERS

Many thanks to the travellers who used the last edition and wrote to us with helpful hints, useful advice and interesting anecdotes:

Annette Vögele, Billy Morton & Callum Blackburn, Boukje de Gooijer, Bruno Shirley, Carmen Cristurean, Cathelijne & Rene van Weelden, Catherine Lee, Chris Candler, Christina Gousetis, Christine Cullen, Cilia Hoogmartens, Daniel Lindley, Dorette Kouwenhoven, Fran Rowe, Gerry Buitendag, Gregory Kipling, Gregory Rose, Hugo Quaedvlieg, Irina Helmke, Isabel Rijo, James Paynter, Jane Rusalen, Janetta Malan, Jeanne MacInnes, Jerome Camier, Julie Woods, laura delizonna, Lorin Veltkamp, Magdalena Ceglowska, Marcy Newman, Marina Naomi Noack, Mark Tilbury, Marlon Goos, Martin Hellwagner, Mia Ruby, Michael Dragon, Robert King, Roger Wort, Ryne James, Sarath de Alwis, Sooha Kim, Steve Burke, Susanne Wimmer, Tara Frediani, Thomas Neaum, Viktoria Wegener, Wietse Sennema,

WRITER THANKS

Joe Bindloss

I'd like to send particular thanks to my partner Linda and boys Benji and Tyler for putting up with me being away as a global crisis started to build. In Sri Lanka, thanks to Milroy Fernando for driving over and above the call of duty and for hospitality at a time when my getting home was not assured. Thanks also to the many helpful Sri Lankans and travellers who chipped in with tips and advice.

Stuart Butler

To my old friends Dimuthu Priyadarshana, Milroy Fernando and Sena Hewage thank you for everything. Huge thanks also too Sue and Faiesz, Stephanie and Palitha, Suraweera Wickramasinghe, Jai and Sumana, Some, Sampath and Janaka, as well as all the team at the Mangrove Cabanas, Back of Beyond and Aga Surf View. Finally, but most importantly, thank you again to Heather, Jake and Grace for all that you do and for being such perfect Sri Lankan travel companions.

Bradley Mayhew

Thanks to Roy for all his help and for the use of his scooter. Best wishes to Dimuthu and family. Thanks to Udaya Karunaratne for sharing his knowledge of Mannar Island.

Jenny Walker

It's always a joy to return to Sri Lanka – a country I first visited as a teenager 40 years ago and have been returning to ever since. In conducting the research for this volume, I have enjoyed the help of numerous people, including 'Mrs Kumari' (for cultural insights), Manjula Fernando (for safe travels) and Sam Owen (beloved husband and co-researcher).

ACKNOWLEDGEMENTS

Climate map data adapted from Peel MC, Finlayson BL & McMahon TA (2007) 'Updated World Map of the Köppen-Geiger Climate Classification', *Hydrology and Earth System Sciences*, 11, 1633–44.

Cover photograph: Monkey on the Thuparama Dagoba, Anuradhapura, Luigi Vaccarella/4Corners ©

THIS BOOK

This 15th edition of Lonely Planet's *Sri Lanka* guidebook was researched and written by Joe Bindloss, Stuart Butler, Bradley Mayhew and Jenny Walker. The previous edition was curated by Anirban Mahapatra and researched and written by Ryan Ver Berkmoes, Bradley, and Iain Stewart. This guidebook was produced by the following:

Senior Product Editors Grace Dobell, Sandie Kestell

Regional Senior Cartographer Valentina Kremenchutskaya

Product Editor Amy Lynch

Book Designer Gwen Cotter

Assisting Editors Ronan Abayawickrema, Sarah Bailey, Victoria Harrison, Anne Mulvaney, Claire Rourke, Gabrielle Stefanos, Saralinda Turner, Simon Williamson

Cartographer Julie Sheridan

Cover Researcher Naomi Parker

Thanks to Daniel Bolger, Fergal Condon, Amy Lysen

Index

Map Pages **000**
Photo Pages **000**

Map Pages **000**
Photo Pages **000**

Map Legend

Sights

- Beach
- Bird Sanctuary
- Buddhist
- Castle/Palace
- Christian
- Confucian
- Hindu
- Islamic
- Jain
- Jewish
- Monument
- Museum/Gallery/Historic Building
- Ruin
- Shinto
- Sikh
- Taoist
- Winery/Vineyard
- Zoo/Wildlife Sanctuary
- Other Sight

Activities, Courses & Tours

- Bodysurfing
- Diving
- Canoeing/Kayaking
- Course/Tour
- Sento Hot Baths/Onsen
- Skiing
- Snorkelling
- Surfing
- Swimming/Pool
- Walking
- Windsurfing
- Other Activity

Sleeping

- Sleeping
- Camping
- Hut/Shelter

Eating

- Eating

Drinking & Nightlife

- Drinking & Nightlife
- Cafe

Entertainment

- Entertainment

Shopping

- Shopping

Information

- Bank
- Embassy/Consulate
- Hospital/Medical
- Internet
- Police
- Post Office
- Telephone
- Toilet
- Tourist Information
- Other Information

Geographic

- Beach
- Gate
- Hut/Shelter
- Lighthouse
- Lookout
- Mountain/Volcano
- Oasis
- Park
- Pass
- Picnic Area
- Waterfall

Population

- Capital (National)
- Capital (State/Province)
- City/Large Town
- Town/Village

Transport

- Airport
- Border crossing
- Bus
- Cable car/Funicular
- Cycling
- Ferry
- Metro/MTR/MRT station
- Monorail
- Parking
- Petrol station
- Skytrain/Subway station
- Taxi
- Train station/Railway
- Tram
- Underground station
- Other Transport

Routes

- Tollway
- Freeway
- Primary
- Secondary
- Tertiary
- Lane
- Unsealed road
- Road under construction
- Plaza/Mall
- Steps
- Tunnel
- Pedestrian overpass
- Walking Tour
- Walking Tour detour
- Path/Walking Trail

Boundaries

- International
- State/Province
- Disputed
- Regional/Suburb
- Marine Park
- Cliff
- Wall

Hydrography

- River, Creek
- Intermittent River
- Canal
- Water
- Dry/Salt/Intermittent Lake
- Reef

Areas

- Airport/Runway
- Beach/Desert
- Cemetery (Christian)
- Cemetery (Other)
- Glacier
- Mudflat
- Park/Forest
- Sight (Building)
- Sportsground
- Swamp/Mangrove

Note: Not all symbols displayed above appear on the maps in this book

OUR STORY

A beat-up old car, a few dollars in the pocket and a sense of adventure. In 1972 that's all Tony and Maureen Wheeler needed for the trip of a lifetime – across Europe and Asia overland to Australia. It took several months, and at the end – broke but inspired – they sat at their kitchen table writing and stapling together their first travel guide, *Across Asia on the Cheap*. Within a week they'd sold 1500 copies. Lonely Planet was born.

Today, Lonely Planet has offices in Tennessee, Dublin and Beijing, with a network of over 2000 contributors in every corner of the globe. We share Tony's belief that 'a great guidebook should do three things: inform, educate and amuse'.

OUR WRITERS

Joe Bindloss
Joe first got the travel bug on a grand tour of Asia in the early 1990s, and he's been roaming around its temples and paddy-fields ever since on dozens of assignments for Lonely Planet and other publishers, covering everywhere from Myanmar and Thailand to India and Nepal. Joe was Lonely Planet's Destination Editor for the Indian Subcontinent until 2019. See more of his work at www.bindloss.co.uk.

Stuart Butler
Stuart has been writing for Lonely Planet for a decade and during this time he's come eye to eye with gorillas in the Congolese jungles, huffed and puffed over snow bound Himalayan mountain passes, interviewed a king who could turn into a tree, and had his fortune told by a parrot. Today, as well as guidebook writing work, Stuart writes often about conservation and environmental issues (mainly in eastern and southern Africa), wildlife watching and hiking. He also works as a photographer and was a finalist in both the 2015 and 2016 Travel Photographer of the Year Awards. When not on the road for Lonely Planet he lives on the beautiful beaches of Southwest France with his wife and two young children. His website is www.stuartbutlerjournalist.com

Bradley Mayhew
Bradley has been writing guidebooks for 20 years now. He started travelling while studying Chinese at Oxford University, and has since focused his expertise on China, Tibet, the Himalaya and Central Asia. He is the co-author of Lonely Planet guides to Tibet, Nepal, Trekking in the Nepal Himalaya, Bhutan, Central Asia and many others. Bradley has also fronted two TV series for Arte and SWR, one retracing the route of Marco Polo via Turkey, Iran, Afghanistan, Central Asia and China, and the other trekking Europe's 10 most scenic long-distance trails. Bradley has also written for Rough Guides, has contributed chapters to *Silk Road: Monks, Warriors & Merchants* and is a co-author of Insight Guide's *Silk Road*.

Jenny Walker
A member of the British Guild of Travel Writers, Jenny has travelled to over 125 countries and has been writing for Lonely Planet for more than 20 years. Currently working in Oman as Deputy CEO of a government agency responsible for the quality assurance of education, her MPhil thesis focused on the Arabian Orient in British Literature (Oxford University) and her PhD thesis (Nottingham Trent University) on the Desert as trope in Anglophone travel writing since 1950. A frequent visitor to Sri Lanka, she made her first trip to the island as a teenager in the 1970s and has returned many times over the years, including to source hand-crafted items in the 1990s in support of the country's cottage industries.

Published by Lonely Planet Global Limited
CRN 554153
15th edition – Oct 2021
ISBN 978 1 78701 659 0
© Lonely Planet 2021 Photographs © as indicated 2021
10 9 8 7 6 5 4 3 2 1
Printed in Singapore

Although the authors and Lonely Planet have taken all reasonable care in preparing this book, we make no warranty about the accuracy or completeness of its content and, to the maximum extent permitted, disclaim all liability arising from its use.

All rights reserved. No part of this publication may be copied, stored in a retrieval system, or transmitted in any form by any means, electronic, mechanical, recording or otherwise, except brief extracts for the purpose of review, and no part of this publication may be sold or hired, without the written permission of the publisher. Lonely Planet and the Lonely Planet logo are trademarks of Lonely Planet and are registered in the US Patent and Trademark Office and in other countries. Lonely Planet does not allow its name or logo to be appropriated by commercial establishments, such as retailers, restaurants or hotels. Please let us know of any misuses: lonelyplanet.com/ip.